DELIUS KLASING

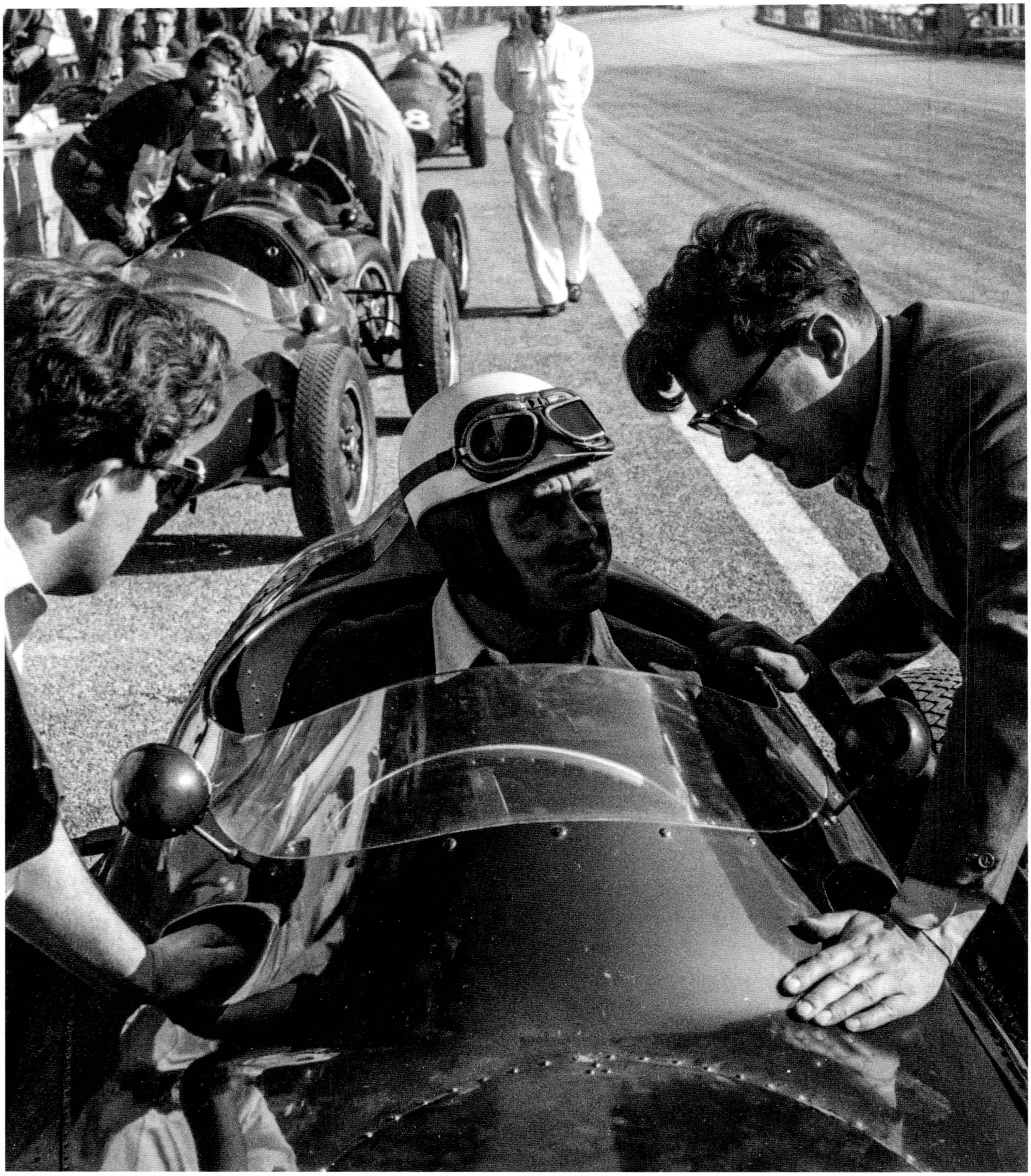

MONACO
MOTOR RACING

Edward Quinn
Motorsport
1950 – 1965

Edited by
Wolfgang Frei

Delius Klasing Verlag

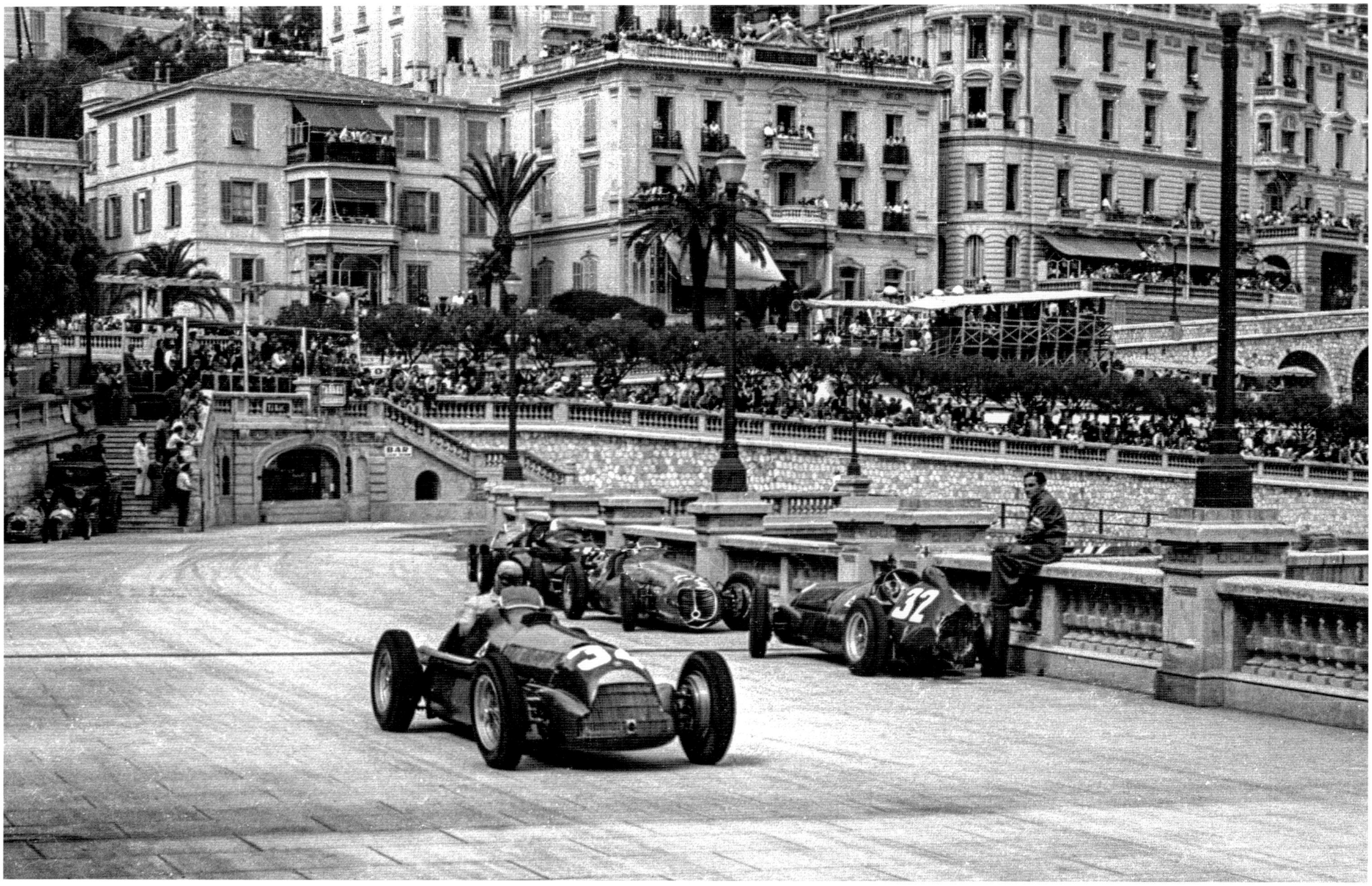

Eines von Quinns ersten Grand-Prix-Fotos 1950: Juan Manuel Fangio passiert vier Rennwagen, die am Unfall in der ersten Runde beteiligt waren, und fährt auf seinem Alfa Romeo „Alfetta“ N° 34 dem Start-Ziel-Sieg entgegen.

One of Quinn's first Grand Prix photos in 1950: Juan Manuel Fangio, Alfa Romeo 158 "Alfetta" N° 34, in first place, was not affected by the accident behind him. He won his first Grand Prix in Monaco with a start-to-finish victory.

MEINE ERSTEN GRAND-PRIX-FOTOS

Der erste Grand Prix von Monaco wurde im Mai 1929 ausgetragen und wurde als „Rund-um-die-Häuser"-Rennen bekannt. Damals waren Autorennen noch ein Sport für Privatfahrer, die meisten kauften sich ihre eigenen Autos. Gleich das erste auf dem gewundenen Rundkurs von Monte Carlo ausgetragene Rennen war 1929 ein erstaunlicher Erfolg, obwohl die Strecke keineswegs für den Rennsport konstruiert war. Alle Champions der damaligen Zeit nahmen daran teil. Gewonnen wurde das Rennen vom geheimnisumwitterten William Grover, genannt „Williams", in einem Bugatti, der die 100 Runden in 3h 56 zurücklegte. 1980 war es 1h 55. Ein anderer Bugatti schaffte es auf den zweiten Platz, knapp vor dem Rennfahrer-As Caracciola auf Mercedes.

Von 1929 an kamen die besten Rennfahrer und Autos der Welt nach Monaco, um sich beim Grand Prix zu messen, und das Rennen wurde zum Höhepunkt der internationalen sportlichen und gesellschaftlichen Ereignisse in Monaco. Kriegsbedingt fanden zwischen 1937 und 1948 keine Rennen statt. Als sie wieder aufgenommen wurden, gab es eine Welle des Interesses, und von den Fünfzigerjahren an war das Rennen wieder ein Spitzenereignis.

Als ich 1950 zum ersten Mal zum Grand Prix fuhr, erlebte ich so etwas wie eine Feuertaufe. Ich hatte mir die spektakulärste und für die Fahrer mühsamste Kurve für meine Fotos ausgesucht. Das war gleich nach der „Schikane" neben dem Hafen, die Kurve war als „Tabac" bekannt, da die Strecke direkt vor einer Bar Tabac vorbeiführte.

Der Start mit dem lauten Dröhnen und Knattern der donnernden Motoren war ein überwältigendes Erlebnis. Als die Autos auf die Stelle zurasten, an der ich stand, waren sie noch im Pulk und ich wusste, dass sie nicht alle zusammen durchkommen konnten. Drei Autos beschleunigten gleichzeitig mit heulenden Motoren. Sie lagen Nase an Nase und keiner wollte ausweichen. Als ich die Autos auf mich zurasen sah, hielt ich meine Kamera so ruhig wie möglich.

Das erste Auto, das die Kurve erreichte – ich weiss nicht mehr, wer es war, wahrscheinlich Nino Farina –, schrammte an der Mauer entlang und prallte direkt unter meinen Füßen in die Mauer. Dann prallten die anderen Autos gegen das erste, jedes krachte in das Heck des anderen und überall lief Benzin aus. Ich drückte so schnell ich konnte auf den Auslöser meiner Kamera, obwohl es mir durch den Schock fast unmöglich war, die Kamera ruhig zu halten. Glücklicherweise wurde niemand schwer verletzt, obwohl der Unfall spektakulär aussah. Das Rennen gewann der große Manuel Fangio. Als ich den Film entwickelte, waren die meisten Bilder dieses Unfalls unscharf, da ich so stark gezittert hatte.

Nach dieser unglücklichen Erfahrung fotografierte ich dennoch die meisten anderen Grand-Prix-Rennen von Monaco in den 50er- und 60er-Jahren und lernte die Fahrer recht gut kennen. Aber in fast jeder Saison wurde in jenen Tagen ein Fahrer Opfer dieses sogenannten „Grand-Prix-Zirkus". Einer nach dem anderen starben die großen Rennchampions, die ich kannte: der „Goldjunge" Peter Collins, Mike Hawthorn, der vor seinem Tod 40-mal verletzte Jean Behra, die Italiener Musso und Ascari. Dann später Jim Clark, „der Stille" Wolfgang von Trips, Joachim Bonnier. Alle verzeichneten große Formel-1-Siege und dann fuhren sie eines Tages zu schnell oder waren zu erschöpft oder wurden Opfer eines mechanischen Defekts. Aber in der Woche danach gab es immer einen Newcomer, der bereit war, ihren Platz einzunehmen.

Edward Quinn, Nizza 1980

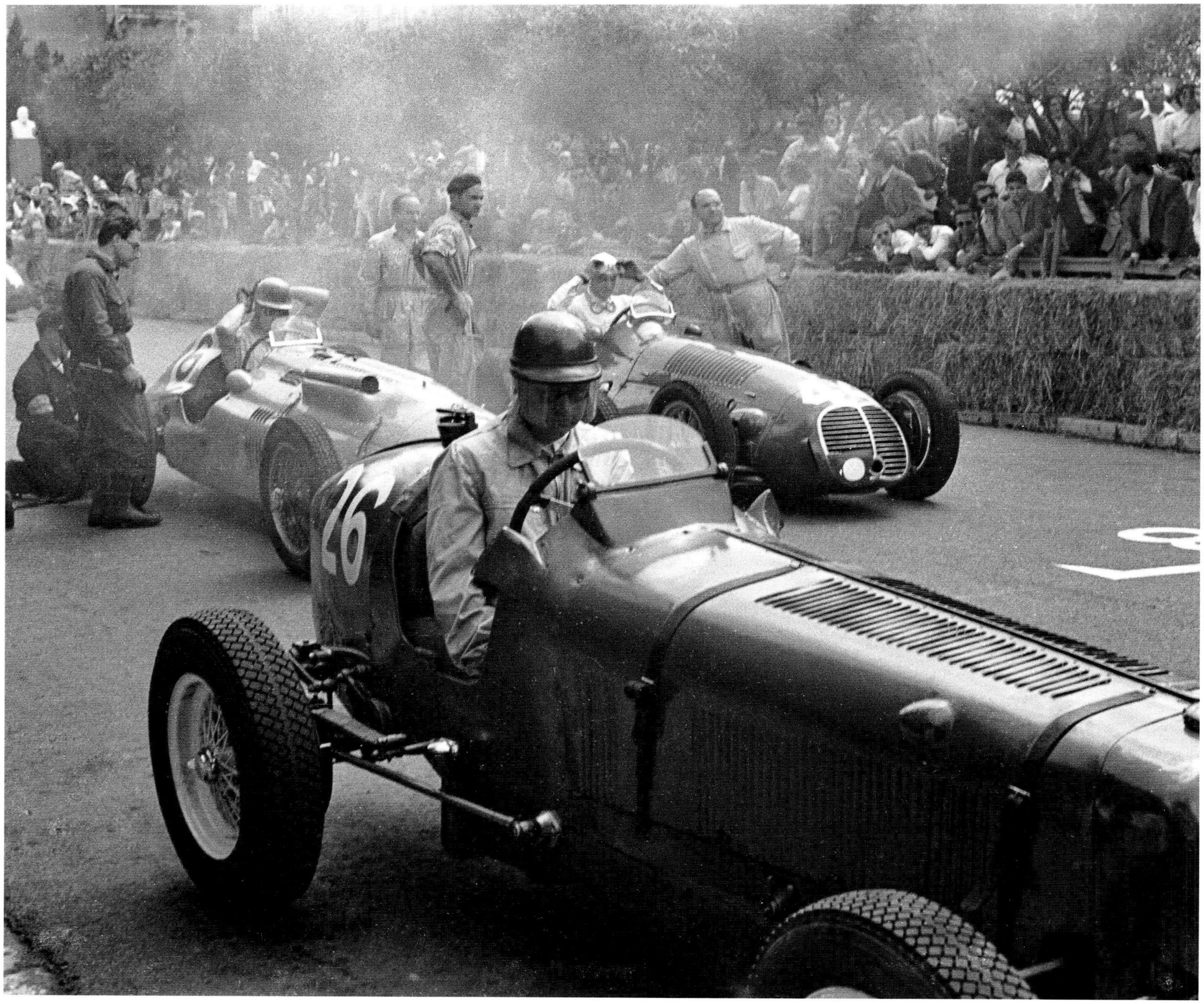

1950, kurz vor dem Start des Grand Prix von Monaco: Bob Gerard, ERA R4A N° 26, Johnny Claes, Talbot Lago T26C N° 6, Louis Chiron, Maserati 4CLT N° 48.

The start of the Monaco Grand Prix 1950 is imminent. Bob Gerard, ERA R4A N° 26, Johnny Claes, Talbot Lago T26C N° 6, Louis Chiron, Maserati 4CLT N° 48.

MY FIRST GRAND PRIX PHOTOS

The first Monaco Grand Prix race was held in May 1929 and at once it became known as the "round-the-houses" race. In those days car racing was very much a gentleman's sport and most of the drivers owned their own cars. The first race in Monte Carlo in 1929 around the tortuous circuit, in no way constructed for racing, was a resounding success. All the champions of the time took part. The race was won by the enigmatic William Grover, known as "Williams" in a Bugatti that completed the 100 laps in 3h 56. The time in 1980 was 1h 55. Another Bugatti scraped through into second place, just beating the crack driver Caracciola who was driving a Mercedes.

From 1929 on all the world's best racing drivers and cars came to compete in the Monaco Grand Prix and the race became the highlight of Monaco's international sporting and social events. There were no races held between 1937 and 1948, so when racing recommenced there was a surge of interest and by the fifties the race was again a top event.

When I went to the Monaco Grand Prix for the first time in 1950, I had what could be called a baptism of fire. I had chosen the most spectacular and worst corner for the drivers as the spot where I would take my photos. This was just after the "chicane" beside the harbour, the corner was known as the "Tabac" as the course passed right in front of a bar called Tabac.

The roar and crackling of the thundering engines at the start of the race was a terrific, mind-blowing experience. The cars were still in a pack when they came speeding towards the place where I stood, so I knew they could not get through all at the same Three cars screeched and screamed forward as they accelerated. They were nose to nose and nobody wanted to give way. When I saw the cars rocketing towards me I held my camera as steady as I could. The first car to get to the corner, I can't remember who it was, probably Nino Farina scraped along the wall and hit the corner right under my feet. Then with a tearing of metal the other cars piled up against the first car, each one smashing into the rear of the other and petrol was spurting out everywhere. I pressed the button of my camera as quickly as I could although the shock made it nearly impossible for me to keep the camera steady. Fortunately although the accident looked spectacular, no one was badly hurt. The race was won by the great Manuel Fangio. When I came to develop the film I found that most of the pictures of this accident were out of focus because my hands had been shaking so much.

However after this unfortunate experience I still went back to photograph most of the other Monaco Grand Prix races during the fifties and sixties and I got to know the drivers quite well. But nearly every season in those days some driver fell victim of what was known as the "Grand Prix Circus". One by one the great racing champions I knew died: Peter Collins, "the golden boy", Mike Hawthorn, Jean Behra who before he died had been injured 40 times, the Italians Musso and Ascari. Then later Jim Clark, "the quiet man" Wolfgang von Trips, Joachim Bonnier. All had great Formula 1 victories and then, one day, they would go too fast or they were over-tired or there was a mechanical failure. But the week after there was always some newcomer willing to take their place.

Edward Quinn, Nice 1980

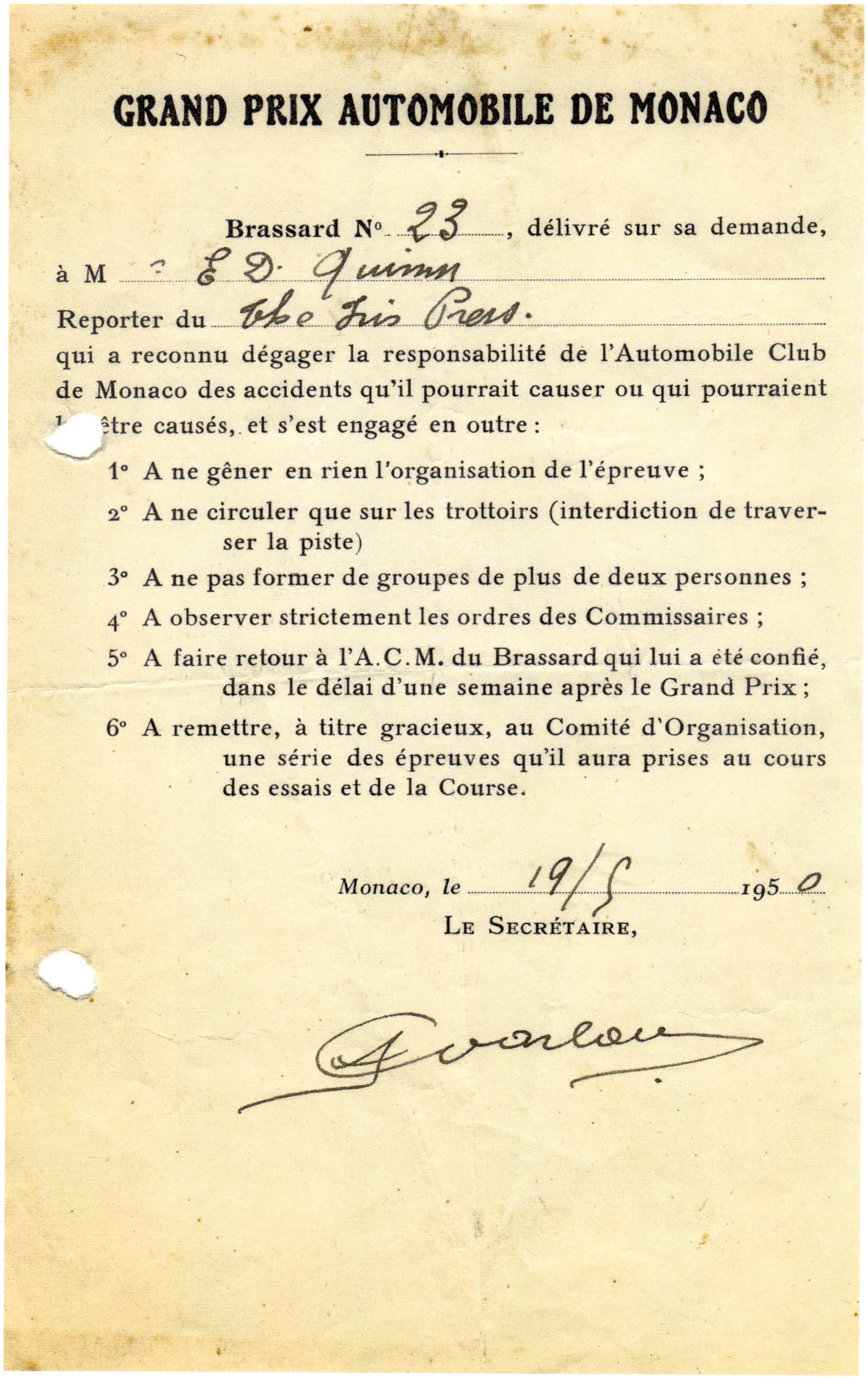

GRAND PRIX AUTOMOBILE DE MONACO

Brassard N° 23, délivré sur sa demande,

à M E. D. Quinn

Reporter du the Iris Press.

qui a reconnu dégager la responsabilité de l'Automobile Club de Monaco des accidents qu'il pourrait causer ou qui pourraient l[illegible]être causés, et s'est engagé en outre :

1° A ne gêner en rien l'organisation de l'épreuve ;

2° A ne circuler que sur les trottoirs (interdiction de traverser la piste)

3° A ne pas former de groupes de plus de deux personnes ;

4° A observer strictement les ordres des Commissaires ;

5° A faire retour à l'A.C.M. du Brassard qui lui a été confié, dans le délai d'une semaine après le Grand Prix ;

6° A remettre, à titre gracieux, au Comité d'Organisation, une série des épreuves qu'il aura prises au cours des essais et de la Course.

Monaco, le 19/5 1950

LE SECRÉTAIRE,

Quittung für die Pressearmbinde von Edward Quinn mit Verhaltensregeln für den Grand Prix von Monaco 1950.

The receipt for the press armband worn by Edward D. Quinn for the Monaco Grand Prix 1950 with rules of conduct.

EDITORIAL

Seit den 50er- und 60er-Jahren, von denen dieses Buch handelt, hat nie ein anderes Autorennen einen ähnlichen Glamour wie der Monaco Grand Prix ausgestrahlt. Der ungewöhnliche Rundkurs mitten durch die Stadt wurde bis heute nur wenig verändert: Bei der Kirche Sainte Dévote wurde eine Schikane hinzugefügt, die Strecke um das neue Schwimmbad herumgeführt, der Tunnel verlängert und die Gasometer-Kurve durch die Rascasse ersetzt. Alles andere hat sich grundlegend verändert: Damals waren die italienischen Autos rot, die britischen grün und die französischen blau, Werbung auf Autos und Overalls gab es nicht, auch kein TV, keine kommerziellen Sponsoren, das Preisgeld war knapp, die Autos mechanische Boliden statt fahrender Computer mit Aerodynamik aus dem Windkanal. Die Fahrer waren noch nicht völlig versteckt hinter Überrollstrukturen und geschlossenen Helmen mit schmalen Visieren; sie waren auch während des Rennens an ihren Gesichtern zu erkennen. Aber sie lebten ungemein gefährlich. Ein großer Teil der Rennfahrer dieser Zeiten hat das Leben beim Motorsport verloren. Ihre Sicherheit – und auch die der Zuschauer – wurde erst Mitte der 60er-Jahre ein wichtiges Thema und führte schrittweise zu einer strengen Reglementierung des Rennsports.

Scheint es nur so, oder waren die Rennfahrer von damals andere Typen als die heutigen? Eher gestandene Haudegen als junge Burschen? Jedenfalls wäre es heute kaum mehr möglich, dass ein 46-Jähriger den Monaco Grand Prix gewinnt, wie das „Simply the Best“ Juan Manuel Fangio geschafft hat. Und undenkbar, dass ein Fahrer in Monaco Formel-1-Rennen, Rallyes, Formel-3- und Sportwagenrennen bestreitet, wie „Mr. Motor Racing“ Stirling Moss. Und wahrscheinlich war auch die Beziehung unter den Fahrern enger als sie es heute ist. Dazu sagte Moss: „In den 60er-Jahren waren die Formel-1-Piloten eine befreundete kleine Bande – so ganz anders als die unnahbaren Superstars von heute.“

Das ist es, was wir in diesem Buch zeigen wollen. Edward Quinn war nah dran. Es ging ihm nicht einfach darum, fahrende Rennwagen vor dieser einmaligen Kulisse im Amphitheater von Monaco mit dem Casino, dem Hôtel de Paris und dem Hafen zu fotografieren; ihn interessierten vor allem die Fahrer, ihre Entourage, ihr Verhältnis zueinander und einfach ihr oft unbeschwerter Spaß an einem gefährlichen Sport. Damals war der Zugang zu den Boxen kaum geregelt, es gab keine Geheimnistuerei und keine Public-Relations-Agenten als unumgängliche Mittelsmänner, man hat sich einfach gekannt. Das spürt man in den Bildern dieses Bandes.

Der erste Monaco Grand Prix fand 1929 statt, aber schon 1911 war Monaco Zentrum des anderen legendären Motorsport-Ereignisses, das bis heute weiterlebt: der Rallye Monte-Carlo. Auch diese Rennen hat Edward Quinn schon in den 50er-Jahren als freier Fotojournalist für Zeitungen und Zeitschriften verfolgt.

Wir haben einige seiner Rallye-Bilder in dieses Buch aufgenommen; sie werden nicht nur bei den Renn-Enthusiasten sondern auch den Oldtimer-Liebhabern Interesse finden und unser Thema Monaco Motor Racing abrunden.

Wolfgang Frei, Zürich 2021

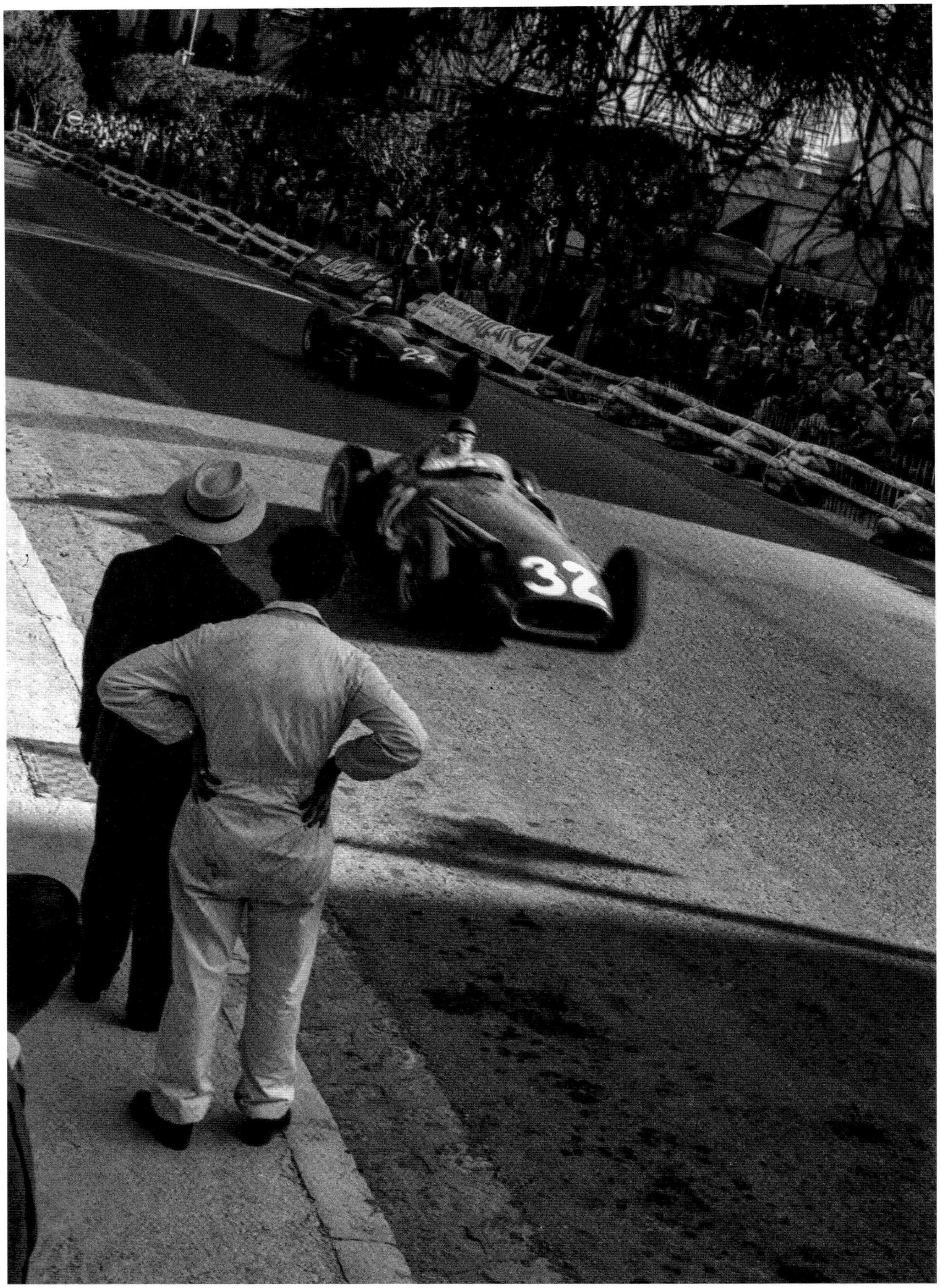

Monaco Grand Prix 1957: Juan Manuel Fangio, Maserati 250F N° 32, und Wolfgang von Trips, Ferrari 801 N° 24. Der Mann mit weißem Hut ist Tony Vandervell, Gründer des Vanwall Formel-1-Teams.

Monaco Grand Prix 1957: Juan Manuel Fangio, Maserati 250F N° 32, and Wolfgang von Trips, Ferrari 801 N° 24. With white hat Tony Vandervell, founder of the Vanwall Formula 1 team.

EDITORIAL

Since the 1950s and 1960s, the period covered by this book, no other motor race has ever exuded the same glamour as the Monaco Grand Prix. The unusual circuit through the middle of the city has changed very little since: A chicane was added at Sainte Dévote, the circuit was rerouted around the new swimming pool, the tunnel was lengthened and the Gasometer hairpin replaced with the Rascasse bend. Everything else has changed radically. Back then, the Italian cars were simply red, the British green and the French blue, there were no advertisements on cars and overalls, no TV either, no commercial sponsors, the prize money was modest, the cars were mechanical workhorses instead of driving computers with aerodynamics from the wind tunnel. The drivers were not yet completely hidden behind roll bars and closed helmets; they could be recognised by their faces even during the race. But they lived incredibly dangerously. A large proportion of the racing drivers of those times lost their lives in motor sport. Their safety – and that of the spectators – only became an important issue in the mid-1960s and gradually led to strict regulation of the sport.

But it seems like racing drivers back then were a different breed from those of today – more like seasoned warriors than young lads. In any case, it would hardly be possible today for a 46-year-old to win the Monaco Grand Prix as "Simply the Best" Juan Manuel Fangio did. Likewise it is astounding that the same driver would contest Formula 1 races, rallies, Formula 3 and sports car races in Monaco as "Mr Motor Racing" Stirling Moss did. And probably relationships among the drivers were closer than they are today as Moss said: "In the 60s, Formula 1 drivers were a friendly little gang – so different from the aloof superstars of today." That is what we want to show in this book.

Edward Quinn was close to them. He was not simply interested in photographing racing cars in front of this unique setting in the amphitheatre of Monaco with the Casino, the Hôtel de Paris and the harbour. Above all he was interested in the drivers, their entourage, their relationship to each other and simply their often lighthearted sense of fun in a dangerous sport. In those days, access to the pits was hardly regulated, there was no secrecy and no public relations advisors as unavoidable middlemen, people simply knew each other. You can feel that in the photos in this volume.

The first Monaco Grand Prix took place in 1929, but as early as 1911 Monaco was the centre of the other legendary motorsport event that lives on to this day: the Monte Carlo Rally. Edward Quinn also followed these events as a freelance photojournalist for newspapers and magazines back in the 1950s. We have included some of these Rally pictures in this book. They will interest not only racing enthusiasts but also classic car lovers and round off our theme of Monaco Motor Racing.

Wolfgang Frei, Zurich 2021

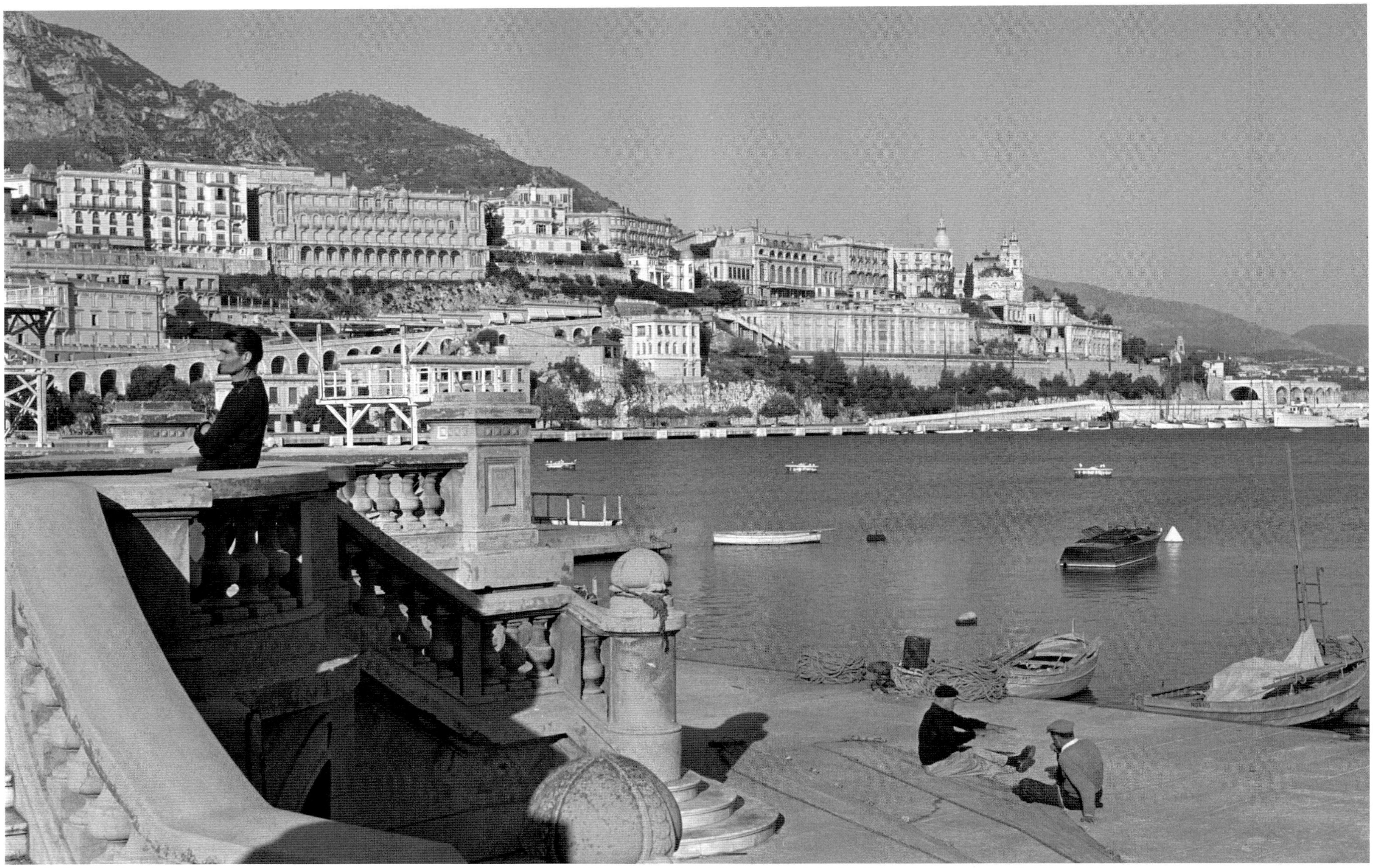

Der idyllische Hafen von Monaco 1950, wo heute unzählige Yachten liegen, nicht nur während des Grand Prix. Gegenüber rechts das Casino mit zwei Türmen, daneben das Hôtel de Paris mit seinem Turm. Ganz links die kleine Kuppel des Hôtel Beau-Rivage, davor die Montée Beau-Rivage, die Auffahrt von Sainte Dévote zum Casino. Gut sichtbar der Ausgang des Tir-aux-Pigeons-Tunnels.

Monaco's idyllic harbour in 1950, where today countless yachts are moored not only during the Grand Prix. On the other side, on the right, the Casino with its twin towers, next to it the Hôtel de Paris with its characteristic turret. On the far left, the small dome of the Hôtel Beau-Rivage, in front of it the Montée Beau-Rivage, the access from Sainte Dévote to the Casino. The exit from the Tir-aux-Pigeons tunnel is also clearly visible.

1950

Die „Drei Fs“

Monaco im ersten Jahr der neuen Formel-1-Weltmeisterschaft. Für die Motoren gilt eine Mischformel: Entweder 1.500 cm³ mit Kompressor oder 4,5 Liter mit Saugmotor. Die legendären, konkurrenzlosen und PS-starken Alfa Romeo „Alfetta“ mit 8-Zylindern und Kompressor sind nach einem Jahr Pause zurück, gefahren von den „Drei F“, Farina, Fagioli und Fangio, der erstmals in Monaco teilnimmt. Konkurrenz kommt von der Scuderia Ferrari und den Talbot-Lago, die als einzige mit den großen Motoren bestückt sind. Die veralteten Maserati scheinen abgeschlagen.

In der ersten Runde hatte eine vom Wind getragene Gischt die Tabac-Kurve rutschig gemacht. Einer der „Drei F“, Nino Farina, erwischte die Kurve nicht und versperrte mit seiner Alfetta die Strecke. In der Folge krachten neun Wagen ineinander, eine der bemerkenswertesten Massenkarambolagen der Grand-Prix-Geschichte.

So wurde gleich zu Beginn des Rennens die gesamte Ausgangslage verändert.

The “Three Fs”

Monaco in the first year of the new Formula 1 World Championship. A mixed formula applies to the engines: either 1500cc with supercharger or 4.5 litre unsupercharged. The high horsepower 8-cylinder supercharged Alfa Romeo “Alfetta” are back after a year’s break, driven by the “Three Fs”, Farina, Fagioli and Fangio, the latter competing at Monaco for the first time. Competition comes from Scuderia Ferrari and Talbot-Lago, the only cars with big engines. The outdated Maseratis seem to have been beaten off.

On the first lap, a spray carried by the wind had made the Tabac left-hander slippery. One of the “Three Fs”, Nino Farina, missed the corner and blocked the way with his Ferrari.

As a result, nine cars crashed into each other in one of the most remarkable pile-ups in Grand Prix history. Thus everything changed right at the start of the race.

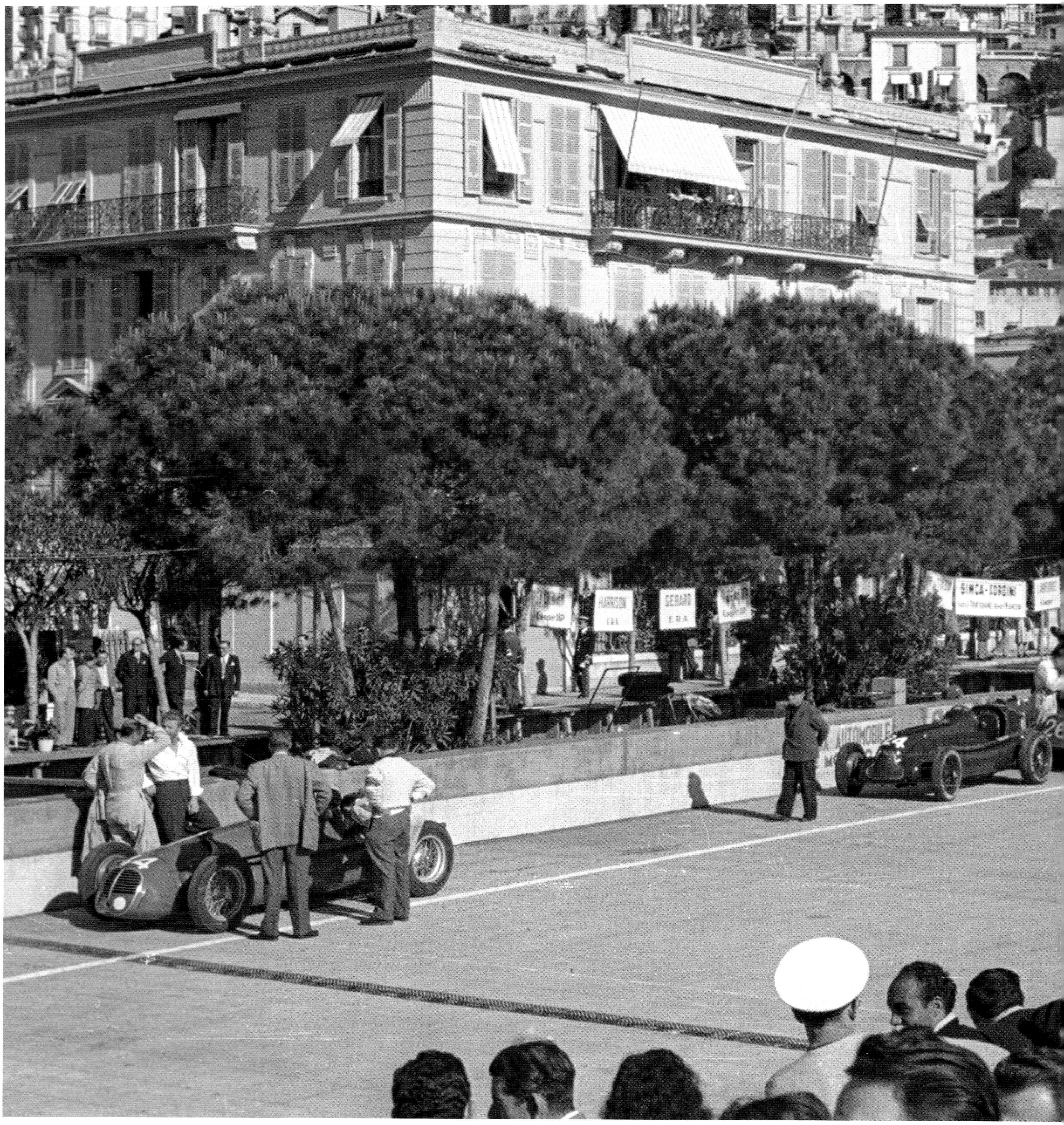
HARRISON
ERA
GERARD
ERA
SIMCA-GORDINI
AUTOMOBILE

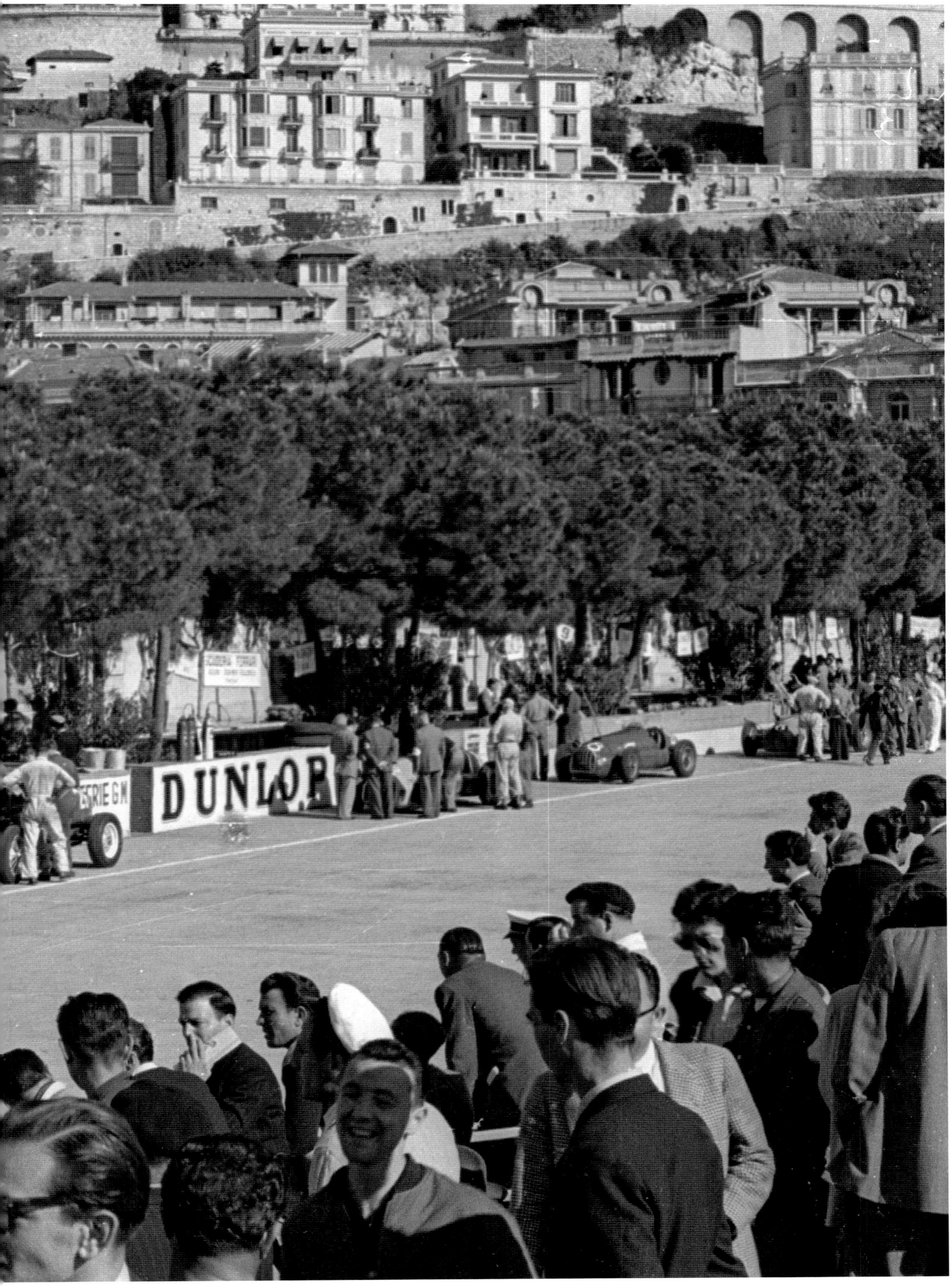

An den „Boxen“, von links:
Franco Rol, Maserati 4CLT N° 44,
Cuth Harrison, ERA R8C N° 24,
Bob Gerard, ERA R4A N° 26.

In the “pits” from left:
Franco Rol, Maserati 4CLT N° 44,
Cuth Harrison, ERA R8C N° 24,
Bob Gerard, ERA R4A N° 26.

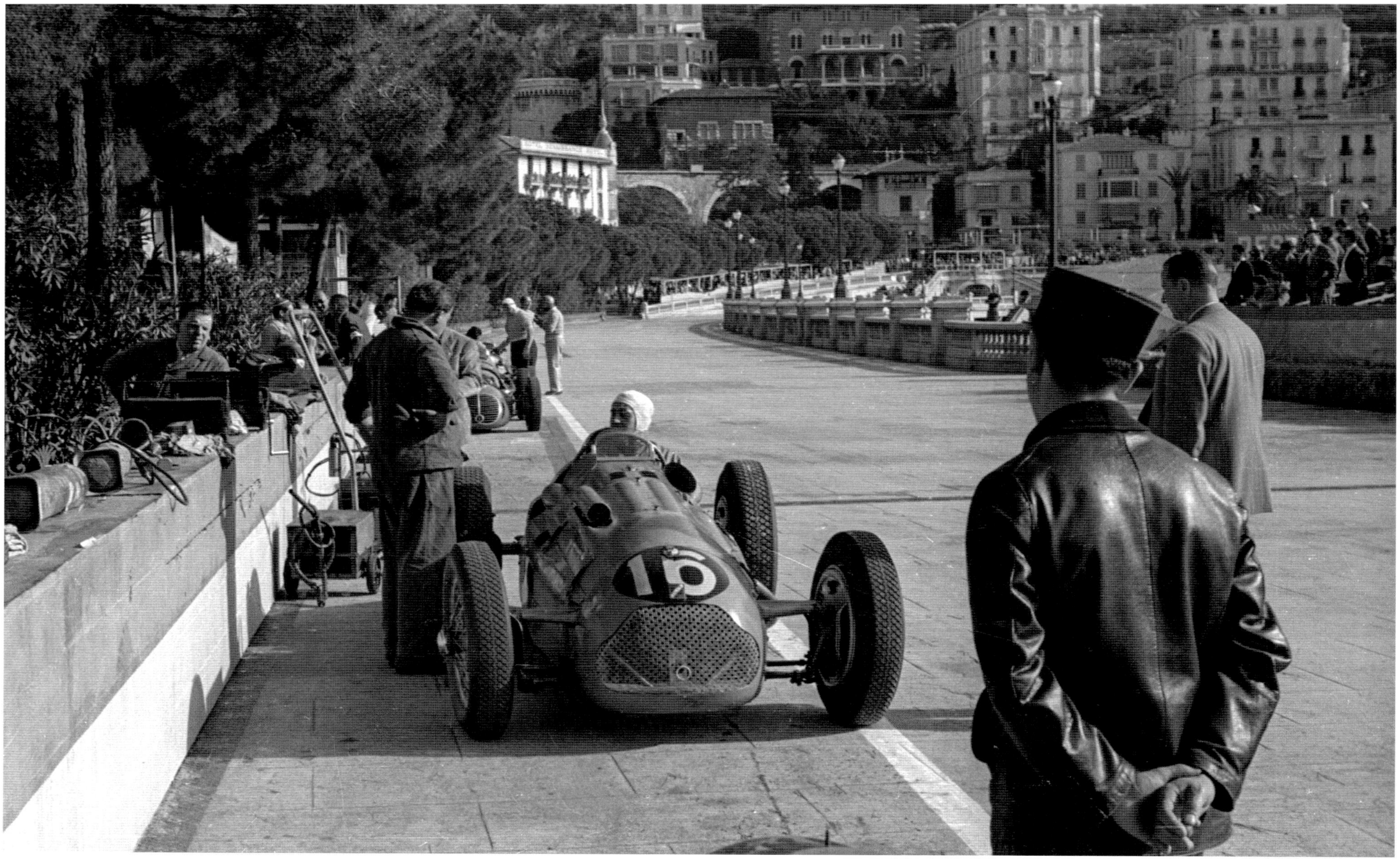

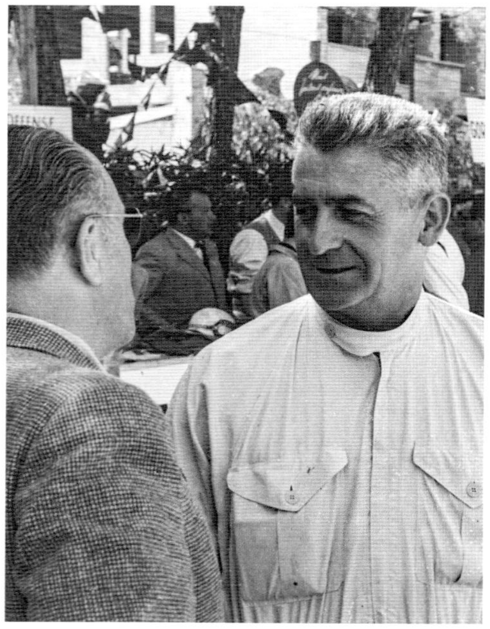

Louis Rosier, Talbot-Lago T26C N° 16.

Rosier kam erst mit 40 Jahren zum ersten F1-Rennen und nahm an 38 Grands Prix teil. Er war davor bekannt als Motorradrennfahrer, fuhr Sportwagenrennen und gewann die 1.100-cm³-Kategorie der Rallye Monte-Carlo 1949.
Legendär war sein Sieg 1950 beim 24-Stunden-Rennen von Le Mans, wo er es schaffte, auf einem Talbot-Lago T26GS allein 23 Stunden am Steuer zu sitzen. Rosier starb nach einem Unfall bei einem Rennen in Montlhéry 1956.

Rosier came to F1 racing for the first time at the ripe old age of 40 and participated in 38 Grands Prix. He was known before that as a motorcycle racer, raced sports cars and won the 1100cc category of the 1949 Monte Carlo Rally.
His victory in the 24 Hours of Le Mans in 1950 was legendary, when he managed to drive a Talbot-Lago T26GS single-handedly for 23 hours. Rosier died after an accident during a race in Montlhéry 1956.

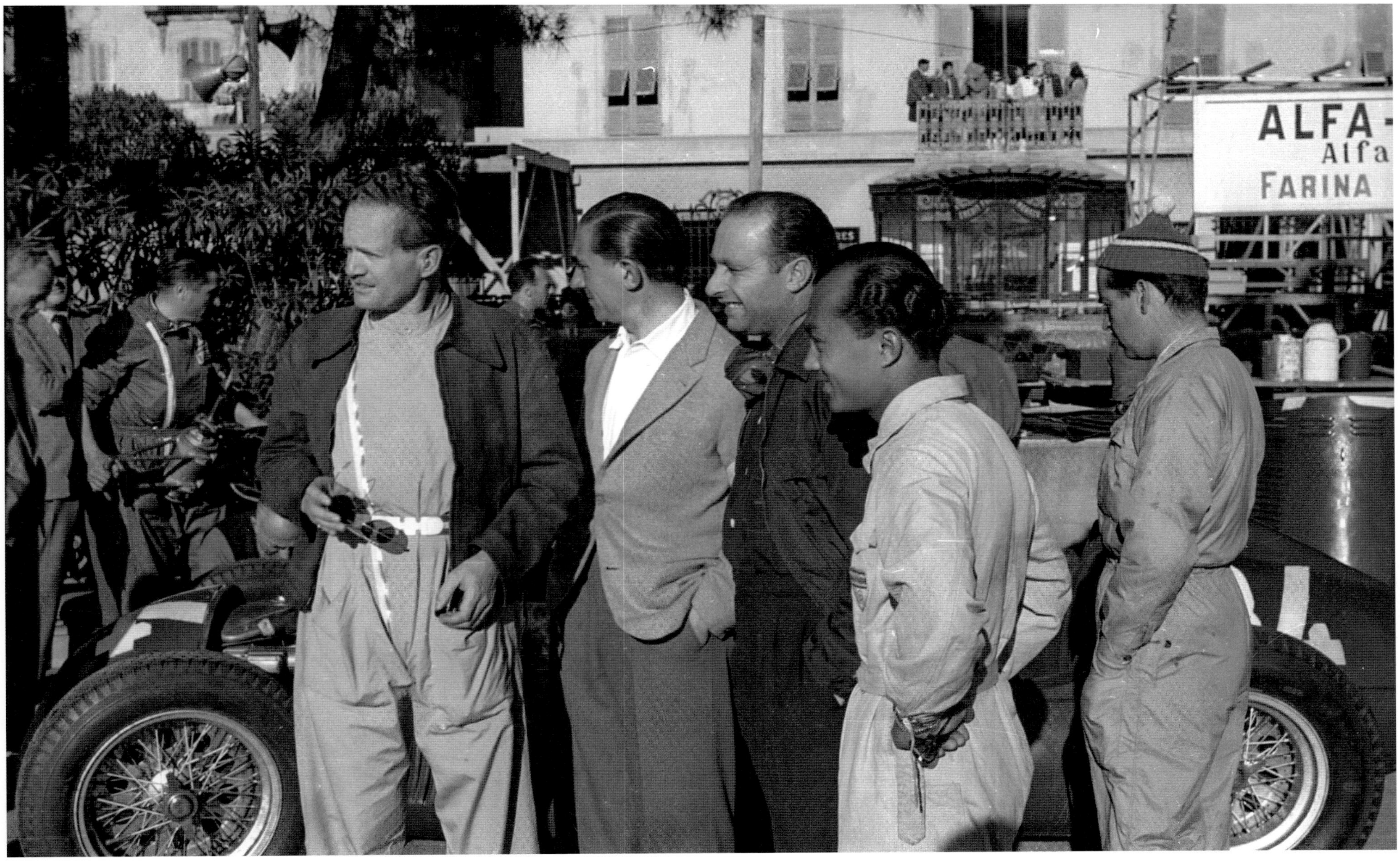

GP-Piloten, von links: Toulo de Graffenried, Vorkriegs-Rennfahrer Goffredo „Freddie“ Zehender, Juan Manuel Fangio, Prinz Bira und Maurice Trintignant mit seiner bekannten Pudelmütze.

GP drivers, from the left: Toulo de Graffenried, pre-war driver Goffredo "Freddie" Zehender, Juan Manuel Fangio, Prince Bira and Maurice Trintignant with his bobble hat.

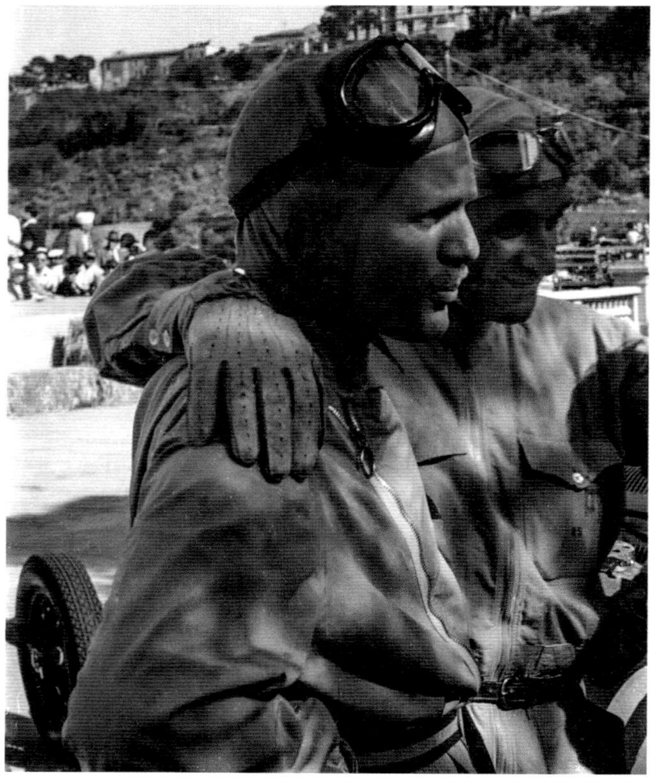

Zwei Freunde: Emmanuel „Toulo“ de Graffenried, „De Graff“ (links), Maserati 4CLT N° 52, und Raymond Sommer, Ferrari 125 N° 42.

Two friends: Emmanuel "Toulo" de Graffenried, "De Graff" (left), Maserati 4CLT N° 52, and Raymond Sommer, Ferrari 125 N° 42.

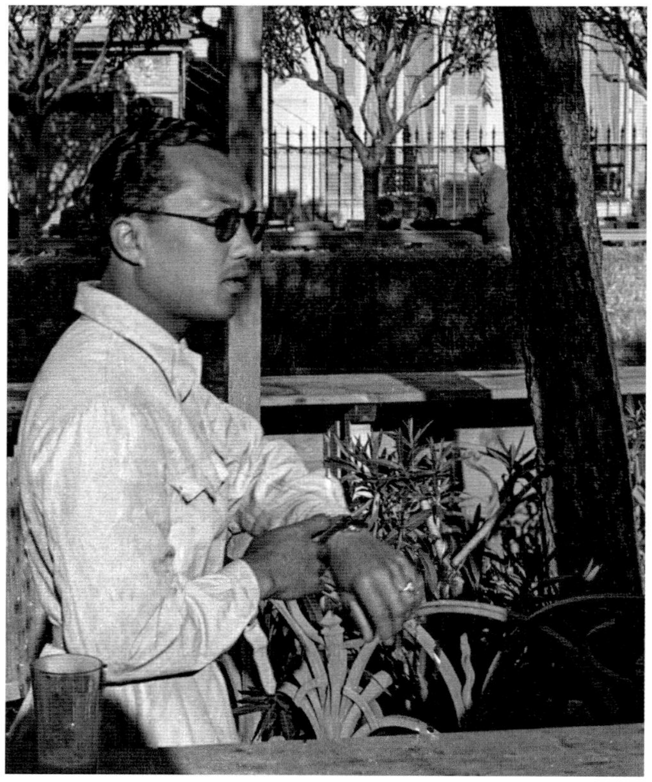

Einer der vielen Adligen, die – meist als Privatfahrer – an der F1-Weltmeisterschaft teilnahmen. Prince Bira von Siam (heute Thailand), eigentlich Prinz Birabongse Bhanutej Bhanubhandhu, Maserati 4CLT N° 50.

One of the many aristocrats who took part in the F1 World Championship – mostly as private drivers. Prince Bira of Siam (today Thailand), actually Prince Birabongse Bhanutej Bhanubhandhu, Maserati 4CLT N° 50.

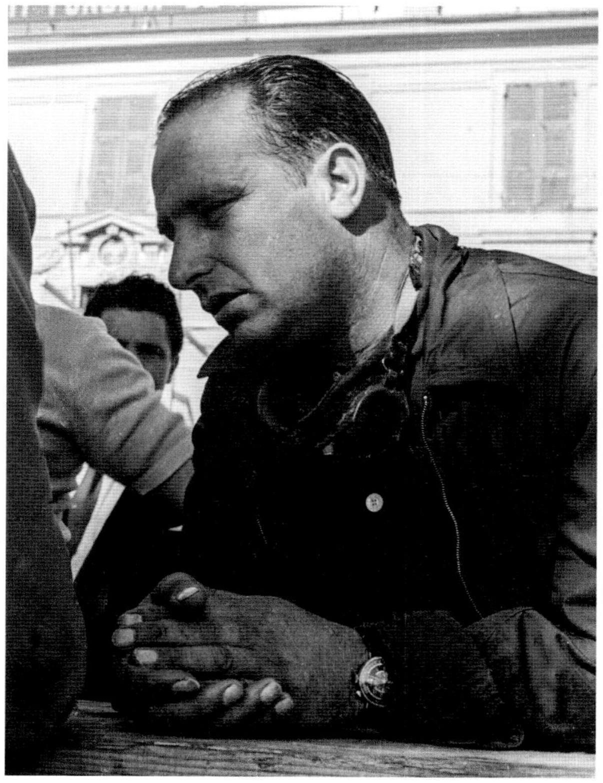

Juan Manuel Fangio, Sieger des Grand Prix 1950 auf Alfa Romeo 158 „Alfetta“ N° 34. Der Argentinier gilt für viele Fachleute als bester Rennfahrer in der Geschichte des Grand-Prix-Sports. Er wurde fünfmal Weltmeister.

Juan Manuel Fangio, winner of the Grand Prix 1950, Alfa Romeo 158 "Alfetta" N° 34. The Argentine is considered by many experts to be the best racing driver in the history of Grand Prix sport. He was five times world champion.

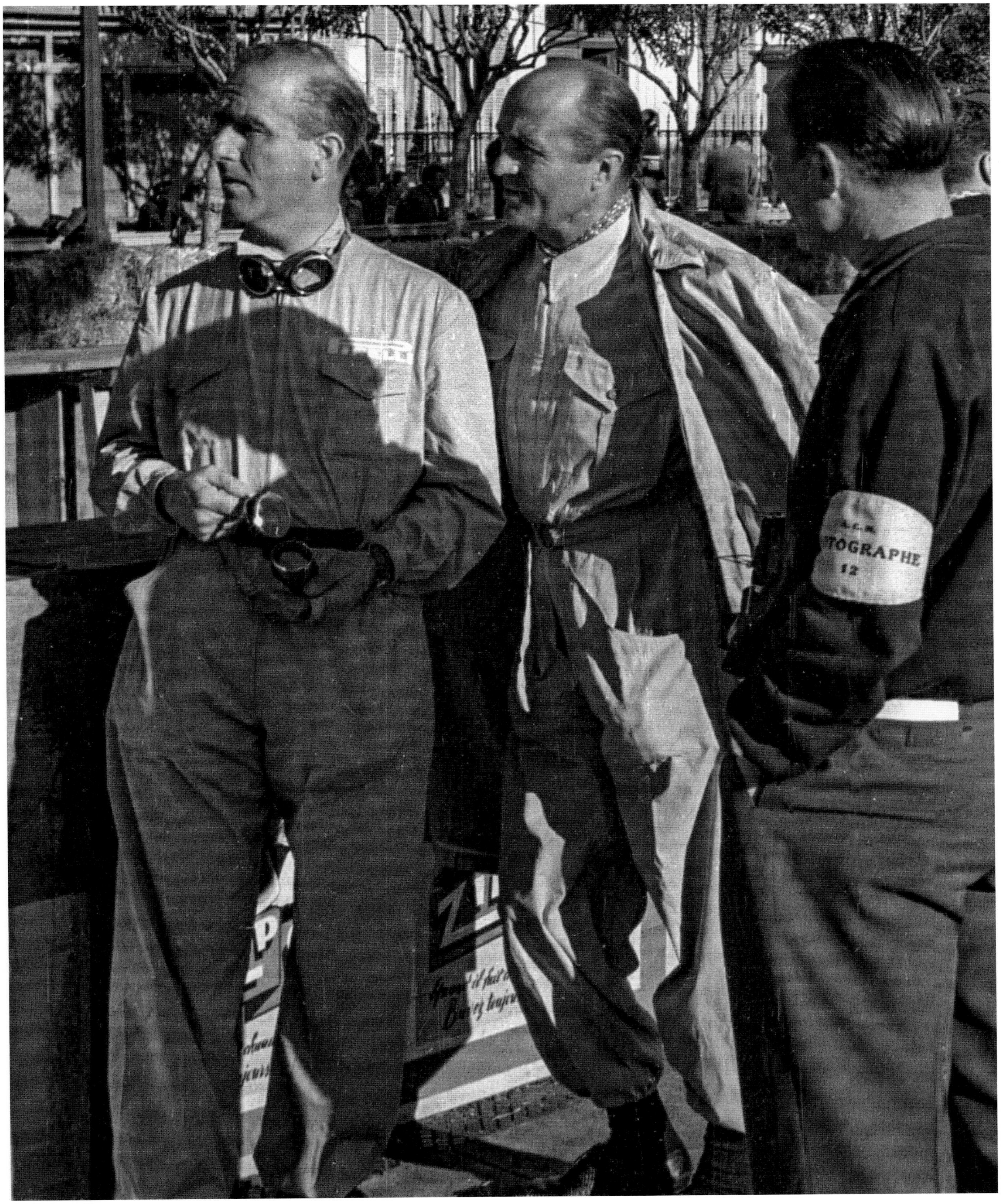

Gestandene Herren: Giuseppe „Nino“ Farina (links), 51-jährig, Alfa Romeo 158 „Alfetta“ N° 32, and Louis Chiron, 44-jährig, Maserati 4CLT N° 48.

Two gentlemen: Giuseppe “Nino” Farina (left), 51-year-old, Alfa Romeo 158 “Alfetta” N° 32, and Louis Chiron, 44-year-old, Maserati 4CLT N° 48.

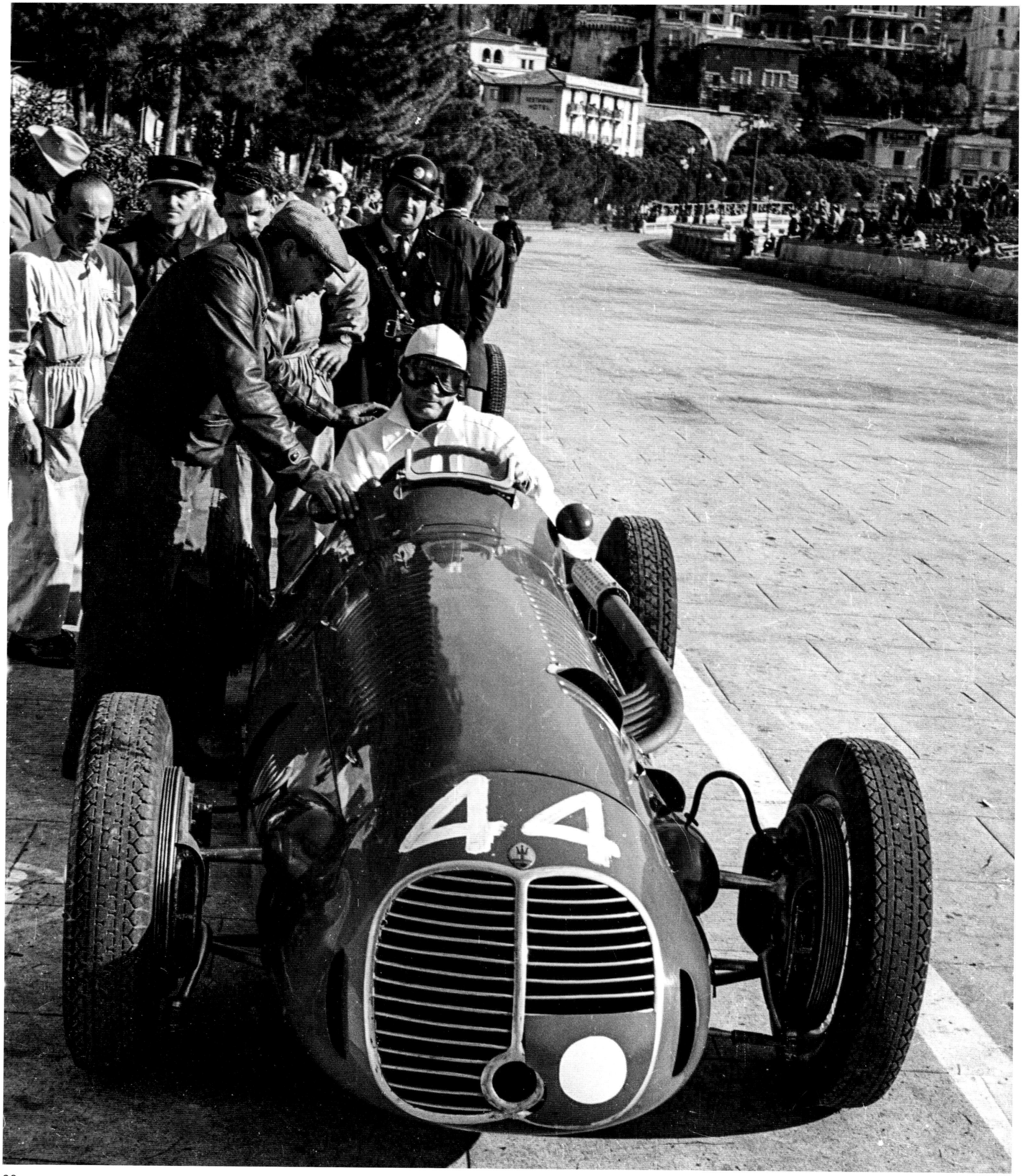
44

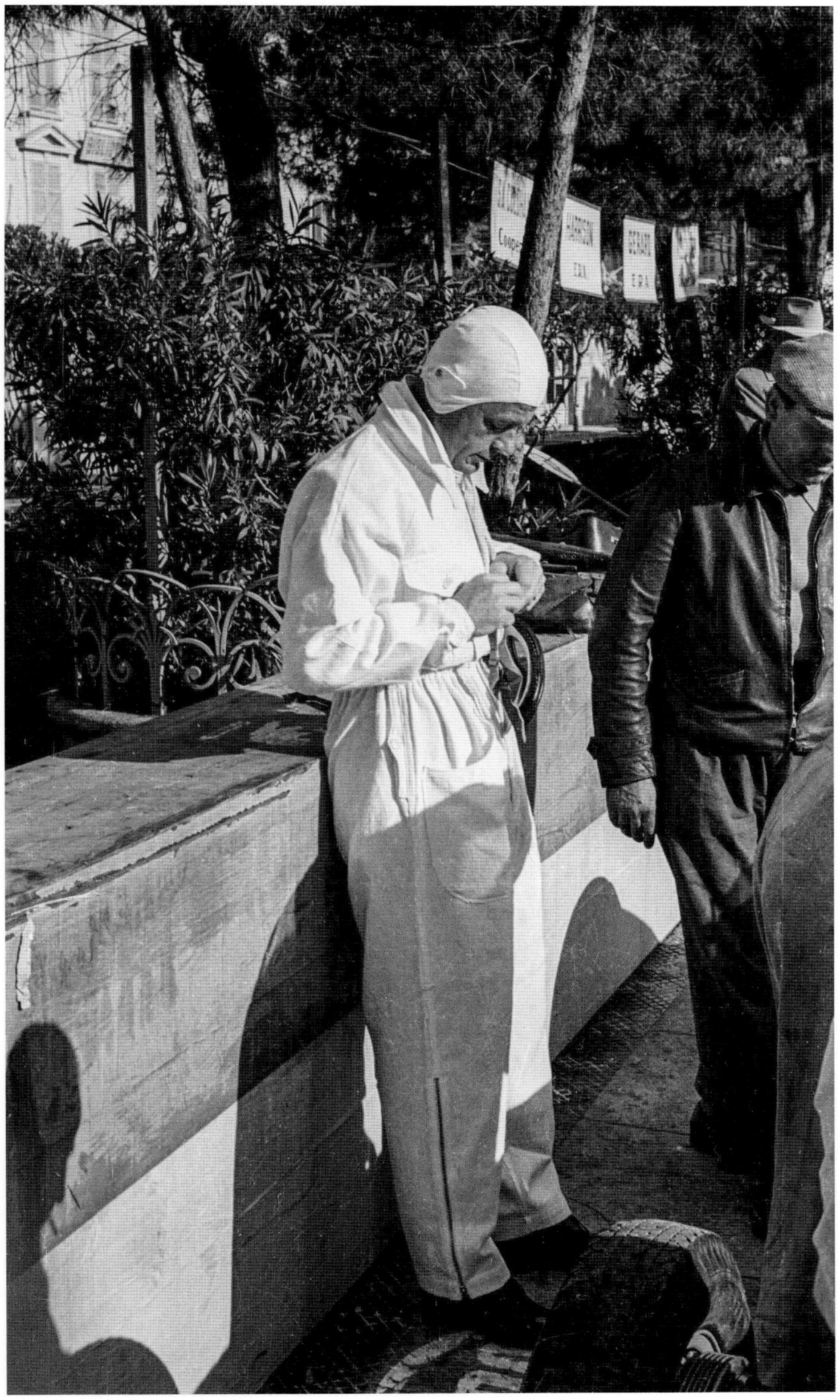

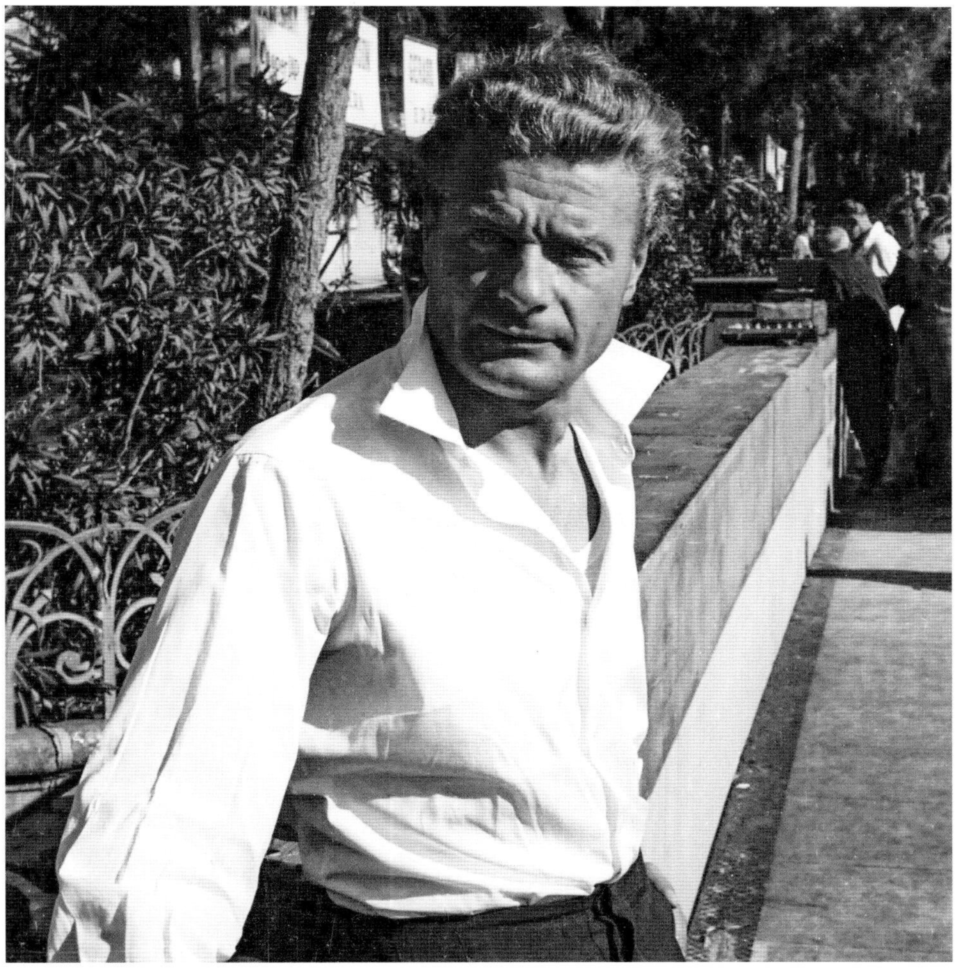

Ein typisches Beispiel für die Gentleman-Rennfahrer dieser Zeit: Franco Rol, Maserati 4CLT N° 44. Er war ein wohlhabender italienischer Aristokrat, der sich mehr in Sportwagen als in Einsitzern einen Namen machte. Er schätzte es, mit Seidenhemd unter blütenweißem Rennoverall zu fahren.
1950 kam Rol in die Formel 1. Er wurde Teamkollege von Louis Chiron bei den Officine Alfieri Maserati S.A. Beim Monaco Grand Prix 1950 gab er sein Debüt, wo er in die Startkollision der ersten Runde verwickelt war.

A typical example of the gentleman racers of the time: Franco Rol, Maserati 4CLT N° 44. He was a wealthy Italian aristocrat who made more of a mark in sports cars than in single-seater competition. He liked to drive in a silk shirt under a pristine white racing suit. In 1950 Rol entered Formula 1, becoming a teammate of Louis Chiron at Officine Alfieri Maserati S.A. He made his debut at the 1950 Monaco Grand Prix, where he was involved in the first lap starting collision.

Juan Manuel Fangio, Alfa Romeo 158 „Alfetta" N° 34.

Luigi Fagioli, Spitzname der „Abruzzen-Räuber", Alfa Romeo 158 „Alfetta" N° 36. Er starb nach einem Unfall im Training zum Großen Preis von Monaco 1952. Sein Lancia Aurelia touchierte im Tunnel den rechten Randstein, prallte gegen die Felsen und überschlug sich.

Luigi Fagioli, nicknamed the "Abruzzi robber", Alfa Romeo 158 "Alfetta" N° 36. He died after an accident during practice for the 1952 Monaco Grand Prix. His Lancia Aurelia hit the right-hand kerb in the tunnel, crashed into the rocks and overturned.

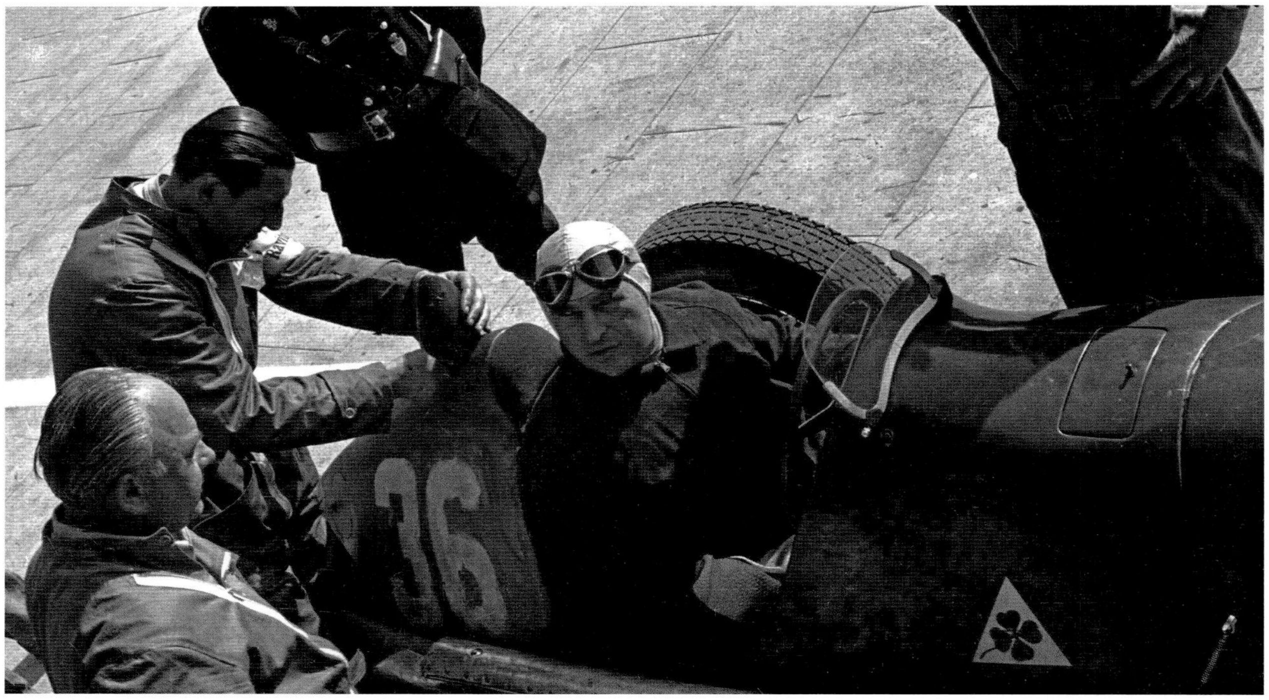

Sicherheit hatte damals eine geringe Bedeutung, man ging hohe Risiken ein. Drei Viertel aller Rennfahrer starb in dieser Periode auf einer Rennstrecke. Und gerade auf dem Stadtkurs von Monaco waren Randsteine, Bäume, Mauern und Häuser ein großes Sicherheitsproblem. Es gab lange keine Leitplanken und nur an einigen Orten dienten Strohballen, Sandsäcke oder Baumstämme einem zweifelhaften Schutz der Fahrer oder Zuschauer. Die Strohballen konnten zudem in Brand geraten, wie das beim schrecklichen Flammentod von Lorenzo Bandini beim Grand Prix 1967 geschah.

Safety was of little importance at that time and people took big risks. Three quarters of all racing drivers died on a race circuit during this period. And especially on the street circuit of Monaco, curbs, trees, walls and houses were a big safety problem. There were no crash barriers for a long time and only in some places did bales of straw, sandbags or tree trunks provide dubious protection for drivers or spectators. The straw bales could also catch fire, as happened in the shocking death of Lorenzo Bandini in the flames at the 1967 Grand Prix.

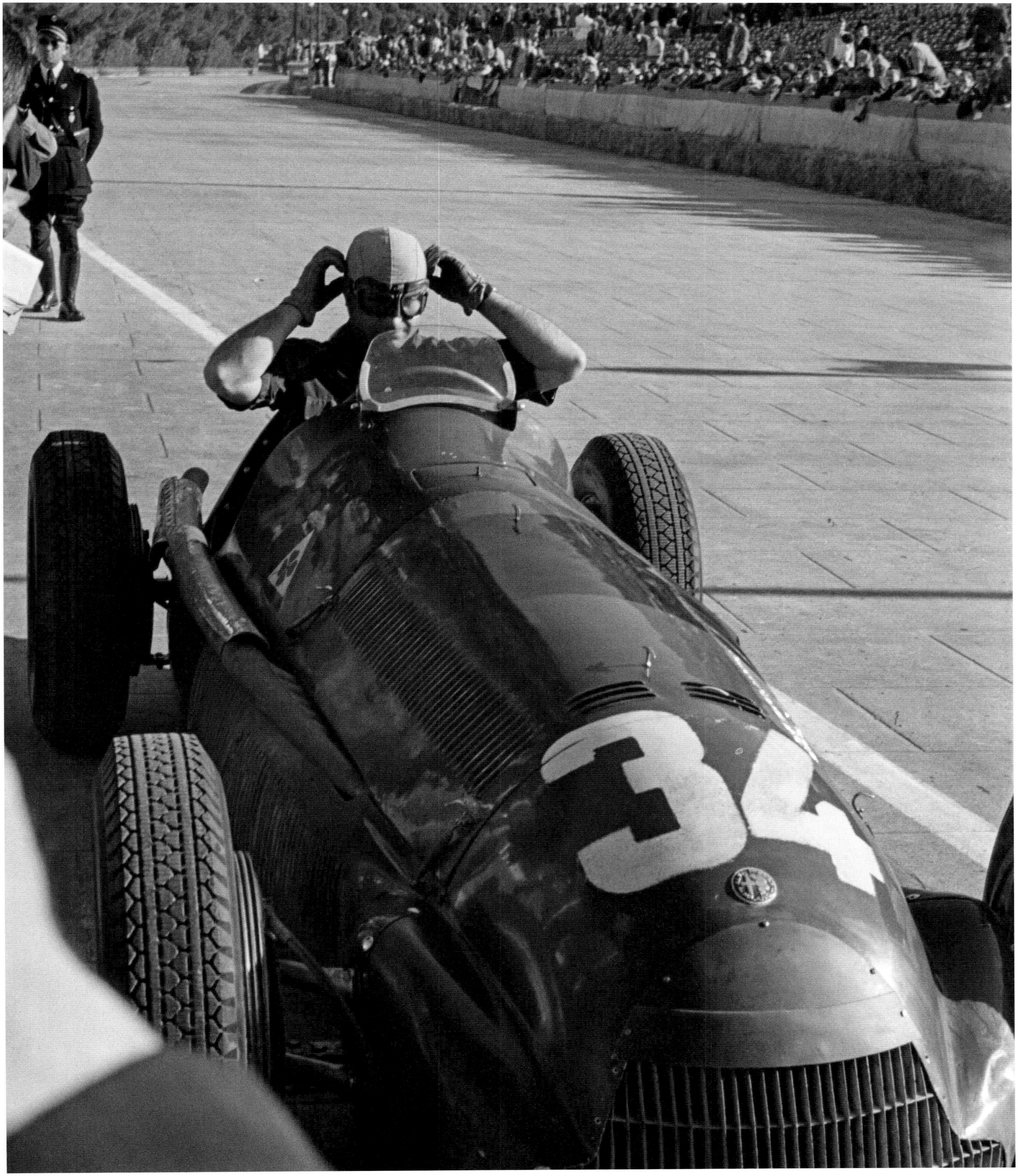

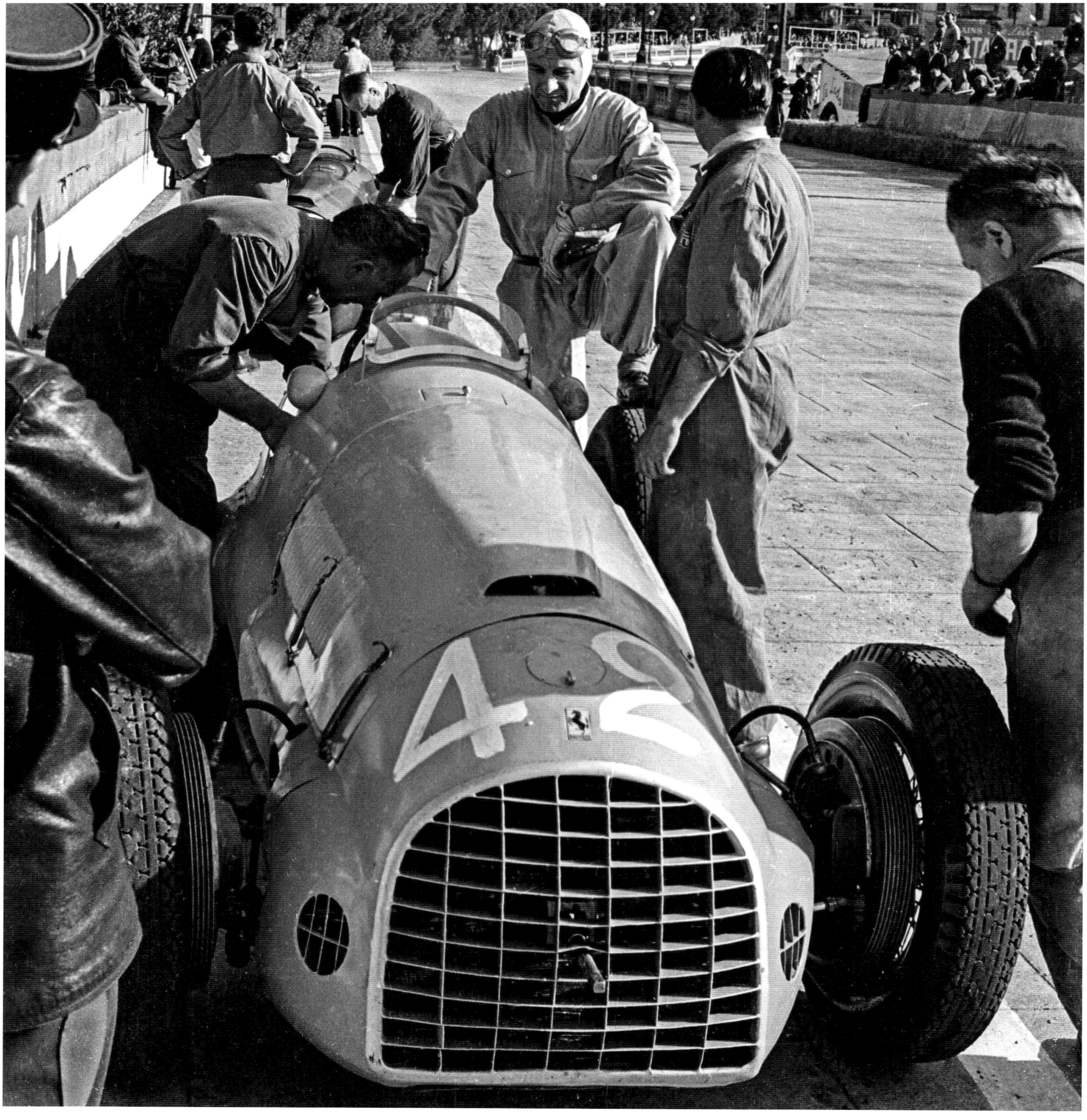

Raymond Sommer,
Ferrari 125 N° 42 mit 4½ Liter V12 Saugmotor.

Raymond Sommer,
Ferrari 125 N° 42 with 4½ litre V12 unsupercharged engine.

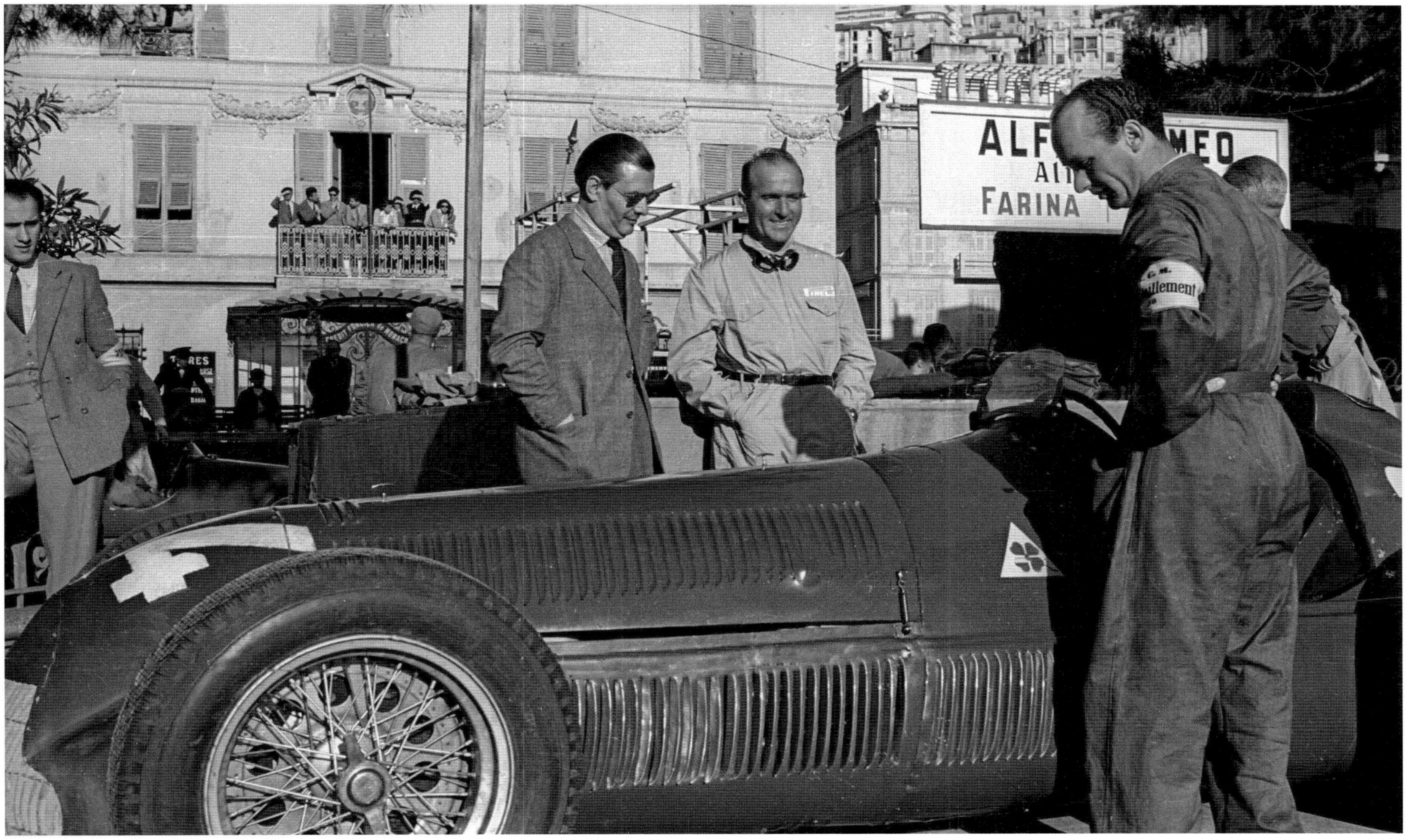

Der erste Formel-1-Weltmeister 1950: Giuseppe „Nino“ Farina, 1½ Liter Alfa Romeo 158 „Alfetta“ N° 34 mit Kompressor. Die Abkürzung 158 bezieht sich auf den Hubraum von 1.500 cm³ und acht Zylinder.

The first Formula 1 world champion 1950: Giuseppe “Nino” Farina, 1½ litre supercharged Alfa Romeo 158 “Alfetta” N° 34. The abbreviation 158 refers to the engine capacity of 1½ litre and eight cylinders.

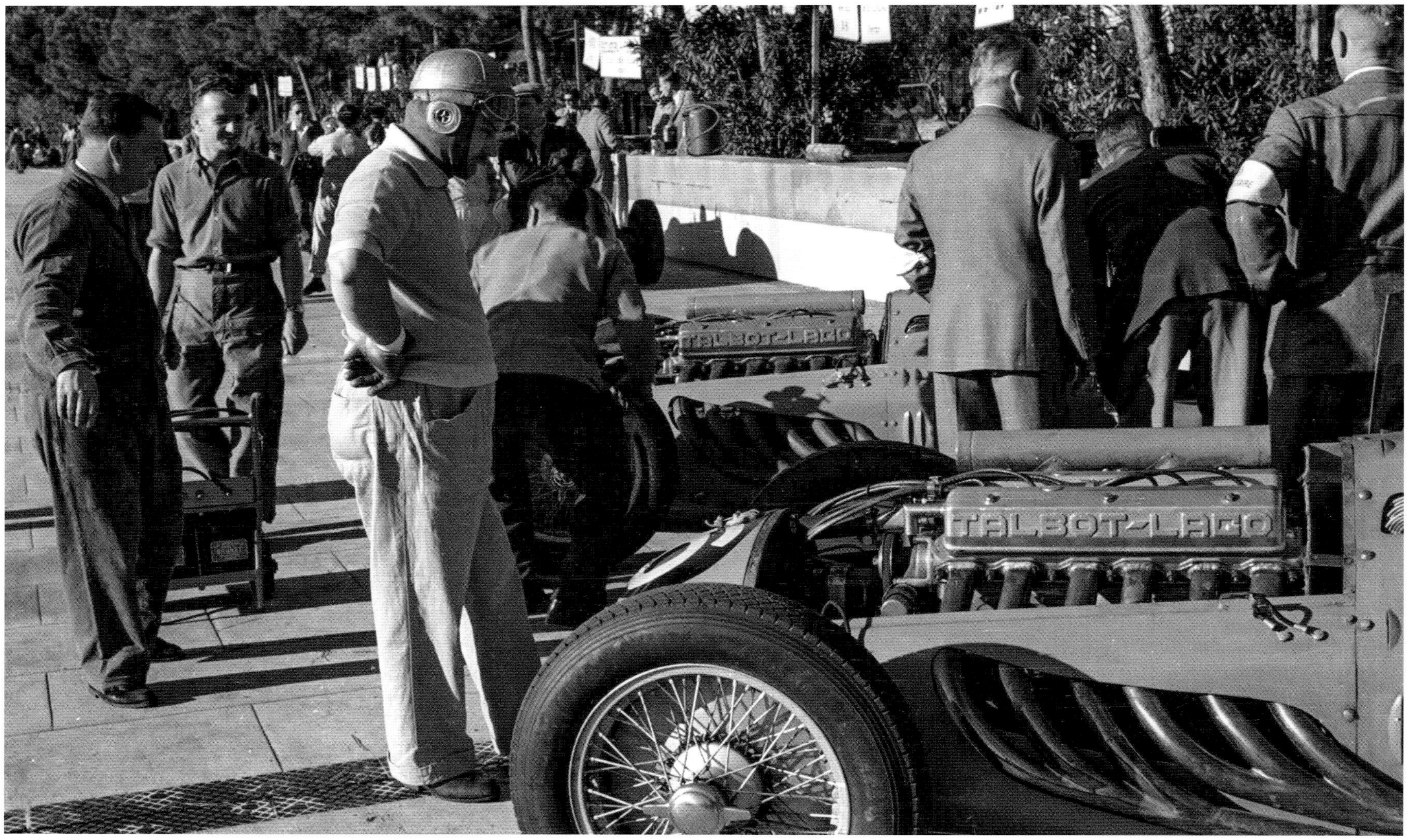

Der Maserati-Pilot Alfredo Pián interessiert sich für die beiden Talbot-Lago T26C N° 16 von Louis Rosier und Johnny Claes N° 6. Er selbst fuhr den Maserati 4CLT N° 4. Am zweiten Tag des Trainings hatte er einen Unfall, wurde aus dem Auto geschleudert und brach sich das rechte Wadenbein.

Maserati driver Alfredo Pián inspects the two Talbot-Lago T26C N° 16 belonging to Louis Rosier and Johnny Claes N° 6. Pian was in Maserati 4CLT/48 N° 4. On the second day of practice he had an accident, was flung from his car and fractured his right fibula.

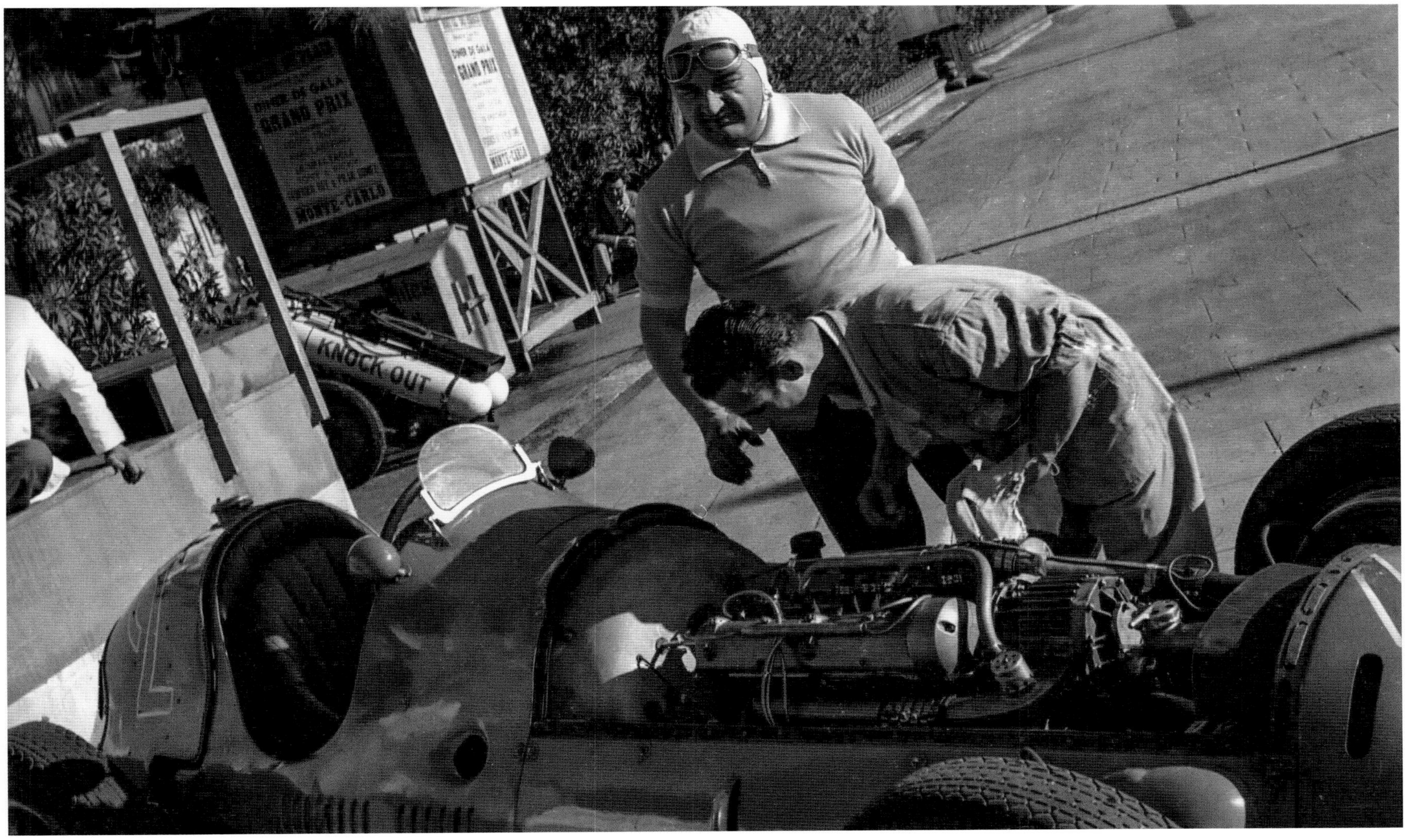

José Froilán González „El Cabezon“ (Großkopf) mit seinem Maserati 4CLT N° 2.

José Froilán González “El Cabezon” (Big Head) with his Maserati 4CLT N° 2.

Eine Neuerung in diesem Jahr ist die Organisation eines Formel-3-Grand-Prix mit Namen „Prix de Monte Carlo“ im Rahmenprogramm. Nicht weniger als 30 kleine 500-cm^3-Einsitzer hatten sich für das Rennen angemeldet.
Ein junger, damals kaum bekannter englischer Fahrer vollbringt in diesen kleinen Autos wahre Wunder. Sein Name ist Stirling Moss, der mit seinem Cooper JAP N° 22 natürlich die Bestzeit aufstellen wird. Moss bricht mehrfach den Rundenrekord und gewinnt mit fast 7 Sekunden auf Harry Schell. Dies ist der erste große Sieg für den talentierten englischen Fahrer.

An innovation this year was the organization of a Supporting Race, a 500cc Formula 3 Grand Prix called the Prix de Monte Carlo. No fewer than 30 of the little single seaters entered the race.
A little-known young English driver drove one of these small cars. His name was Stirling Moss. He would naturally set the best time with his Cooper JAP N° 22. Moss broke the lap record repeatedly and won with almost 7 seconds over Harry Schell. This was the first major win for the talented English driver.

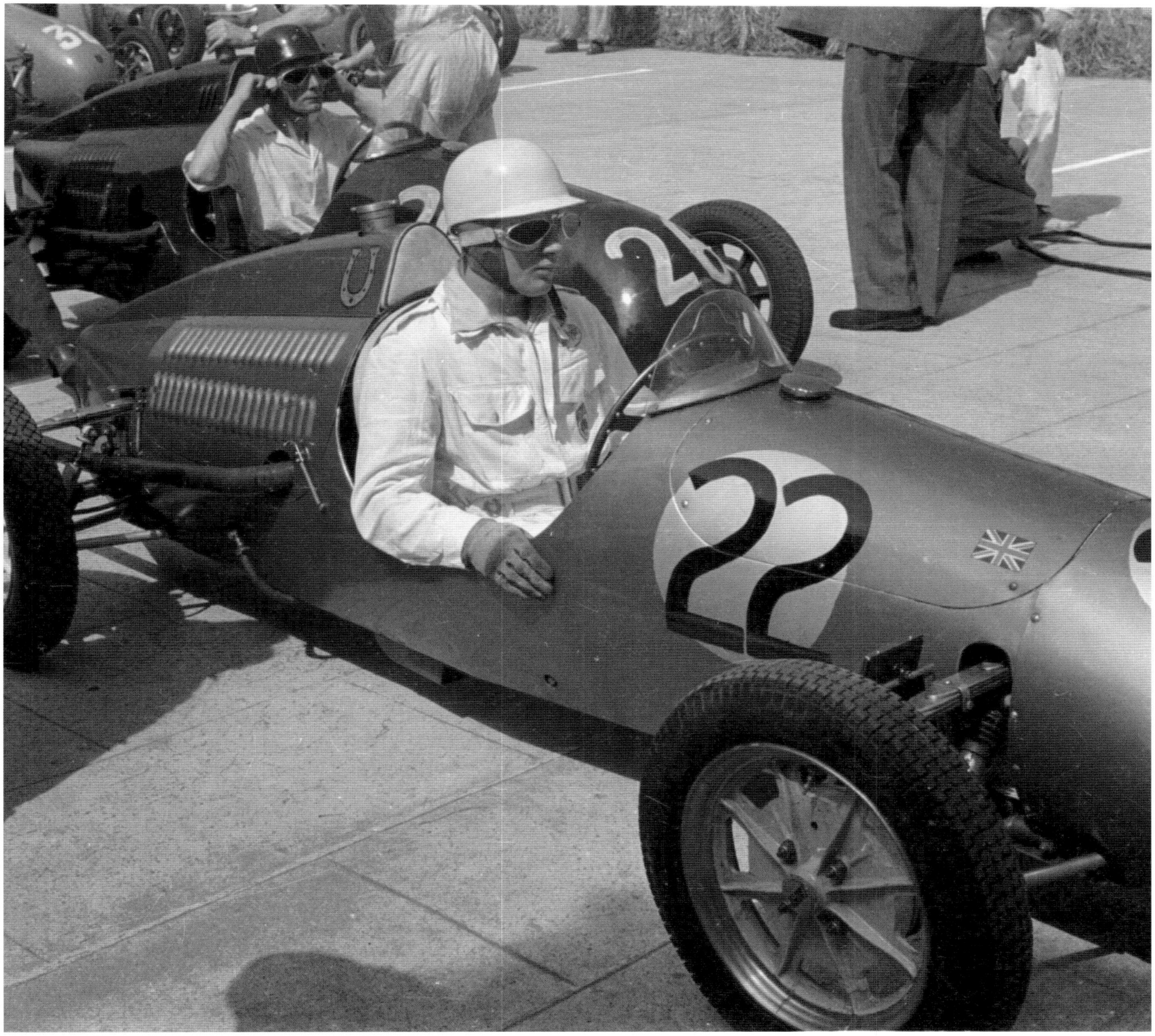
22

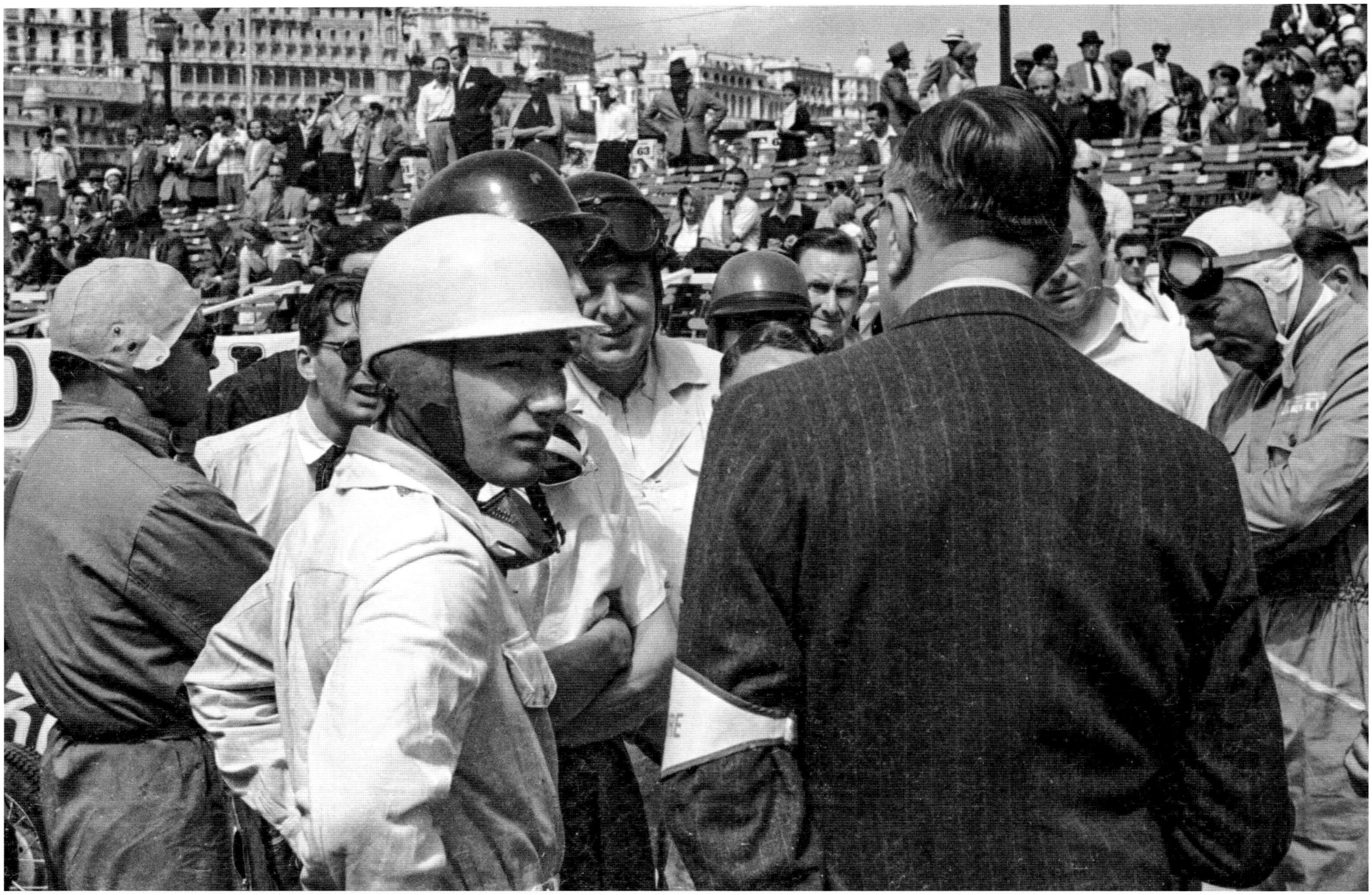

Fahrerbesprechung. SCM (Stirling Craufurd Moss)
mit weißem Helm. Hinter ihm (mit Sonnenbrille) Bob Gerard.

*Drivers' briefing. SCM (Stirling Craufurd Moss) wearing a
white helmet. Behind him (in sunglasses) Bob Gerard.*

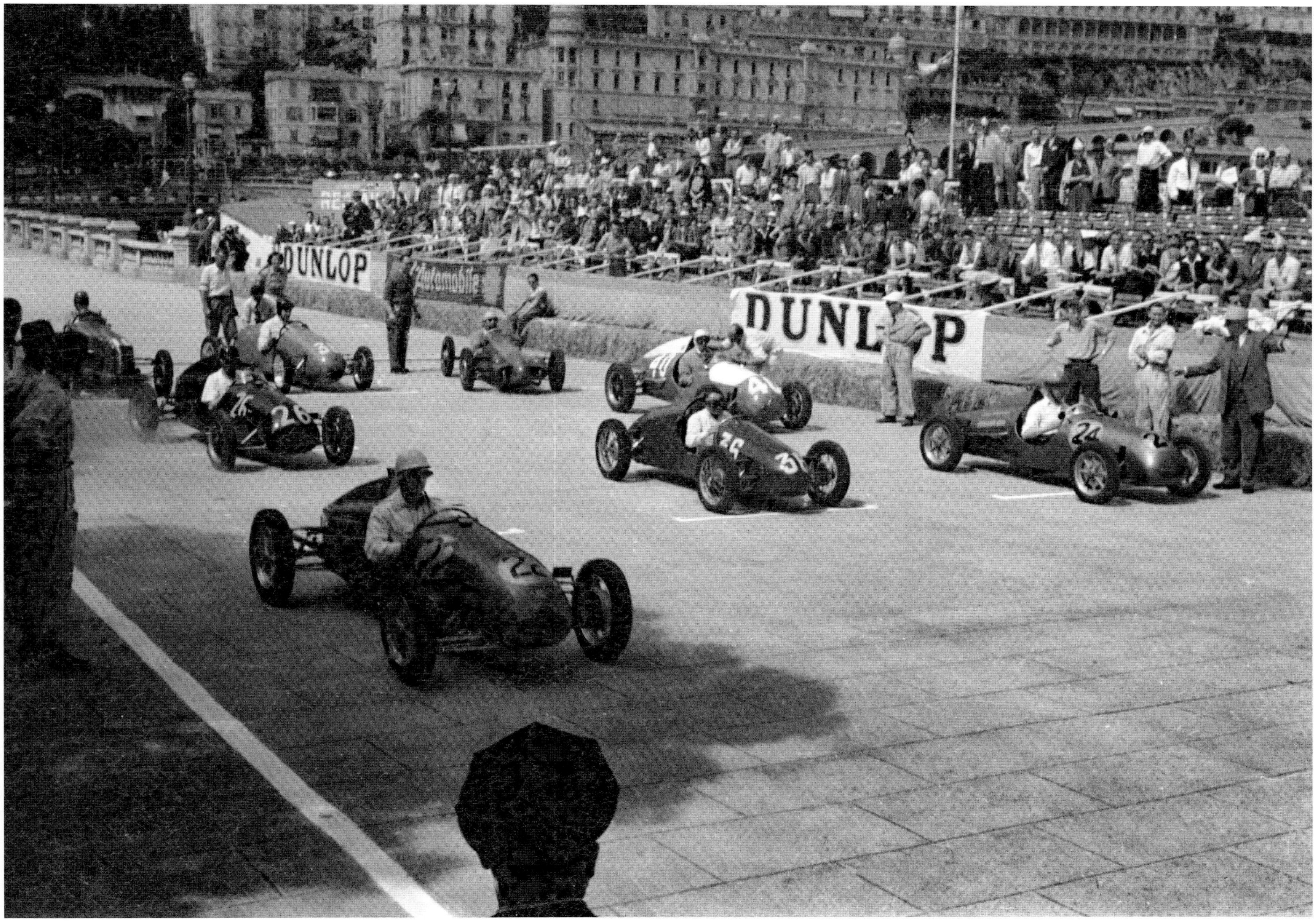

In der ersten Reihe der ersten Serie: Stirling Moss, Cooper JAP N° 22.

On the front row of the first heat: Stirling Moss, Cooper JAP N° 22.

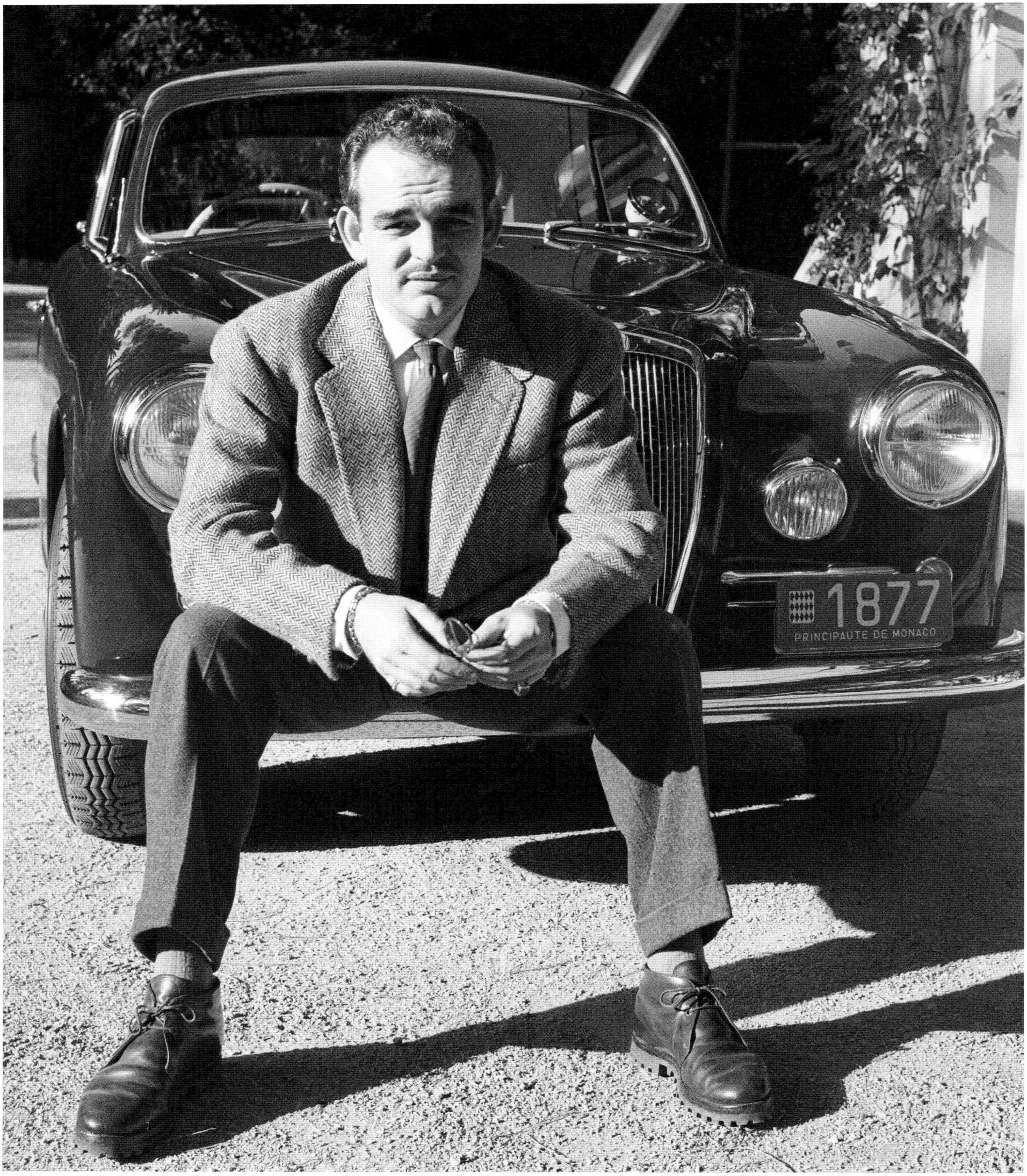
1877
PRINCIPAUTE DE MONACO

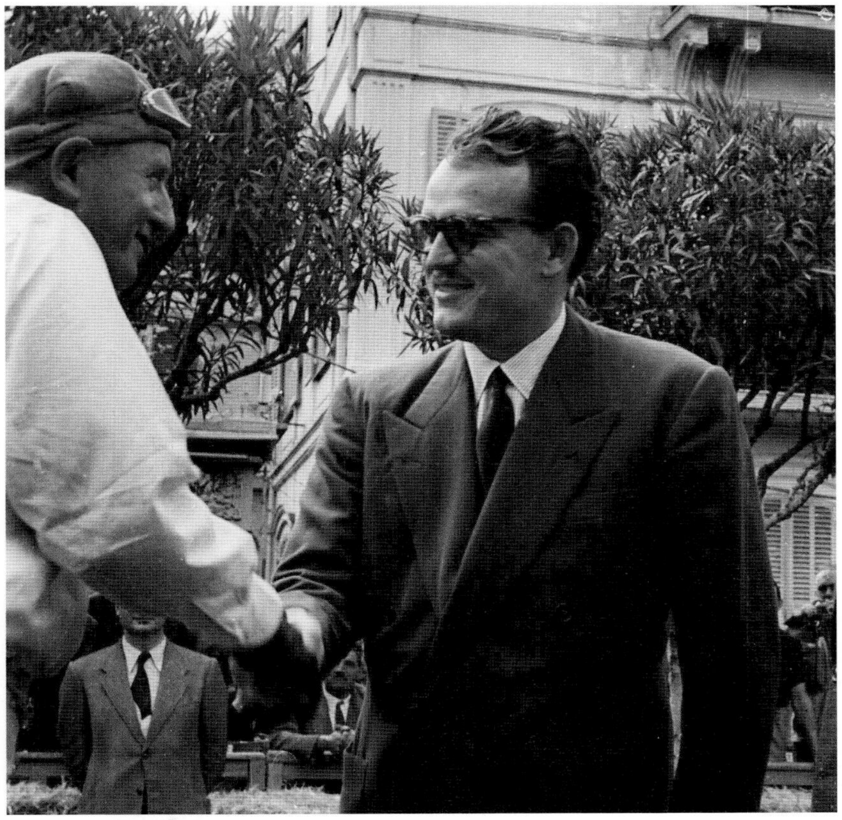

Fürst Rainier begrüßt Philippe Etancelin, Fahrer des Talbot-Lago T26C N° 14.

Prince Rainier welcomes Philippe Etancelin, driver of the Talbot-Lago T26C N° 14.

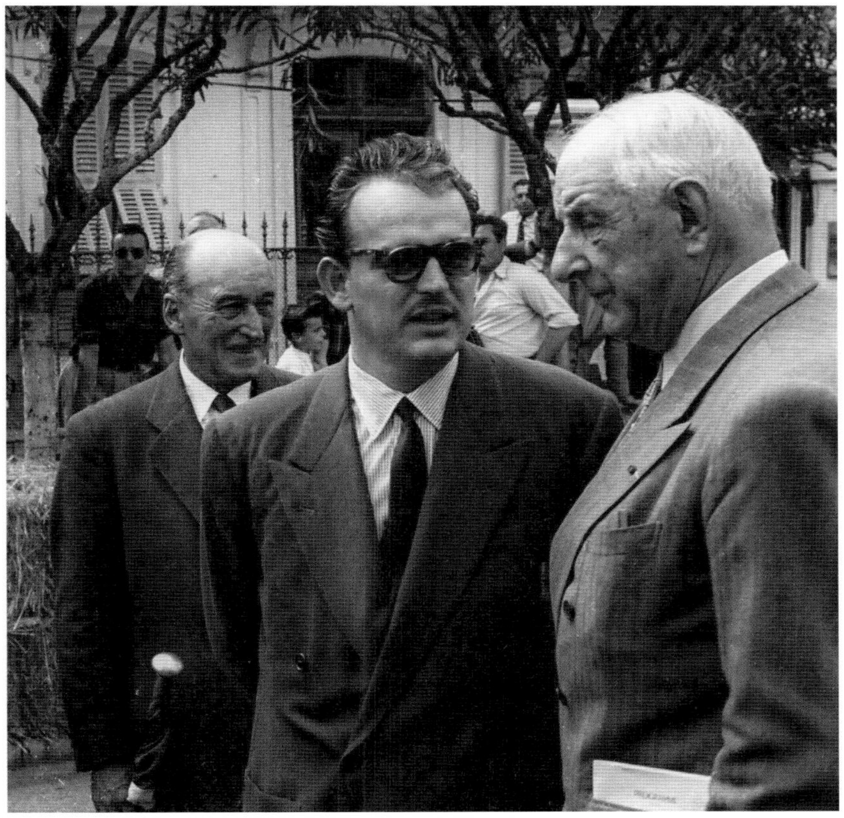

Fürst Rainier und Charles Faroux, Rennleiter seit dem ersten Rennen 1929. Hinter Rainier (mit Flagge) der Gründer des Grand Prix, Antony Noghès. Er war auch an der Gründung der Rallye Monte-Carlo im Jahr 1911 beteiligt. Er schlug die karierte Flagge zum Beenden von Rennen vor.

Prince Rainier and Charles Faroux, Clerk of the Course since the first race in 1929. Behind Rainier with the flag is the founder of the Grand Prix Antony Noghès. He also helped create the Monte-Carlo Rally in 1911. In addition he suggested the international adoption of the chequered flag to end races.

Der Autoenthusiast Fürst Rainier von Monaco 1954 vor seiner Villa Iberia in Saint-Jean-Cap-Ferrat mit seinem Lancia Aurelia B20 Gran Turismo 2500. Er nahm unter dem Pseudonym Louis Carladès mit einem Panhard DB Frua coupé an der Tour de France Automobile 1953 teil. Auf der Nordroute verlor er die Kontrolle über den Wagen und beendete das Rennen in einem Graben.

Car enthusiast Prince Rainier of Monaco in 1954 in front of his Villa Iberia in Saint-Jean-Cap-Ferrat with his Lancia Aurelia B20 Gran Turismo 2500. He competed with a Panhard DB Frua coupé in the Tour de France Automobile 1953 under the pseudonym of Louis Carladès. On the northern route, he lost control of the car and ended up in a ditch.

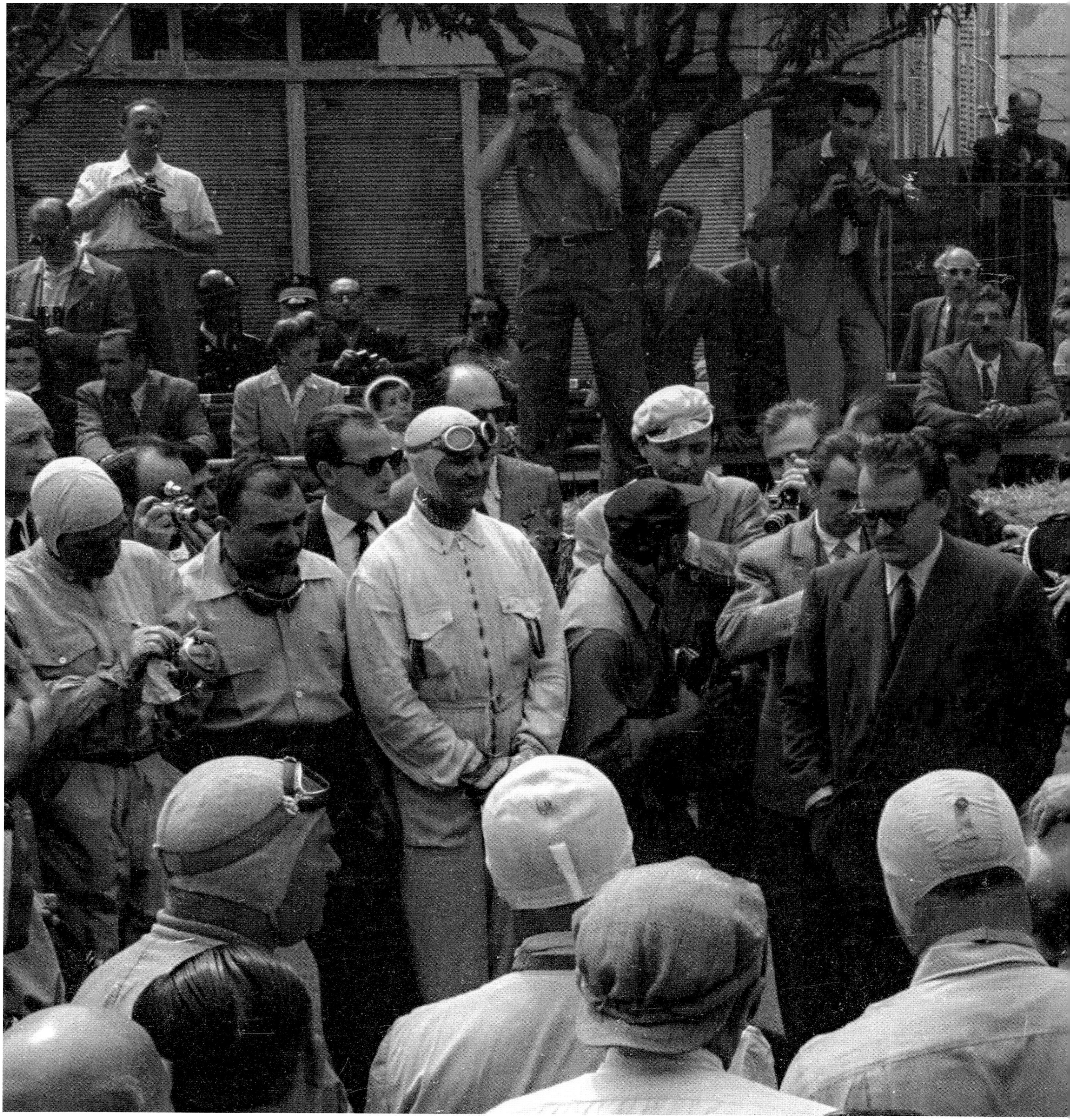

Fürst Rainier bei der Fahrerbesprechung. Charles Faroux, Rennleiter, erinnert an die Streckenregeln, die Pflichten jedes Fahrers, die Regeln für das Überholen und die Bedeutung der verschiedenen Flaggen.

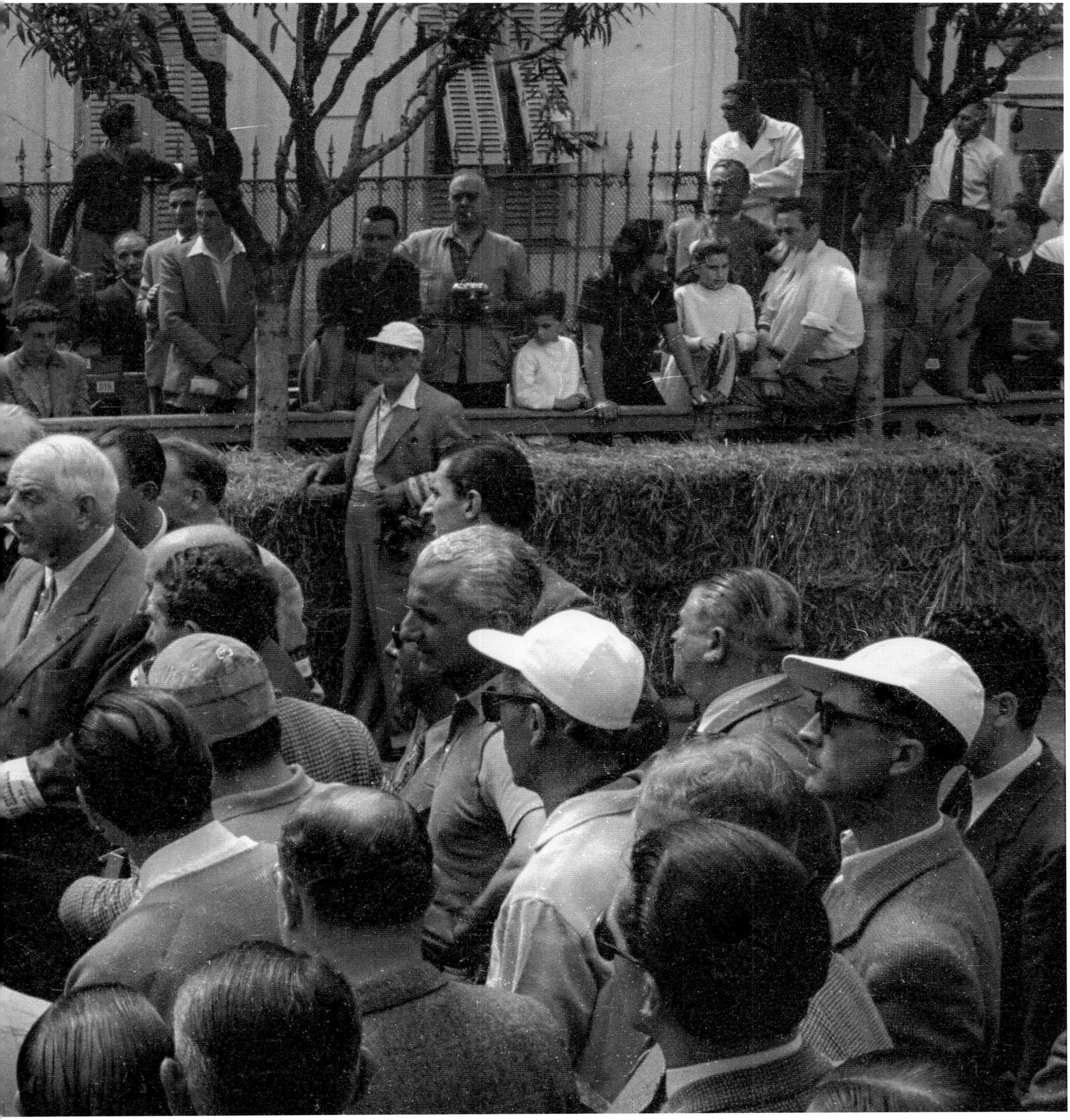

Prince Rainier at the drivers' briefing. Charles Faroux, Clerk of the Course, reminds the competitors of the course rules, the duties of each driver, the rules for overtaking and the meaning of the different flags.

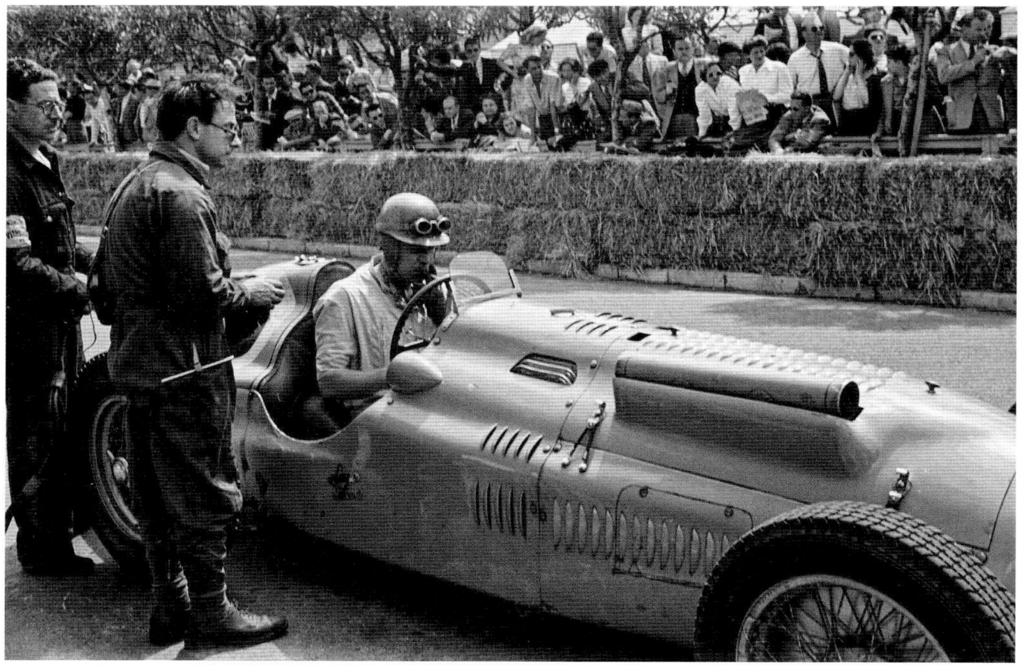

Johnny Claes, Talbot-Lago T26C N° 6.

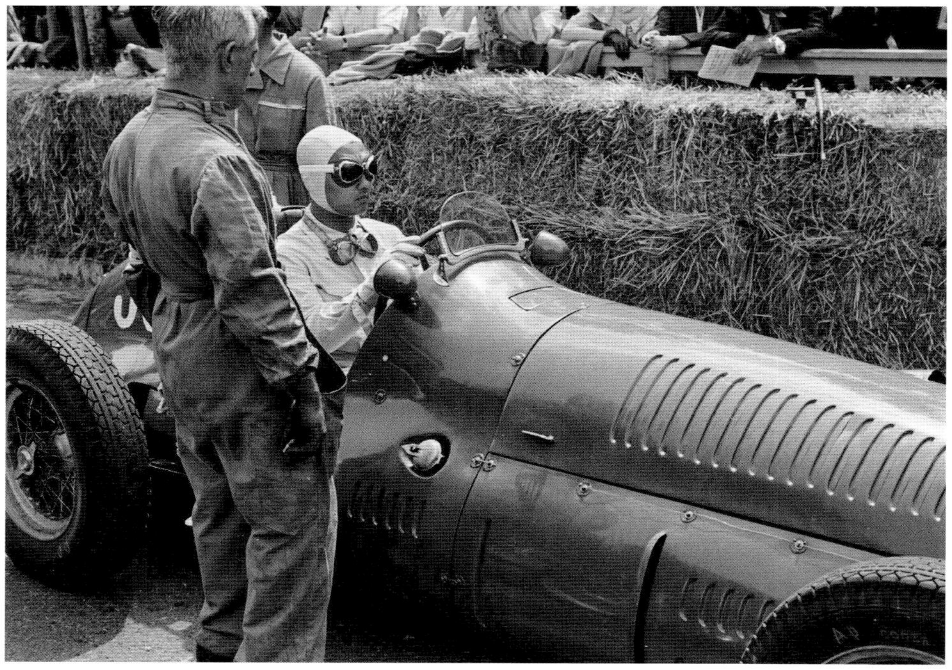

Prince Bira, Maserati 4CLT N° 50.

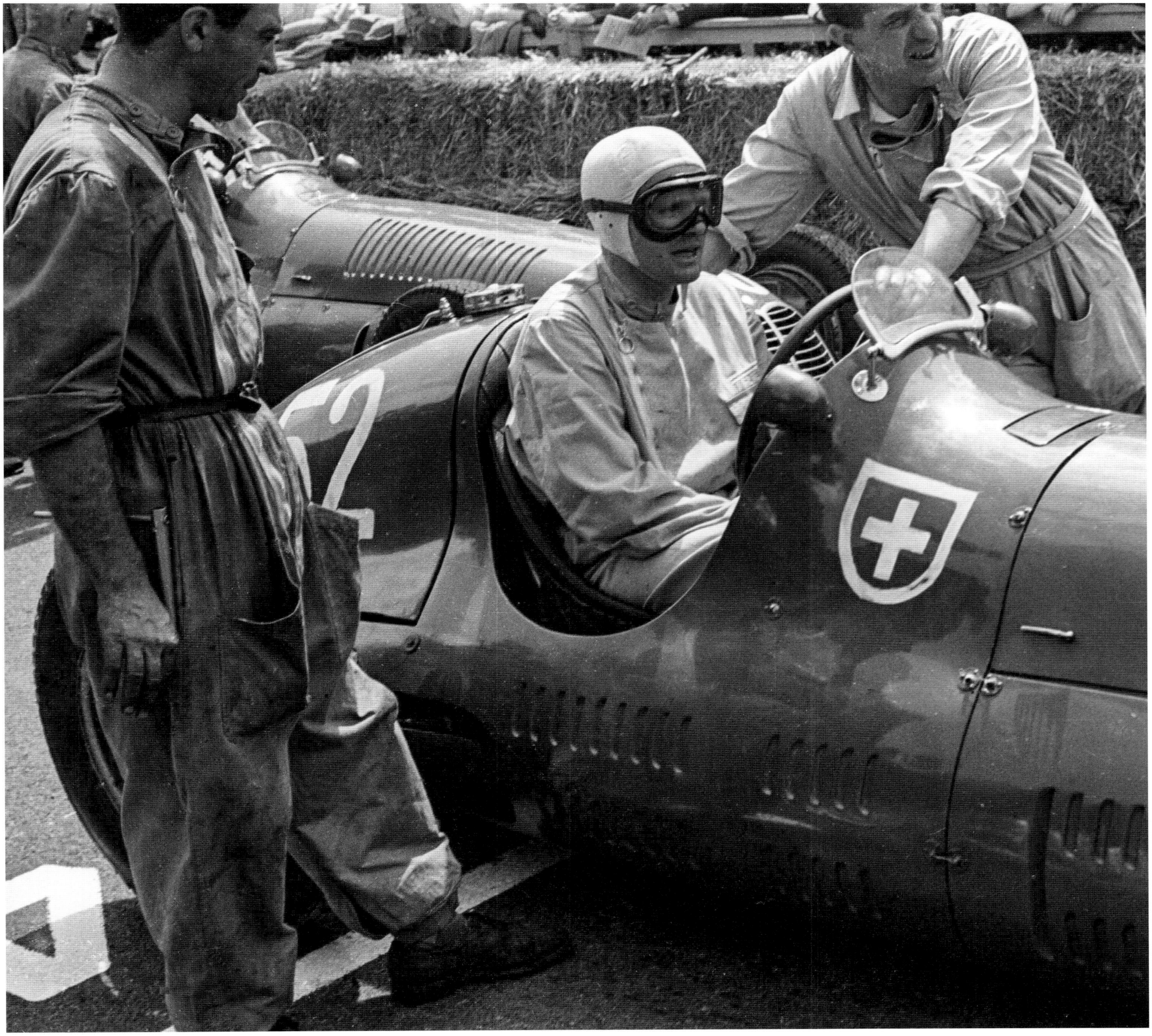

Toulo de Graffenried, Maserati 4CLT N° 52.

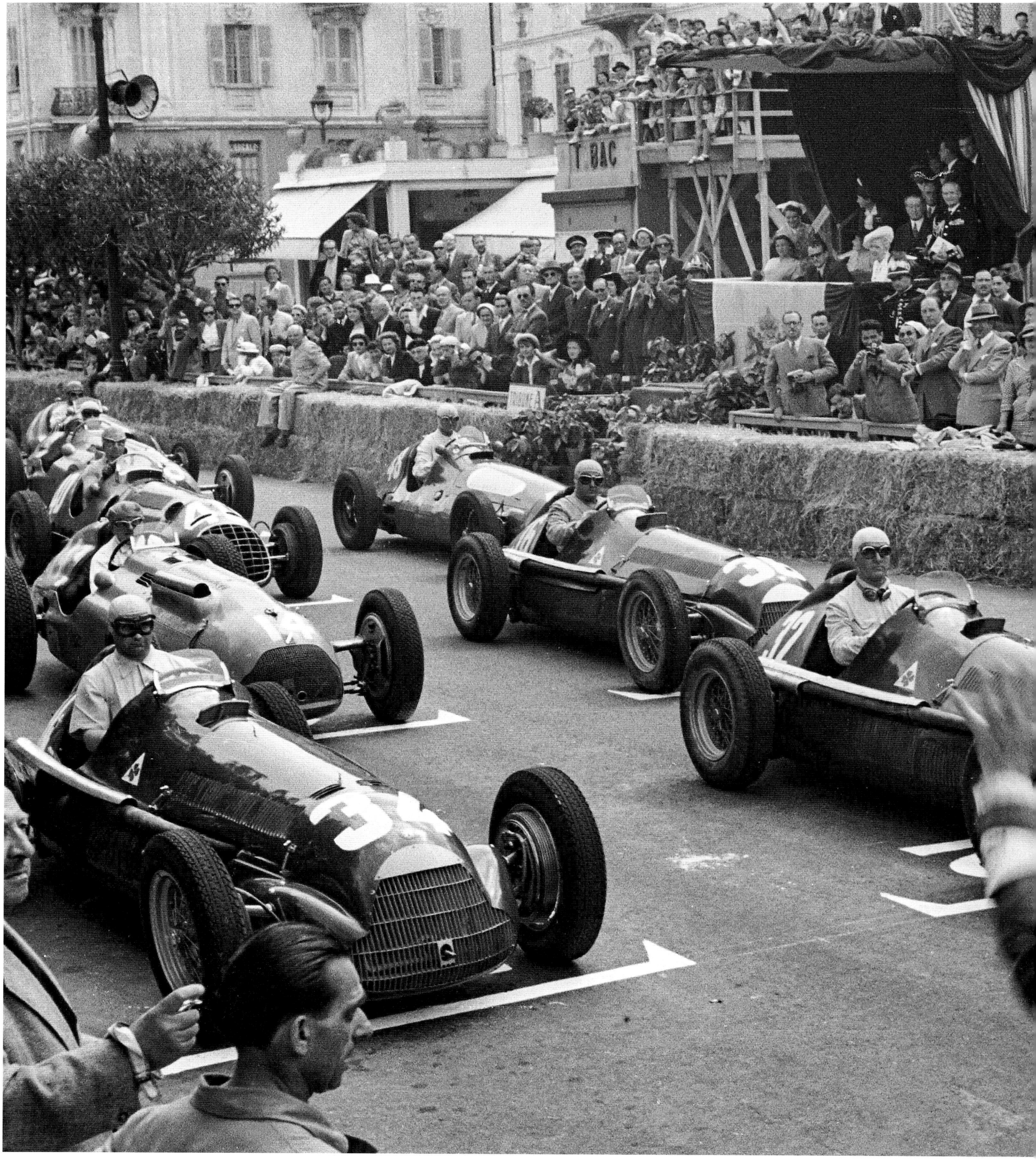

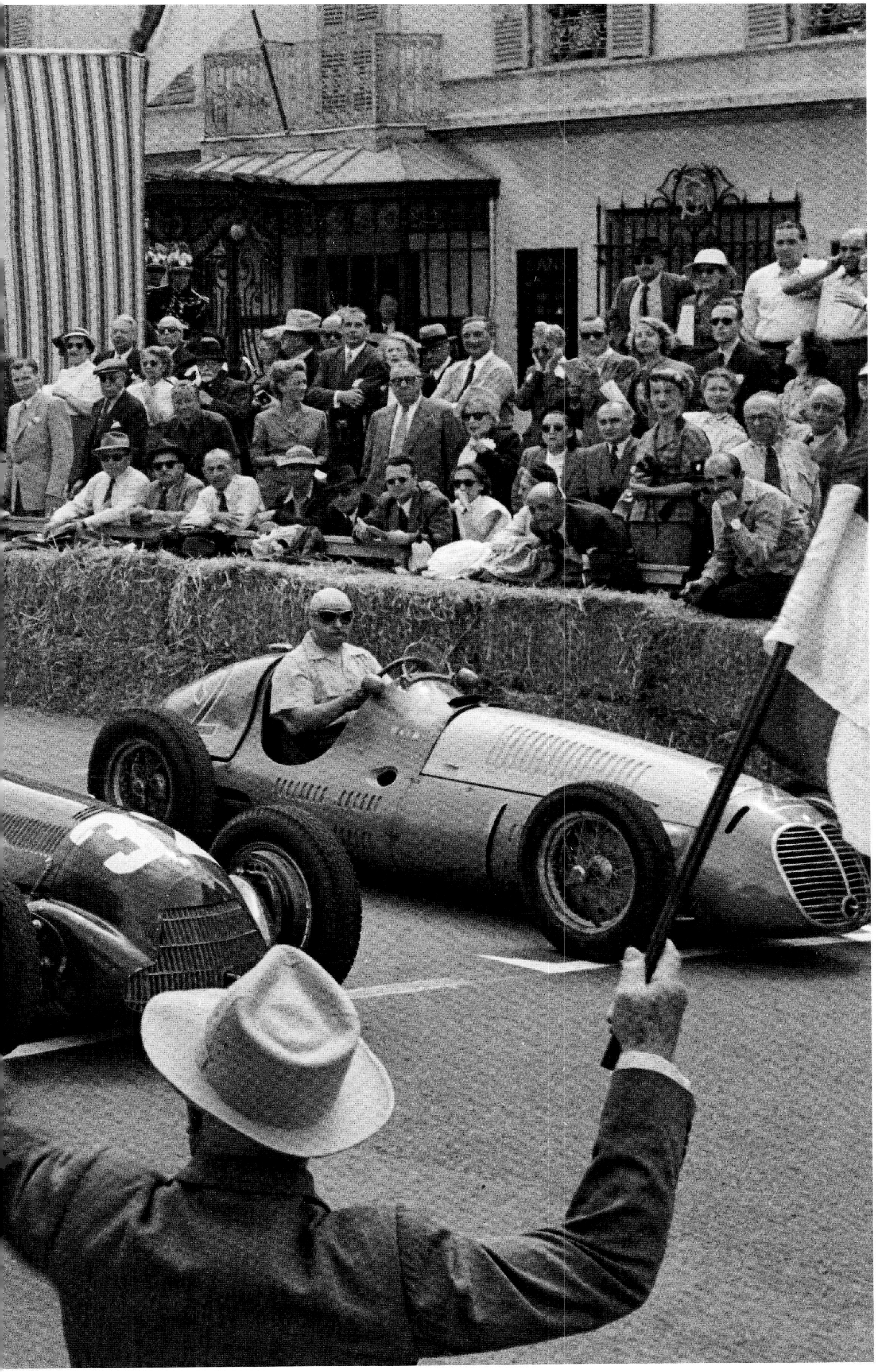

Grand Prix 1950

Mit der Fahne in der Hand gibt Charles Faroux, seit der ersten Ausgabe Rennleiter, den Start. Juan Manuel Fangio, Alfa Romeo 158 „Alfetta“ N° 34, Sieger des Grand Prix, Giuseppe „Nino“ Farina, Alfa Romeo 158 N° 32, José Froilán González, Maserati 4CLT N° 2, Philippe Etancelin, Talbot-Lago T26C N° 14, Luigi Fagioli, Alfa Romeo 158 N° 36, Alberto Ascari, Ferrari 125 N° 40, Louis Chiron, Maserati 4CLT N° 48.

With flag in hand, Charles Faroux, race director since the first edition of the race, gives the start. Juan Manuel Fangio, Alfa Romeo 158 "Alfetta" N° 34, winner of the Grand Prix, Giuseppe "Nino" Farina, Alfa Romeo 158 N° 32, Jose Froilan Gonzales, Maserati 4CLT N° 2, Philippe Etancelin, Talbot-Lago T26C N° 14, Luigi Fagioli, Alfa Romeo 158 N° 36, Alberto Ascari, Ferrari 125 N° 40, Louis Chiron, Maserati 4CLT N° 48.

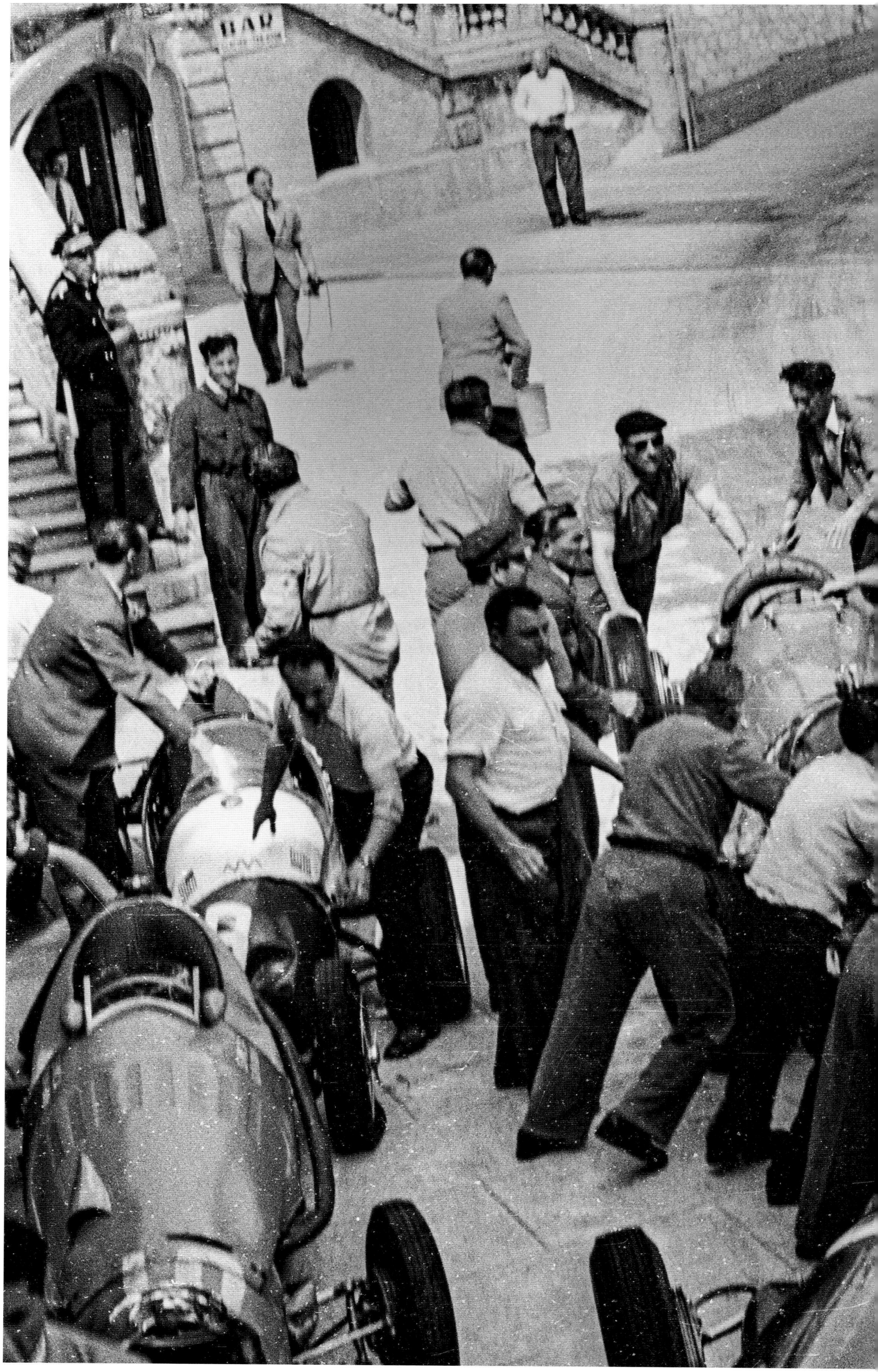

Teurer Schrottplatz: Die erste Runde war für viele Fahrer die einzige. Beim Bureau de Tabac fordert der Kurs seine ersten Opfer. Gischt, die über die Hafenmauer schwappt, verändert die gesamte Ausgangslage. Giuseppe „Nino“ Farina, Alfa Romeo 158 „Alfetta“ N° 32, Robert Manzon, Simca Gordini N° 10, Cuth Harrison, ERA R8C N° 24, Harry Schell, Cooper JAP N° 8, Franco Rol, Maserati 4CLT N° 44.

An expensive scrapyard: the first lap was the only one seen by many of the drivers. At the Bureau de Tabac, the accident on the first lap claimed its first victims. Spray from the waves hitting the harbour wall changed the whole race order. Giuseppe "Nino" Farina, Alfa Romeo 158 "Alfetta" N° 32, Robert Manzon, Simca Gordini N° 10, Cuth Harrison, ERA R8C N° 24, Harry Schell, Cooper JAP N° 8, Franco Rol, Maserati 4CLT N° 44.

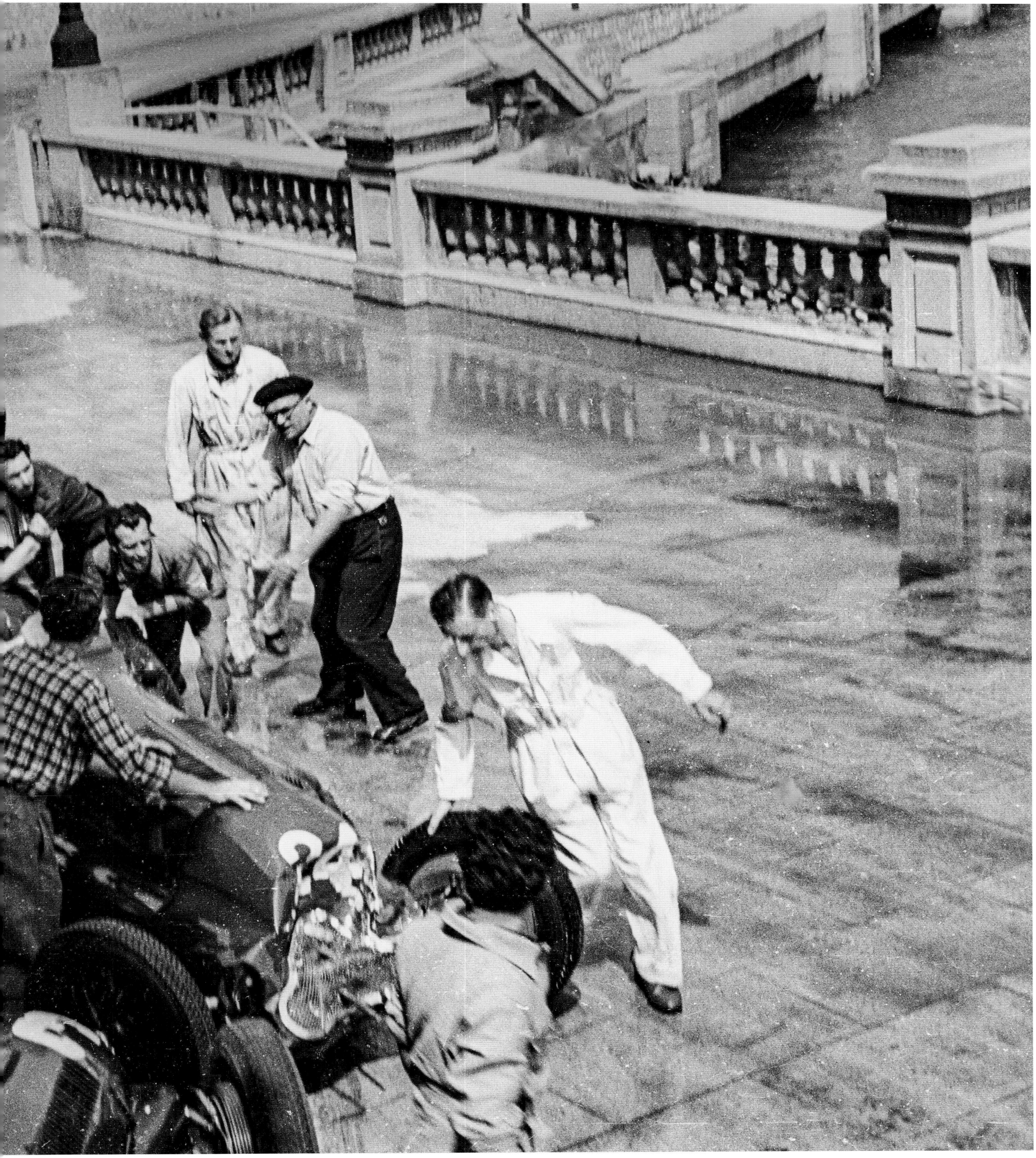

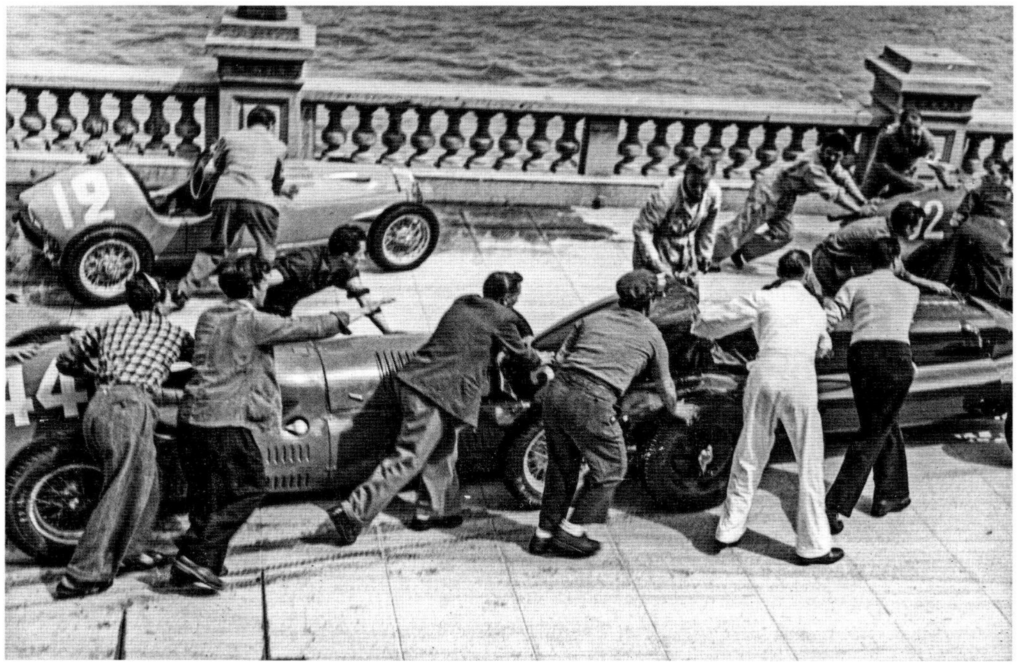

Die Schrottfahrzeuge von Franco Rol, Maserati 4CLT N° 44, Cuth Harrison, ERA R8C N° 24, Toulo de Graffenried, Maserati 4CLT N° 52, und Maurice Trintignant, Simca Gordini N°12.

The damaged cars belonging to Franco Rol, Maserati 4CLT N° 44, Cuth Harrison, ERA R8C N° 24, Toulo de Graffenried, Maserati 4CLT N° 52, and Maurice Trintignant, Simca Gordini N° 12.

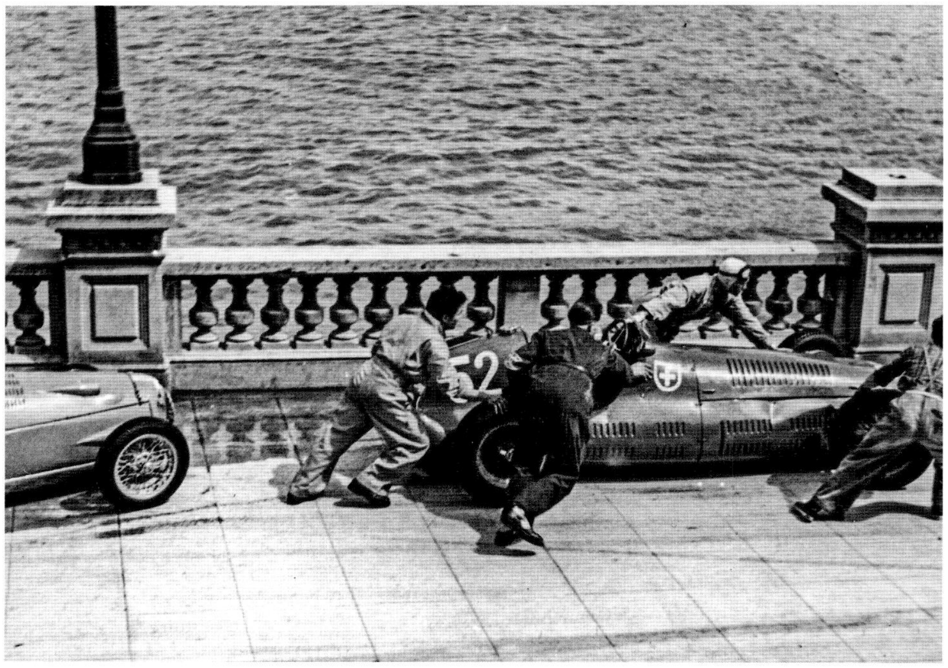

Toulo de Graffenried, schiebt seinen Maserati 4CLT/48 N° 52 mithilfe von freiwilligen Streckenposten zur Seite.

Toulo de Graffenried pushes his Maserati 4CLT N° 52 aside with the help of volunteer marshals.

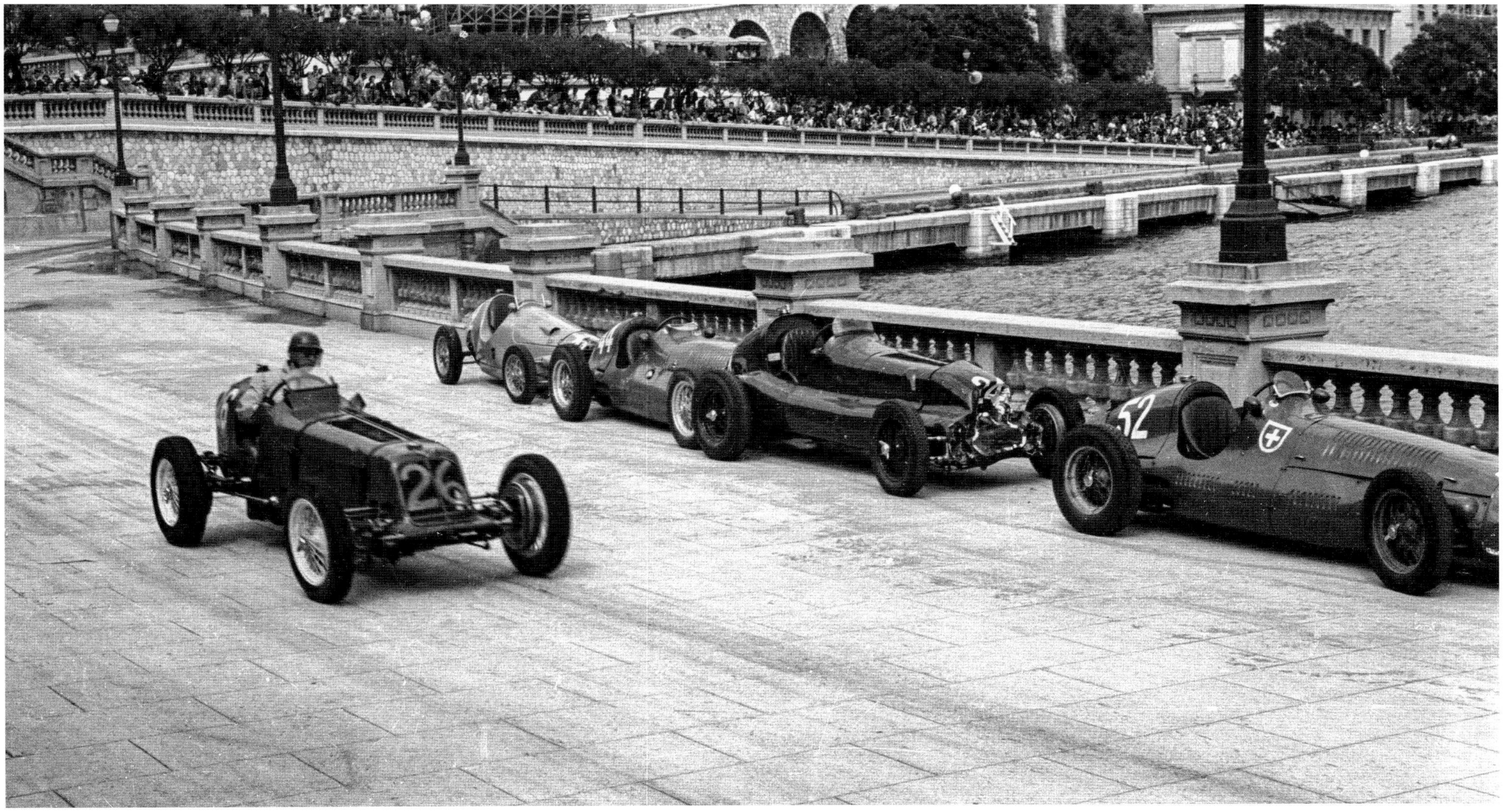

Bob Gerard, ERA R4A N° 26, passiert die geparkten Fahrzeuge von Toulo de Graffenried, Maserati 4CLT N° 52, Cuth Harrison, ERA R8C N° 24, Franco Rol, Maserati 4CLT N° 44 und Maurice Trintignant, Simca Gordini N° 12.

Bob Gerard, ERA R4A N° 26, passes the abandoned cars of Toulo de Graffenried, Maserati 4CLT N° 52, Cuth Harrison, ERA R8C N° 24, Franco Rol, Maserati 4CLT N° 44 and Maurice Trintignant, Simca Gordini N° 12.

Grand Prix 1950

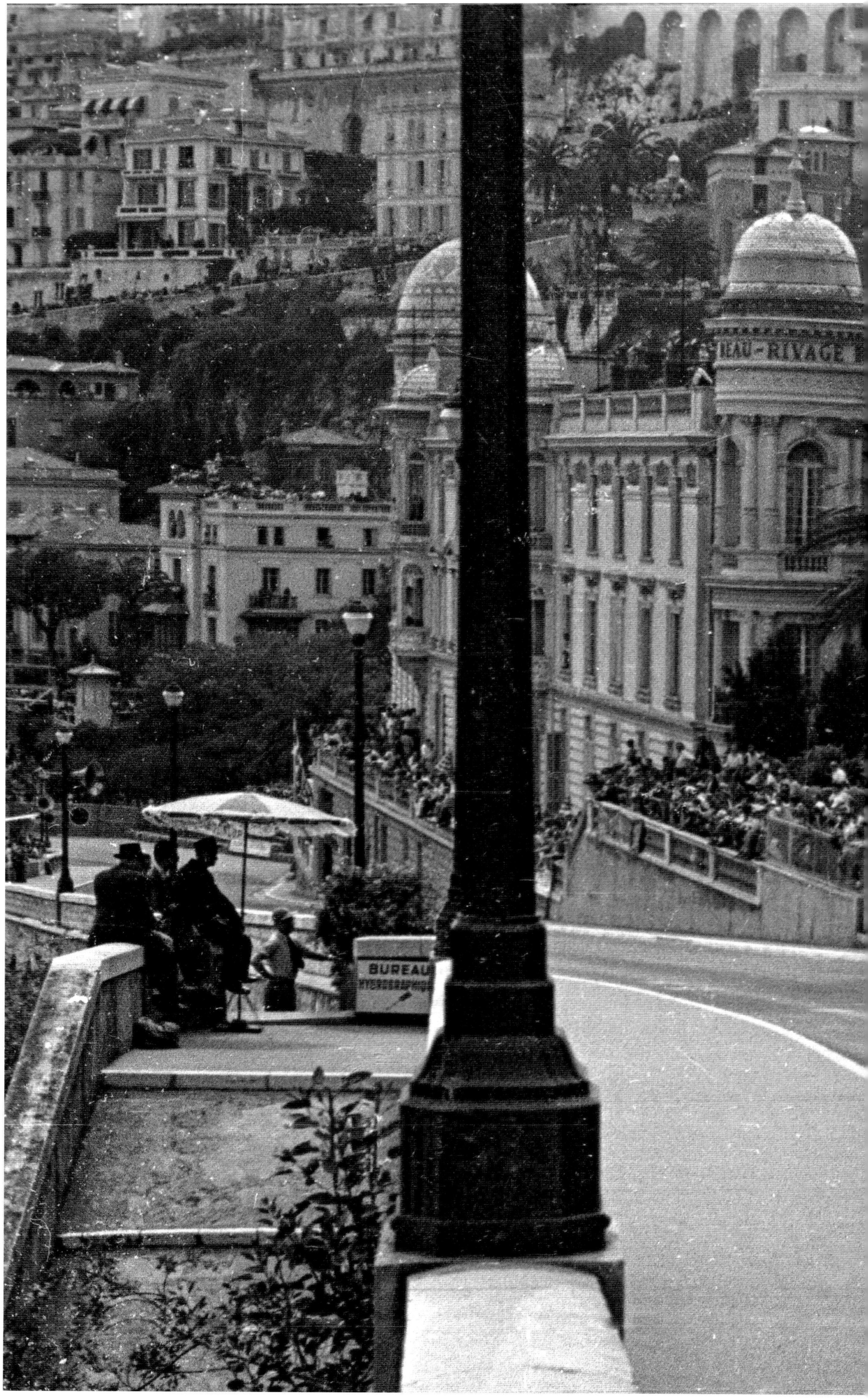

Die Avenue d'Ostende hinauf am Hôtel Beau Rivage vorbei: Luigi Villoresi, Ferrari 125 N° 38.

Up the Avenue d'Ostende past the Hôtel Beau Rivage: Luigi Villoresi, Ferrari 125 N° 38.

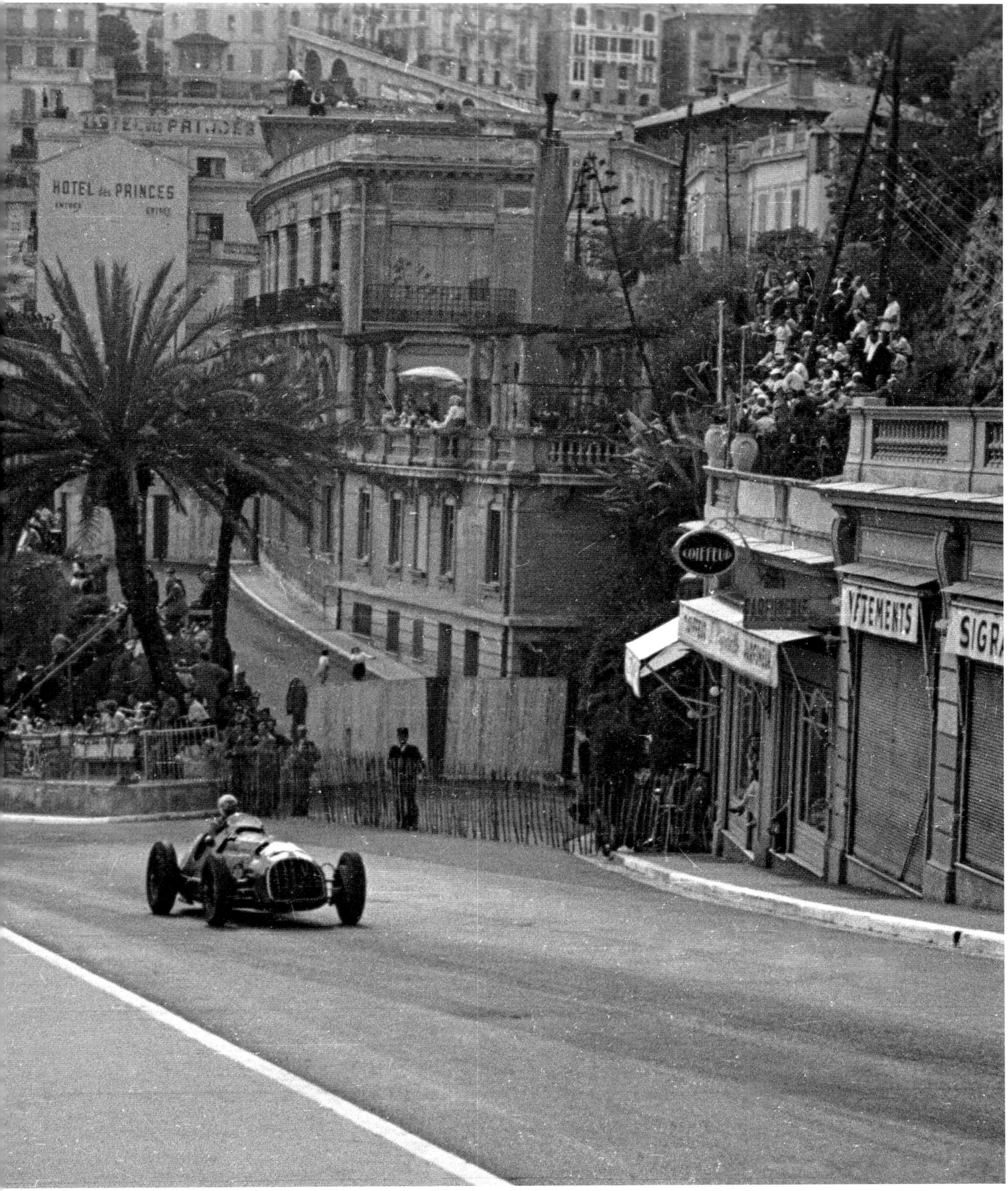
HOTEL des PRINCES

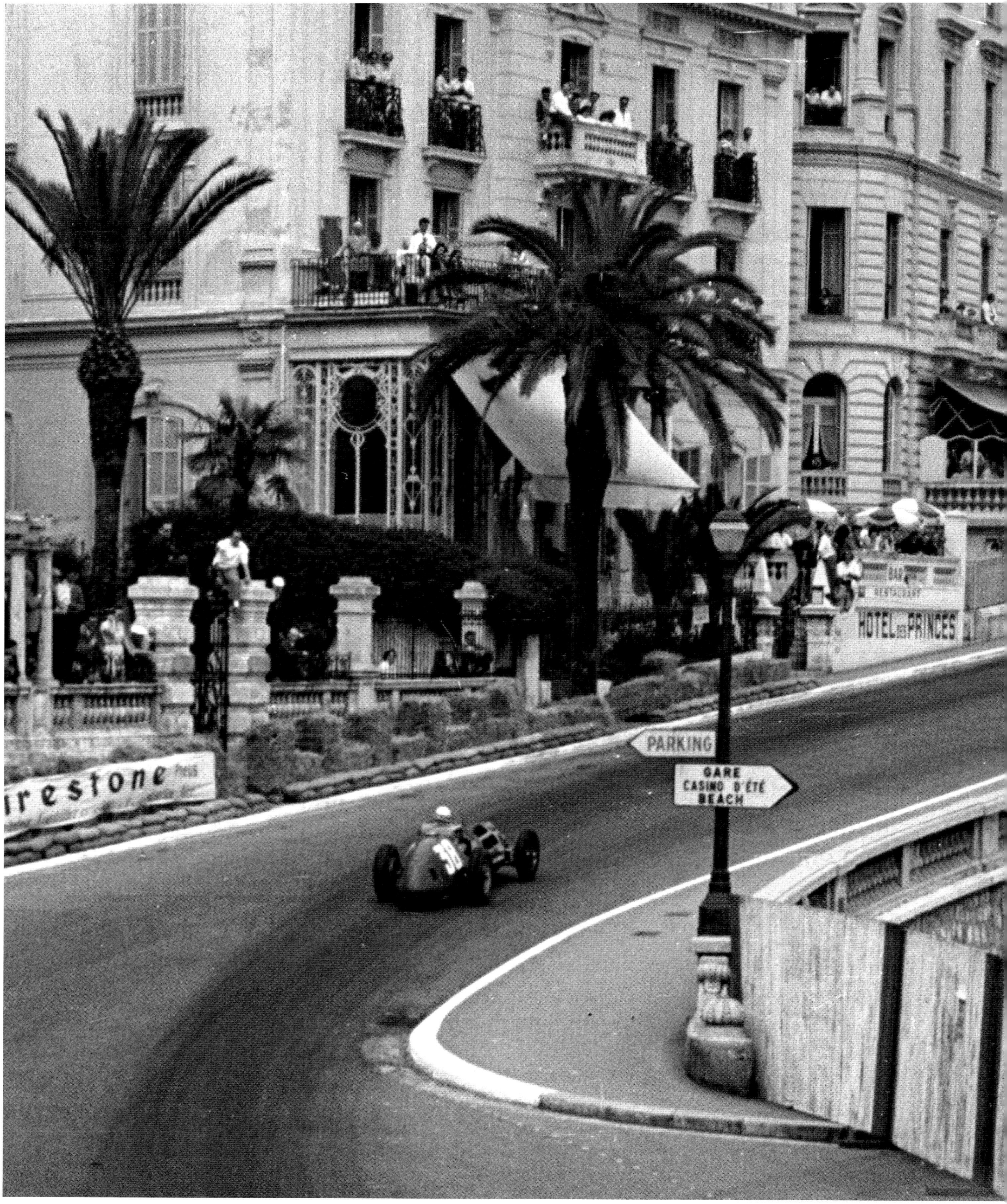
irestone
HOTEL DES PRINCES
PARKING
GARE
CASINO D'ÉTÉ
BEACH

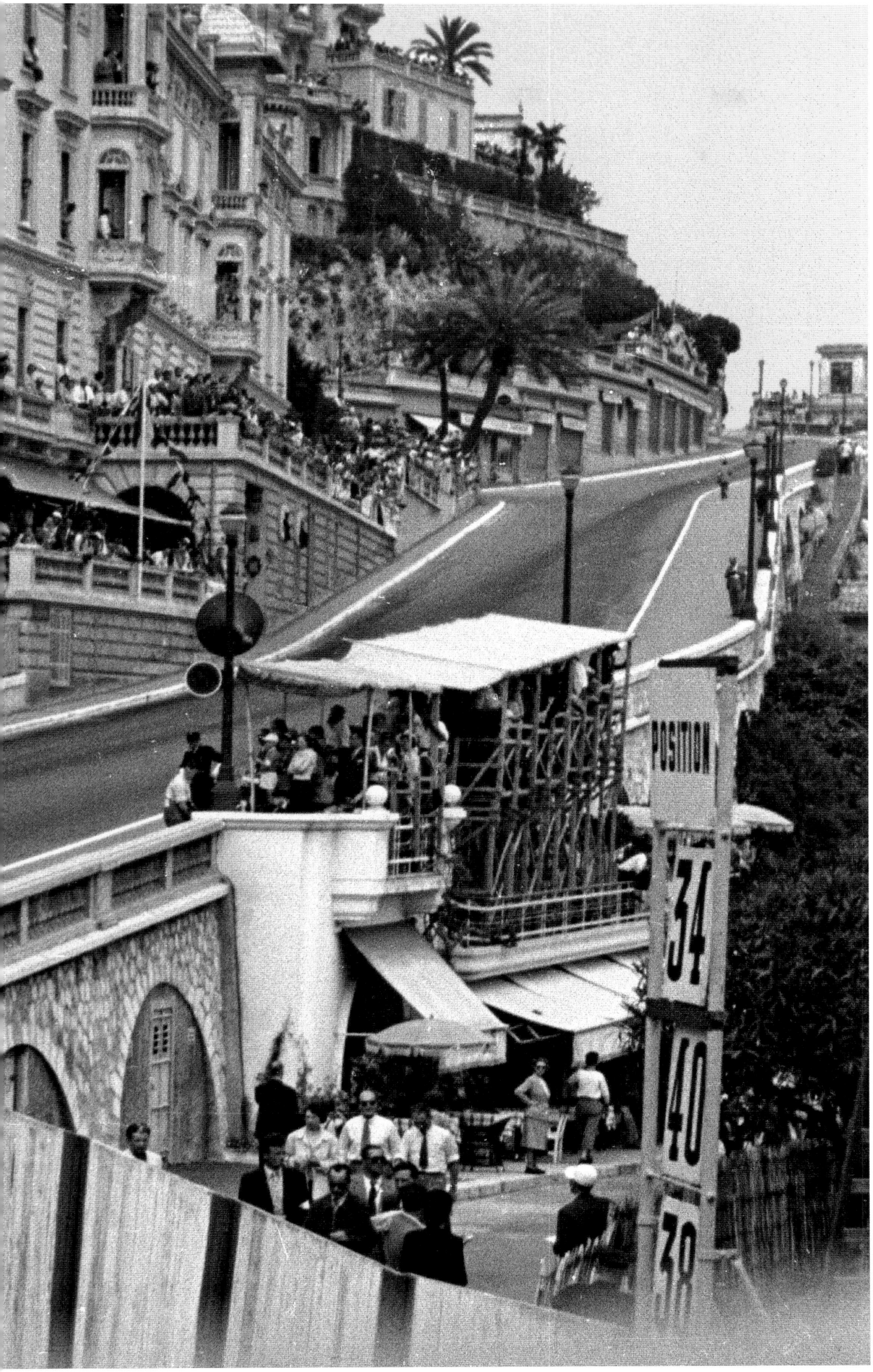

Sainte-Dévote-Kurve: Luigi Villoresi, Ferrari 125 N° 38, mit beträchtlichem Abstand Dritter hinter Fangio und Ascari.

Sainte Dévote corner: Luigi Villoresi, Ferrari 125 N° 38, third by a considerable margin behind Fangio and Ascari.

Grand Prix 1950

Final result Monaco Grand Prix 1950

1. Juan Manuel Fangio,
   Alfa Romeo 158 „Alfetta“
2. Alberto Ascari, Ferrari 125
3. Louis Chiron, Maserati 4CLT

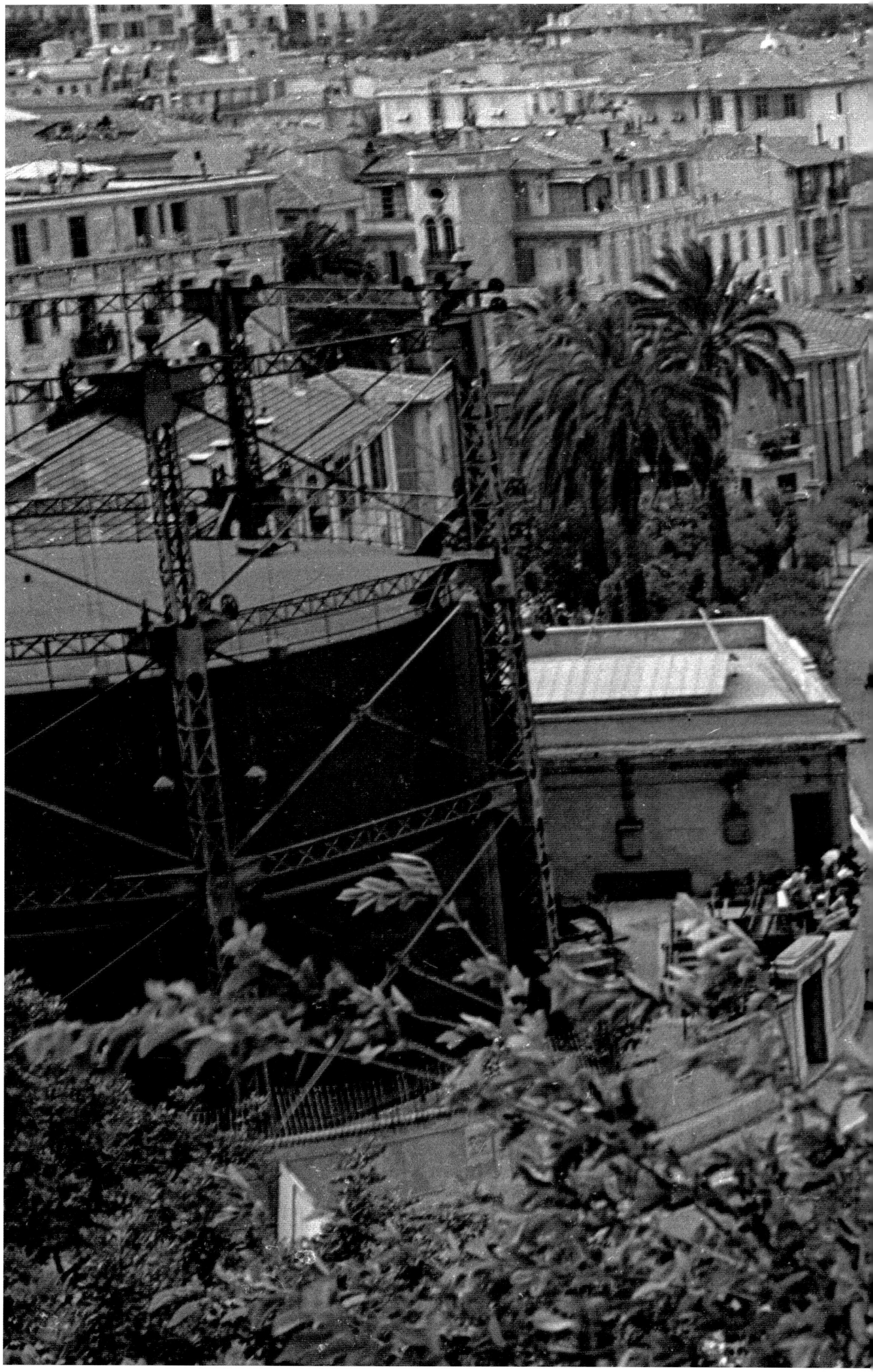

Die Gasometer-Haarnadelkurve mit dem Gasometer links, der ihr den Namen gegeben hat. Die spektakuläre Kurve wurde später nach dem Bau des Schwimmbades ersetzt durch die zwei Kurven „La Rascasse“ und „Antony Noghès“.

The Gasometer hairpin with the gasometer on the left which gave it its name. The spectacular corner was later replaced by the two corners "La Rascasse" and "Antony Noghès" after the construction of the swimming pool.

.

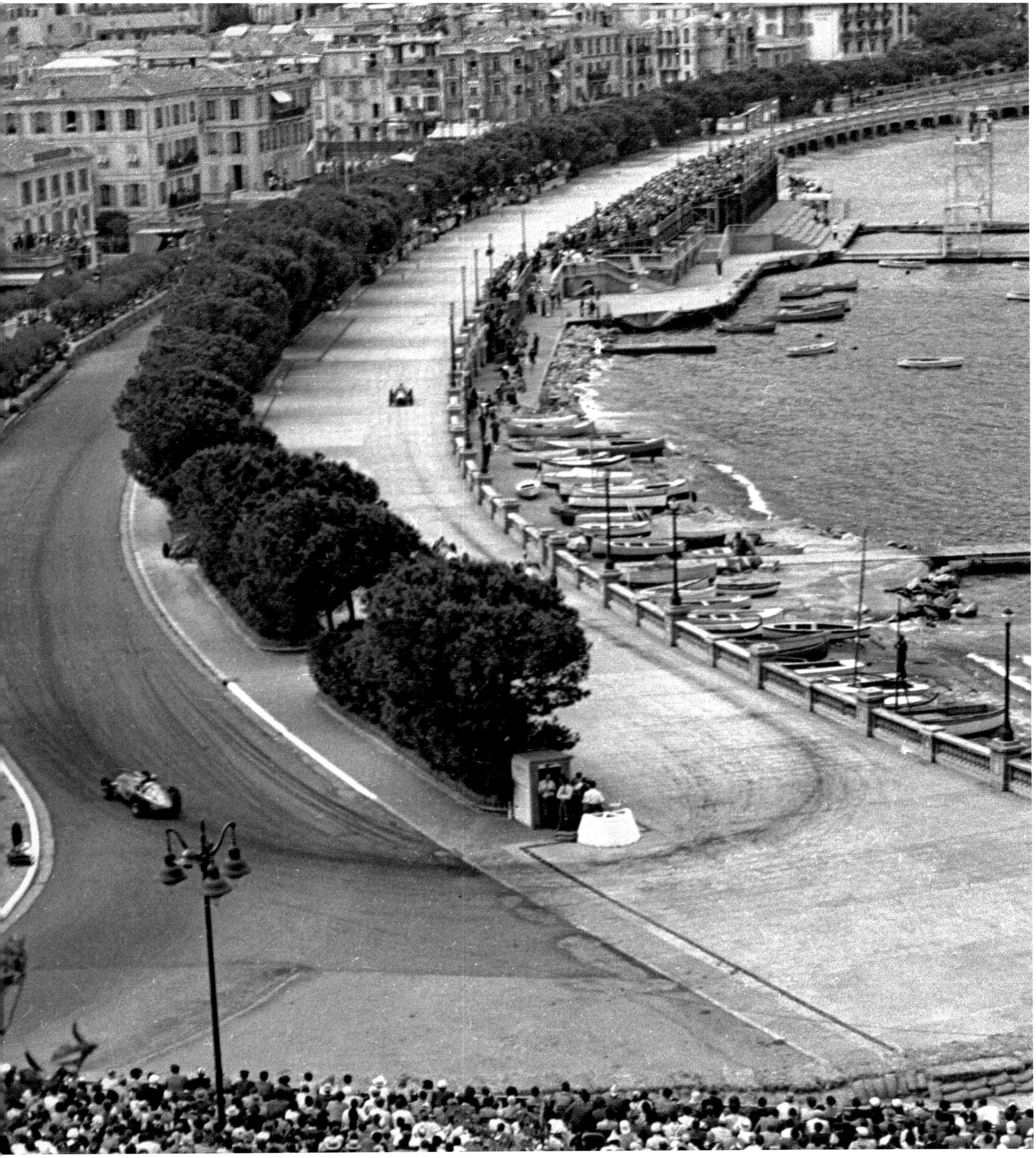

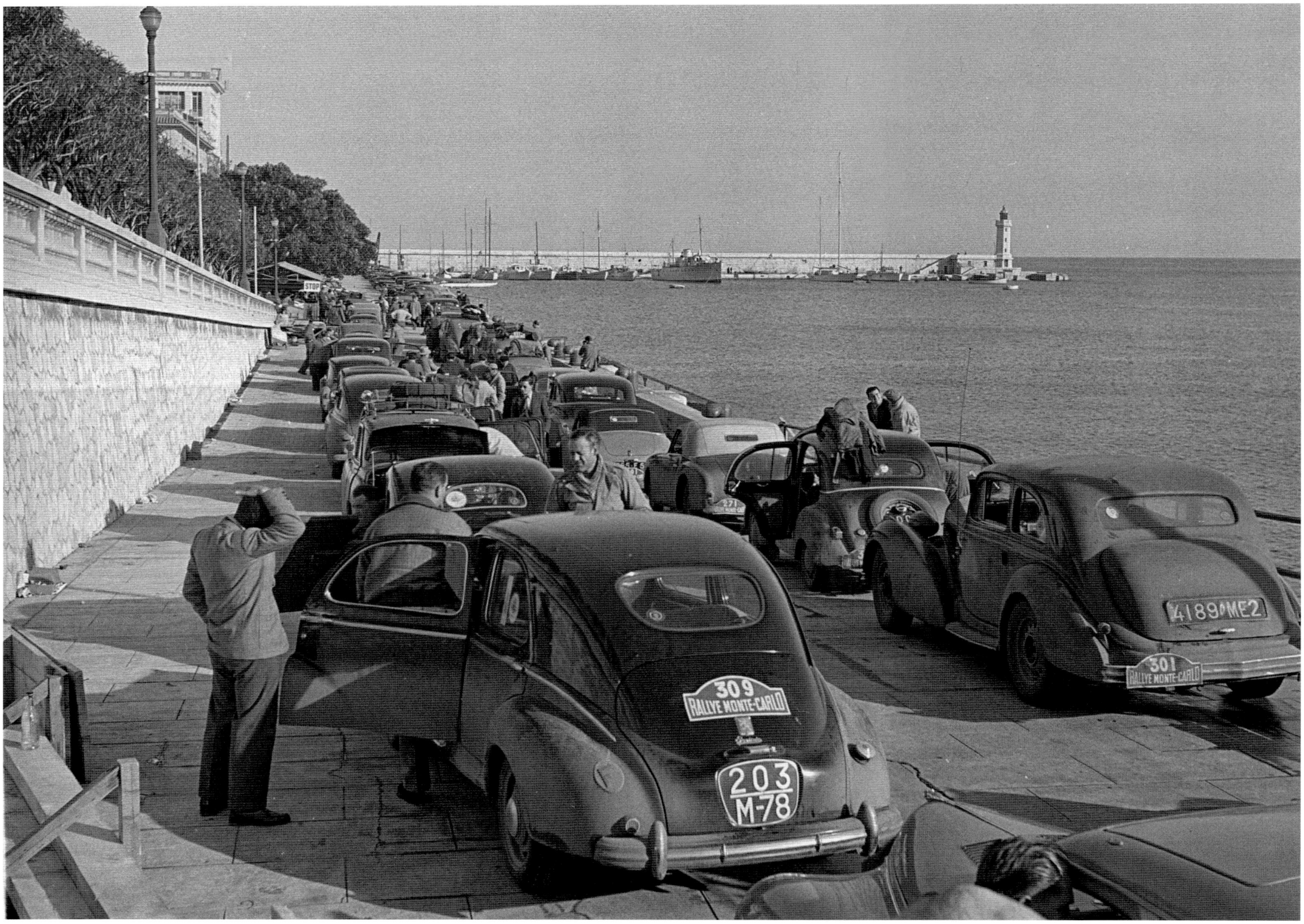

Ankunft der Rallye-Teilnehmer
in Monte Carlo 1951.

*The competitors arrive for the rally,
Monte Carlo 1951.*

1951

Die Rallye geht auf die Grand-Prix-Strecke

In diesem Jahr gibt es keinen Grand Prix in Monaco, wohl aber das andere motorsportliche Großereignis: die Rallye. Die „Monte", die Rallye Monte-Carlo, gilt als die Mutter des heutigen Rallyesports. Deren Anfänge werden auf die erste Austragung im Jahr 1911 datiert, die vom lokalen Zigarettenhersteller Antony Noghès und Fürst Albert I. initiiert wurde.

Das Rennen war von Anfang an als große Sternfahrt (im Englischen „rally") angelegt: Sie startete von verschiedenen Städten in Europa aus und endete in Monte Carlo. 1951 waren das Glasgow, Lissabon, Oslo, Palermo, Stockholm und Monte-Carlo. In Monte-Carlo oder in der Nähe wurden dann Sonderprüfungen durchgeführt, die sich fast jedes Jahr änderten, zum Beispiel Gleichmäßigkeit der Geschwindigkeit auf Bergstrecken, Beschleunigung, Bremsen, langsames Fahren und Rückwärtsfahren oder kurze Bergrennen.

1951 wird zum ersten Mal eine Gleichmäßigkeitsprüfung auf der Originalstrecke des Grand Prix durchgeführt. Es galt, vier Runden so schnell wie möglich, aber jede Runde so gleichmäßig wie möglich zu fahren.

The Rally moves to the Grand Prix circuit

There is no Grand Prix in Monaco this year, but there is a Rally. The Monte Carlo Rally, the "Monte", is considered the mother of today's rallying. Its beginnings date back to the first event in 1911, which was initiated by local cigarette manufacturer Antony Noghès and Prince Albert I.

From the beginning, the event was designed as a major rally: it started from various cities in Europe and ended in Monte Carlo. In 1951, these were Glasgow, Lisbon, Oslo, Palermo, Stockholm and Monte Carlo. Special tests were then held in or around Monte Carlo which changed almost every year, for example speed regularity on mountain routes, acceleration, braking, reversing, slow driving and short hill climbs.

In 1951, a regularity test was held for the first time on the original Grand Prix circuit. The aim was to drive four laps as fast as possible but each lap as evenly as possible.

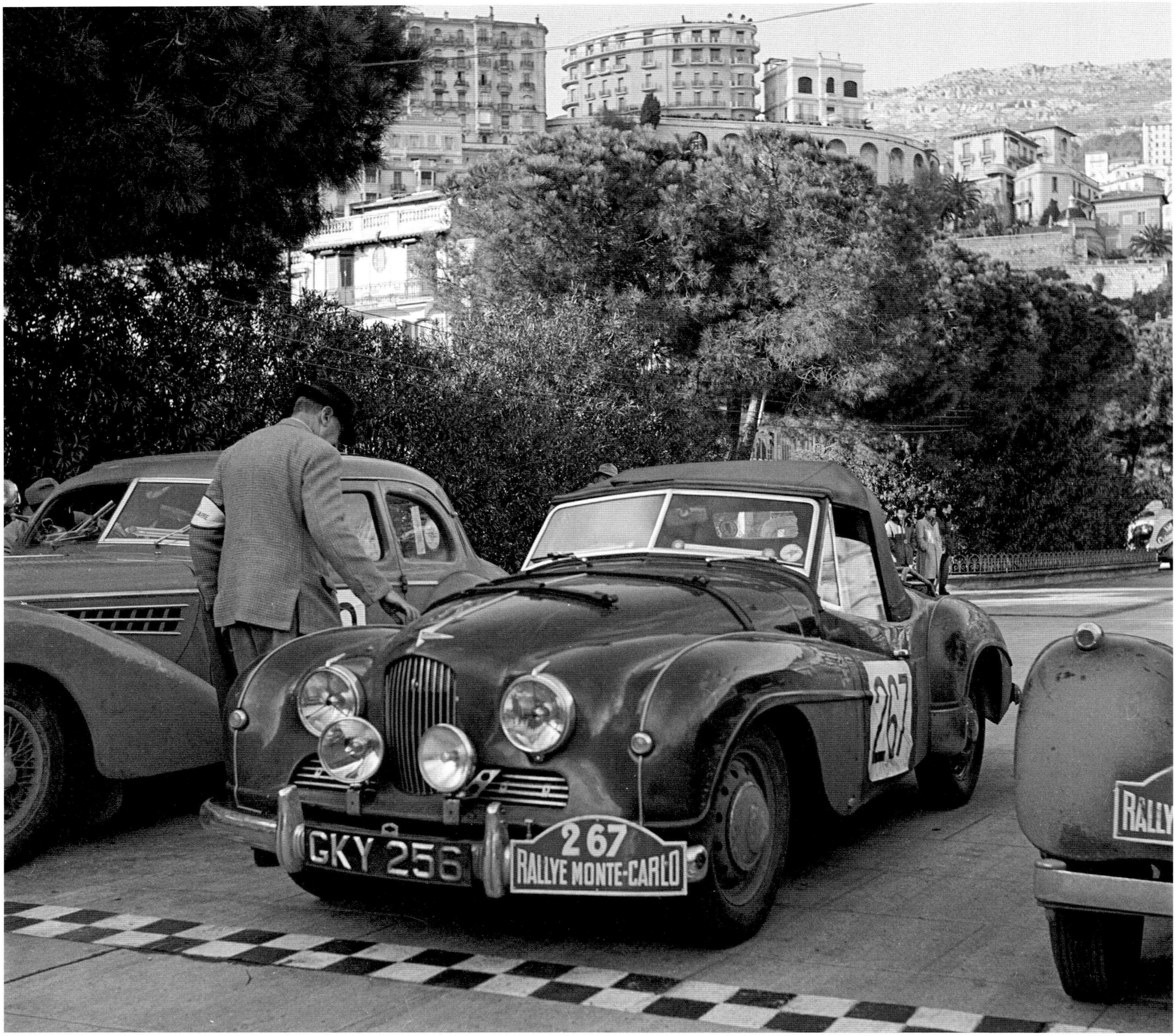

Sieger in der 1.500-cm³-Kategorie Ellison/Robinson, Jowett Jupiter N° 267, die an der Gleichmäßigkeitsprüfung auf der Strecke des Monaco Grand Prix teilnehmen.

Winner in the 1500cc class Ellison/Robinson, Jowett Jupiter N° 267, taking part in the regularity speed test on the circuit of the Monaco Grand Prix.

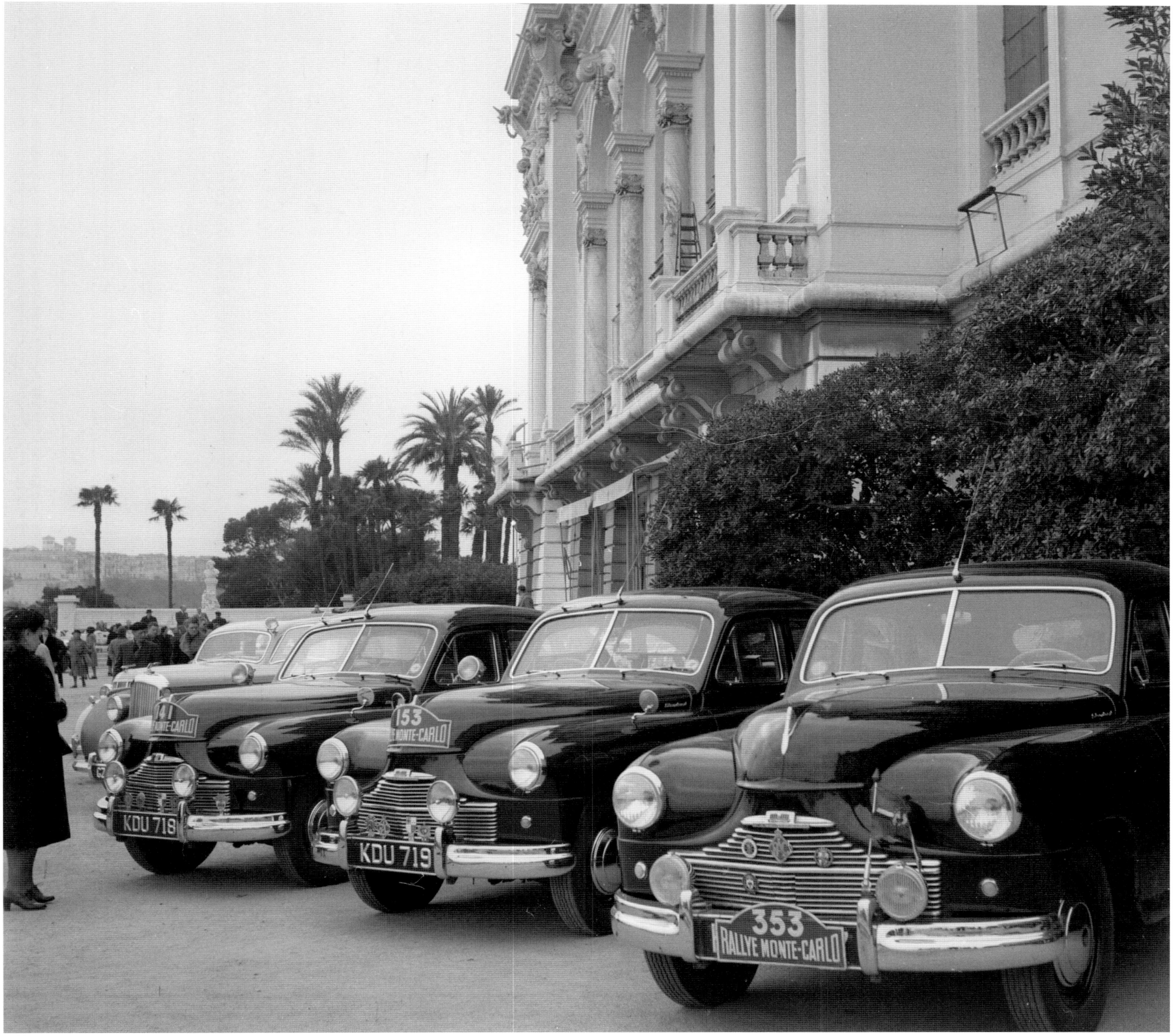

Hinter dem Casino: Eine Armada von Standard Vanguard: N° 141 Edge/Tyrer, N° 153 Rawlings/Tracey, N° 353 Mylonadis/Alvigini.

Behind the Casino: A Standard Vanguard Armada: N° 141 Edge/ Tyrer, N° 153, Rawlings/Tracey, N° 353 Mylonadis/Alvigini.

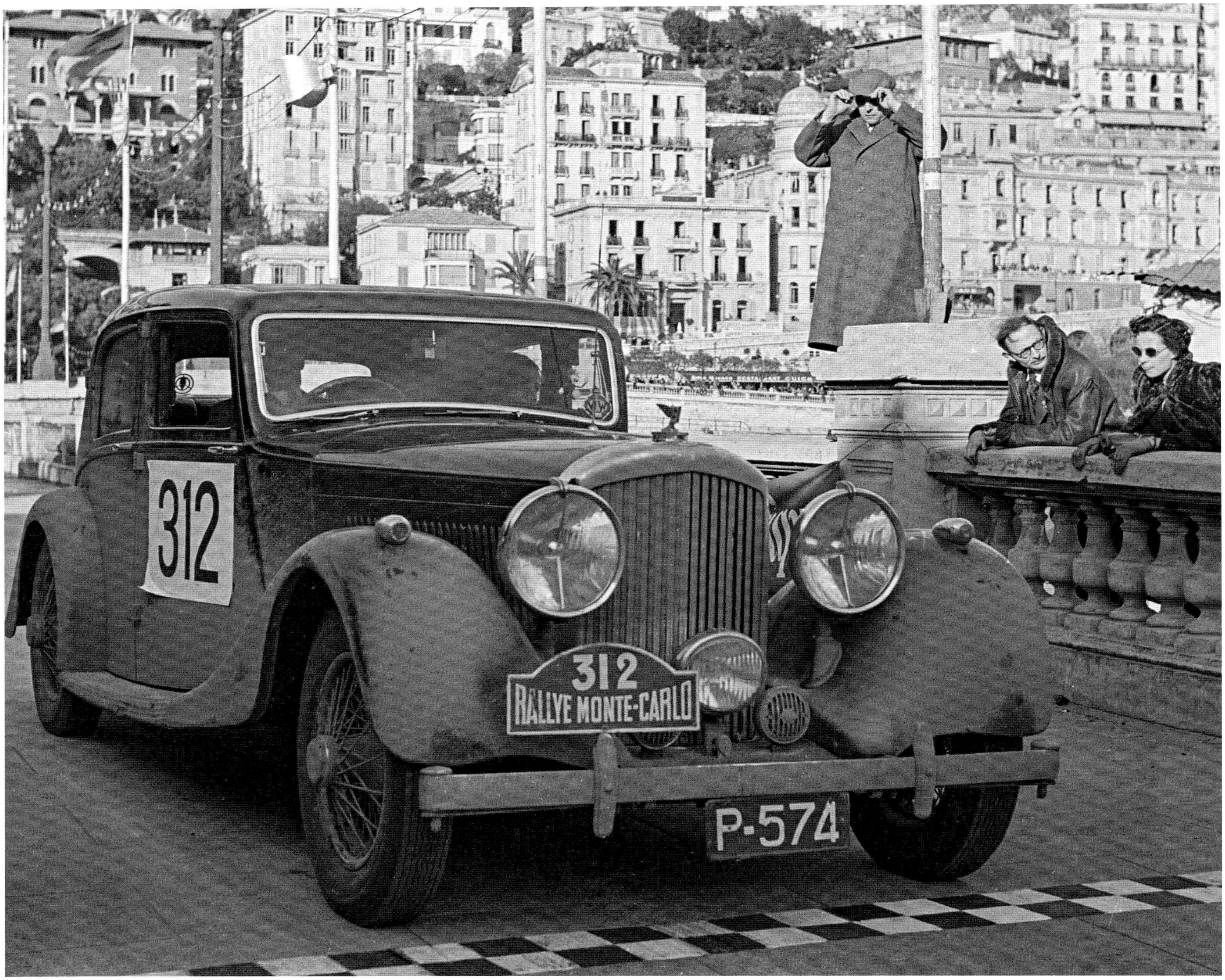

Polis/Sevenstern, Bentley 4¼-Liter, 4-türige Sportlimousine von Park Ward N° 312, beim Start zur Gleichmäßigkeitsprüfung auf der Strecke des Grand Prix.

Polis/Sevenstern, Bentley 4¼-litre 4-door sports saloon by Park Ward N° 312, at the start to the regularity speed test on the circuit of the Grand Prix.

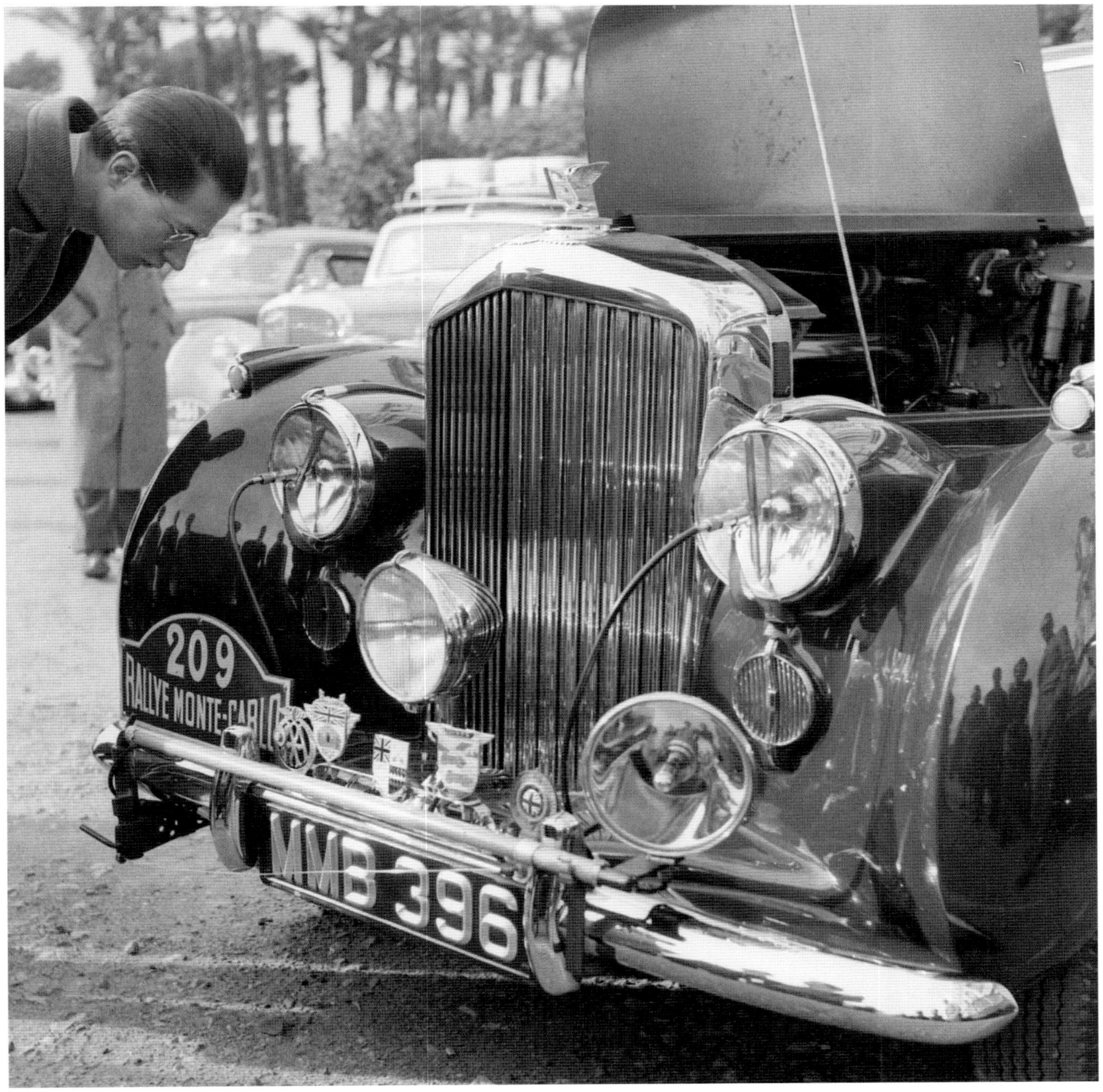

Ehrenpreis für „Rallye-Trimm“ mit Rotationswischern, um die Scheinwerfer sauber zu halten. Couper/Eastwood, Bentley Mark VI, #B235GT, Standard Steel Sports Saloon N° 209.

Grand Prix d'Honneur for "Rally-Trim" with rotary wipers fitted to keep the headlamps clean for Couper/Eastwood, Bentley Mark VI, #B235GT, Standard Steel Sports Saloon N° 209.

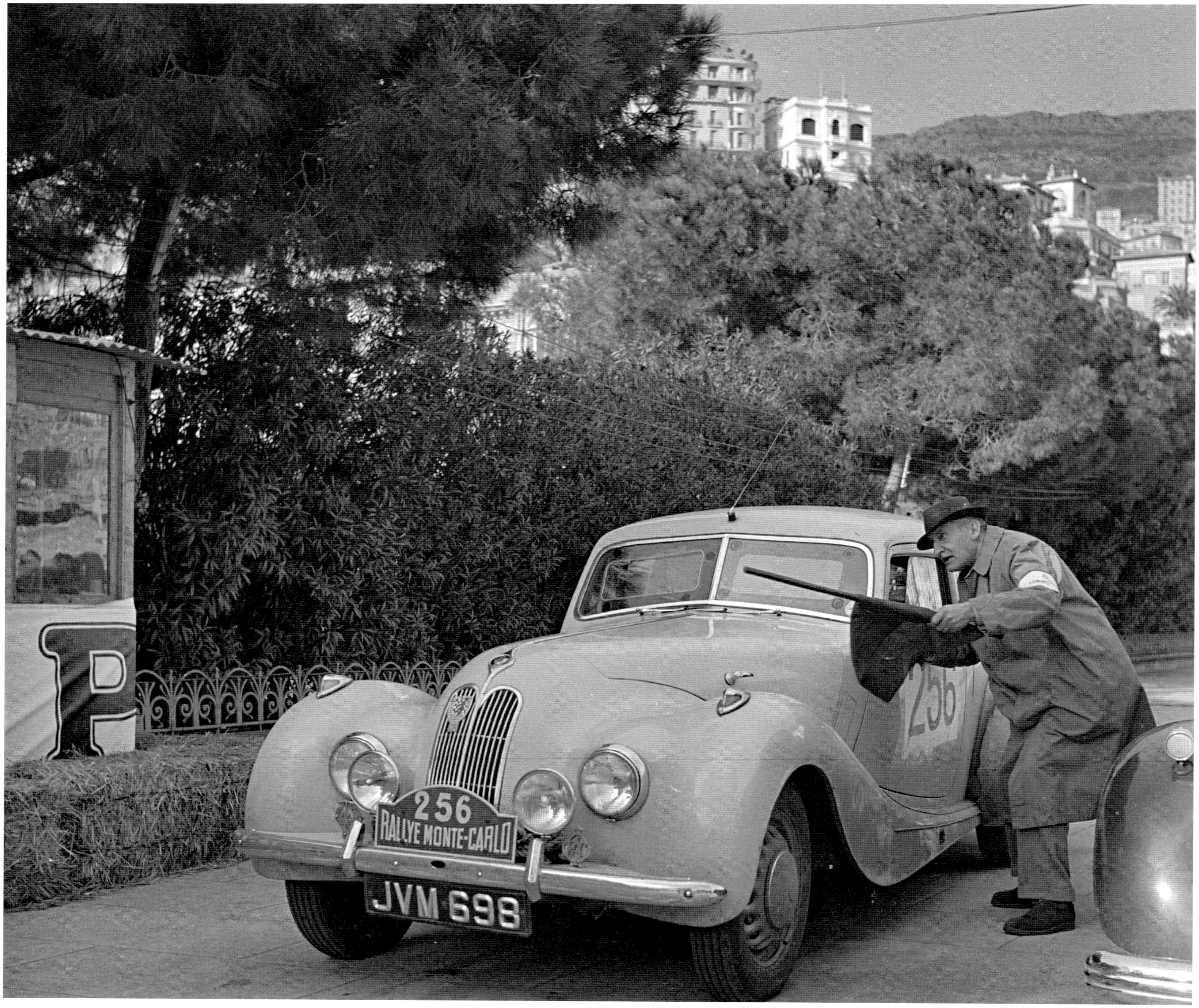

Bolton/Morrell, Bristol 400 N° 256, beim Start zur Gleichmäßigkeitsprüfung auf der Strecke des Großen Preises von Monaco.

Bolton/Morrell, Bristol 400 N° 256, at the start to the regularity speed test on the Monaco Grand Prix circuit.

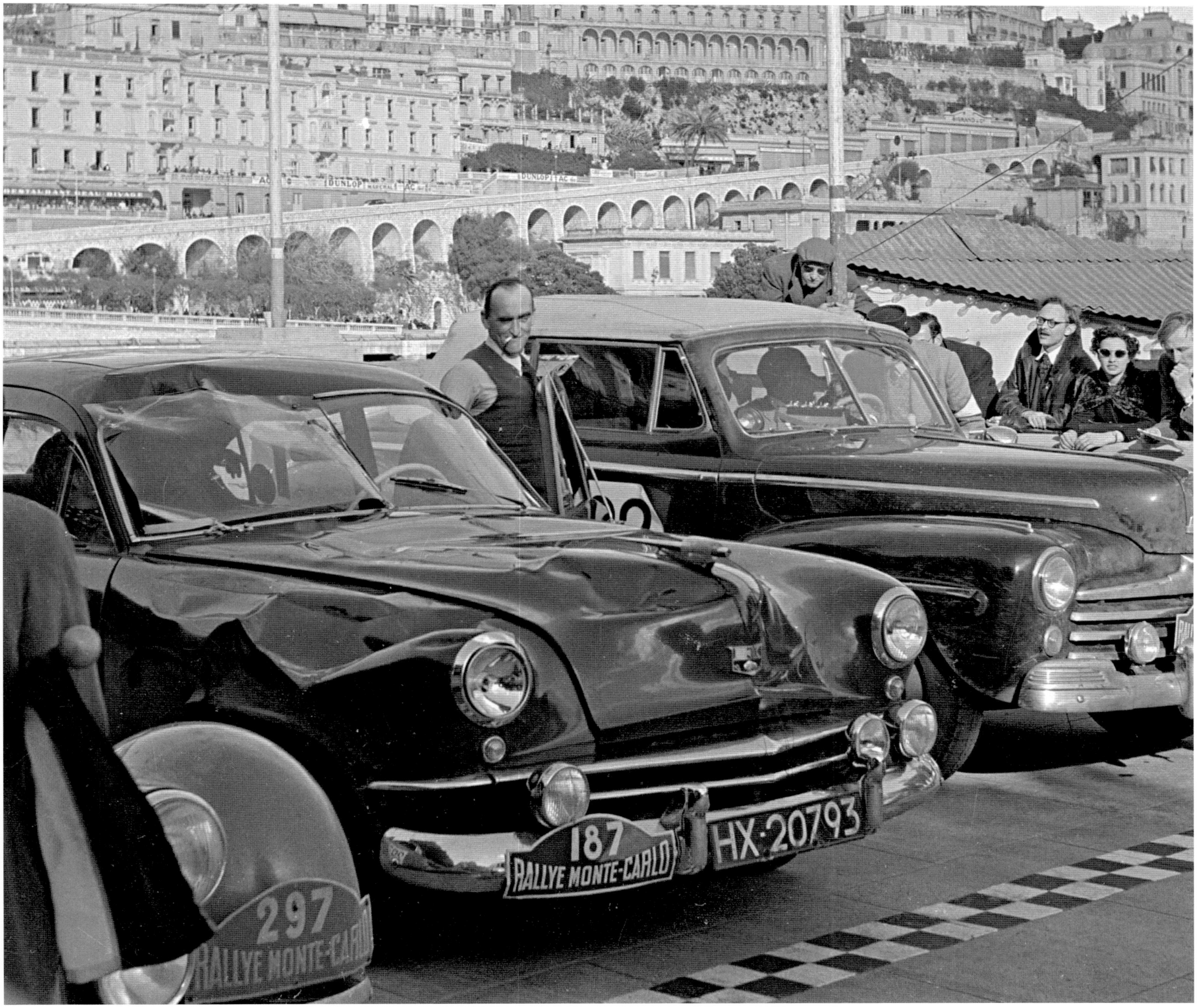

Gute Stimmung trotz leicht modifiziertem Fahrzeug: Barendregt/Beekman, Kaiser N° 187, und Comte de Montreal/Palama, Ford N° 332, bei der Gleichmäßigkeitsprüfung auf der Strecke des Großen Preises von Monaco.

High spirits despite a "slightly modified" vehicle: Barendregt/Beekman, Kais er N° 187, and Comte de Montreal/Palama, Ford N° 332, taking part in the regularity speed test on the circuit of the Monaco Grand Prix.

LISTE DES ENGAGES AU XIIme GRAND PRIX AUTOMOBILE DE MONACO LUNDI 2/6/52

Concurrents	Voitures	Pilotes
ESPAGNE		
L. COATELEN	Pegaso	PALACIO
J. JOVER	Pegaso	JOVER
FRANCE		
TALBOT	Talbot	ROSIER
TALBOT	Talbot	TRINTIGNANT
TALBOT	Talbot	LEVEGH
P.MEYRAT	Talbot	MEYRAT
R.COTTON	Delahaye	COTTON
A. GORDINI	Simca Gordini	MANZON
P. PAGNIBON	Ferrari	PAGNIBON
L. CHINETTI	Ferrari	CHINETTI
GRANDE-BRETAGNE		
ASTON-MARTIN	Aston-Martin	PARNELL
ASTON-MARTIN	Aston Martin	ABECASSIS
ASTON-MARTIN	Aston-Martin	MACKLIN
JAGUAR	Jaguar	MOSS
T.H.WISDOM	Jaguar	WISDOM
S.H.ALLARD	Allard	HUME
ITALIE		
SCUDERIA COTRONE	Ferrari	BUANOCORSI
SCUDERIA MARZOTTO	Ferrari	CARINI
SCUDERIA DELLA GUASTELLA	Ferrari	BRACCO
SCUDERIA DELLA GUASTELLA	Ferrari	STAGNOLI
SCUDERIA DELLA GUASTELLA	Ferrari	CASTELLOTTI
Comte V.MARZOTTO	Ferrari	Comte MARZOTTO
A. SIMON	Ferrari	SIMON
PORTUGAL		
F. MASCARENHAS	Allard	MASCARENHAS

Für Pressezwecke: originale Meldeliste für den Monaco Grand Prix 1952.

Original list of entries for the Monaco Grand Prix 1952 for the press.

1952

Sportwagen statt Monoposto

Die Weltmeisterschaft wird aus Kostengründen in diesem Jahr mit der Formel 2 durchgeführt, mit wesentlich schwächeren Motoren. Die Organisatoren von Monaco sind aber der Meinung, dass die Sportwagen vom Typ Le Mans ein vielfältigeres und spektakuläreres Teilnehmerfeld anziehen, als dies bei einem Formel-2-Rennen der Fall wäre. Deshalb ist der diesjährige Grand Prix ein Rennen für Sportwagen und nicht für Monoposto ohne Kotflügel. Die Veranstaltung findet an zwei Tagen statt: am Sonntag der Prix de Monte Carlo für Wagen bis 2 Liter Hubraum, am Montag der Grand Prix von Monaco für die größeren Motoren. Die resultierenden Rennen sind höchst attraktiv ...

Wieder dabei ist auch Stirling Moss. Er nimmt an beiden Veranstaltungen teil und hat in diesem Jahr schon die Rallye Monte-Carlo bestritten. Wahrscheinlich hat es nie mehr einen Fahrer gegeben, der in so vielen Kategorien so erfolgreich war.

Sports cars instead of monopostos

For cost reasons, the World Championship was held this year for Formula 2 cars with smaller engines. However, the Monaco organisers felt that the Le Mans type sports cars would attract a more diverse and spectacular field of participants than would be the case with a Formula 2 race. They therefore changed this year's Grand Prix into a race for sports cars instead of the open wheeler monopostos. It was a two-day event, Sunday for the cars up to 2 litres, as the Prix de Monte Carlo, and the Monaco Grand Prix on Monday for the bigger engines. And the races became really attractive...

Stirling Moss was also back. He took part in both competitions and had already contested the Monte Carlo Rally this year. There has probably never been another driver who has been so successful in so many categories.

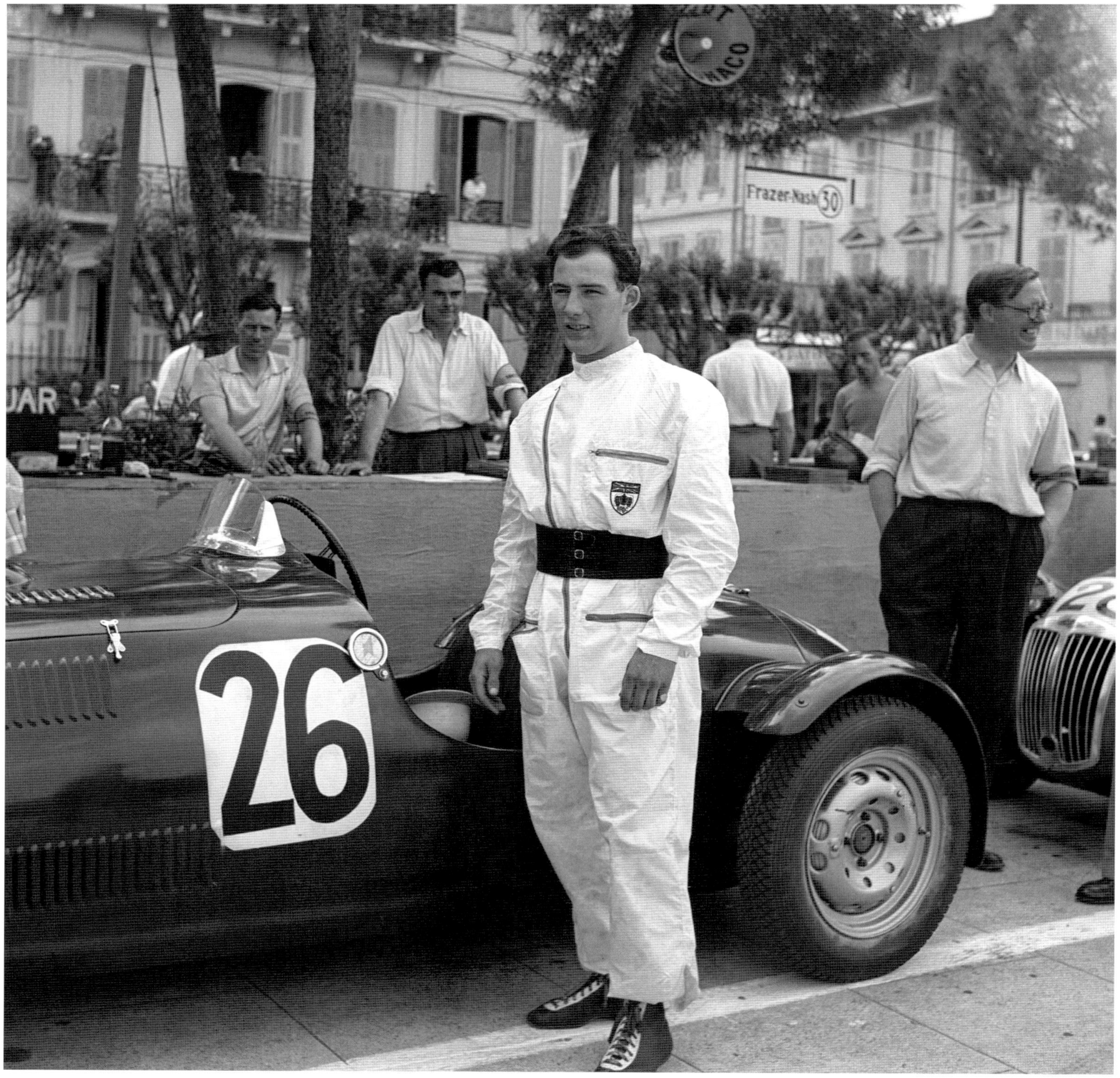

Stirling Moss
mit frisch gebügeltem Overall.

Stirling Moss
in freshly pressed overalls.

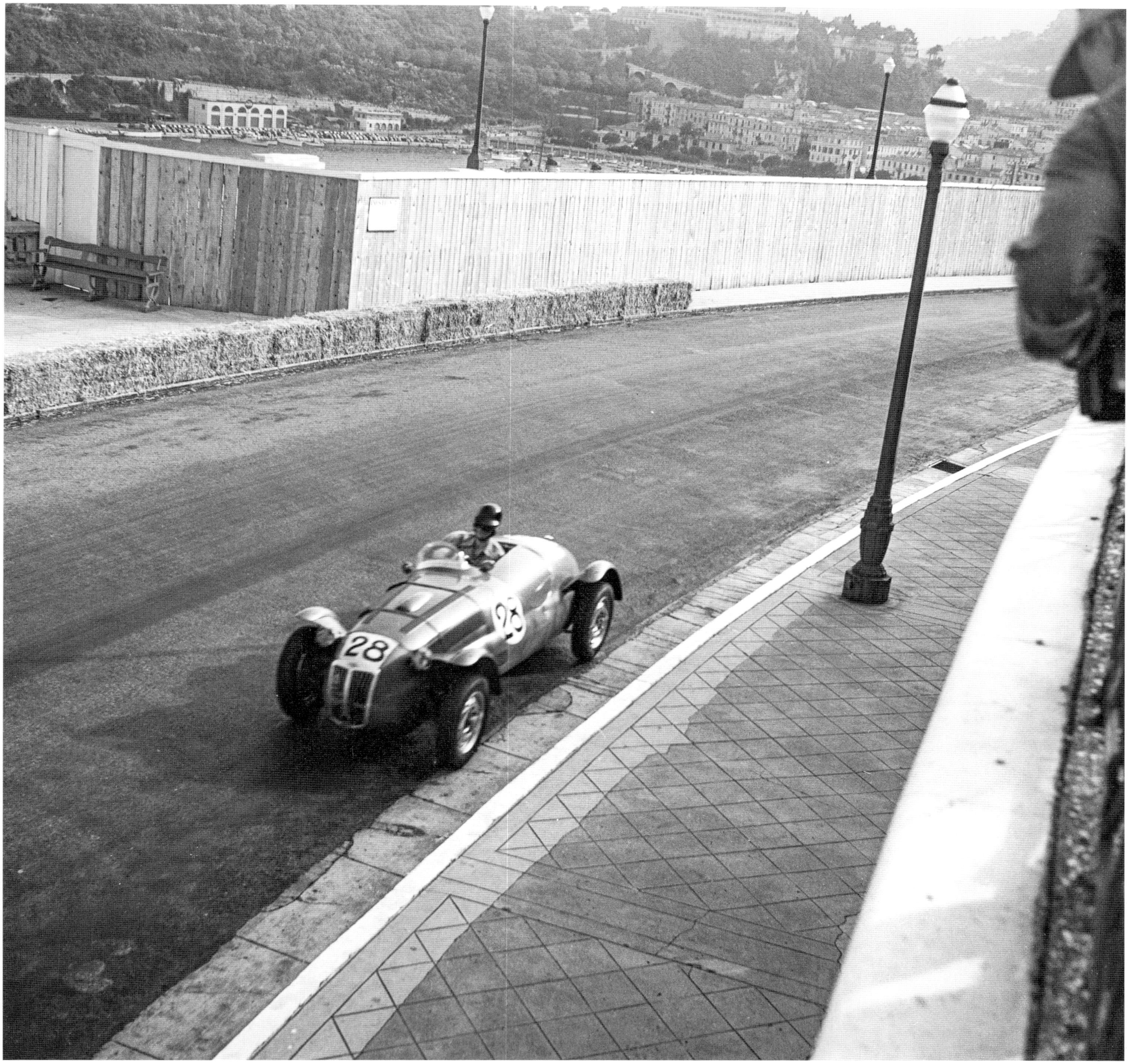

Tony Crook, Frazer Nash Le Mans Replica Mk II N° 28,
Rennen der Kategorie bis 2 Liter.

Tony Crook, Frazer Nash Le Mans Replica Mk II N° 28, race for sports cars up to 2 litre.

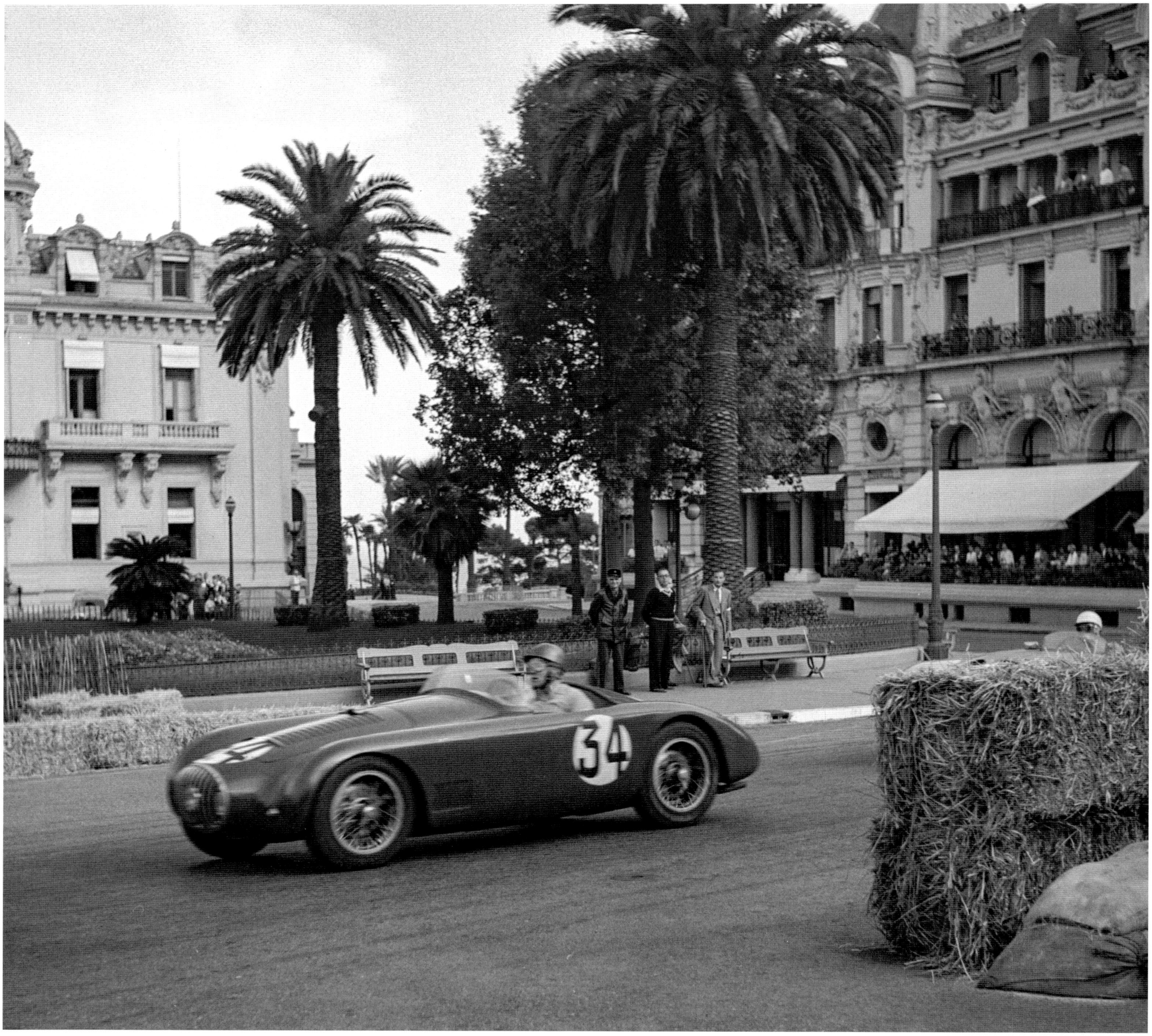

Auf der Place du Casino mit dem Hôtel de Paris:
Franco Bordoni, Osca MT4 1350 N° 34.

*On the Place du Casino with the Hôtel de Paris:
Franco Bordoni, Osca MT4 1350 N° 34.*

Final Result Prix de Monte Carlo 1952

1. Robert Manzon, Gordini N° 14
2. Franco Bordoni, Osca N° 34
3. Tony Crook, Frazer Nash N° 28

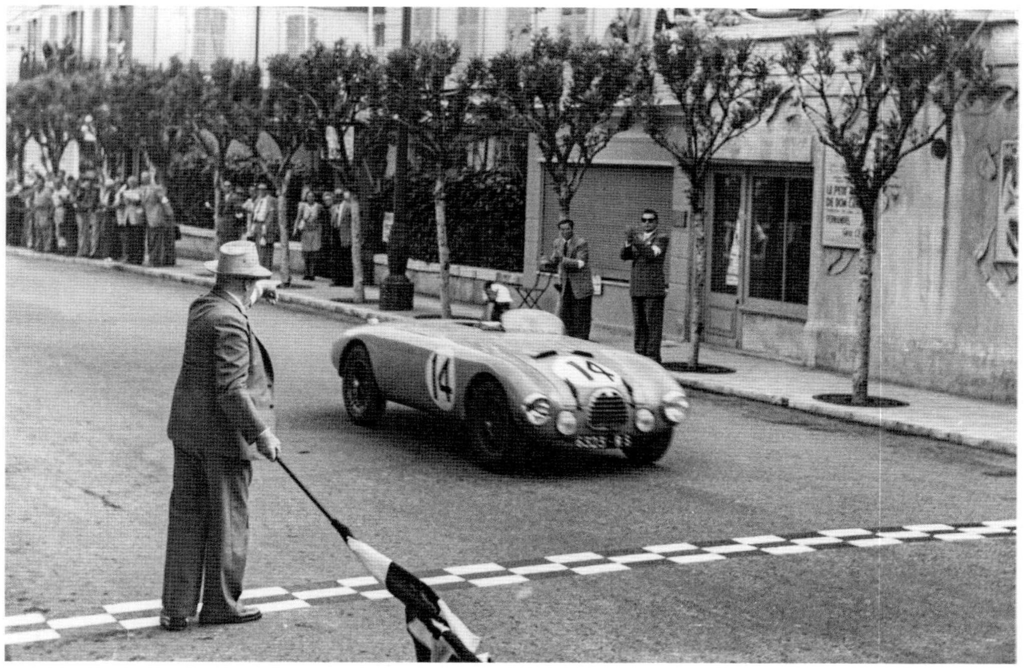

Charles Faroux, Rennleiter, schwenkt die Flagge für Robert Manzon, den Sieger des Prix de Monte Carlo, Gordini T15S 1.5 N° 14.

Charles Faroux, Clerk of the Course, waves the flag for Robert Manzon, winner of the Prix de Monte Carlo, Gordini T15S 1.5 N° 14.

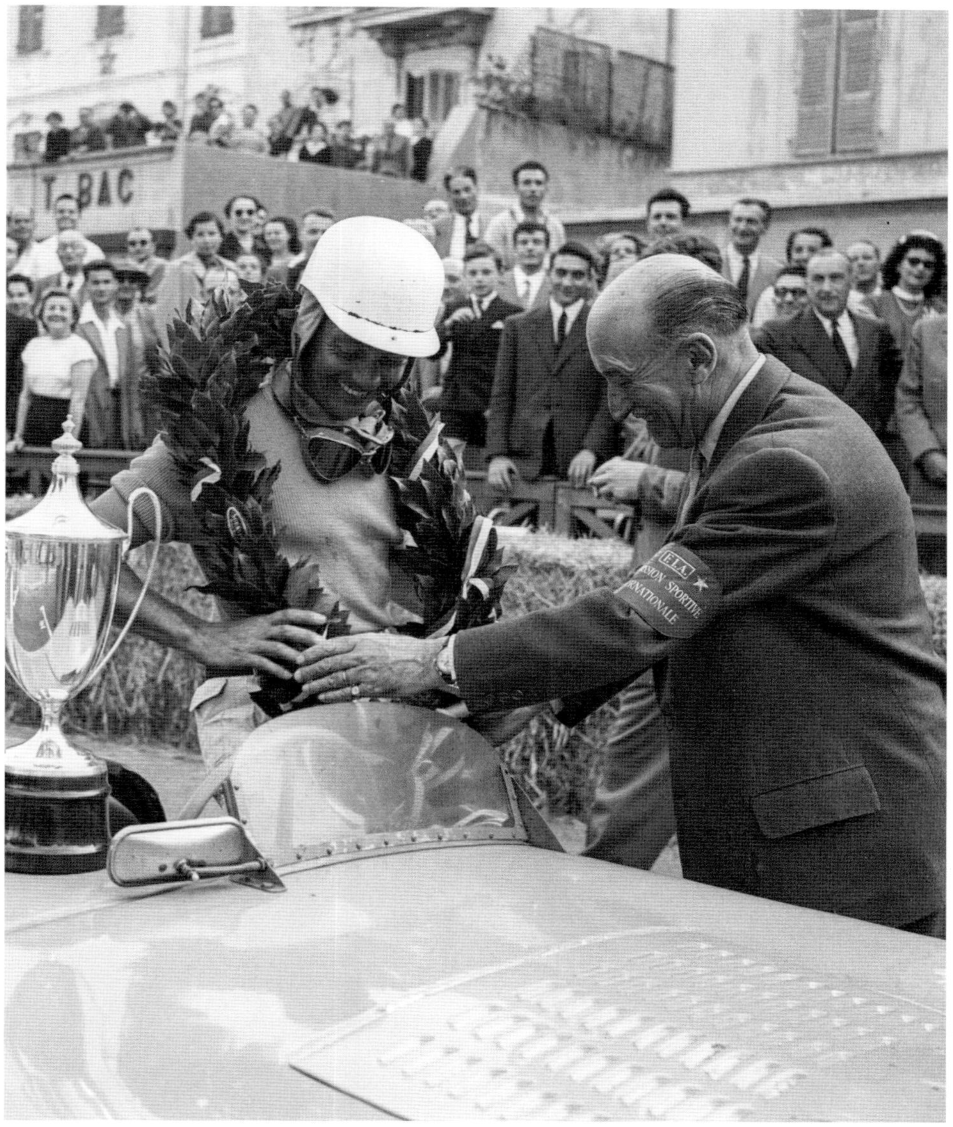

Der Gründer des Grand Prix, Antony Noghès, überreicht Robert Manzon den Siegerkranz im Rennen der Kategorie bis 2 Liter.

The founder of the Grand Prix, Antony Noghès, presents the winner's wreath of the race for sports cars up to 2 litre to Robert Manzon.

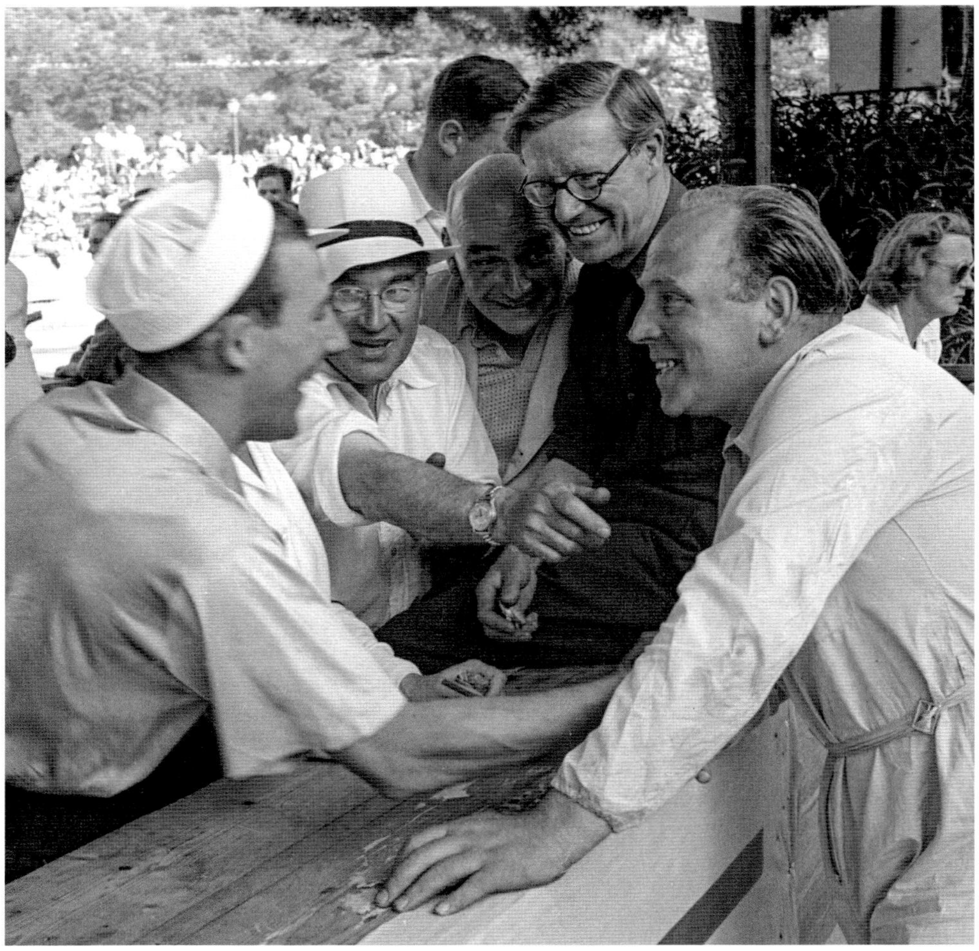

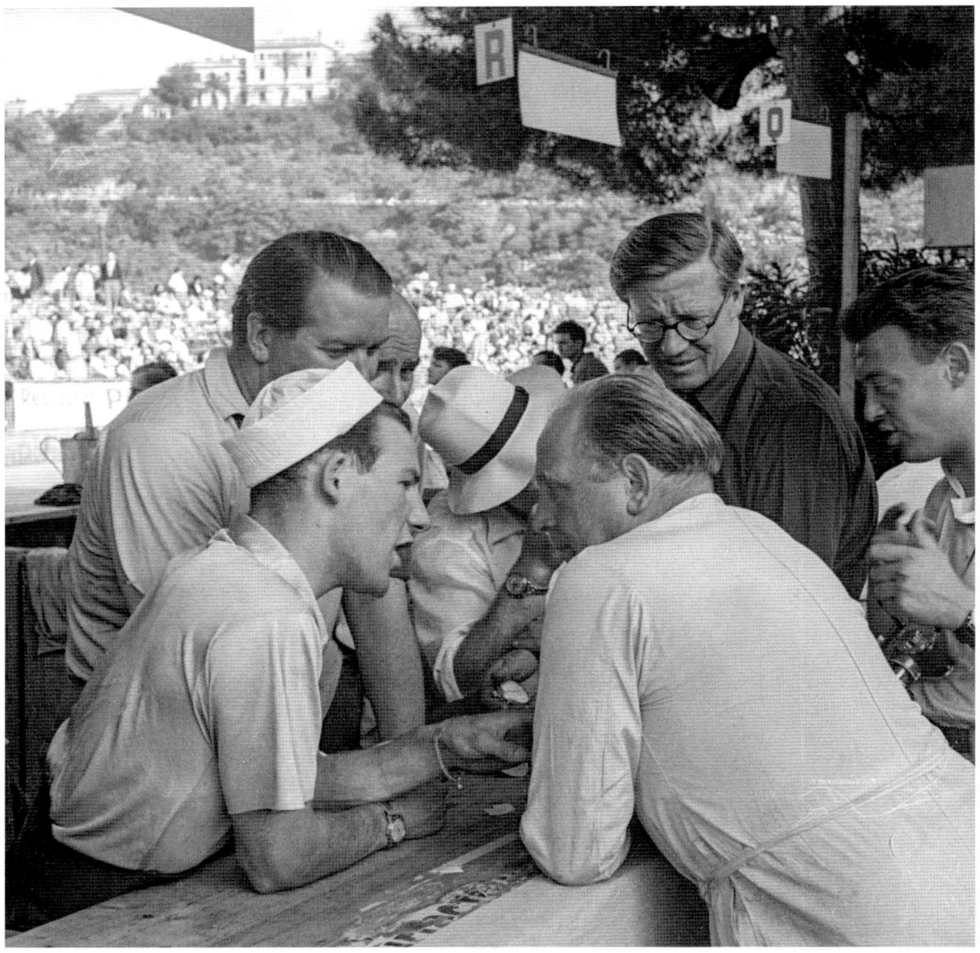

Stirling Moss beim Fachsimpeln und Scherzen mit Fahrerkollegen, ganz links Anthony Hume, im Overall Reginald Parnell, mit Hut Vater Moss, im dunklen Hemd HJ „Aldy“ Aldington.

Stirling Moss talking shop and joking with fellow drivers, far left Anthony Hume, in overalls Reginald Parnell, with hat father Moss, with dark shirt HJ "Aldy" Aldington.

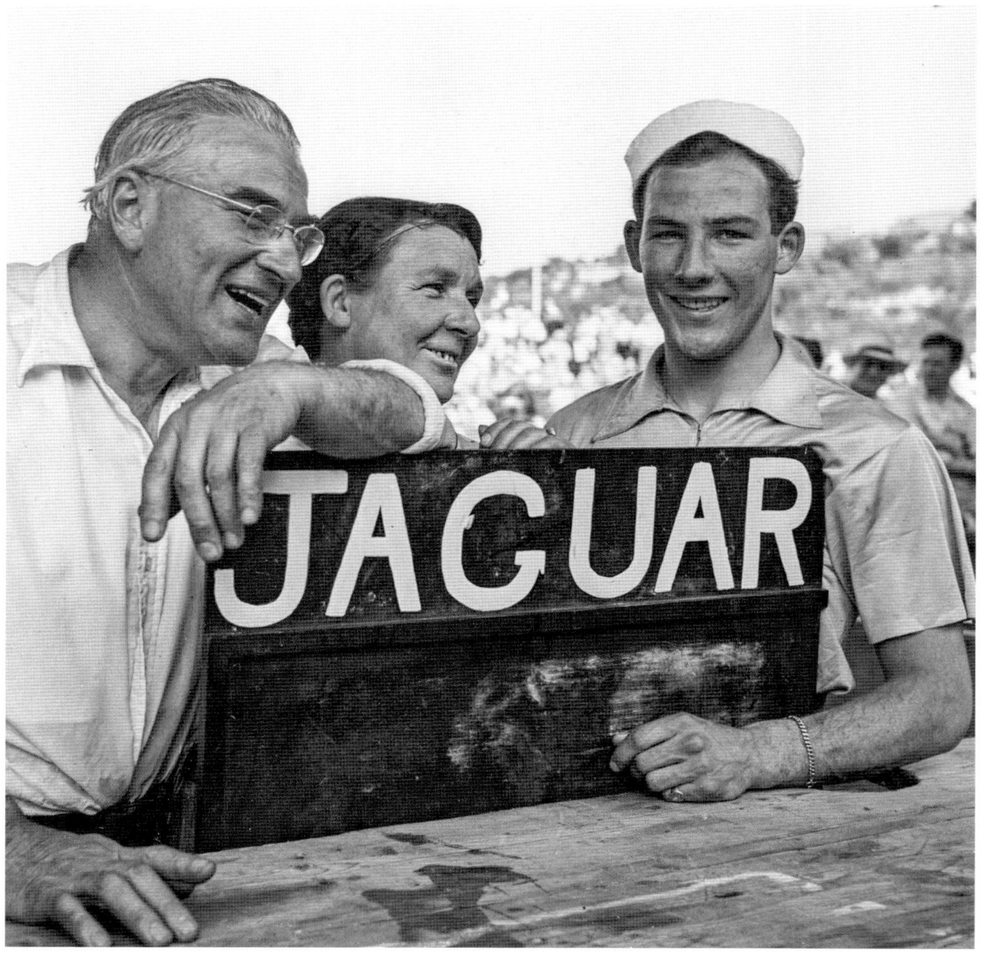

Die Mosses, eine Familie mit Benzin im Blut: Stirlings Vater, ein Zahnarzt, war Rennen in Brooklands und Indianapolis gefahren, seine Mutter war Ambulanzfahrerin im Ersten Weltkrieg. Moss war in Monaco Grand-Prix-Sieger in den Jahren 1956, 1960 und 1961.

The Mosses, a family with petrol in their veins: Stirling's father, a dentist, had raced at Brooklands and Indianapolis, his mother was an ambulance driver in the First World War. Moss was Grand Prix winner in 1956, 1960 and 1961.

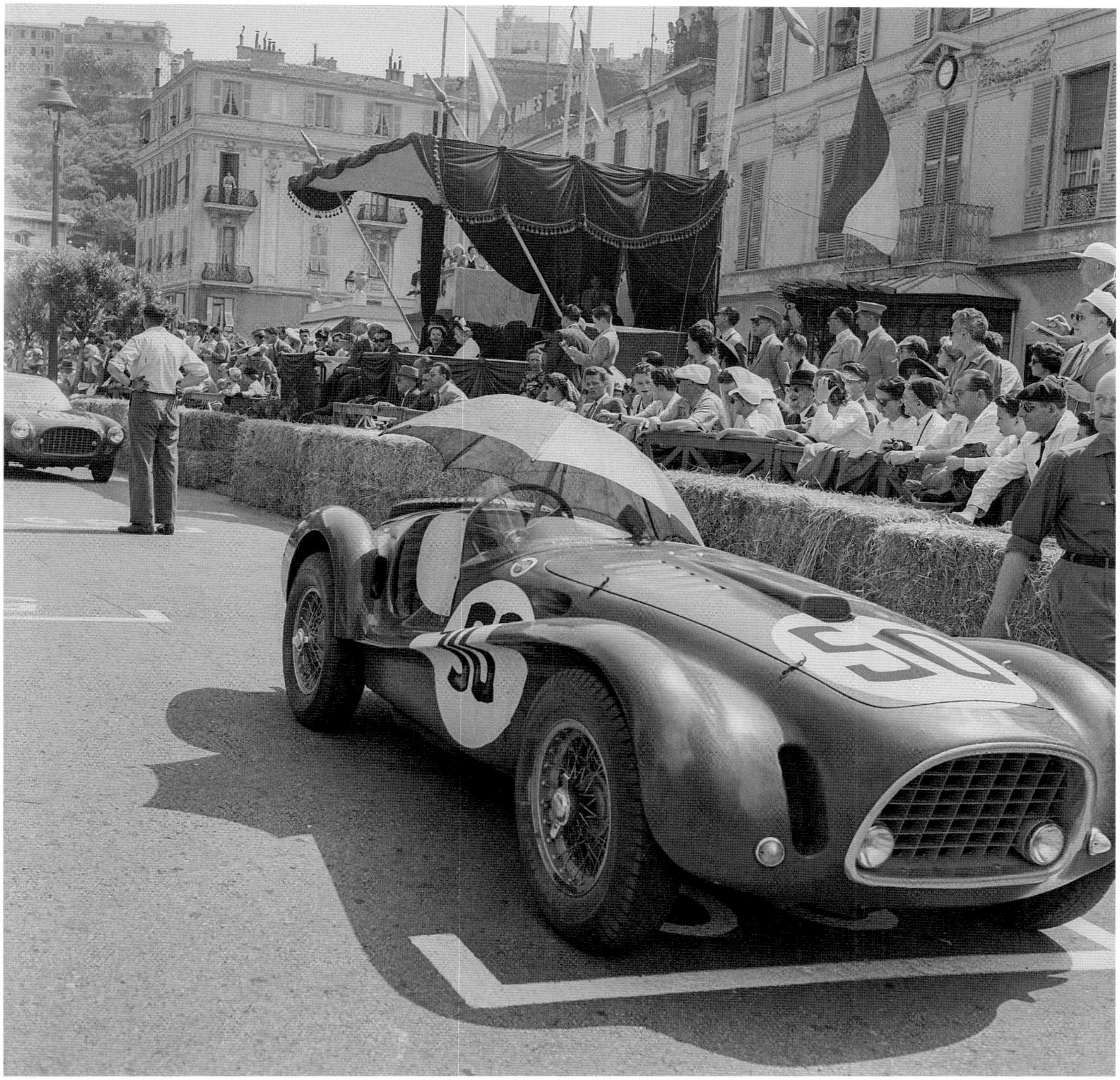

Rennwagen mit Sonnenschirm: der Ferrari 225S Spider Vignale N° 50 von Stagnoli/Biondetti, 3. im Rennen. Im Hintergrund Ferrari 225S Berlinetta Vignale N° 60, von „Pagnibon“, 5. Rang.

Racing car with parasol: the Ferrari 225S Spider Vignale N° 50 of Stagnoli/Biondetti, 3rd in race. In the background Ferrari 225S Berlinetta Vignale N° 60, of "Pagnibon", which was placed fifth.

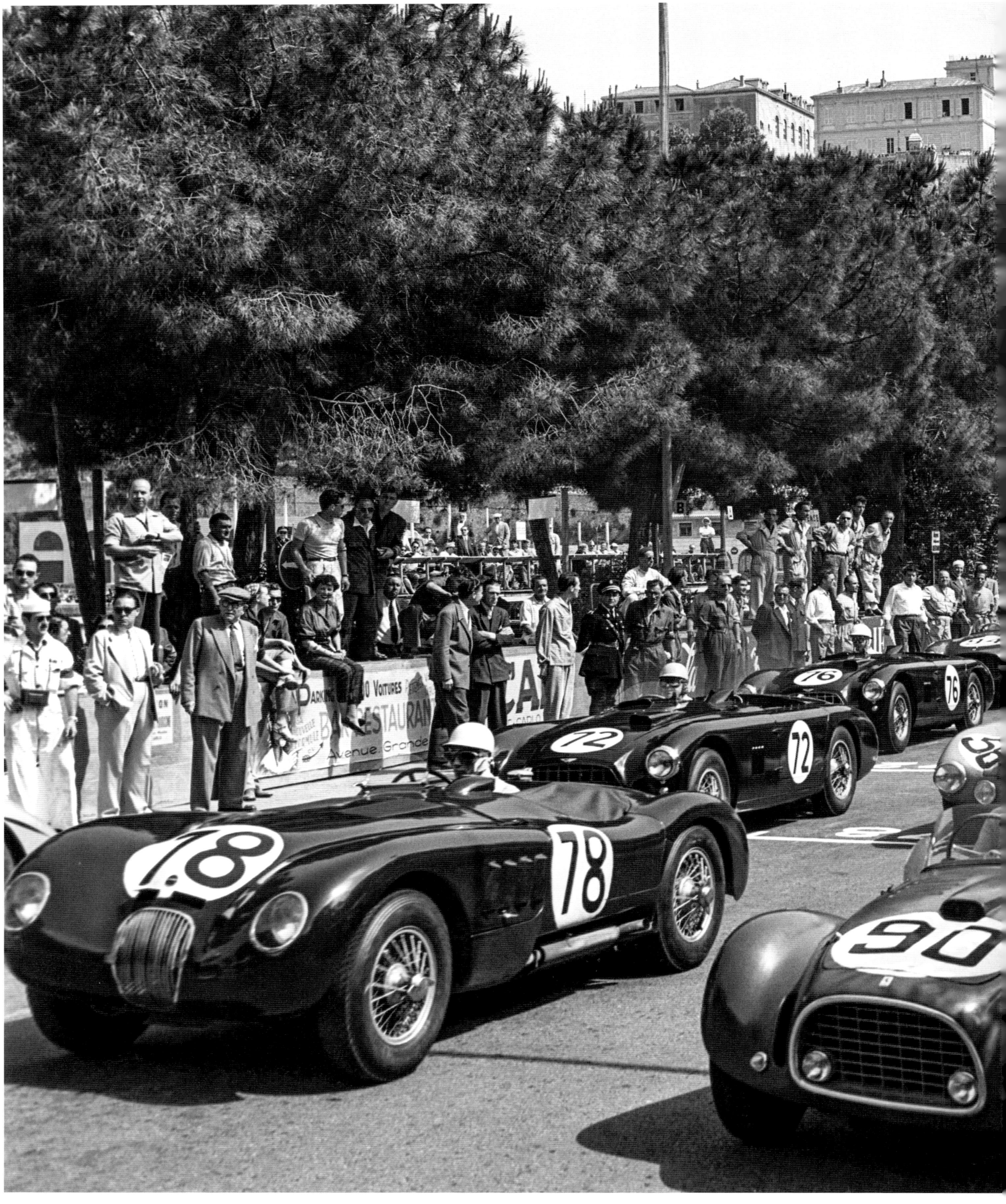
Avenue Grande
78
72
76
90

Grand Prix 1952

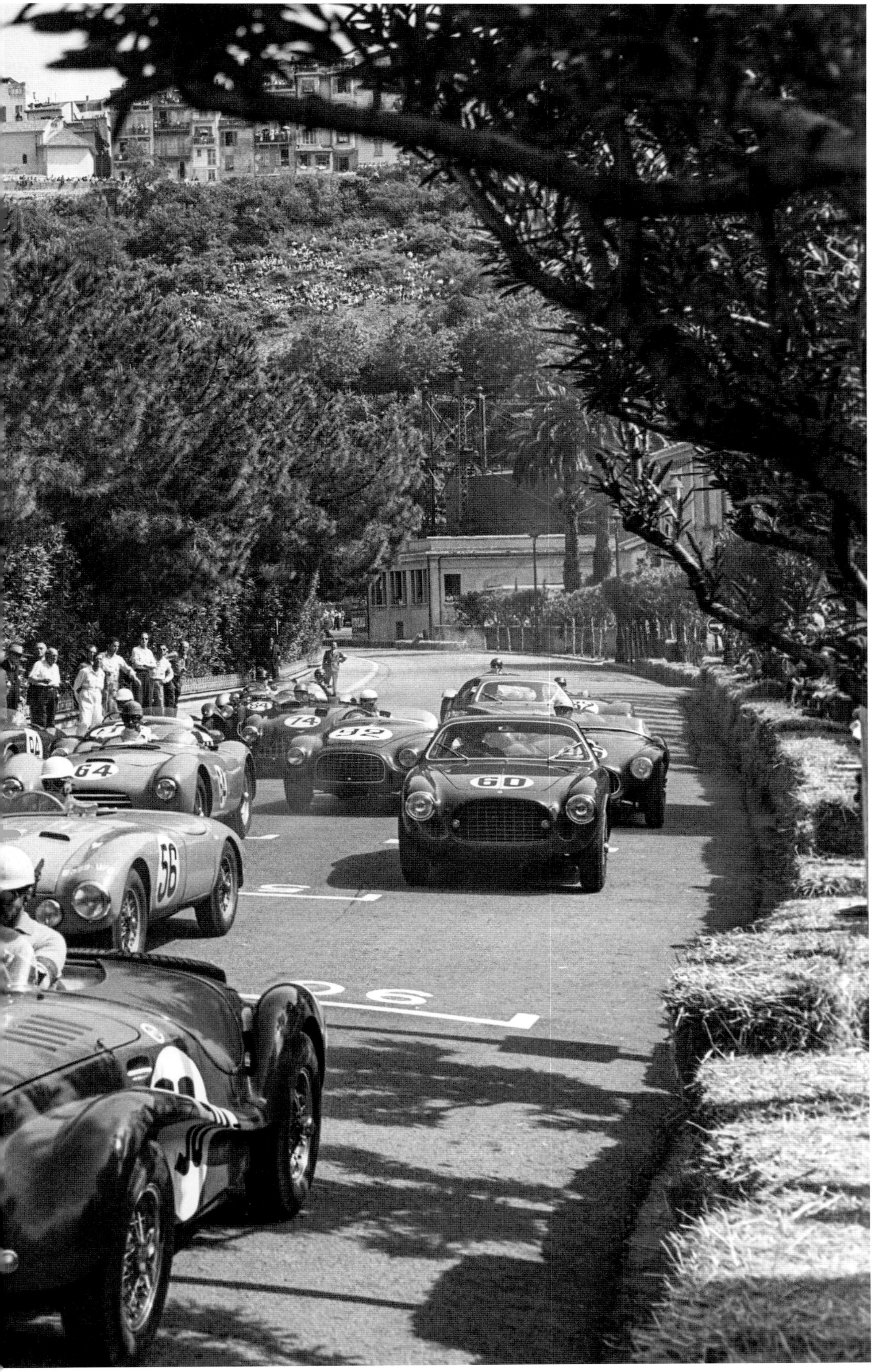

Start!
Stirling Moss, Jaguar C-Type N° 78,
Luigi Stagnoli, Ferrari 225S N° 90,
Robert Manzon, Gordini T15S 2.3 N° 56,
Reg Parnell, Aston Martin DB3 N°72,
„Pagnibon“, Ferrari 225S N° 60,
Lance Macklin, Aston Martin DB3 N° 76,
Louis Rosier, Talbot Lago T26 GS N° 64,
Vittorio Marzotto, Ferrari 225S N° 94,
Eugenio Castellotti, Ferrari 225S N° 92,
Peter Collins, Aston Martin DB3 N° 74,
Anthony Hume, Allard J2 N° 84.

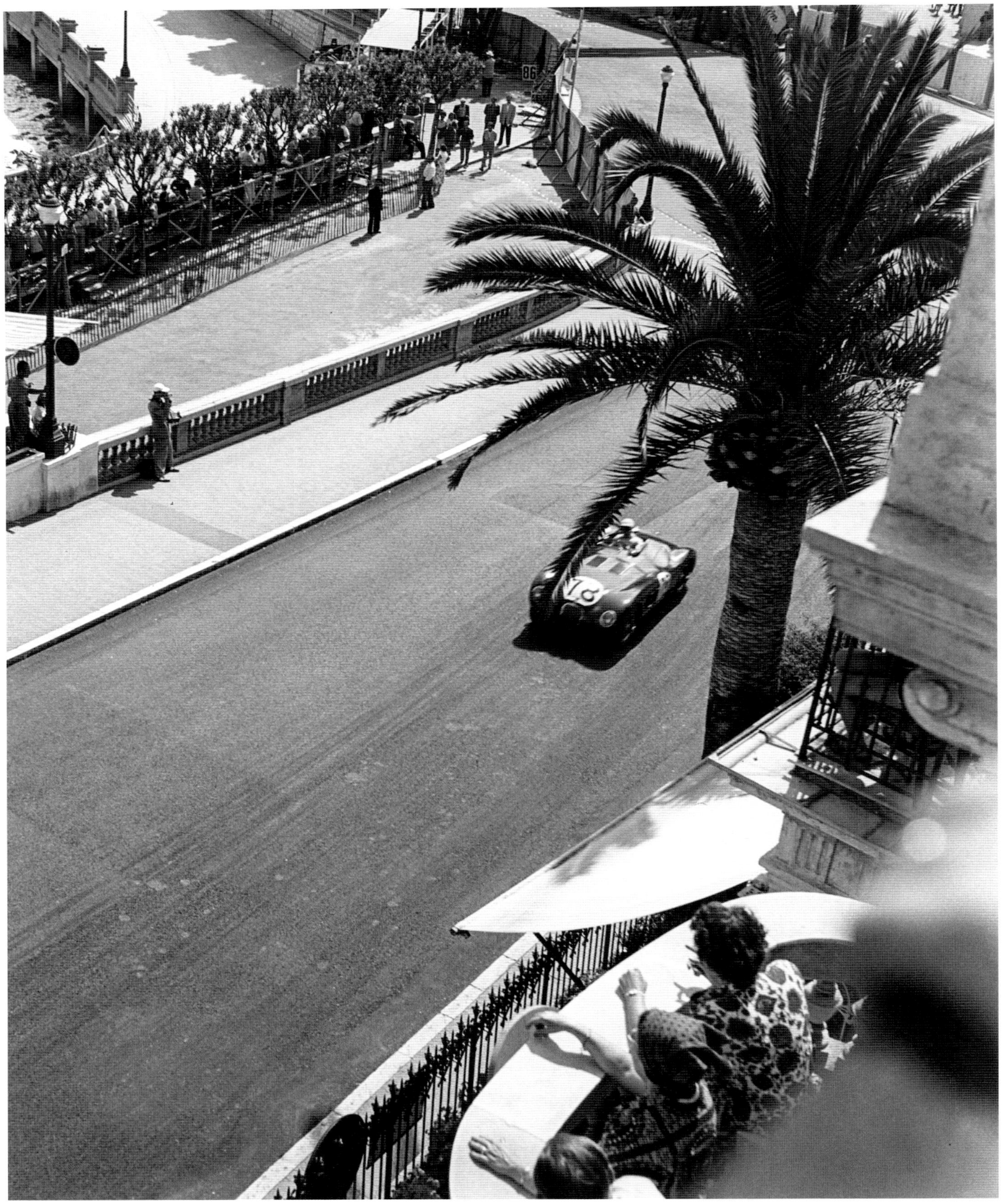

Der Spitzenreiter beim Beau-Rivage-Aufstieg:
Stirling Moss, Jaguar C-Type N° 78.

*The leader on the climb up the Beau Rivage:
Stirling Moss, Jaguar C-Type N° 78.*

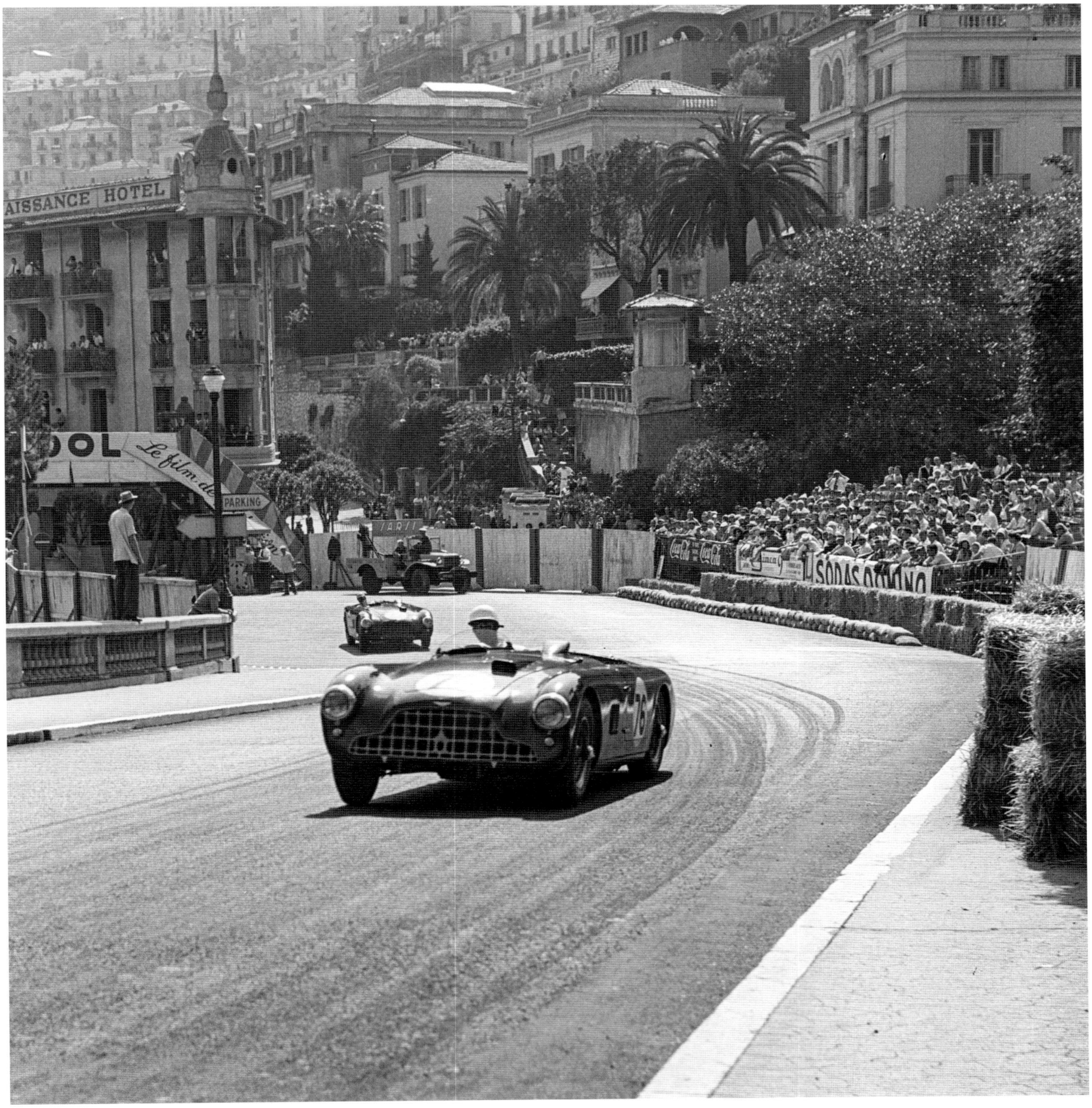

Aus der Sainte-Dévote-Kurve hinaus:
Lance Macklin, Aston Martin DB3 N° 76.
Hinter ihm Peter Collins, Aston Martin DB3 N° 74.

Emerging from the Sainte Dévote corner:
Macklin, Aston Martin DB3 N° 76.
Behind him Peter Collins, Aston Martin DB3 N° 74.

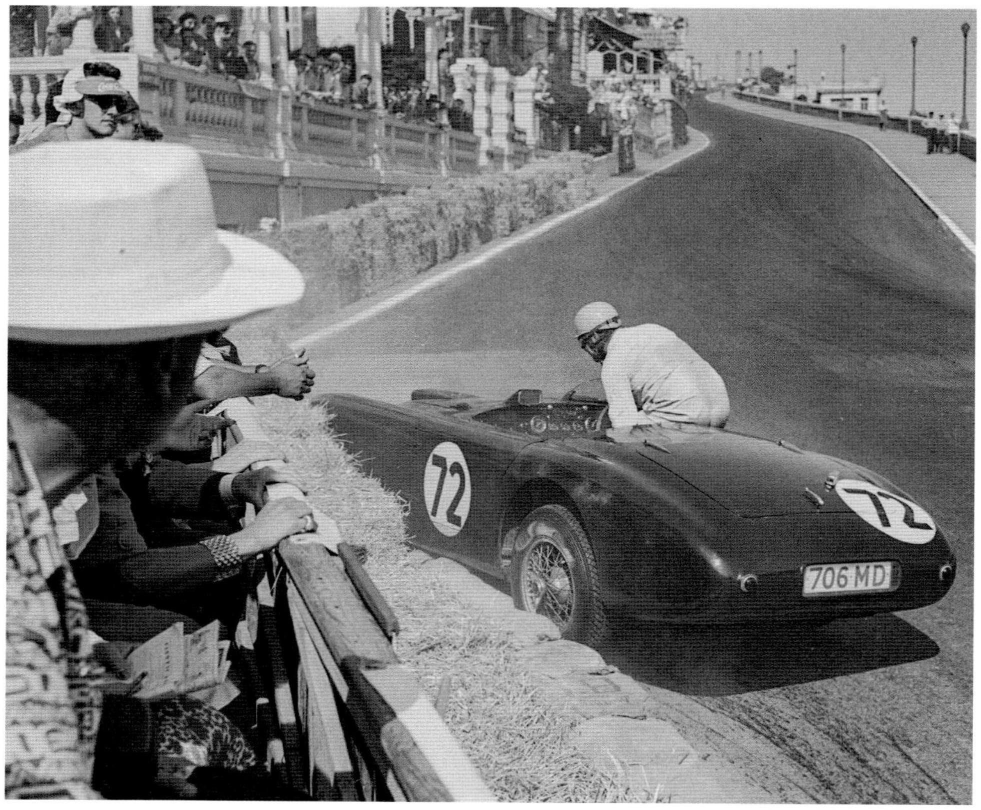

Der spektakuläre Unfall in der Sainte-Dévote-Kurve: Der Aston Martin N° 72 von Reg Parnell hat einen Motorschaden und verliert Öl auf der ganzen Straße. Er rutscht in die Strohballen an der Außenseite der Kurve. Das Auto war in der Mitte der Strecke geparkt …

The spectacular accident on the Sainte Dévote corner: Reg Parnell's Aston Martin N° 72 blows its engine and spills oil all over the road. He collides with the straw bales on the outside of the corner. The car ends up in the middle of the course…

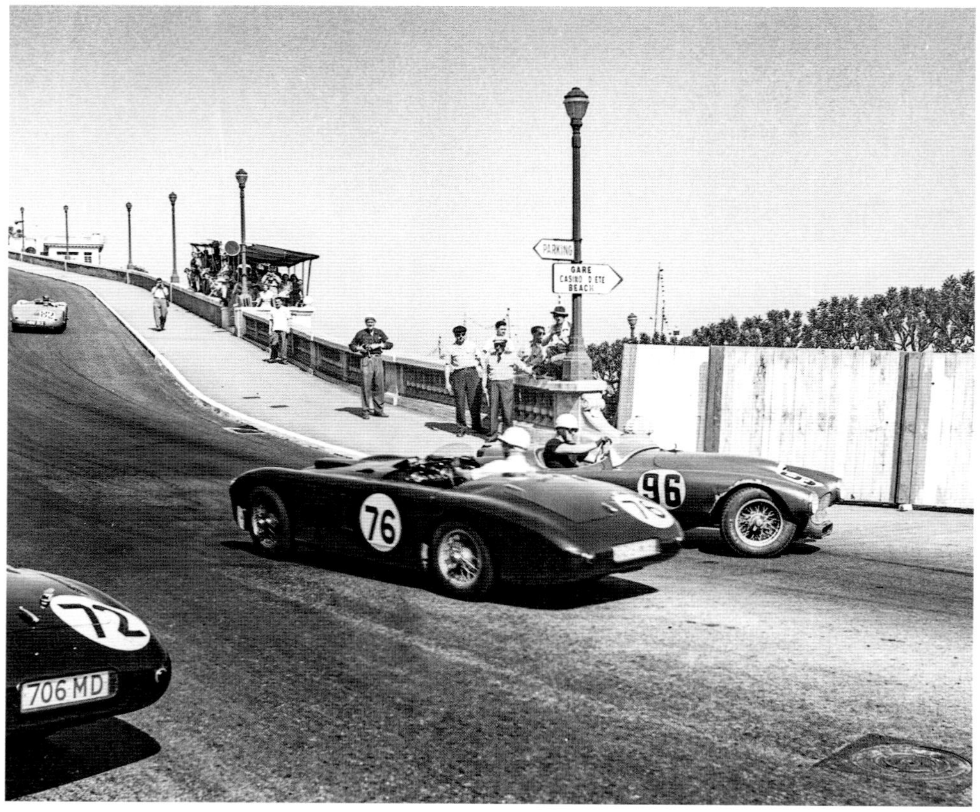

… während Piero Carini, Ferrari 340 N° 96, hart bremst, sich dreht und gegen die Absperrung fährt. Er startet wieder, aber mit beschädigter Hinterachse. Lance Macklin, Aston Martin N° 76, schafft es zu überholen.

…while Piero Carini, Ferrari 340 N° 96, brakes hard, spins to stop against the barrier. He will start again, but with a damaged rear axle. Lance Macklin, Aston Martin N° 76, manages to slip past.

Dann finden Stirling Moss, Jaguar N° 78, und Robert Manzon, Gordini T15S N° 56 die um den ersten Platz kämpfen, die Durchfahrt versperrt, und drehen sich. Manzon trifft den Aston von Parnell mit dem Heck. Wenige Augenblicke später rammt Anthony Hume mit seinem Allard N° 84 die anderen Autos rückwärts.

Then Stirling Moss, Jaguar N° 78, and Robert Manzon, Gordini T15S N° 56, fighting for first place, find the way blocked and both spin. Manzon hits the Aston of Parnell stern-first. A few moments later, Anthony Hume, with his Allard N° 84, rams the other cars from behind.

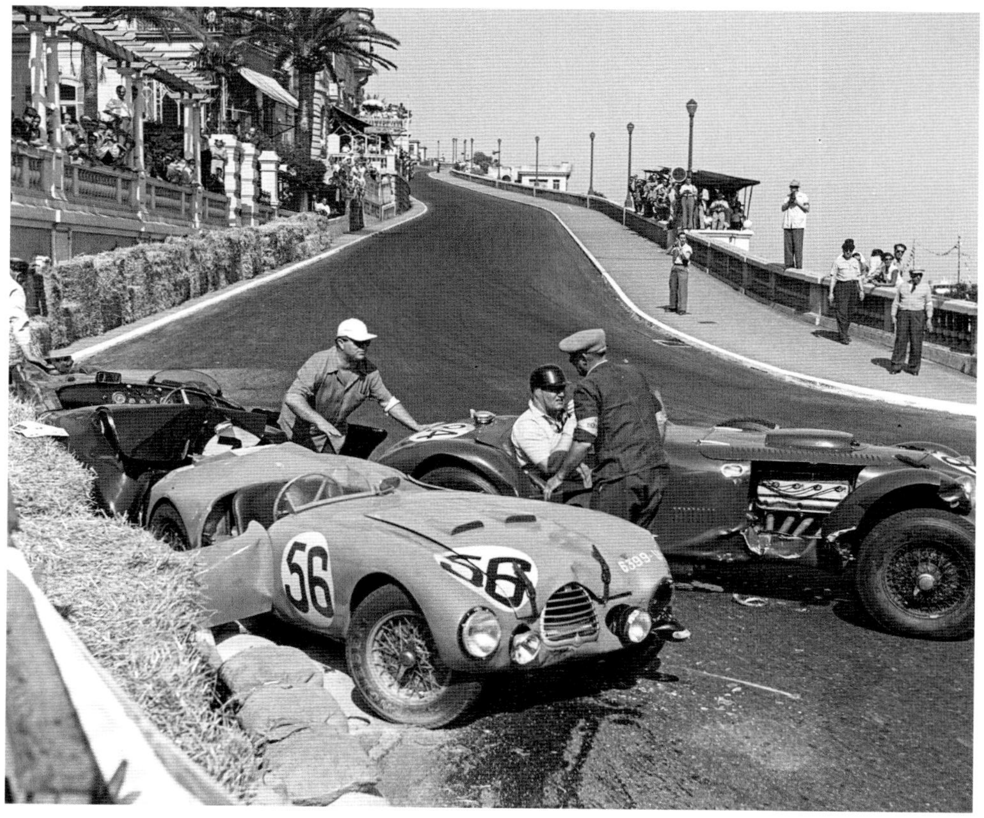

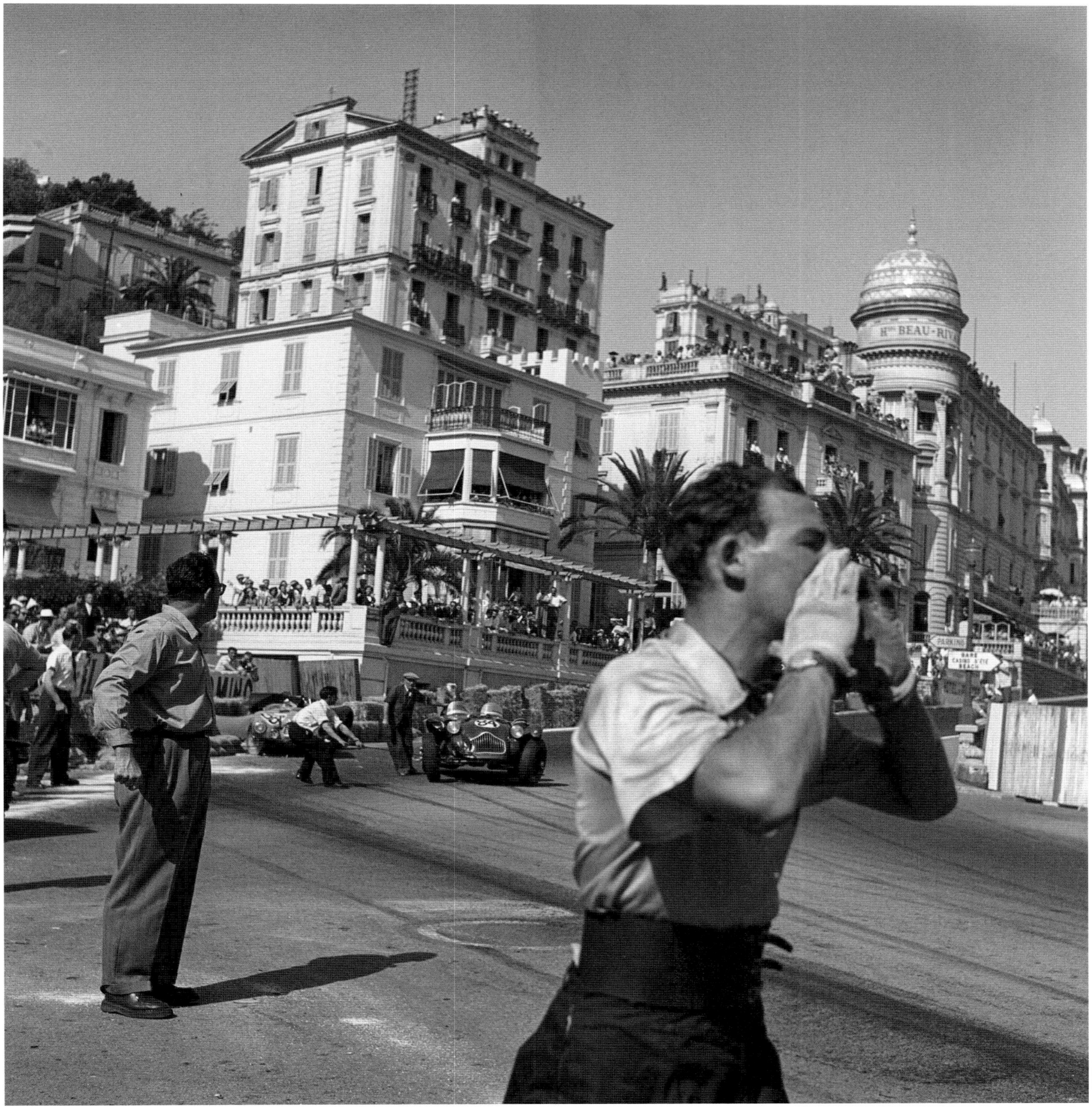

Stirling Moss ruft nach Unterstützung, während im Hintergrund der Allard N° 84 von Hume weggeräumt wird.

Stirling Moss calls for support, while in the background Hume's Allard N° 84 is cleared away.

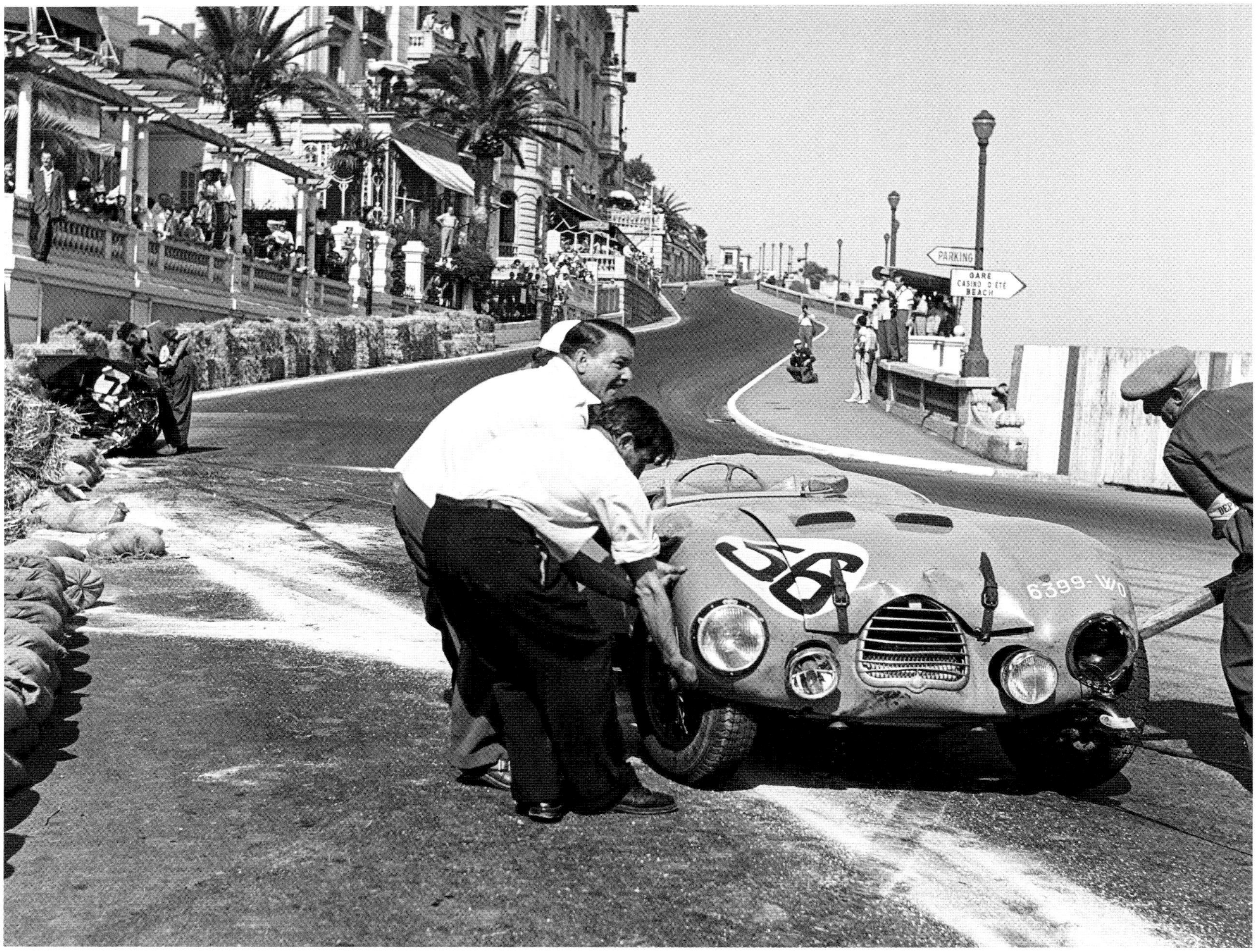

Die Streckenposten versuchen den Gordini N° 56
von Manzon von der Strecke zu räumen.

*The marshals try to clear Manzon's Gordini N° 56
from the course.*

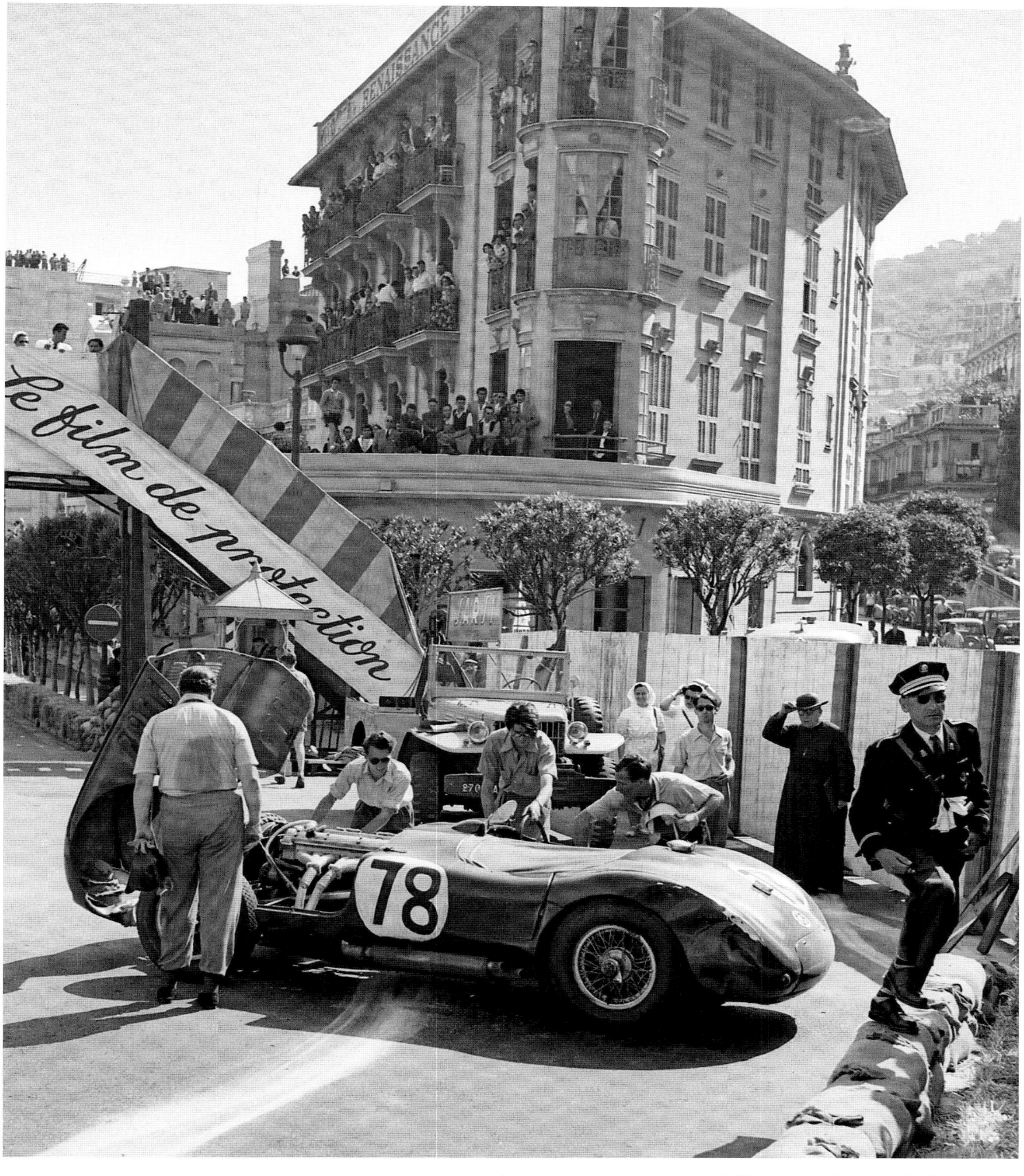

Moss versucht, seinen Jaguar mithilfe von Tony Crook wieder flott zu machen. Das notwendige Personal für alle Fälle ist auch bereit: Polizei, Krankenschwester und Pfarrer.

Moss tries to get his Jaguar back on track with the help of Tony Crook. The necessary personnel for all eventualities are also on hand: a policeman, a nurse and a priest.

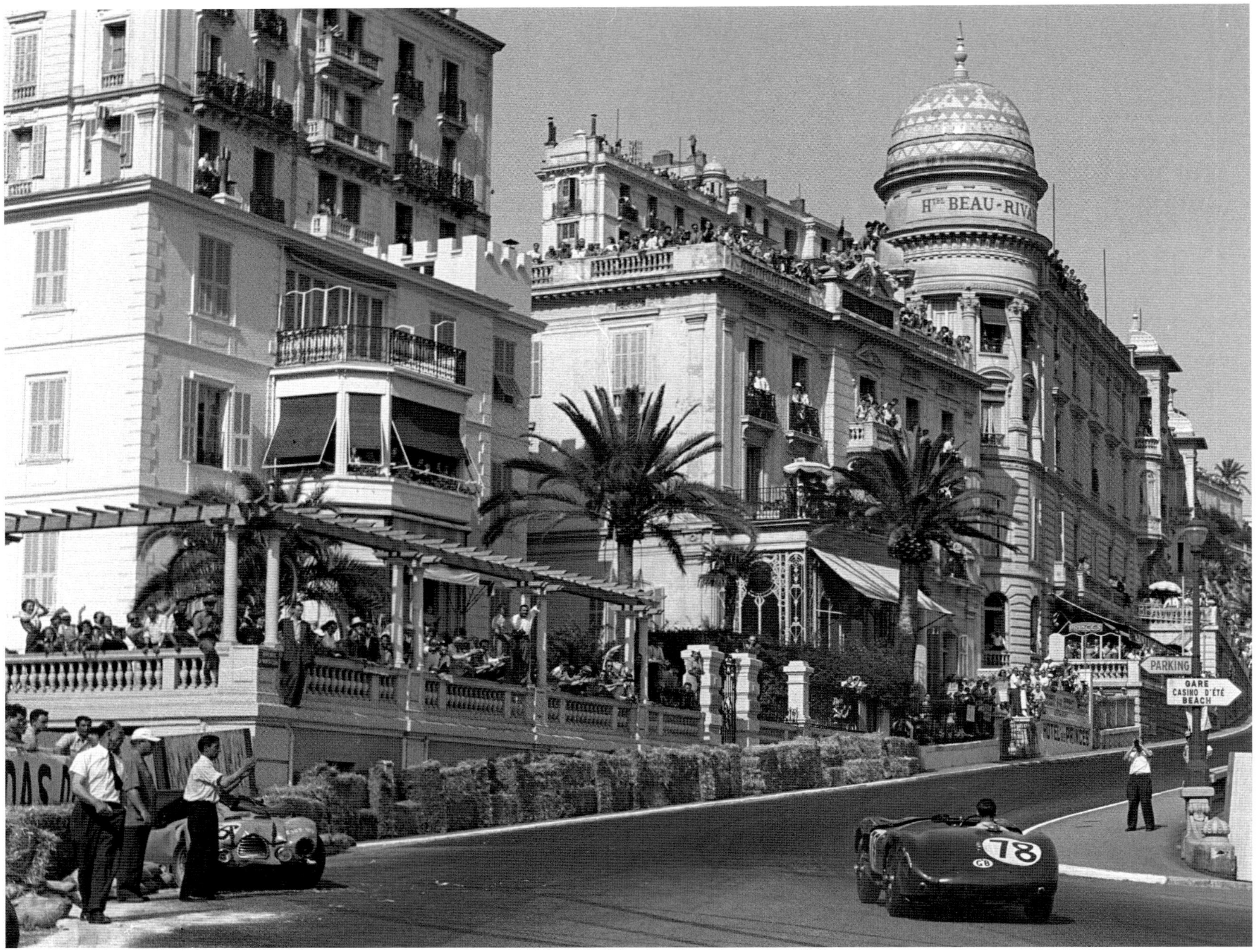

Unter großem Beifall der Zuschauer kann Moss das Rennen
mit einem beschädigten, aber fahrbaren Jaguar fortsetzen.

*To appreciative applause from the spectators, Moss gets away
with a damaged but drivable Jaguar.*

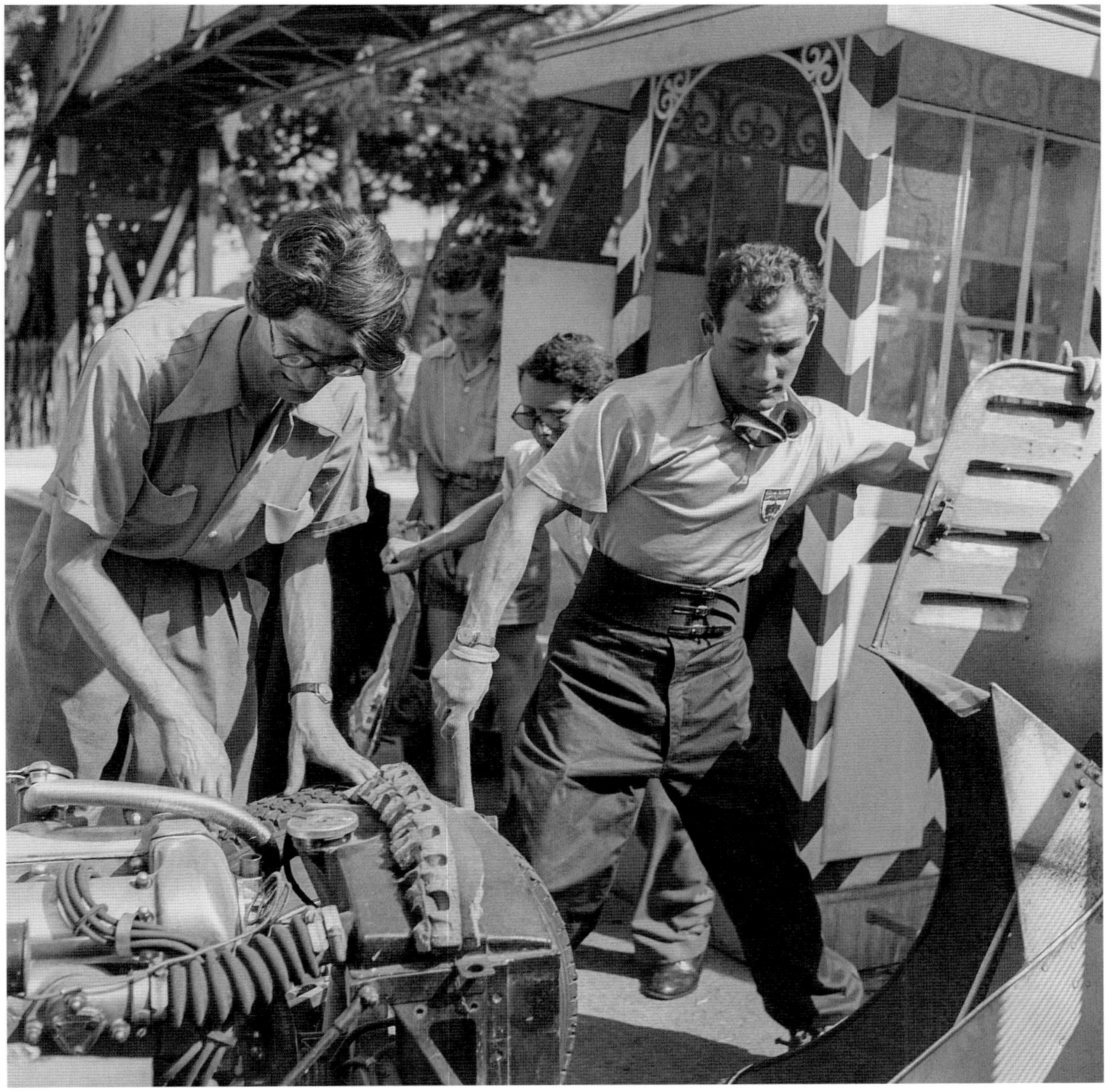

An den Boxen hilft Moss den Mechanikern mit einem großen Hammer, den Jaguar wieder etwas in Form zu bringen. Links Tony Crook. Die Hinterräder werden gewechselt und Moss ist wieder im Rennen. Er wird noch Fünfter – wird aber disqualifiziert, weil ihm zwei britische Zuschauer nach dem Unfall geholfen hatten.

In the pits, Moss uses a large hammer to help the mechanics knock the Jaguar back into shape. Tony Crook on the left. The rear wheels are changed and Moss is back in the race. He still finishes fifth – but is disqualified because two British spectators helped him after the accident.

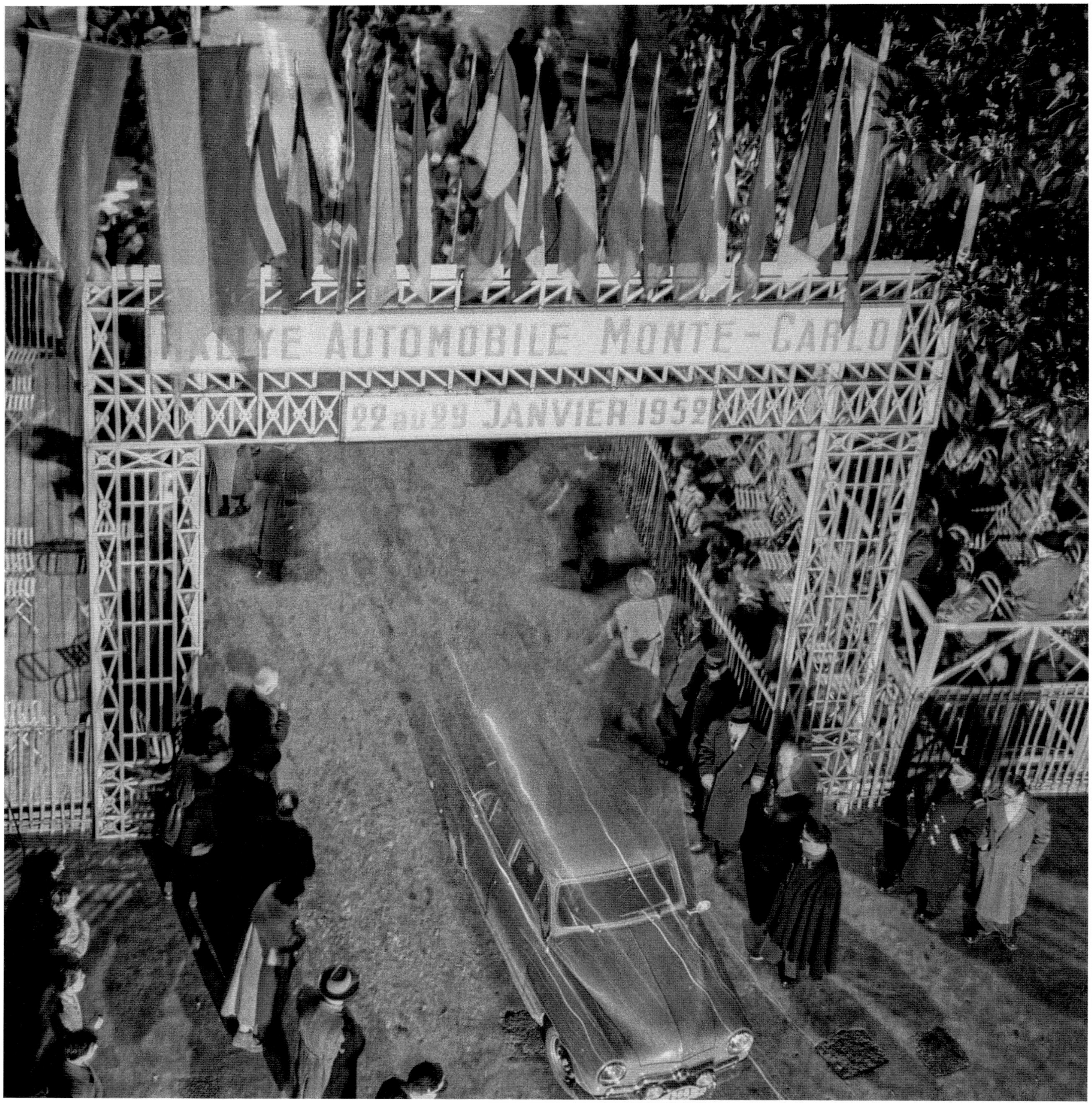

Start zur Rallye-Runde von Monte-Carlo aus.
Bonnet/Monnet, Simca Aronde N° 368.

Start of the Rally section in Monte Carlo.
Bonnet/Monnet, Simca Aronde N° 368.

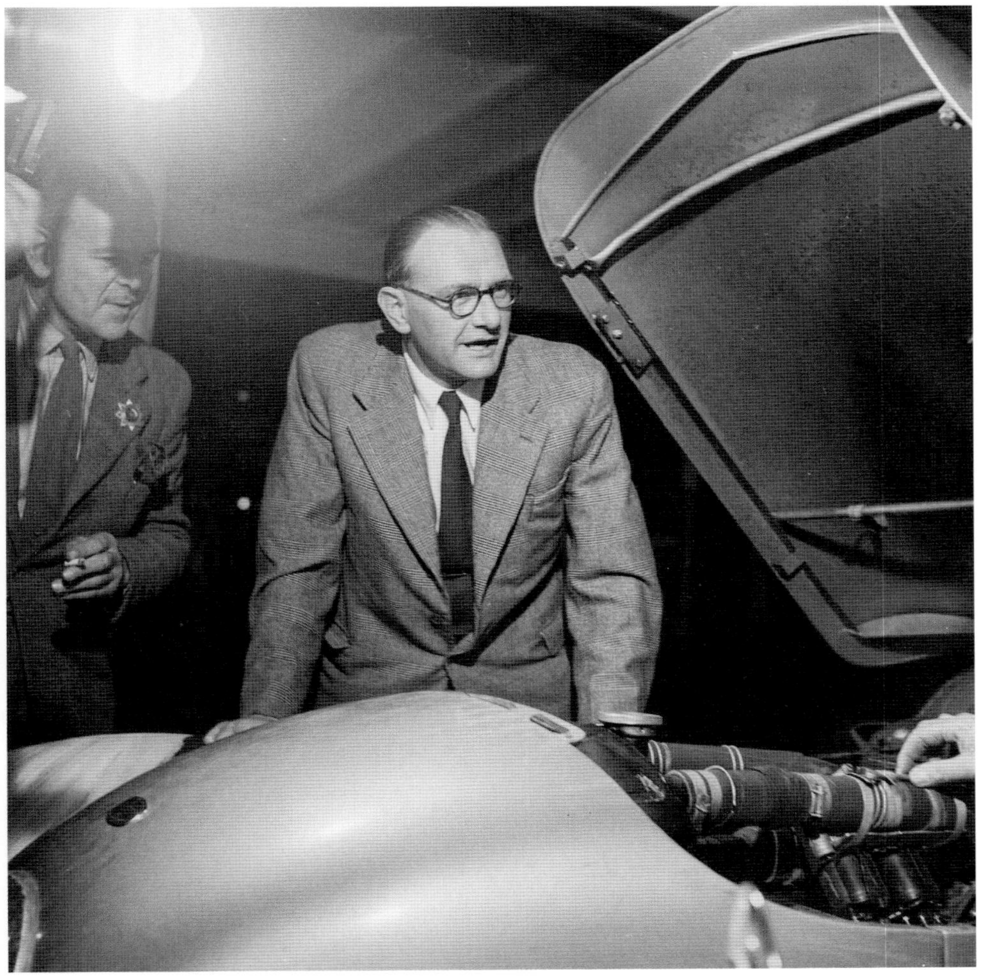

Sydney H. Allard, Sieger dieser Rallye, mit seinem Allard P1 N° 146. Er war der Gründer der Autofirma Allard und ein erfolgreicher Rennfahrer in Autos aus eigener Konstruktion.

Sydney H. Allard, winner of the Rally, with his Allard P1 N° 146. He was the founder of the Allard car company and a successful racing driver in cars of his own construction.

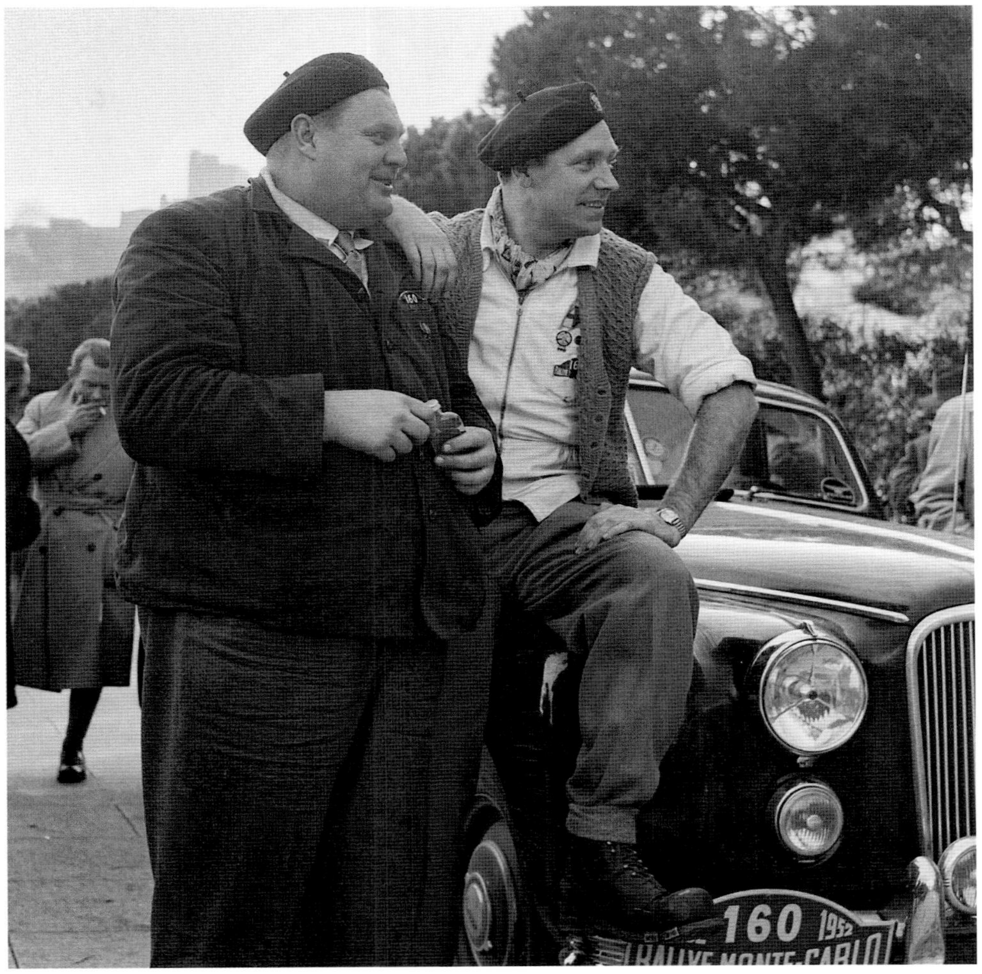

Gute Stimmung, leichtes Übergewicht: 160 Korpoo/Pulkkinen, Jaguar Mark VII N° 160.

Light-hearted heavy-weights: Korpoo/Pulkkinen, Jaguar Mark VII N° 160.

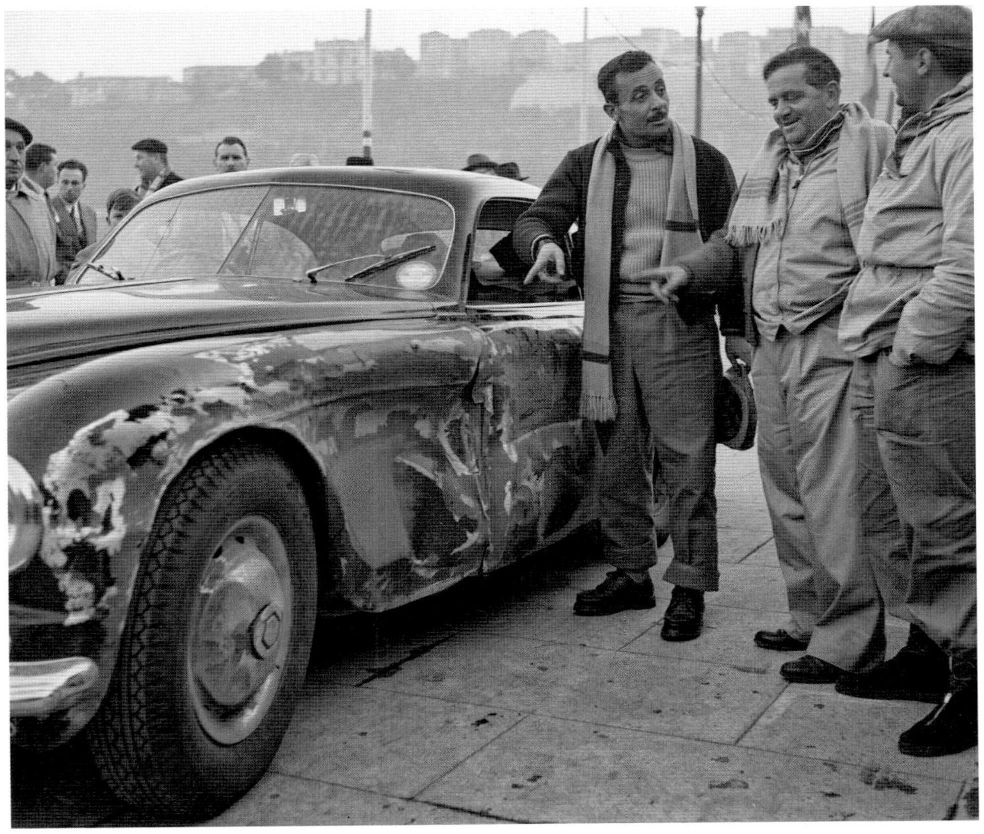

Gute Stimmung, schwerer Schaden: Ferrario/Pellecchia, Alfa Romeo 6c N° 194. Blechschäden hatten bis 1961 noch Strafpunkte zur Folge.

Light-hearted discussion of damaged bodywork: Ferrario/Pellecchia, Alfa Romeo 6c N° 194. Until 1961, so-called "fender benders" still resulted in penalty points.

Rallye 1952

Ein Monat später, 100 Kilometer weiter im Süden an der Côte d'Azur: Am Ziel der 13. Rallye Paris – Saint-Raphaël Féminin, einer Rallye nur für weibliche Teilnehmer in Frankreich. Sie fand über einen Zeitraum von 45 Jahren statt, beginnend im Jahr 1929.

A month later, 100 kilometres further south on the Côte d'Azur: At the finish of the 13th Rally Paris – Saint-Raphaël Féminin, a rally exclusively for female participants in France. It took place over a period of 45 years, starting in 1929.

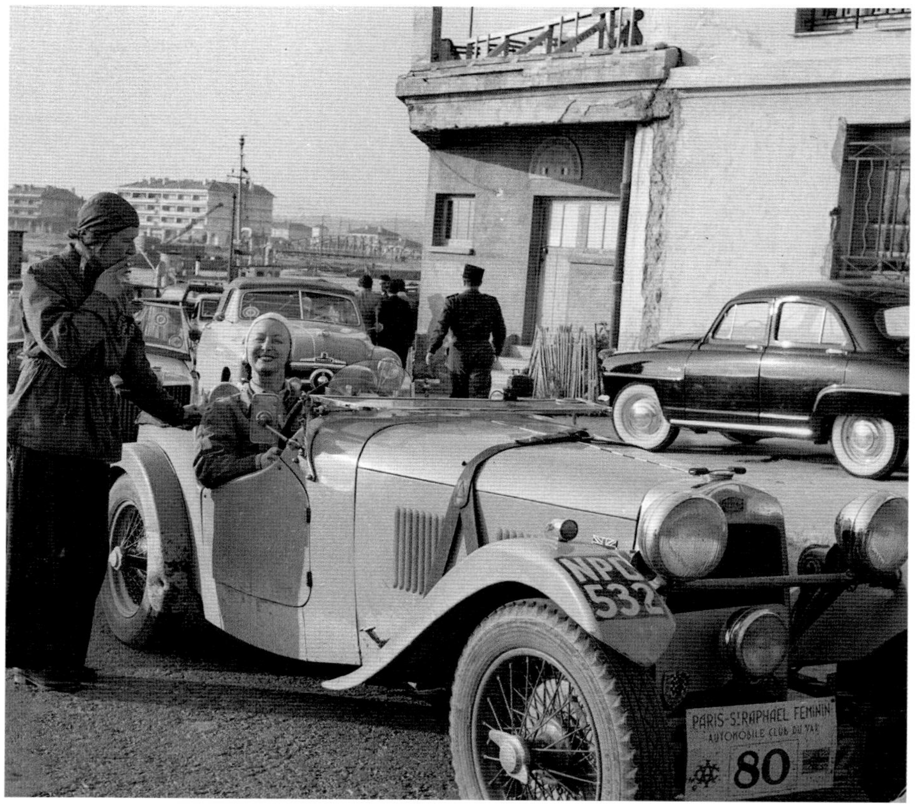

Nancy Mitchell, erste in ihrer Kategorie, fröhlich am Steuer des Cabrios N° 80 der heute längst vergessenen britischen Marke HRG. Von den 241 produzierten HRG sollen 225 überlebt haben.

Nancy Mitchell, first in class, cheerfully at the wheel of the N° 80 convertible of the now long-forgotten British marque HRG. Of the 241 cars made, it is estimated that 225 survive.

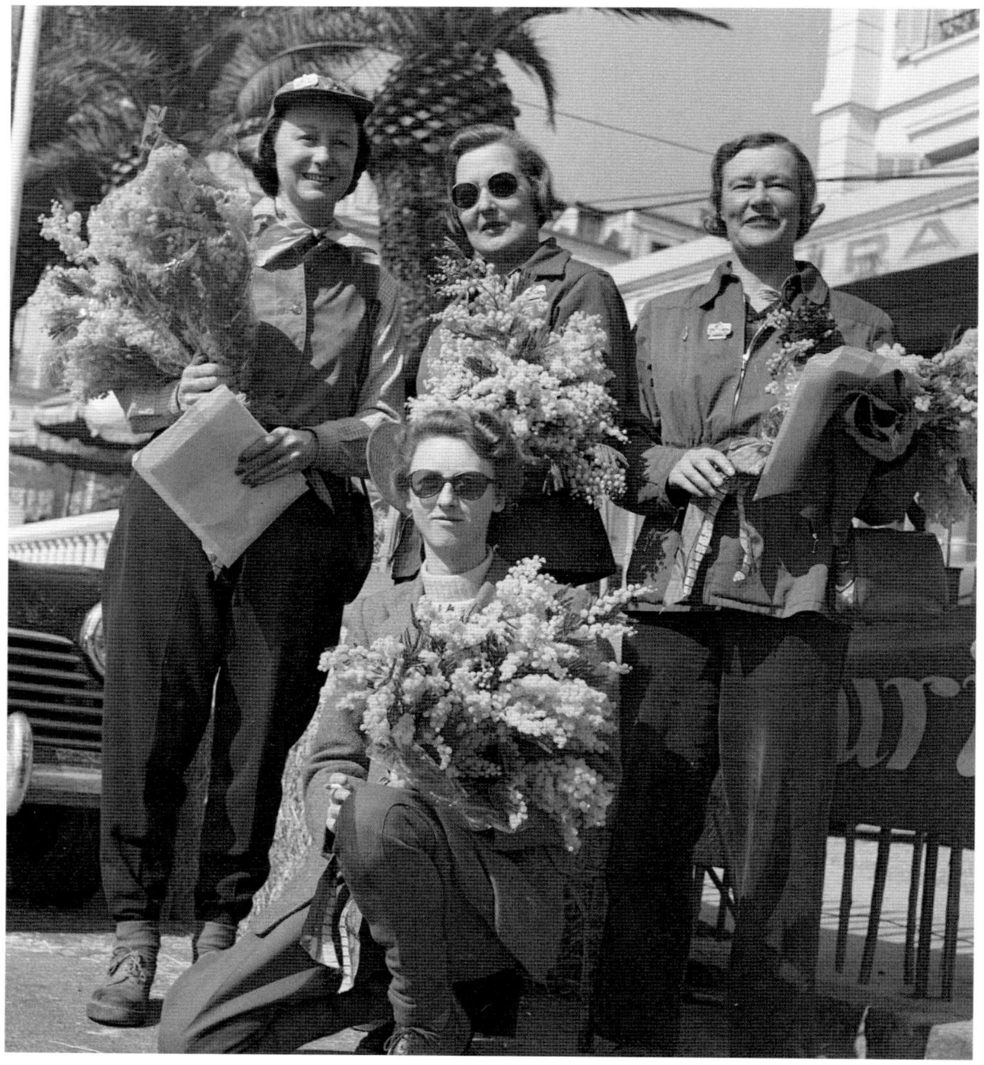

Vier gewinnende Frauen. *Four winning women.*

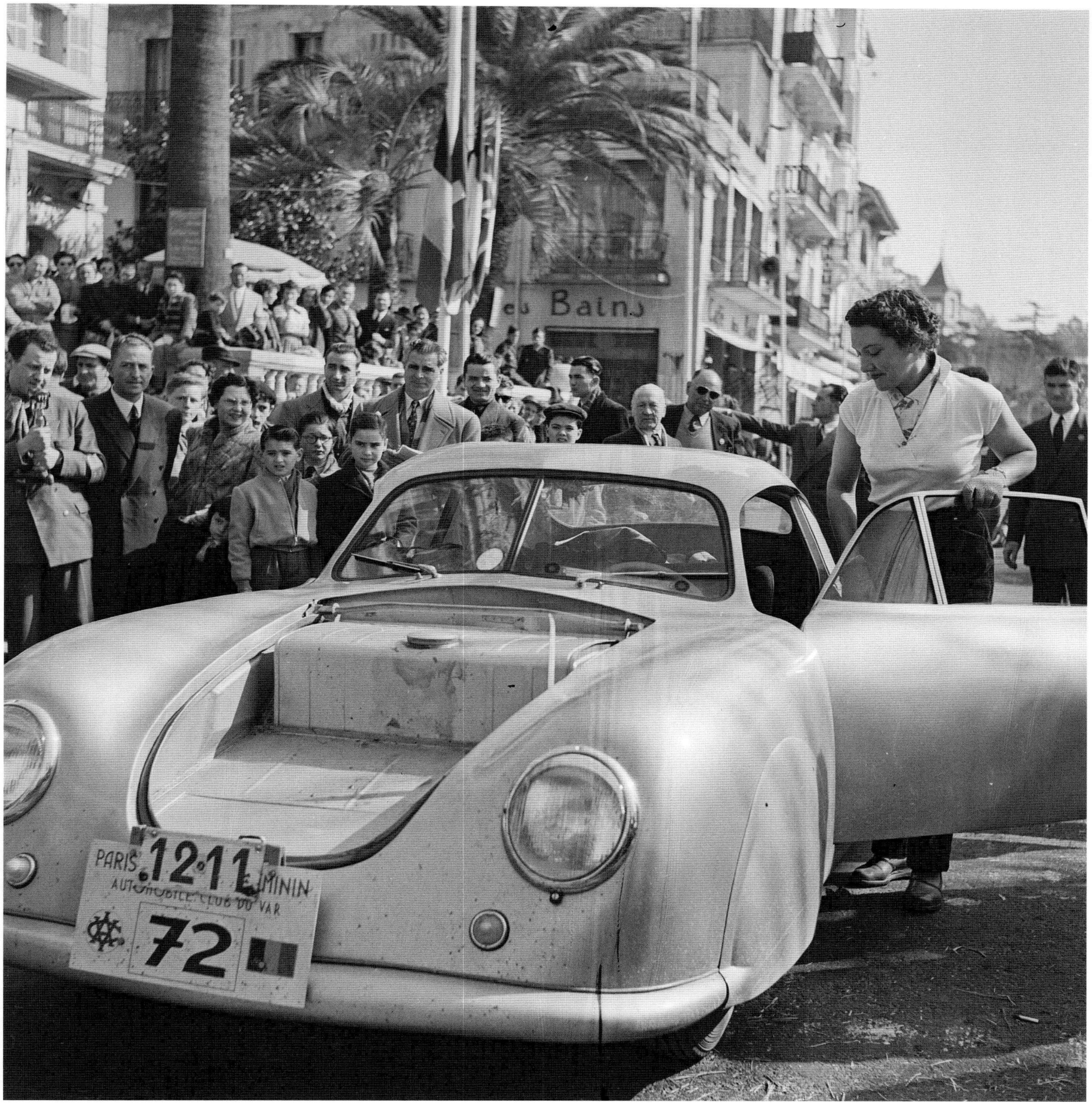

Gilberte Thirion, Zweite in ihrer Kategorie, Porsche 356 SL („Super Leicht“) N° 72, auch genannt „Alubüchsle“, wegen der Aluminiumkarosserie. Der Aerodynamik-Effekt der Radabdeckung wurde hier wohl kompensiert durch die fehlende Haube. Sollte so das Gewicht nochmals reduziert werden?

Gilberte Thirion, second in class, Porsche 356 SL ("Super Leicht") N° 72, also called "Alubüchsle" (little tin box) because of its aluminium body. The aerodynamic effect of the wheel cover was probably compensated here by the missing bonnet. Was this possibly an attempt to further reduce the weight?

Nachtruhe in Monaco. *All calm in Monaco by night.*

1953 – 1954

Rallye mit Teilnahmerekord

1953 und 1954 werden keine Grand Prix ausgetragen. Die Rallye Monte-Carlo dagegen erlebt 1953 einen Teilnahmerekord mit 404 Teams, von denen 346 das Rennen beenden. Wie immer seit der Gründung 1911 beginnt das große Motorsportereignis mit einer Sternfahrt der Equipen nach Monte Carlo von verschiedenen europäischen Städten über tausende von Kilometern: 112 Teams von Lissabon, 103 von Glasgow, 42 von Stockholm, 37 von München, 15 von Oslo, und 11 von Palermo. Für Fahrer von Monaco aus ist die Anfahrt als Rundkurs organisiert.

Wegen des guten Wetters kommen 253 Teams ex aequo klassiert ohne Strafpunkte in Monte Carlo an. Der Brems-/Beschleunigungswettbewerb entscheidet dann, welche 100 Equipen noch an der Gleichmäßigkeitsprüfung am Col de Braus teilnehmen dürfen: Die Autos sollen aus dem Stand 200 Meter so schnell wie möglich erreichen und dann so bremsen, dass der Wagen auf einer Linie zwischen den zwei Achsen stehen bleibt. Nach weiteren 50 Metern wird die Zeit gestoppt. Dass eine so kurze Prüfung, bei der die starken Autos im Vorteil sind, nach so vielen tausend Kilometern letztlich entscheidet, stößt auf große Kritik von Fahrern und Presse. Die Organisatoren werden heftig angegriffen, man spricht von einer unsportlichen Lotterie und die Fortführung der Rallye wird infrage gestellt.

Die Organisatoren reagieren: 1954 wird der Brems-/Beschleunigungswettbewerb nicht mehr durchgeführt und zusätzliche Prüfungen werden eingeführt: ein Bergrennen über 3,7 km auf den Mont Agel und ein Rennen über fünf Runden auf der originalen Grand-Prix-Strecke in Monaco.

Rally with record participation

There was no Grand Prix held in 1953 and 1954. The Monte Carlo Rally, on the other hand, attracted record numbers of participants in 1953, with 404 teams, 346 of whom finished the race. As always since its inception in 1911, the great motorsport event began with a rally of teams to Monte Carlo from various European cities over thousands of kilometres: 112 teams from Lisbon, 103 from Glasgow, 42 from Stockholm, 37 from Munich, 15 from Oslo, and 11 from Palermo. For drivers from Monaco, the journey was organised as a circuit.

Because of the good weather, 253 teams arrived in Monte Carlo ex aequo classified without penalty points. The braking/acceleration competition then decided which 100 teams were still allowed to take part in the regularity test on the Col de Braus: the cars had to reach 200 metres from a standing start as quickly as possible and then brake in such a way that the car stopped on a line between the two axles. After another 50 metres, the time was stopped. The fact that such a short test, in which the strongest cars had an advantage, became the ultimate decider after so many thousands of kilometres was met with a great deal of negativity from drivers and the press. The organisers were heavily criticised – there was talk of an unsporting lottery and the continuation of the Rally was called into question.

The organisers responded in 1954, the braking/acceleration competition was abandoned and additional tests were introduced: a 3.7 km hill climb up Mont Agel and a five-lap race on the original Grand Prix circuit in Monaco.

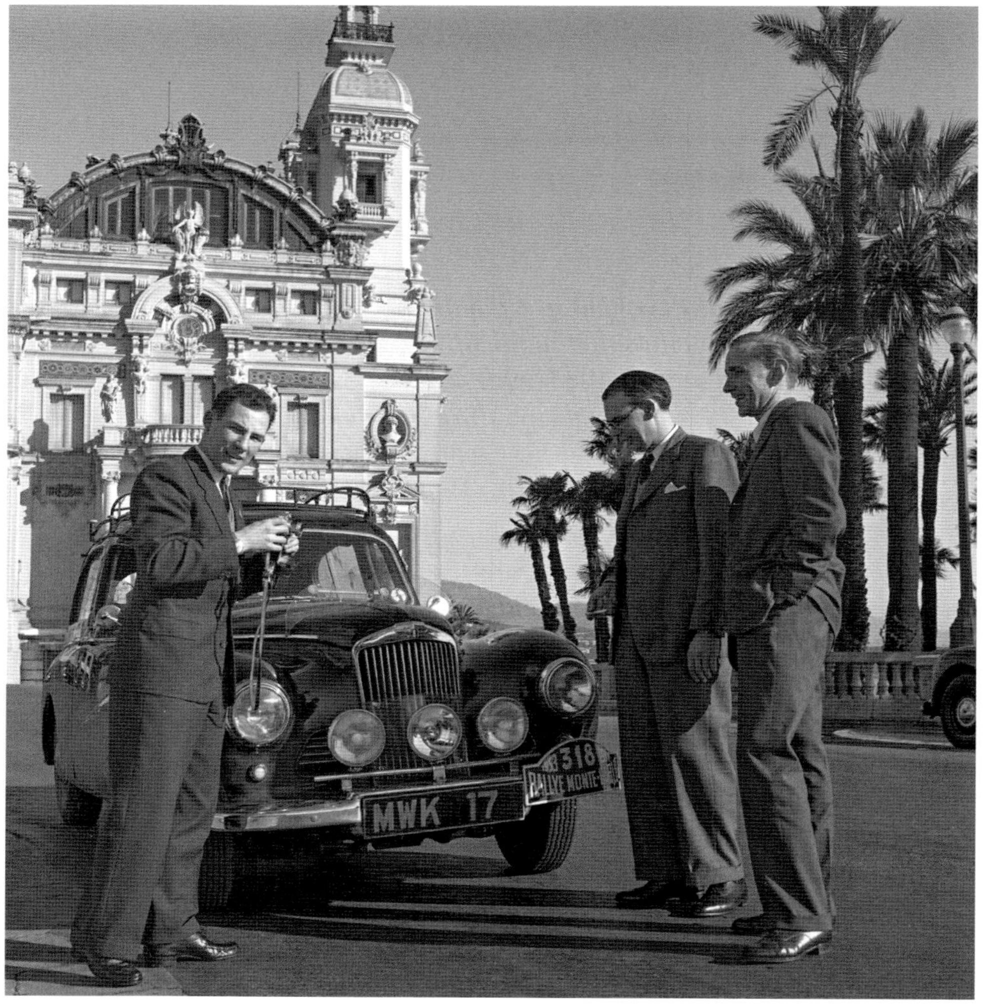

Stirling Moss fotografiert sein Team im Sonntagsanzug vor dem Casino, vor dem Cocktail zu Ehren der Fahrer im Jardin Exotique. Stirling Moss/John Cooper/Desmond Scannell, Sunbeam Talbot 90 N° 318, 6. Rang.

Stirling Moss taking a photo of his team in their Sunday best in front of the Casino, before the cocktail reception in honour of the drivers in the Jardin Exotique. Stirling Moss/John Cooper/Desmond Scannell, Sunbeam Talbot 90 N° 318, 6th in race.

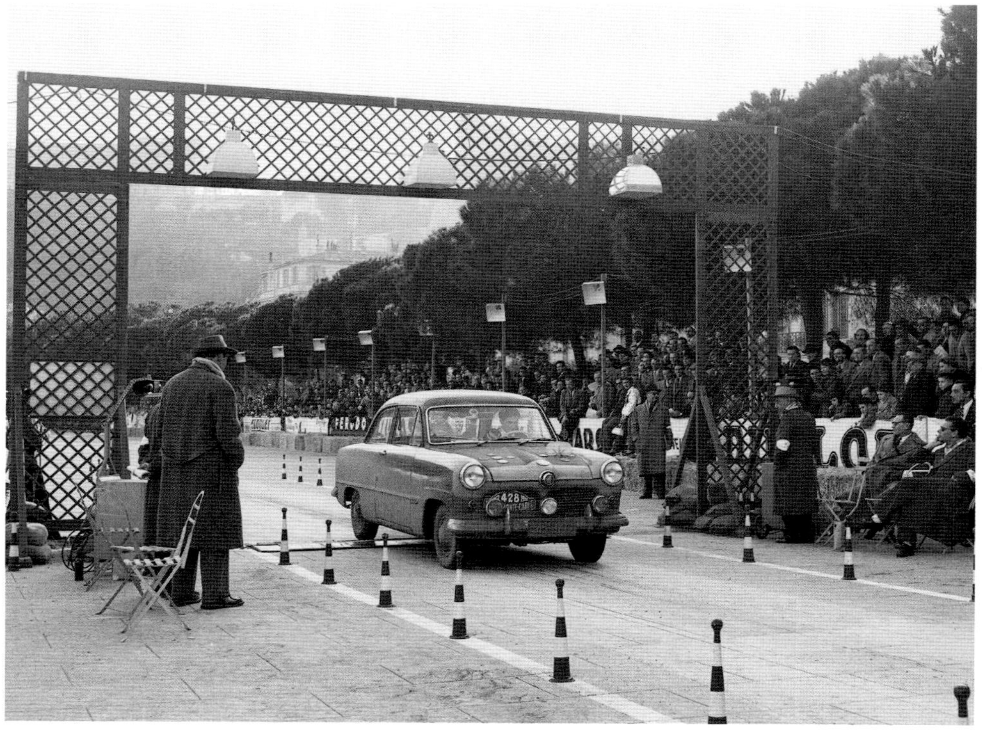

Krull/Vidal, Ford Taunus N° 428, beim Brems-/Beschleunigungswettbewerb. Die Linie, die sich nach dem Bremsen zwischen den Achsen befinden muss, ist deutlich sichtbar.

Krull/Vidal, Ford Taunus N° 428, completing the braking/acceleration competition. The line that must be between the axles after braking is clearly visible.

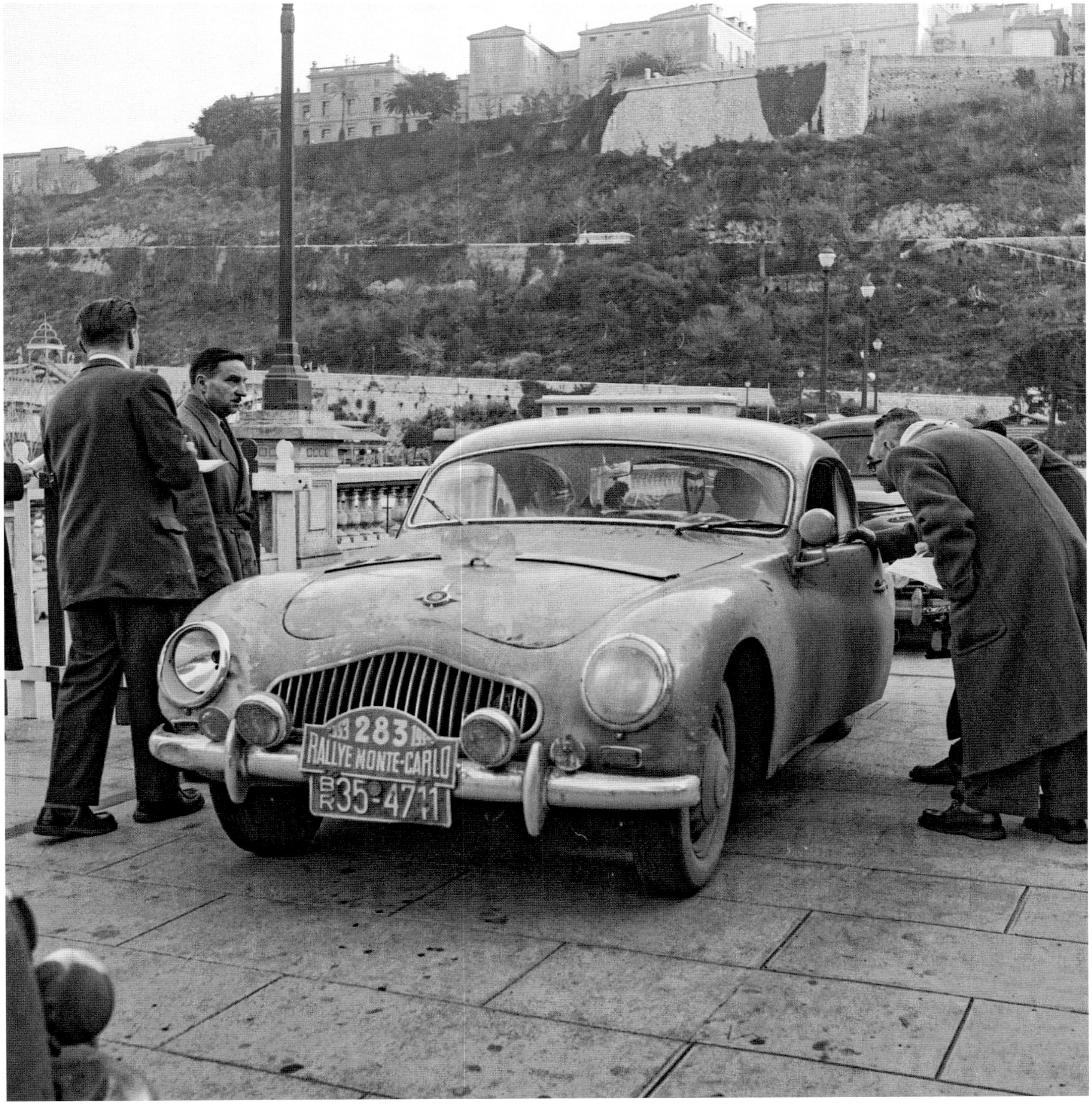

Cremer/Loof, Veritas-Nürburgring C 3/52 N° 283. Ein dreisitziger sportlicher Luxuswagen. Sechs Stück sollen gebaut worden sein, drei existieren noch, darunter dieser Wagen.

Cremer/Loof, Veritas-Nürburgring C 3/52 N° 283. A three-seater luxury sports car. Six are said to have been built, three still exist, including this car.

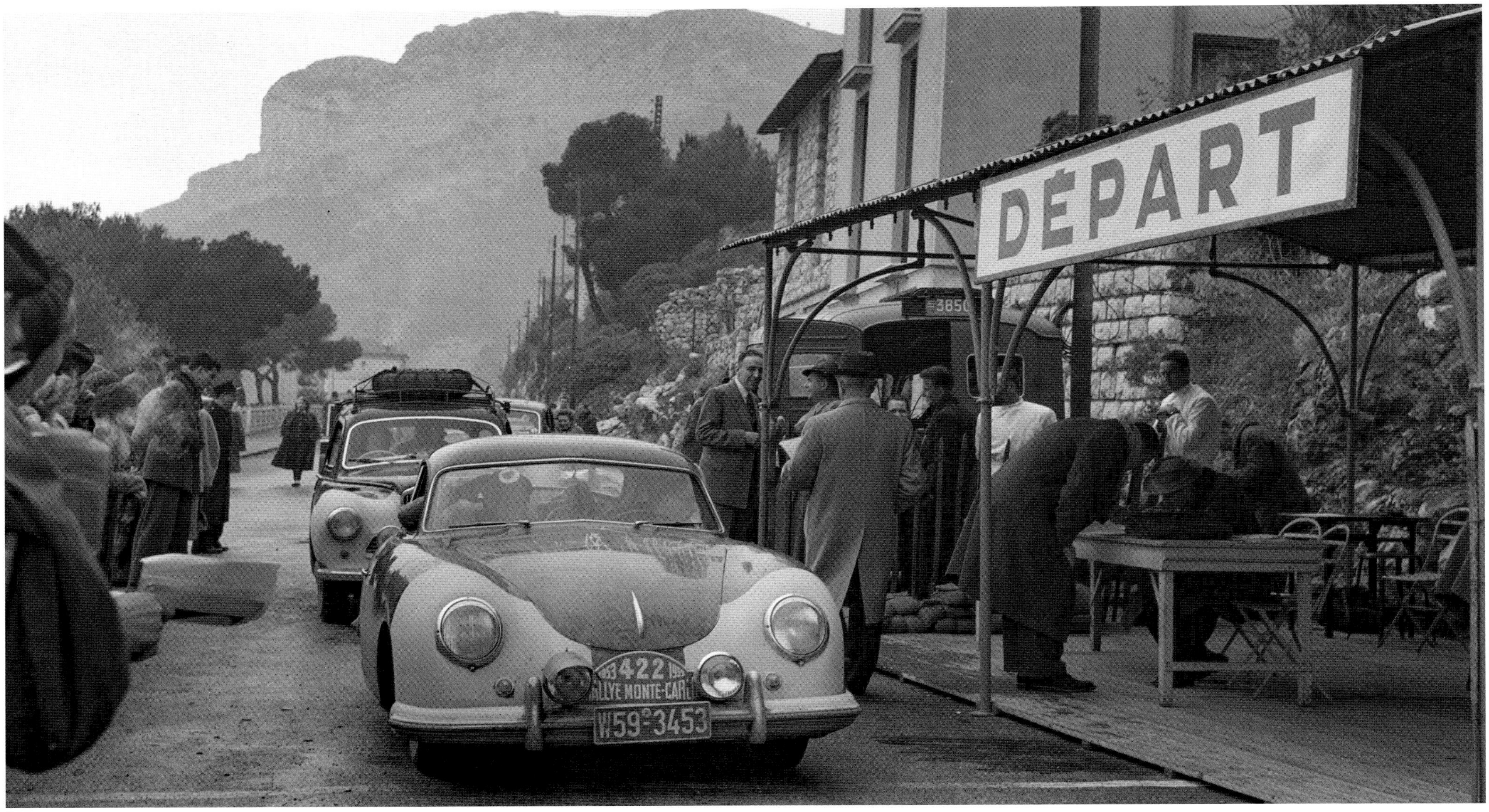

Um zu verhindern, dass die Teilnehmer unbemerkt an den Zeitnehmern vorbeifahren, beschlossen die Organisatoren, die vorderen Kotflügel der Autos mit abwaschbarer Farbe weiß zu streichen. So konnten die Offiziellen sie schon von Weitem identifizieren, auch wenn ihre Rallye-Schilder aufgrund von Schmutz oder ihrer Position am Auto nicht gut sichtbar waren.

To prevent the competitors from taking the time-keepers by surprise and passing without being spotted the organisers decided to paint the front wings of the cars white with washable paint. This enabled the officials to try to identify them a long way off even if their rally plates were not easily visible because of dirt or their position on the car.

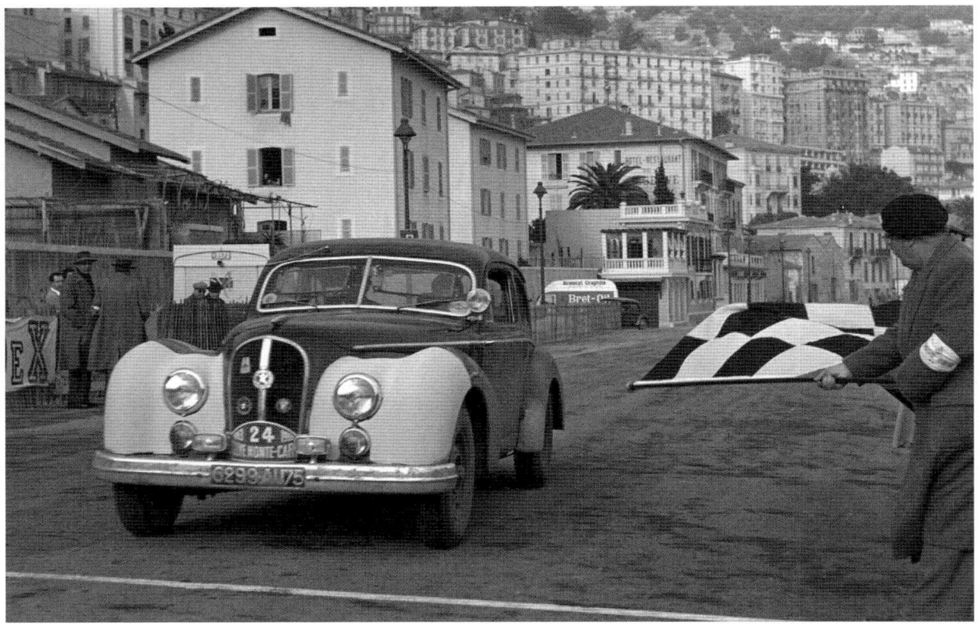

Cohade/Monjo, Hotchkiss N° 24.

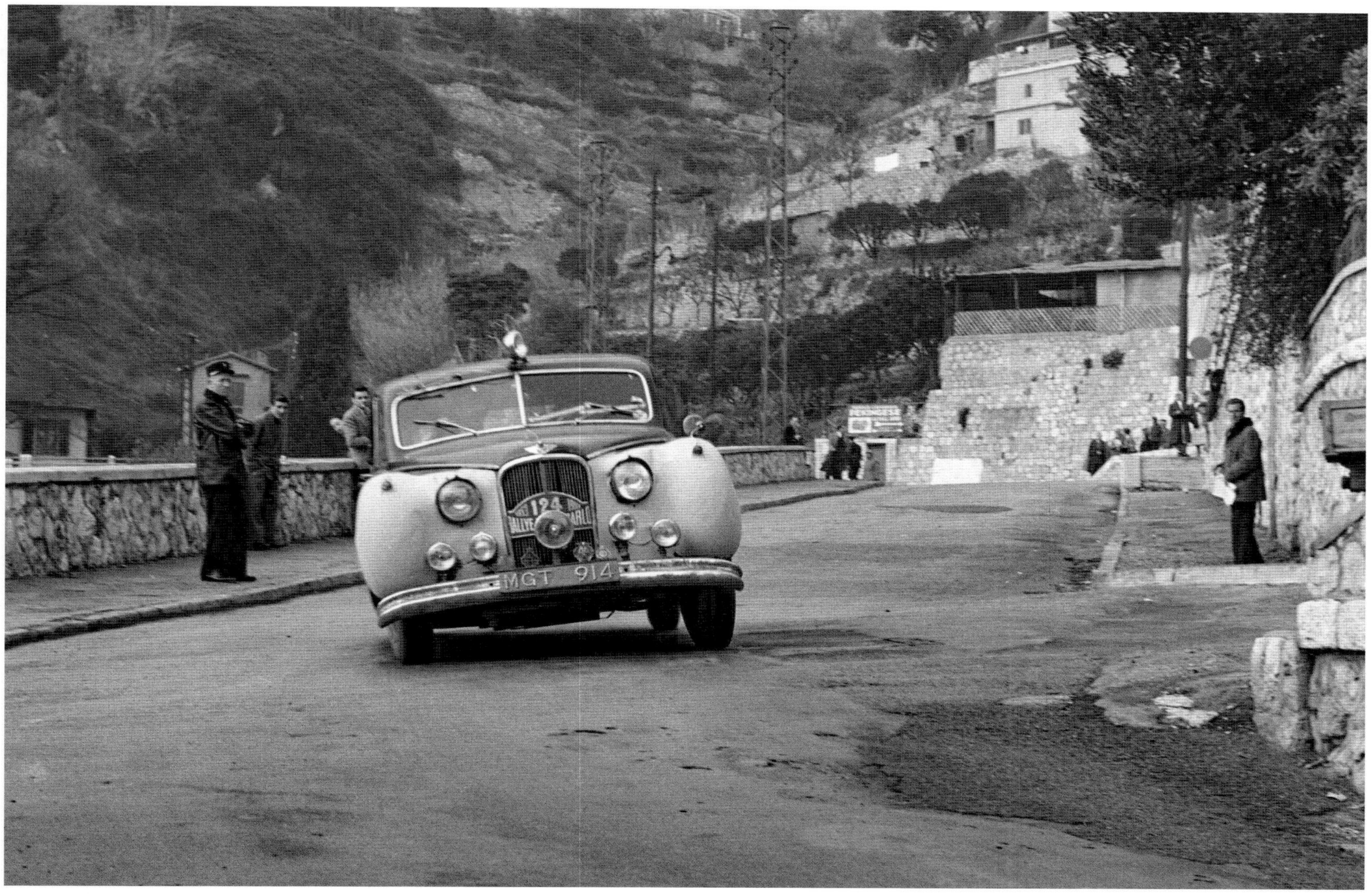

Wick/Levy, Jaguar Mk VII N° 124. Circuit du Col de Braus.

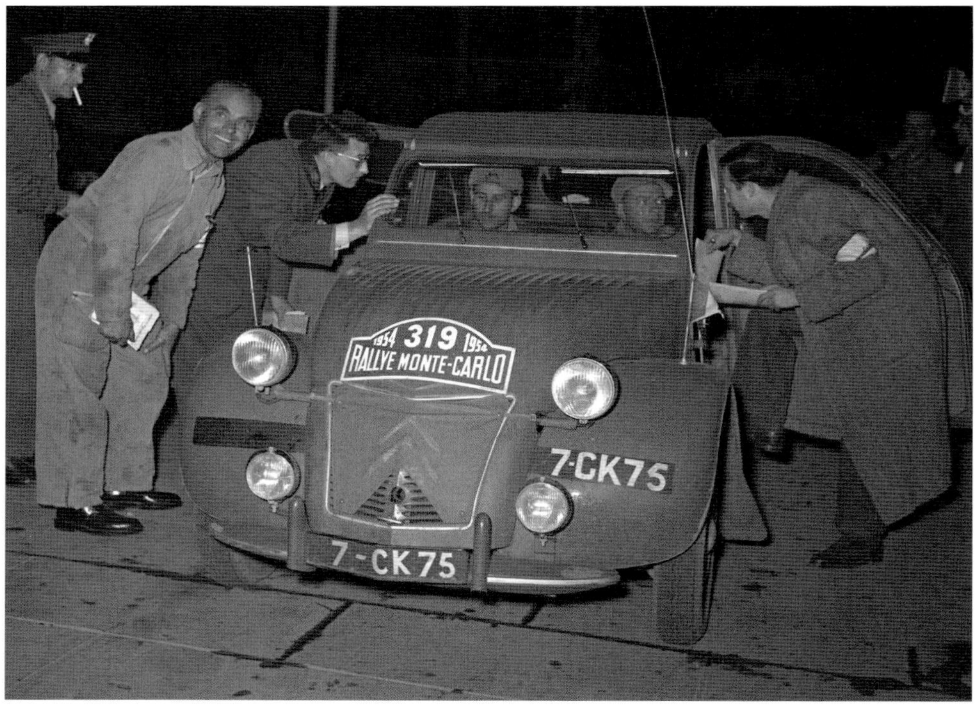

Sensationell: Michel Berbier/Jacques Duvey starteten mit ihrem Citroën 2CV N° 319 mit 375cm³ Hubraum und 9 PS von Oslo aus. Davor waren sie von Kapstadt nach Oslo mit demselben Wagen gefahren. Insgesamt 23.000 km! Sie erreichten Rang 323 von 329 Klassierten.

Sensational: Michel Berbier/Jacques Duvey started from Oslo in their Citroën 2CV N° 319 with 375cm³ engine capacity and 9 hp. Before that, they had driven from Cape Town to Oslo in the same car. A total of 23,000 km! They finished 323rd out of 329 competitors.

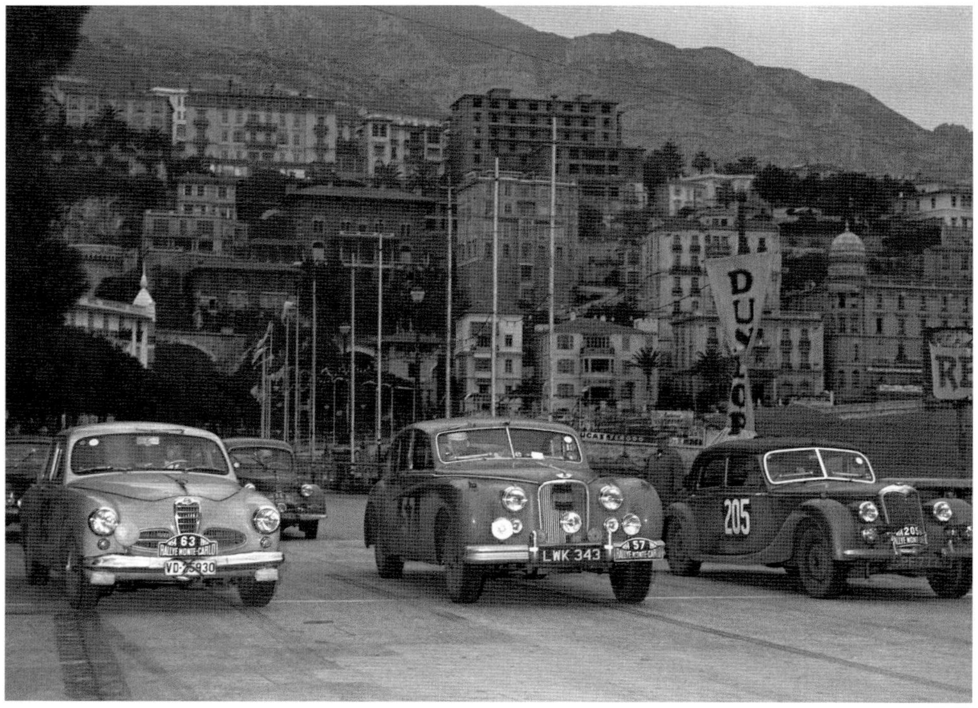

Alle mit Helm: Bornand/Spiliotakis, Alfa Romeo, N° 63, Vard/Jolley, Jaguar MK VII, N° 57, Riley Pathfinder N° 205. Der Alfa Romeo N° 63 war zu schnell und landete auf den Sandsäcken.

Helmets on: Bornand/Spiliotakis, Alfa Romeo, N° 63, Vard/Jolley, Jaguar MK VII, N° 57, Riley Pathfinder N° 205. The Alfa Romeo N° 63 was too fast and ended up on the sandbags.

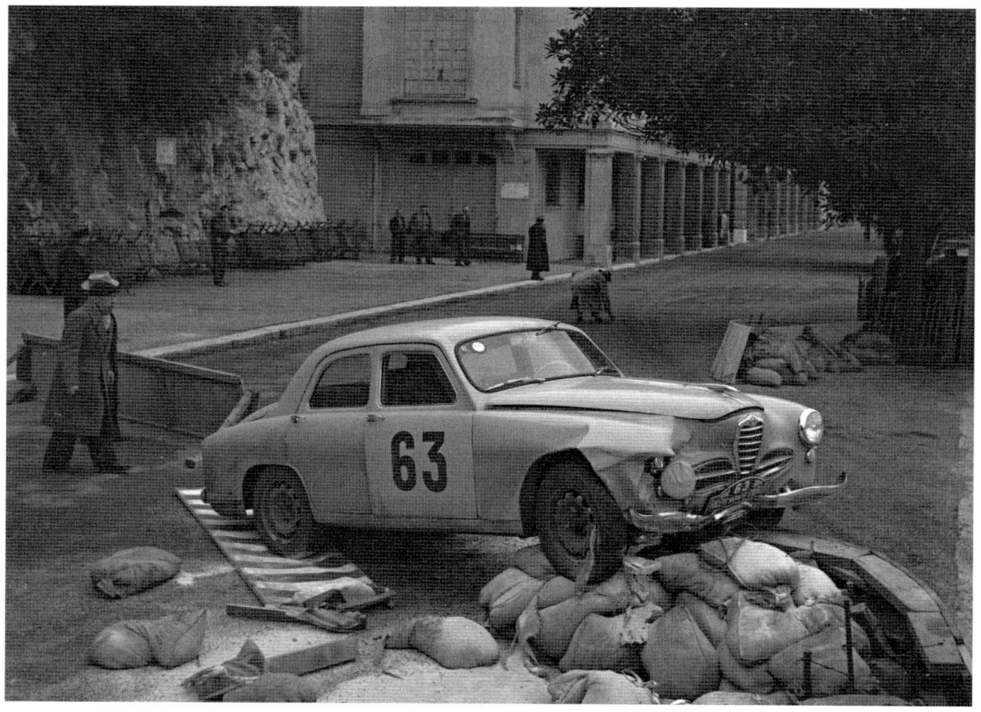

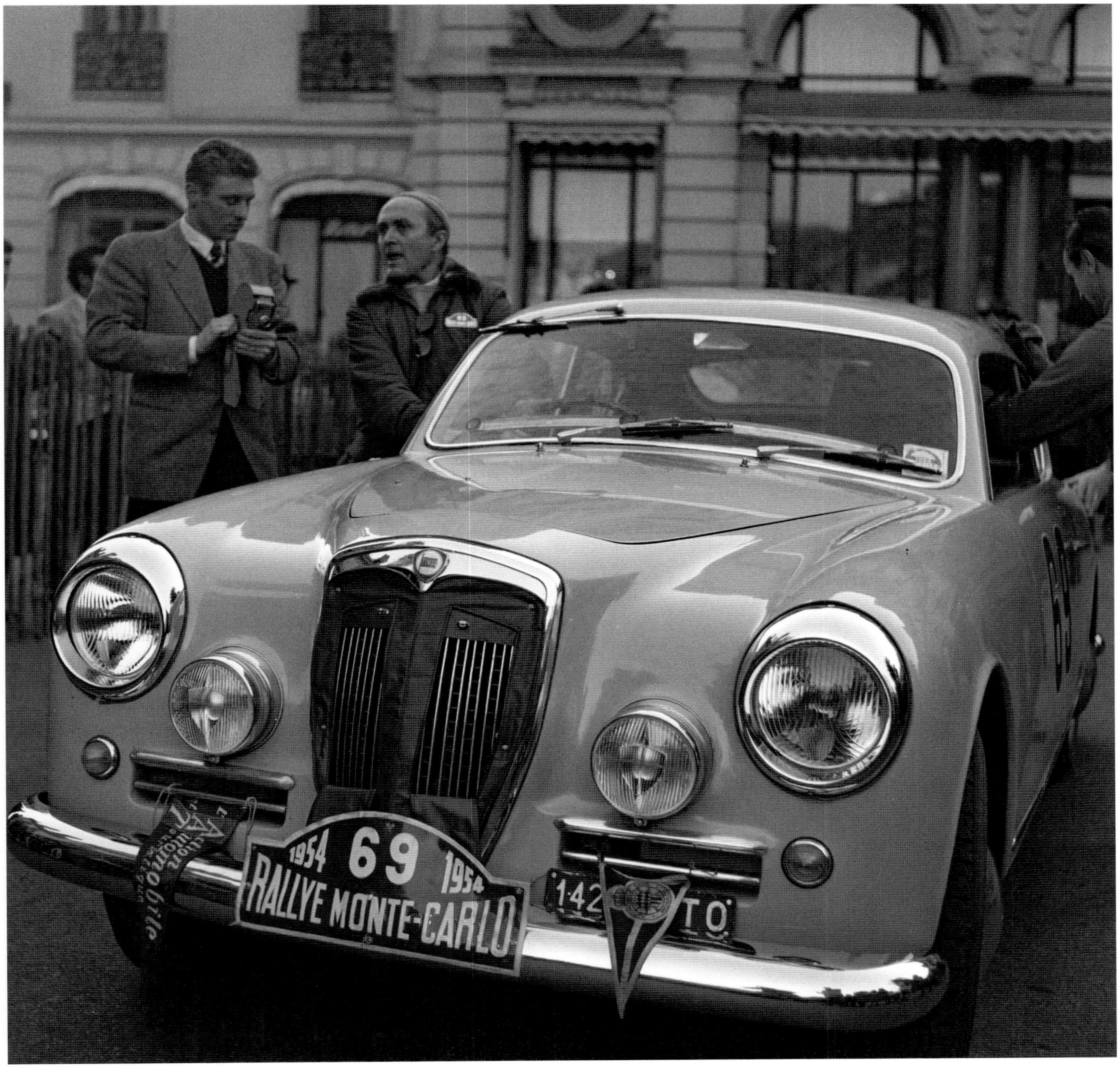

Vor dem Casino: Louis Chiron, Lancia Aurelia GT N° 69, Sieger der Rallye Monte-Carlo 1954 zusammen mit seinem Copilot Basadonna. Chiron ist der einzige Fahrer, der in Monaco sowohl Rallye als auch Grand Prix (1931) gewann.

Louis Chiron, Lancia Aurelia GT left-hand drive N° 69, winner of Monte Carlo Rally 1954 with his co-driver Basadonna, in front of Casino Monte Carlo. He was the only driver who won both the Rally and Grand Prix (in 1931) at Monaco.

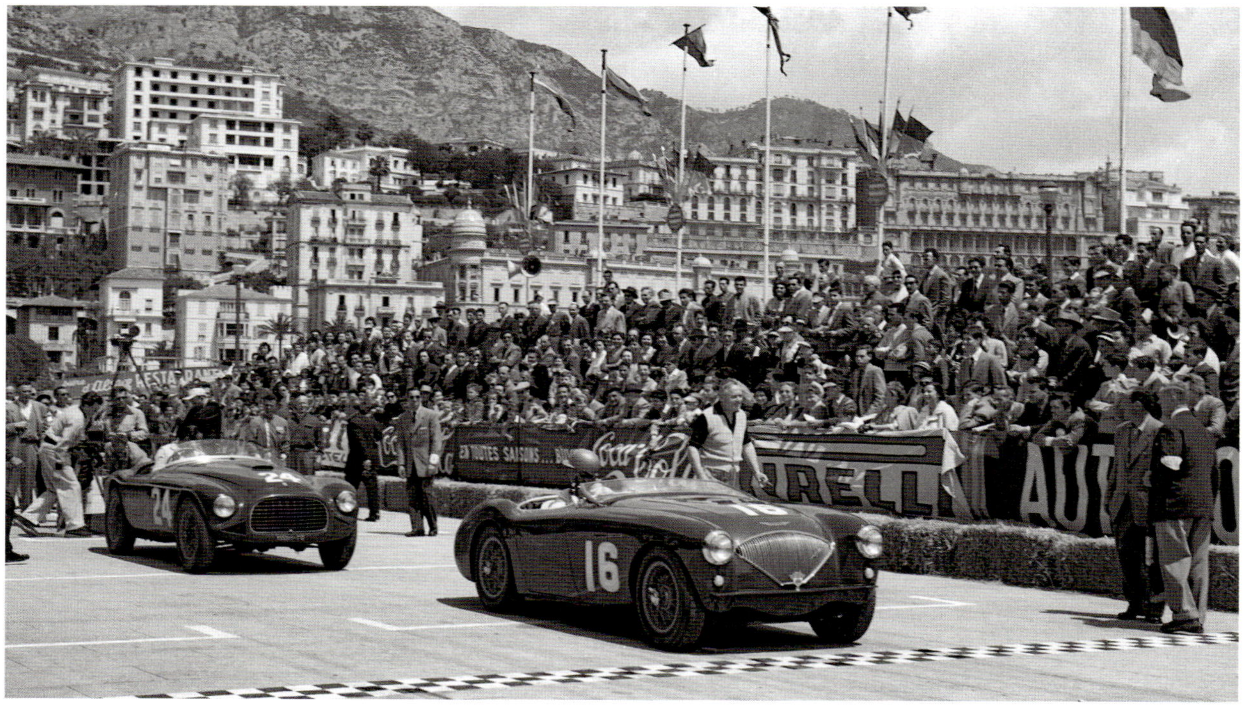

Während der Dreharbeiten zu *The Racers:* Lance Macklin, Austin-Healey 100/4 N° 16, Ferrari 212 Export Touring Barchetta. Hinter dem Healey Regisseur Henry Hathaway.

On the film set of The Racers: *Lance Macklin, Austin-Healey 100/4 N° 16, Ferrari 212 Export Touring Barchetta. Director Henry Hathaway can be seen behind the Healey.*

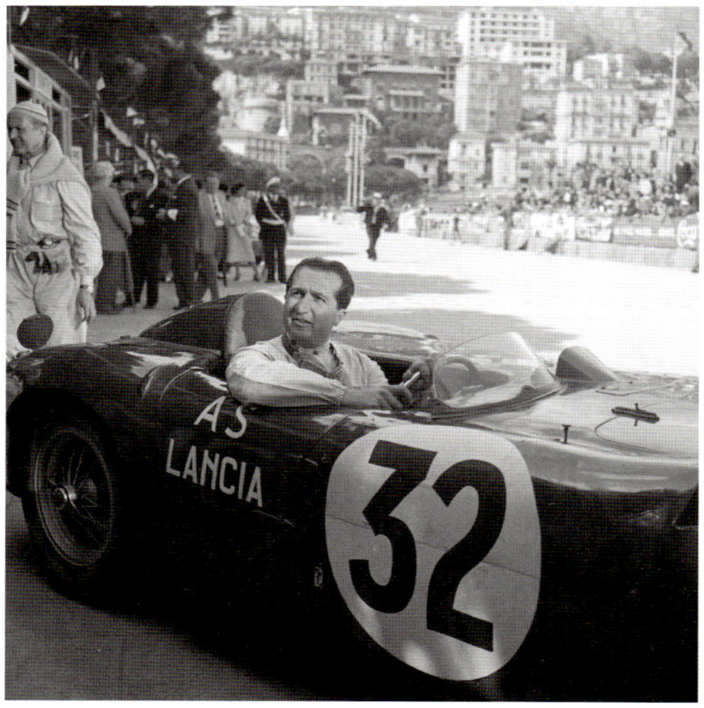

In einer 5-Sekunden-Sequenz in *The Racers:* Alberto Ascari in Lancia D24 Spider Sport. Links Louis Chiron.

In a 5-second sequence in The Racers*: Alberto Ascari in a Lancia D24 Spider Sport. On the left Louis Chiron.*

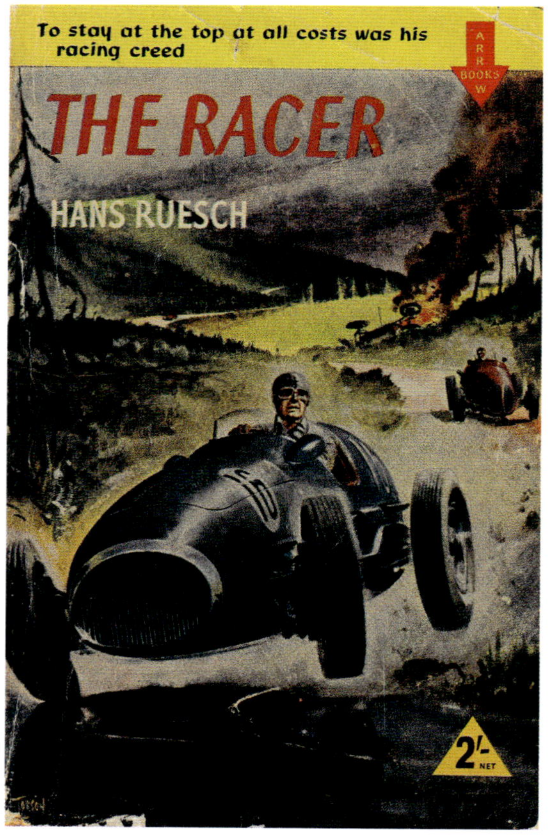

Cover des Taschenbuchs *The Racer.* Das Buch war die Vorlage für den Film.

Cover of the paperback The Racer. *The book provided the inspiration for the film.*

The Racers (Der Favorit) war einer der ersten von vielen Rennfahrer-Spielfilmen. Monaco war der Schauplatz der Eröffnungsszenen. Regie führte Henry Hathaway, die Hauptrolle spielte Kirk Douglas, der aber für den Film nicht in Monaco war, sondern hier von John Fitch gedoubelt wurde.

The Racers (Le cercle infernal) *was one of the first of many car racing feature films. Monaco was the setting for the opening scenes. Directed by Henry Hathaway, starring Kirk Douglas, who was not in Monaco for the film, but was doubled by John Fitch.*

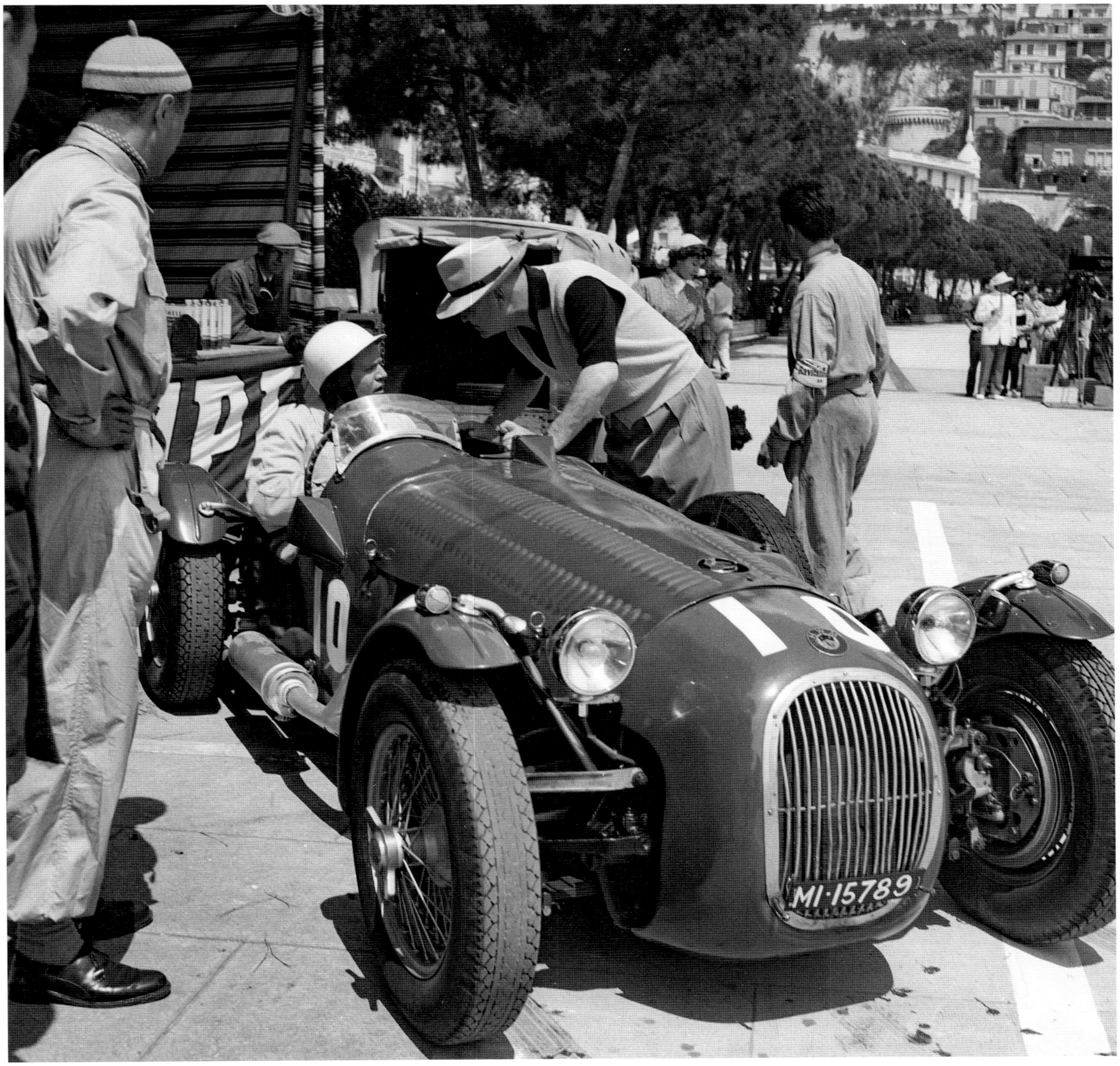

Toulo de Graffenried sitzt im HWM Alta. Rechts, mit Hut, Regisseur Henry Hathaway, links schaut Louis Chiron zu. Aus dem Wagen, ex-Stirling Moss, entstand später der Stovebolt Special, nachdem MGM die Autos nach Abschluss der Dreharbeiten verkauft hatte.

Toulo de Graffenried in the HWM Alta, with director Henry Hathaway, in the hat, left Louis Chiron. The car, ex-Stirling Moss, was later turned into the Stovebolt Special after MGM sold the cars off once filming finished.

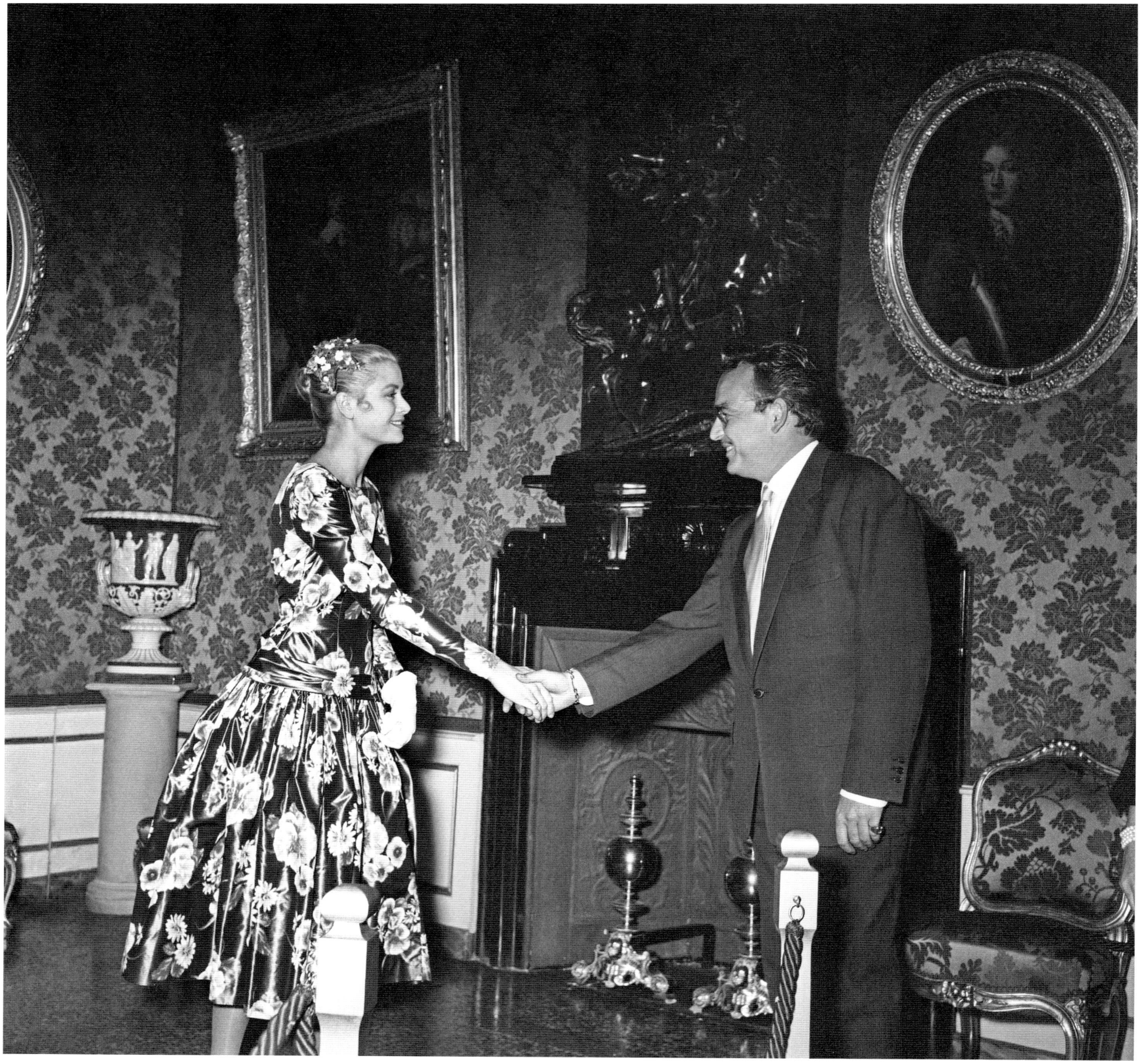

Das andere 1955 für Monaco bedeutsame Ereignis, wie sich erst später herausstellte: Zwei Wochen vor dem Grand Prix treffen sich Grace Kelly und Fürst Rainier zum ersten Mal. Ein Jahr später war ihre Hochzeit.

The other significant event for Monaco in 1955, as it turned out later: Two weeks before the Grand Prix, Grace Kelly and Prince Rainier met for the first time. They married a year later.

1955

Der Grand Prix kehrt zurück

„Wenn Sie die besten Fahrer der Welt auf Europas härtester Rennstrecke sehen wollen, packen Sie Ihren Koffer und nehmen Sie ein Flugzeug oder den Zug nach Monte Carlo. Wenn Ihr Herz nicht während des ganzen Rennens wie ein Vorschlaghammer schlägt und Sie nach dem Rennen nicht erschöpft in Ihren Sitz sinken, überwältigt von Emotionen und um einen Schnaps bittend, müssen Sie gefühllos sein." So steht es etwas dramatisch im Grand-Prix-Programmheft 1955. Für dieses Erlebnis zahlt man auf dem besten Platz für das Rennen inklusive aller Trainings 2.500 alte Francs, verglichen mit heute knapp 60 Euro. 2020 kostete das gleiche Angebot rund 1.200 Euro.

Am 22. Mai wird der Grand Prix zum ersten Mal seit 1952 wieder durchgeführt. Er trägt zudem den ehrenvollen Namen „Grand Prix d'Europe".

Das Starterfeld mit allen großen Marken und Fahrern ist erstklassig. Für die Formel sind seit 1954 entweder 2,5-Liter-Saugmotoren oder aufgeladene 750-cm³-Motoren zugelassen. Gemeldet sind Teams von Mercedes, Ferrari, Lancia, Maserati and Gordini, dazu zwei private Vanwalls. Es ist der erste Auftritt des Mercedes Benz W196 in Europa. Moss und Fangio scheiden mit ihren Mercedes zwar wegen technischer Probleme aus, dominieren aber 1955 die Weltmeisterschaft mit Abstand.

The Grand Prix returns

"If you want to see the best drivers in the world on Europe's toughest circuit, pack your suitcase and take a plane or train to Monte Carlo. If your heart doesn't beat like a sledgehammer throughout the race and you don't sink into your seat exhausted after the race, overwhelmed with emotion and asking for a drink, you must be totally lacking in feeling." So it says somewhat dramatically in the 1955 Grand Prix programme booklet. The cost of this experience was 2,500 old francs for the best seat for the race, including all practice sessions, compared with just under 60 Euros today. In 2020, the same offer cost around 1,200 euros.

On 22 May, a Grand Prix was held for the first time since 1952. It also bore the venerable name "Grand Prix d'Europe".

The starting field with all the big maker names and drivers was first class. Teams from Mercedes, Ferrari, Lancia, Maserati and Gordini were entered, plus two private Vanwalls. Either 2.5 litre unsupercharged or supercharged 750cc engines have been permitted for the formula since 1954. It was the first appearance of the Mercedes Benz W196 in Europe. Moss and Fangio both retired with their Mercedes due to technical problems, but easily dominated the 1955 World Championship.

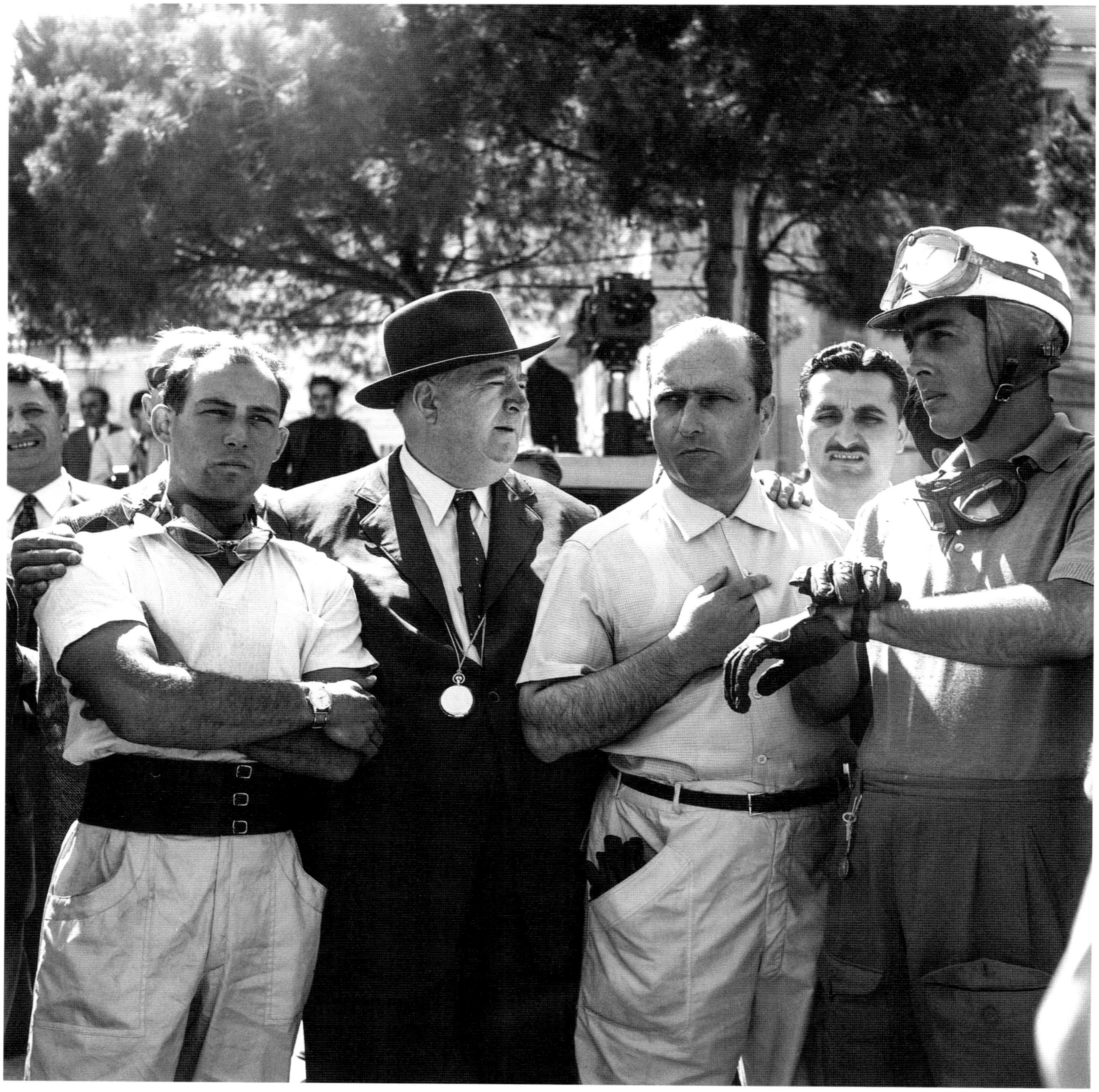

Gruppenbild mit Mercedes-Rennleiter: von links Stirling Moss, Alfred Neubauer, Juan Manuel Fangio, Luigi Musso. Musso wurde 1958 beim Großen Preis von Frankreich in Reims tödlich verletzt.

Group photo with Mercedes race director: From left Stirling Moss, Alfred Neubauer, Juan Manuel Fangio, Luigi Musso. Musso was fatally injured during the French Grand Prix at Reims in 1958.

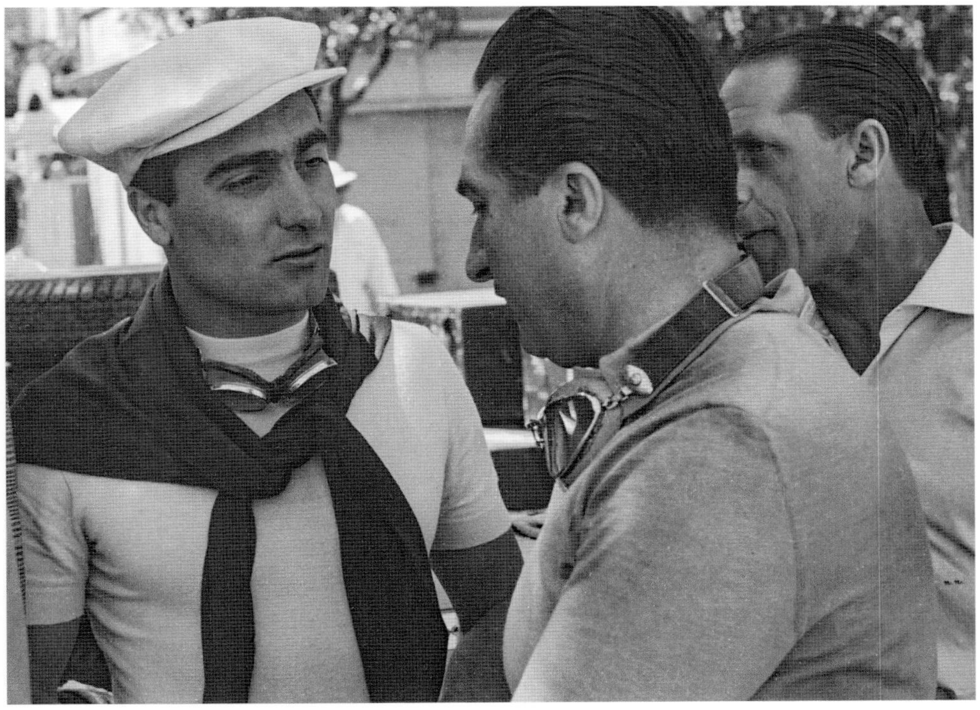

Enge Freunde: Alberto Ascari und Eugenio Castellotti (links). Ascari kommt vier Tage nach diesem Rennen bei einer Ferrari-Testfahrt ums Leben, so wie auch Castellotti zwei Jahre später beim Test eines Ferrari.

Close friends: Alberto Ascari and Eugenio Castellotti (left). Ascari died four days after this race during a Ferrari test drive; Castellotti died two years later while testing a Ferrari.

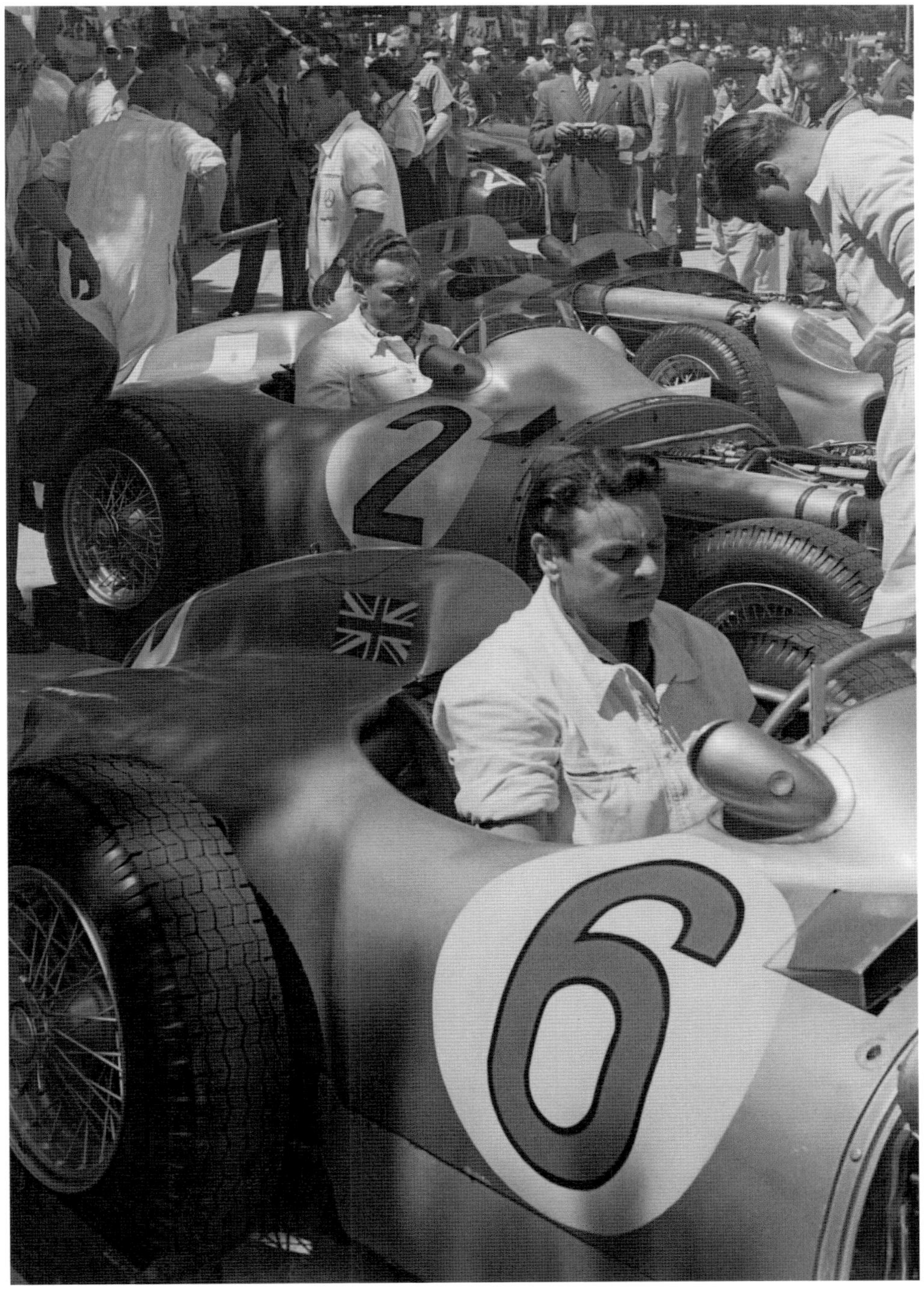

Die Mechaniker mit den beiden Mercedes W196 von Moss, N° 6, Fangio, N° 2, und ganz hinten Herrmann, N° 9. Für die engen Kurven von Monaco hatten die Stuttgarter zwei spezielle Versionen des W196 mit kürzerem Radstand für Moss und Fangio gebaut. Herrmann brach sich bei einem Trainingsunfall das Bein und konnte am Rennen nicht teilnehmen.

The mechanics with the three Mercedes W196 of Moss, N° 6, Fangio, N° 2, and Herrmann, N° 9. Herrmann injured himself during practice and was unable to take part in the race. For the tight corners of Monaco, the Stuttgart company had built two special versions of the W196 with a shorter wheelbase for Moss and Fangio. Herrmann broke his leg in a practice accident and was forced to drop out of the race.

Die Fahrer sind Flirts und Spaß nicht abgeneigt … Bella Darvi, eine der Hauptdarstellerinnen im Film *The Racers*, besucht das Training. Sie ist in Monaco für die Premiere des Films in der Opéra de Monte-Carlo. Der Film wurde teilweise hier gedreht (s. Seiten 88/89 in diesem Buch).

Drivers are not averse to flirting and fun… Bella Darvi, one of the leading actresses in the film The Racers, *visited a practice session. She was in Monaco for the premiere of the movie at the Opéra de Monte-Carlo. The film was partly shot here (see pages 88/89 of this book).*

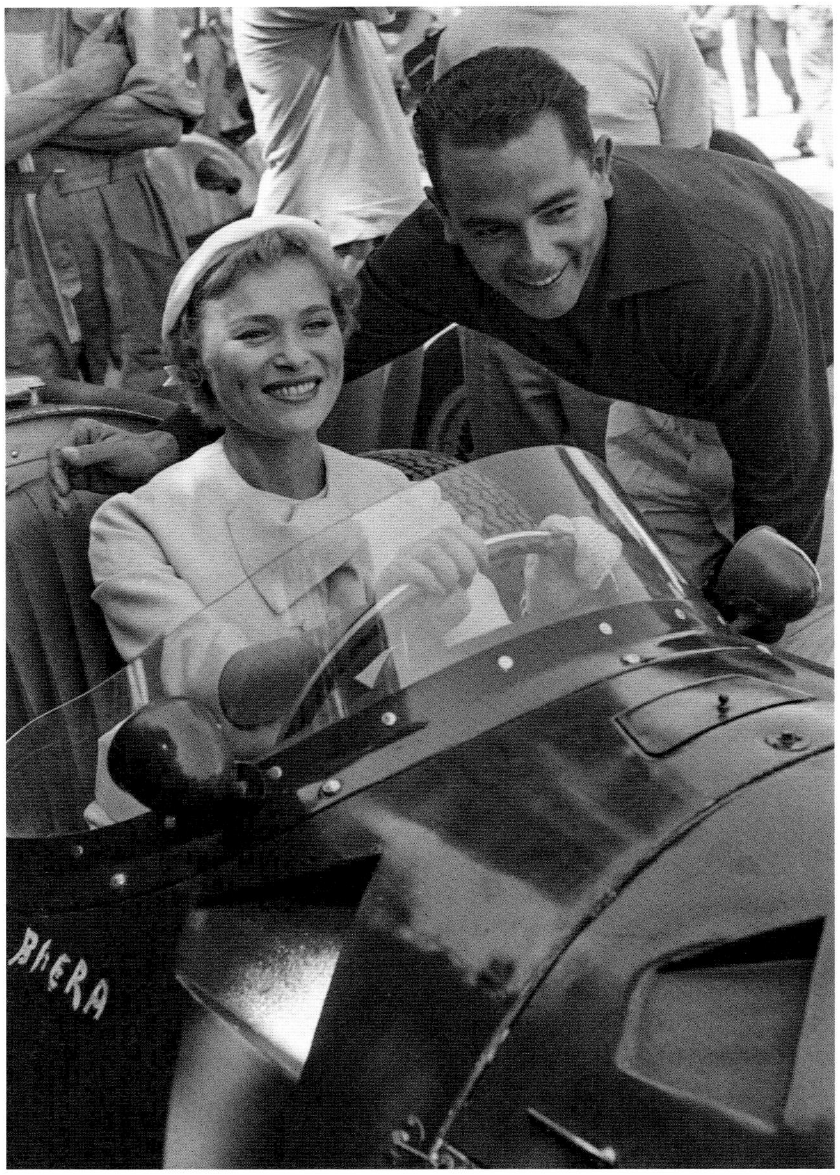

… mit Jean Behra, in seinem Maserati 250F.
(Man beachte die falsche Schreibweise „Bhera“ für Behra.)

…with Jean Behra, in his Maserati 250F.
(Note the misspelling of "Bhera" for Behra)

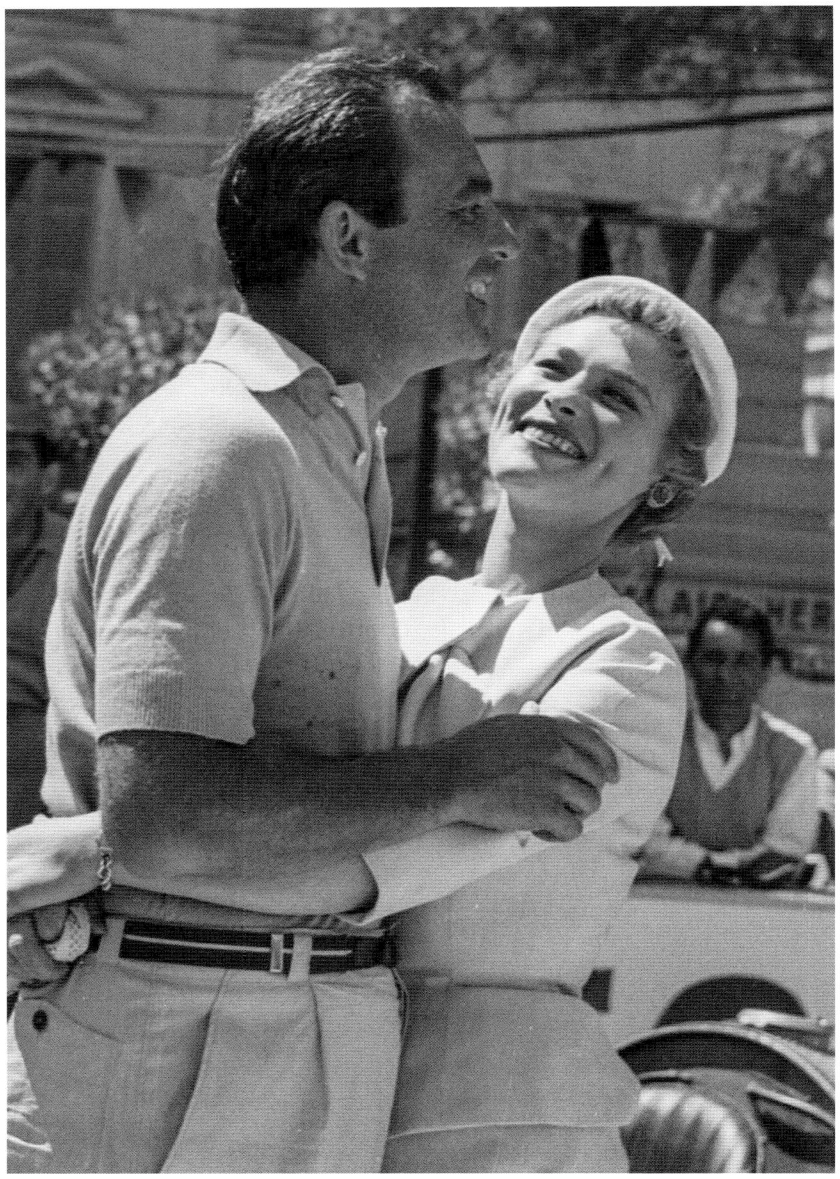

… mit Harry Schell.

…with Harry Schell.

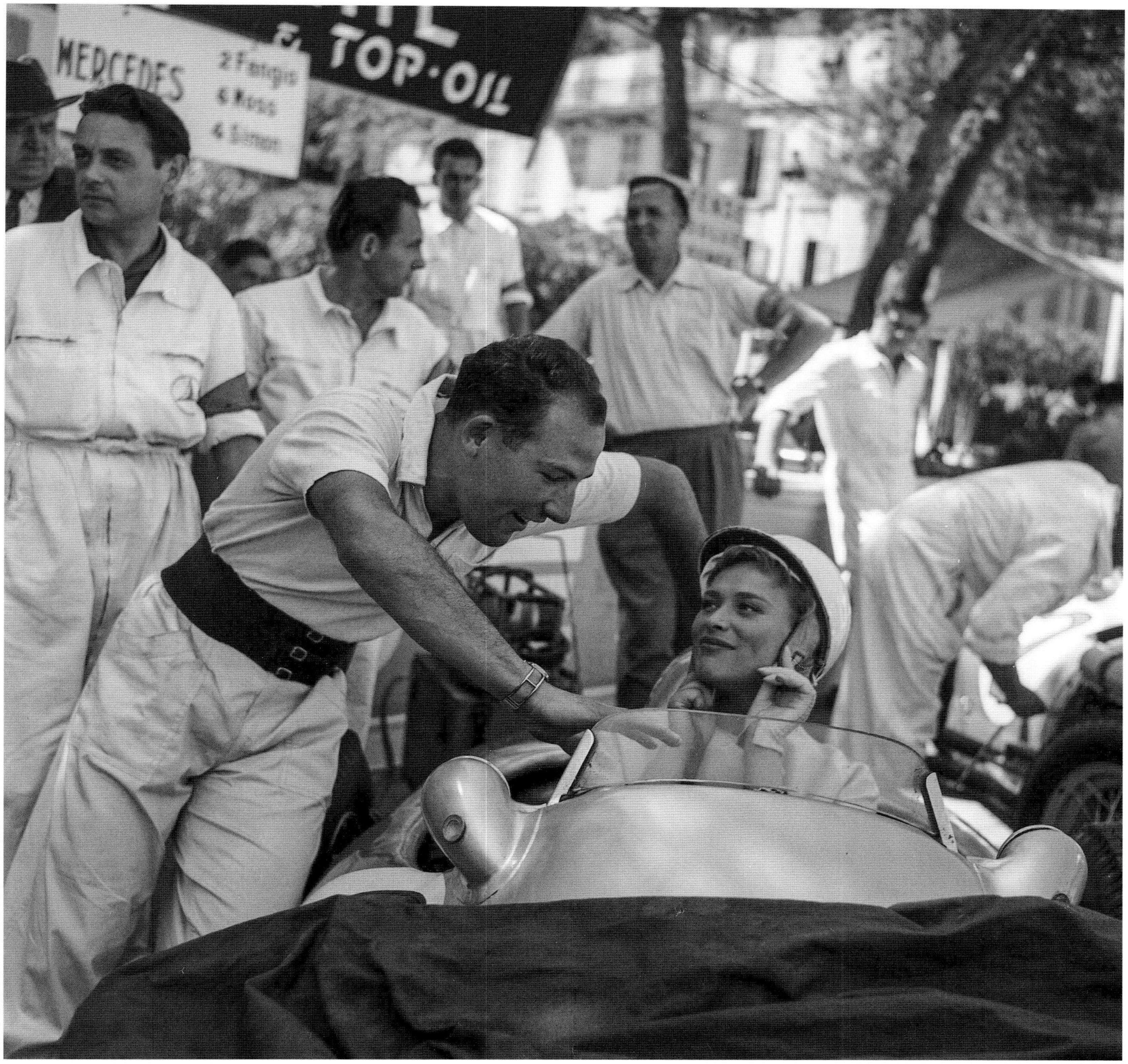

... mit Stirling Moss,
in seinem Mercedes W196 N° 6.

...with Stirling Moss,
in his Mercedes W196 N° 6.

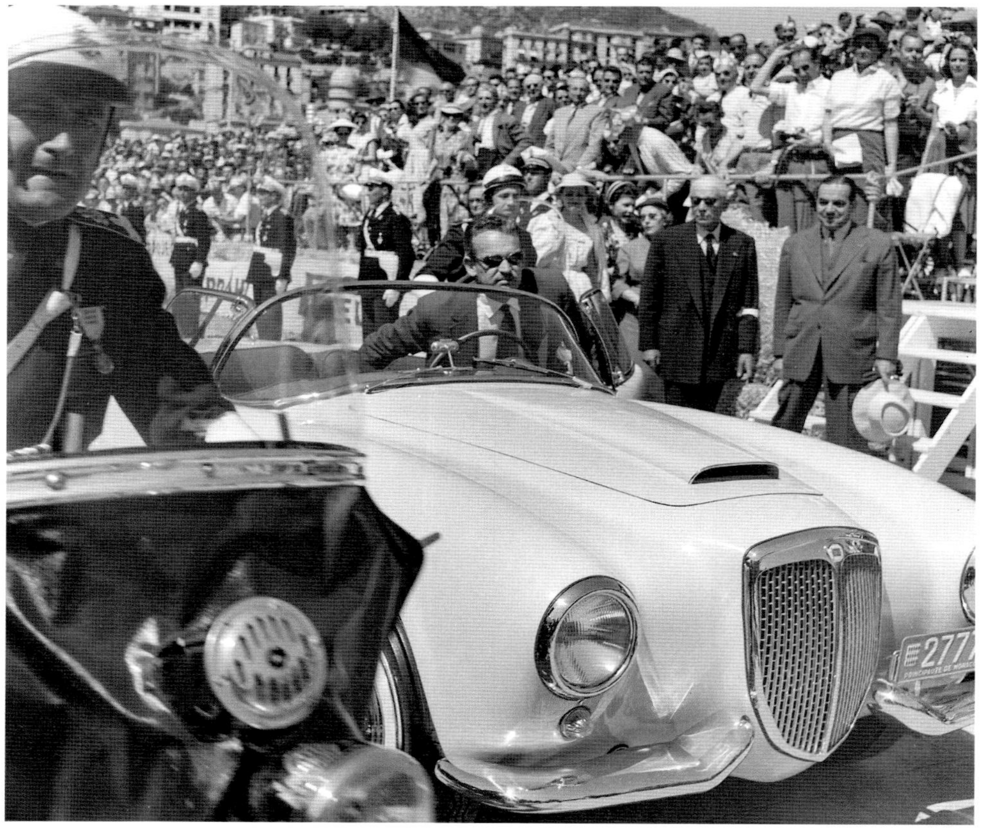

Fürst Rainier III. von Monaco vor der Paraderunde mit seinem Lancia Aurelia B24 Spider America Cabriolet 1955.

Prince Rainier III of Monaco with his Lancia Aurelia B24 Spider America Cabriolet 1955 immediately before closing the track before the start.

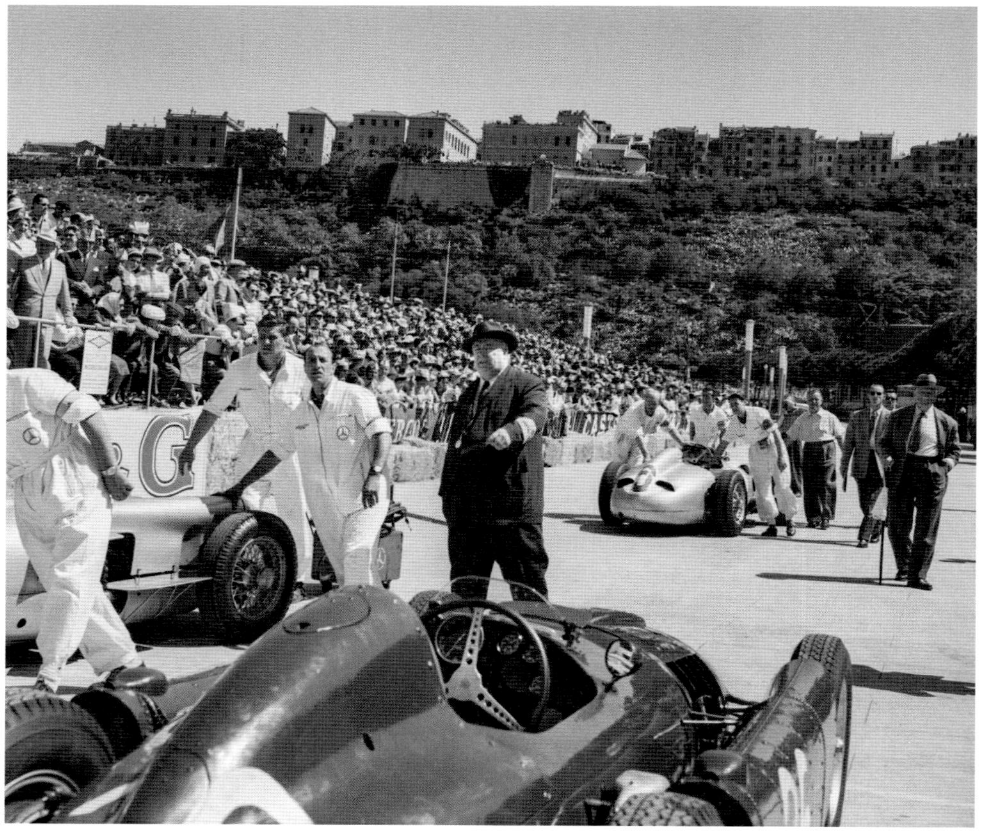

Alfred Neubauer, Mercedes-Rennleiter. Die Wagen von Alberto Ascari, N° 26, Stirling Moss, Mercedes-Benz W196 N° 6, und Juan Manuel Fangio, Mercedes-Benz W196 N° 2. „Le Rocher“ im Hintergrund.

Alfred Neubauer, Mercedes racing manager. The cars driven by Alberto Ascari, N° 26, Stirling Moss, Mercedes-Benz W196 N° 6, and Juan Manuel Fangio, Mercedes-Benz W196 N° 2. “Le Rocher” can be seen in the background.

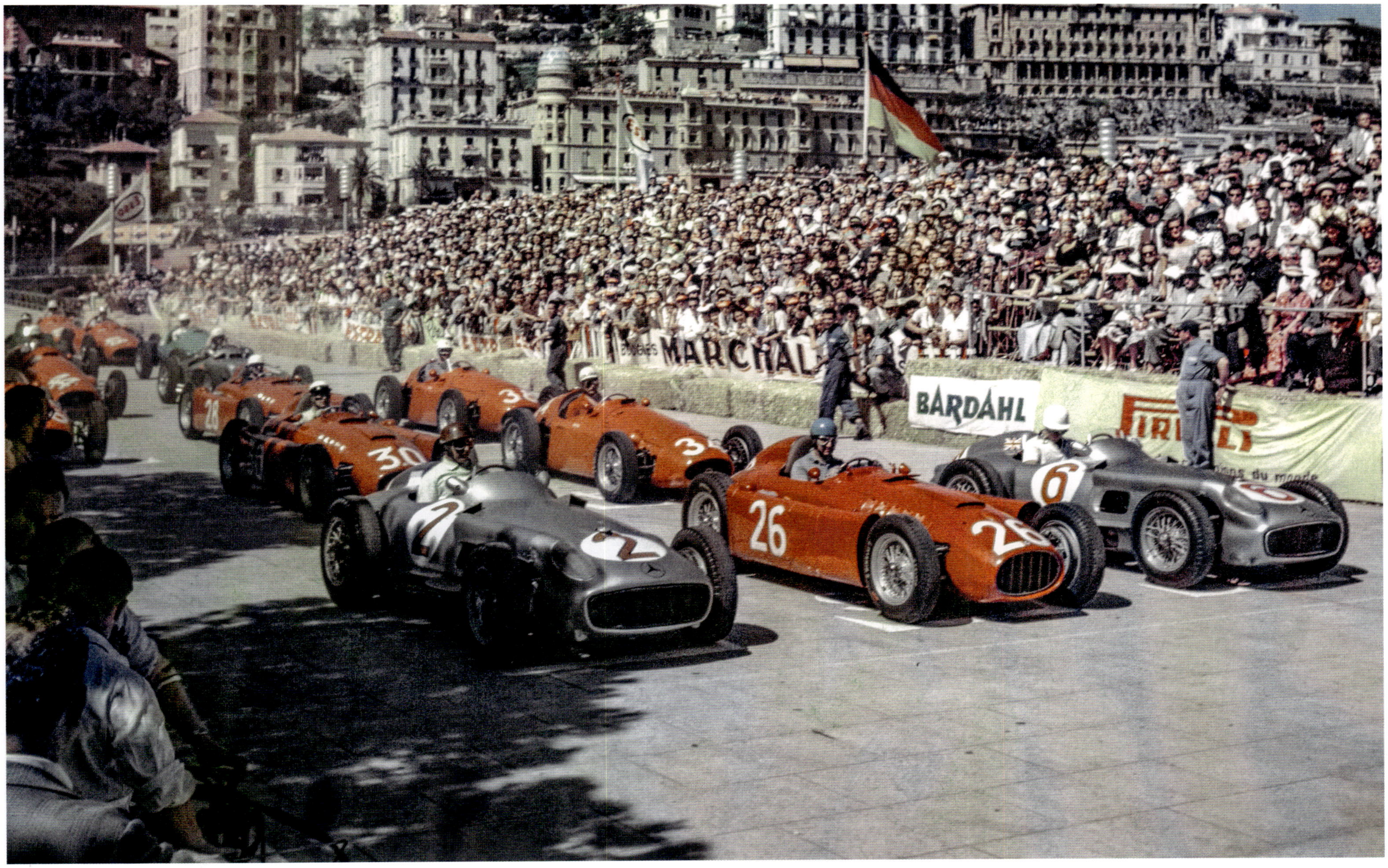

Der Start ist nun direkt am Hafen. Juan Manuel Fangio, Mercedes-Benz W196 N° 2, Alberto Ascari, Lancia D50 N° 26, Stirling Moss, Mercedes-Benz W196 N° 6, Eugenio Castellotti, Lancia D50 N° 30, Jean Behra, Maserati 250F N° 34, Luigi Villoresi, Lancia D50 N° 28, Luigi Musso, Maserati 250F N° 38, Maurice Trintignant, Ferrari 625 N° 44.

The race now next to the harbour. Juan Manuel Fangio, Mercedes-Benz W196 N° 2, Alberto Ascari, Lancia D50 N° 26, Stirling Moss, Mercedes-Benz W196 N° 6, Eugenio Castellotti, Lancia D50 N° 30, Jean Behra, Maserati 250F N° 34, Luigi Villoresi, Lancia D50 N° 28, Luigi Musso, Maserati 250F N° 38, Maurice Trintignant, Ferrari 625 N° 44.

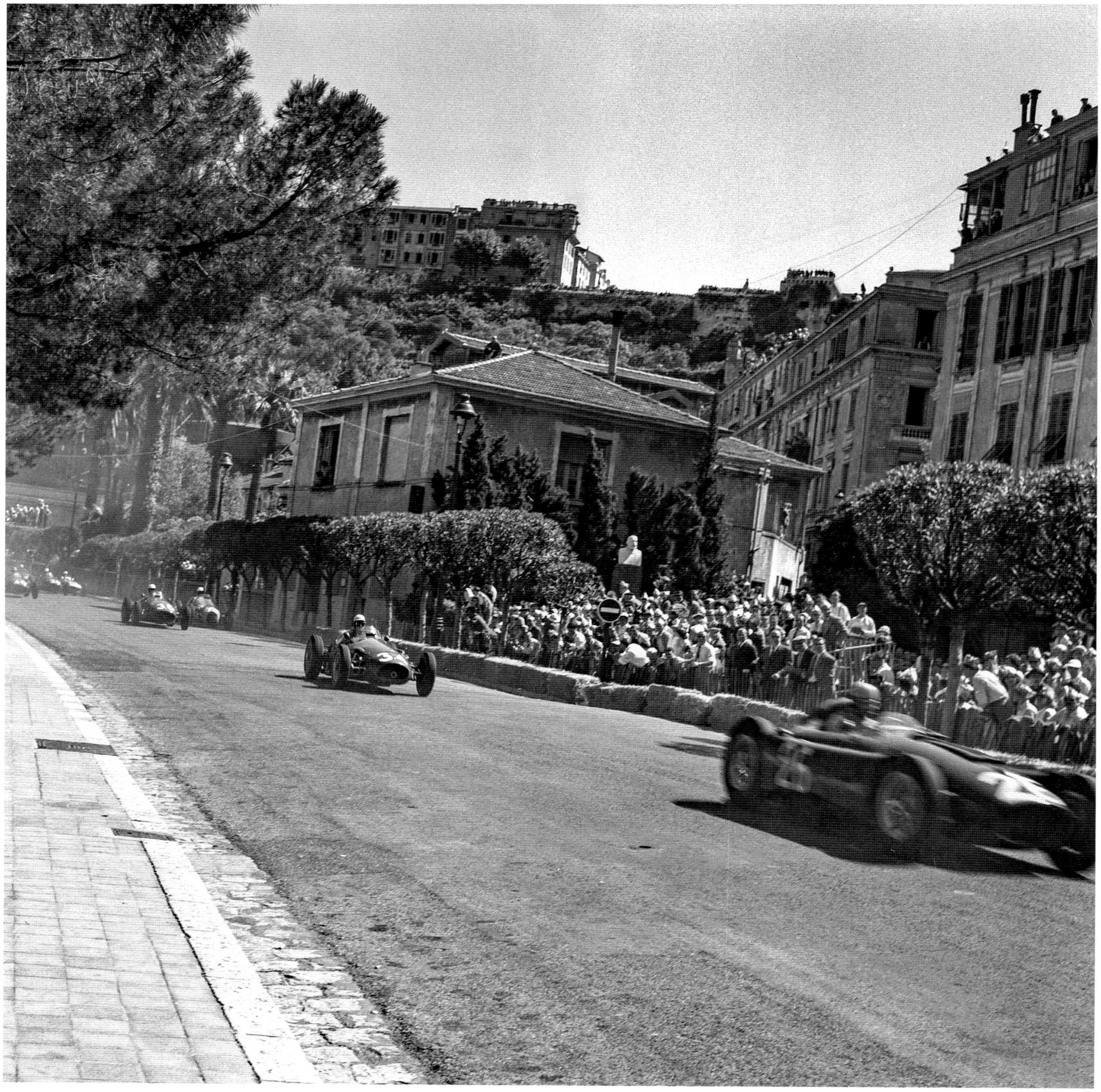

Auf der Gegengeraden, wo seit 1963 gestartet wird. Alberto Ascari, Lancia D50 N° 26, Jean Behra, Maserati 250F N° 34, Roberto Mieres, Maserati 250F N° 36, Robert Manzon, Gordini T16 N° 8.

On the back straight, where the race has been started since 1963. Alberto Ascari, Lancia D50 N° 26, Jean Behra, Maserati 250F N° 34, Roberto Mieres, Maserati 250F N° 36, Robert Manzon, Gordini T16 N° 8.

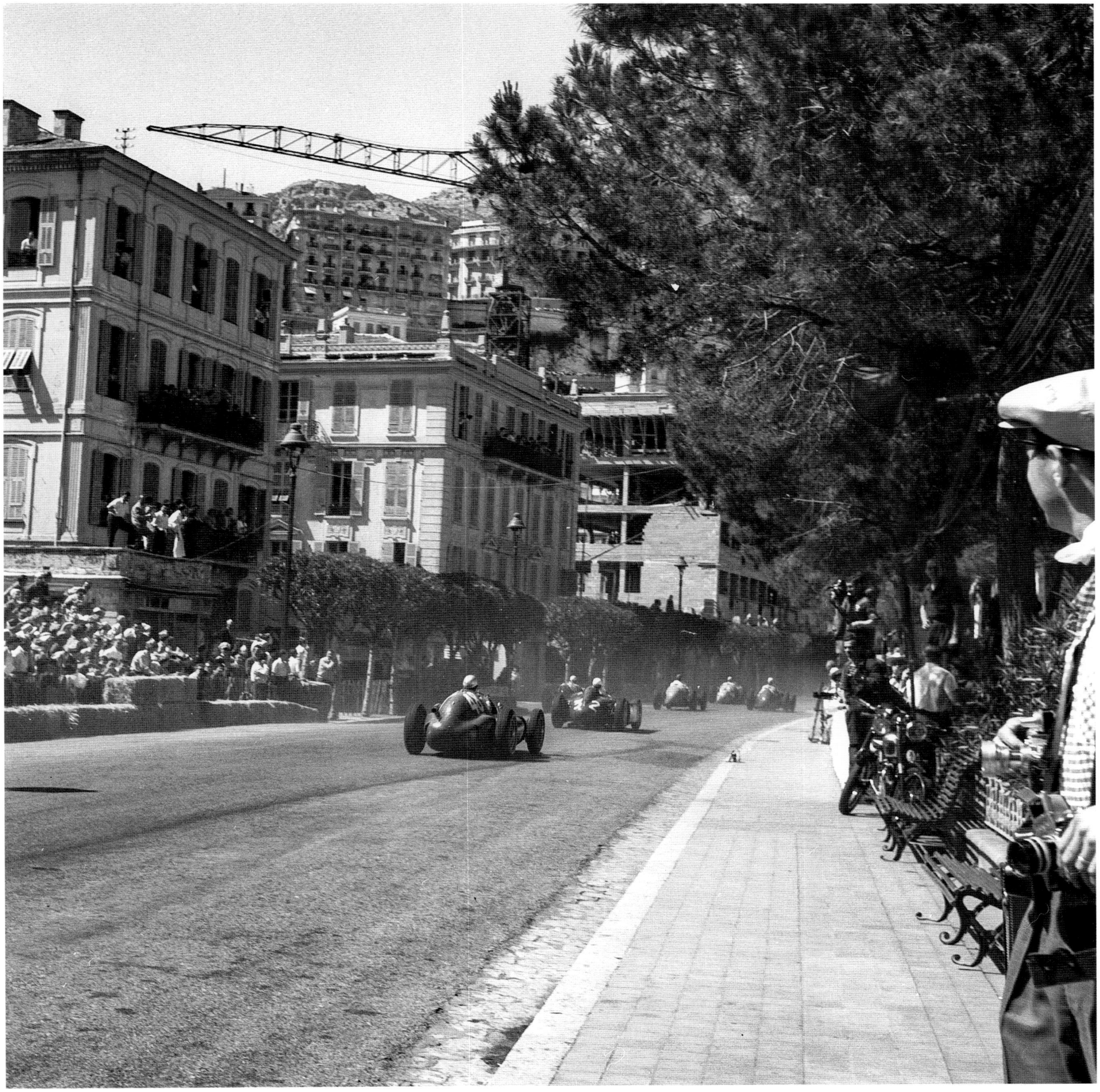

Piero Taruffi, Ferrari 555 N° 48, Louis Chiron, Lancia D50 N° 32, wurde sechster und war mit 56 Jahren der älteste Fahrer, der je am Grand Prix teilgenommen hatte.

Piero Taruffi, Ferrari 555 N° 48, Louis Chiron, Lancia D50 N° 32, finished sixth and at 56 was the oldest driver ever to compete in the Grand Prix.

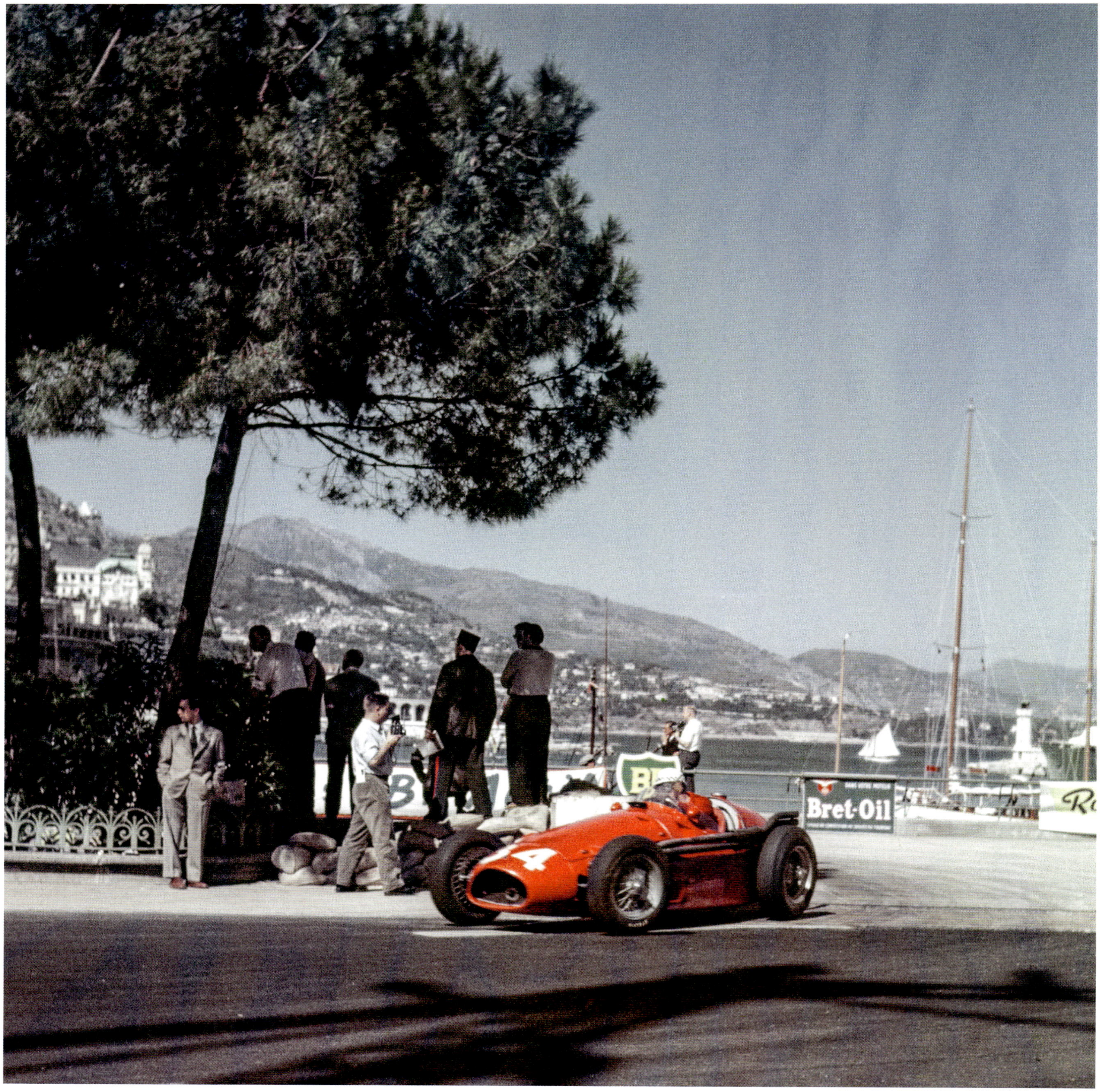

Jean Behra, Maserati 250F N° 34, umrundet die Gasometer-Kurve. „Jeannot" Behra aus Nizza, ein Idol in Frankreich, war ursprünglich Radrennfahrer, dann mehrfacher französischer Motorradmeister auf seiner roten Moto-Guzzi, bevor er zu den Autos wechselte.

Jean Behra, Maserati 250F N° 34, rounding the Gasometer hairpin. "Jeannot" Behra from Nice, an idol in France, was originally a competitive cyclist, then a multiple French motorbike champion on his red Moto-Guzzi before switching to cars.

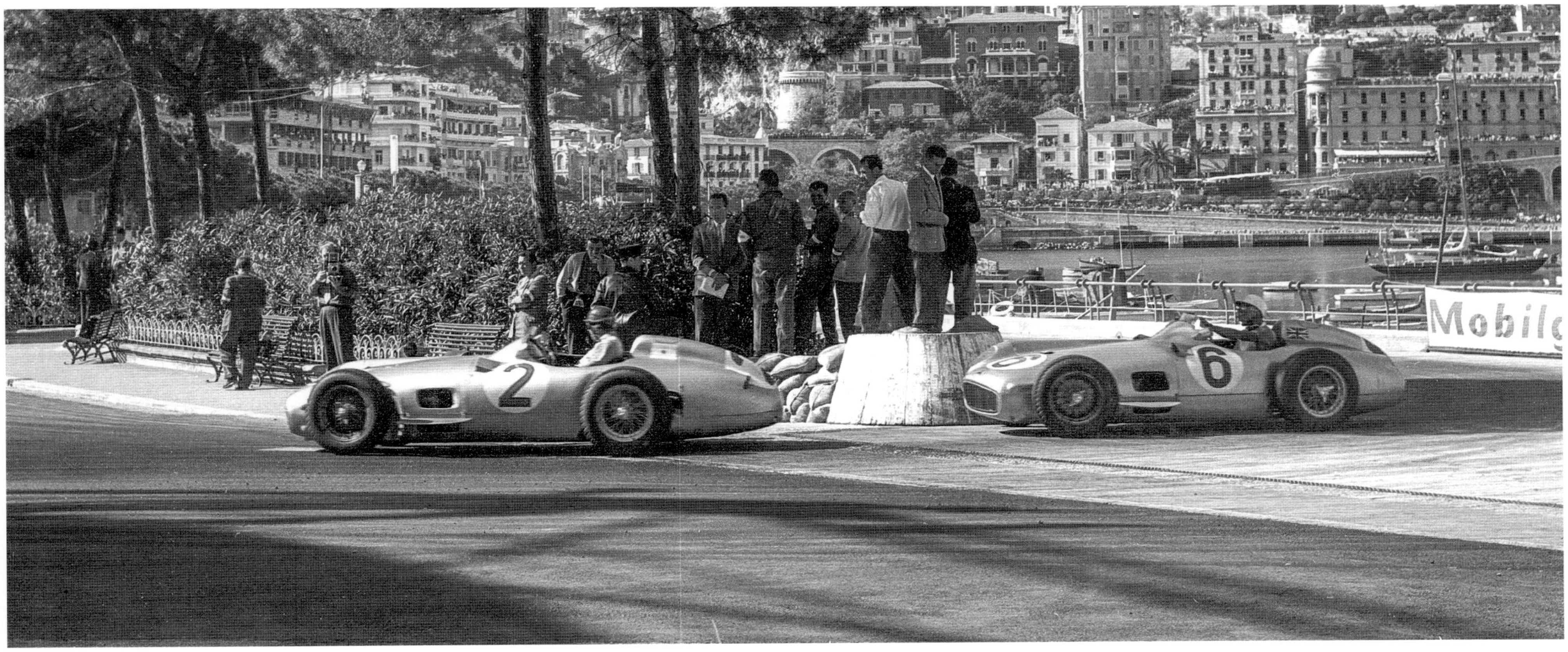

Warum 1955 Fangio N° 2 und Moss N° 6 oft als „the train" („der Zug") bezeichnet wurden, illustriert dieses Bild. Moss über Fangio: „Ich habe in Fangios Spuren unschätzbar viel gelernt. Er war eine Vaterfigur für mich."

This photo explains why Fangio N° 2 and Moss N° 6 were often referred to as "the train". Moss said of Fangio: "I learned an inestimable amount from following in Fangio's wheeltracks. He was a father figure to me."

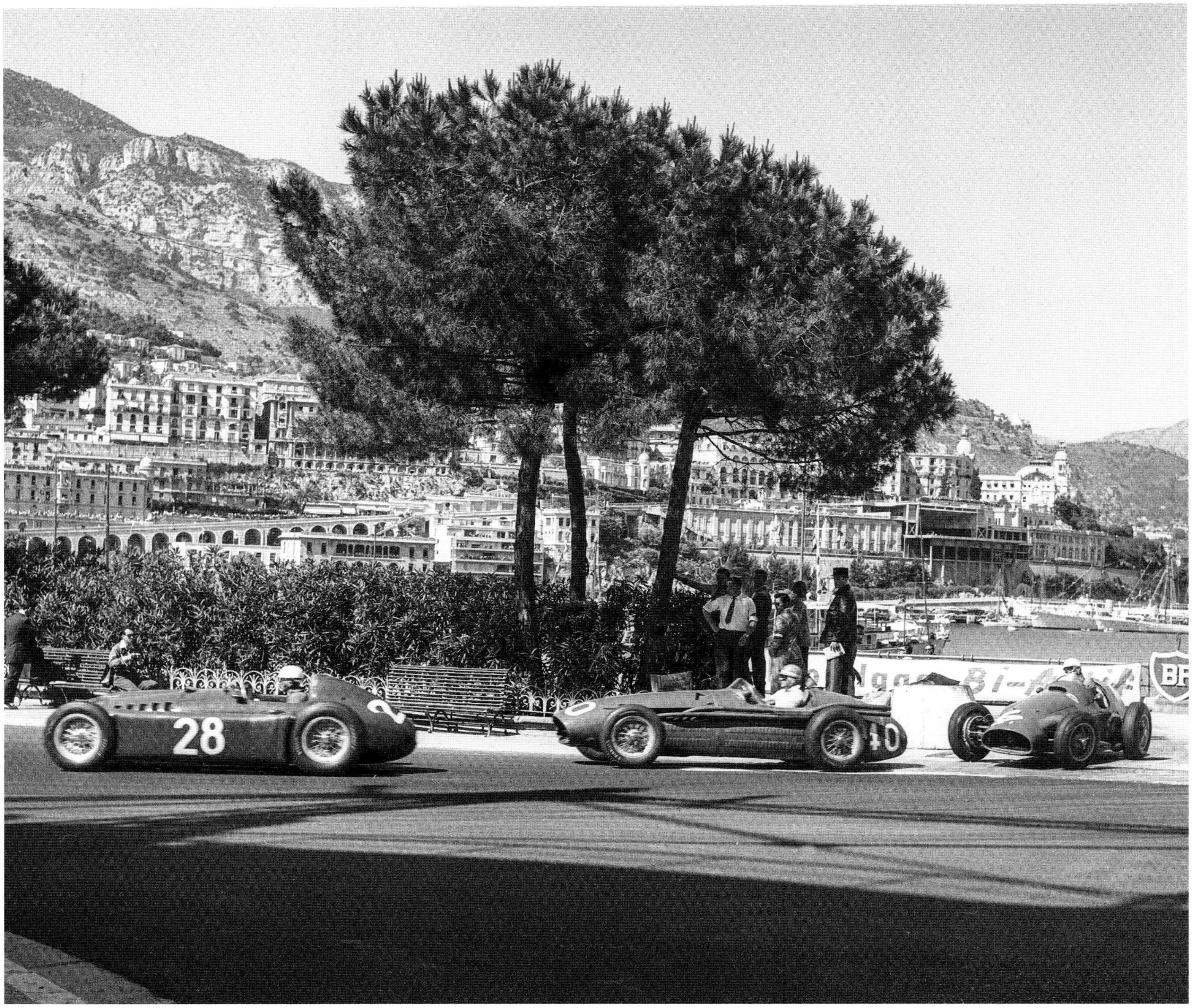

Luigi Villoresi, Lancia D50 N° 28, Cesare Perdisa, Maserati 250F N° 40, dahinter Maurice Trintignant, Ferrari 625 N° 44, der wegen der vielen Ausfälle überraschender Sieger auf dem eigentlich nicht konkurrenzfähigen älteren Ferrari wurde.

Luigi Villoresi, Lancia D50 N° 28, Cesare Perdisa, Maserati 250F N° 40. Behind them Maurice Trintignant, Ferrari 625 N° 44, who became the surprising winner in the rather uncompetitive older Ferrari due to the many retirements.

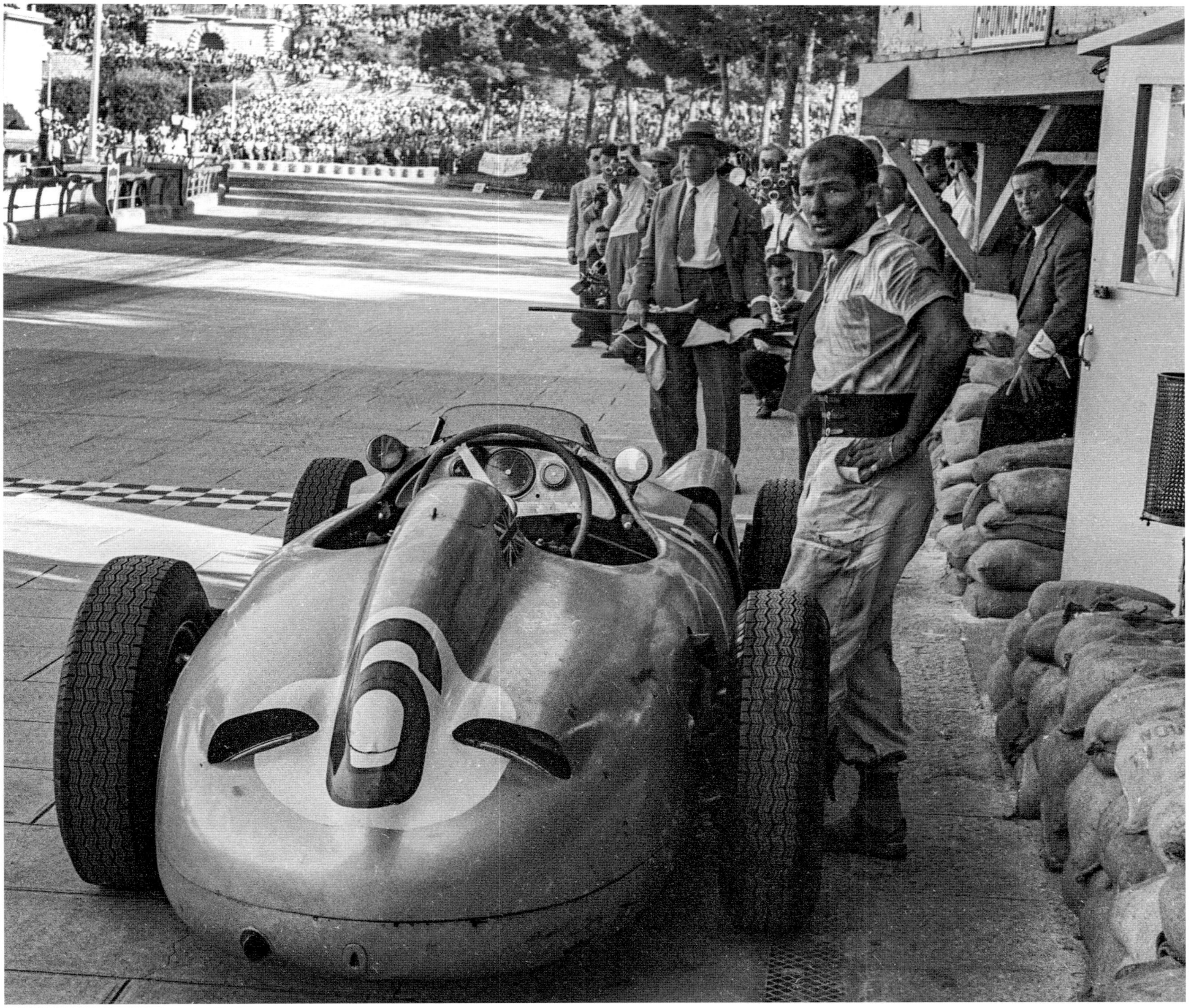

Stirling Moss, Mercedes-Benz W196 N° 6, schied wegen einer gebrochenen Ölleitung aus, nachdem er das Feld zusammen mit Fangio fast das ganze Rennen über angeführt hatte. Es gelang ihm, vor der Box anzuhalten. Um das Rennen dennoch zu beenden und als Neunter klassiert zu werden, wartete er darauf, sein Auto über die Ziellinie zu schieben.

Stirling Moss, Mercedes-Benz W196 N° 6, retired, after leading the field together with Fangio for nearly the whole race, because of a broken oil line. He managed to stop in front of the pits and in order nevertheless to finish the race he waits to push his car over the finishing line to be declared 9th.

Final Result of the Monaco Grand Prix 1955

1. Maurice Trintignant, Ferrari 625
2. Eugenio Castellotti, Lancia D50
3. Jean Behra/Cesare Perdisa, Maserati 250F

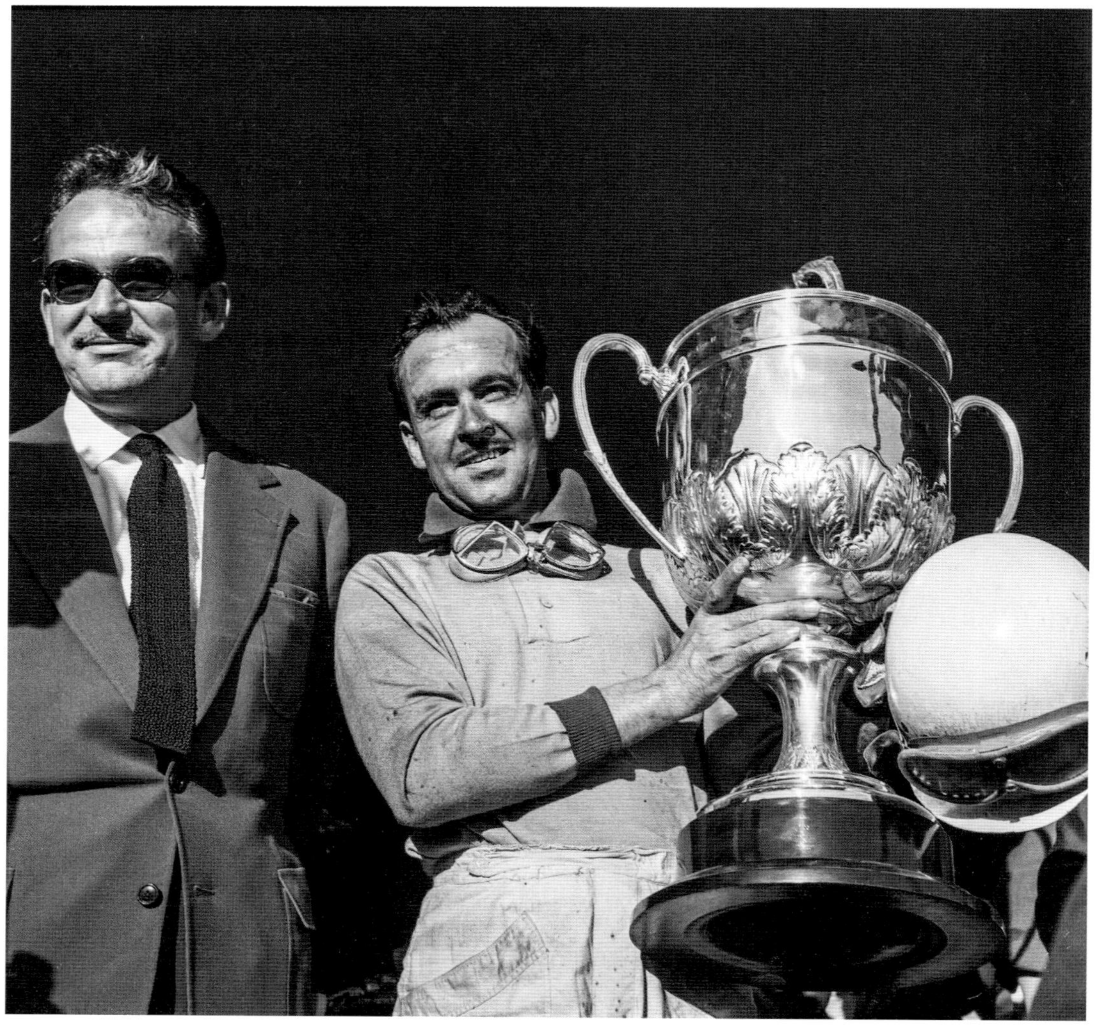

Fürst Rainier überreicht dem Sieger Maurice Trintignant den riesigen „Coupe du Grand Prix“. Trintignant gewann wegen der vielen Ausfälle überraschend auf dem eigentlich nicht konkurrenzfähigen Ferrari 625. Erst 20 Jahre später gewann wieder ein Ferrari den Grand Prix – mit Niki Lauda am Steuer.

Prince Rainier presents winner Maurice Trintignant with the splendid "Coupe du Grand Prix". Trintignant's victory in his rather uncompetitive Ferrari 625 came as a surprise due to the many retirements. It would take another twenty years before a Ferrari (with Niki Lauda at the wheel) won the Monaco Grand Prix again.

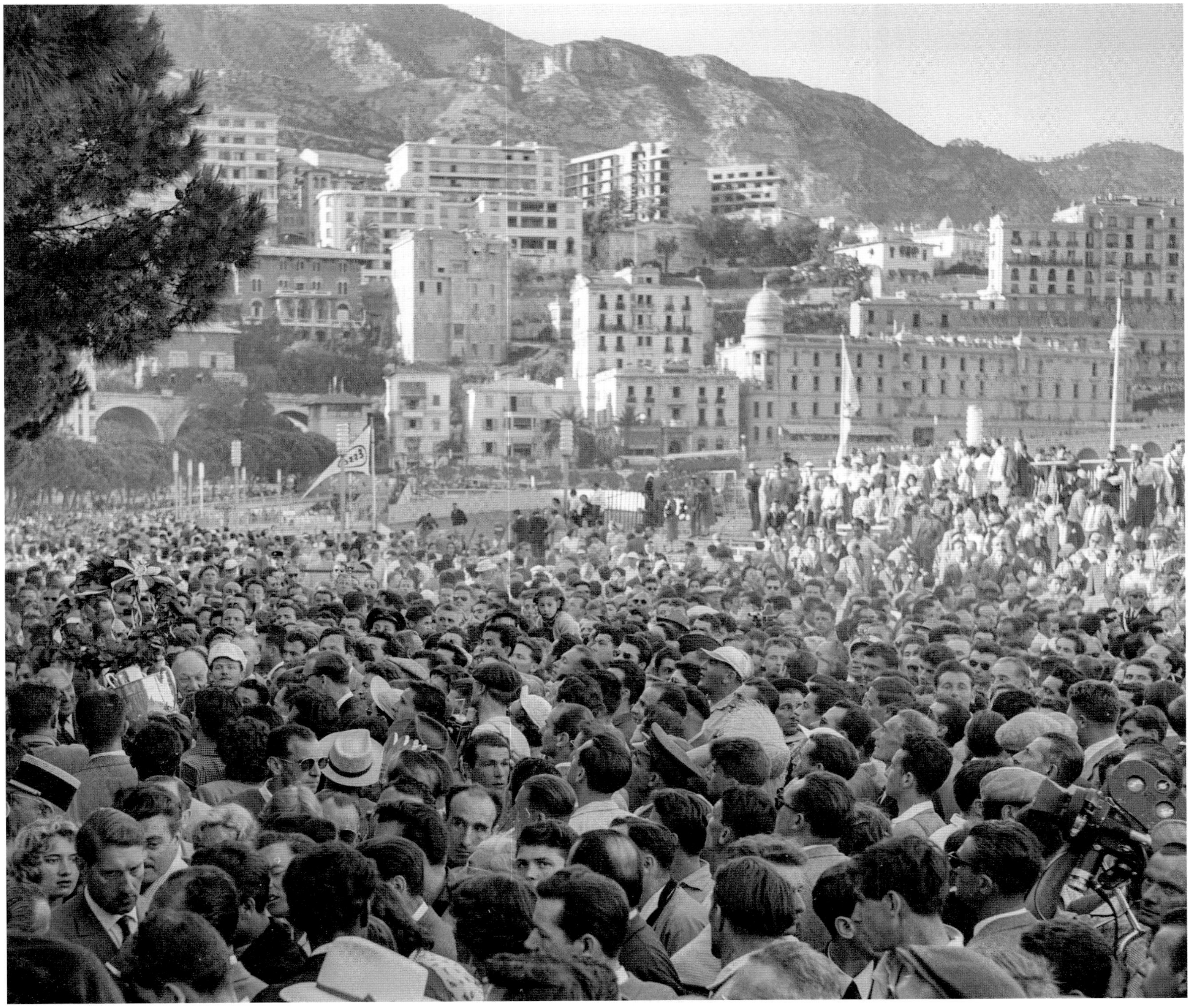

Vexierbild: Wo ist der Sieger? Irgendwo in der Menge steht Maurice Trintignant, umringt von Enthusiasten, nur der Pokal und der Siegerkranz sind zu sehen. Wunderbare Zeiten, als die Zuschauer noch Tuchfühlung mit einem Grand-Prix-Sieger aufnehmen konnten.

Conundrum: Where is the winner? Somewhere in the crowd is Maurice Trintignant, completely surrounded by fans. Only the trophy and the winner's wreath can be seen in the crowd. Those were the good old days when spectators could still get up close and personal with a Grand Prix winner.

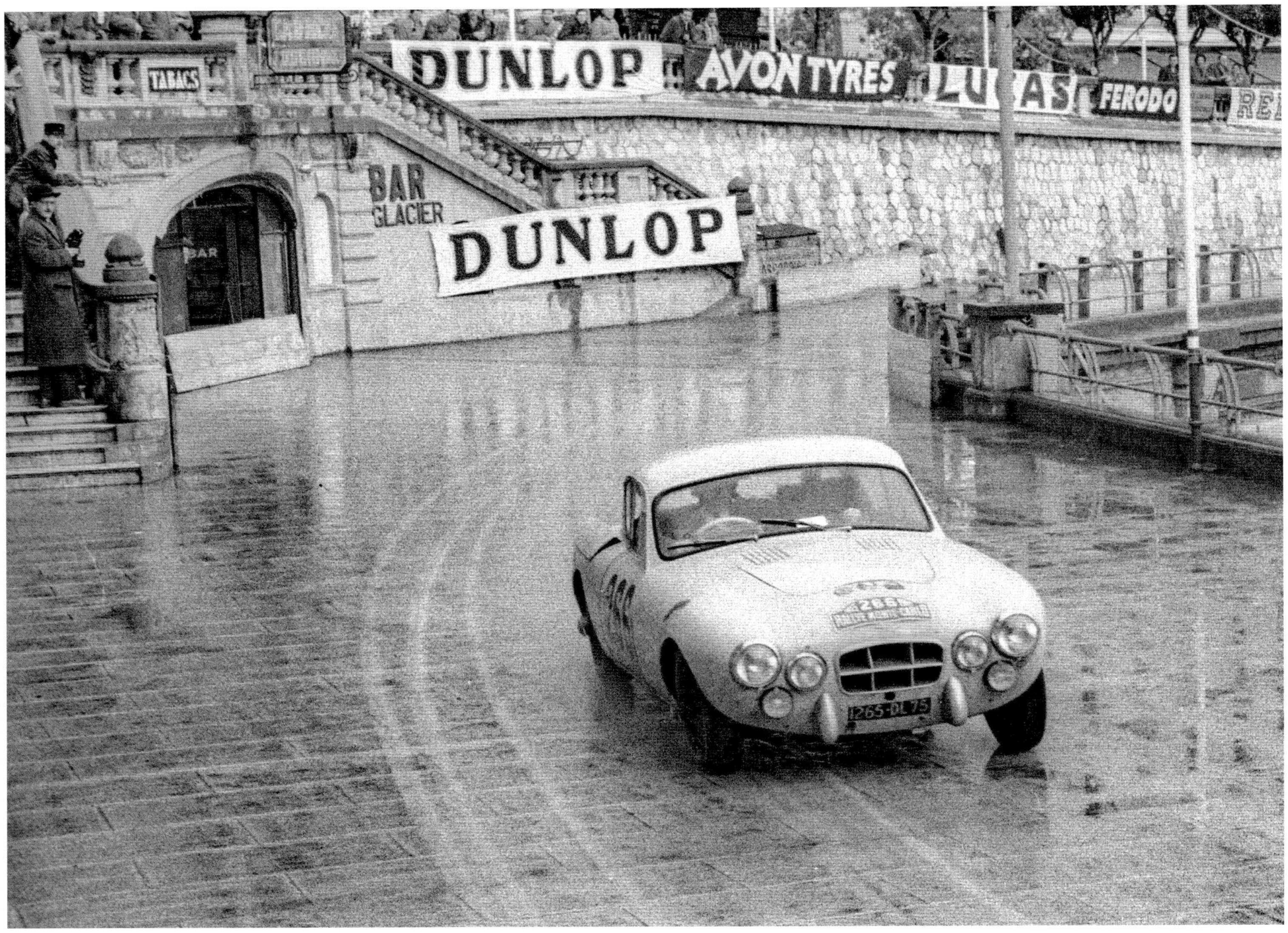

Cotton/Lemerle, N° 266 Salmson 2300 S, mit Karosserie von Pichon-Parat, ein Unikat.
Links die Bar-Tabac, die der Kurve den Namen gegeben hat: Bis heute lautet ihr Name Tabac.

Cotton/Lemerle, N° 266 Salmson 2300 S, special bodied by Pichon-Parat, a one-off car.
On the left the Bar-Tabac, which gave the name to the corner: to this day it is the Tabac Corner.

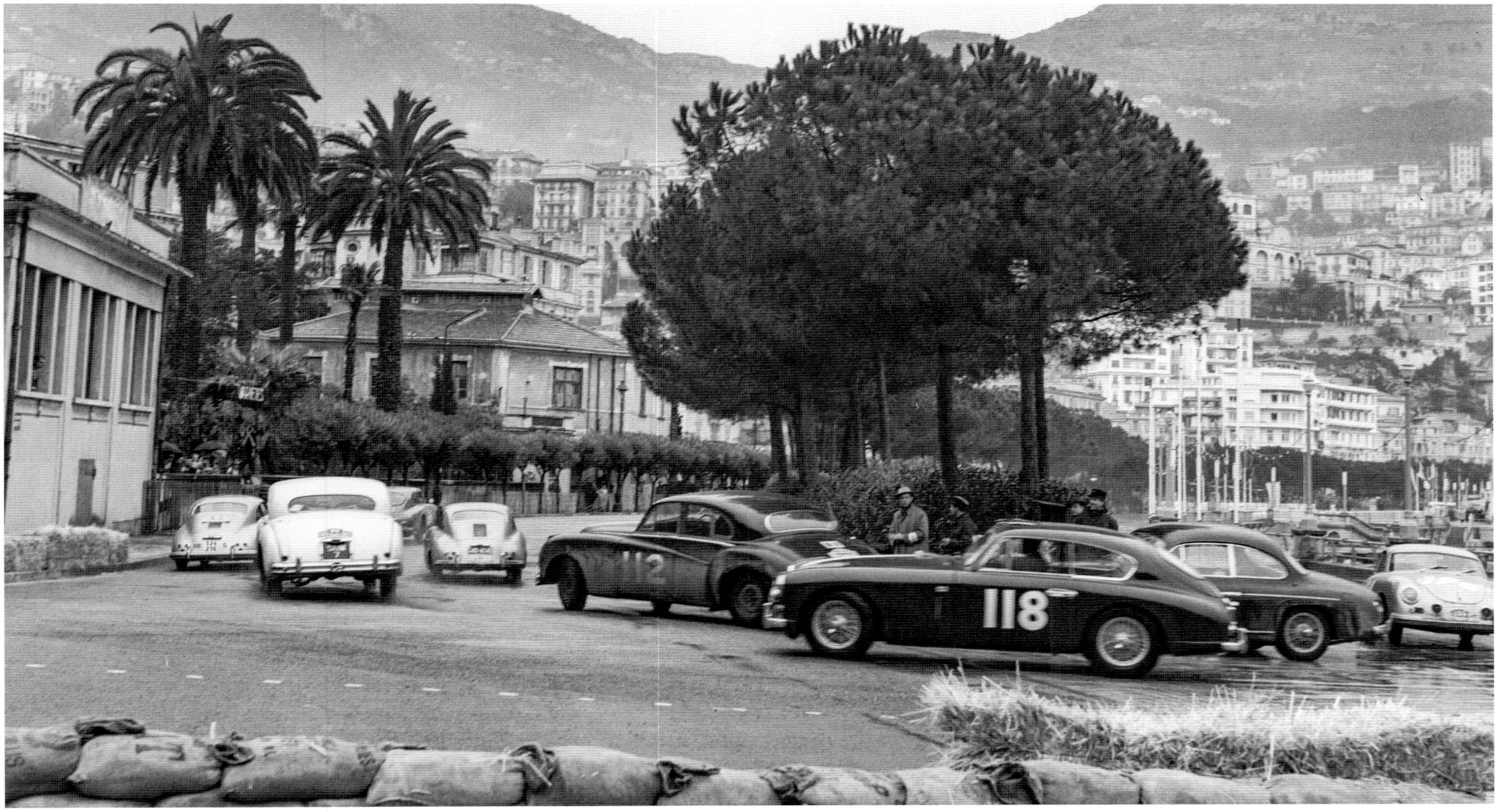

Dichter Verkehr in der Gasometer-Kurve. Faulkner/Silverthorne, Aston Martin DB2-4 N° 118, Appleyard/Appleyard, Jaguar Mk VII N° 90, Vard/Jolley, Jaguar MK VII N° 112, und drei Porsche 356.

Crowded traffic at the Gasometer hairpin. Faulkner/Silverthorne, Aston Martin DB2-4 N° 118, Appleyard/Appleyard, Jaguar Mk VII N° 90, Vard/Jolley, Jaguar MK VII N° 112 and three Porsche 356.

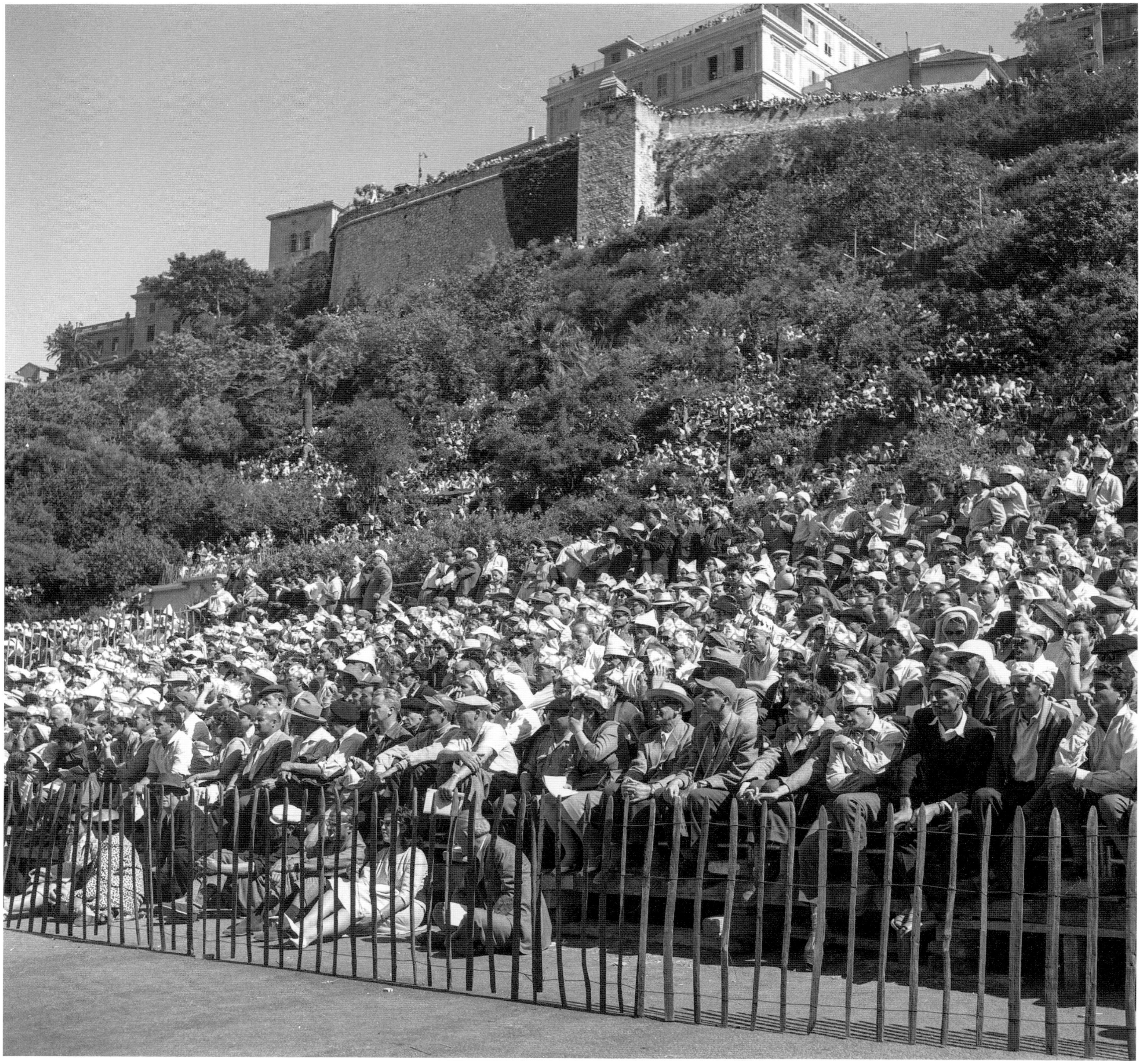

Natürliche Tribüne: dichtgedrängte Zuschauer an den Hängen des „Le Rocher", der Altstadt von Monaco mit dem fürstlichen Palast.

Natural grandstand: a densely packed group of spectators on the slopes of "Le Rocher" (The Rock), the Old Town of Monaco with the Royal Palace.

1956

Moss gegen Fangio

Nachdem sich Mercedes aus der Formel 1 zurückgezogen hat, wechselt Fangio zu Ferrari und Moss, sein Partner 1955, wird die Nr. 1 beim großen italienischen Konkurrenten Maserati. Nur 14 Wagen sind in diesem Jahr am Start: neben den Lancia-Ferrari D50 – Lancia hatte sich 1955 aus finanziellen Gründen aus dem Rennsport zurückgezogen – und den Maserati 250F nur noch die schwächeren Gordini und Vanwall.

Moss erwischt einen guten Start und fährt von Anfang an vorneweg. Für Fangio hingegen, gestartet von der Pole-Position, ist es ein Rennen zum Vergessen. Mit einer ungewohnt wilden Fahrweise dreht er sich in der dritten Runde und verursacht den Ausfall von Musso und Schell. In der 32. Runde verpasst er die Schikane und beschädigt ein Rad seines D50 und muss an die Box.

Dann profitiert er von einer Regel, die bis 1957 galt: Es ist erlaubt, während des Rennens die Fahrer eines Autos zu wechseln. Die erreichten Punkte werden dann geteilt. Deshalb kann ein Fahrer auch gleichzeitig auf zwei Rängen platziert sein. So übernimmt Fangio den Ferrari seines Teamkollegen Collins, der mit 45 Sekunden Rückstand an zweiter Stelle liegt. Er holt Runde um Runde auf, fährt die schnellste Runde und wird am Ende mit 6 Sekunden hinter Moss Zweiter.

So gewinnt Moss als erster britischer Fahrer seit „Williams“ 1929 den Grand Prix. Aber Fangio wird 1956 zum dritten Mal hintereinander Weltmeister.

Moss vs. Fangio

After Mercedes withdrew from Formula 1, Fangio switched to Ferrari and Moss, his partner in 1955, became No. 1 at the big Italian competitor Maserati. There were only 14 cars on the grid this year. Besides the Lancia-Ferrari D50 – Lancia had withdrawn from Racing in 1955 for financial reasons – and the Maserati 250F the weaker three Gordini and two Vanwall.

Moss got off to a good start and took the lead from the outset. For Fangio, however, who started from pole position, it was a race to forget. With an unusually wild driving style he spun in the third lap and forced the retirement of Musso and Schell. On the 32nd lap he missed the chicane and damaged one of the wheels of his D50, necessitating a pit stop.

He benefitted from a rule that held until 1957, allowing a change of drivers during the race. The points scored were then shared. This meant that a driver could be placed on two ranks at the same time. Fangio took over the Ferrari of his team mate Collins, who was 45 seconds behind in second place. He caught up lap after lap, set the fastest lap time and ended up second, six seconds behind Moss.

Thus Moss became the first British driver since "Williams" to win the Grand Prix in 1929. But Fangio became world champion for the third time in a row in 1956.

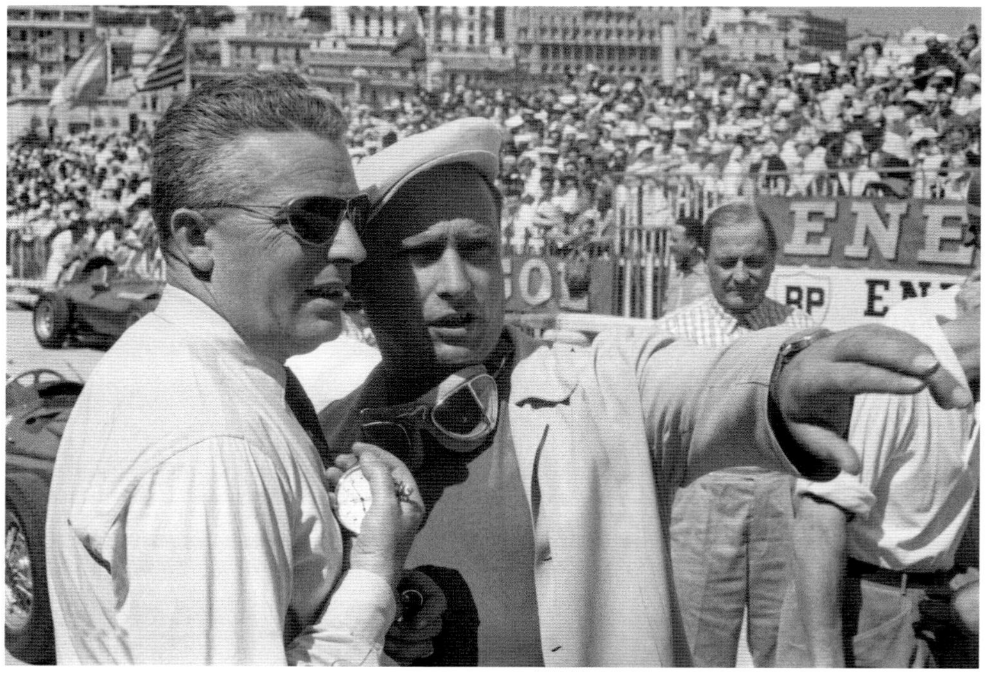

Juan Manuel Fangio and „Maestro“ Nello Ugolini, sportlicher Leiter der Scuderia Ferrari bis 1955, dann 1956 bei Maserati.

Juan Manuel Fangio and “Maestro” Nello Ugolini, sporting director until 1955 of Scuderia Ferrari, then from 1956 of Maserati.

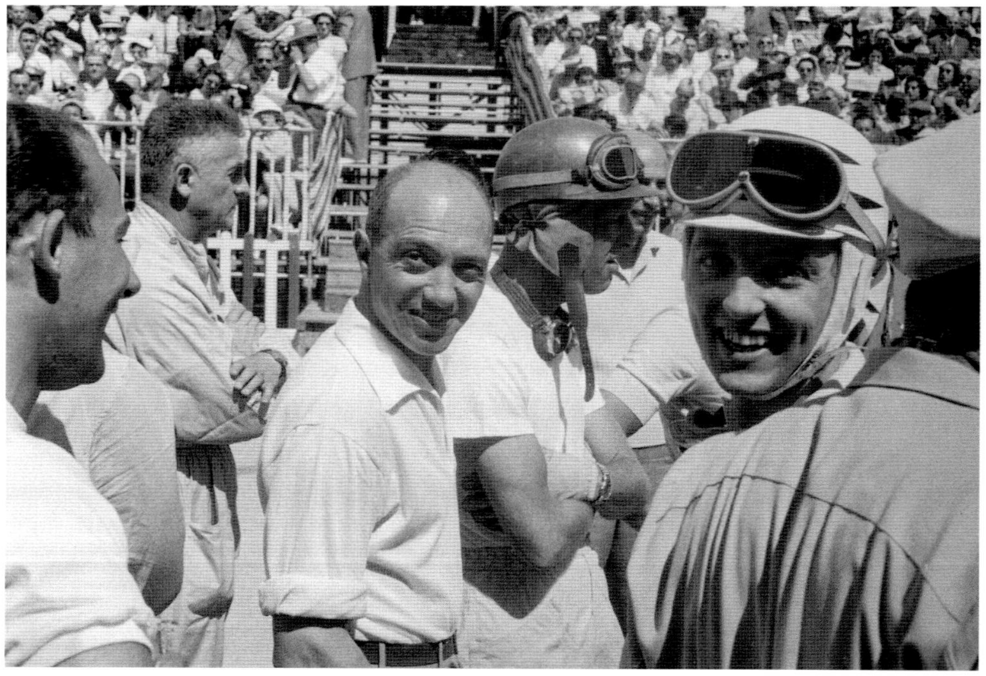

Letzte Scherze vor dem Start bei der Fahrerbesprechung. Stirling Moss, Louis Rosier, Robert Manzon, Peter Collins, Cesare Perdisa (von links).

One last joke before the start at the drivers’ briefing. Stirling Moss, Louis Rosier, Robert Manzon, Peter Collins, Cesare Perdisa (from left).

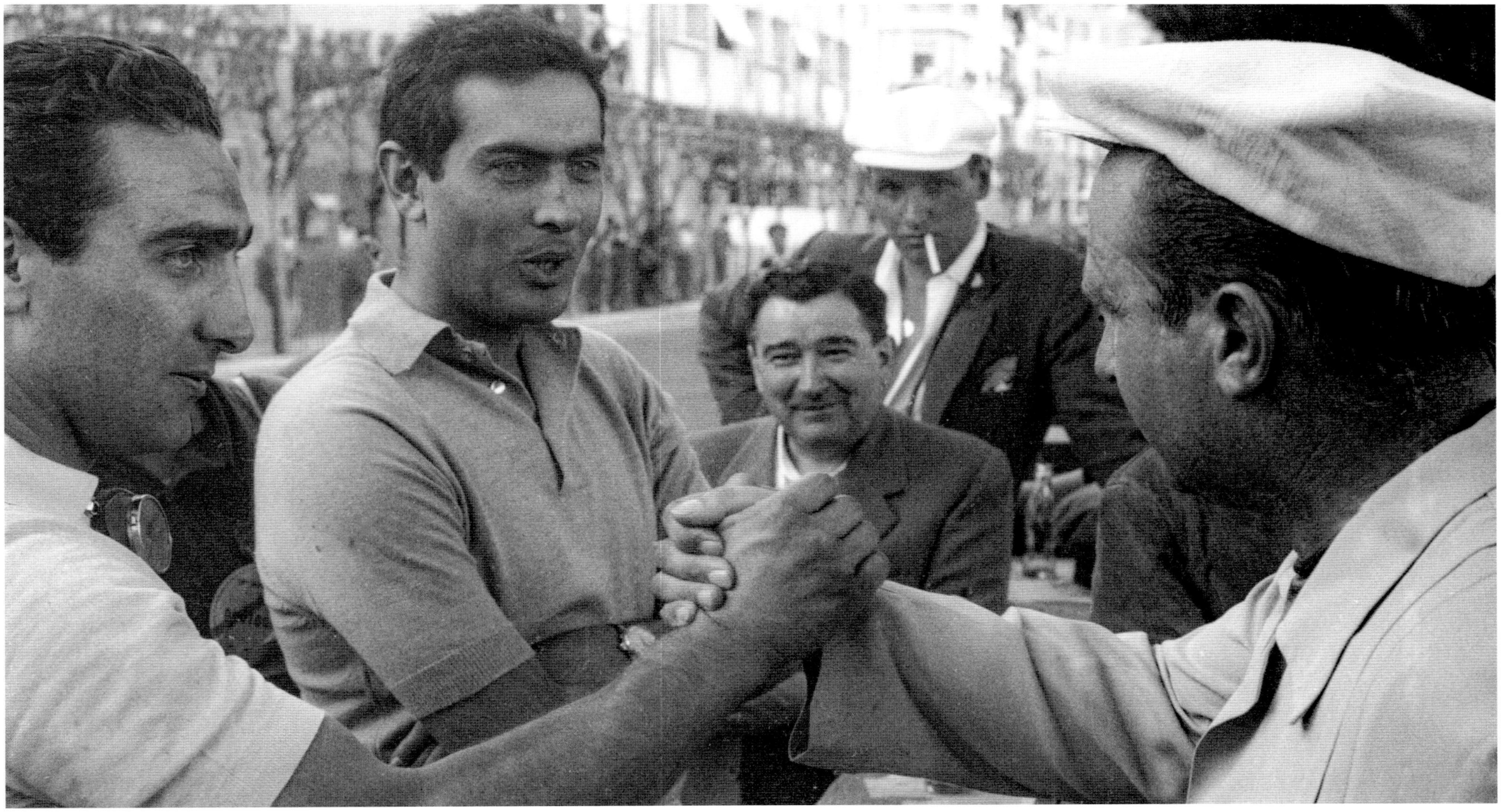

Drei von der Scuderia Ferrari:
Eugenio Castellotti und Luigi Musso, zwei heftige Rivalen, und Juan Manuel Fangio (von links).

Three members of the Scuderia Ferrari team: Eugenio Castellotti and Luigi Musso, two fierce rivals, and Juan Manuel Fangio (from left).

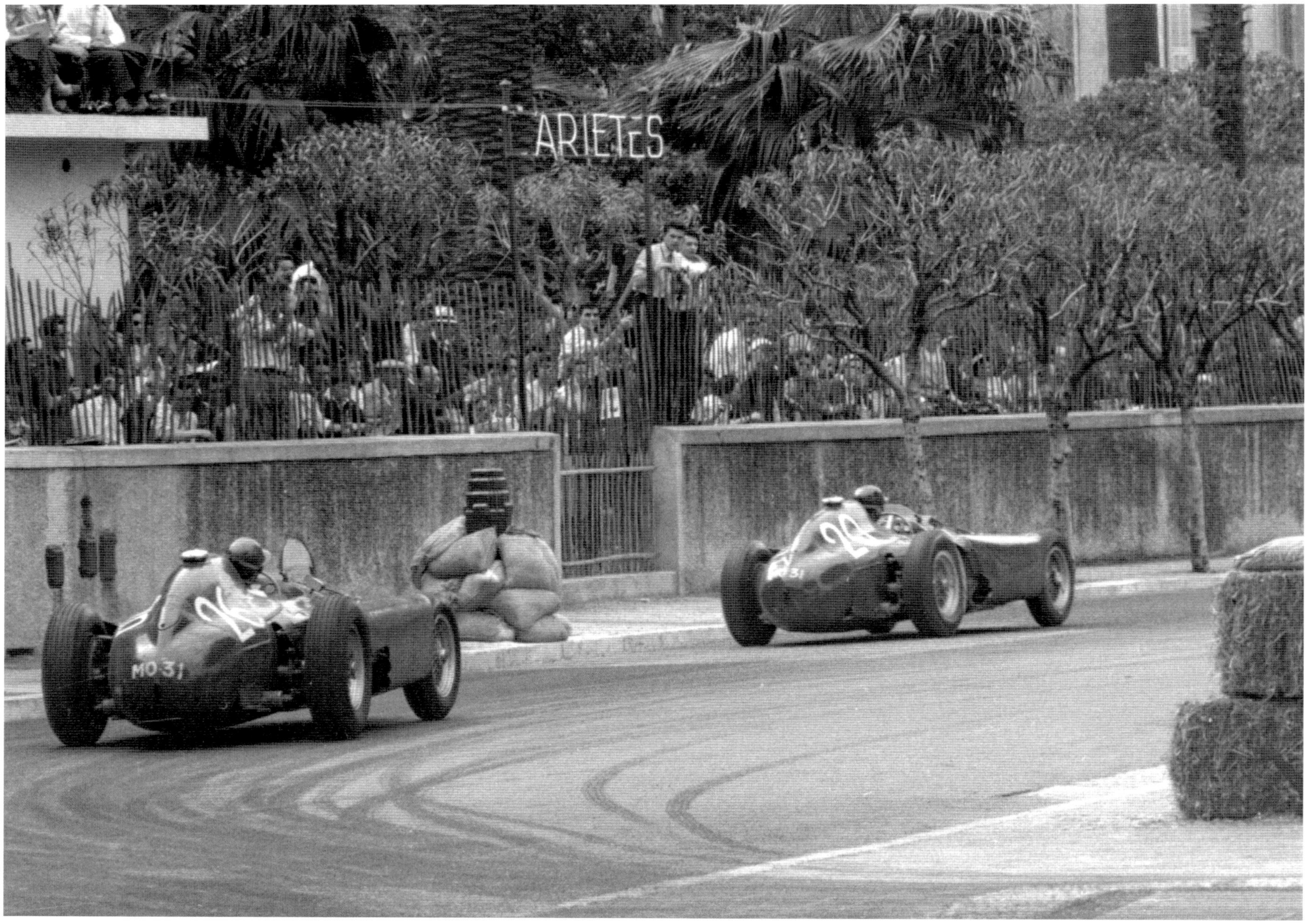

Juan Manuel Fangio, Lancia-Ferrari D50 N° 20,
Peter Collins, Lancia-Ferrari D50 N° 26.

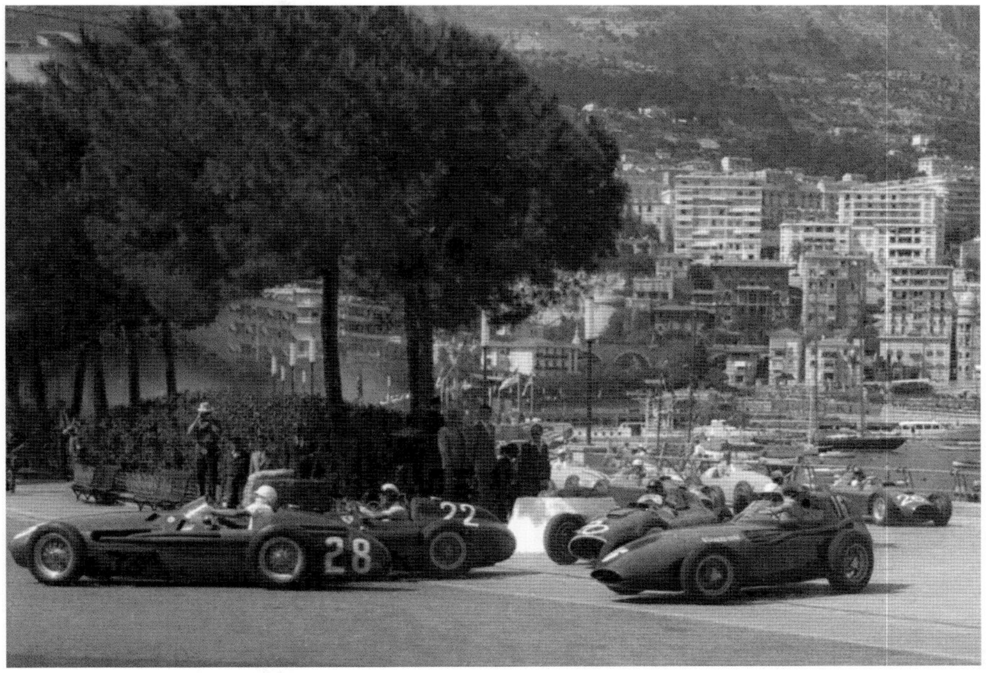

Stirling Moss, Maserati 250F N° 28,
Eugenio Castellotti, Lancia-Ferrari D50 N° 22,
Harry Schell, Vanwall N° 16,
Juan M. Fangio, Lancia-Ferrari D50 N° 20,
Peter Collins, Lancia-Ferrari D50 N° 26.

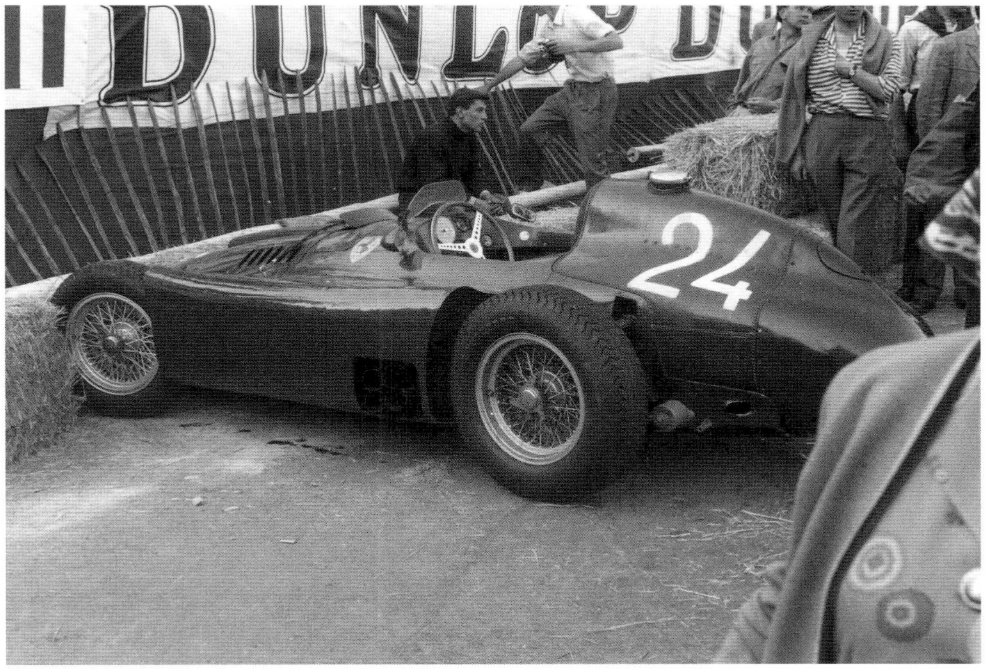

Luigi Musso, Lancia-Ferrari D50 N° 24, rammte in der dritten Runde an der Sainte Dévote die Abschrankung, behindert von Fangio.

Luigi Musso, Lancia-Ferrari D50 N° 24, hit the bales at Sainte Dévote on the third lap, hindered by Fangio.

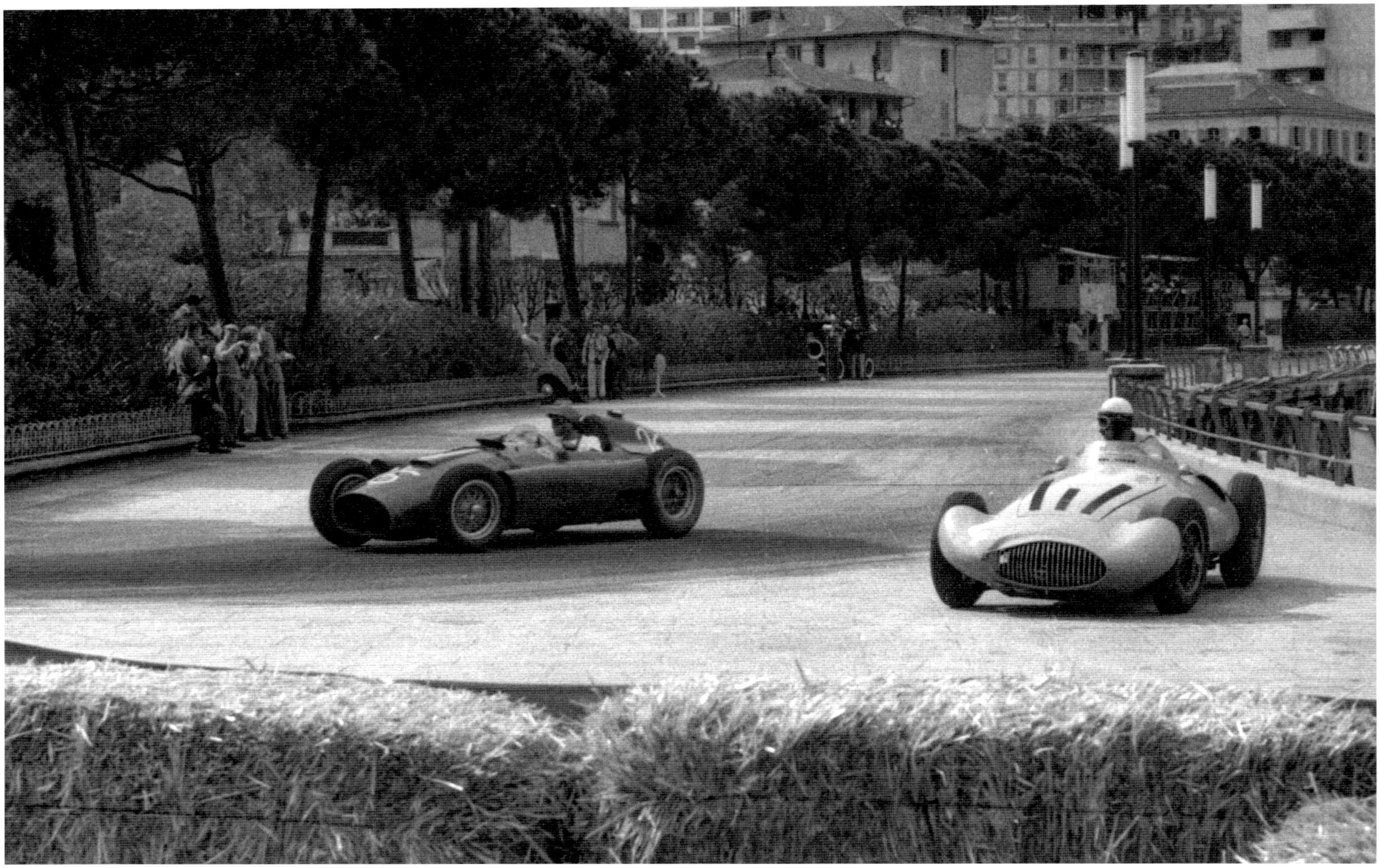

Peter Collins, Lancia-Ferrari D50 N° 26, und Elie Bayol mit dem neuen 8-Zylinder Gordini T32 N° 4 mit einer speziellen aerodynamischen Karosserie.

Peter Collins, Lancia-Ferrari D50 N° 26, and Elie Bayol with the new 8 cylinder Gordini T32 N° 4 with a special aerodynamic body.

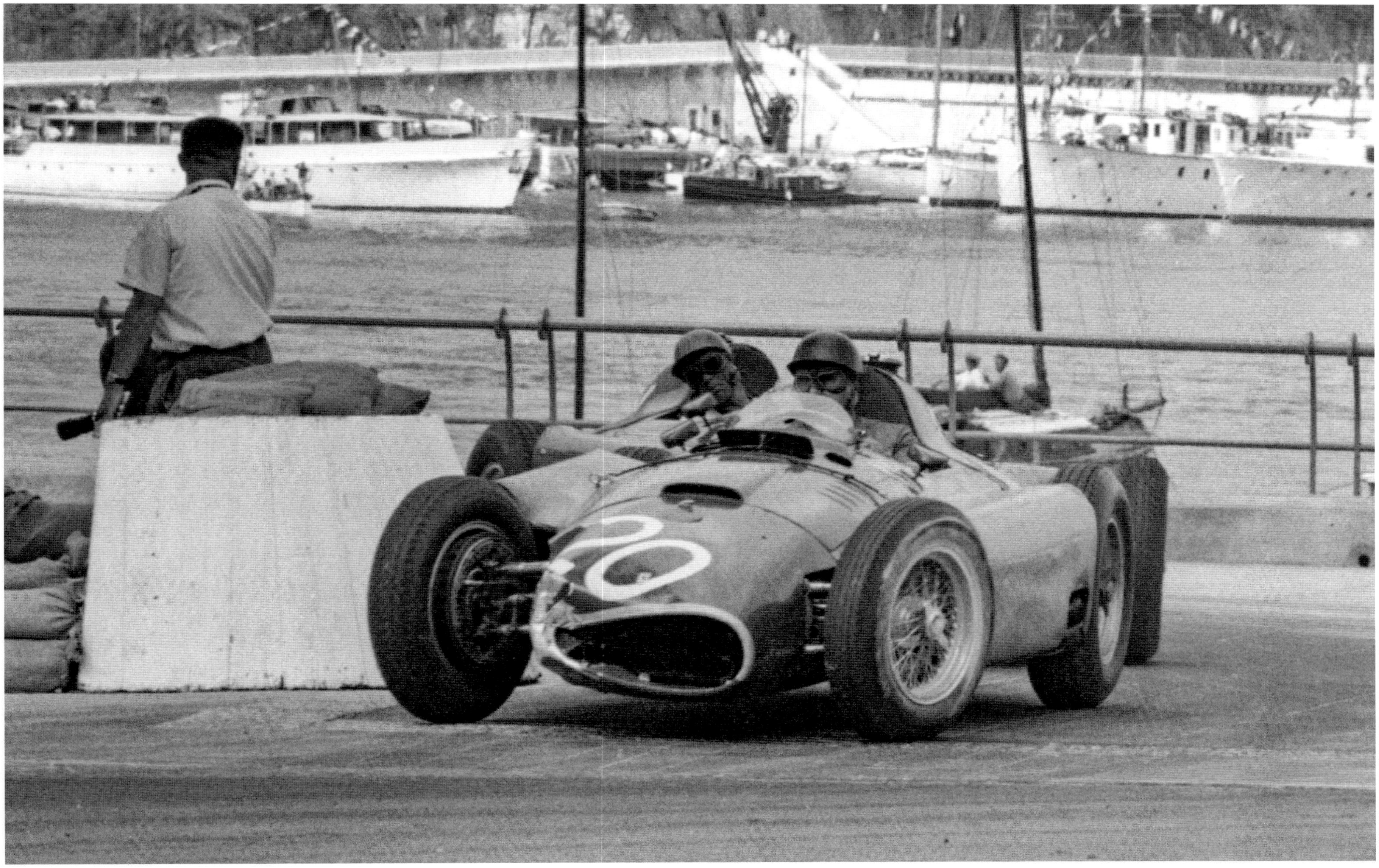

Juan Manuel Fangio beschädigte die Nase seines Lancia-Ferrari D50 N° 20. Hinter ihm Peter Collins, Lancia-Ferrari D50 N° 26.

Juan Manuel Fangio damaged the nose of his Lancia-Ferrari D50 N° 20. Behind him Peter Collins, Lancia-Ferrari D50 N° 26.

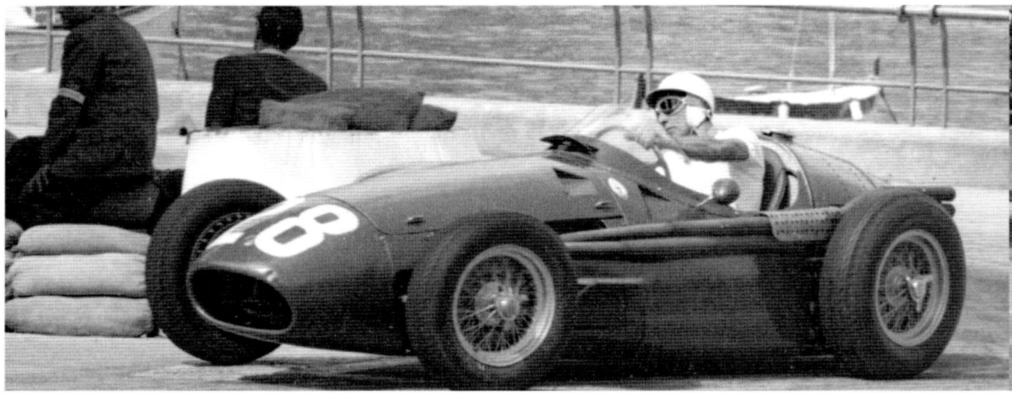

1. Stirling Moss, Maserati 250F N° 28.

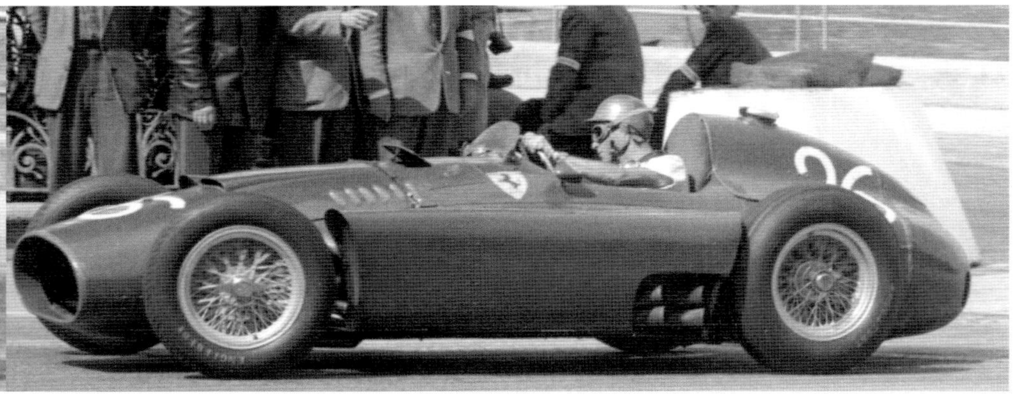

2. Peter Collins, Lancia-Ferrari D50 N° 26 mit Fangio (with Fangio).

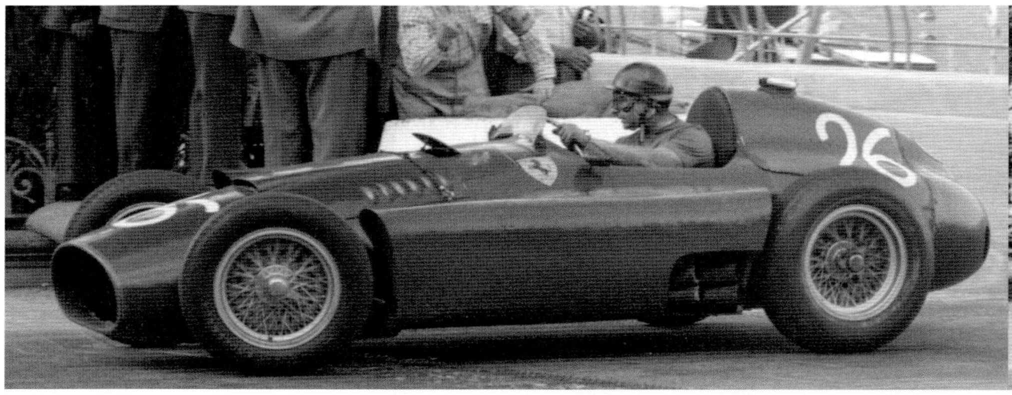

2. Juan Manuel Fangio in Peter Collins' Lancia D50 N° 26.

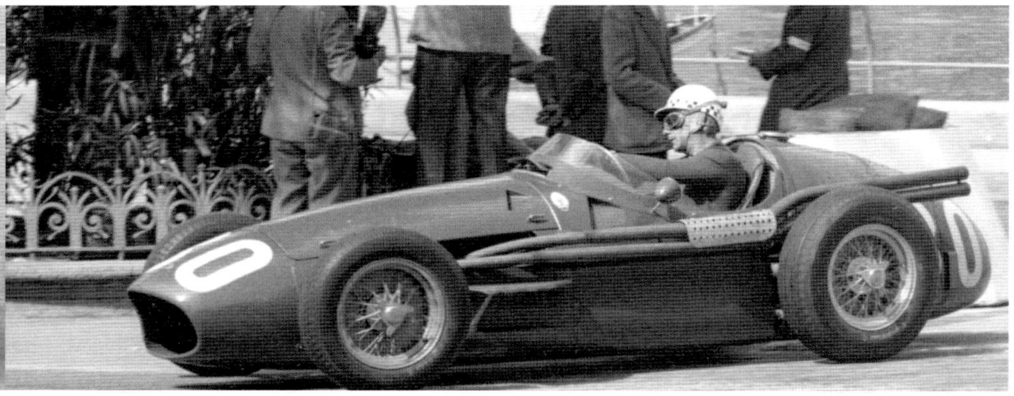

3. Jean Behra, Maserati 250F N° 30.

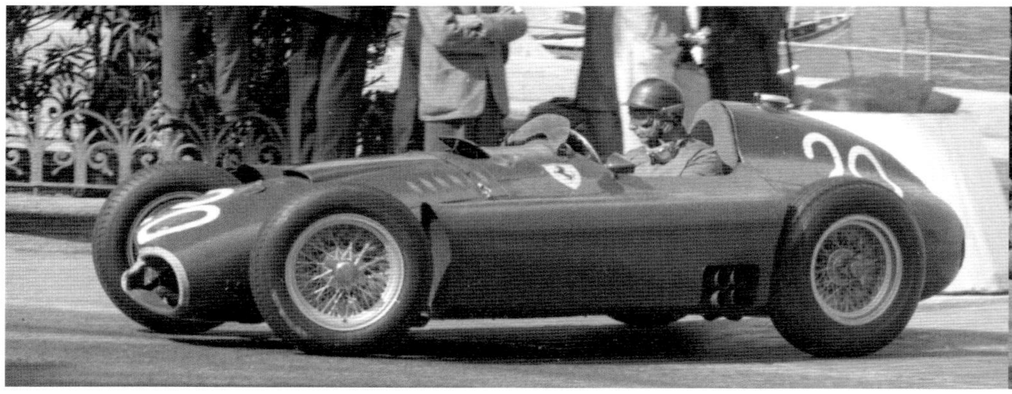

4. Juan Manuel Fangio, Lancia-Ferrari D50 N° 20 mit Castellotti (with Castellotti).

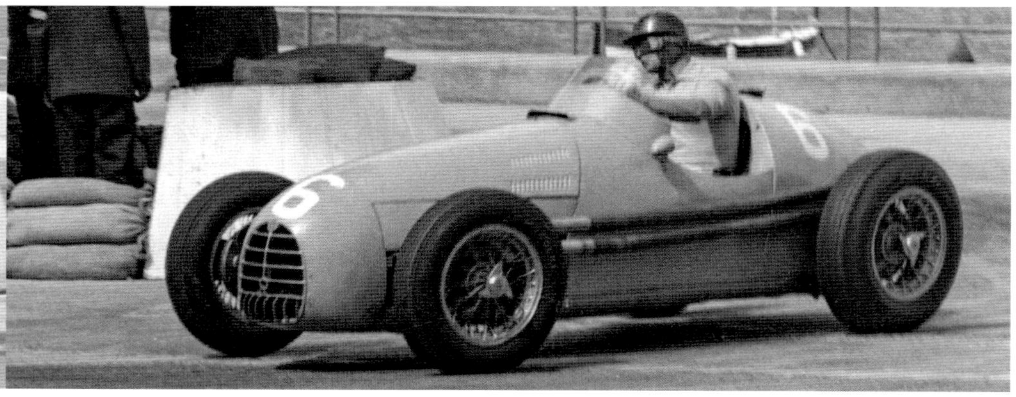

5. „Nano" da Silva Ramos, Gordini T16 N° 6.

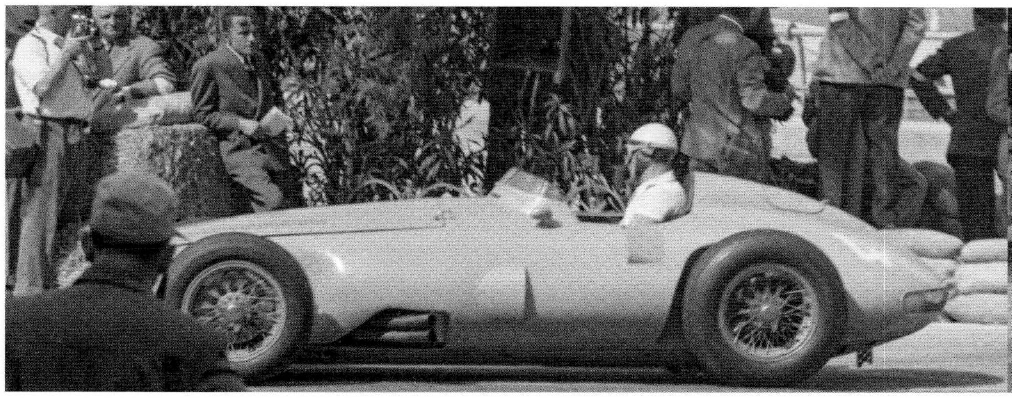

6. Elie Bayol, Gordini T32 N° 4.

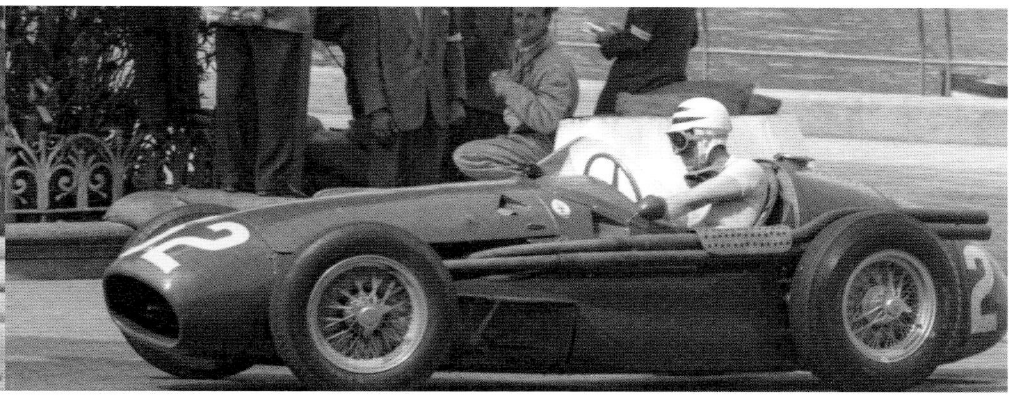

7. Cesare Perdisa, Maserati 250F N° 32.

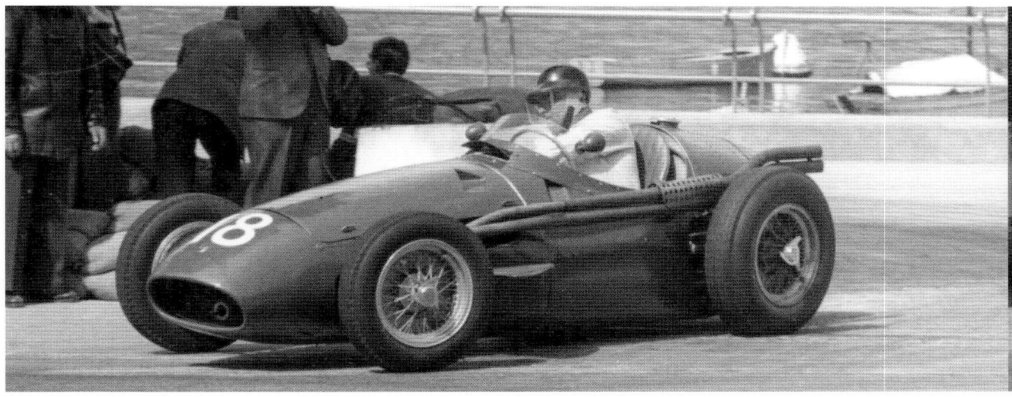

8. Horace H. Gould, Maserati 250F N° 18.

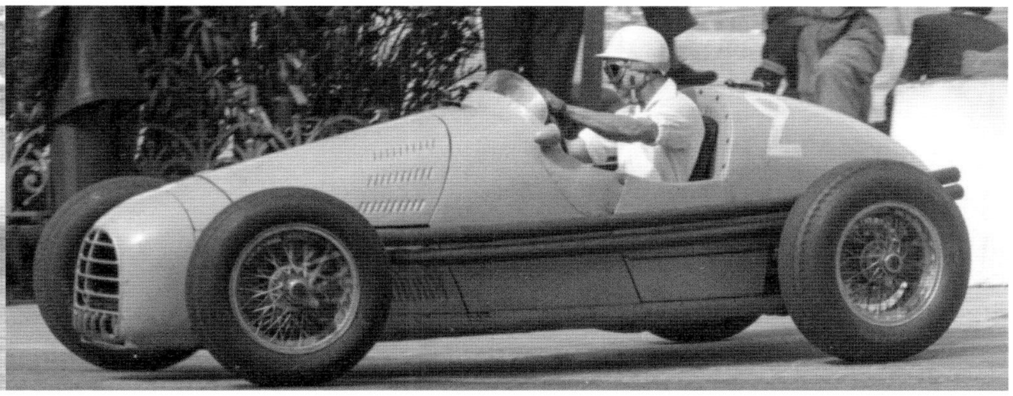

Robert Manzon, Gordini T16 N° 2. Ausfall (überhitzt). *Retired (overheating).*

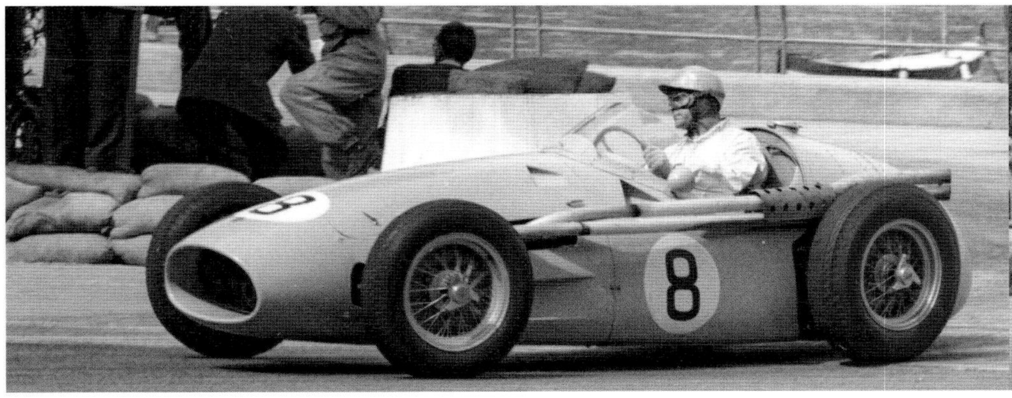

Louis Rosier, Maserati 250F N° 8. Ausfall (Motorschaden). *Retired (engine).*

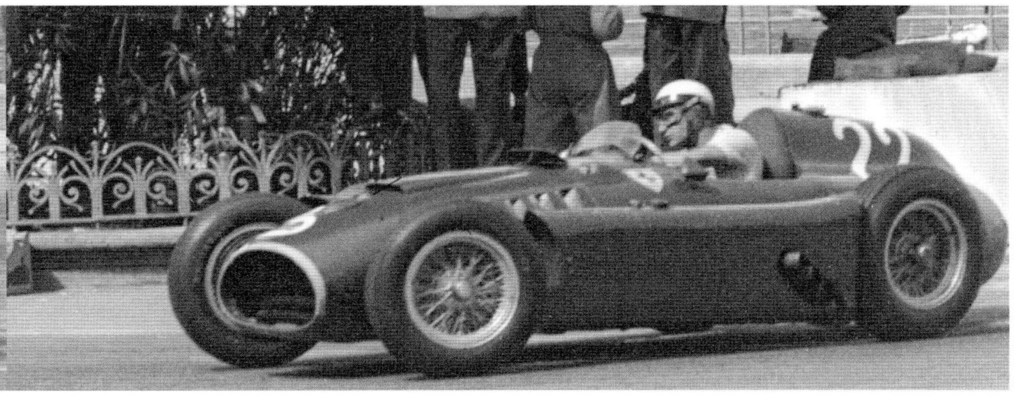

Eugenio Castellotti, Lancia-Ferrari D50 N° 22. Ausfall (Kupplung). *Retired (clutch).*

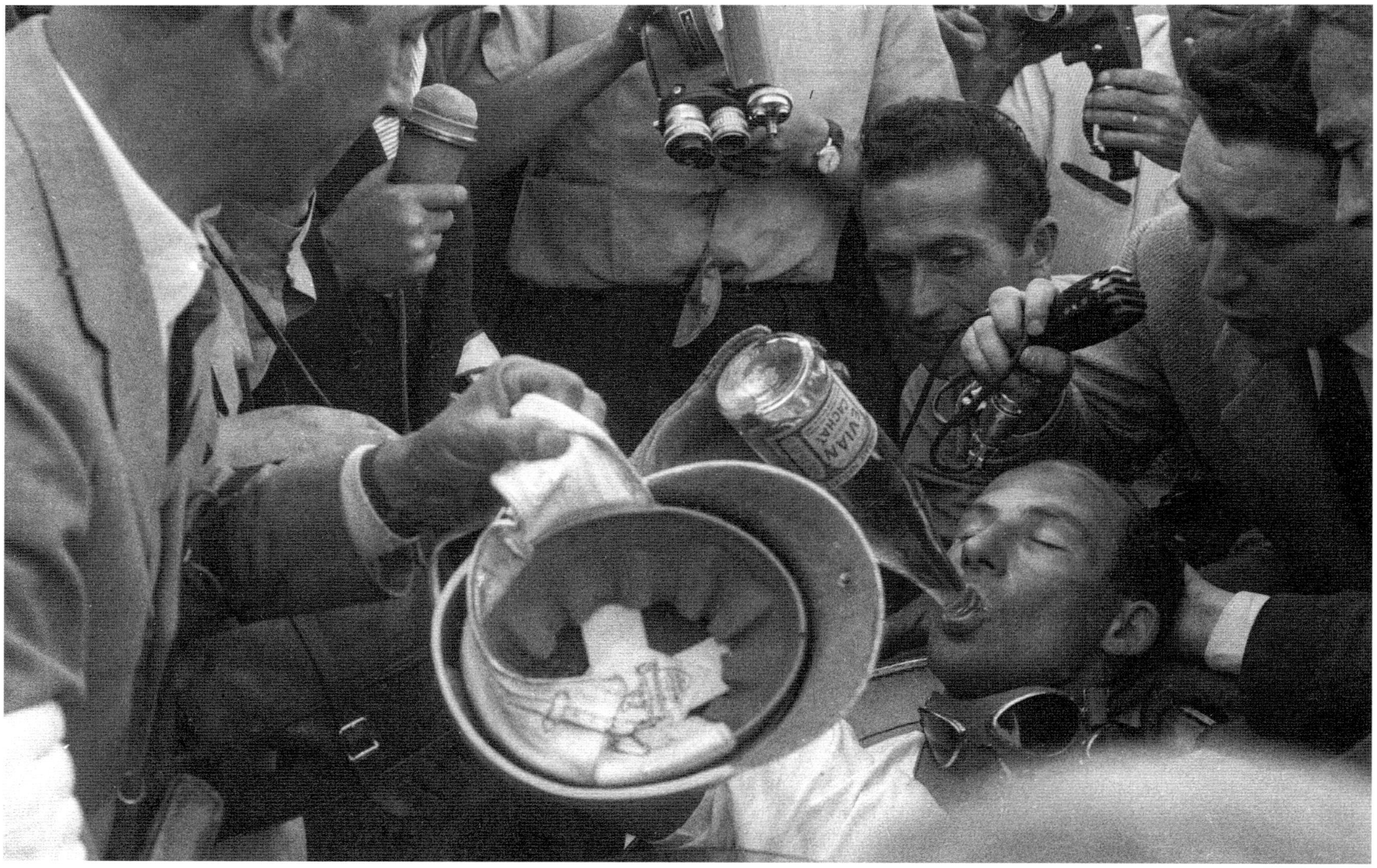

Stirling Moss nach 100 Runden in 3 Stunden und 32 Sekunden mit der Durchschnittsgeschwindigkeit von 104,514 km/h.

Stirling Moss after 100 laps in 3 hours and 32 seconds with an average speed of 104.514 km/h.

Final Result of the Monaco Grand Prix 1956

1. Stirling Moss, Maserati 250F
2. Peter Collins/Juan Manuel Fangio, Lancia-Ferrari D50
3. Jean Behra, Maserati 250F

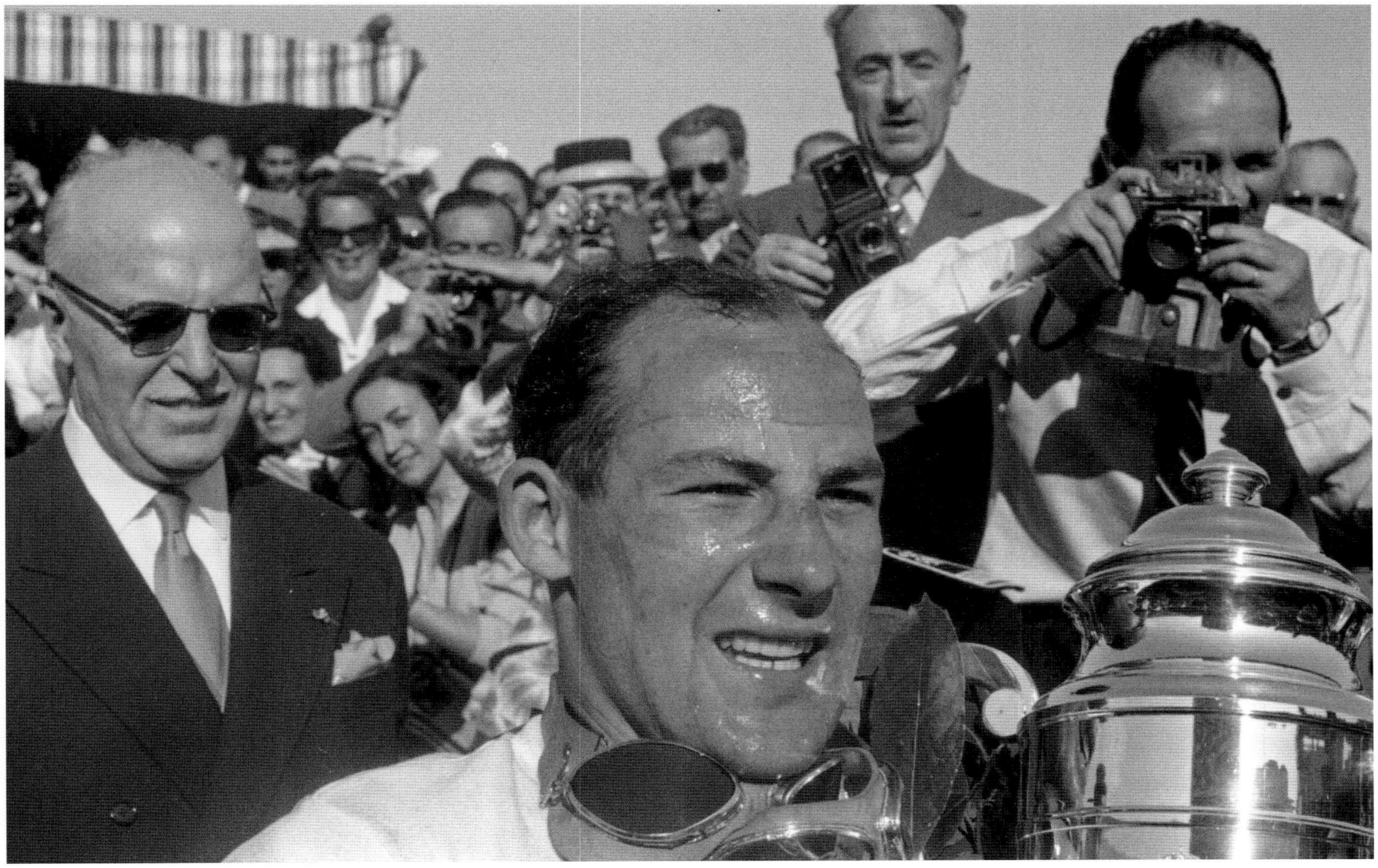

Der Sieger: Stirling Moss, Maserati 250F.
Hinter ihm Fürst Pierre.

The winner: Stirling Moss, Maserati 250F.
Behind him Prince Pierre.

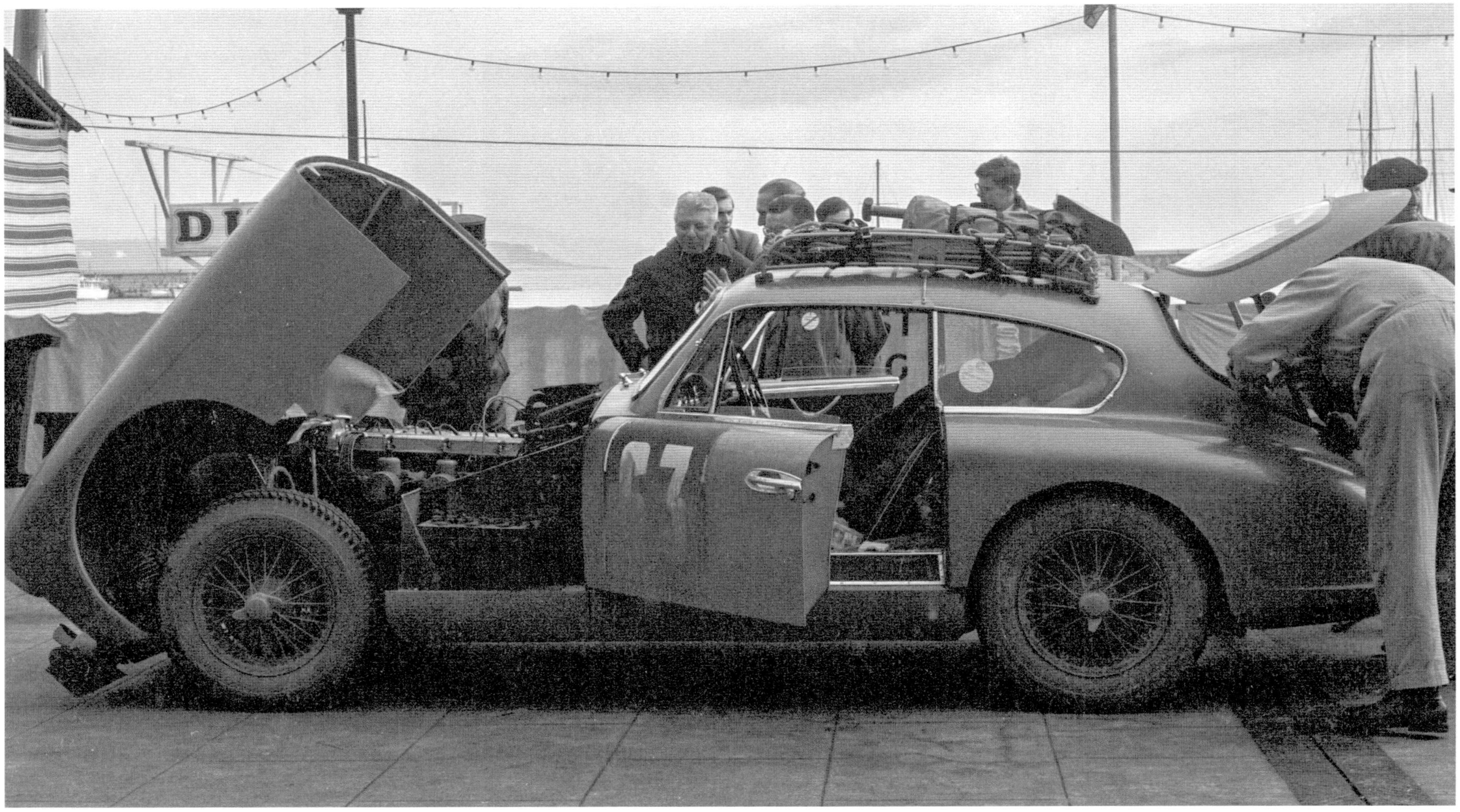

Carter/Rohner in Aston Martin DB2-4 N° 63.

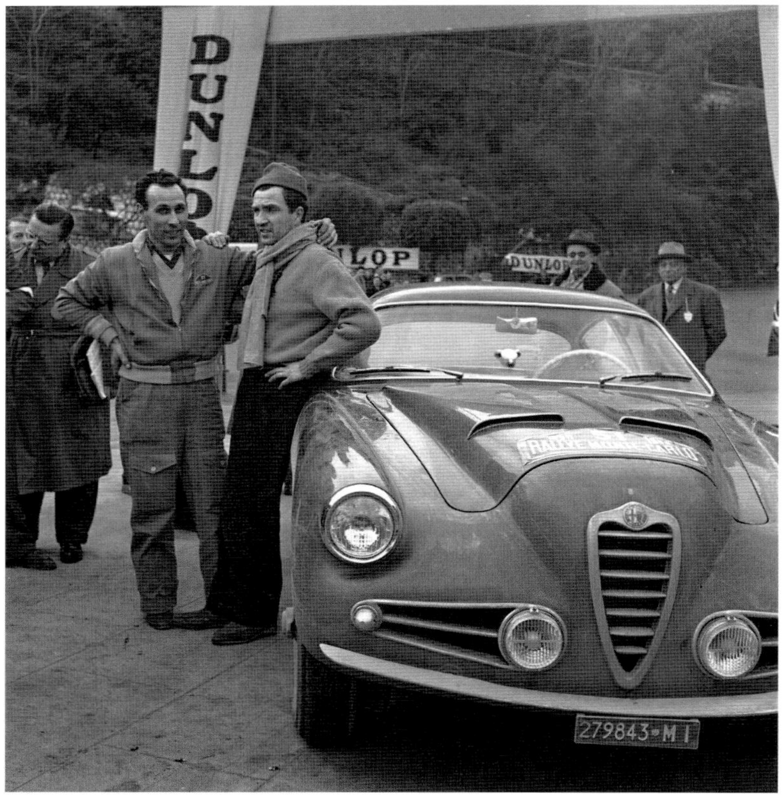

Boilet/Chany auf Alfa Romeo 1900 Super Zagato mit Spezialkarosserie N° 51.

Boilet/Chany in special bodied Alfa Romeo 1900 Super Zagato N° 51.

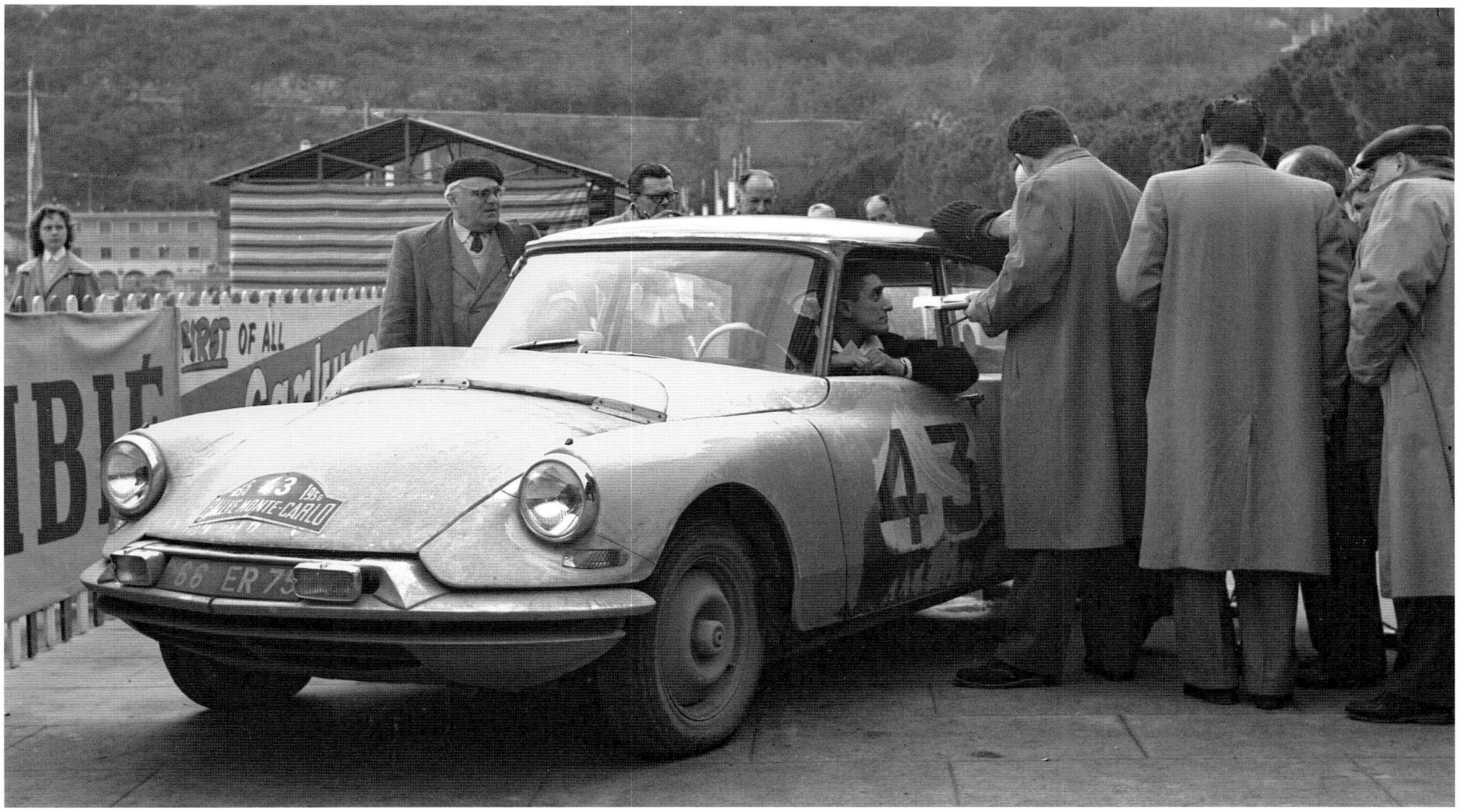

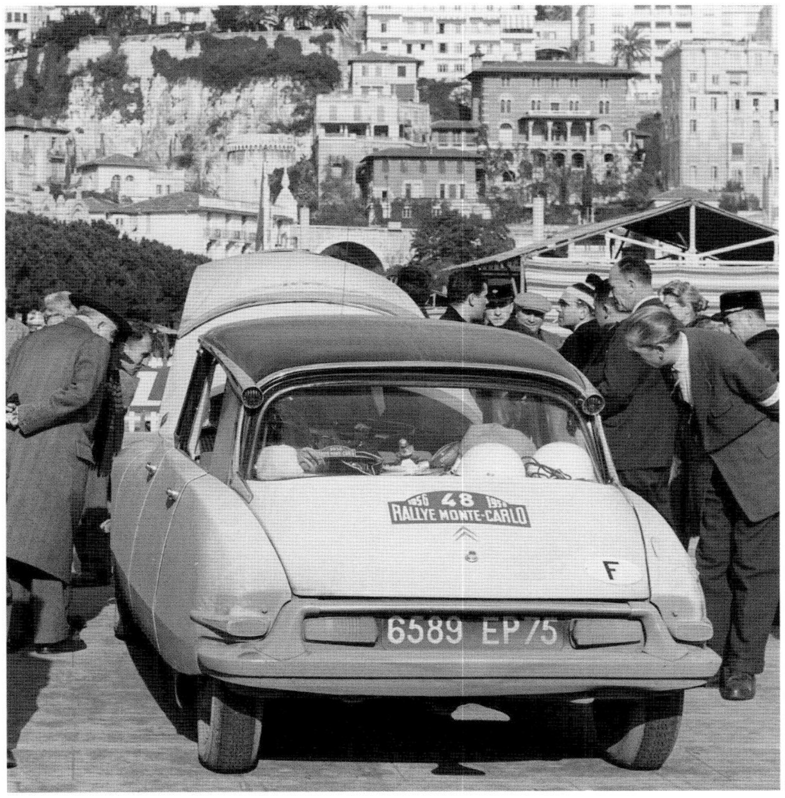

Bestaunt von allen Seiten: zwei der neuen, futuristischen Citroën DS, die einzigen im Feld mit Scheibenbremsen. Capravesne/Alexandre, N° 43, and Rozze/Dubassay, N° 48.

Admired from all sides: two examples of the new, futuristic Citroën DS, the only cars fitted with disc brakes. Capravesne/Alexandre, N° 43, and Rozze/Dubassay, N° 48.

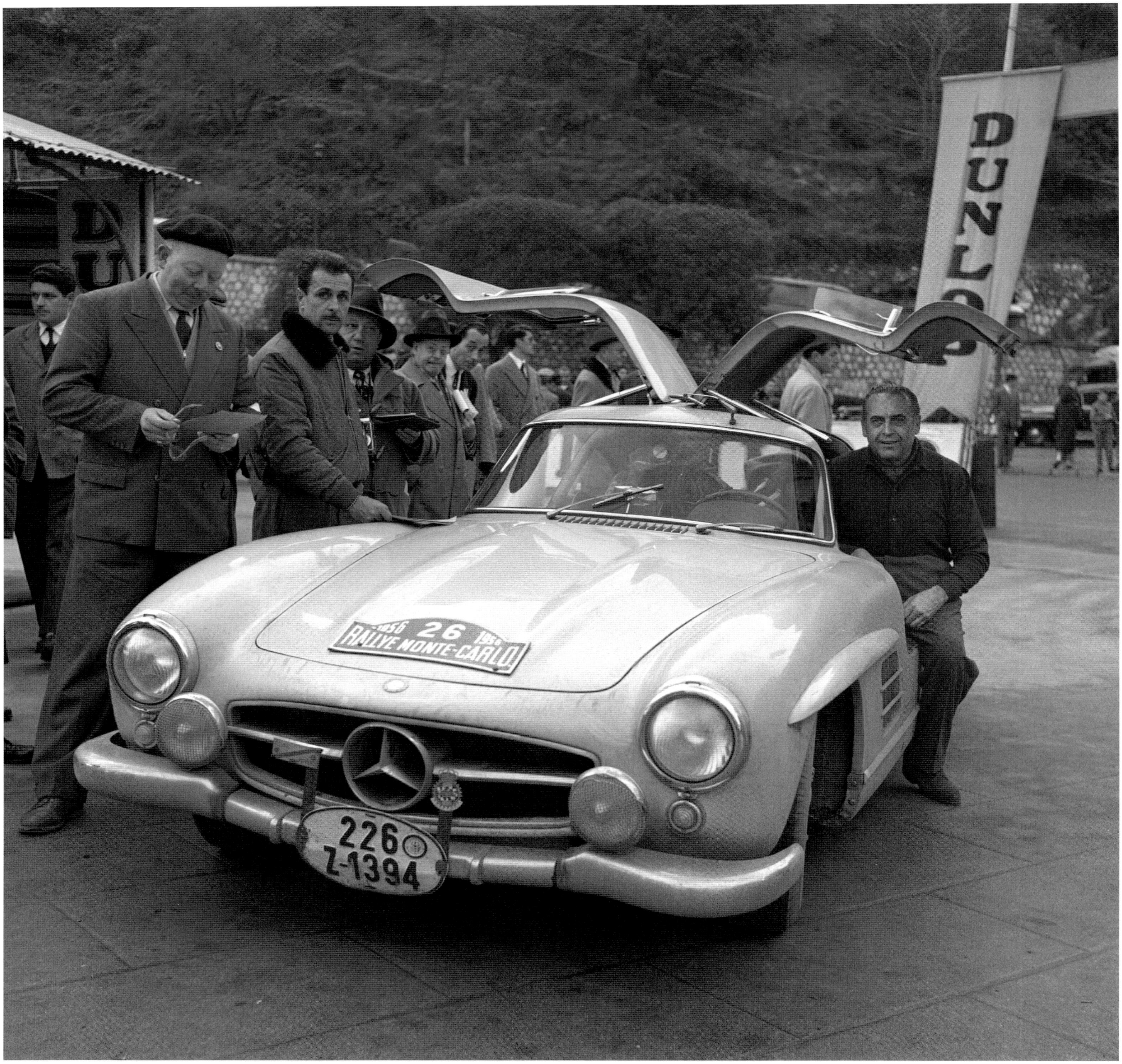

Noch unbeschädigt: Mercedes-Benz 300 SL Flügeltürer N° 26
von Fabregas/Basadonna.

*Still intact: Mercedes-Benz 300 SL Gullwing N° 26
of Fabregas/Basadonna.*

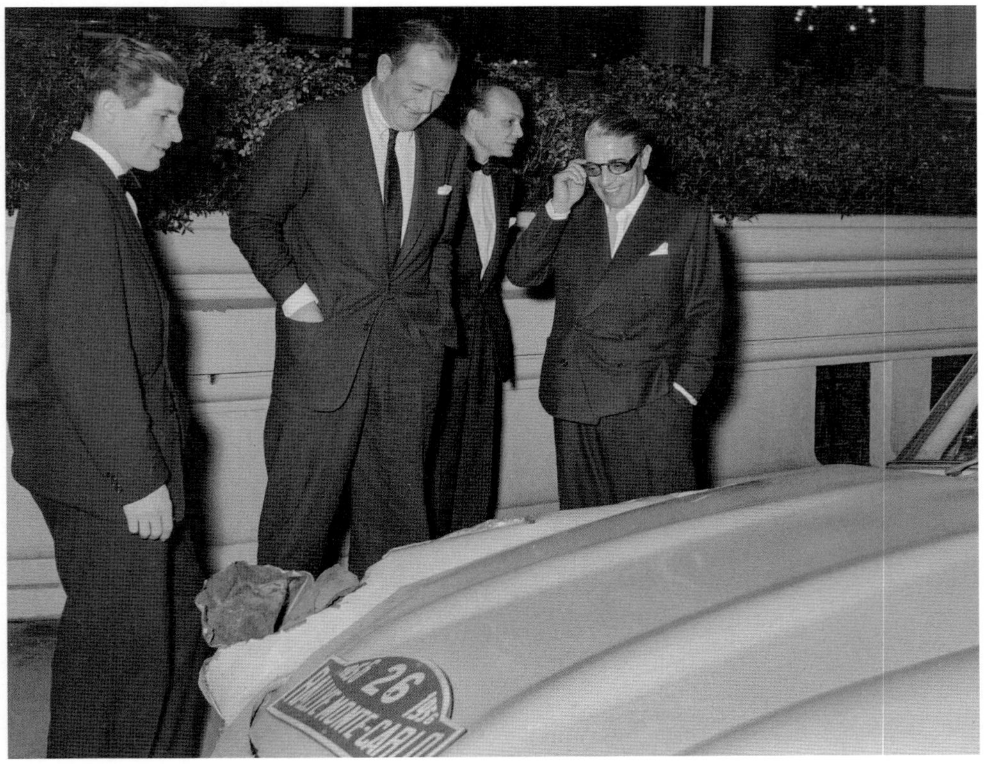

John Wayne und Aristoteles Onassis.
Gut gelaunt studieren sie den beschädigten
Mercedes-Benz 300 SL N° 26.

*John Wayne and Aristotle Onassis smile
as they study the damaged
Mercedes-Benz 300 SL N° 26.*

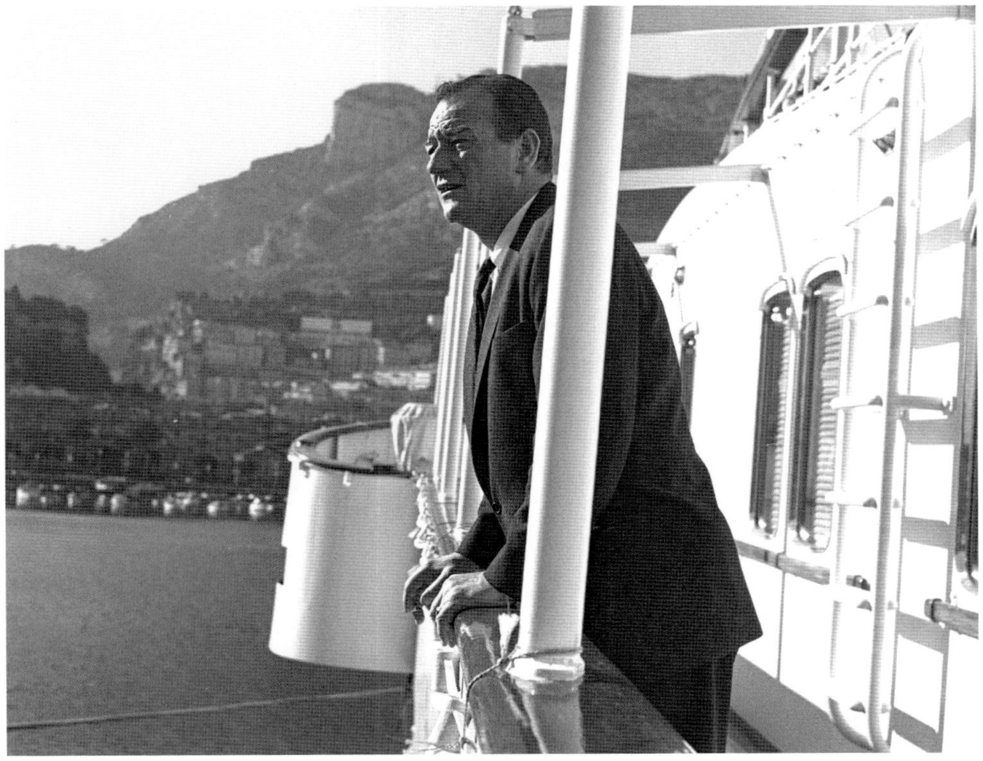

John Wayne war Gast auf Onassis' Superyacht Christina
im Hafen von Monaco.

*John Wayne was a guest on the Onassis superyacht
Christina in Monaco's harbour.*

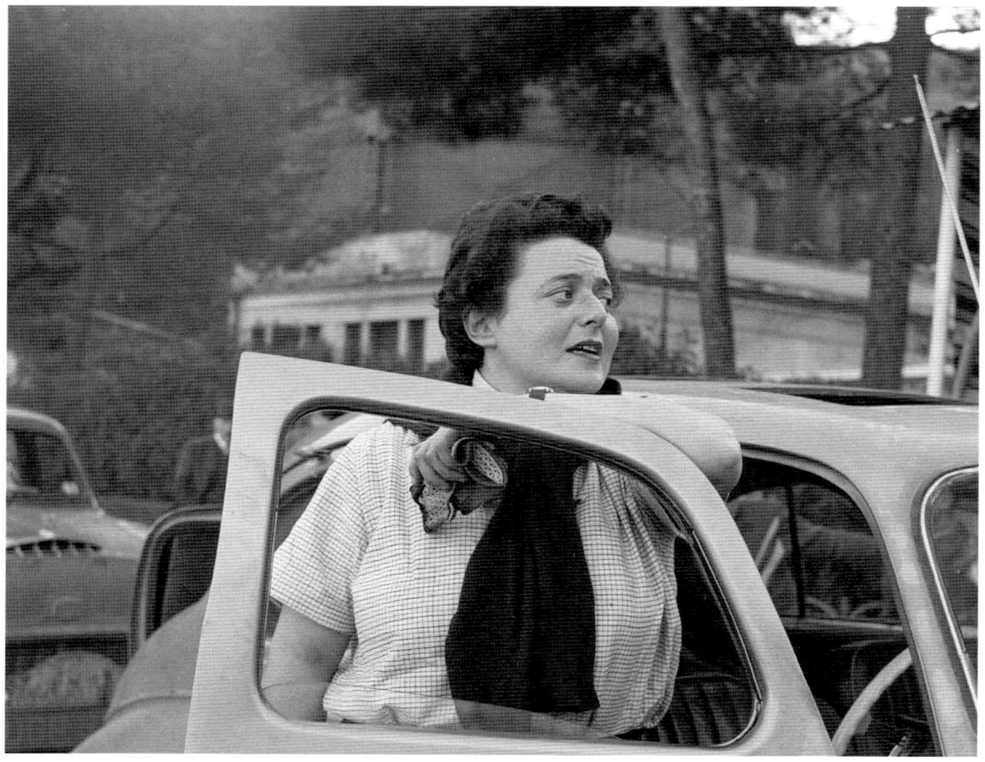

Sheila van Damm, Sunbeam Mk III N° 284, Großbritanniens Top-Rallyefahrerin in den 50er-Jahren. Ihr Vater war der Manager des berühmten Londoner Windmill Theatre.

Sheila van Damm, Sunbeam Mk III N° 284, Britain's top woman rally driver in the 1950s. Her father was the manager of the famous London Windmill Theatre.

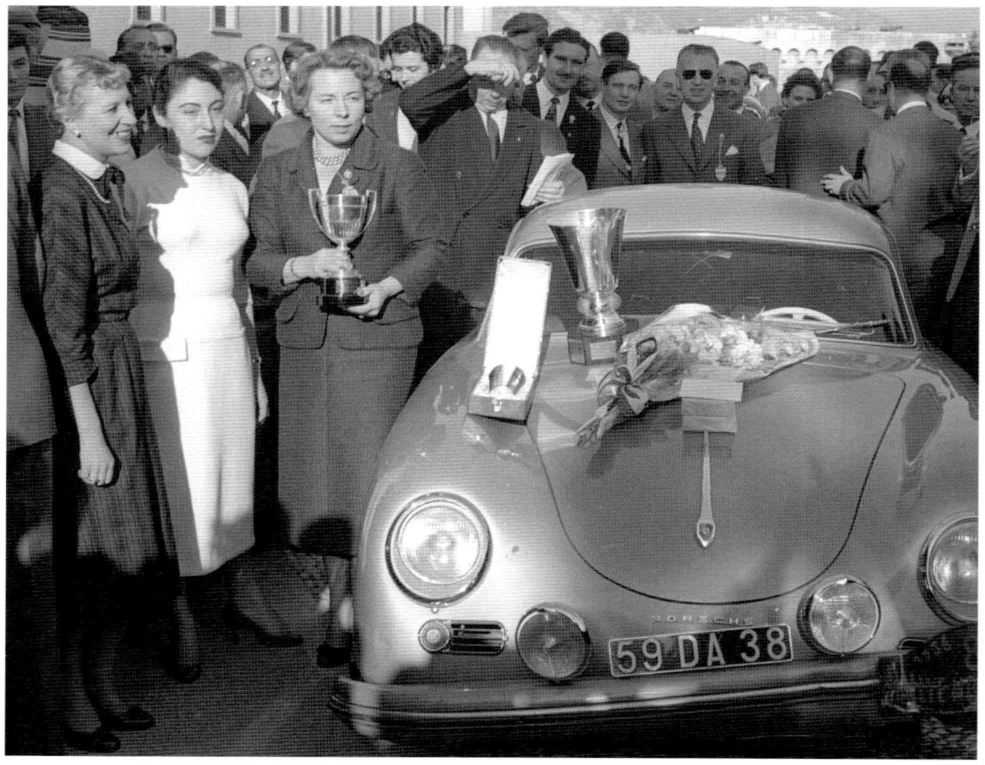

Madeleine Blanchoud/Lucienne Alziary,
Porsche 356 N° 83, Erste im „Coupe des Dames".

Madeleine Blanchoud/Lucienne Alziary,
Porsche 356 N° 83, Winner of the Coupe des Dames.

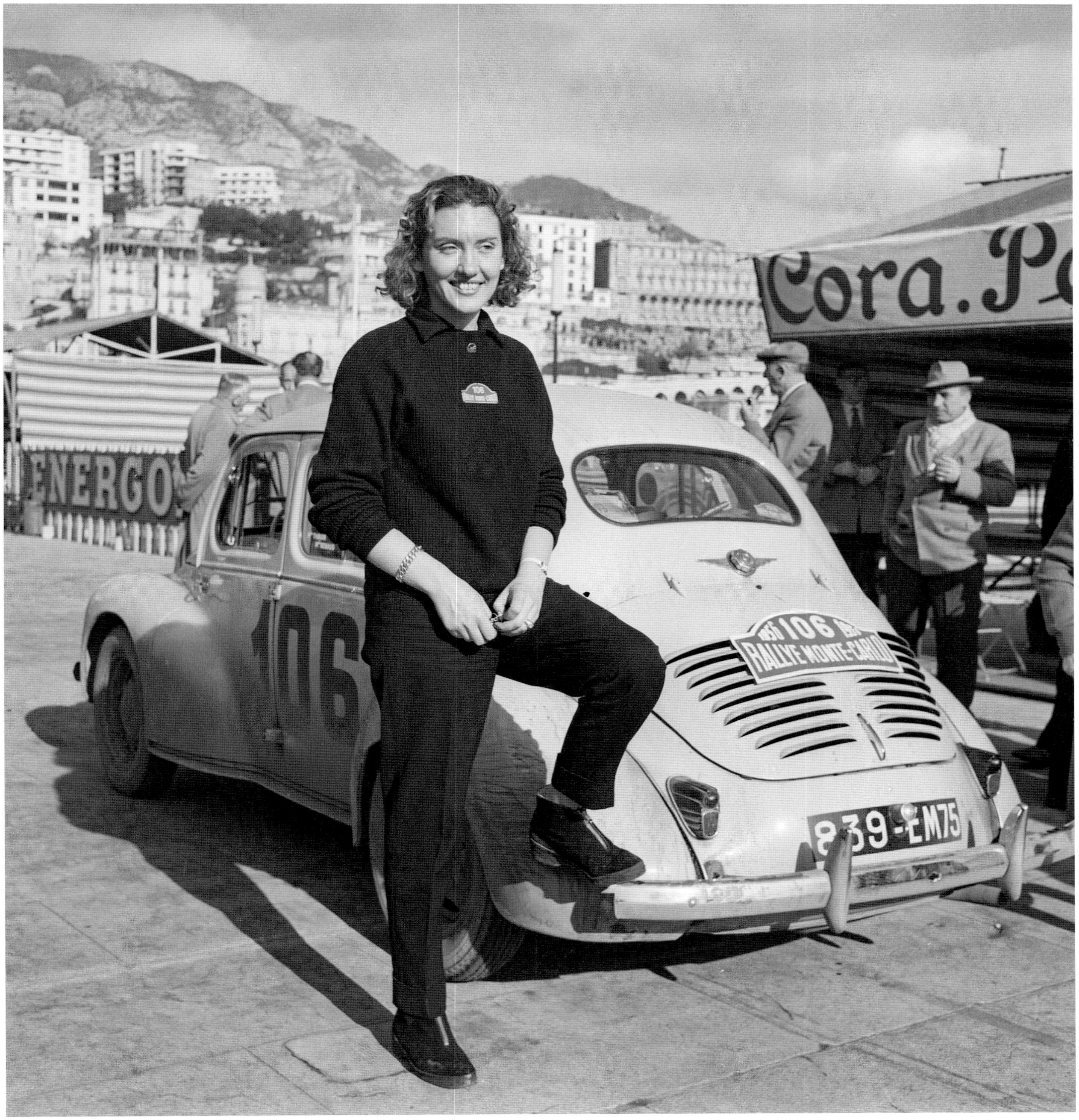

Gilberte Thirion, Renault 4CV N° 106. Sie hatte an vielen Rallyes und Sportwagenrennen erfolgreich teilgenommen. Bei der Mille Miglia von 1956 war sie im Dauphine-Werksteam wesentlich schneller als ihre Kollegen Louis Rosier, Paul Frère und Maurice Trintignant, alles Grand-Prix-Fahrer.

Gilberte Thirion, Renault 4CV N° 106. She had successfully participated in many rallies and sports car races. At the 1956 Mille Miglia, she was much faster than her colleagues in the Dauphine works team Louis Rosier, Paul Frère and Maurice Trintignant, all Grand Prix drivers.

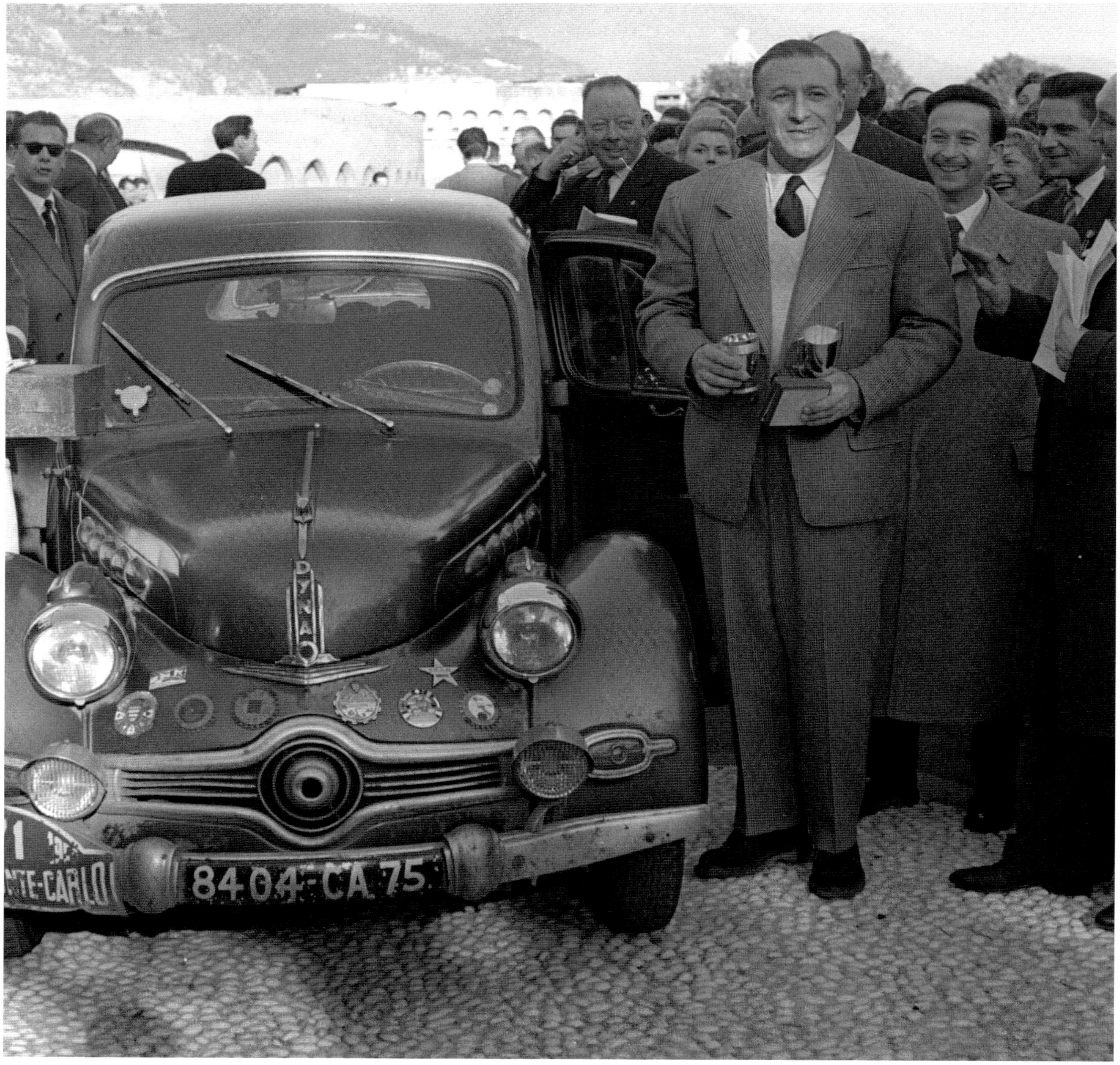

Cotton/Leclerc, Panhard Dyna X N° 71,
ein seit 1948 produziertes Auto. 1. in Kat. 1, Classe 4.

Cotton/Leclerc, Panhard Dyna X N° 71,
a car produced since 1948. 1st in Cat. 1, Class 4.

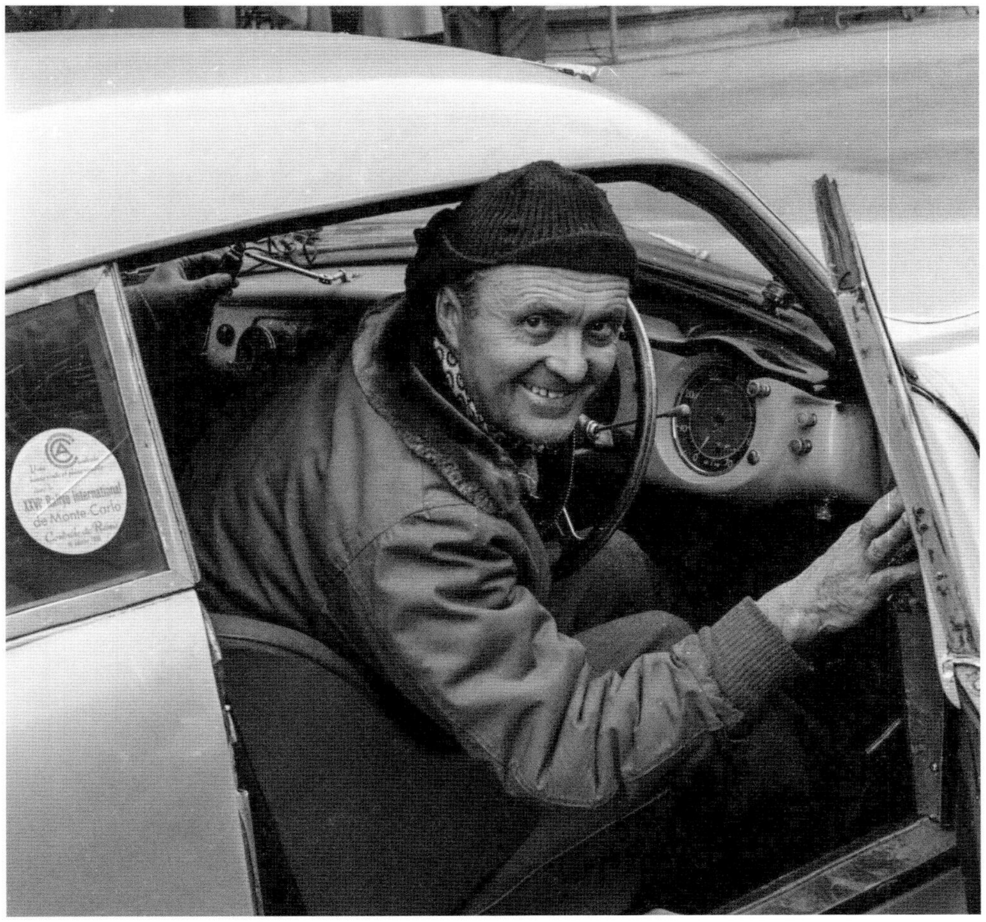

Lokalmatador Louis Chiron im rechtsgesteuerten Lancia Aurelia GT N° 32, Erster in Cat. 2, Classe 1. Es ist nicht das gleiche Lancia-Modell, mit dem er 1954 gewann.

Local hero Louis Chiron in the right-hand drive Lancia Aurelia GT N° 32, 1st in Cat. 2, Class 1. This was not the same model of Lancia with which he won in 1954.

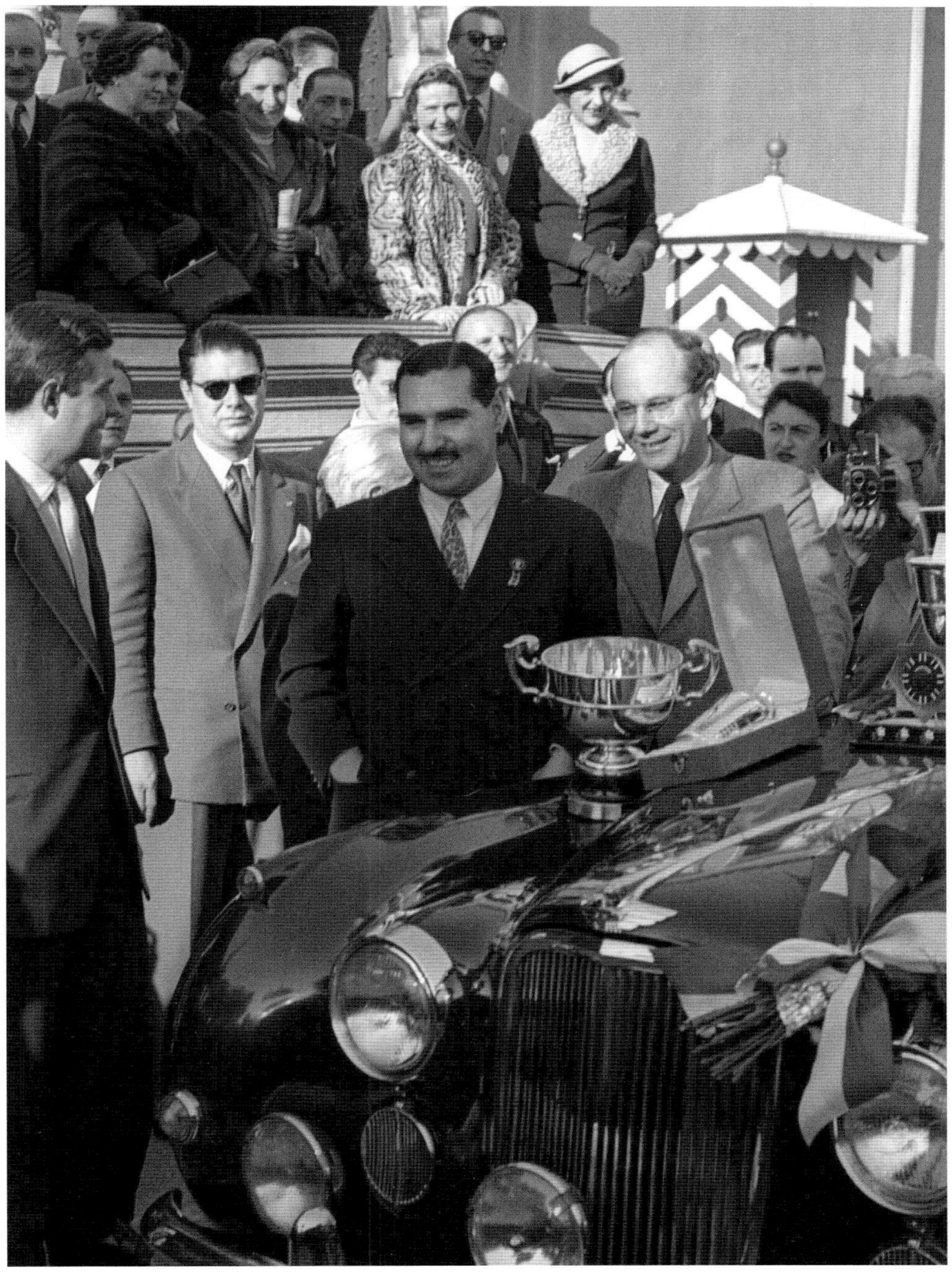

Adams/Bigger, Jaguar MK VII N° 164.
Sieger des Rennens.

Adams/Bigger, Jaguar MK VII N° 164.
The race winner.

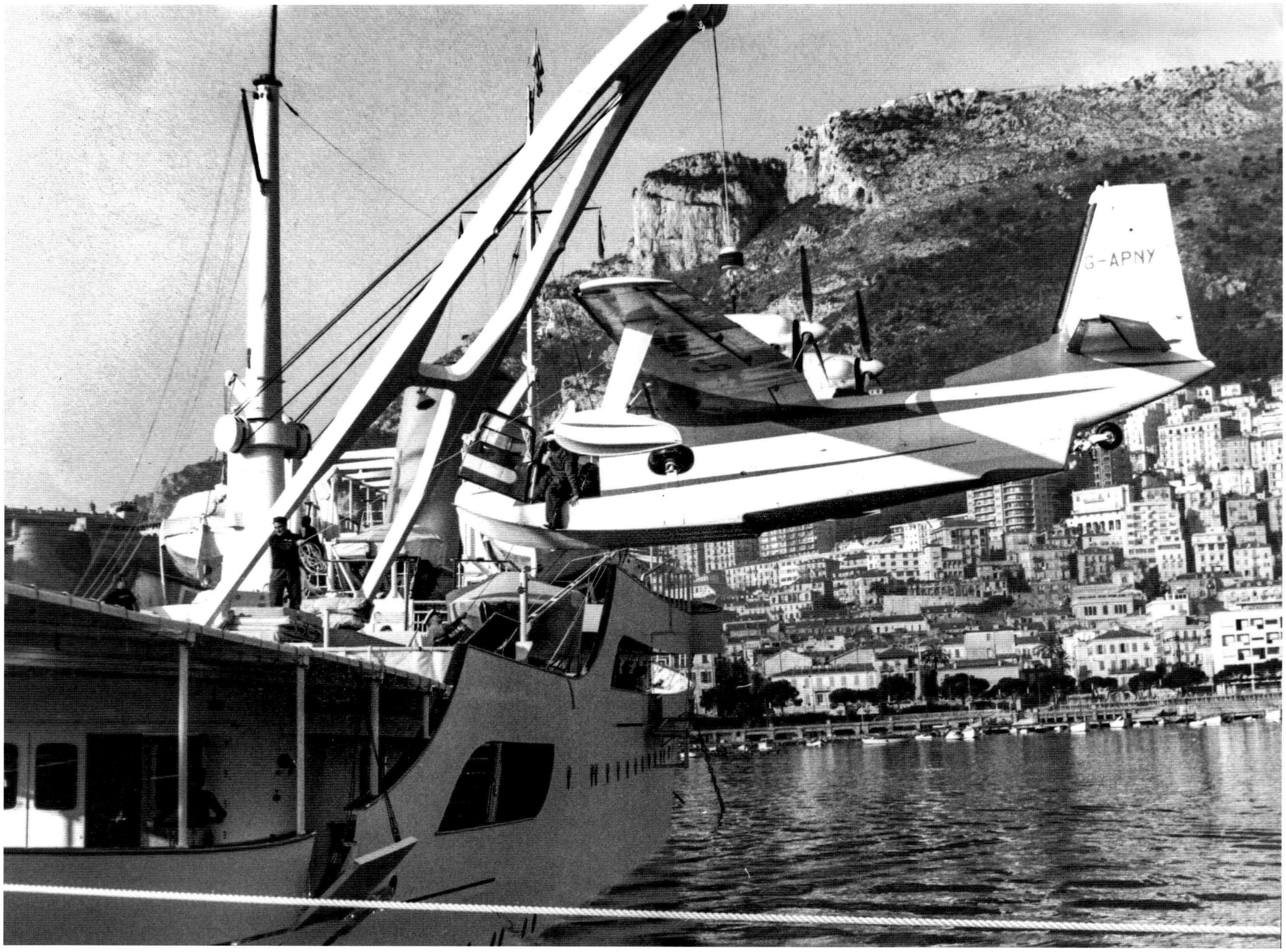

Monaco war immer schon ein beliebter Anlaufhafen für Superyachten, vor allem während des Grand Prix. Aber kaum eine hatte ein Wasserflugzeug an Deck, wie die Christina des griechischen Reeders Onassis.

Monaco has always been a popular port of call for superyachts, especially during the Grand Prix. However, very few had a seaplane on deck, like the Christina, which belonged to Greek shipping magnate Aristotle Onassis.

1957

Zum ersten Mal mit Fürstin Gracia

Die italienische Grand-Prix-Überlegenheit nimmt langsam ab, auch wenn Maserati und Ferrari neue Autos bringen. Die britischen Konstrukteure sind im Vormarsch. Die Vanwall sind eine neue Macht, mit der man rechnen muss, vor allem mit ihren Piloten Moss und Brooks. Connaught und BRM qualifizieren sich zum ersten Mal. Die französischen Gordini sind nicht mehr dabei.

Aber die eigentliche Überraschung ist ein kleiner Wagen mit 100 PS weniger als Fangios Maserati: der Cooper mit Jack Brabham am Steuer.

Es ist das letzte Rennen von Fangio in Monaco und der erste Auftritt von Fürstin Gracia. Und das letzte Jahr der Privatfahrer. Auch wenn es darunter schnelle und erfolgreiche Rennfahrer gibt – sie haben keine Chancen mehr gegen die Werksteams mit ihren Mechanikern, Ingenieuren, Rennleitern, geheimen Ersatzteilen und vor allem viel Geld.

Die Rallye kann in diesem Jahr wegen der Treibstoffbeschränkungen in der Folge der Suez-Krise nicht durchgeführt werden.

Princess Grace makes her first appearance

Italy's supremacy in the Grand Prix was waning, even though Maserati and Ferrari brought along new cars. The British continued to gain ground. The Vanwalls proved a new force to be reckoned with, especially with their drivers Moss and Brooks. Connaught and BRM qualified for the first time. The French Gordini were notable for their absence.

But the real surprise was a little car with 100 bhp less than Fangio's Maserati: the Cooper with Jack Brabham at the wheel.

It was Fangio's last race in Monaco and Princess Grace's first appearance in the royal box. This was also the last year for private drivers. Although there were brilliant racers among them, they no longer stood a chance against the factory teams with their mechanics, engineers, race directors, secret spare parts and, most importantly, plenty of money.

The Rally was not held this year because of fuel restrictions in the wake of the Suez crisis.

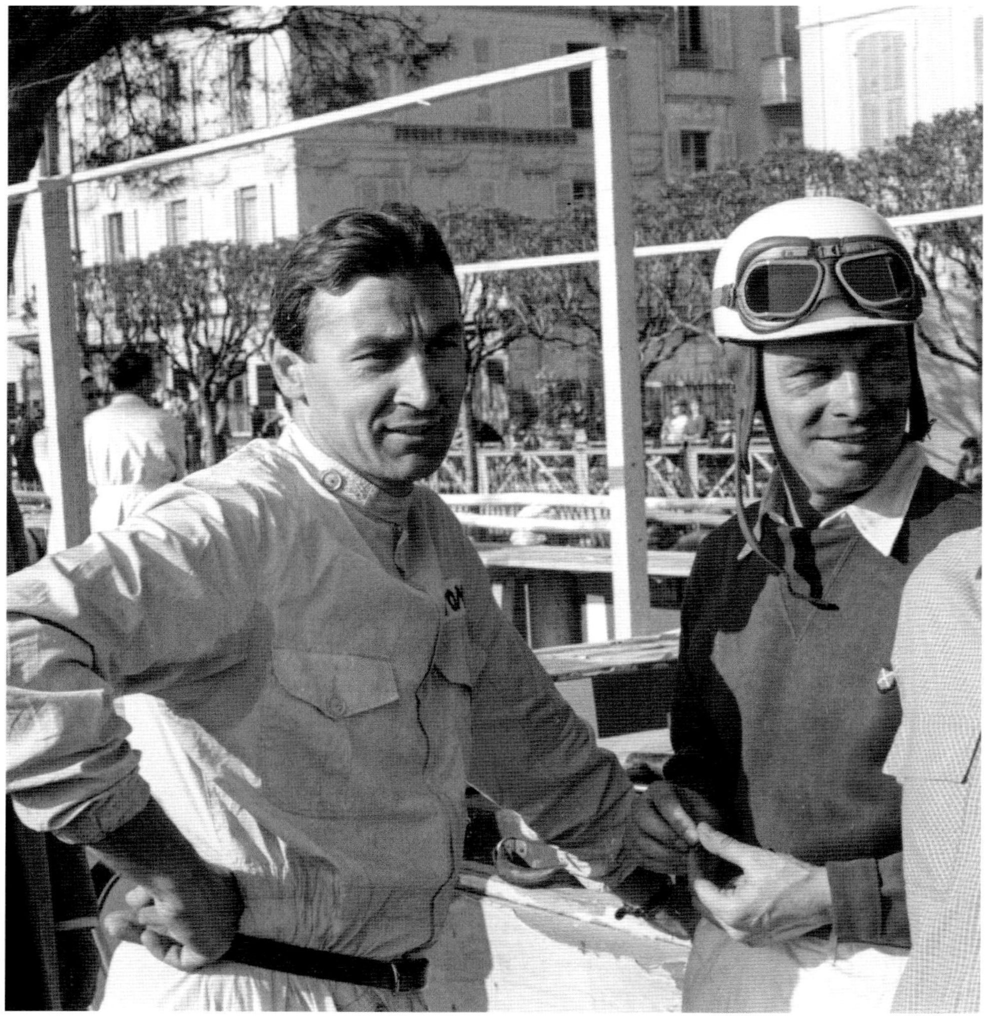

Die BRM-Fahrer Ron Flockhart (rechts) und Roy Salvadori.

BRM drivers Ron Flockhart and on the left Roy Salvadori.

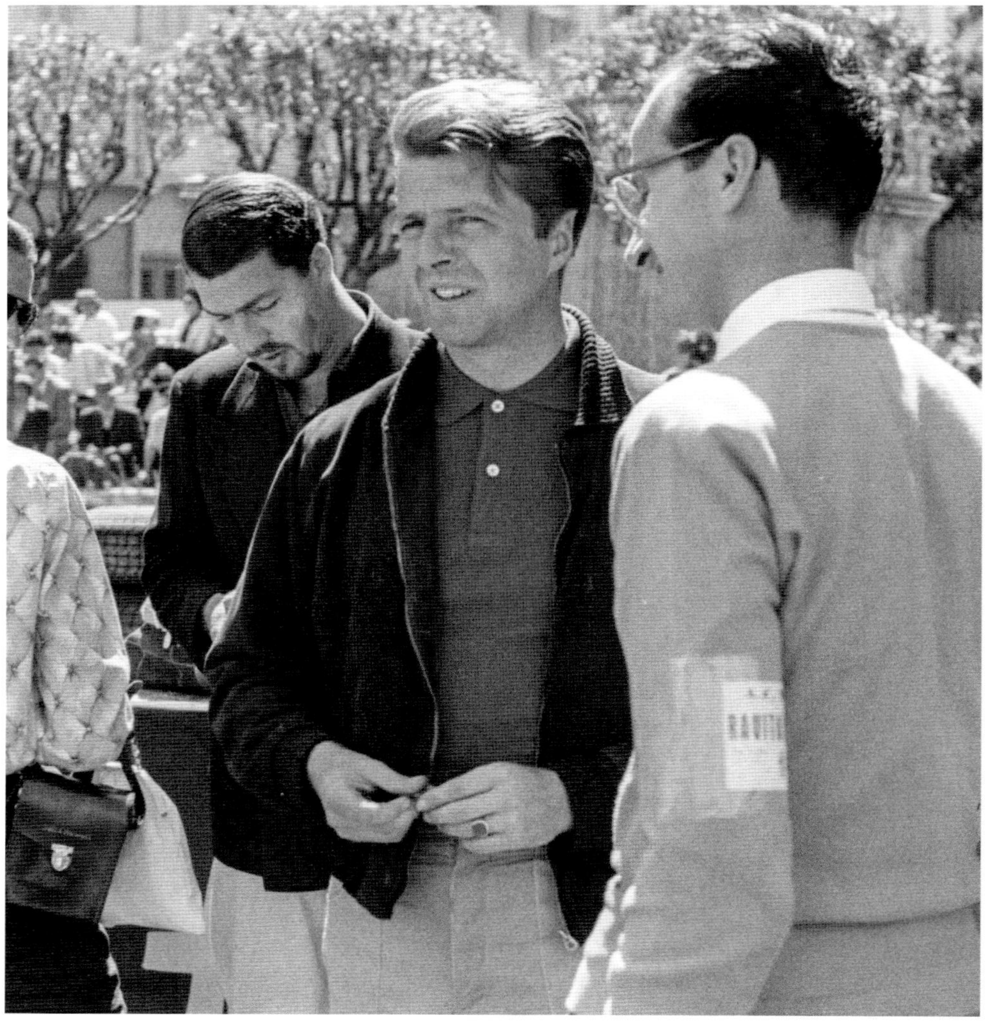

Ferrari-Fahrer Wolfgang „Taffy“ Graf Berghe von Trips (links) mit Ferrari-Rennleiter Romolo Tavoni, im Hintergrund Joakim Bonnier.

Ferrari driver Wolfgang "Taffy" Graf Berghe von Trips (left) with Ferrari racing manager Romolo Tavoni, in the background Joakim Bonnier.

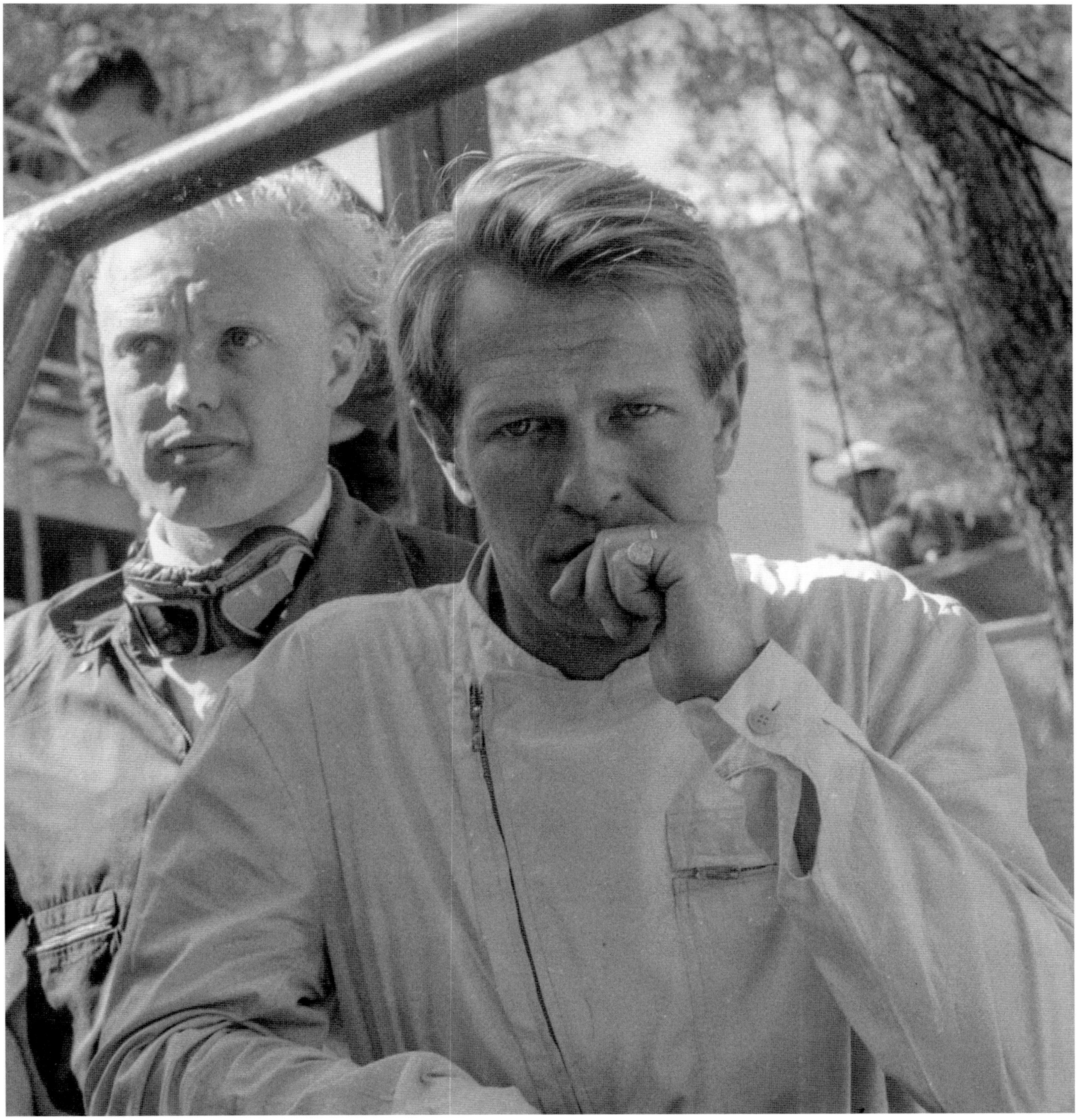

Peter Collins und Mike Hawthorn (links), zwei enge Freunde und 1957 Ferrari-Teamkollegen. Collins war die lässige, unbeschwerte Verkörperung des Rennfahrers der 50er-Jahre: gutaussehend, mit Charme und Witz. Hawthorn war ein ganz anderer Typ, aber auch ein Vorbild für viele junge Fahrer.

Peter Collins and Mike Hawthorn (left), two close friends and Ferrari teammates in 1957. Collins was the casual, easygoing embodiment of the 1950s racing driver. Hawthorn was a different character, but was also role model for many young drivers of the era.

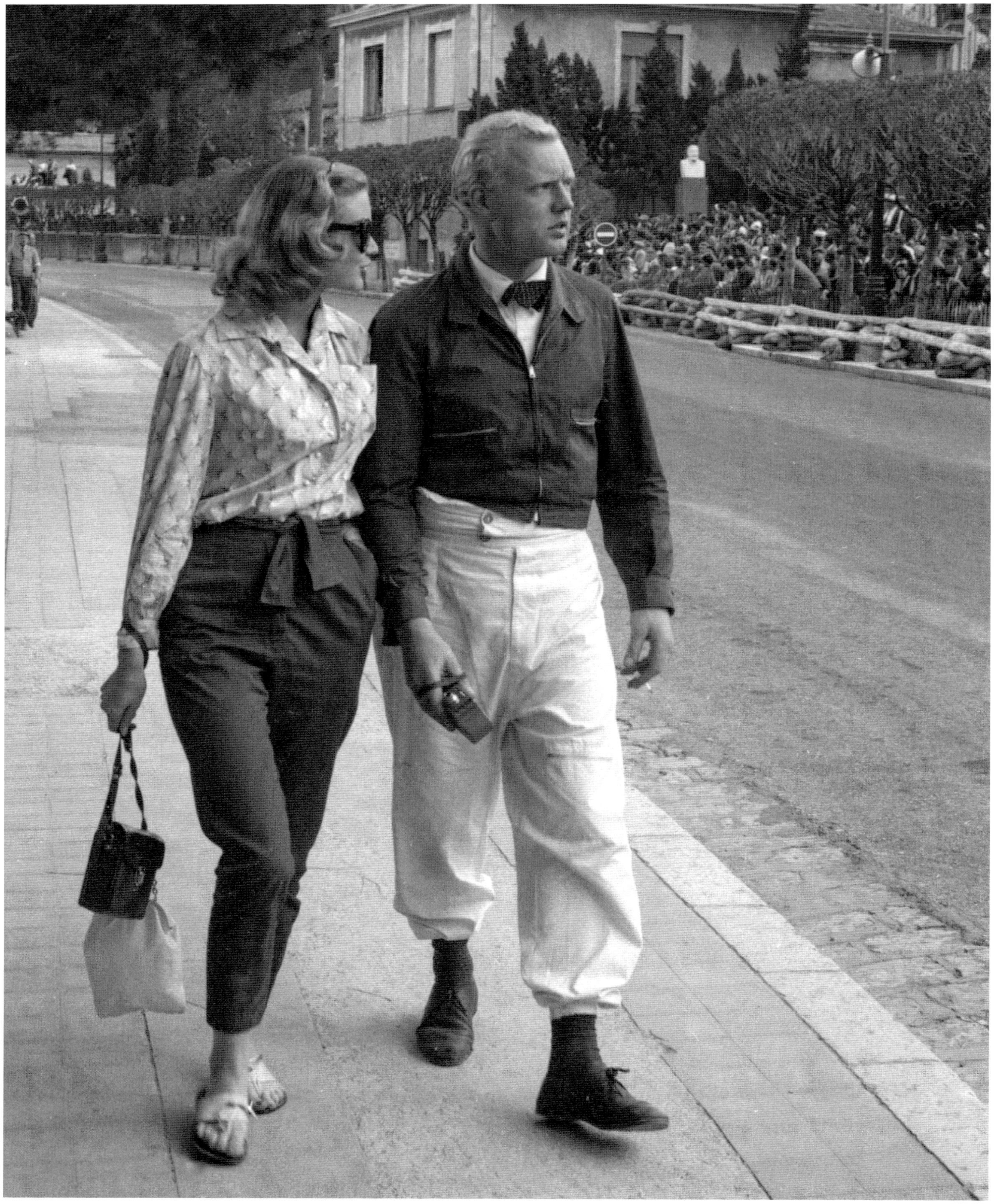

Mike Hawthorn mit seiner amerikanischen Freundin Valerie Witalis.
Er war bekannt dafür, eine Fliege, ein weißes Hemd und einen grünen Lumber zu tragen – im Rennen.

Mike Hawthorn with American girlfriend Valerie Witalis. He was noted for wearing a bow tie, a white shirt and a green jacket – when racing.

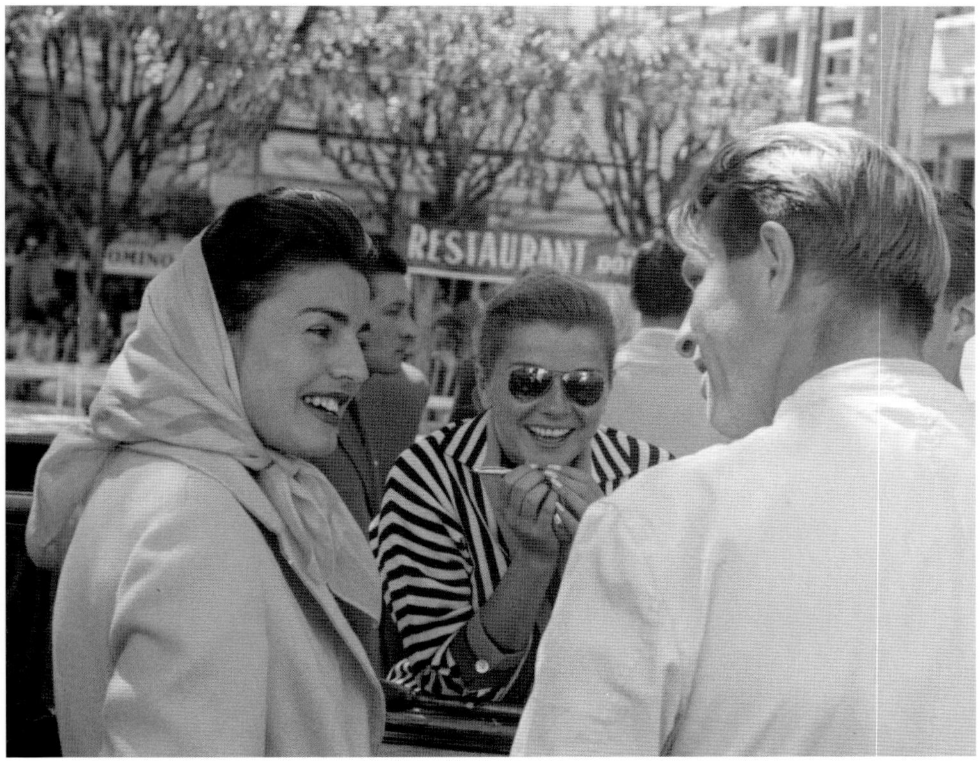

Das Traumpaar der Formel 1: Peter Collins (r.) und seine Frau Louise (M.). Sie heirateten 1957 nach nur einer Woche Bekanntschaft. Die Ehe dauerte eineinhalb Jahre bis zum Tod von Peter auf dem Nürburgring, 1958 beim Grand Prix von Deutschland. Links Celia „Chelita" Howard, Ex-Prinzessin Bira.

Formula 1's dream couple: Peter Collins (r.) and his wife Louise (c.). They married in 1957 after only one week of acquaintance. The marriage lasted one and a half years until Peter's death in 1958 at the Nürburgring during the German Grand Prix. Left Celia "Chelita" Howard, formerly Princess Bira.

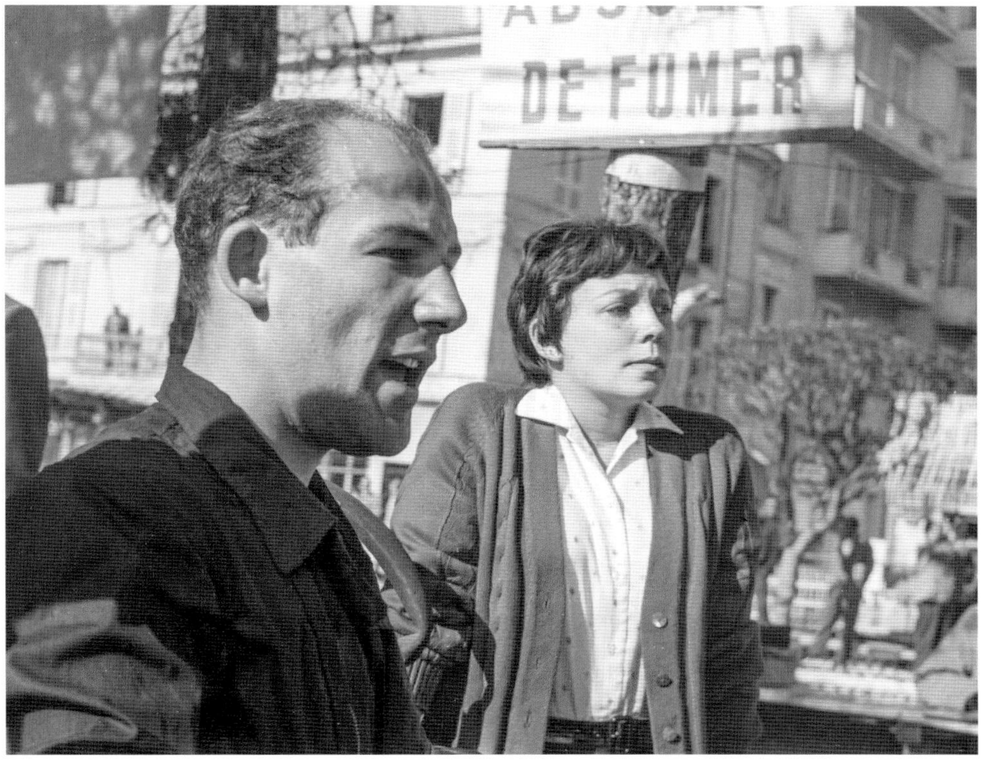

Stirling Moss und seine Verlobte Katie Molson, Erbin einer kanadischen Brauereidynastie.

Stirling Moss and his fiancée Katie Molson, a member of the Canadian brewing dynasty.

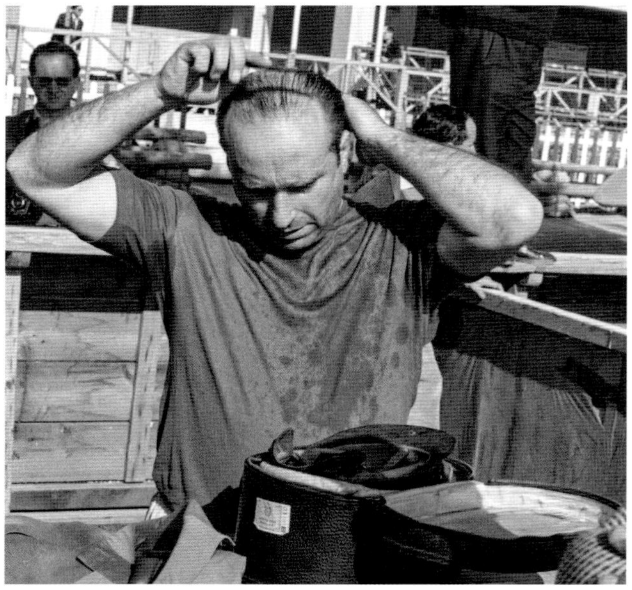

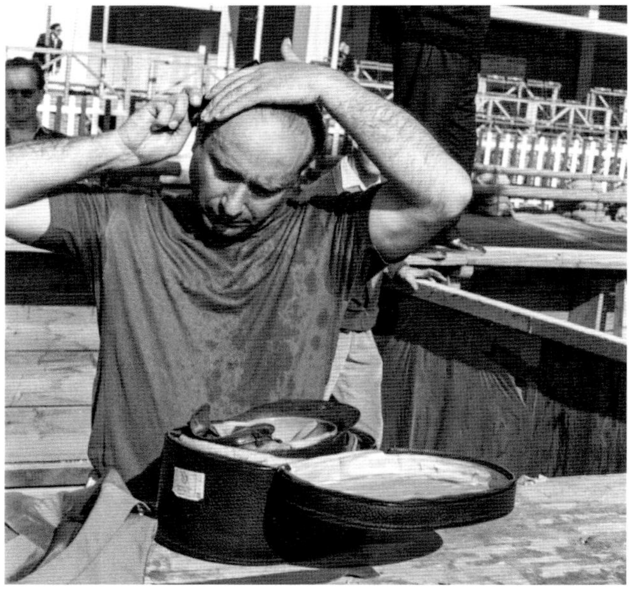

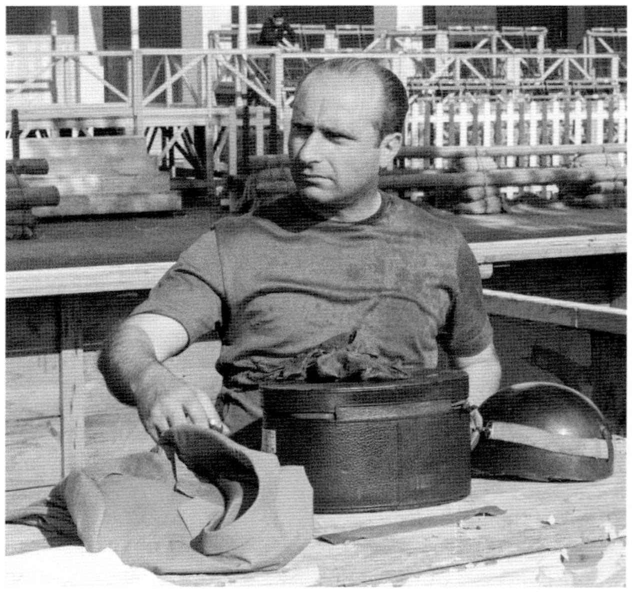

Fangio macht sich schön.
Man beachte die elegante Box für seinen Helm.

Fangio prepares in style.
Note the elegant box for his helmet.

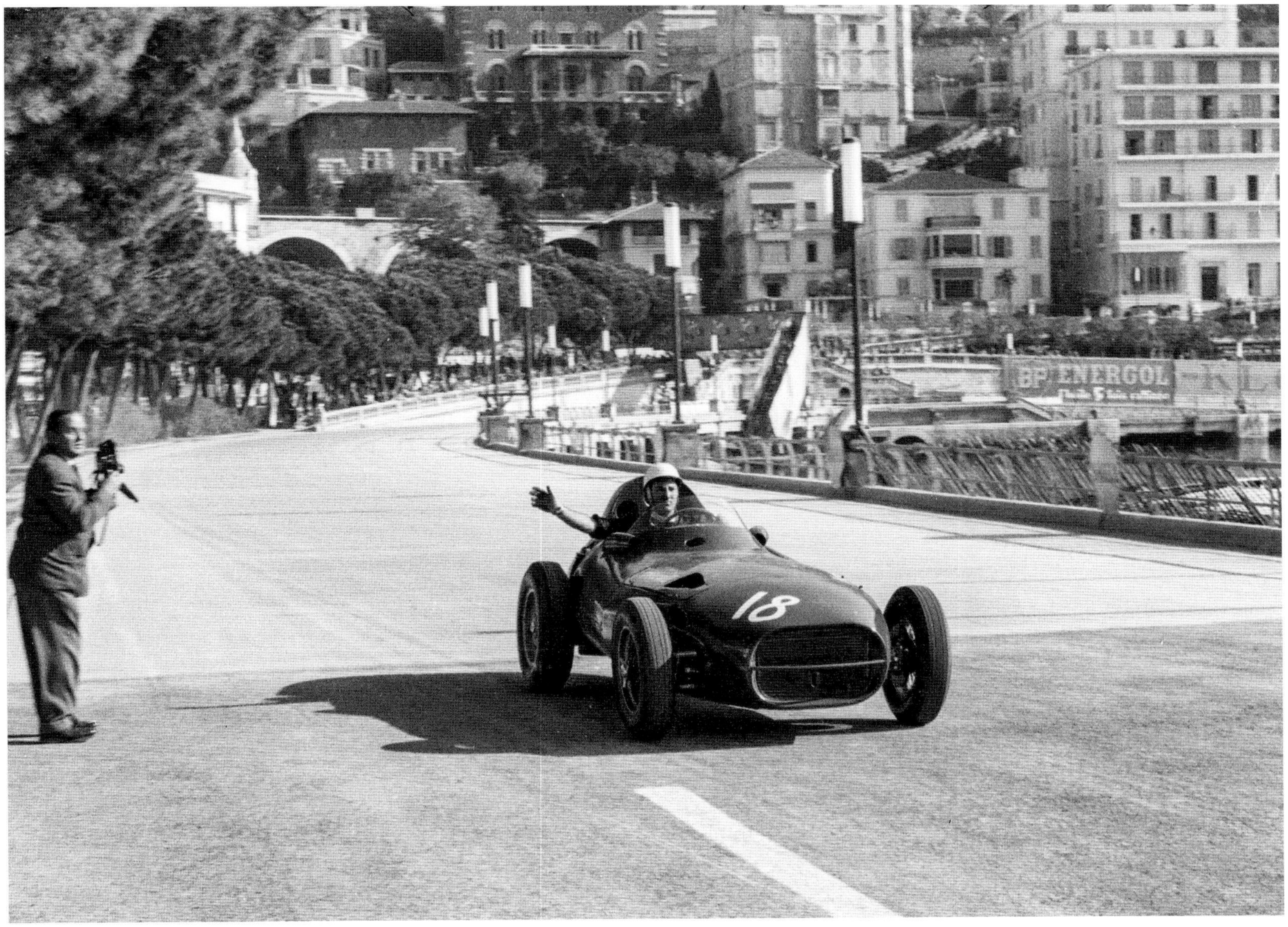

Stirling Moss auf Vanwall VW3/V4 N° 18 kommt mit einem Winken zurück an die Boxen. Der Fotograf ist überrascht.

Stirling Moss in Vanwall VW3/V4 N° 18 returns to the pits with a wave. The photographer seems surprised.

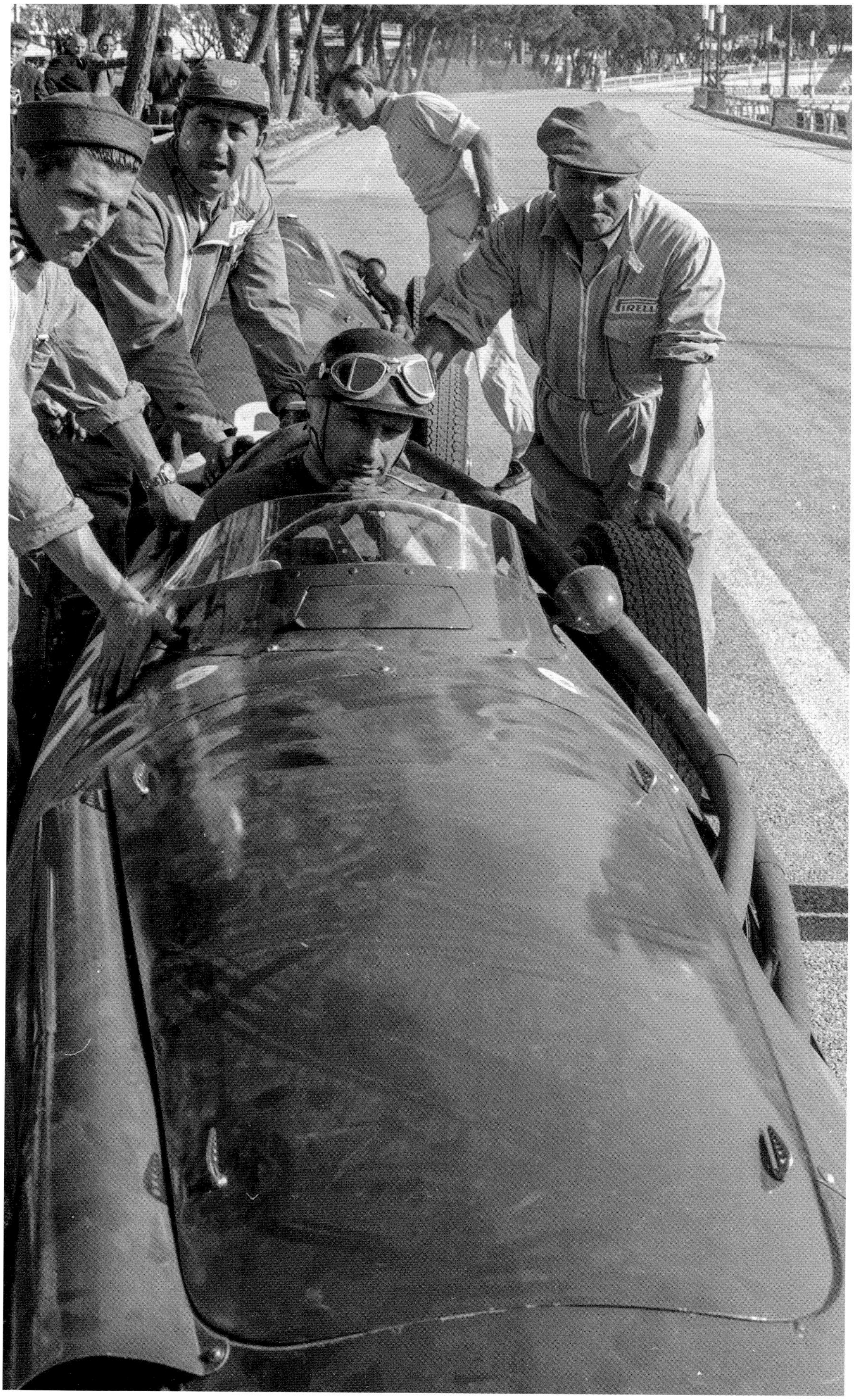

Juan Manuel Fangio auf Maserati 250F
mit seinen Mechanikern.

*Juan Manuel Fangio in his Maserati 250F
with his mechanics.*

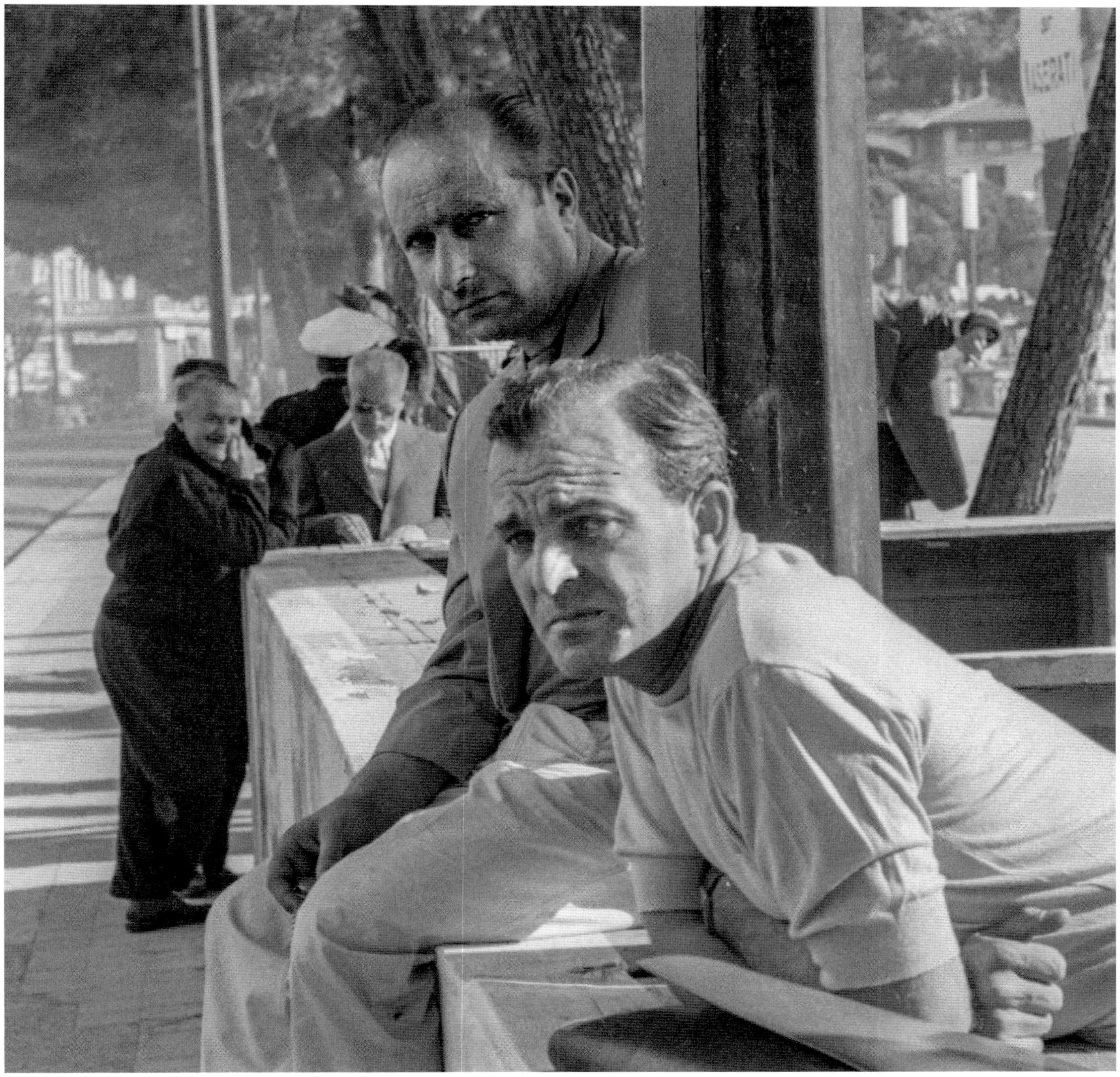

Skeptische Gesichter an der Maserati-Box im Training: die Teamkollegen Juan Manuel Fangio und Harry Schell.

Concerned faces at the Maserati pit during practice: teammates Juan Manuel Fangio and Harry Schell.

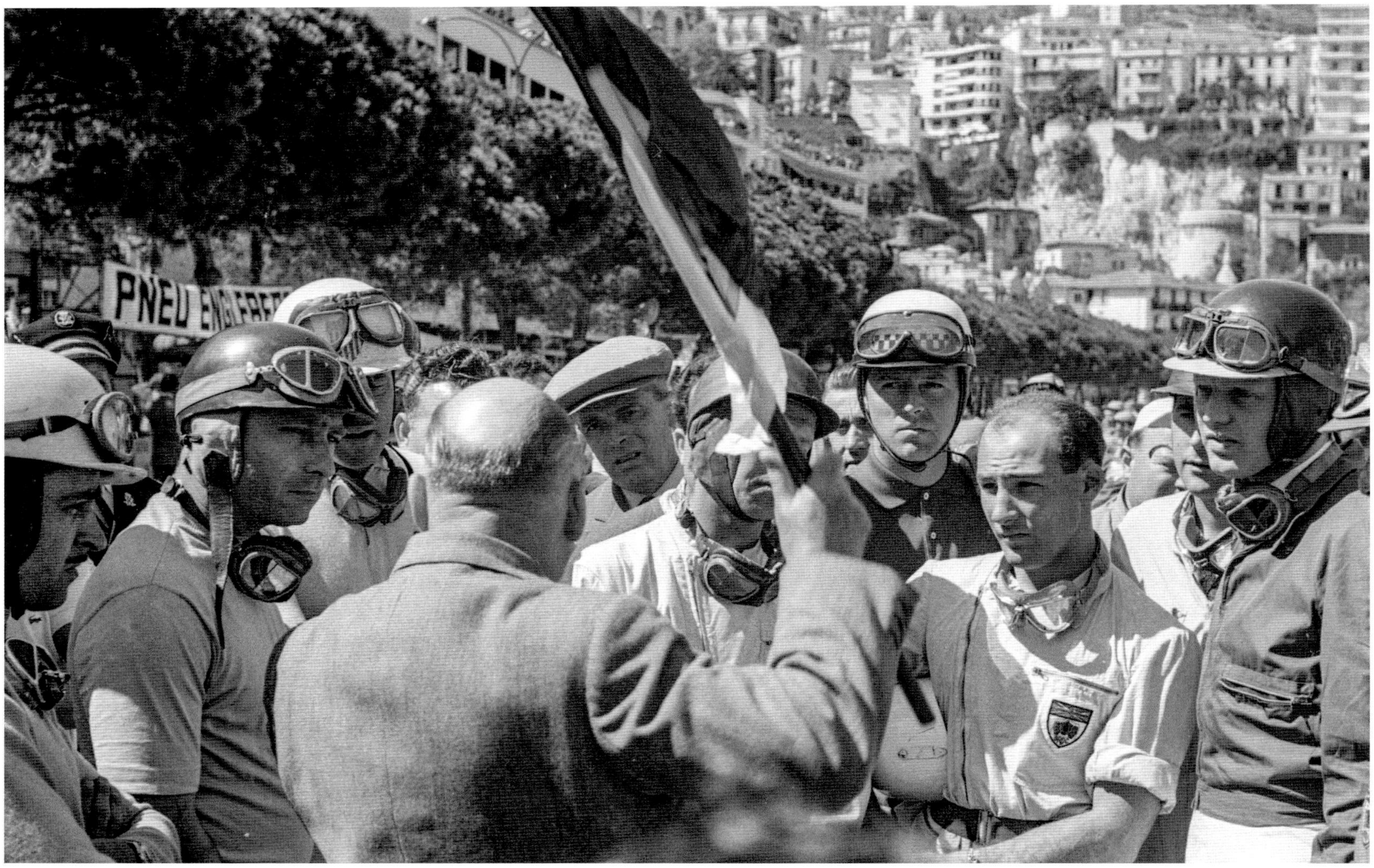

Fahrerbesprechung, von links: Maurice Trintignant, Juan Manuel Fangio, Harry Schell hinter Fangio, Peter Collins verdeckt durch die Flagge, Wolfgang von Trips, Stirling Moss, Jack Brabham, Mike Hawthorn.

Drivers' briefing from left Maurice Trintignant, Juan Manuel Fangio, Harry Schell behind Fangio, Peter Collins hidden by flag, Wolfgang von Trips, Stirling Moss, Jack Brabham, Mike Hawthorn.

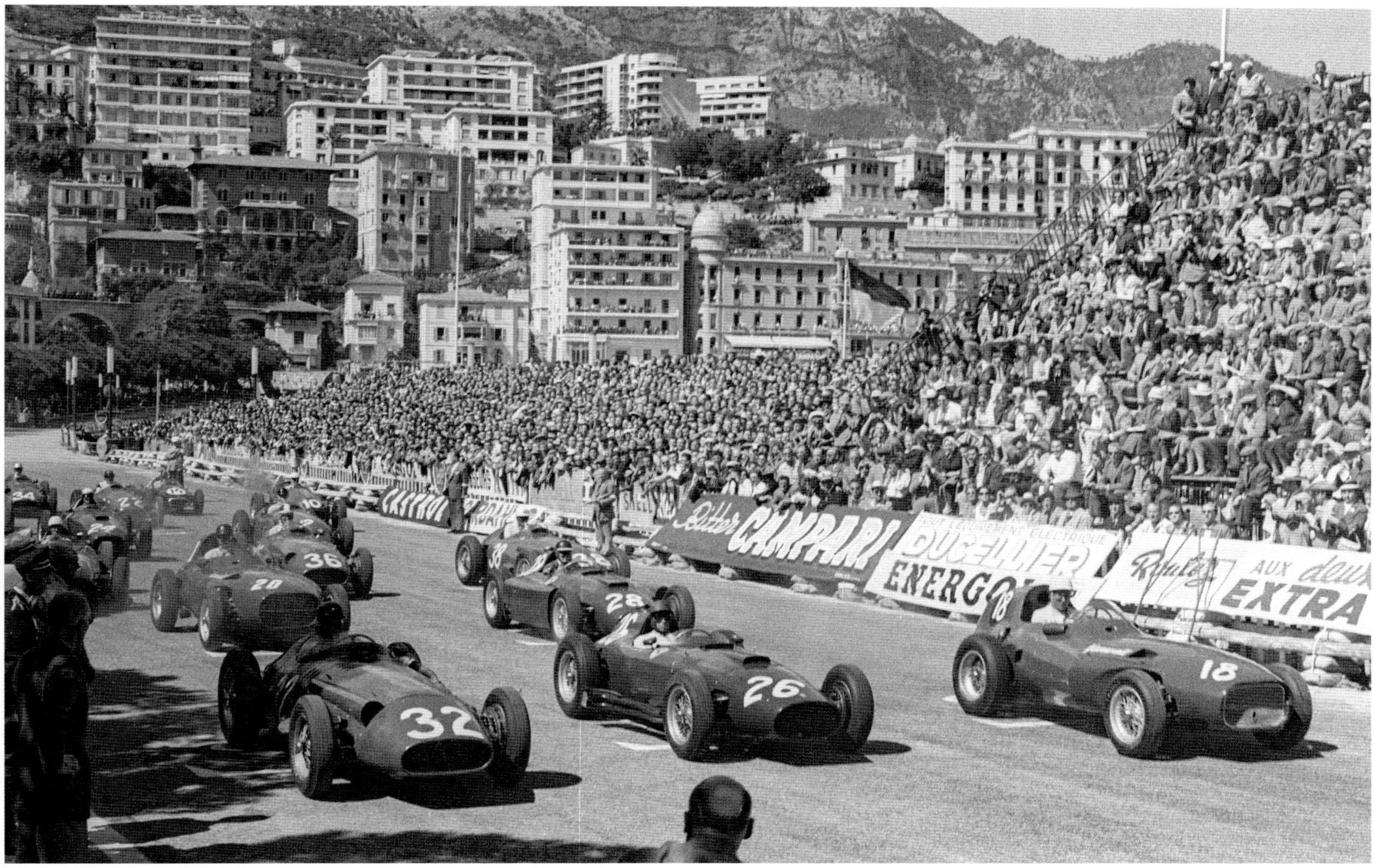

Start des 15. Grand Prix von Monaco.
Start to the 15th Grand Prix de Monaco.

Juan Manuel Fangio, Maserati 250F N° 32,
Peter Collins, Ferrari 801 N° 26,
Stirling Moss, Vanwall VW3/V4 N° 18,
Tony Brooks, Vanwall VW7/V1 N° 20,
Mike Hawthorn, Lancia-Ferrari D50 N° 28,
Carlos Menditéguy, Maserati 250F N° 36,
Harry Schell, Maserati 250F N° 38,
Wolfgang von Trips, Ferrari 801 N° 24,
Masten Gregory, Maserati 250F N° 2,
Ron Flockhart, BRM P25 N° 6,
Horace H. Gould, Maserati 250F N° 22,
Jack Brabham, Cooper T43 N° 14,
Stewart Lewis-Evans, Connaught B N° 10,
Giorgio Scarlatti, Maserati 250F N° 34.

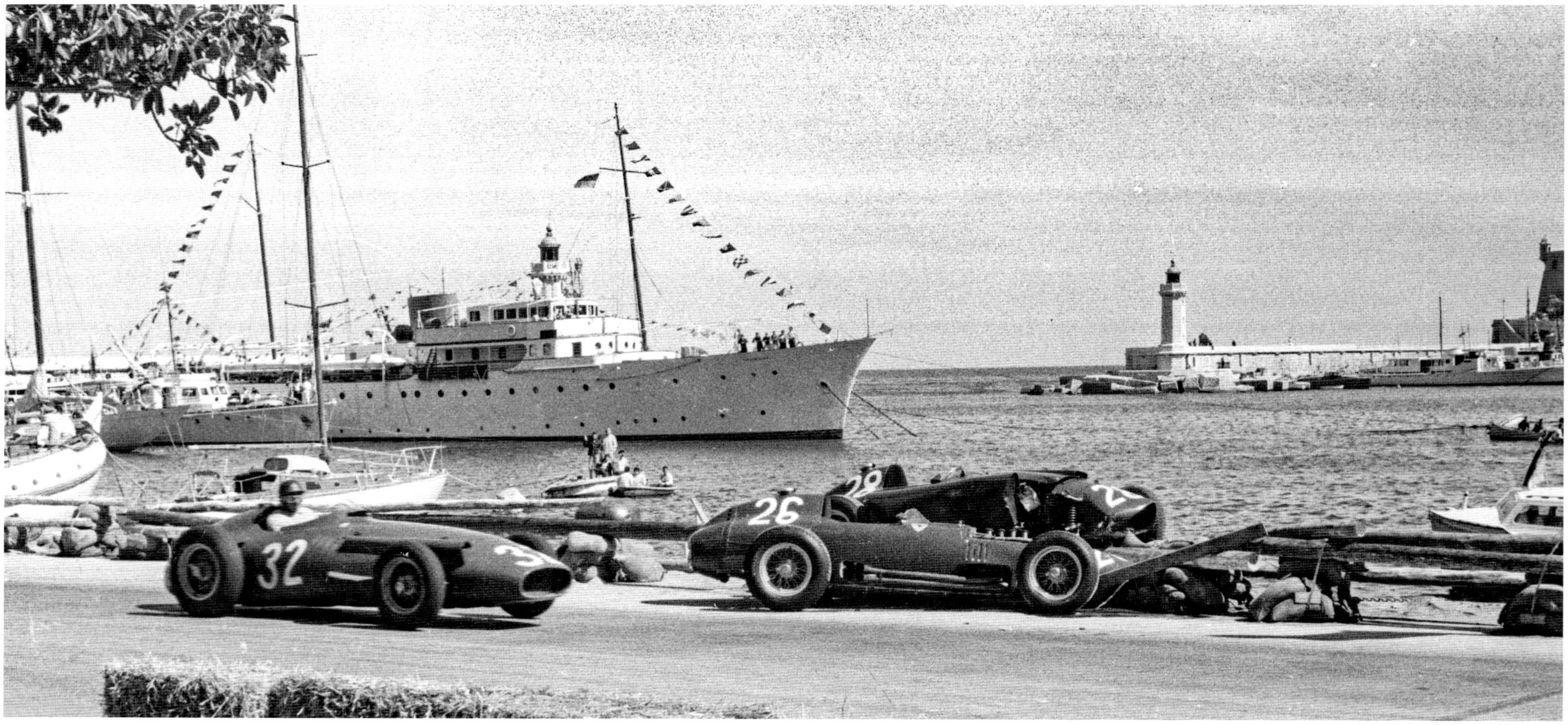

Bereits in der vierten Runde geschieht der Unfall, der drei Top-Fahrer eliminiert: Moss fährt zu schnell in die Schikane und demoliert seinen Vanwall unter einem Baum in der Abschrankung. Die herumfliegenden Holzbalken behindern Collins N° 26, der auf der anderen Straßenseite in die Barriere fährt. Hawthorn N° 28 kann nicht ausweichen und prallt in den Ferrari von Collins. Und wieder einmal fährt Fangio N° 32 unbehelligt vorbei.

The accident which eliminated three top drivers happened on the fourth lap: Moss entered the chicane too fast and demolished his Vanwall against the barrier under a tree. The flying debris hindered Collins N° 26, who hit the barrier on the other side of the road. Hawthorn N° 28 was unable to get out of the way and crashed into Collins' Ferrari. Once again, Fangio N° 32 drove past without a scratch.

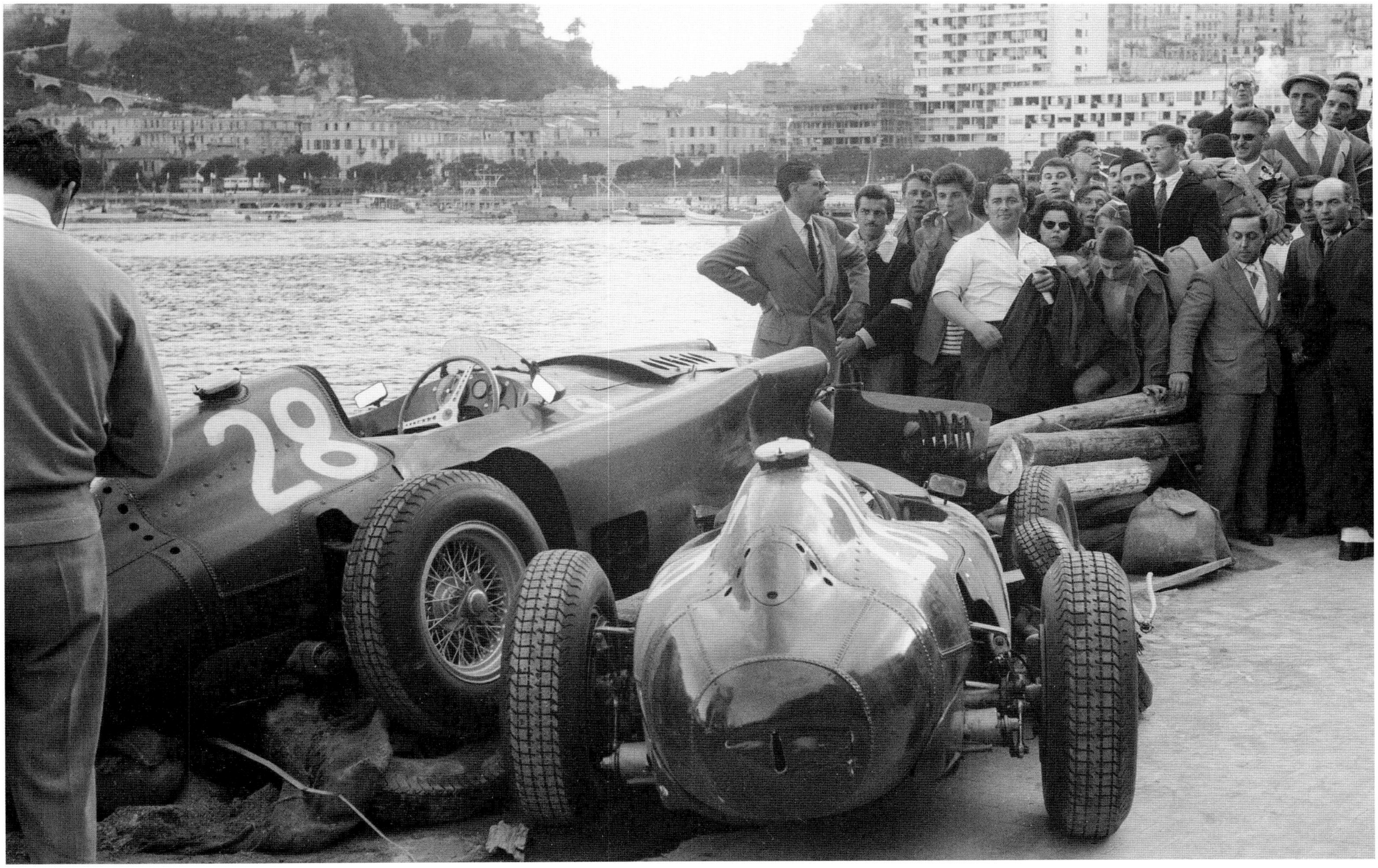

Die schwer beschädigten Ferraris von Collins N° 26 und Hawthorn N° 28.

The badly damaged Ferraris driven by Collins N° 26 and Hawthorn N° 28.

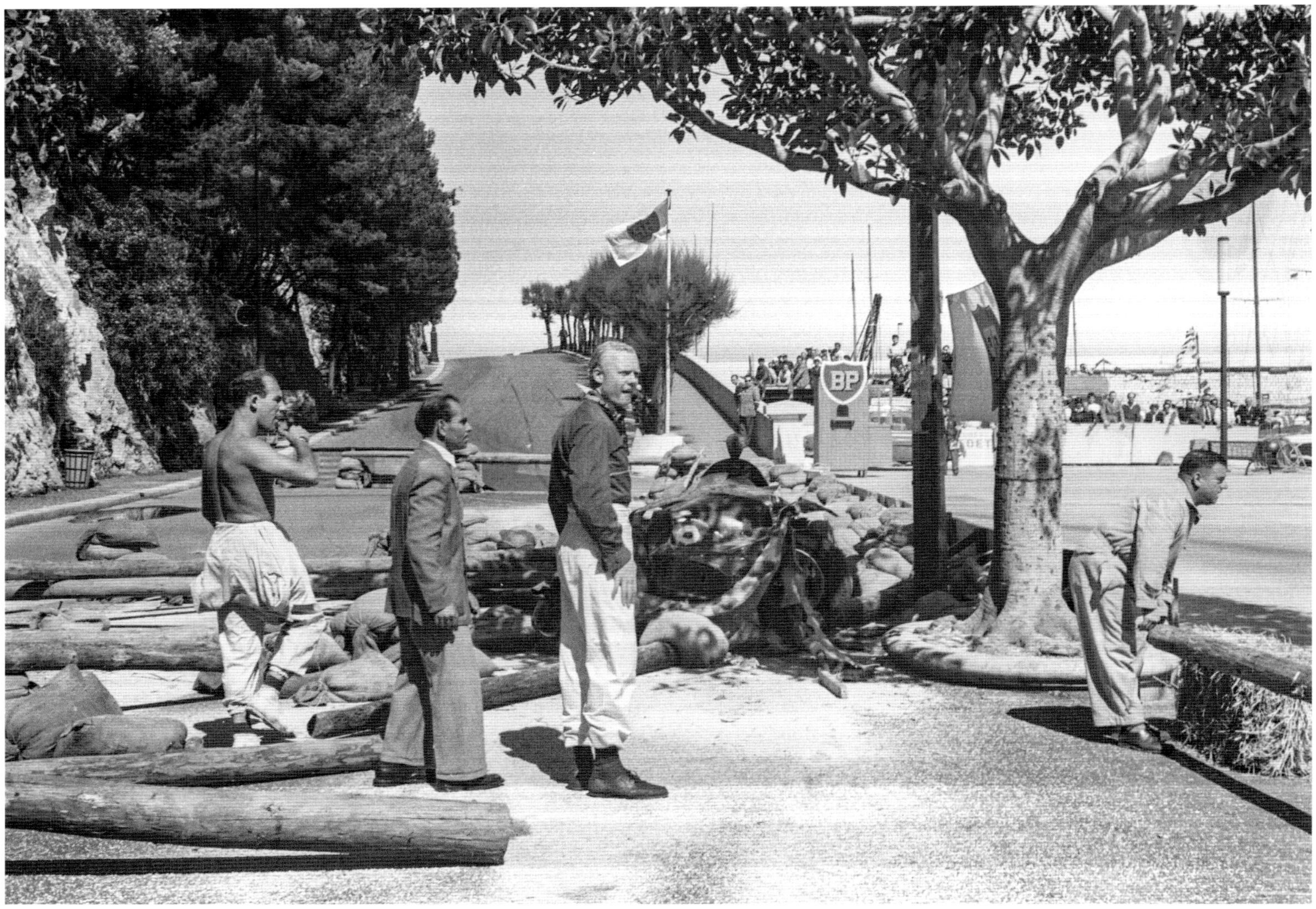

Moss und Hawthorn inspizieren den demolierten Vanwall und gehen zu Fuß in den Erste-Hilfe-Raum. Aber außer ein paar Kratzern gibt es nichts zu verarzten.

Moss and Hawthorn inspect the crashed Vanwall and make their way to first aid room on foot. Apart from a few scratches there were no injuries.

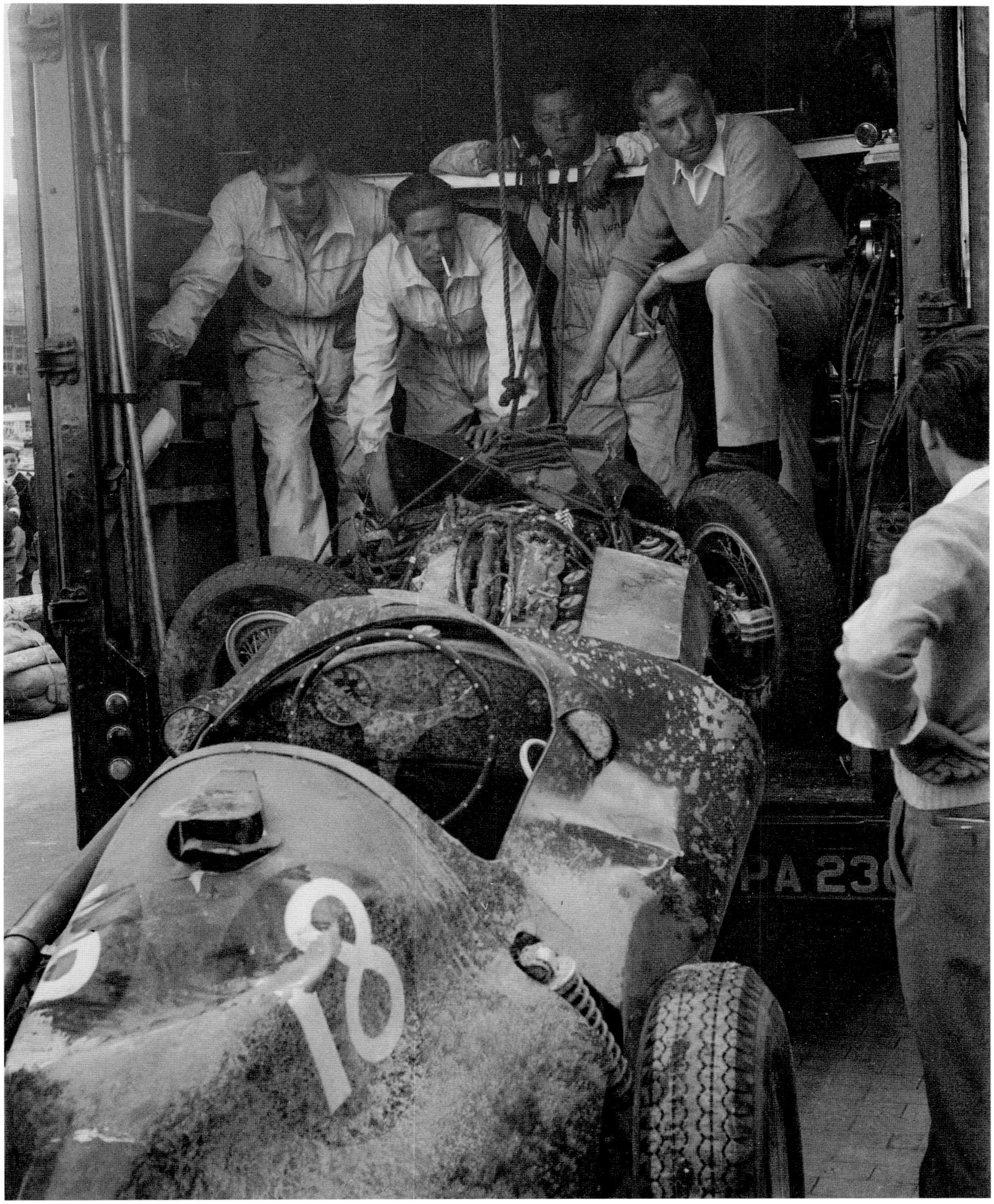

Der Vanwall von Moss wird abtransportiert.

Moss' Vanwall is towed away.

Zurück an den Boxen. Hawthorn will unbedingt den Ferrari von Wolfgang von Trips übernehmen, der auf dem ausgezeichneten dritten Platz liegt. Die Ferrari-Box winkt von Trips herein.

Back in the pits. Hawthorn is eager to take over Wolfgang von Trips' Ferrari, which is in an excellent third place. The Ferrari pit flags von Trips in.

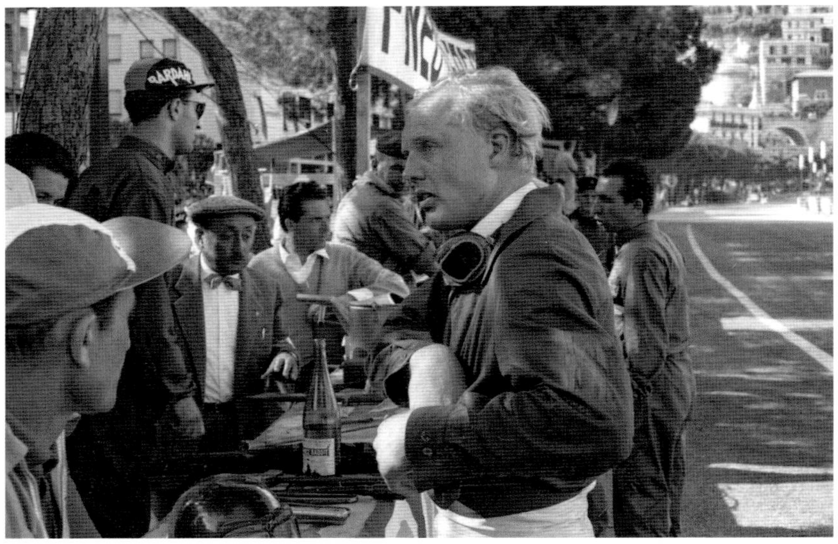

Aber das Cockpit ist für den Briten mit seinen langen Beinen so eng, dass er kaum das Lenkrad drehen und den Schalthebel nicht finden kann.

However the cockpit was so cramped for the Briton with his long legs that he could barely turn the steering wheel and couldn't find the gearshift.

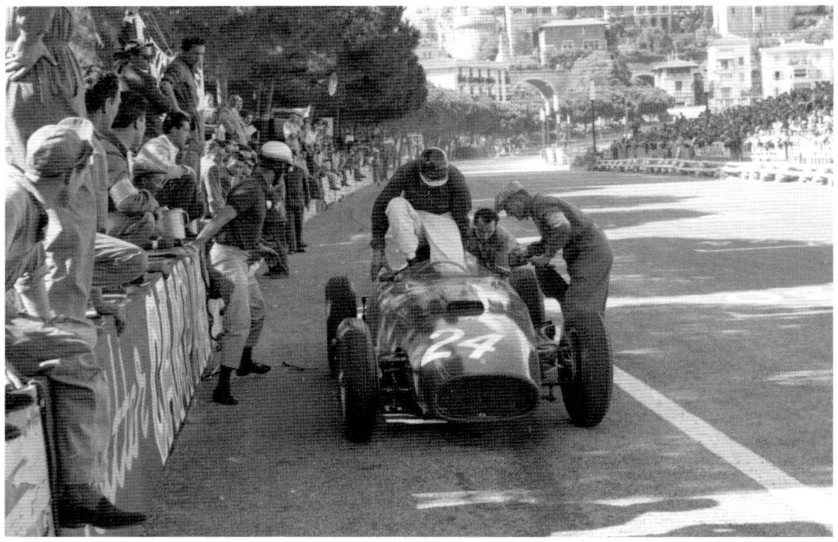

Hawthorn schafft es gerade mal, zwei Runden zu drehen. Aber seine Sitzposition ist so unbequem, dass er nach einem großen Zeitverlust wieder an die Box kommt.

Hawthorn managed to complete just three laps before his position became so uncomfortable that he was forced to return to the pits after losing a considerable amount of time.

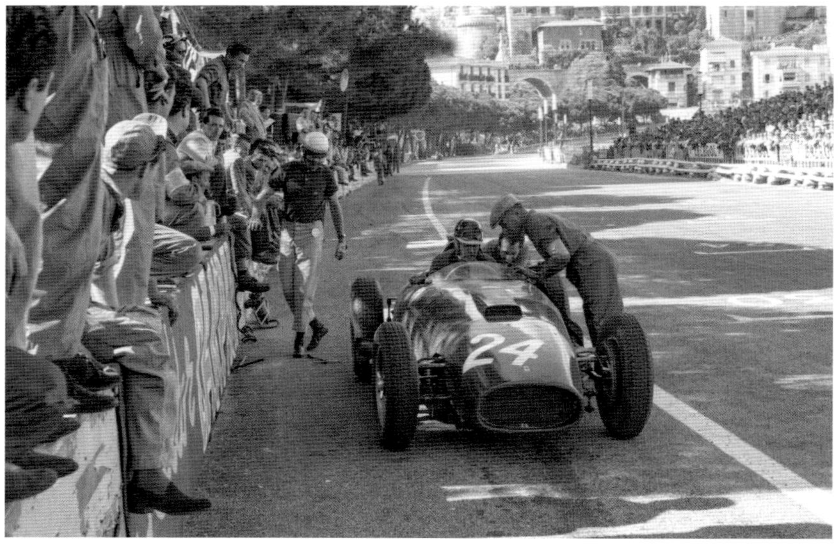

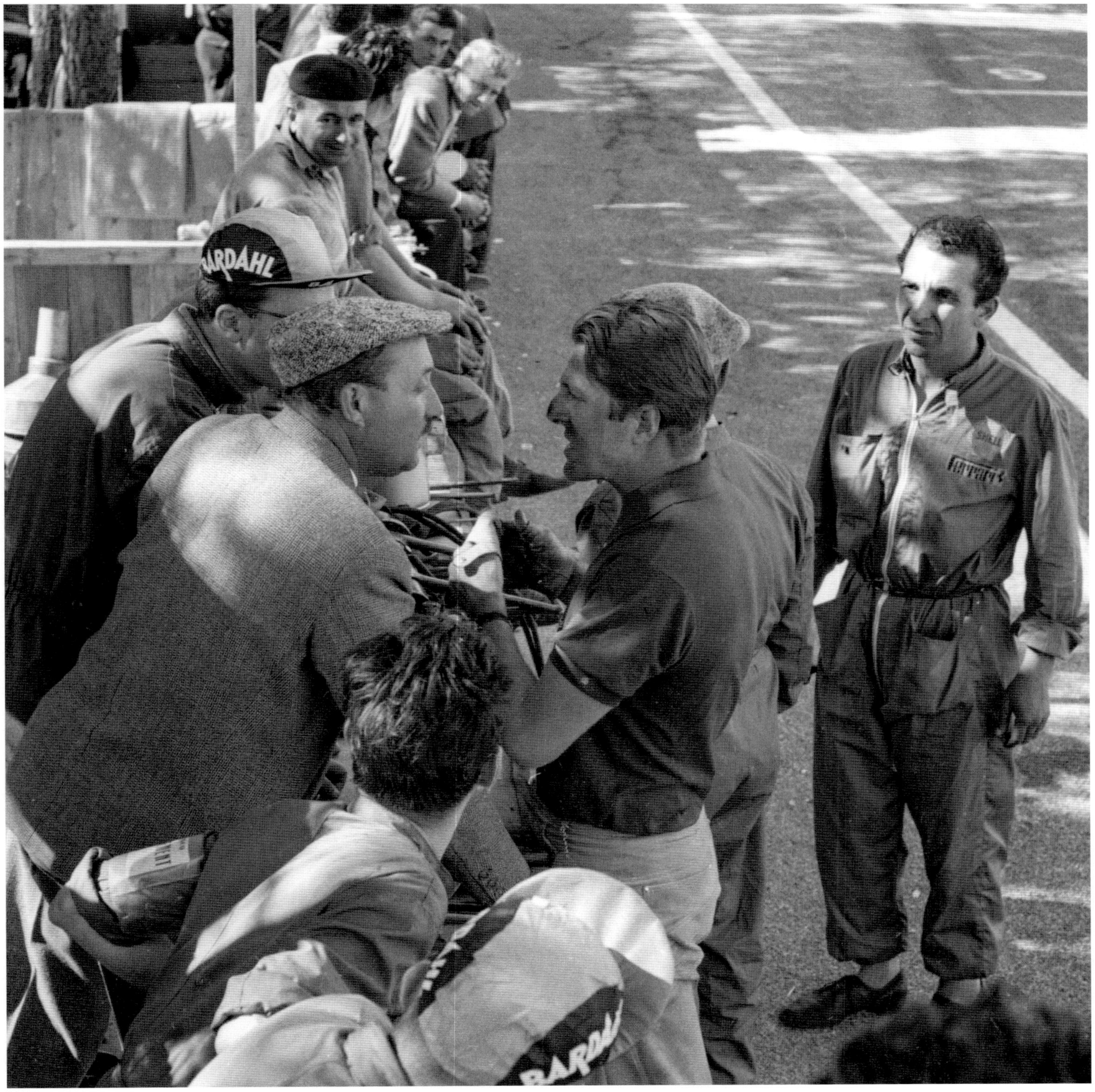

Von Trips ist stinksauer, dass er, an dritter Stelle liegend, seinen Ferrari dem Teamkollegen übergeben musste. Wenig später kommt Hawthorn schon wieder rein, von Trips übernimmt und arbeitet sich erneut an die dritte Position vor. 15 Runden vor Schluss erleidet er einen Motorschaden, schießt seitlich in eine Mauer auf der Zufahrt zum Casino und scheidet aus.

Von Trips was hopping mad that, despite being in third position, he had to hand over his Ferrari to his team mate. A little later Hawthorn returned to the pit and von Trips was able to take over again and worked his way back up to third position. With 15 laps to go, he suffered an engine failure and crashed into the side of a wall on the approach to the Casino, forcing him to retire.

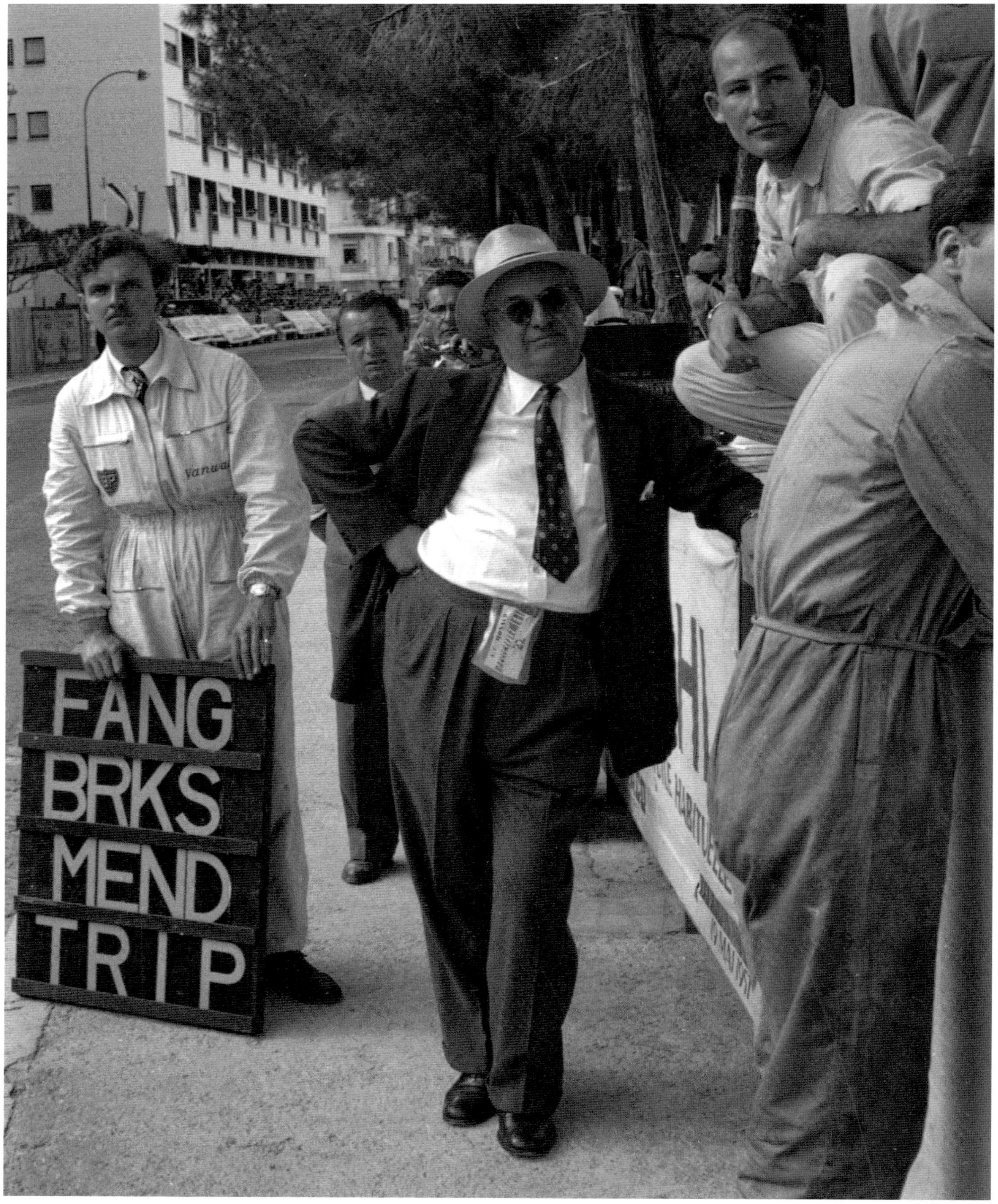

Stirling Moss und Tony Vandervell, Chef des Vanwall-Formel-1-Rennstalls. Ein Mechaniker mit einer Boxentafel, die zeigt, dass von Trips nach dem zweiten Fahrerwechsel schon auf dem vierten Platz hinter Fangio, Brooks und Menditéguy liegt.

Stirling Moss and Tony Vandervell, boss of the Vanwall Formula 1 racing team. A mechanic holds a pit board showing that von Trips is already in fourth place behind Fangio, Brooks and Menditéguy after the second driver changeover.

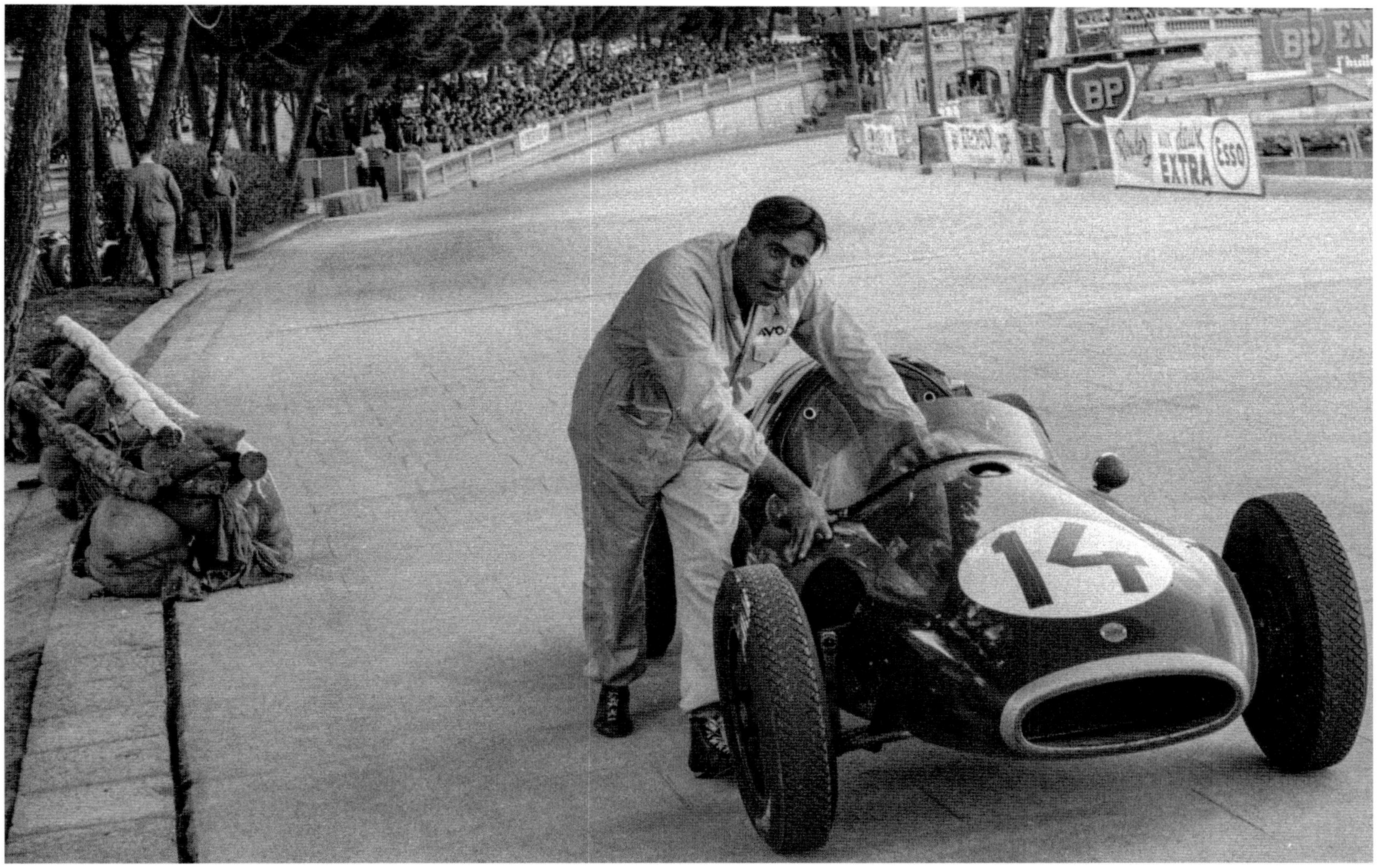

Die Benzinpumpe des Cooper fiel aus, als Jack Brabham, überraschend an vierter Stelle liegend, beim Casino vorbeifuhr. Doch der Australier ließ sich nicht beirren, rollte bis zur Strandpromenade und schob das Auto unter großem Applaus den Rest der Runde bis zur Ziellinie. Leider wurde er dabei von Gregory, Lewis-Evans und Trintignant überholt.
Links gut zu sehen: die wenig vertrauenserweckende Konstruktion der Sicherheitsabschrankung.

The Cooper's fuel pump failed as Jack Brabham, surprisingly in 4th place, passed the Casino. Undaunted, the Australian coasted down to the seafront and pushed the car the rest of the lap to the finish line to great applause. Unfortunately, he was overtaken by Gregory, Lewis-Evans and Trintignant. The construction of the safety barrier is clearly visible on the left, which does not inspire much confidence.

Stirling Moss sagte, wenn er ein F1-Team leiten würde und zwei beliebige Fahrer aus der Geschichte haben könnte, wären das Jim Clark und Tony Brooks. *(Motor Sport Magazin 9/2003)*

Stirling Moss said that if he were running an F1 team and could have any two drivers from history, they would be Jim Clark and Tony Brooks. (Motor Sport Magazine 9/2003)

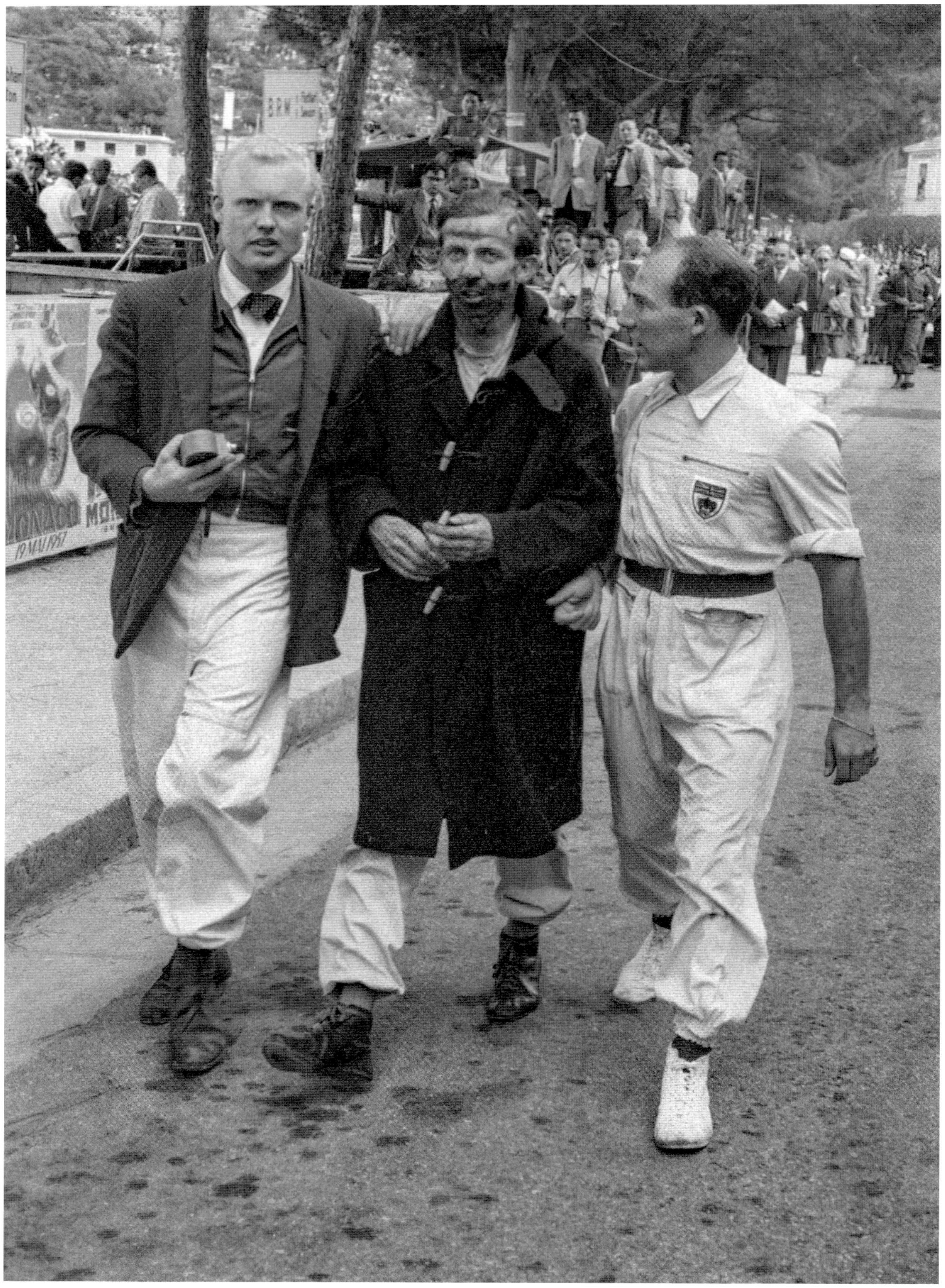

Drei britische Fahrer. Am Ende des Rennens begleiten Hawthorn (links) und Moss (rechts) Tony Brooks. Brooks' Gesicht ist komplett mit Öl und Staub bedeckt.

Three British drivers. At the end of the race Hawthorn (left) and Moss accompany Brooks. Brooks' face is completely covered with oil and dust.

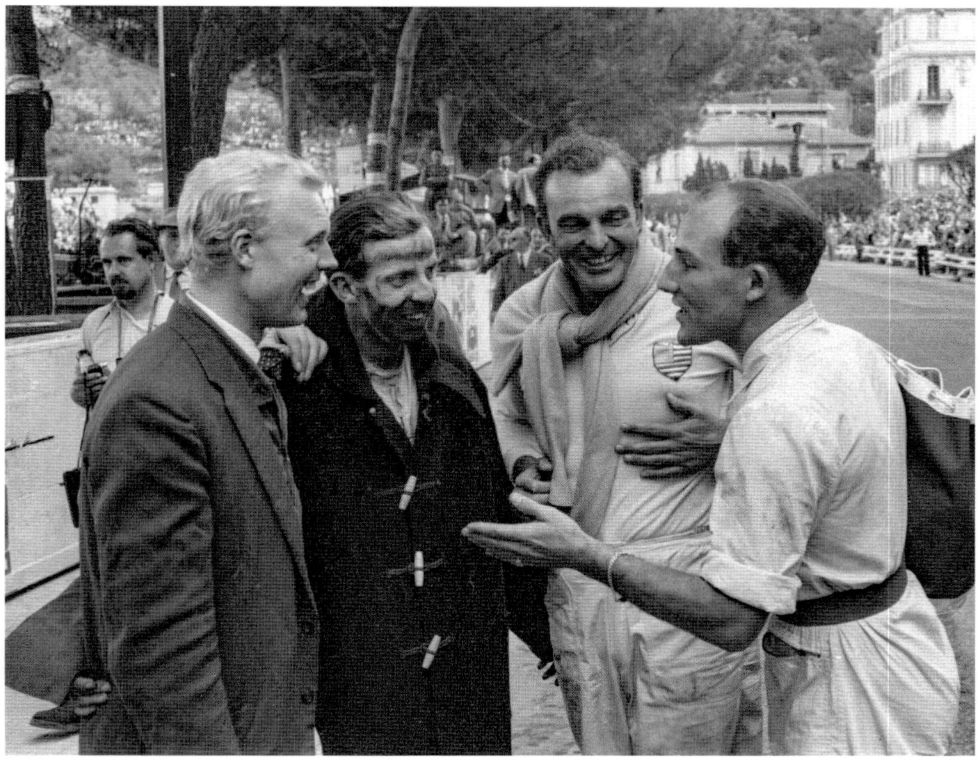

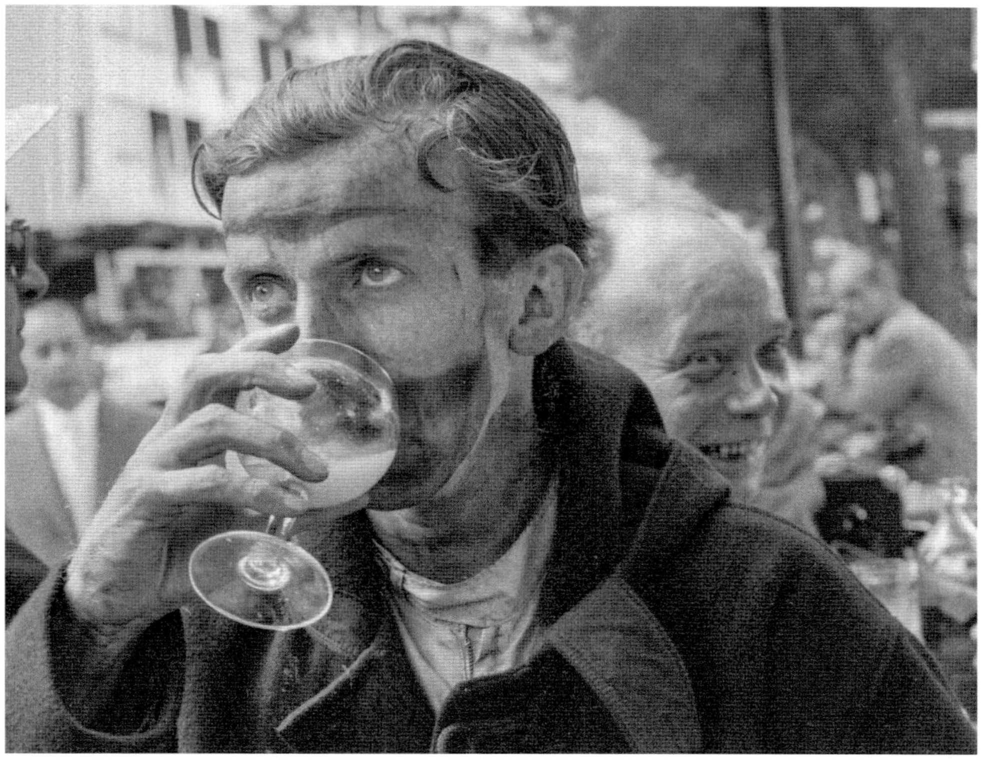

Trotz des Crashs haben die Fahrer immer noch etwas zu lachen.
Von links Hawthorn, Brooks, Harry Schell und Moss.

Despite the crash the drivers are still able to muster a smile.
From left Hawthorn, Brooks, Harry Schell and Moss.

Grand Prix 1957

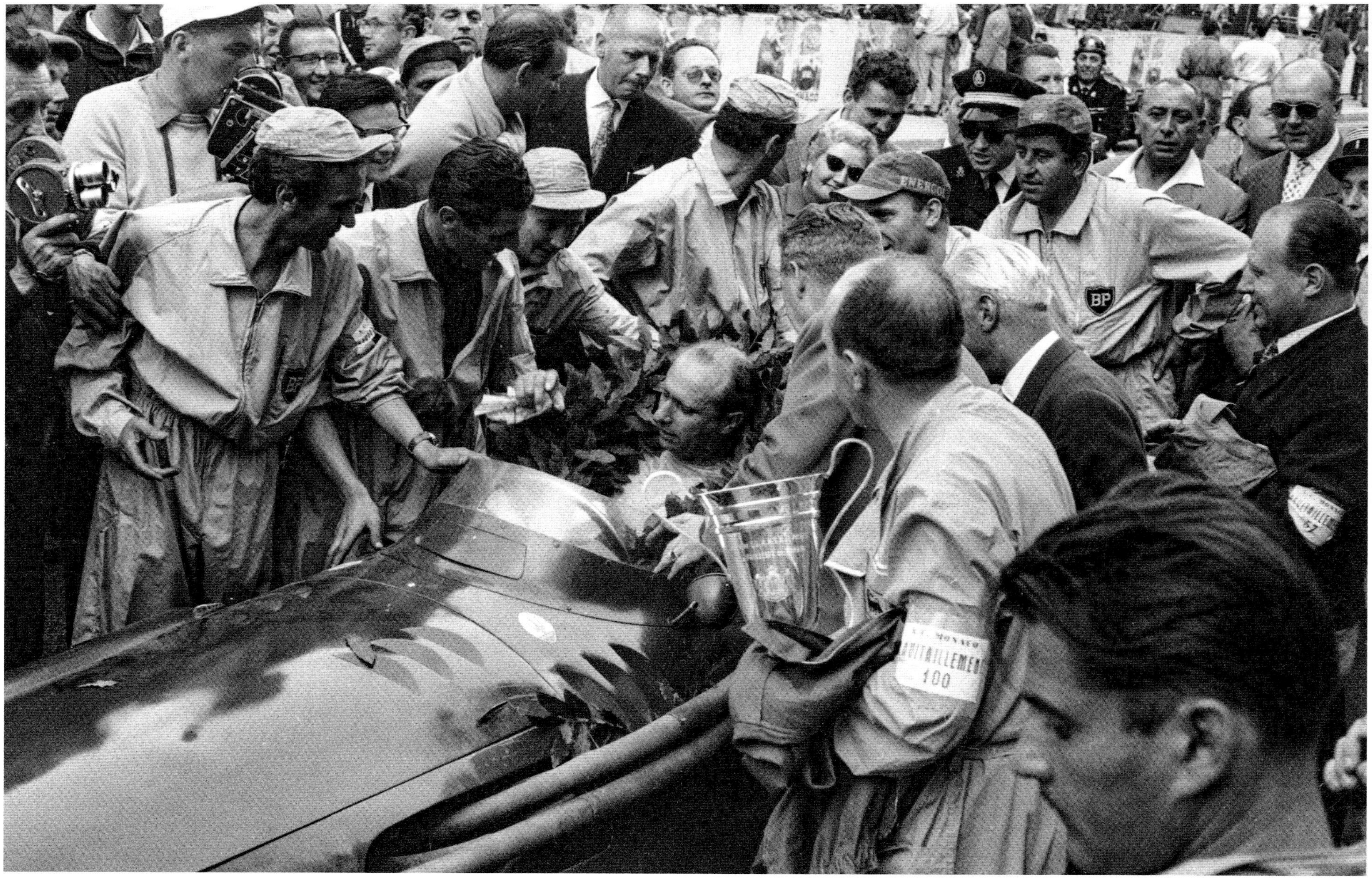

Der letzte Sieg von Fangio und von Maserati in Monaco wird gefeiert. Er gewinnt, obwohl er die letzten 15 Runden ohne 2. Gang auskommen muss.

Celebrations for Fangio and Maserati's last victory in Monaco. The Argentinian won despite having to drive without 2nd gear for the last 15 laps.

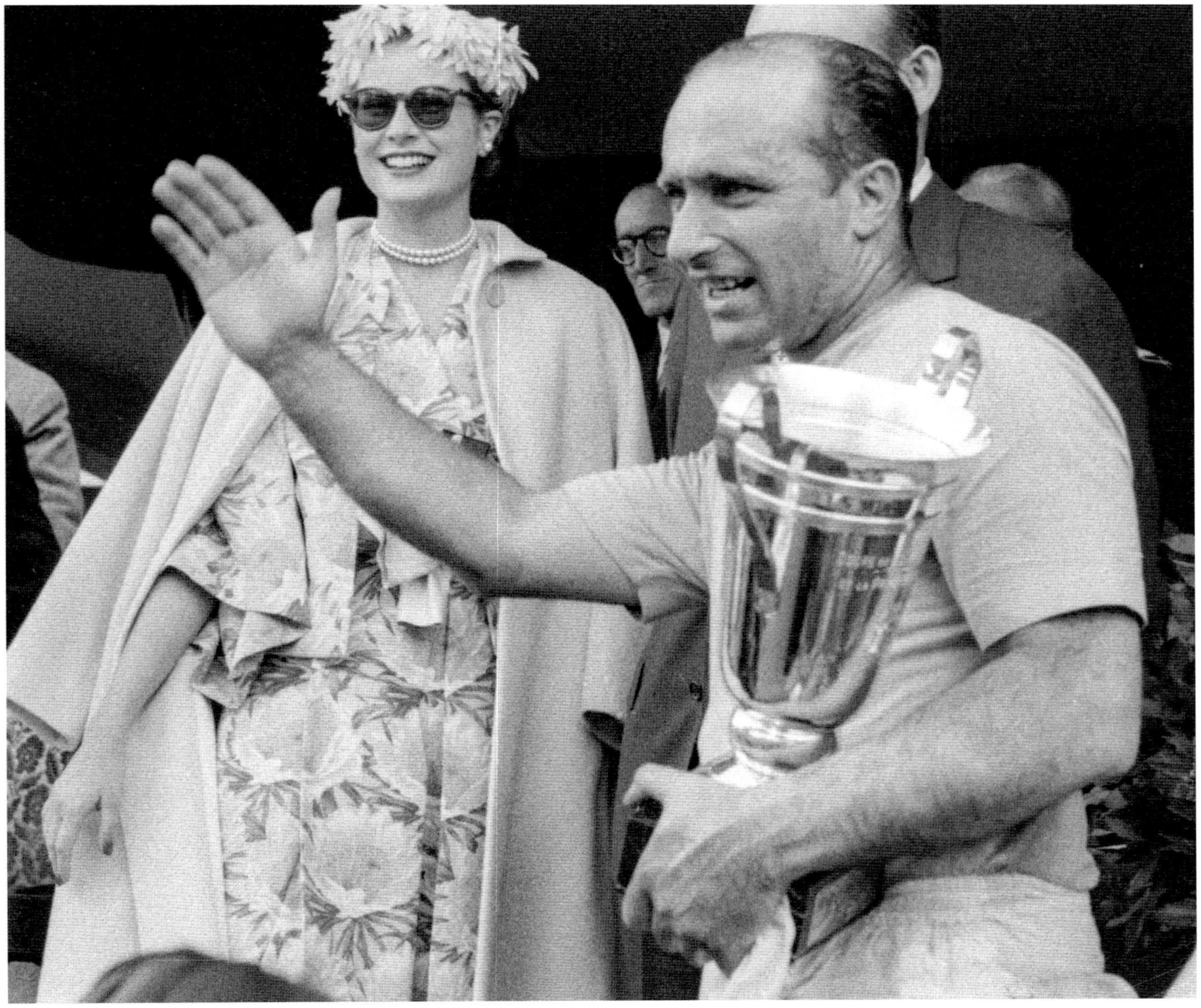

Glamour beim Grand Prix:
Fürstin Gracia hat ihren ersten Auftritt bei der Siegerehrung für Juan Manuel Fangio.

Glamour comes to the Grand Prix:
Princess Grace makes her first appearance at the award ceremony for Juan Manuel Fangio.

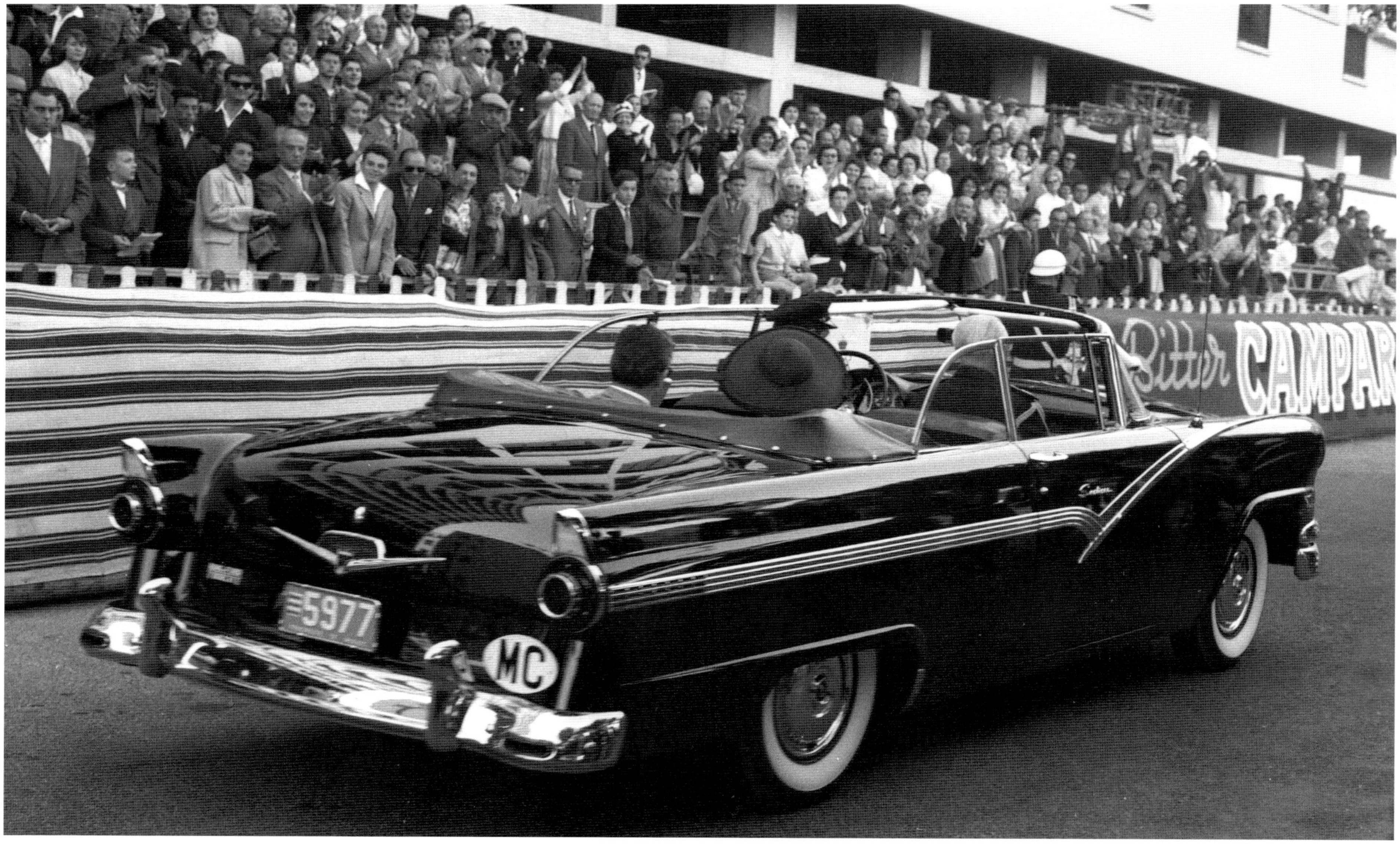

Ankunft an der Rennstrecke mit großem Hut im großen Amerikaner: Fürstin Gracia, daneben Fürst Rainier. Wie dieser Ford Fairlane Sunliner hatten alle Wagen des Fürsten Kennzeichen mit Endzahl 77.

Arriving at the racetrack in a big hat and riding in a big American car, Princess Grace sits next to Prince Rainier. Like this Ford Fairlane Sunliner, all of the Prince's cars had licence plates with the final number 77.

1958

Cooper greift an

Was sich schon letztes Jahr abzeichnete: Die britischen Konstrukteure werden immer stärker. Die fünf trainingsschnellsten Wagen sind alle von der Insel, erst dann folgt ein Ferrari. Maserati rettet sich gerade noch auf die zwei letzten Plätze.

Nach dem sensationellen Formel-1-Debüt 1957 sind die Cooper jetzt voll da, besetzen mit Jack Brabham am Steuer die Poleposition und stellen mit Maurice Trintignant den Sieger. Mit ihren Climax-Heckmotoren sind sie der Ursprung der modernen Formel-1-Konstruktionen. Bereits vor dem Krieg sah man Heckmotoren bei den spektakulären Auto-Union V16 und V12, aber sie hatten sich nicht durchgesetzt. Die klassischen großen Frontmotorwagen dominierten die Nachkriegszeit. Aber nun greifen erfolgreich die kleinen, leichten Cooper an, deren Wendigkeit und hervorragende Straßenlage auf dem engen Monaco-Kurs die eher bescheidene Leistung der Coventry-Climax-Motoren kompensieren. Diese waren ursprünglich für Feuerspritzen im Zweiten Weltkrieg gebaut worden.

Ihren ersten Auftritt in Monaco hat die neue britische Marke Lotus mit Graham Hill, einem bisherigen Mechaniker und Testfahrer für das Team. Er wird einige Jahre später das Rennen zweimal gewinnen.

Cooper goes on the attack

The growing strength of British car builders has already been evident the previous year. This time the five fastest cars in practice were all from Britain, followed by a Ferrari. Maserati just managed to scrape into the last two places.

After the sensational Formula 1 debut in 1957, the Coopers were now in full force, taking pole position with Jack Brabham at the wheel and bringing victory to Maurice Trintignant. With their rear-mounted engines, they were the precursors of modern Formula 1 designs. Even before the war, rear-engined cars were seen in the spectacular Auto-Union V16 and V12, but they had not caught on. The classic large front-engined cars dominated the post-war period. But now the small, lightweight Cooper successfully went on the attack, its manoeuvrability and excellent roadholding on the narrow Monaco circuit compensating for its comparatively weak Coventry-Climax engine. These were originally built for fire pumps during WW II.

The new British marque Lotus made its first appearance in Monaco driven by Graham Hill, previously a mechanic and test driver for the team. He would win the race twice a few years later.

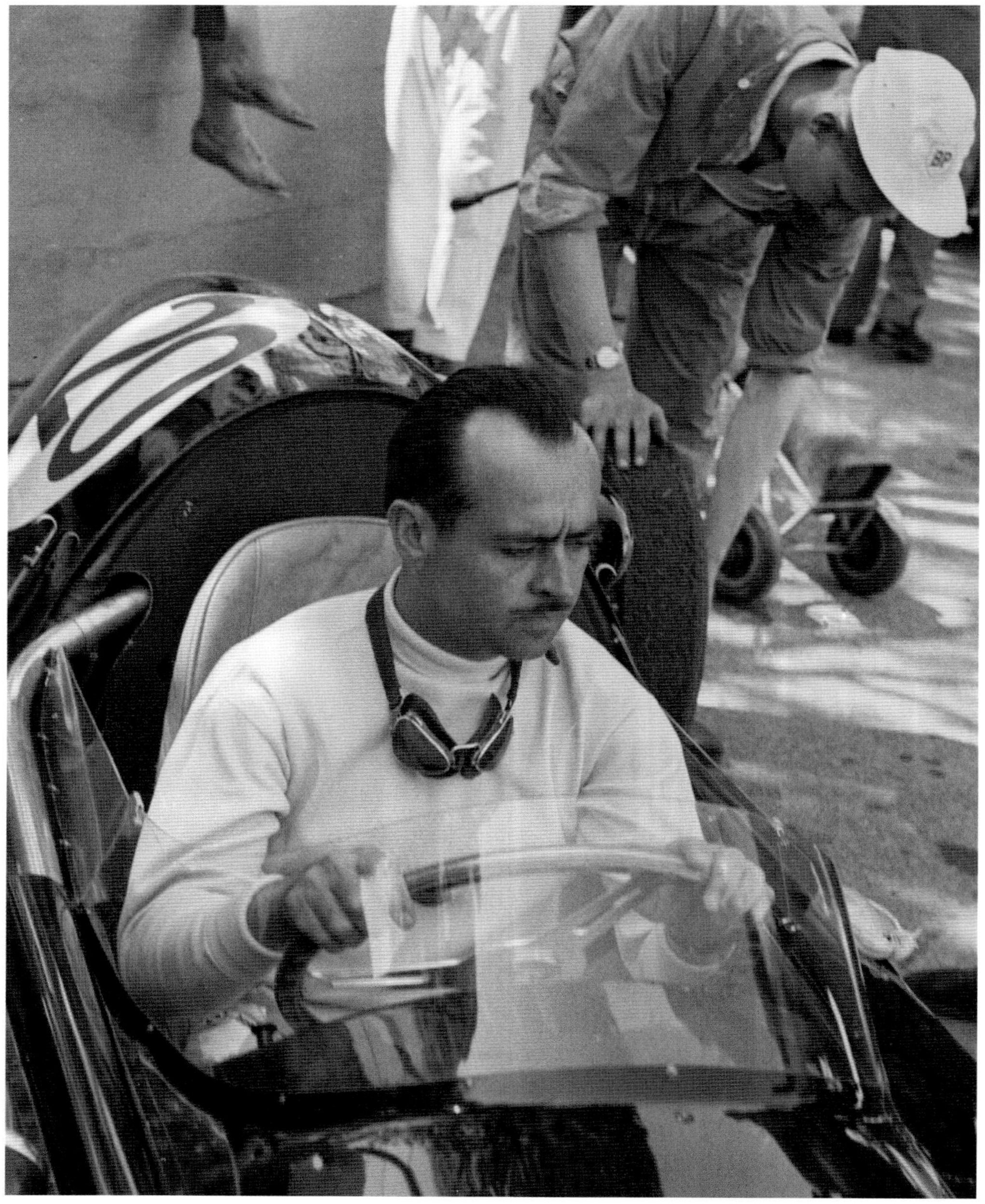

Maurice Trintignant,
der Sieger auf Cooper T45 N° 20.

Maurice Trintignant,
Cooper T45 N° 20, winner of the race.

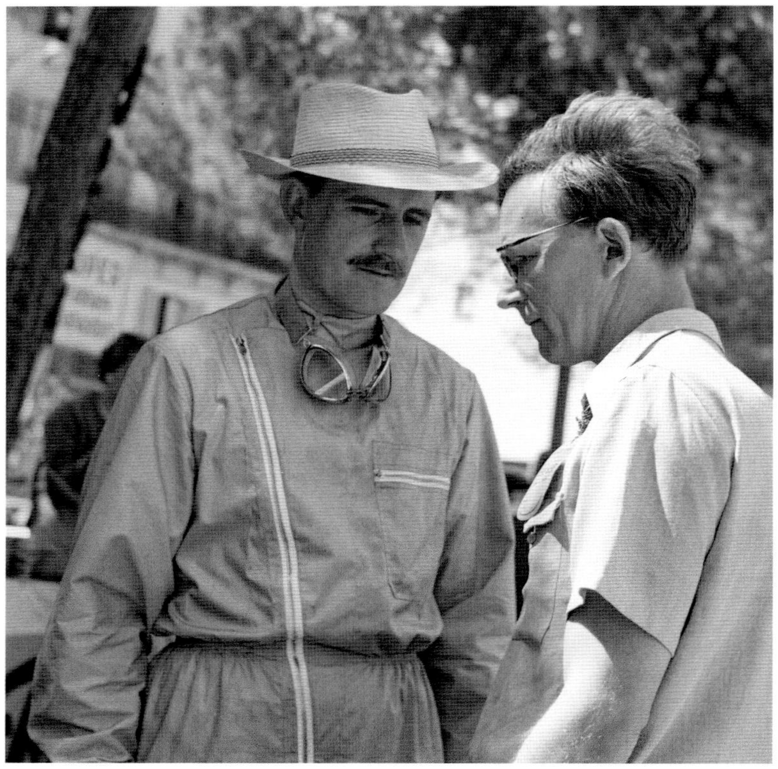

Graham Hill und ein Journalist. Er fährt seinen ersten Grand Prix in Monaco – allerdings ohne den eleganten Hut.

Graham Hill and a journalist. This was Hill's first Grand Prix in Monaco – but not wearing this elegant hat.

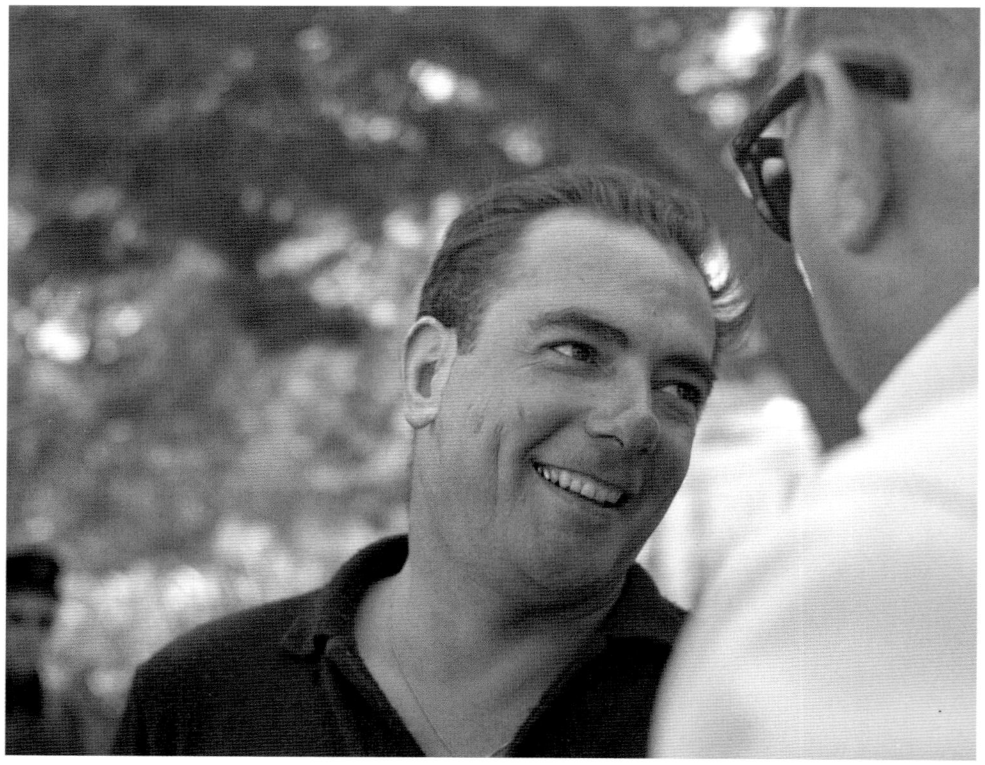

Jean Behra mit dem Plastikohr, das an einen früheren Unfall erinnert. Das französische Rennfahrer-Idol starb 1959 bei einem Sportwagenrennen auf der Berliner Avus.

Jean Behra with his prosthetic ear, a reminder of an earlier accident. The French racing idol died in 1959 during a sports car race on Berlin's Avus race track.

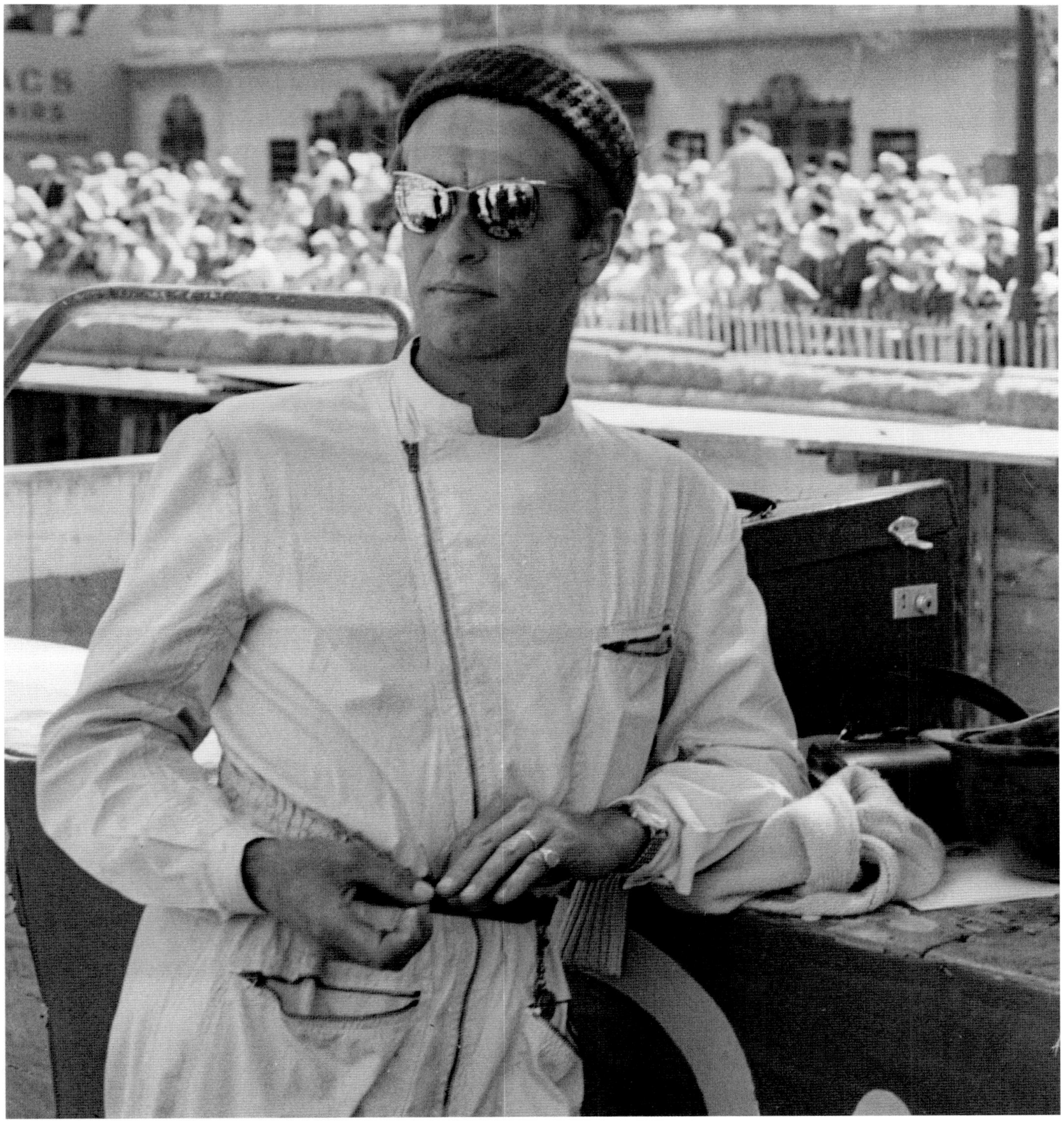

Golden Boy Peter Collins wird Dritter auf Ferrari Dino 246.

Golden Boy Peter Collins finishes third in the Ferrari Dino 246.

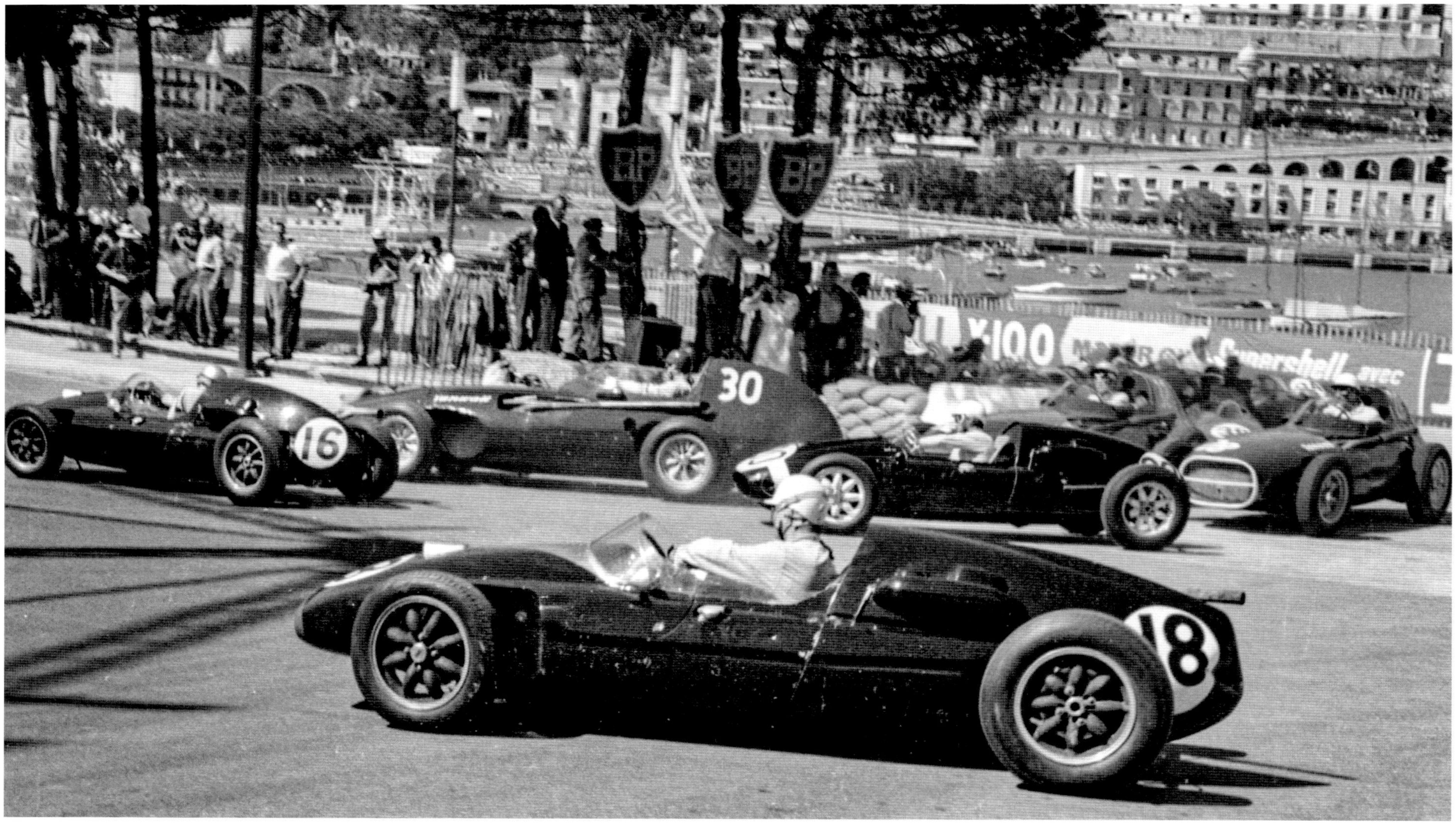

Der nach dem Start an der Spitze liegende Roy Salvadori, Cooper T45 N° 18, verpasst die Gasometer-Kurve. Jack Brabham, Cooper T45 N° 16, Tony Brooks, Vanwall VW10 N° 30, Maurice Trintignant, Cooper T45 N° 20.

Roy Salvadori, Cooper T45 N° 18, leading after the start, misses the Gasometer corner. Jack Brabham, Cooper T45 N° 16, Tony Brooks, Vanwall VW10 N° 30, Maurice Trintignant, Cooper T45 N° 20.

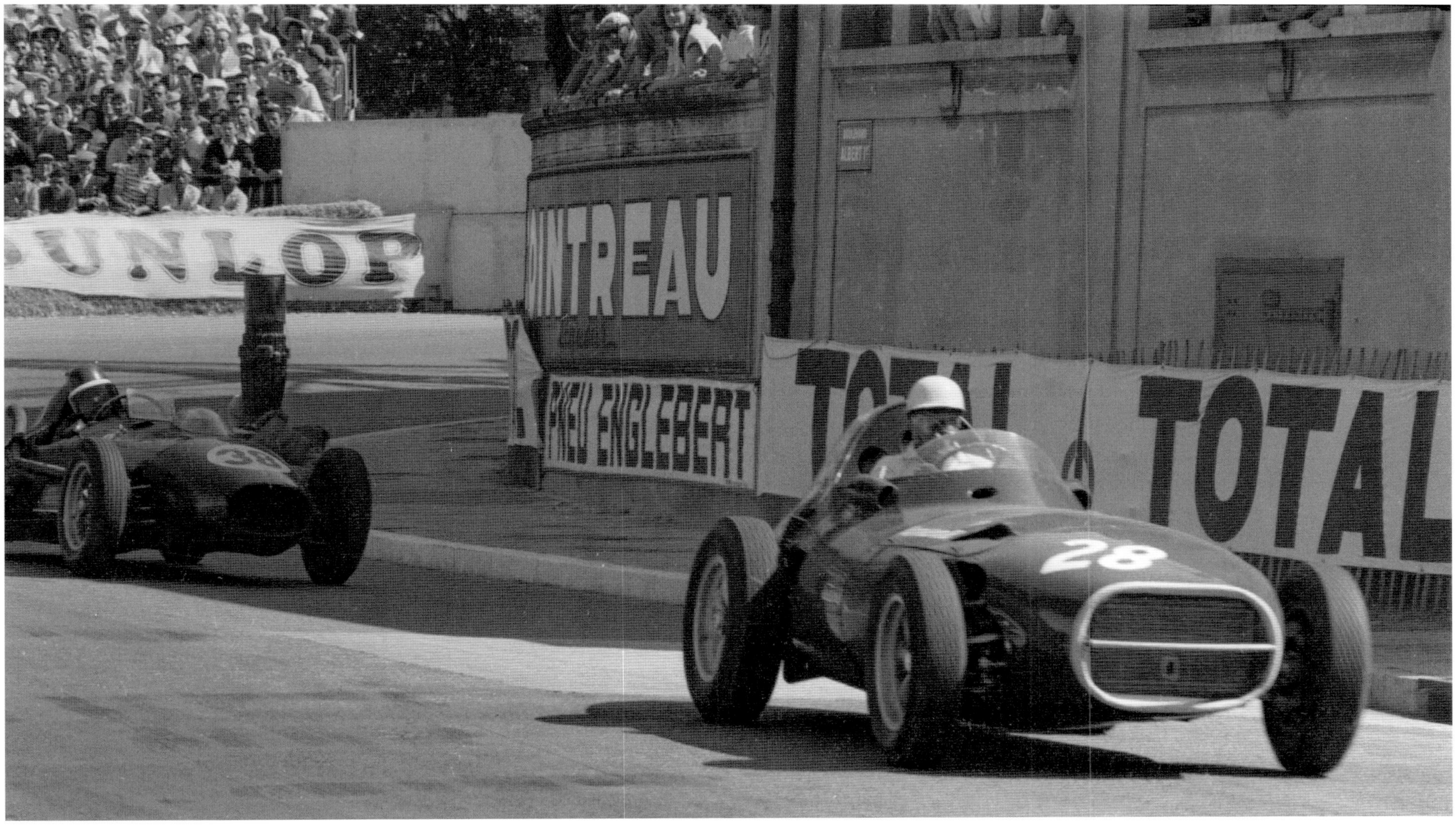

Stirling Moss, Vanwall VW7 N° 28. Mike Hawthorn, Ferrari Dino 246 N° 38. Die Vanwall hatten für Monaco verkürzte Nasen. Damit sollte vermieden werden, dass ein Schaden den Lufteinlass verschließen und für Überhitzung sorgen würde.

Stirling Moss, Vanwall VW7 N° 28. Mike Hawthorn, Ferrari Dino 246 N° 38. The Vanwall cars had shorter noses for Monaco to avoid the possibility of damage in the racing traffic, which might close up the air intake and cause overheating.

Stirling Moss, Vanwall VW7 N° 28, hält mit Ventilproblemen an der Box. Rechts steht Tony Vandervell, Gründer des Vanwall-Formel-1-Rennstalls.

Stirling Moss, Vanwall VW7 N° 28, stops at the pits with valve troubles. Tony Vandervell (white hat), founder of the Vanwall Formula 1 racing team.

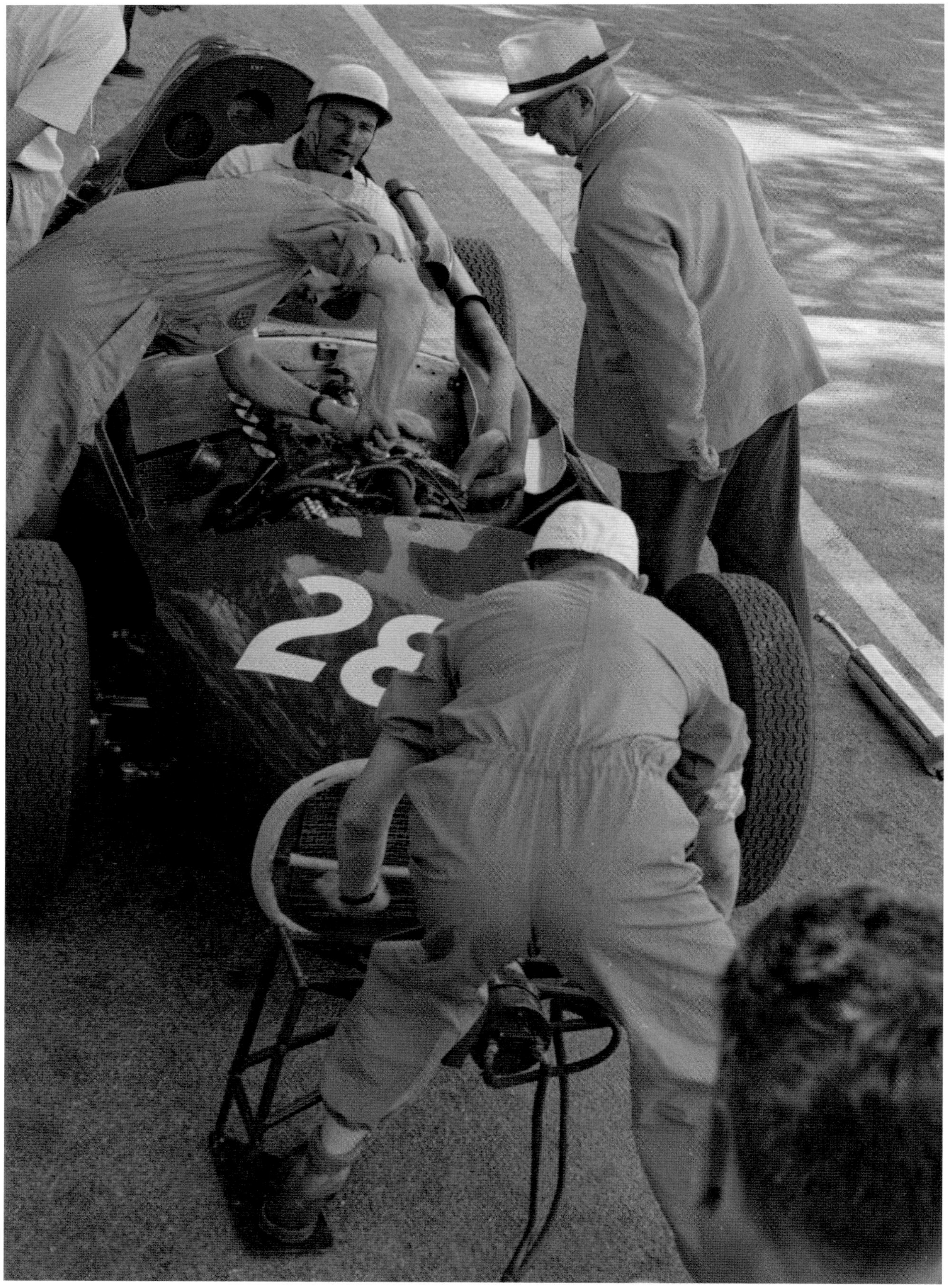

Final Result of the Monaco Grand Prix 1958

1. Maurice Trintignant, Cooper T45
2. Luigi Musso, Ferrari Dino 246
3. Peter Collins, Ferrari Dino 246

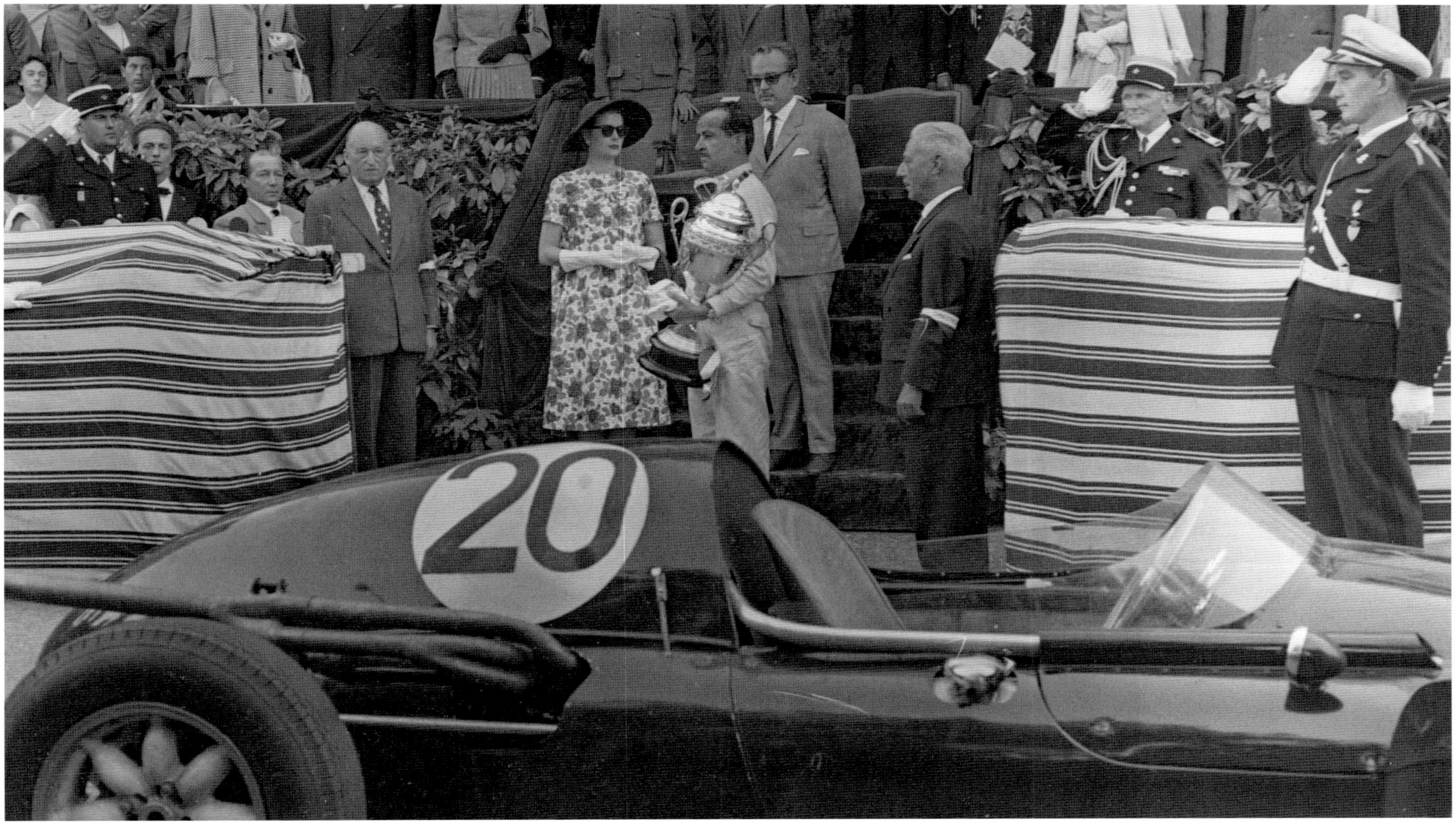

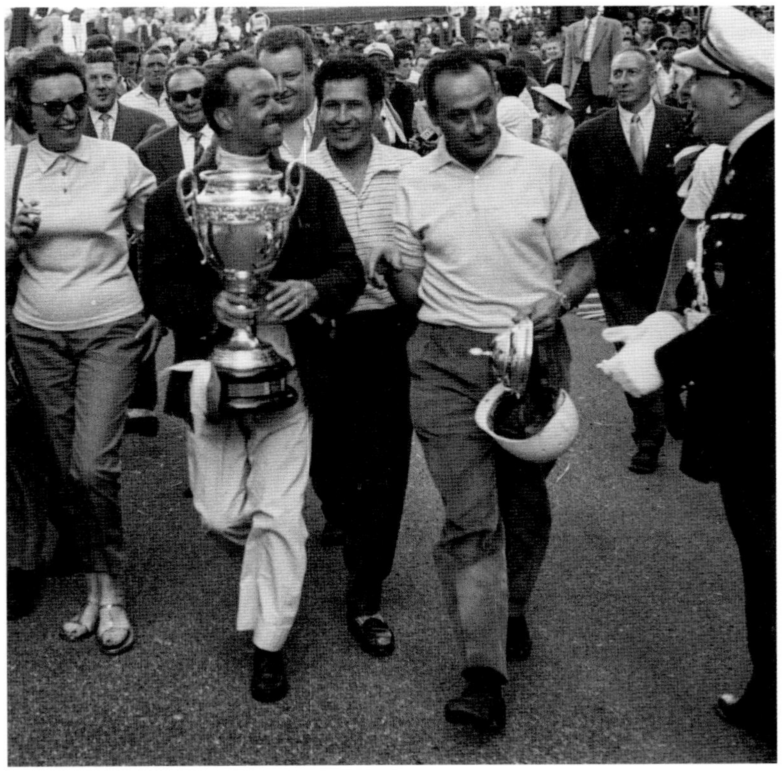

Fürstin Gracia und Fürst Rainier hinter Maurice Trintignant, Cooper T45 N° 20, mit dem Siegerpokal.

Princess Grace and Prince Rainier. Maurice Trintignant, Cooper T45 N° 20, with the winner's trophy.

Die Polizei ist begeistert: Maurice Trintignant, der Sieger des Rennens, Cooper T45 N° 20, und seine Frau Loulou.

An appreciative response from a policeman: Maurice Trintignant the race's winner, Cooper T45 N° 20, and his wife Loulou.

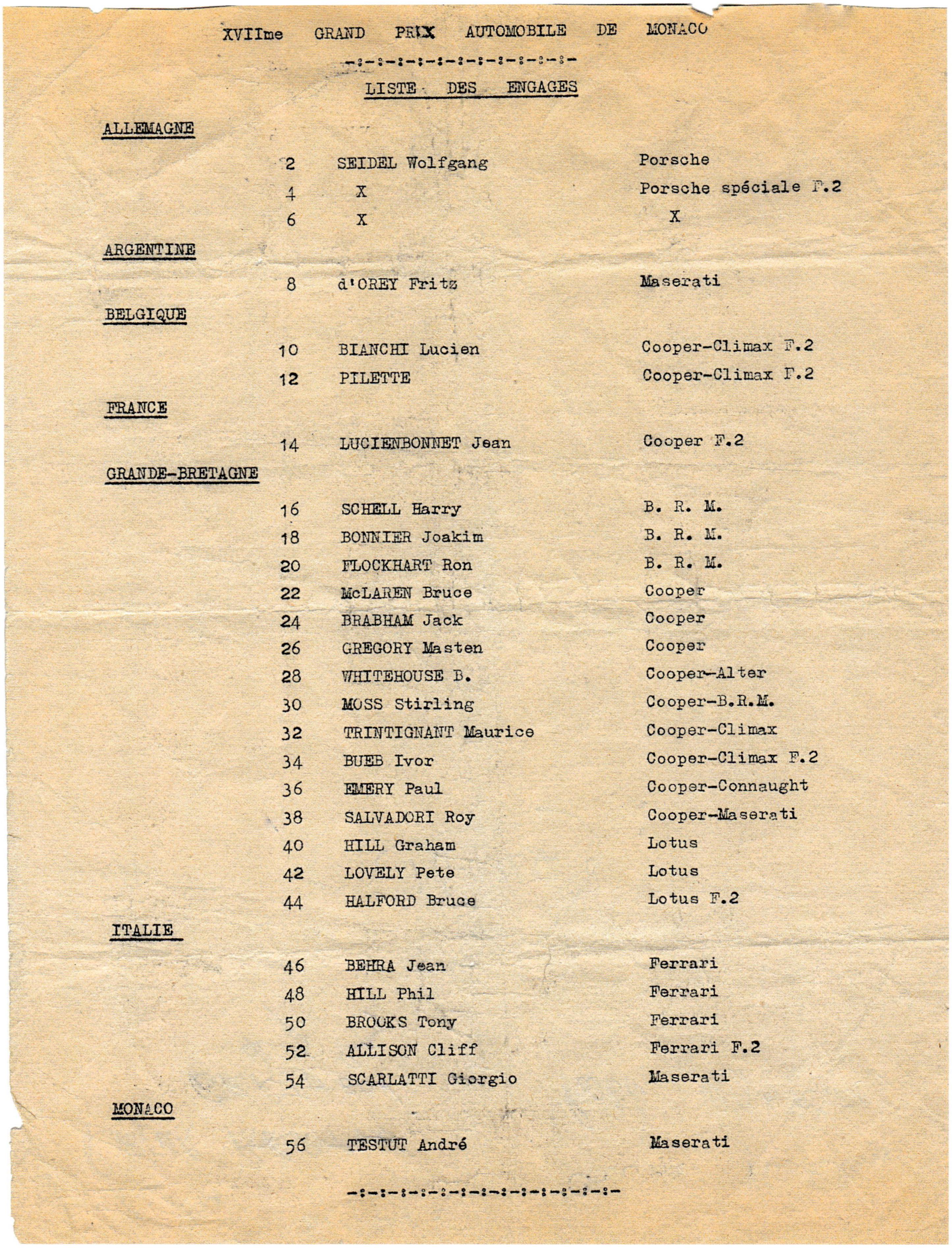

XVIIme GRAND PRIX AUTOMOBILE DE MONACO

-:-:-:-:-:-:-:-:-:-:-:-

LISTE DES ENGAGES

ALLEMAGNE			
	2	SEIDEL Wolfgang	Porsche
	4	X	Porsche spéciale F.2
	6	X	X
ARGENTINE			
	8	d'OREY Fritz	Maserati
BELGIQUE			
	10	BIANCHI Lucien	Cooper-Climax F.2
	12	PILETTE	Cooper-Climax F.2
FRANCE			
	14	LUCIENBONNET Jean	Cooper F.2
GRANDE-BRETAGNE			
	16	SCHELL Harry	B. R. M.
	18	BONNIER Joakim	B. R. M.
	20	FLOCKHART Ron	B. R. M.
	22	McLAREN Bruce	Cooper
	24	BRABHAM Jack	Cooper
	26	GREGORY Masten	Cooper
	28	WHITEHOUSE B.	Cooper-Alter
	30	MOSS Stirling	Cooper-B.R.M.
	32	TRINTIGNANT Maurice	Cooper-Climax
	34	BUEB Ivor	Cooper-Climax F.2
	36	EMERY Paul	Cooper-Connaught
	38	SALVADORI Roy	Cooper-Maserati
	40	HILL Graham	Lotus
	42	LOVELY Pete	Lotus
	44	HALFORD Bruce	Lotus F.2
ITALIE			
	46	BEHRA Jean	Ferrari
	48	HILL Phil	Ferrari
	50	BROOKS Tony	Ferrari
	52	ALLISON Cliff	Ferrari F.2
	54	SCARLATTI Giorgio	Maserati
MONACO			
	56	TESTUT André	Maserati

-:-:-:-:-:-:-:-:-:-:-:-:-

Offizielle Meldeliste mit 28 Fahrzeugen, die um die 16 Startplätze kämpfen.

Official list of entries with 28 cars fighting for 16 places on the grid.

1959

Die britische Phalanx

1959 ist eines der stärksten Jahre für die Briten, wie die Meldeliste zeigt: Von 27 Rennwagen sind allein 18 von der Insel, davon 11 mit Climax-Motoren. Das Rennen wird eine Machtdemonstration für die kleinen Cooper: Sie besetzen die Ränge 1, 3, 5 und 6. Für den zukünftigen dreimaligen Weltmeister Jack Brabham wird es der erste Monaco-Sieg. Auch wenn er von vielen Ausfällen profitiert, ist es doch kein geschenkter Sieg, er fährt immerhin die schnellste Runde.

Große Namen sind in diesem Jahr nicht mehr dabei. Luigi Musso, Peter Collins, Eugenio Castellotti, Alfonso de Portago und Stewart Lewis-Evans sind tödlich verunfallt. Und auch Mike Hawthorn fehlt, der Weltmeister des Vorjahres. Drei Monate vor Monaco ist er bei einem spontanen Rennen mit dem Rennstallbesitzer Rob Walker auf einer englischen Landstraße gestorben, nachdem er mit seinem Jaguar in einen Baum geprallt war. Die genaueren Umstände wurden nie ganz geklärt.

The British are coming

1959 was one of the strongest years for the British, as the entry list showed: of the 27 racing cars entered, 18 alone were from Britain, 11 of them powered by Climax engines. The race was a demonstration of power for the little Coopers: they took 1st, 3rd, 5th and 6th place. This was the first Monaco victory for the future three-time world champion Jack Brabham. Even though he benefited from several retirements, his was still a well-deserved victory; after all, he drove the fastest lap.

Big names were missing this year. Luigi Musso, Peter Collins, Eugenio Castellotti, Alfonso de Portago and Stewart Lewis-Evans had all suffered fatal accidents. Mike Hawthorn, the previous year's world champion, was also absent. Three months before Monaco he was killed when he crashed his Jaguar into a tree. The exact circumstances of the accident were never fully clarified.

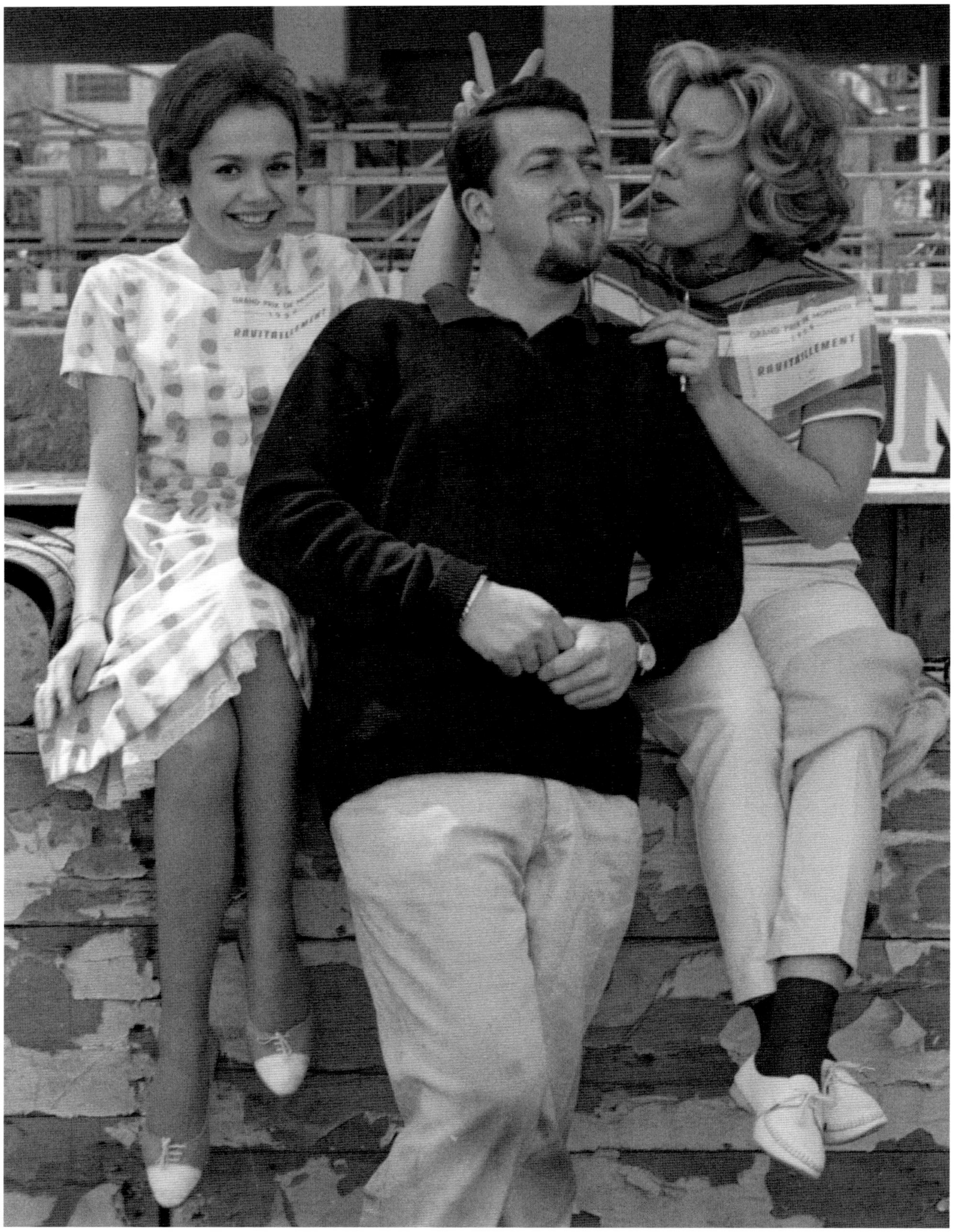

Spaß in der Box. Während Joakim Bonnier für ein Foto posiert, macht Monique Schell, die Frau von Harry Schell, ein verstecktes V-Zeichen.

Fun in the pit. As Joakim Bonnier poses for a picture, Monique Schell, Harry Schell's wife, makes bunny ears behind his head. On the left another racing fan.

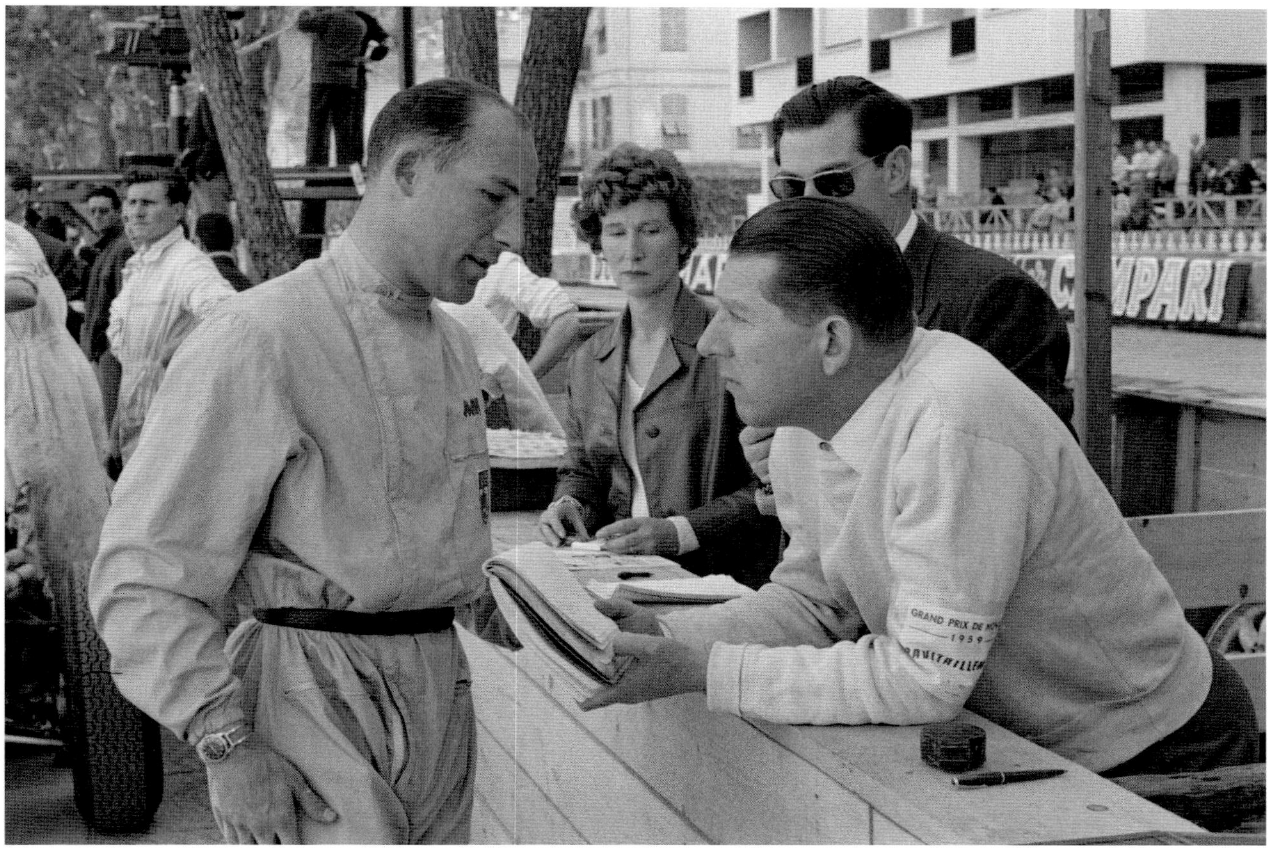

Stirling Moss im Gespräch mit Rob Walker, dem Besitzer des erfolgreichen R.R.C. Walker Racing Teams, das die Monaco-Siegerwagen 1958, 59 und 60 stellte.

Stirling Moss in conversation with Rob Walker, owner of the successful R.R.C. Walker Racing team which provided the Monaco winning cars in 1958, 59 and 60.

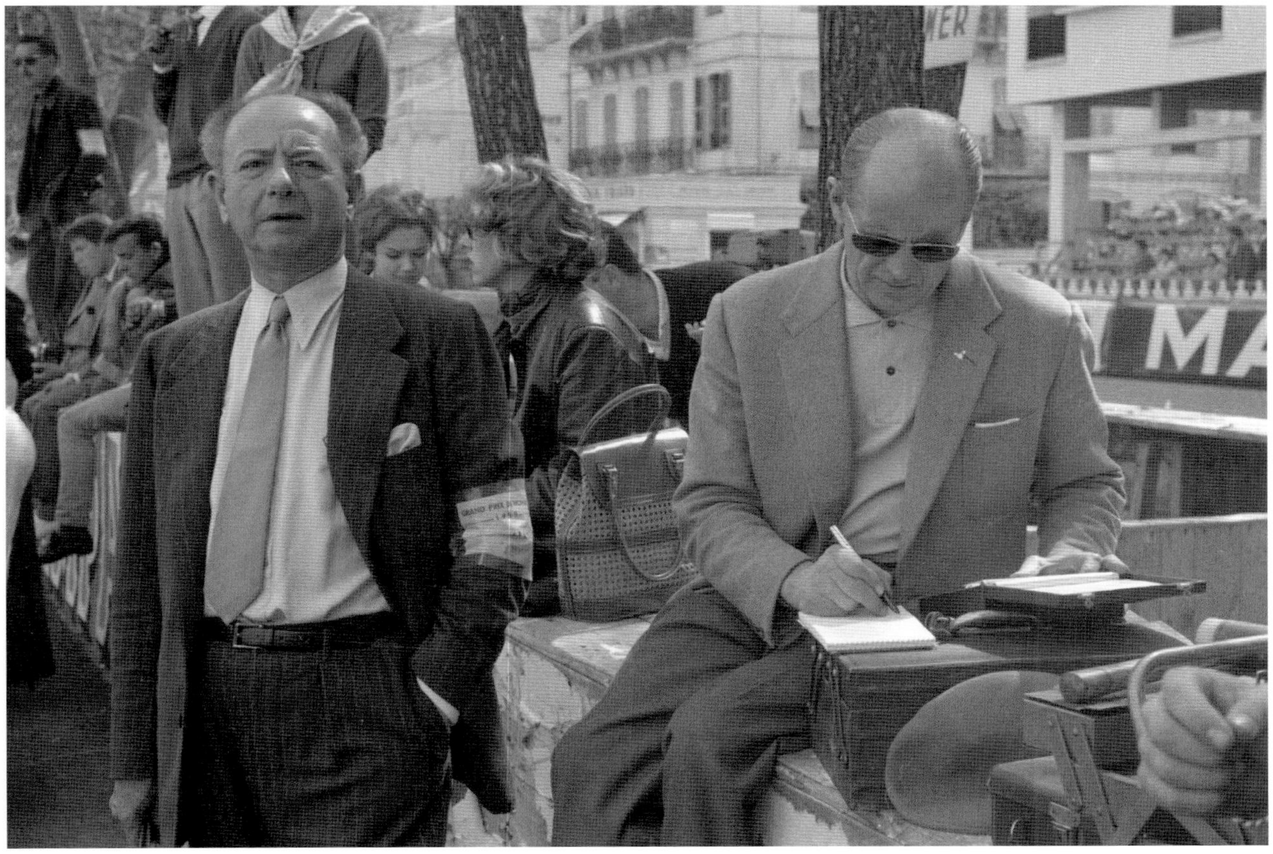

Raymond Mays (links) und Peter Berthon, die Gründer von BRM.

Raymond Mays (left) and Peter Berthon, founders of BRM.

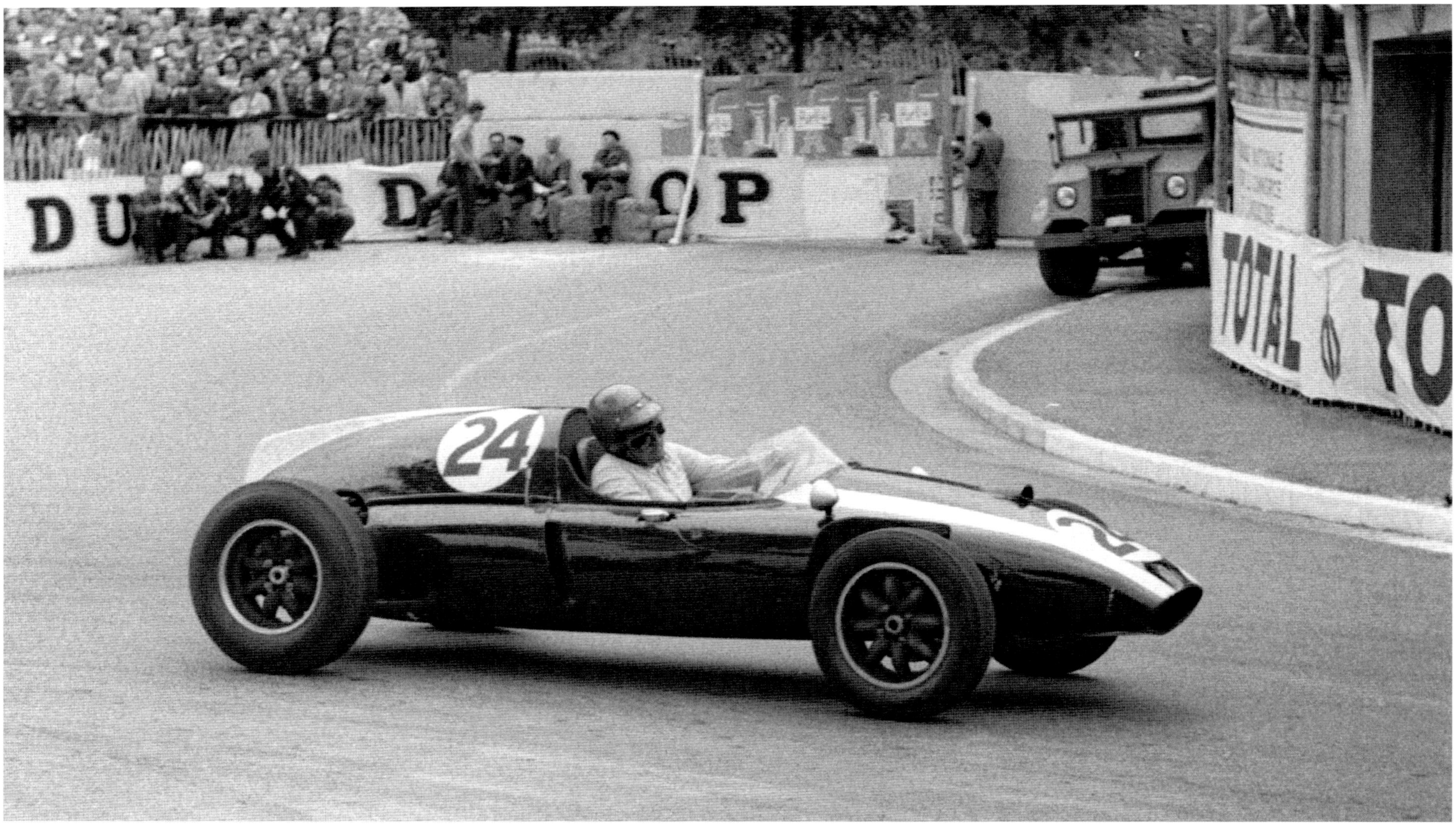

Jack Brabham, Cooper T5I N° 24,
in der Gasometer-Kurve.

*Jack Brabham, Cooper T51 N° 24,
at the Gasometer hairpin.*

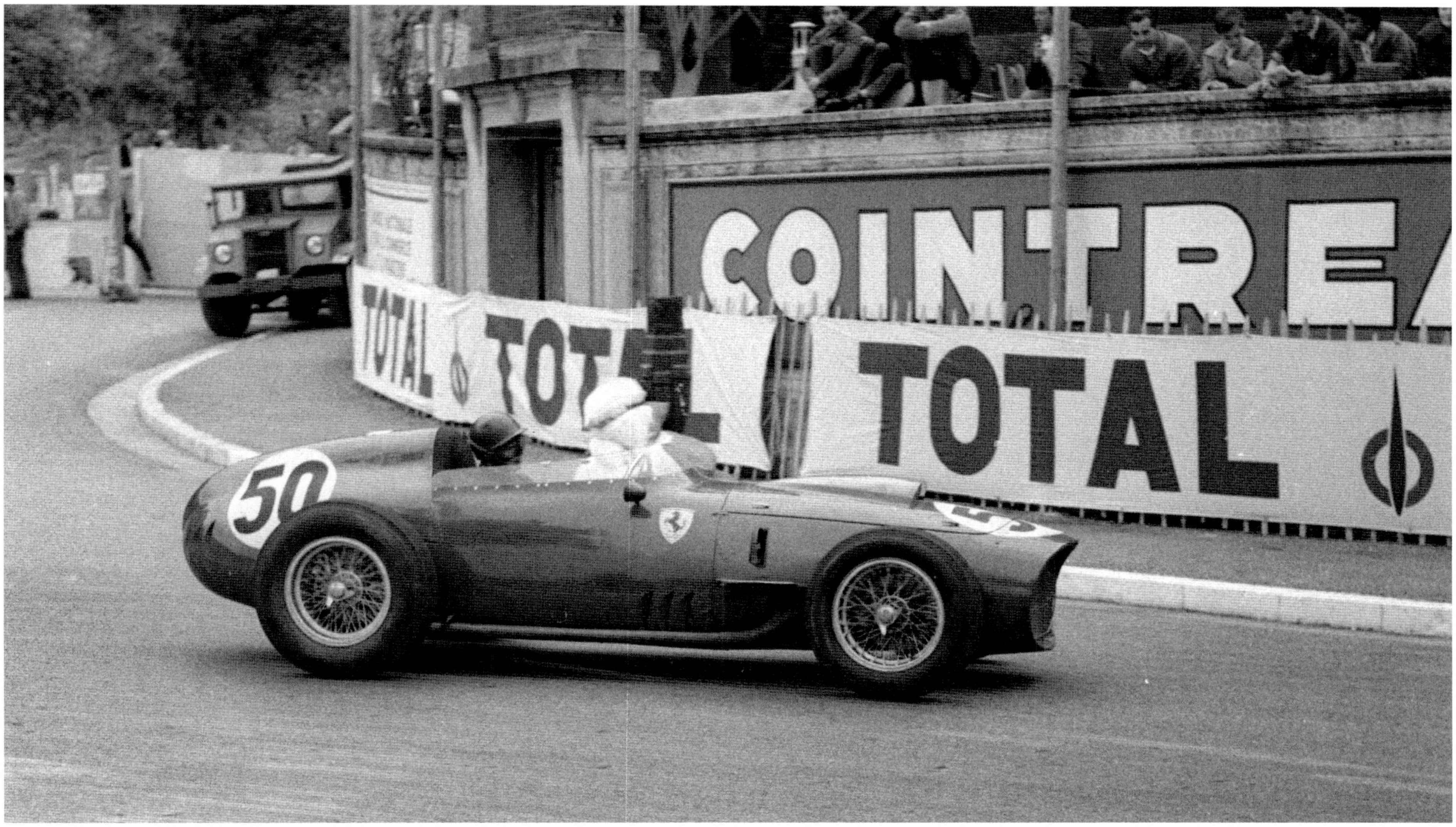

Tony Brooks im Ferrari Dino 246
„short nose“ N° 50 in derselben Kurve.
Er wurde Zweiter.

Tony Brooks cornering his Ferrari Dino 246 "short nose" N° 50 at the Gasometer hairpin. He finished second.

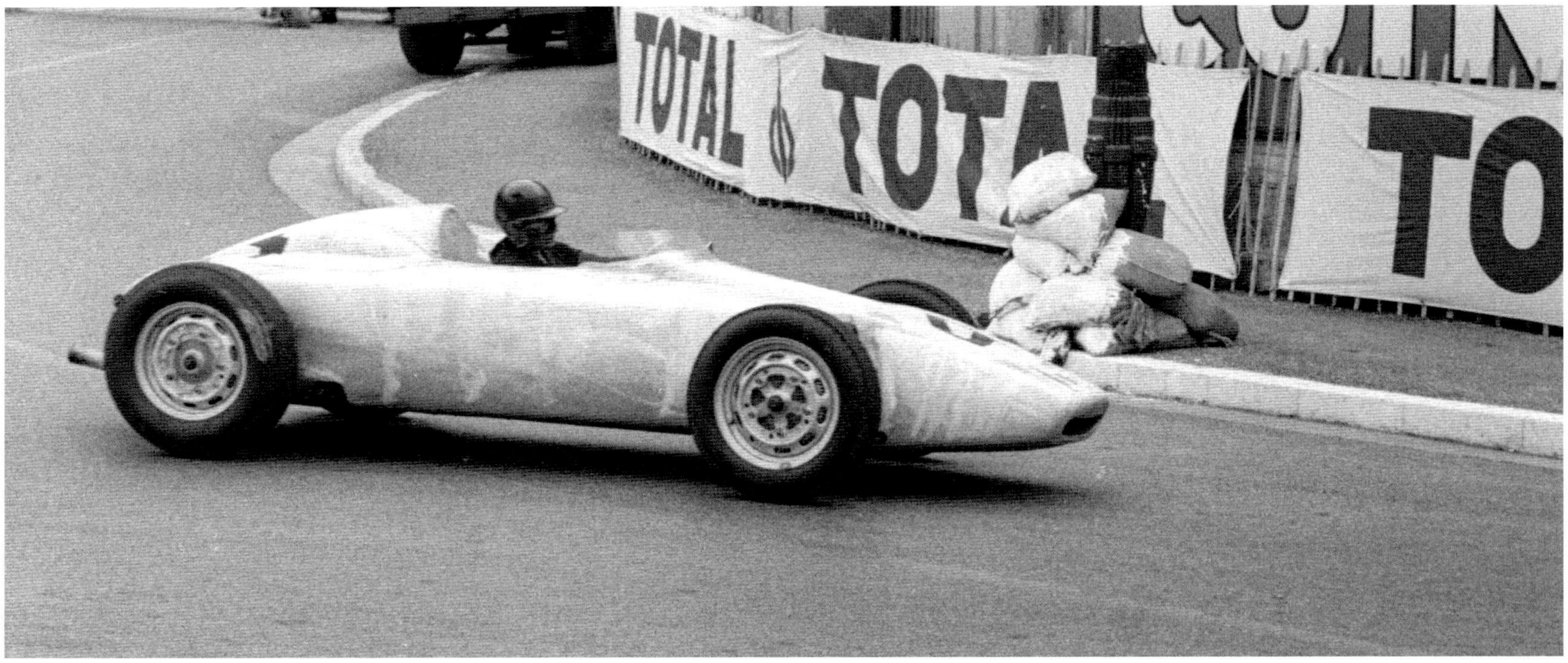

Die italienische Rennfahrerin Maria Teresa de Filippis
auf einem Porsche Special F2 auf RSK-Basis
mit italienischer Karosserie („Behra-Porsche“).

*Italian female motor racing driver Maria Teresa de Filippis
in RSK-based Porsche Special F2 with Italian
body (“Behra-Porsche”).*

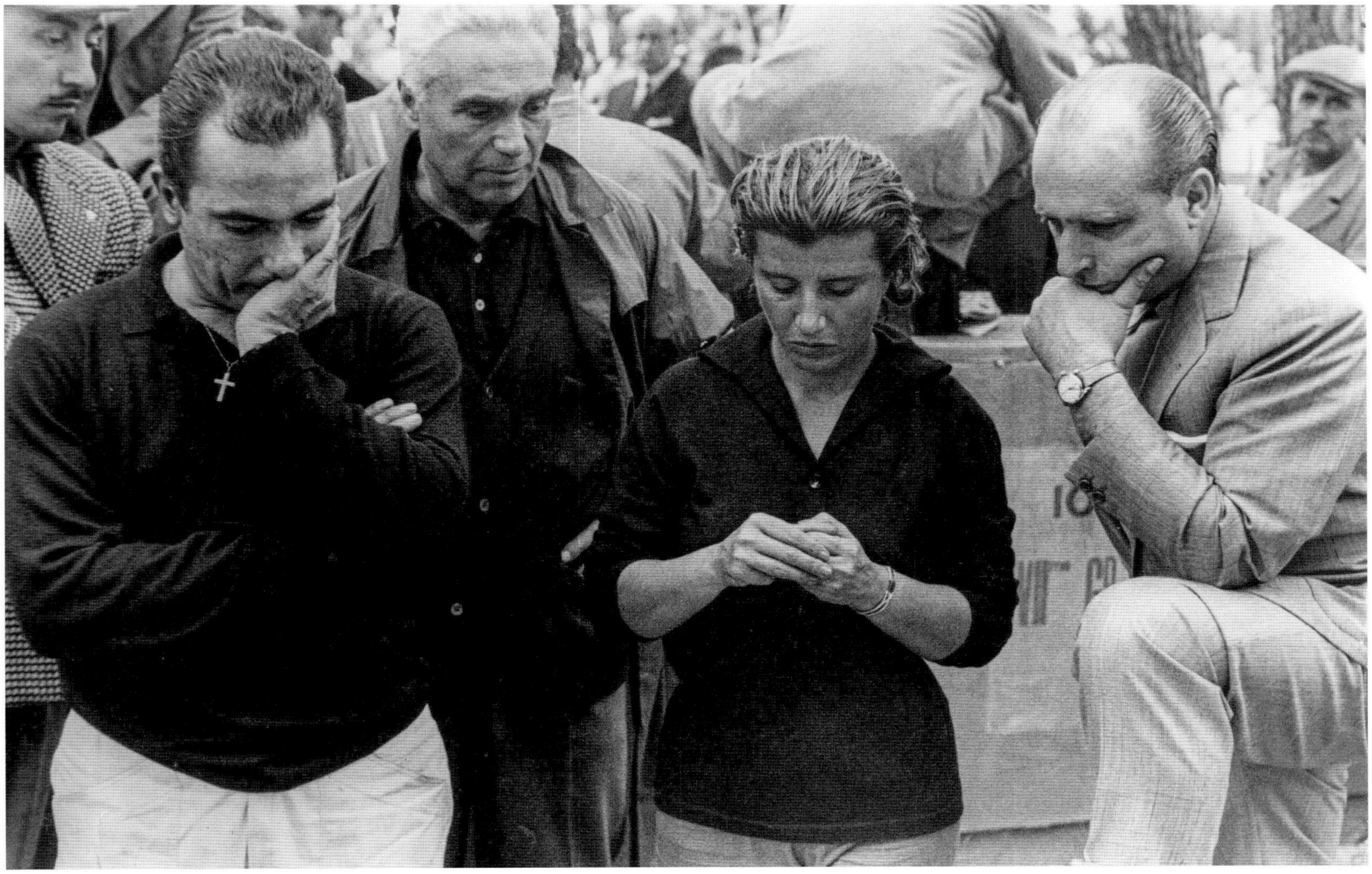

Traurige Gesichter von Jean Behra, Piero Taruffi, Maria Teresa de Filippis und Fangio (von links), als bekannt wurde, dass Maria Teresa sich knapp nicht für den Grand Prix qualifiziert hatte. Behra und Fangio waren ihre Lehrmeister und Vorbilder. Es war das letzte Mal, dass sie an einem Grand Prix teilnahm. Unmittelbar nach dem tödlichen Unfall von Behra auf der AVUS-Strecke in Berlin, drei Monate später, gab sie bekannt, dass sie nie wieder Rennen fahren würde. Um den Hals von Behra ist das kleine Kreuz zu sehen, das er bei seinem Unfall auf der AVUS verlor und das einige Tage später von einem Schüler gefunden wurde.

Sad faces of Jean Behra, Piero Taruffi, Maria Teresa de Filippis and Fangio (from left) when it was announced that Maria Teresa had narrowly failed to qualify for the Grand Prix. Behra and Fangio were her coaches and role models. It was the last time she took part in a Grand Prix. Immediately after Behra's fatal accident on the AVUS circuit in Berlin, three months later, she announced that she would never race again. Around Behra's neck is the small cross he lost in his accident on the AVUS, which was found a few days later by a schoolboy.

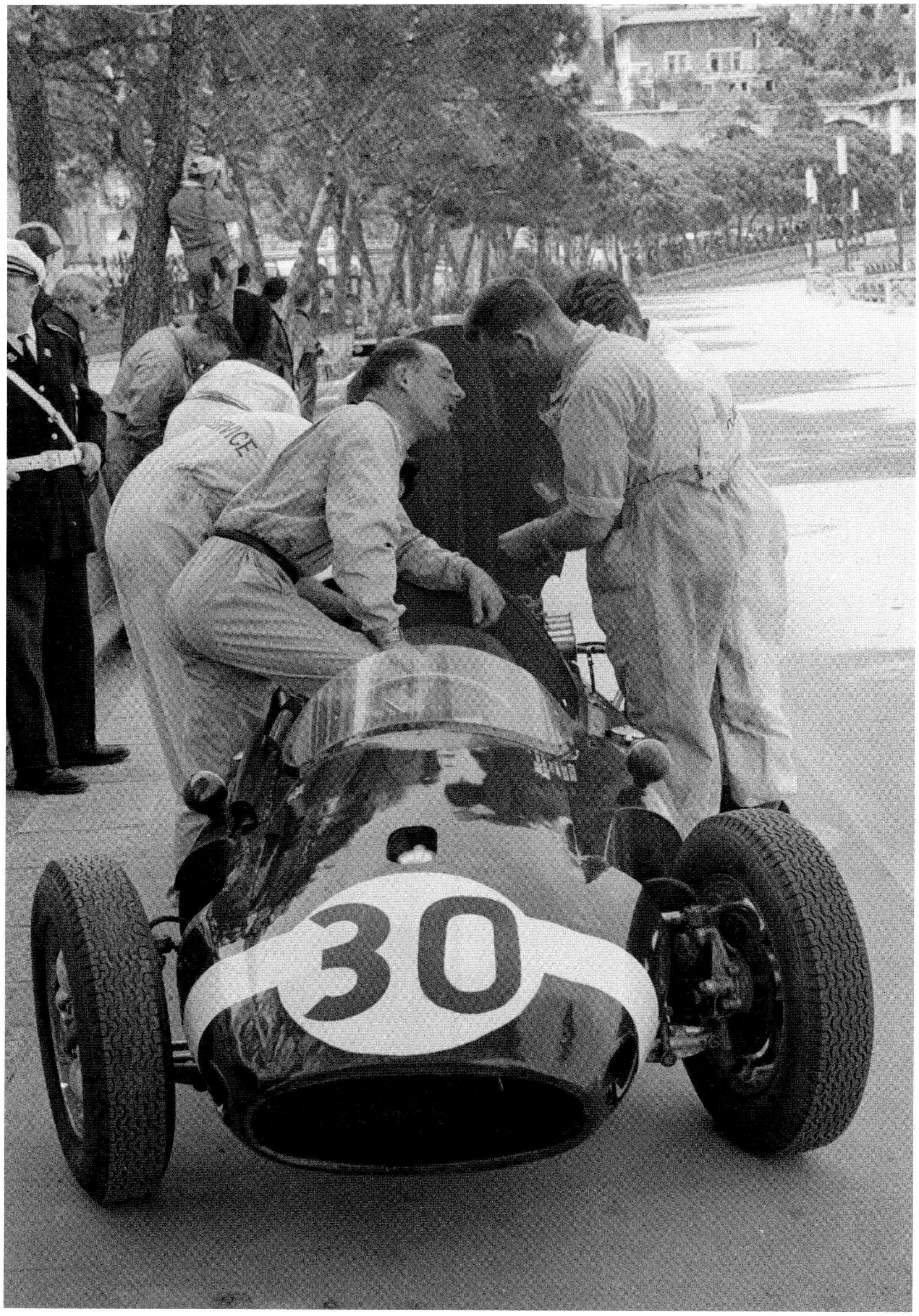

Stirling Moss, Cooper T51 N° 30.

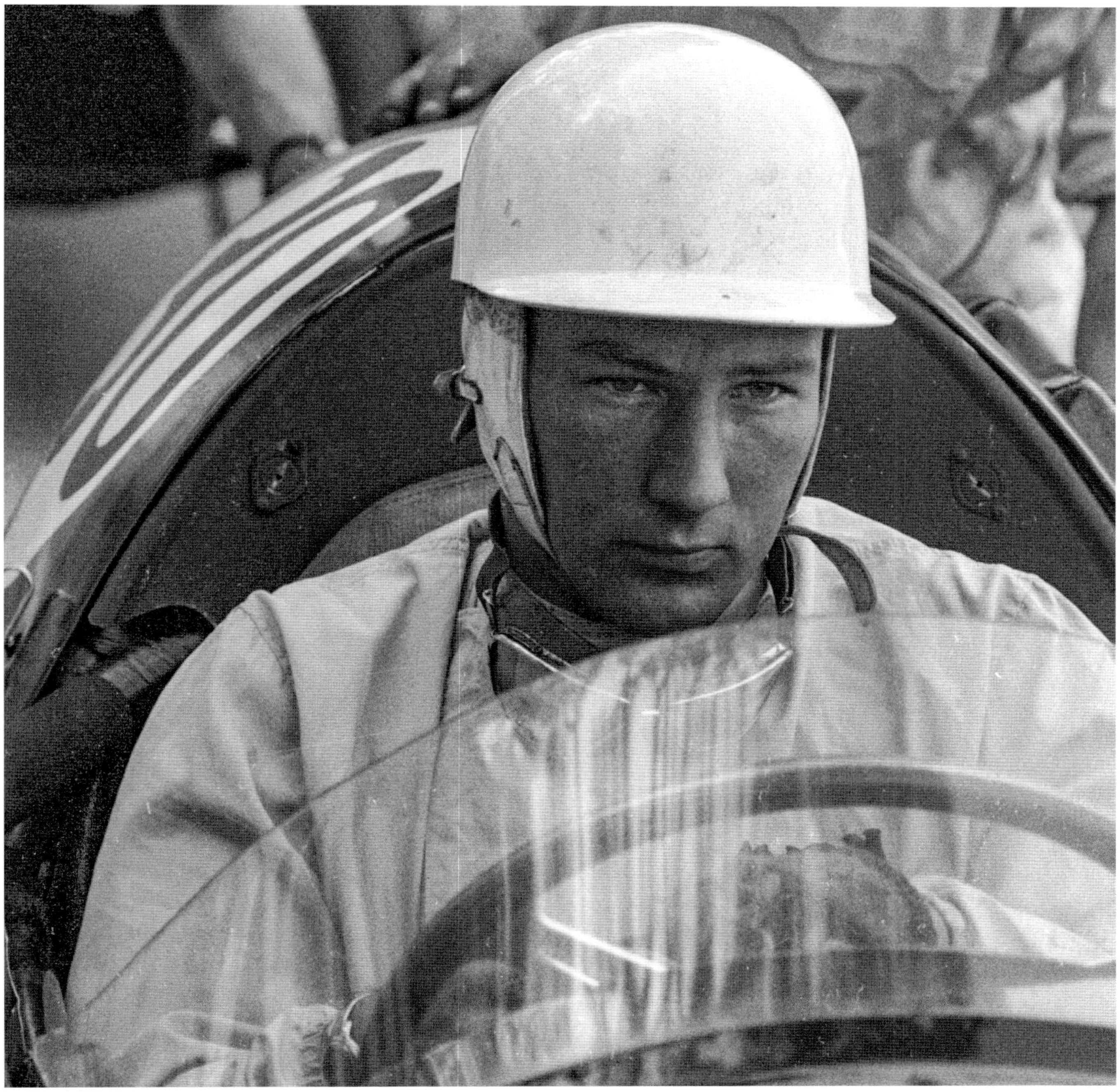

Stirling Moss, Cooper T51 N° 30.

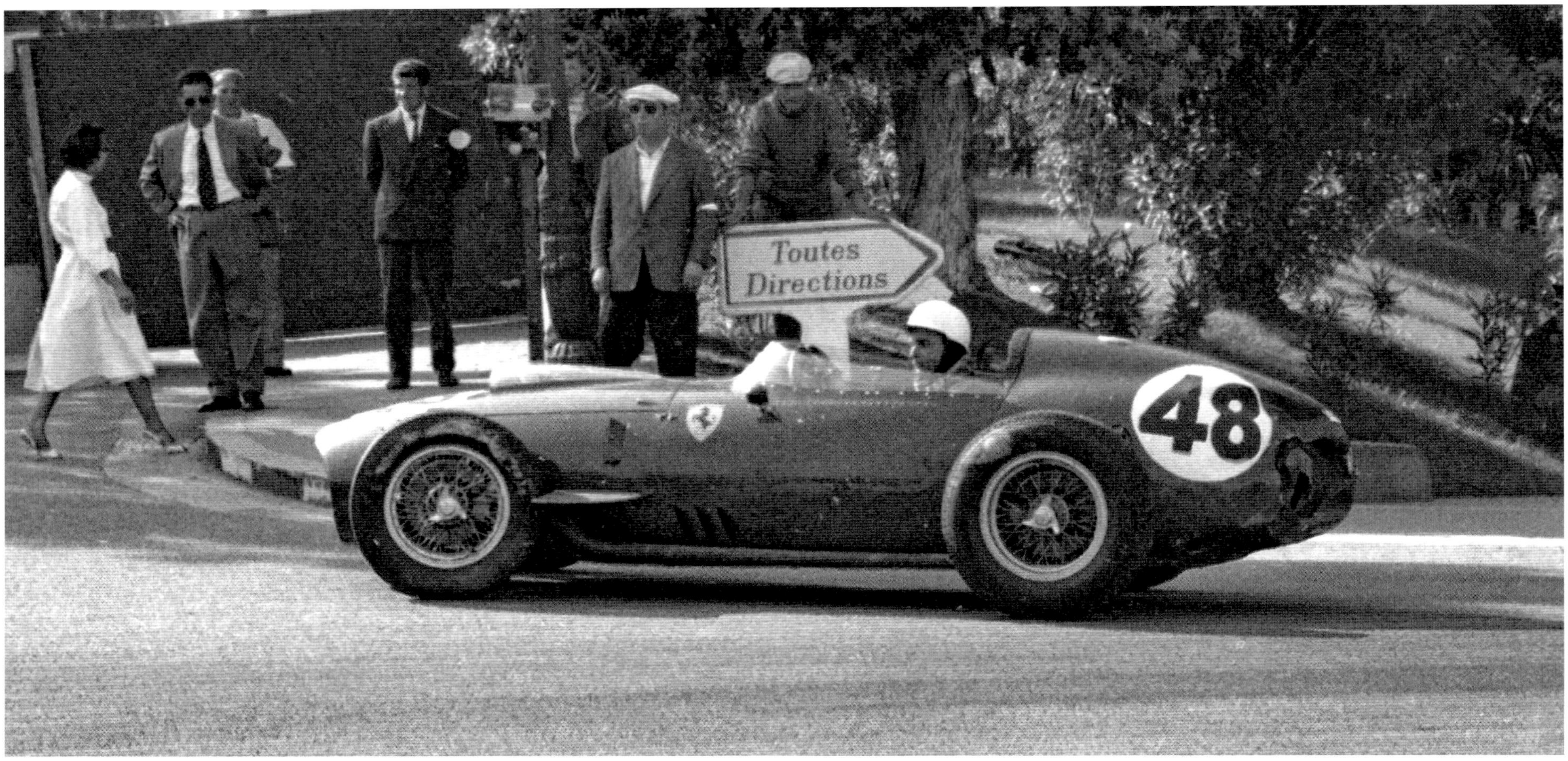

Falsche Richtung: Phil Hill auf einem etwas verbeulten Ferrari Dino 246 „short nose“ N° 48. Sowohl er als auch sein Teamkollege Tony Brooks litten unter Schwindel wegen der Abgase im engen Ferrari-Cockpit.

Wrong direction: Phil Hill in a battered short-nosed Ferrari Dino 246 N° 48. Both he and his teammate Tony Brooks suffered from giddiness because of the exhaust fumes in the cramped Ferrari cockpit.

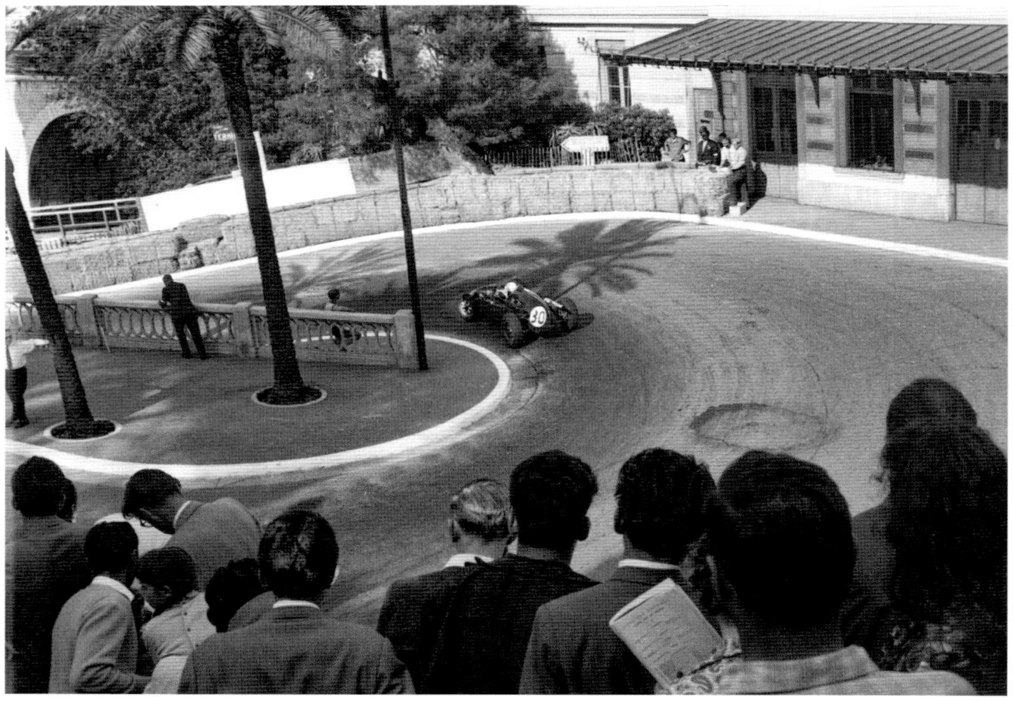

Stirling Moss auf Cooper T51 N° 30 in der Stations-Haarnadel (heute Grand Hotel Hairpin).

Stirling Moss, Cooper T51 N° 30, at the Station Hairpin (today Grand Hotel Hairpin).

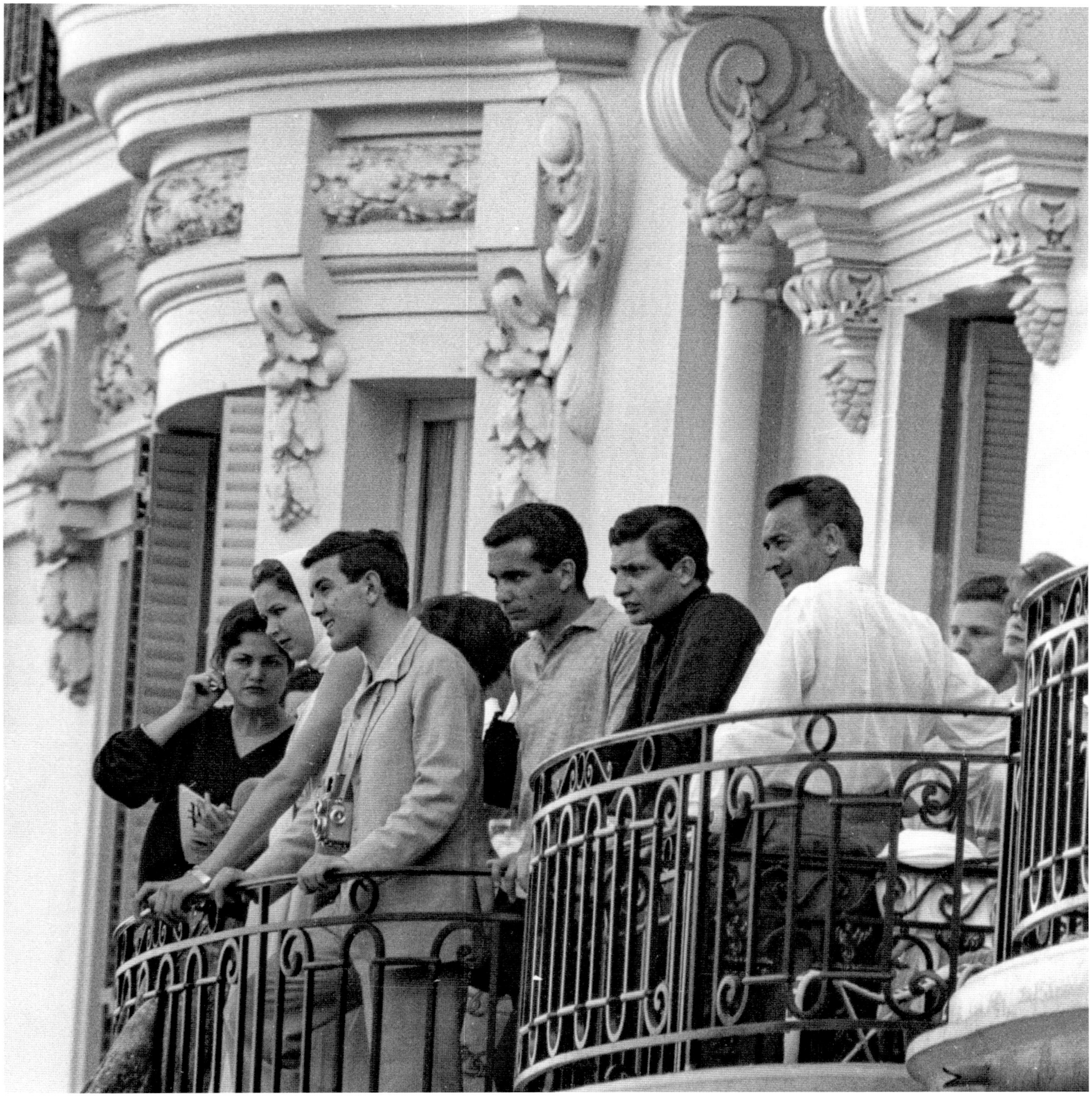

Final Result of the Monaco Grand Prix 1959

1. Jack Brabham, Cooper T51
2. Tony Brooks, Ferrari Dino 246
3. Maurice Trintignant, Cooper T51

Zuschauer auf einer Terrasse des Hôtel de Paris. Gunter Sachs (dunkle Jacke) mit Freunden. Ganz links Prinzessin Maria Pia von Jugoslawien und Gabriella, Prinzessin von Savoyen.

Spectators on a balcony at the Hôtel de Paris: Gunter Sachs (dark jacket) and friends. Far left Princess Maria Pia of Yugoslavia and Gabriella, Princess of Savoy.

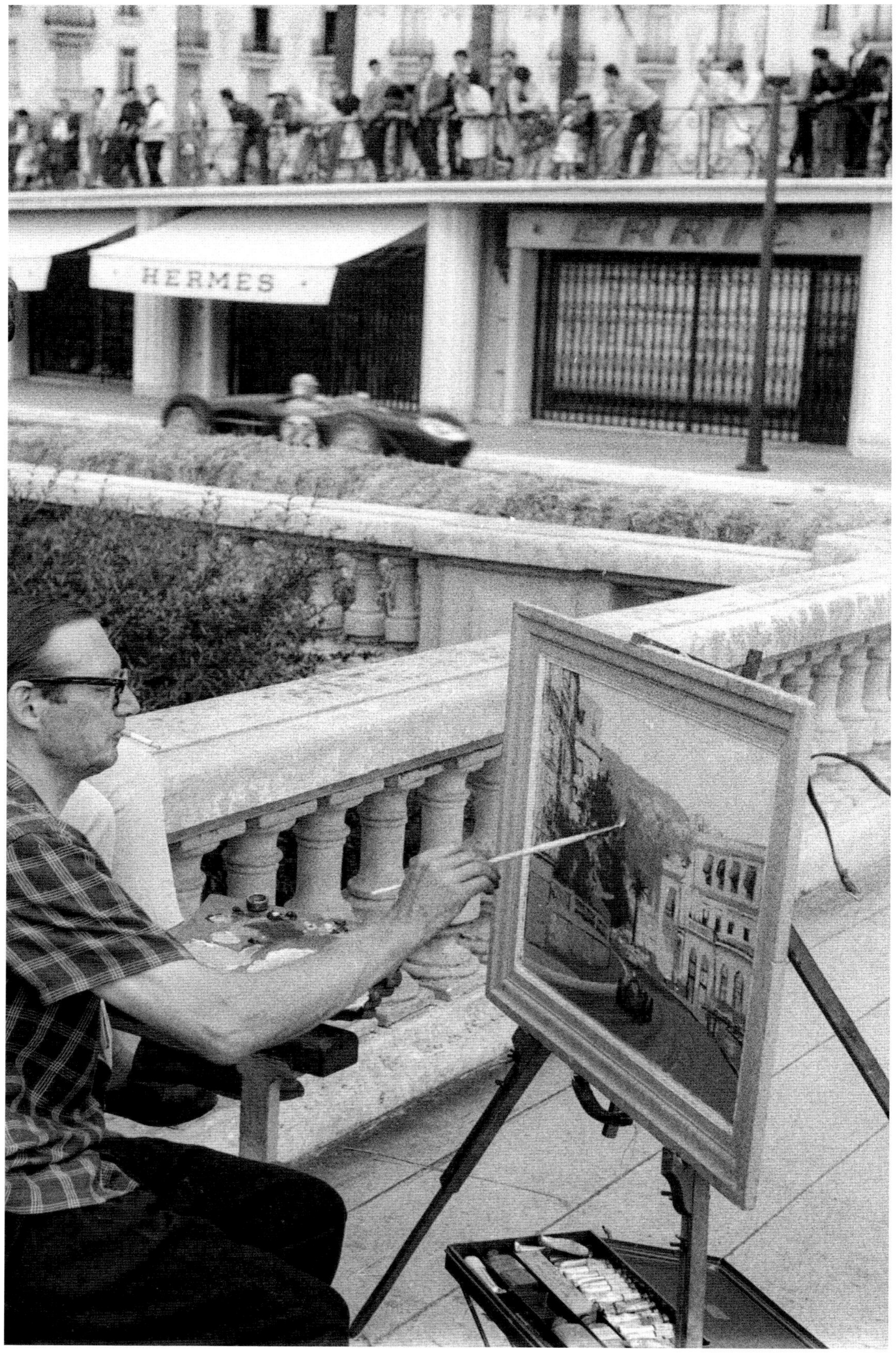

Ein Maler auf dem Weg zu Massenet.
Innes Ireland, Lotus 18 N° 22, vor dem
Hermès-Shop.

*A painter on the way to Massenet.
Innes Ireland, Lotus 18 N° 22, in front of
the Hermès shop.*

1960

Das Ende der Frontmotoren

In diesem Jahr debütieren mehr neue Modelle denn je. Sie läuten das Ende der Frontmotoren in der Formel 1 ein, ausgelöst durch die Erfolge von Cooper. Vier neue Lotus 18 mit Mittelmotoren sind am Start, gefahren von Moss, Ireland, Stacey und Surtees. Das ganze BRM-Team mit Bonnier, Gurney und Graham Hill fährt den neuen P48, Cooper bringt den neuen T53 für McLaren und Brabham. Einzig Ferrari hält noch an den Frontmotoren fest – Phil Hill und von Trips zeigen mit dem Dino 246 den letzten Auftritt dieses Konzepts in Monaco. Aber Ferrari hat auch ein neues Eisen im Feuer: den Mittelmotor Dino 246 P (für posteriore) mit Ginther am Steuer. Etwas veraltet wirkt in diesem Feld der neue Scarab des amerikanischen Millionenerben Lance Reventlow: zu groß, zu schwer und mit Frontmotor – ein Jahr zu spät.

Und wieder gewinnt Stirling Moss. Es ist der erste Sieg von Lotus in einer „grande épreuve“, einem der großen Rennen.

Farewell to front-engines

More new models made their debut this year than ever before. They heralded the end of front-engines in Formula 1, prompted by the successes of Cooper. There were four new mid-engined Lotus 18 cars on the grid, driven by Moss, Ireland, Stacey and Surtees. The entire BRM team with Bonnier, Gurney and Graham Hill drove the new P48, Cooper brought the new T53 for McLaren and Brabham. Only Ferrari stuck with front-engines. Phil Hill and von Trips drove the last exemplars of this concept in Monaco with the Dino 246. However Ferrari also had a new iron in the fire: the mid-engined Dino 246 P (for posteriore) with Ginther at the wheel. The new Scarab of American millionaire heir Lance Reventlow was somewhat outdated in this field: too big, too heavy and – with a front-engine – a year too late.

Stirling Moss was victorious once again. It was Lotus' first win in a "grande épreuve", one of the big races.

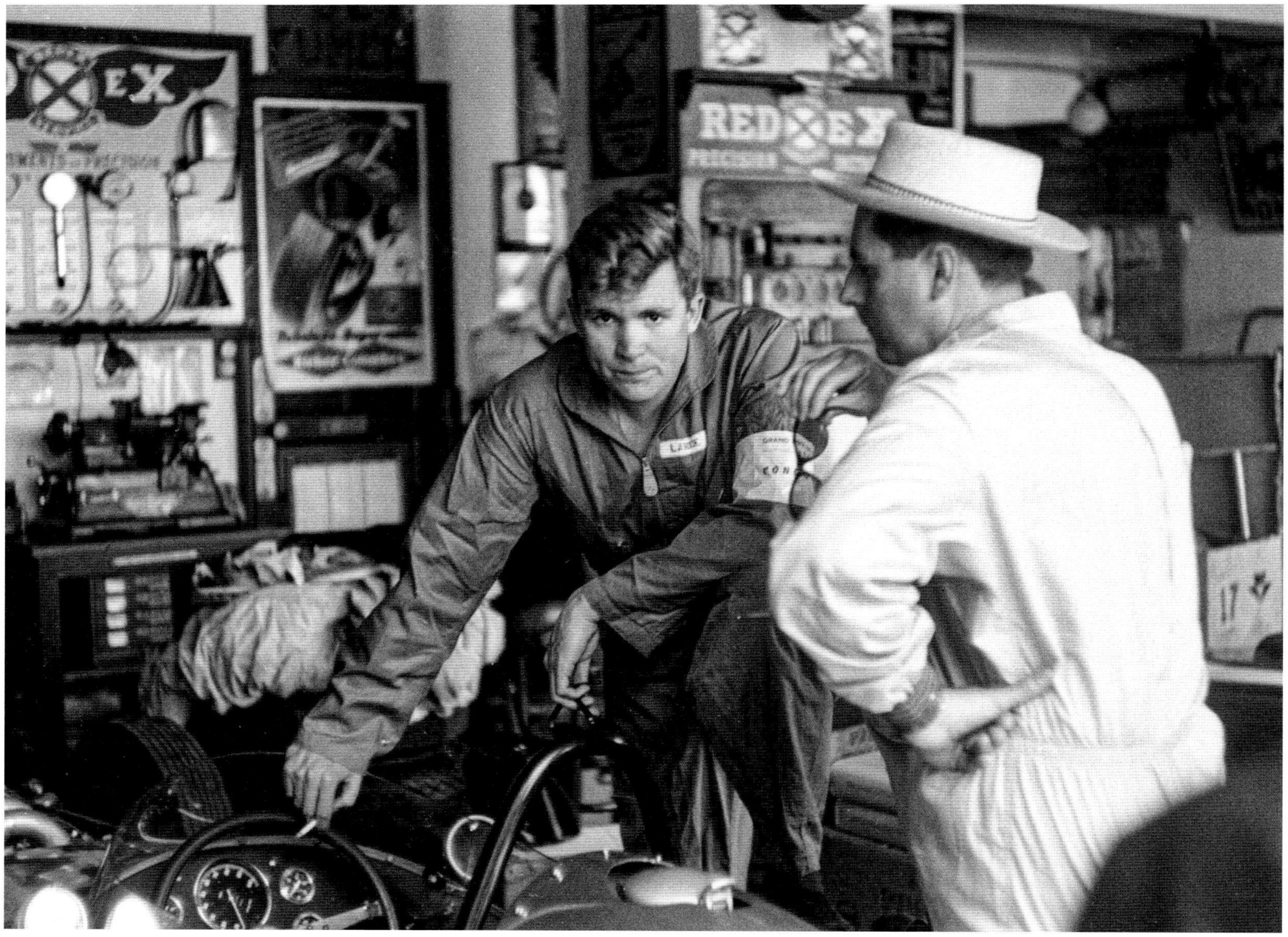

Ein neues Gesicht und ein neuer Wagen in der Formel 1: Lance Reventlow (links), Sohn von Barbara Hutton, der Erbin der Warenhauskette Woolworth. Er entwickelt, finanziert und fährt den Scarab. Mit elegantem Design, mit seinem Frontmotor aber technisch schon veraltet, kommt er mindestens eine Saison zu spät. In einer der Hinterhofgaragen, die in Monte Carlo für die Teams zur Verfügung stehen, unterhält sich Reventlow hier mit Jack Brabham.

A new face and a new car in Formula 1: Lance Reventlow (left), the son of Barbara Hutton, heiress to the Woolworth department store chain. He developed, financed and drove the Scarab, which was beautifully built but with its front engine technically already outdated and thus at least one season too late. Here Reventlow chats with Jack Brabham in one of the backyard garages available to teams in Monte Carlo.

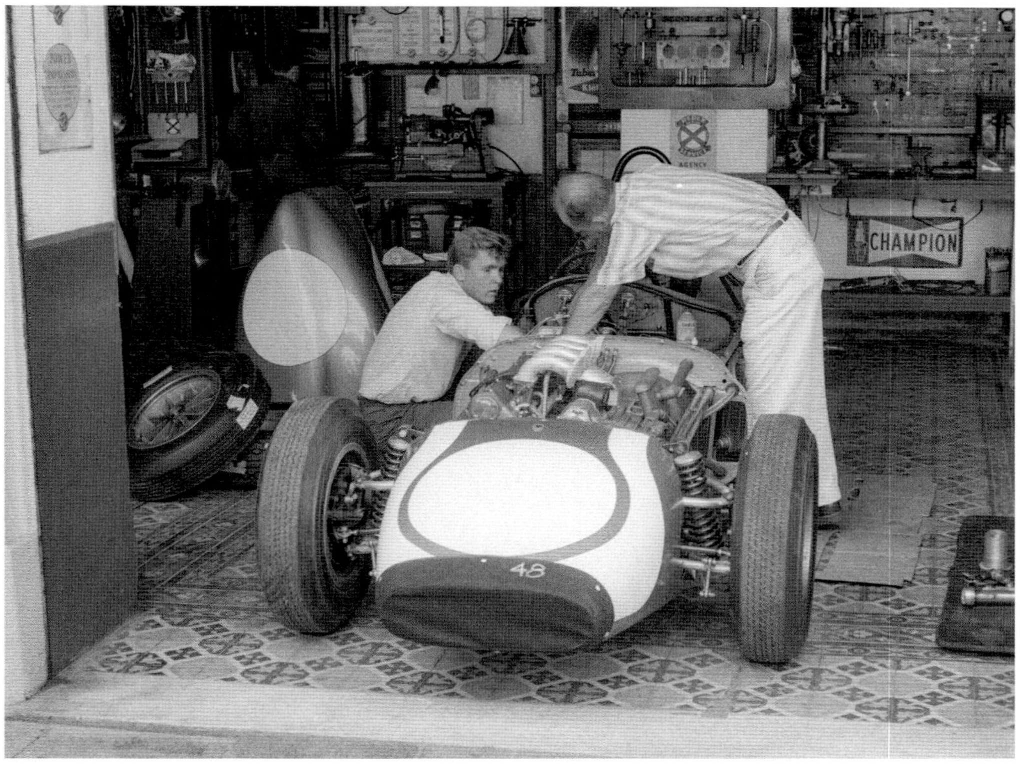

Lance Reventlow und Chefmechaniker
Chuck Daigh arbeiten am Scarab.

*Lance Reventlow and chief mechanic
Chuck Daigh at work on the Scarab.*

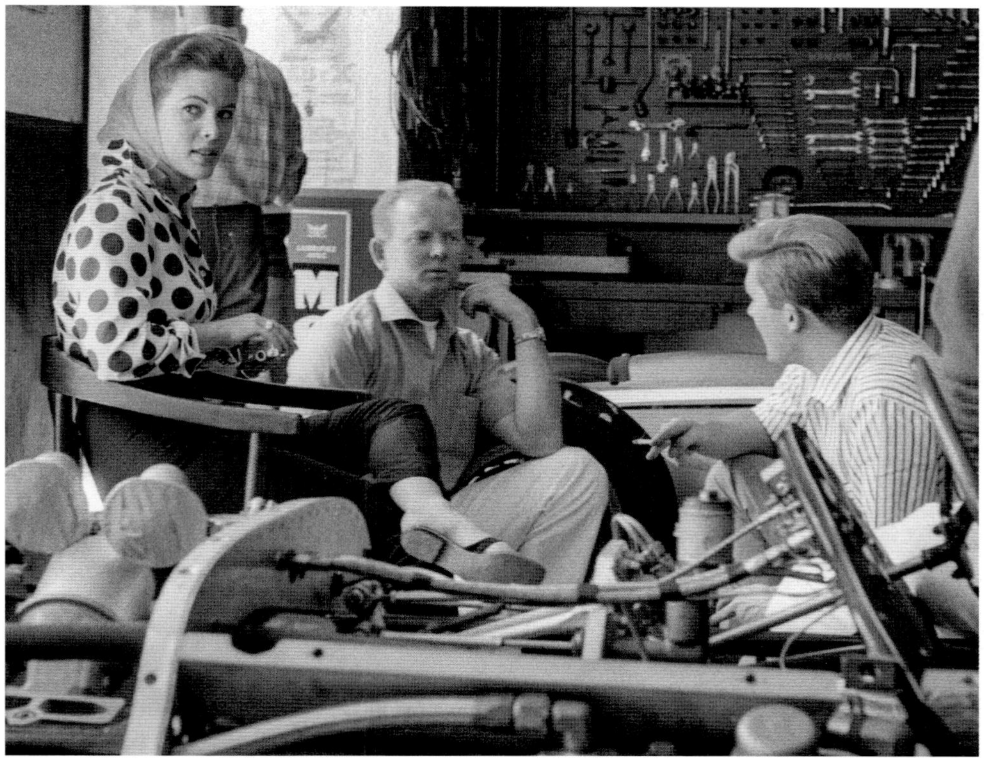

Jill St. John, Schauspielerin und erstes amerikanisches Bond-Girl,
mit Chuck Daigh (Mitte) und ihrem Mann Lance Reventlow (rechts).

*Lance Reventlow and his wife, actress Jill St. John
(the first American Bond girl) and Chuck Daigh.*

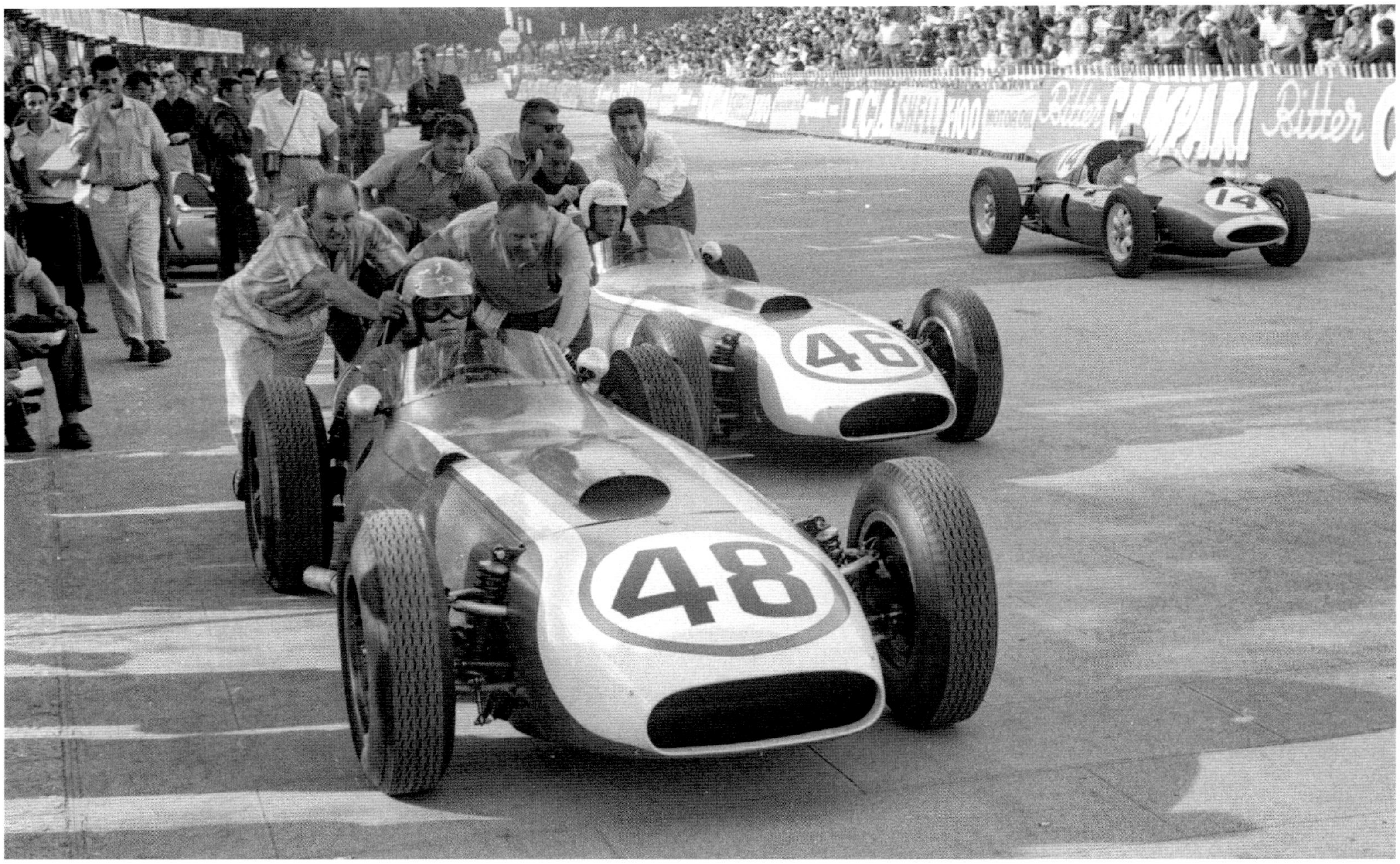

Die mit Spannung erwarteten Scarab-Fahrzeuge erscheinen zum ersten Mal auf einer Rennstrecke in Europa. Lance Reventlow, N° 48, und Chuck Daigh, N° 46, bereiten sich auf Proberunden vor. Reventlow trägt bereits einen in Europa noch ungewohnten Bell-500-Helm, der auch die Ohren bedeckt. Die Scarabs waren außerdem mit Sicherheitsgurten ausgerüstet, die in der Formel 1 erst ab 1972 obligatorisch sind.

The much anticipated Scarab cars appear for the first time on a track in Europe. Lance Reventlow, N° 48, and Chuck Daigh, N° 46, prepare for trial laps. Reventlow wears an unfamiliar Bell 500 helmet that also covers the ears. The Scarabs were already fitted with seat belts, which did not become compulsory in Formula 1 before 1972.

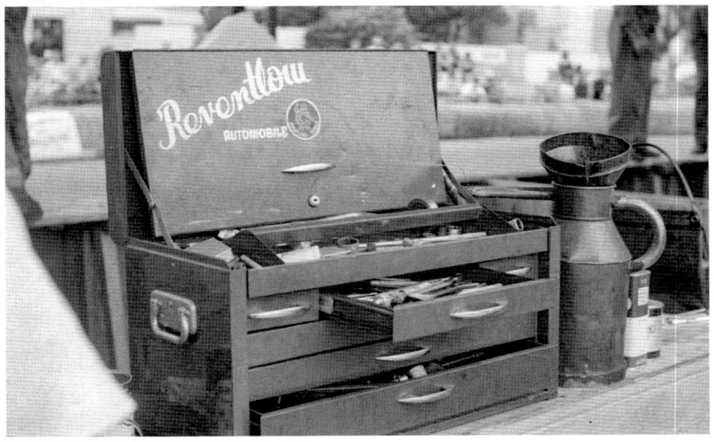

Die etwas chaotische Werkzeugkiste
des Scarab-Teams

*The somewhat chaotic toolbox
of the Scarab team*

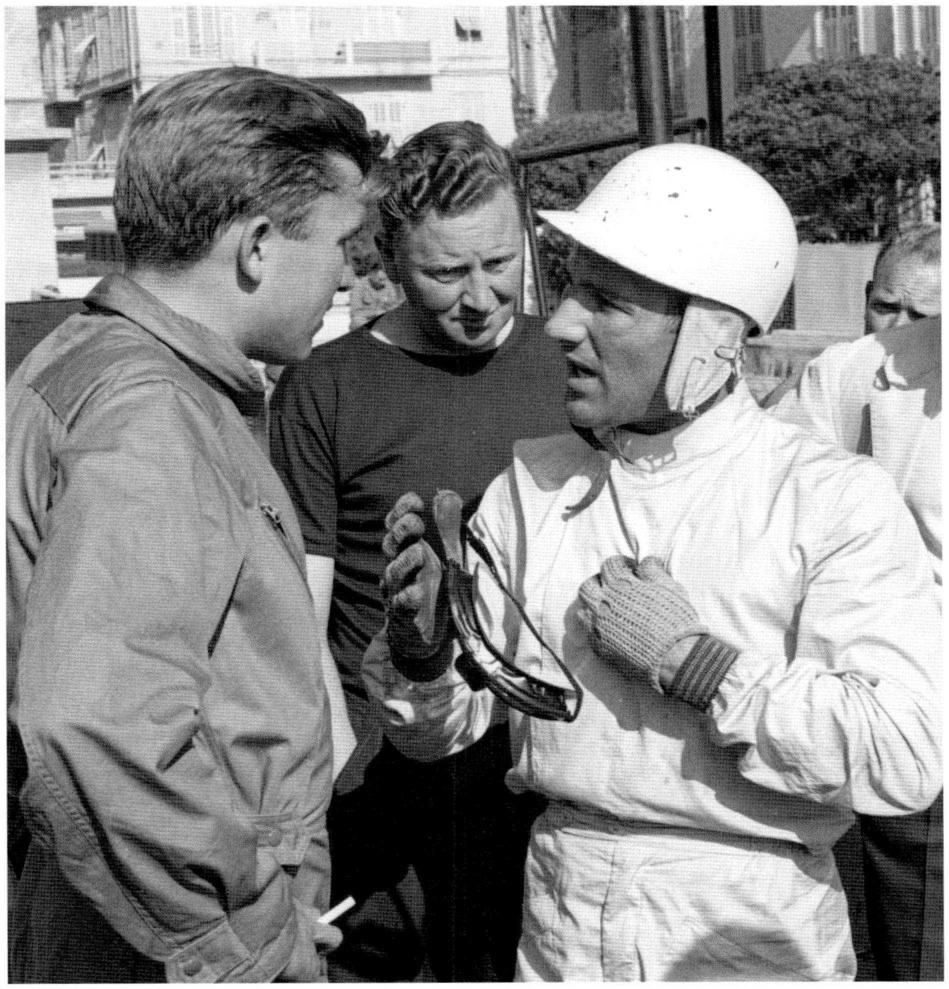

Die Scarabs waren enttäuschend langsam – zu groß, zu schwer und mit Frontmotor. Um herauszufinden, ob es am Fahrer oder am Auto lag, bat Reventlow (links) Stirling Moss um eine Testfahrt. Er fuhr eine bessere Zeit, aber es hätte nicht für die Qualifikation gereicht: Moss blieb neun Sekunden hinter seiner eigenen Lotus-Pole-Zeit.

The Scarabs were disappointingly slow – too big, too heavy and front-engined. To find out if it was the driver or the car, Reventlow (left) asked Stirling Moss to take a test drive. He set a better time, but it still would not have been enough to qualify: 9 seconds slower than his own Lotus pole time.

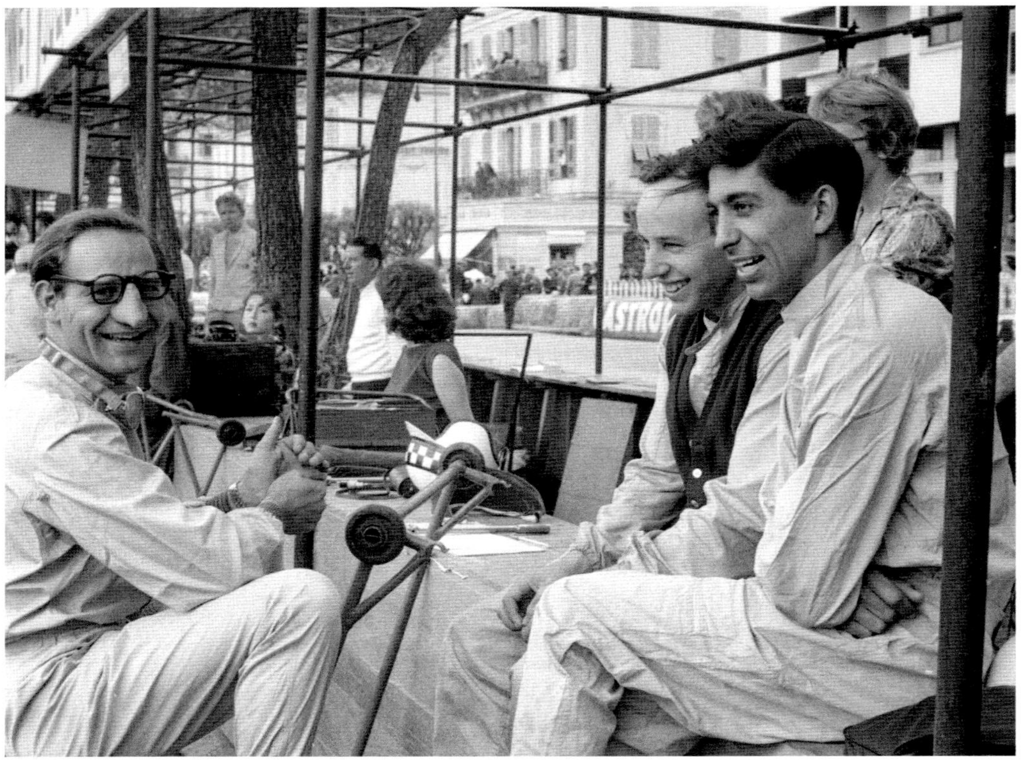

Der Spaßvogel Innes Ireland amüsiert mit falscher Nase und Brille seine Fahrerkollegen John Surtees (M.) und Alan Stacey (r.). Stacey stirbt einen Monat später in Spa-Francorchamps.

The joker in the pack, Innes Ireland, here wearing a false nose and glasses, amuses fellow drivers John Surtees and Alan Stacey. Stacey died a month later at Spa-Francorchamps.

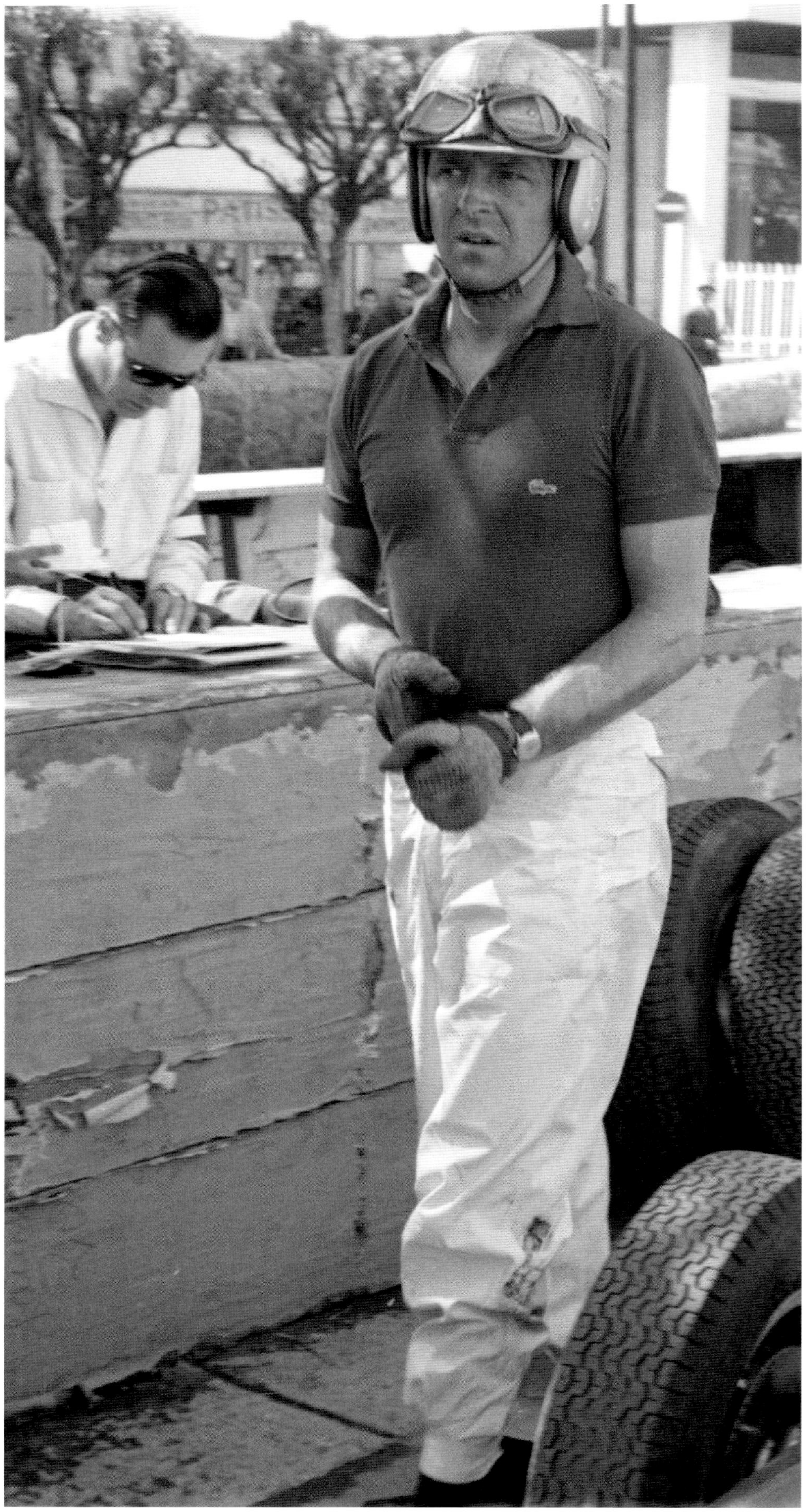

Wolfgang Graf Berghe von Trips. 1961 kollidiert er in Monza mit Jim Clark, wird aus dem Wagen geworfen und stirbt. Sein Ferrari fliegt über die Abschrankung und tötet 14 Zuschauer.

Wolfgang Graf Berghe von Trips. In Monza in 1961 he collided with Jim Clark, was thrown out of the car and died. His Ferrari few over the barrier and killed 14 spectators.

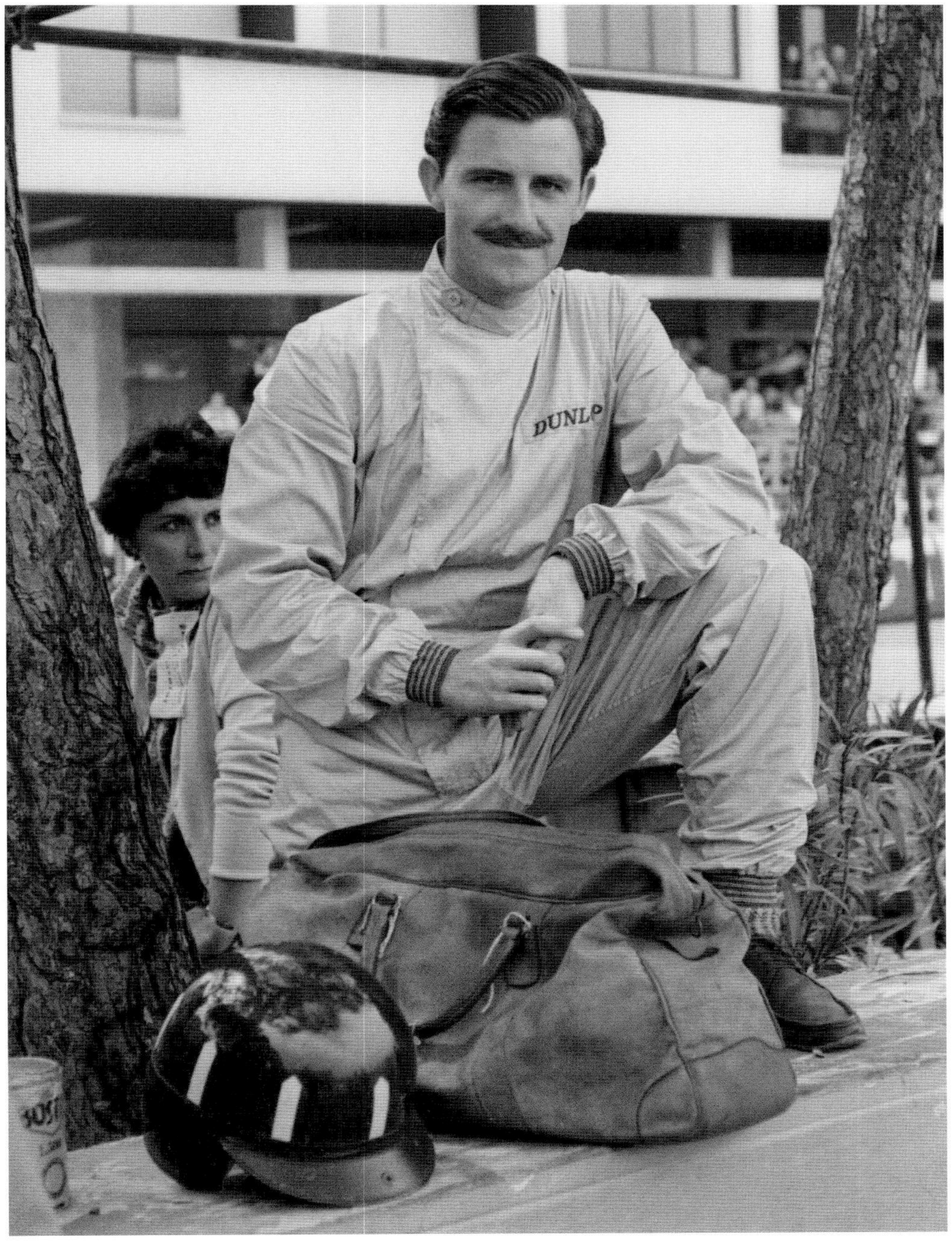

Graham Hill und seine Frau Bette Hill, Großer Preis von Monaco 1960. Hill schaffte den Aufstieg vom Mechaniker zum Fahrer.

Graham Hill and his wife Bette Hill, Monaco Grand Prix 1960. Hill managed the move from mechanic to driver.

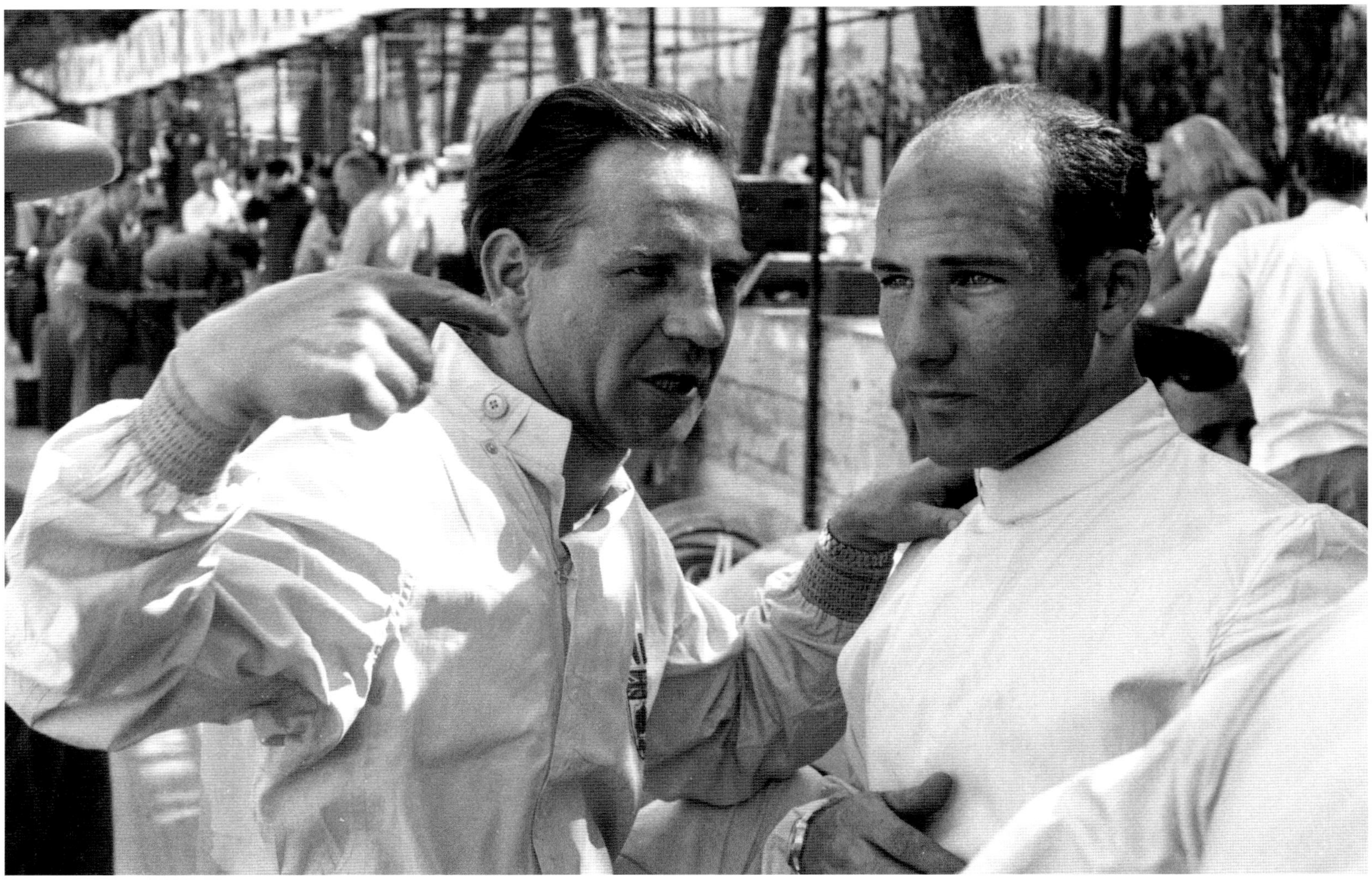

Innes Ireland und
Stirling Moss.

*Innes Ireland and
Stirling Moss.*

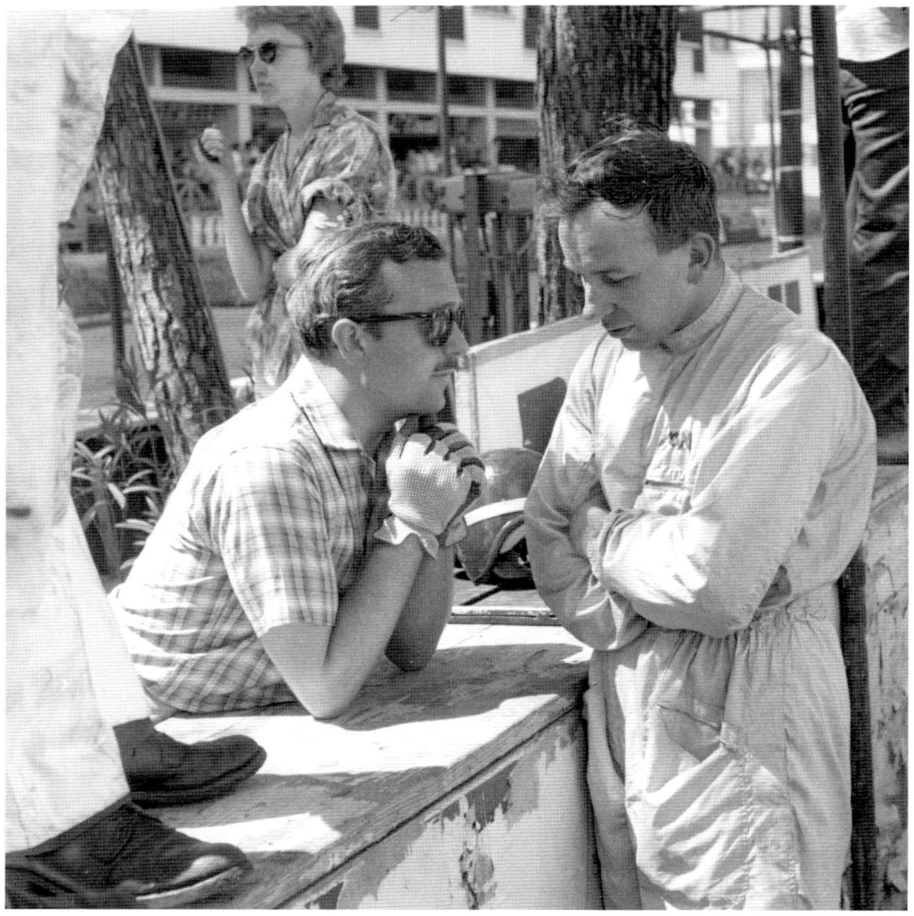

Colin Chapman, Ingenieur und Gründer
von Lotus Cars, und John Surtees.

*Colin Chapman, engineer and founder
of Lotus Cars, and John Surtees.*

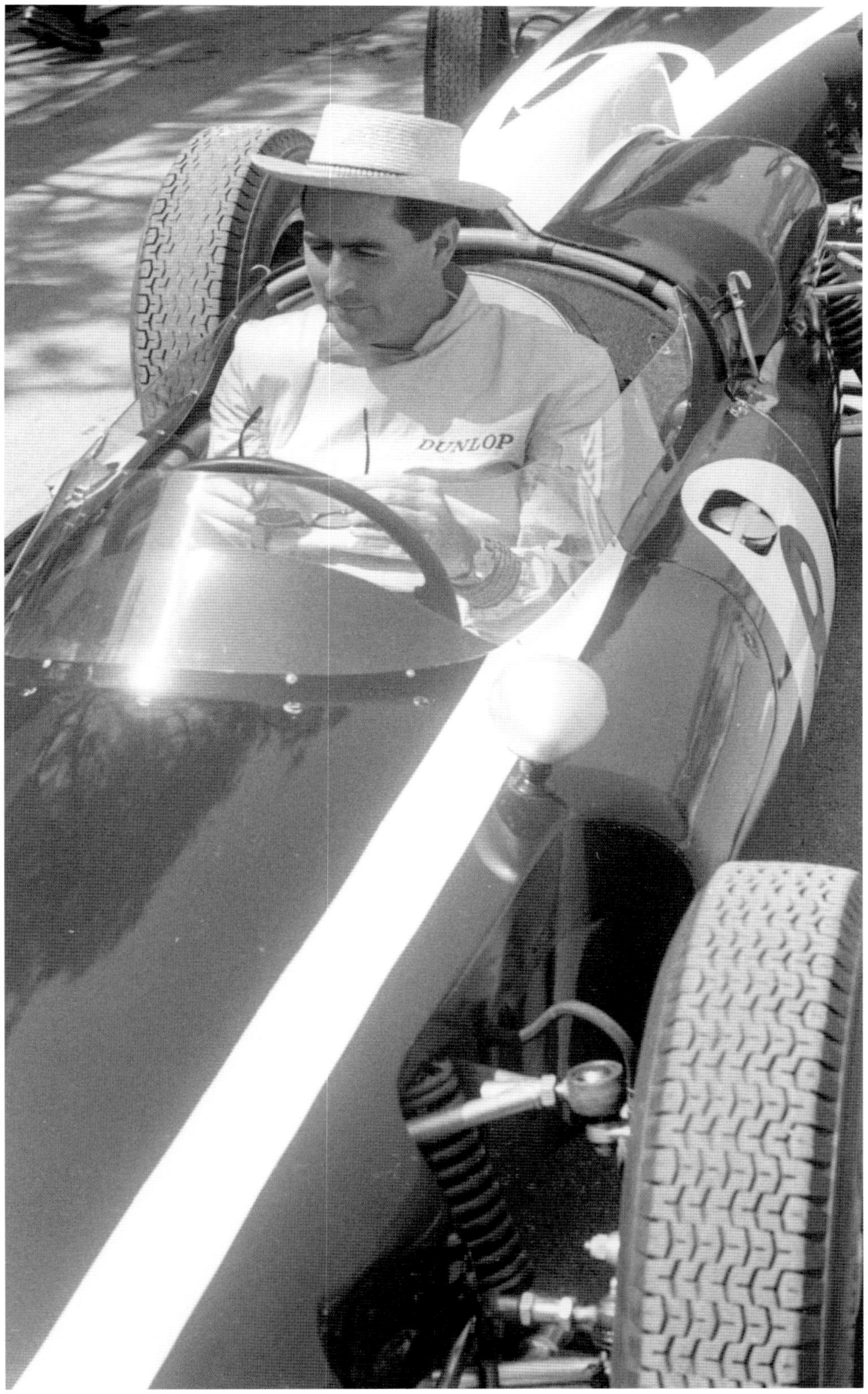

Jack Brabham, Cooper T53 N° 8,
dahinter Bruce McLarens Cooper T53 N° 10.

Jack Brabham, Cooper T53 N° 8,
behind him Bruce McLaren's Cooper T53 N° 10.

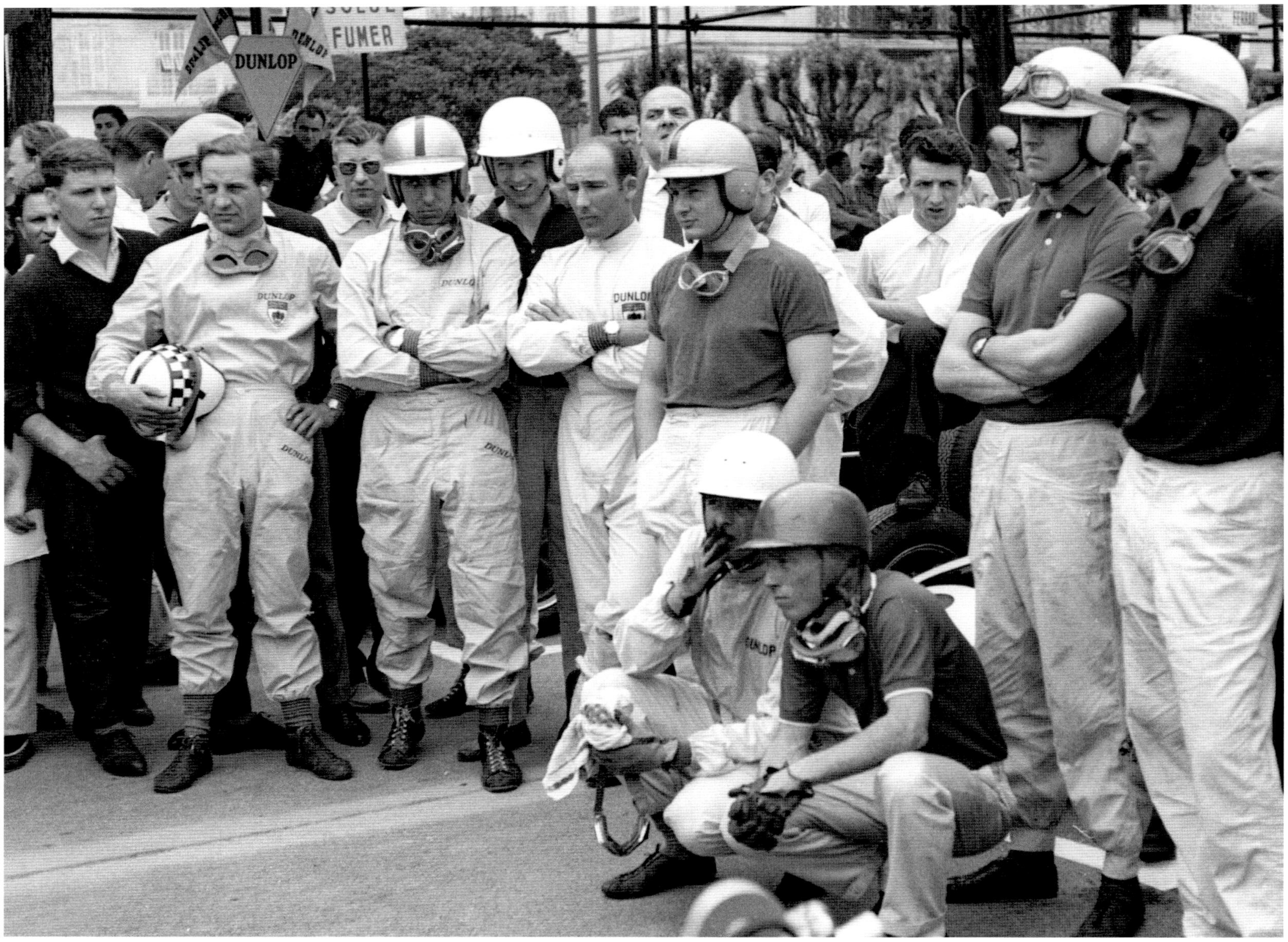

Fahrerbesprechung. Von links: Innes Ireland, Alan Stacey, Tony Brooks, Stirling Moss, Bruce McLaren, dahinter versteckt Chris Bristow, Wolfgang von Trips, Joakim Bonnier, kniend Phil Hill und Richie Ginther.

Drivers' briefing. From Left: Innes Ireland, Alan Stacey, Tony Brooks, Stirling Moss, Bruce McLaren, behind him hidden Chris Bristow, Wolfgang von Trips, Joakim Bonnier, squatting Phil Hill and Richie Ginther.

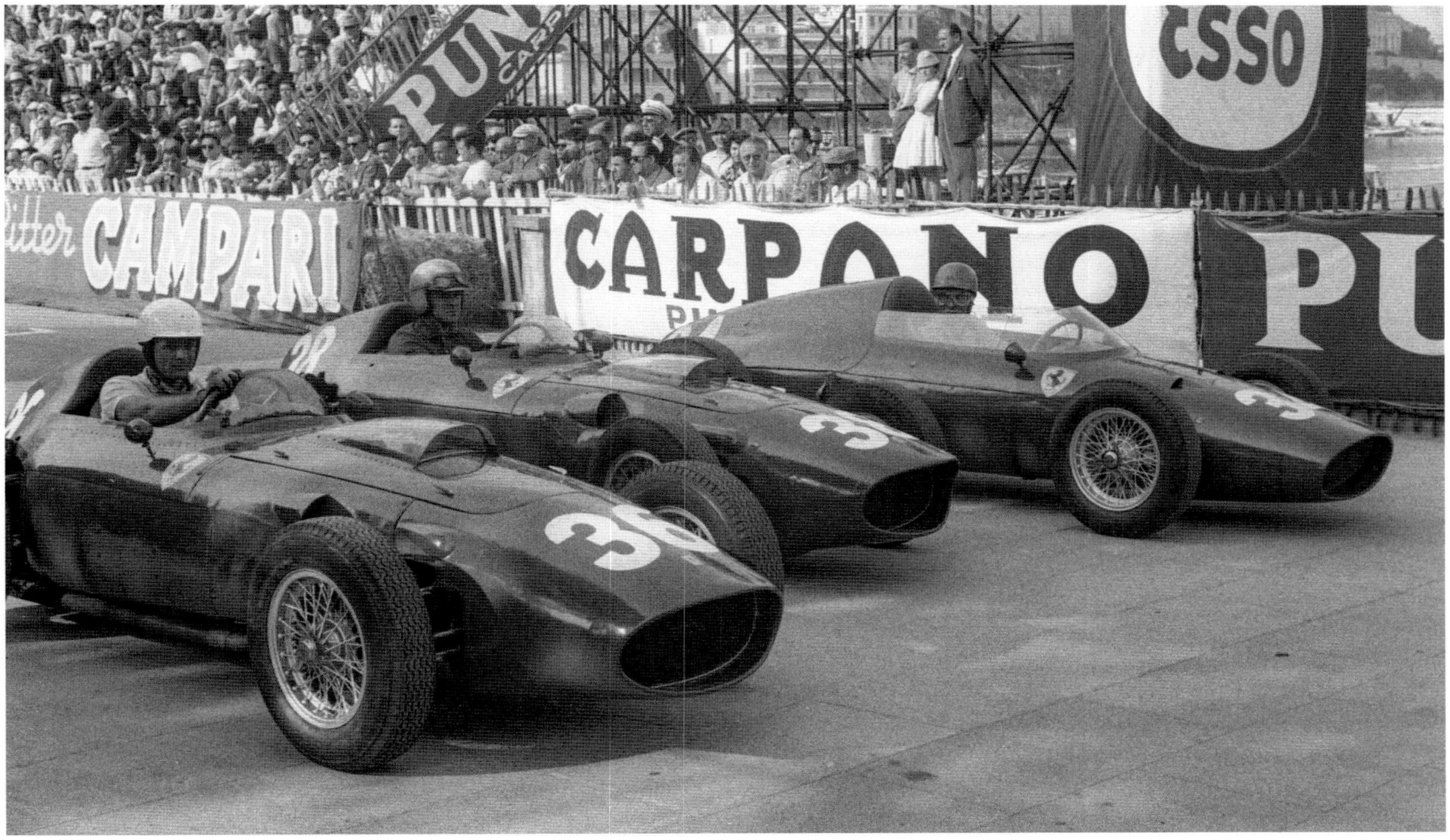

Phil Hill, Ferrari Dino 246 N° 36, Wolfgang von Trips, Ferrari Dino 246 N° 38, und Richie Ginther auf dem experimentellen „motore posteriore“ Ferrari 246/60/MP N° 34 mit Mittelmotor.

Phil Hill, Ferrari Dino 246 N° 36, Wolfgang von Trips, Ferrari Dino 246 N° 38, and Richie Ginther in the mid-engined "motore posteriore" experimental Ferrari 246/60/MP N° 34.

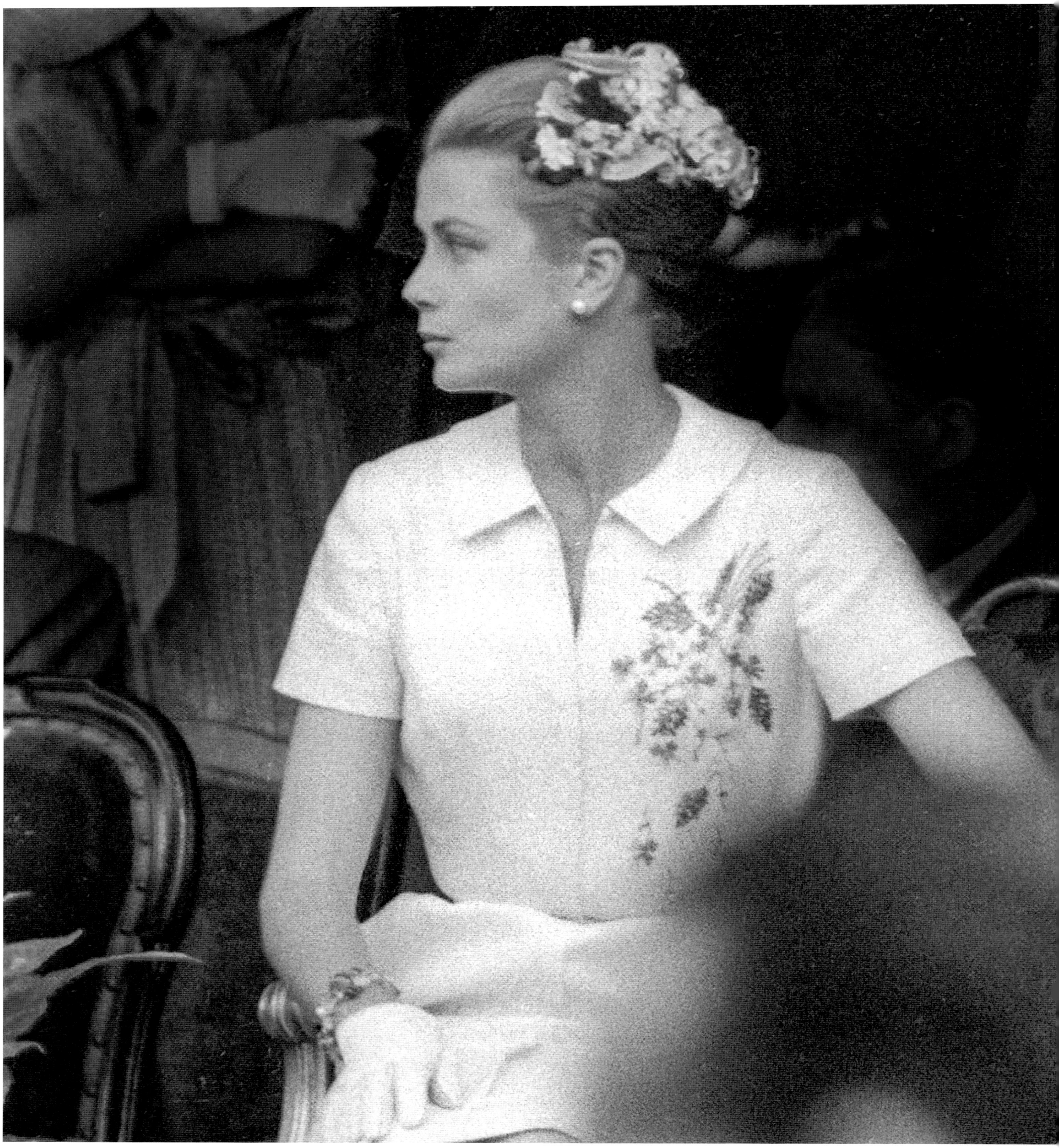

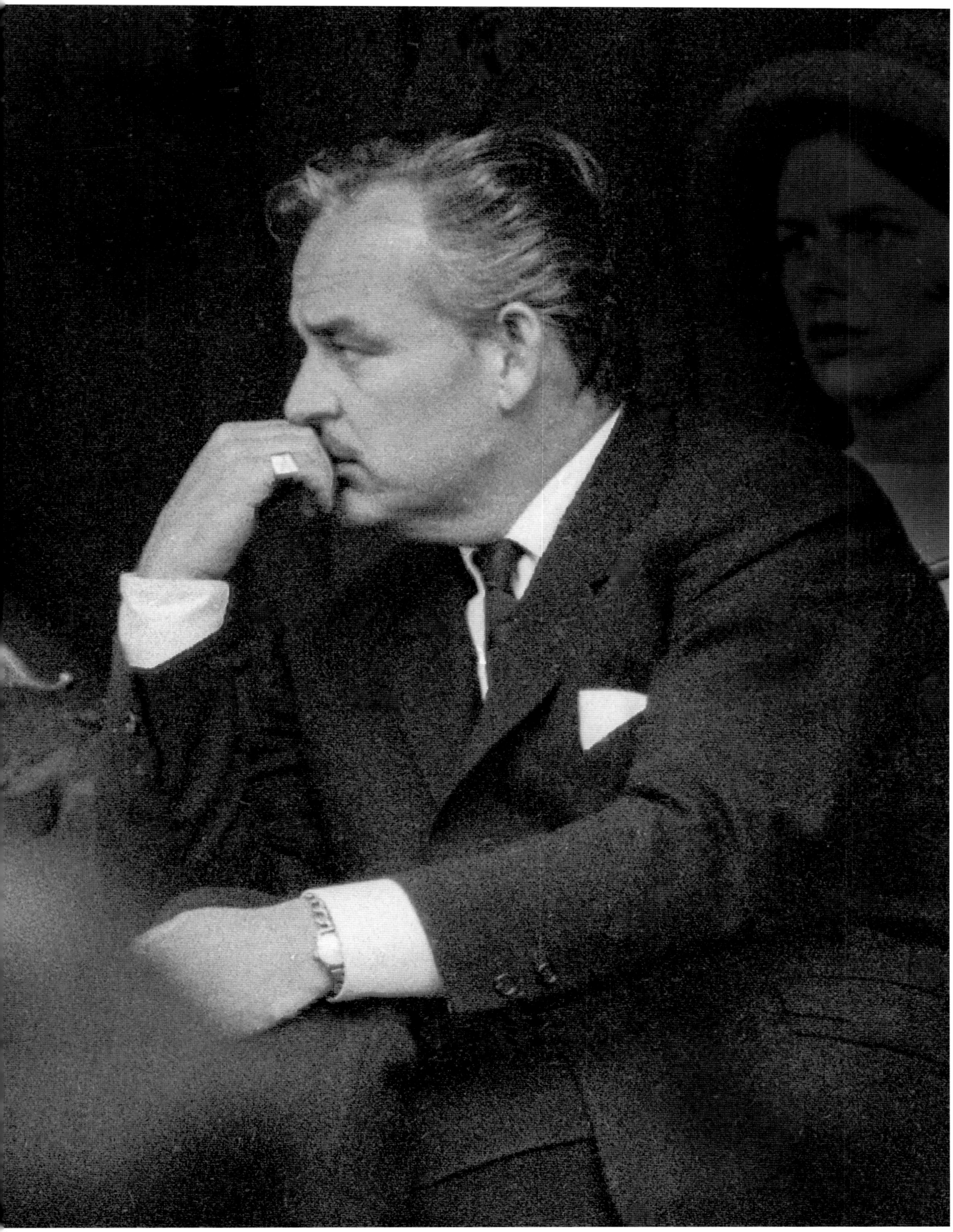

Fürstin Gracia und
Fürst Rainier in ihrer Loge.

*Princess Grace and Prince
Ranier in the Royal Box.*

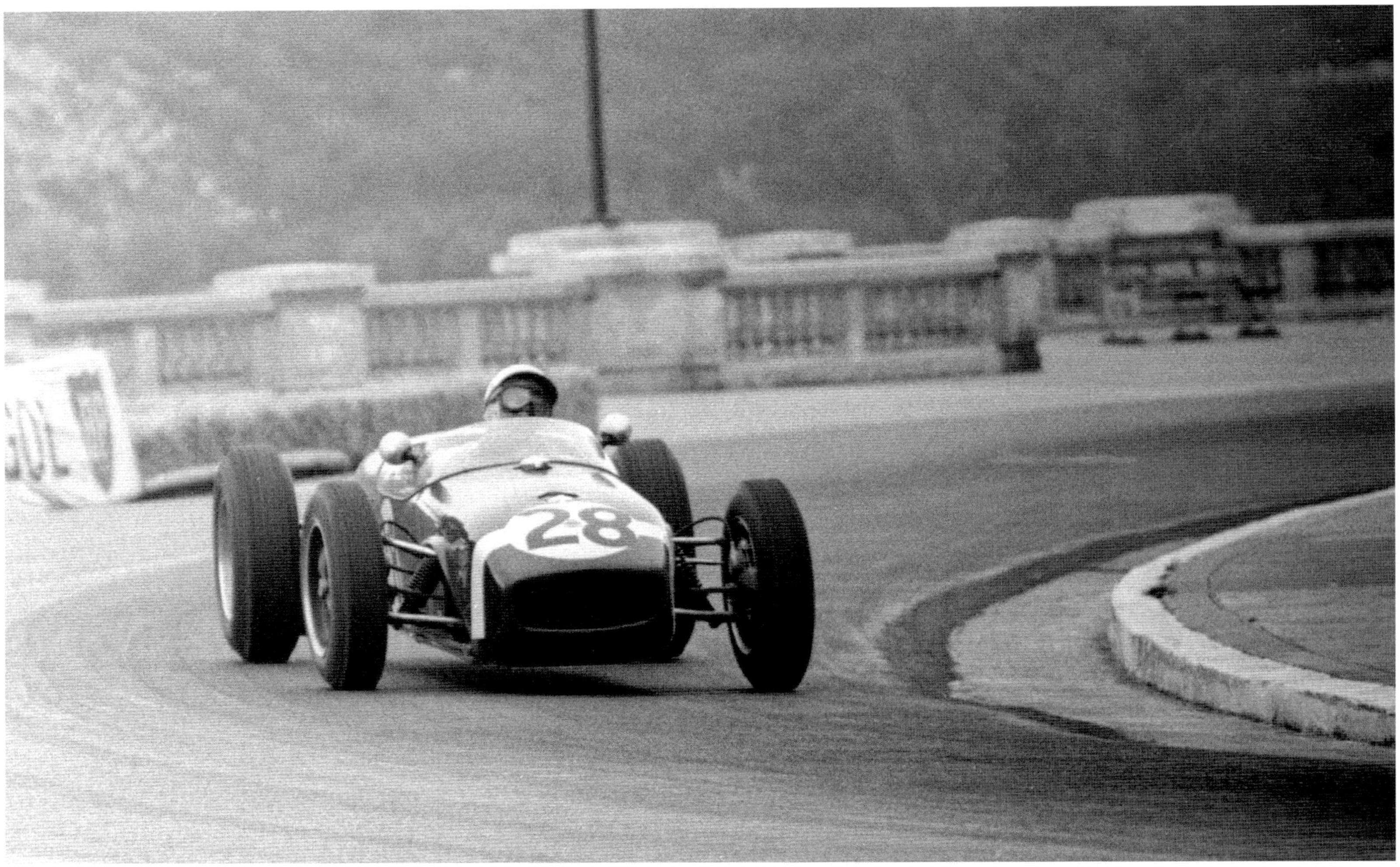

Stirling Moss, Lotus N° 28, bei Massenet.

Stirling Moss, Lotus N° 28 at Massenet.

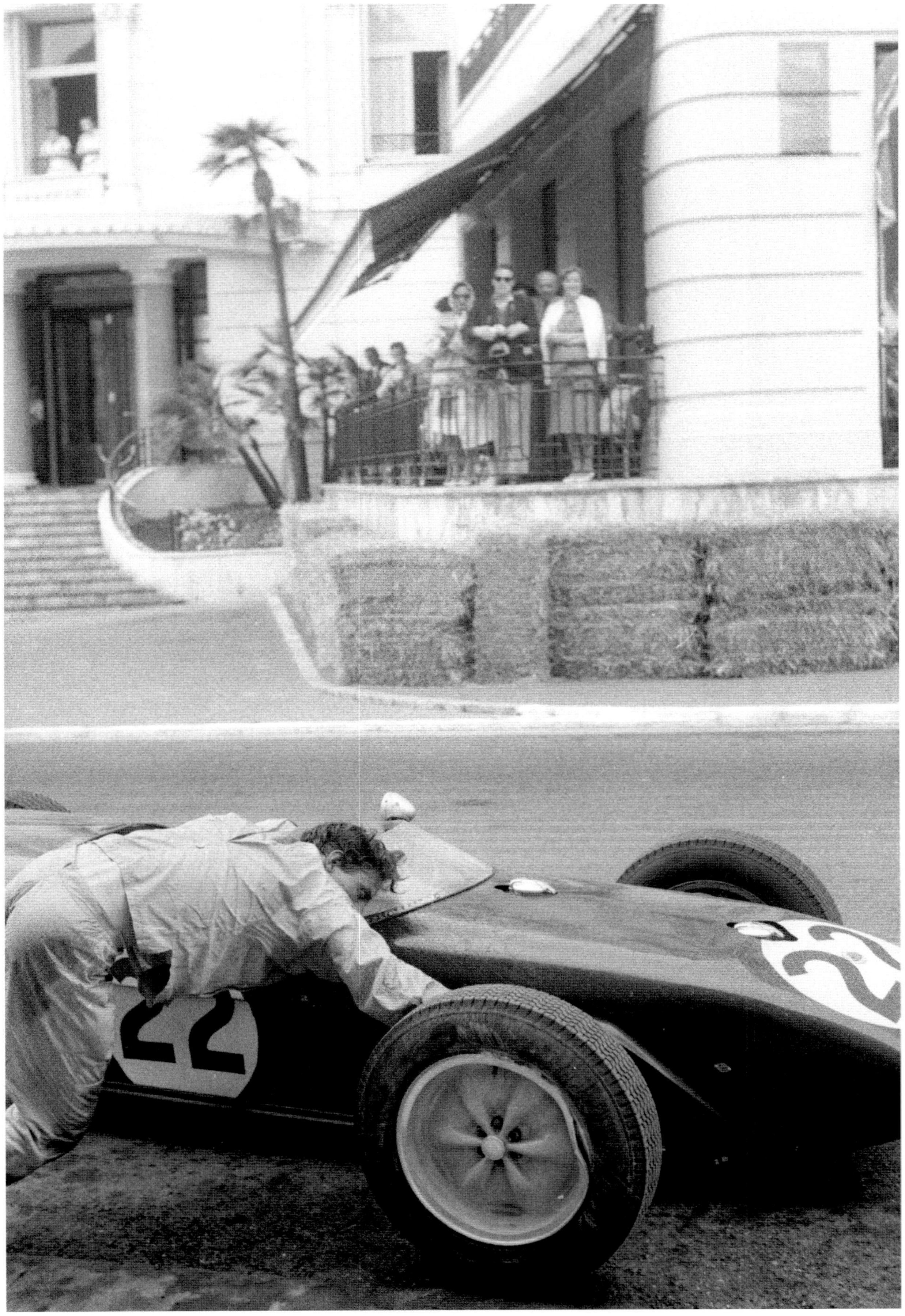

Innes Ireland schiebt seinen Lotus 18 N° 22 bergauf um die kurvenreiche Strecke, damit er das Rennen beenden kann.

Innes Ireland pushes his Lotus 18 N° 22 uphill around the twisting Monaco circuit so that he can finish the race.

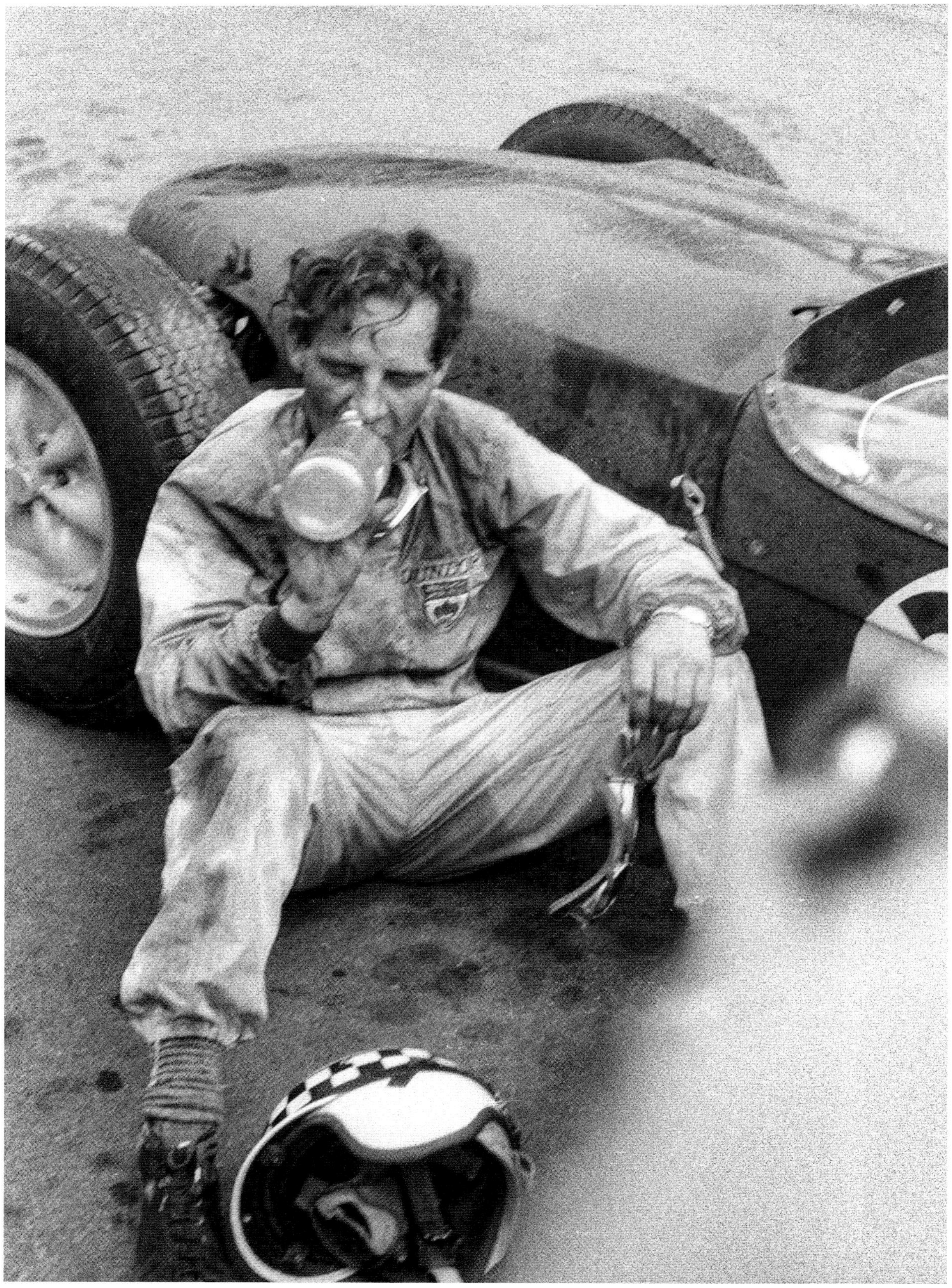

Zwischenhalt für Innes Ireland
bei Massenet.

*A short break for Innes Ireland
at Massenet.*

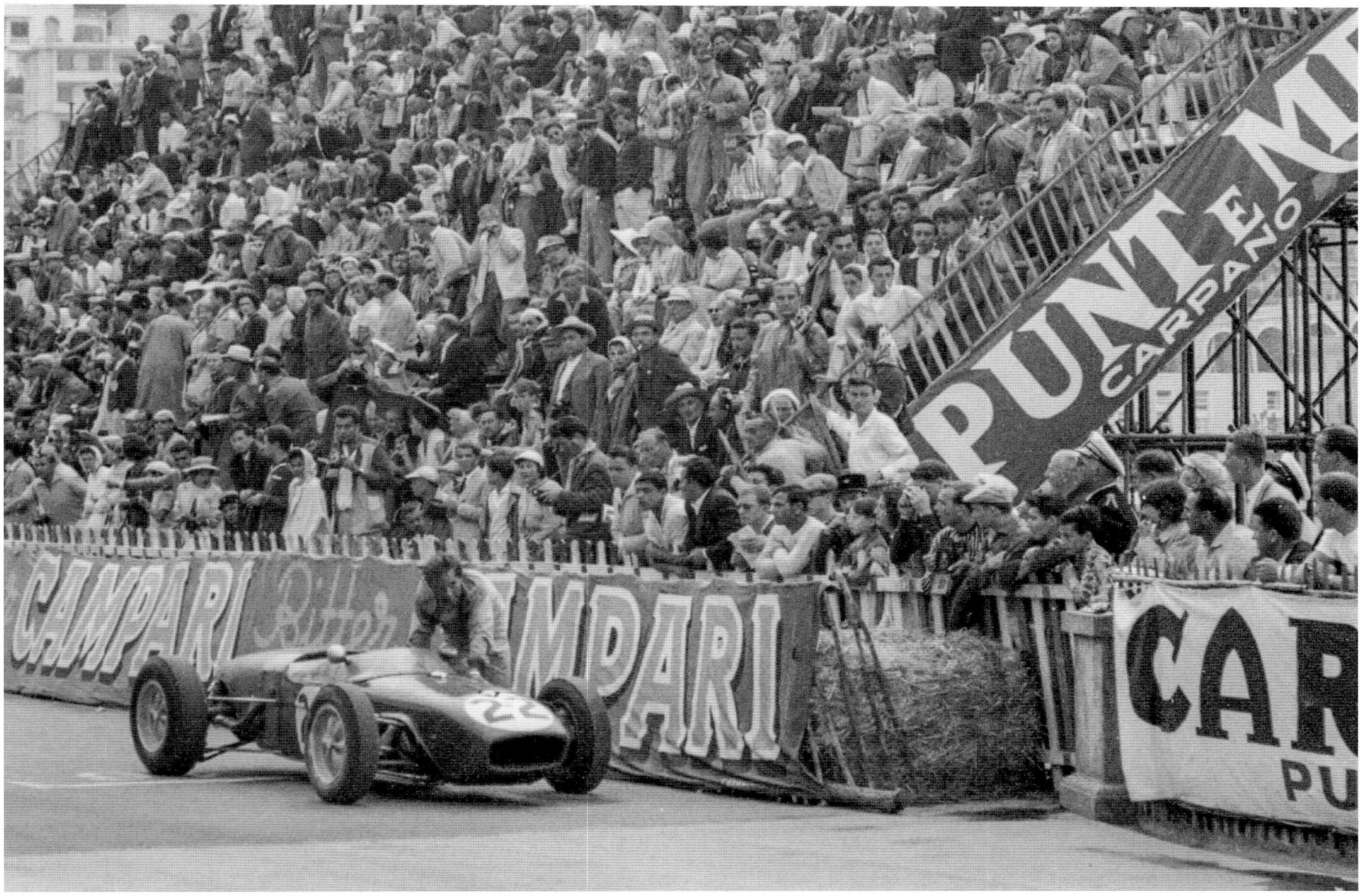

Vor der Haupttribüne die letzten Meter bis zur Ziellinie. Seine Anstrengung wird mit dem 9. Platz belohnt.

The final few metres to the finish line in front of the main grandstand. His effort is rewarded with 9th place.

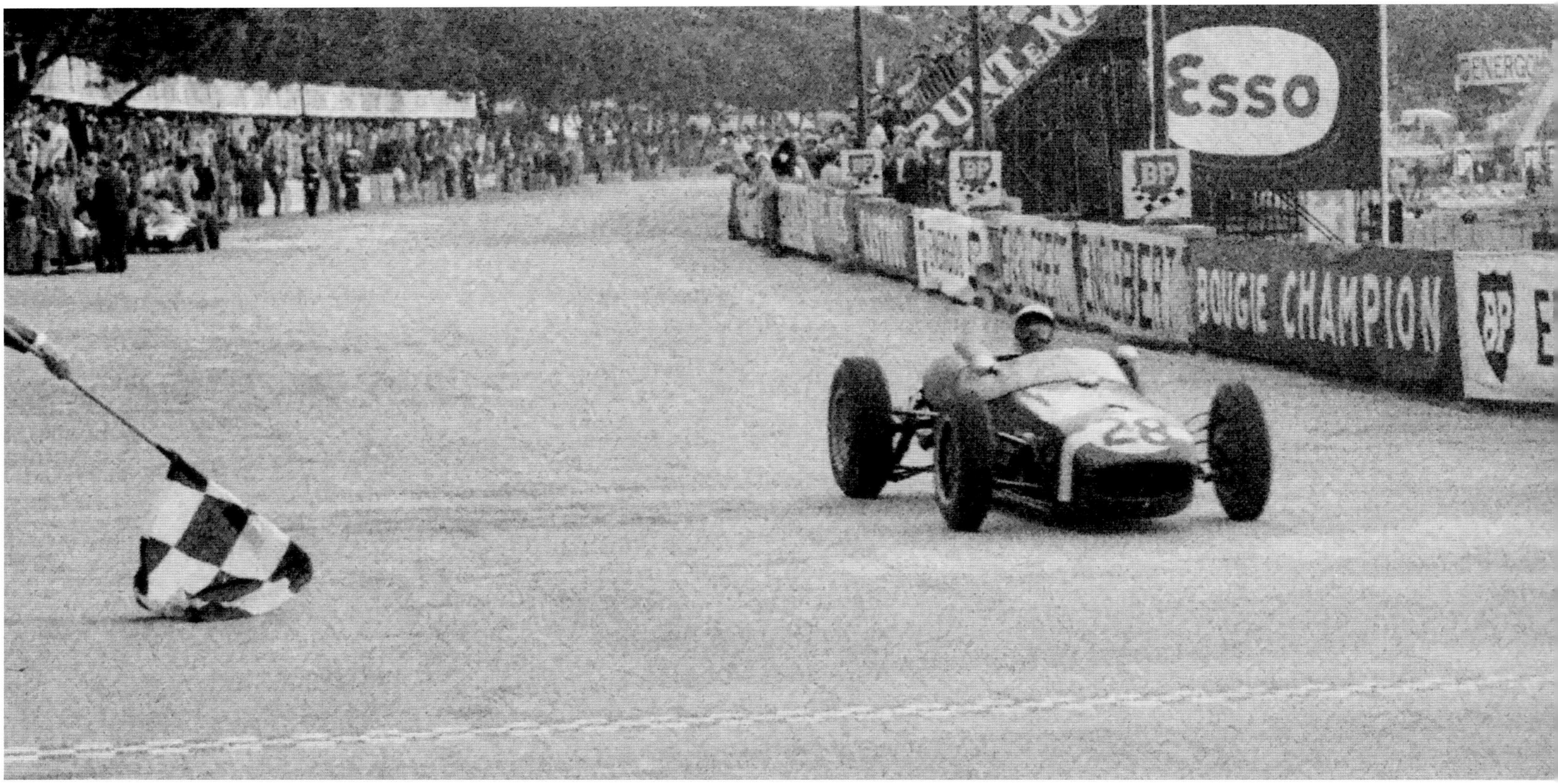
Esso
BOUGIE CHAMPION
BP

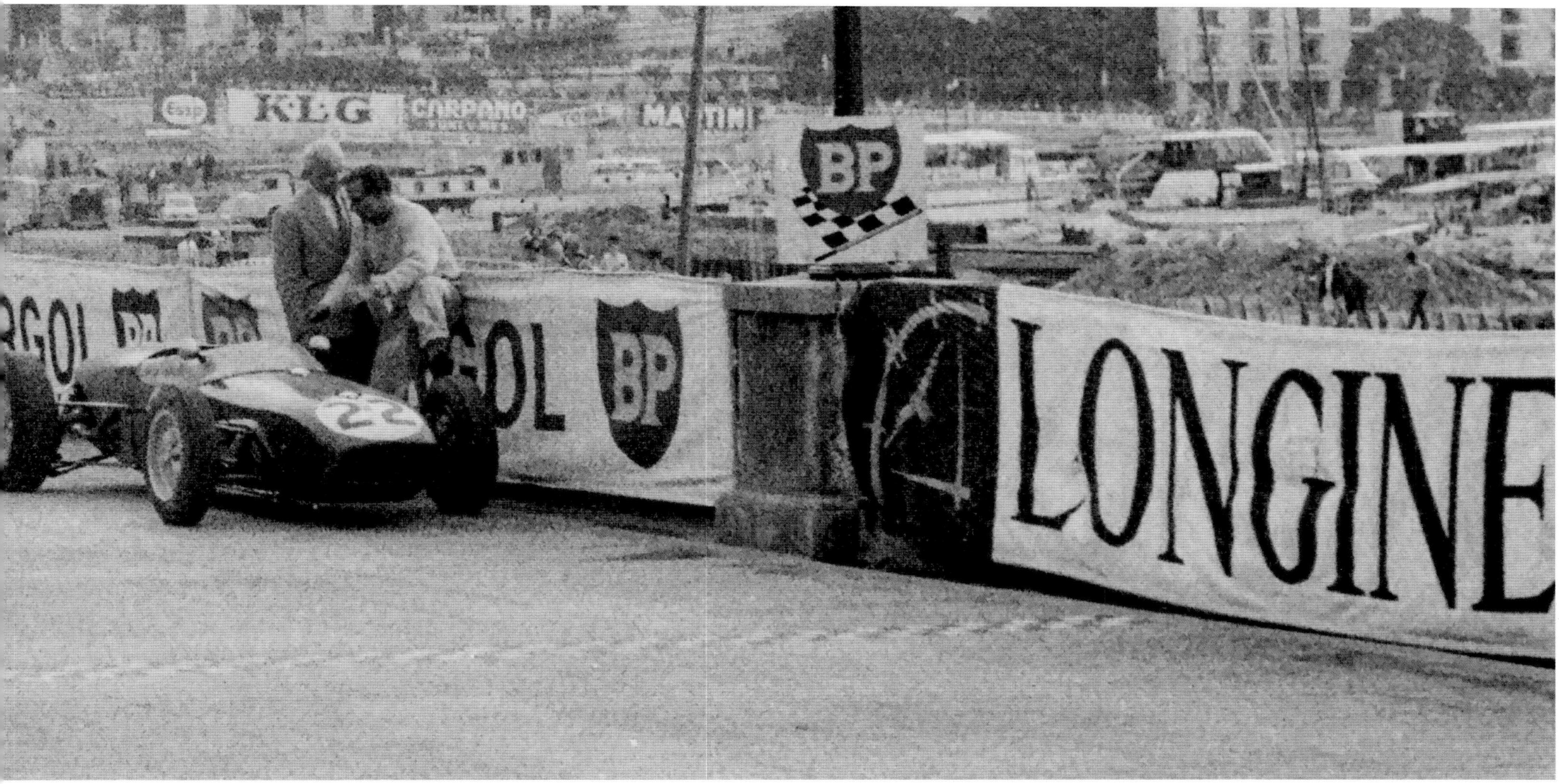

Der Sieger Stirling Moss fährt ins Ziel, vorbei am erschöpften Innes Ireland.

The winner Stirling Moss crosses the finish line, passing the exhausted Innes Ireland.

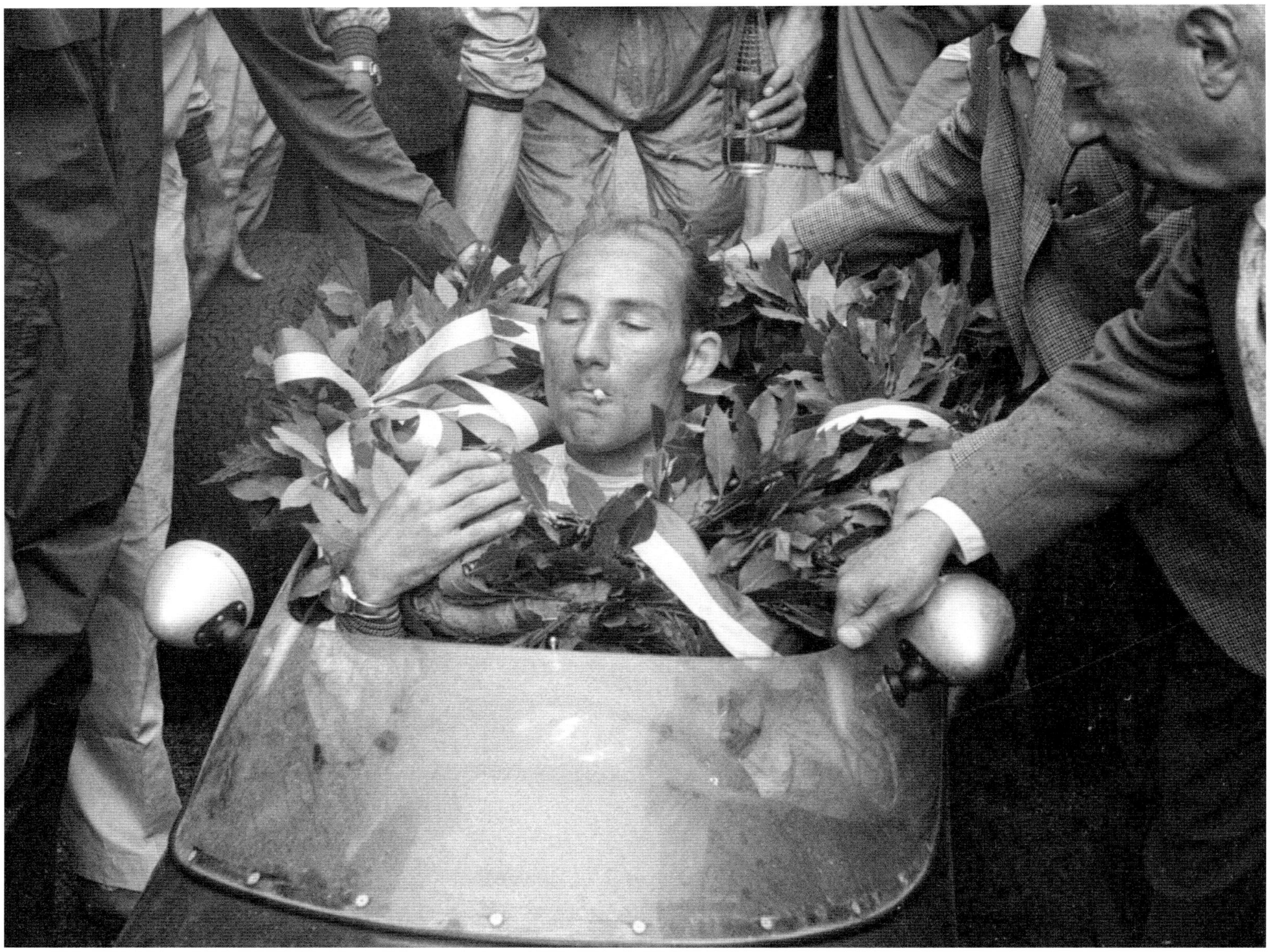

Die erste Zigarette
für den Sieger.

The first cigarette
for the winner.

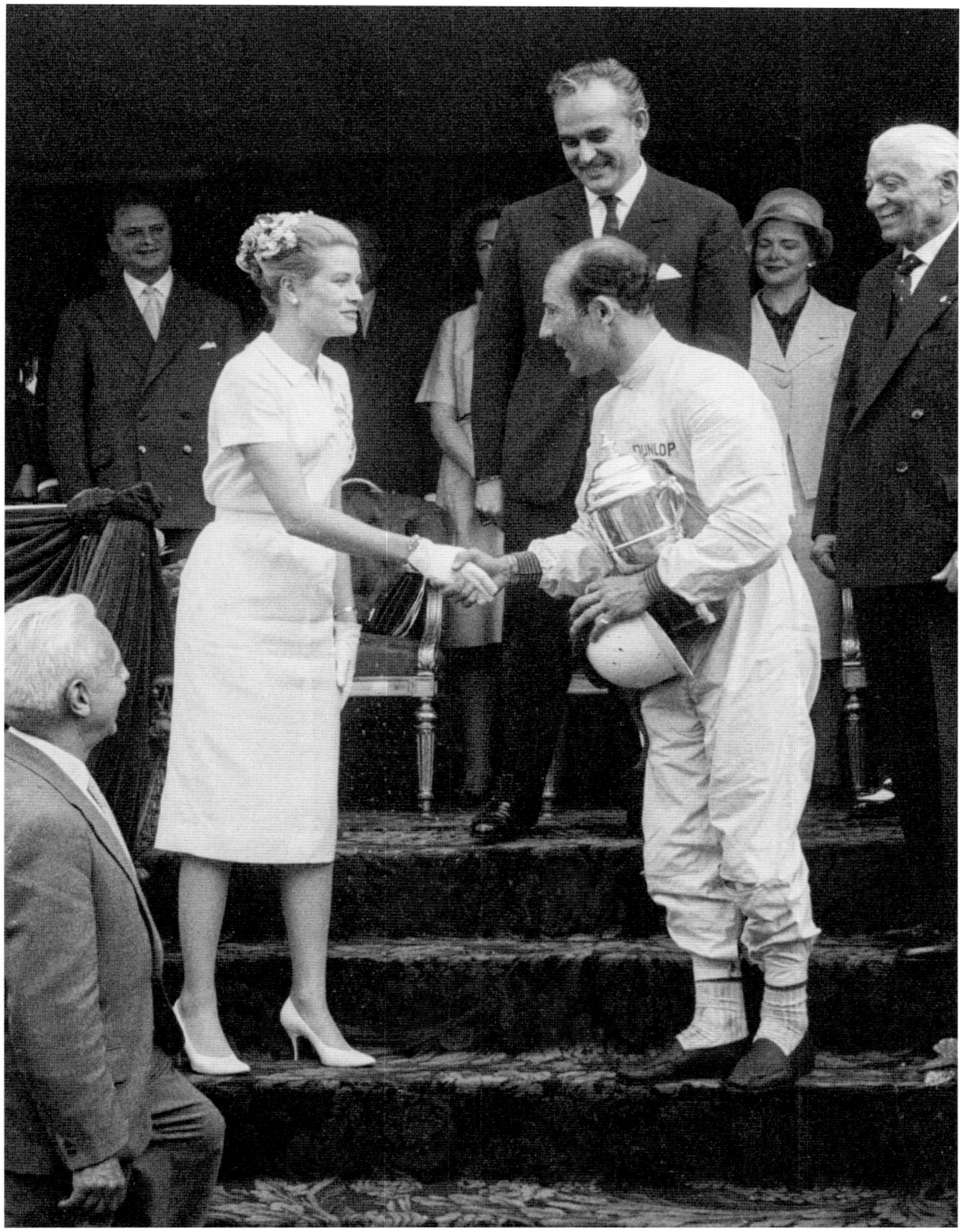

Fürstin Gracia gratuliert dem Sieger des Rennens, Stirling Moss, bei der Preisverleihung auf der Fürstentribüne.

Race winner Stirling Moss is congratulated by Princess Grace in the Royal Box.

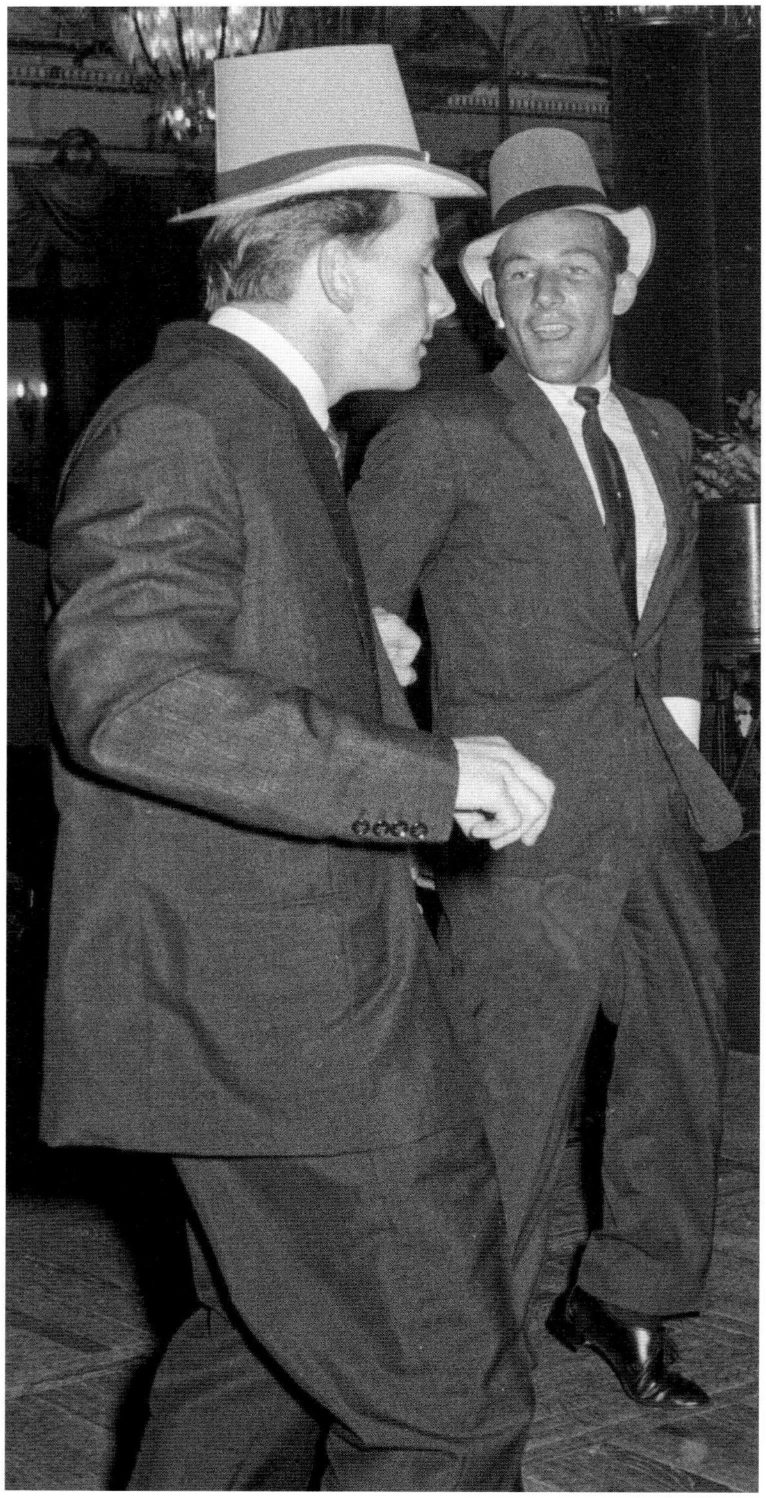

Ausgelassen bei der Grand-Prix-Gala: Stirling Moss und Chris Bristow. Bristow stirbt drei Wochen später bei einem Unfall beim Großen Preis von Belgien.

In exuberant mood at the Grand Prix Gala: Stirling Moss and Chris Bristow. Bristow died three weeks later in an accident at the Belgian Grand Prix.

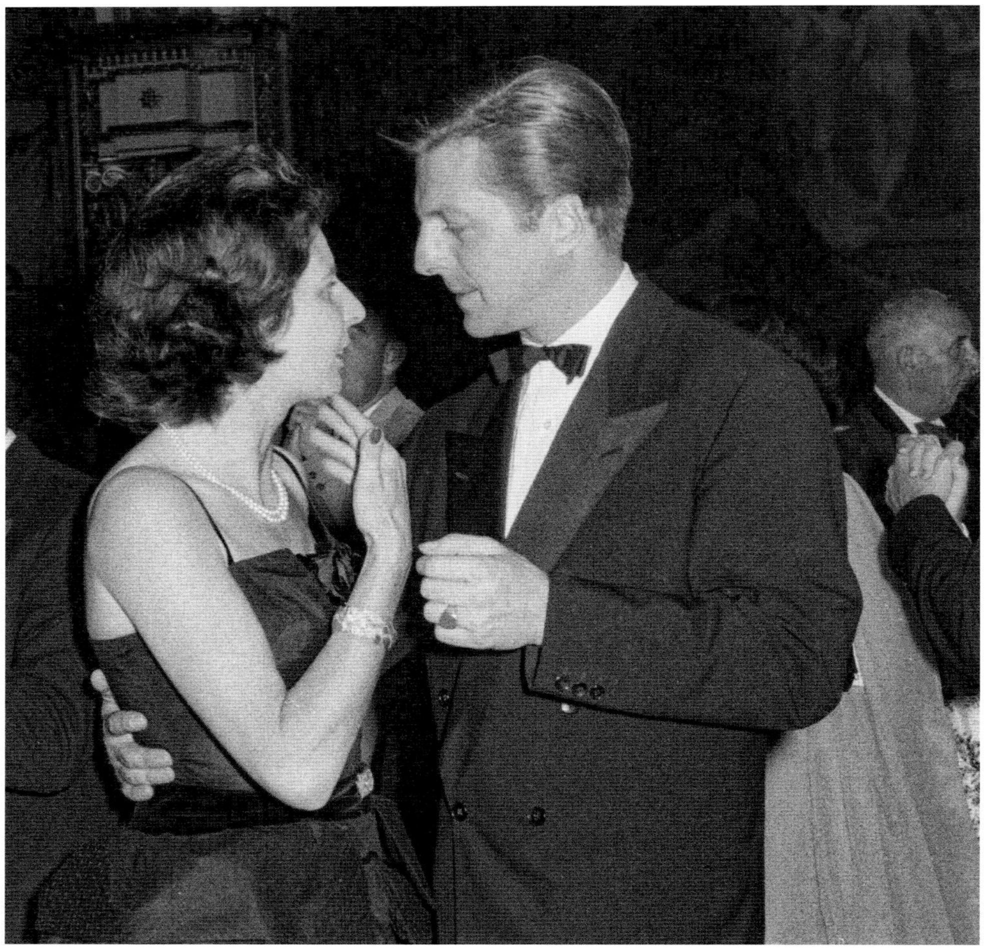

Elegant im Smoking: Wolfgang von Trips.

Black tie elegance: Wolfgang von Trips

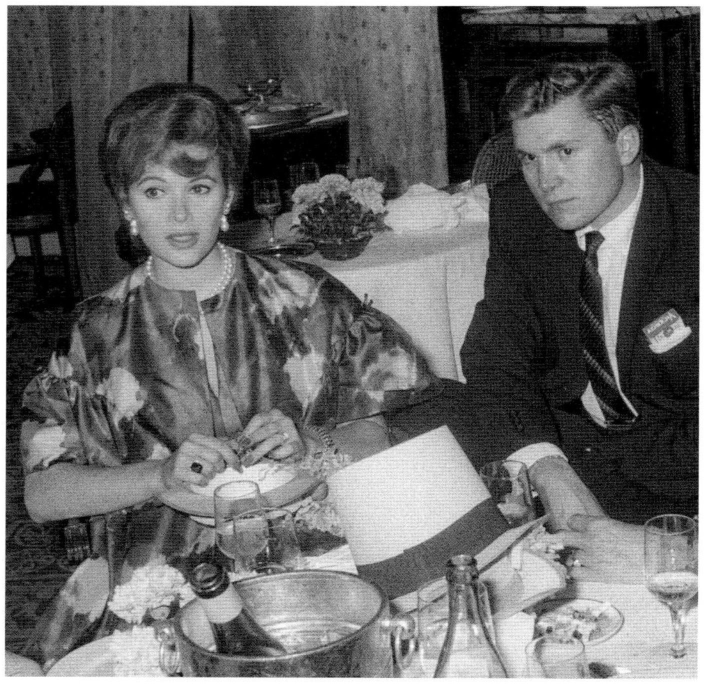

Weniger fröhlich: der erfolglose Lance Reventlow mit seiner Gattin Jill St. John.

In more serious mood: Lance Reventlow with his film star wife, Jill St. John.

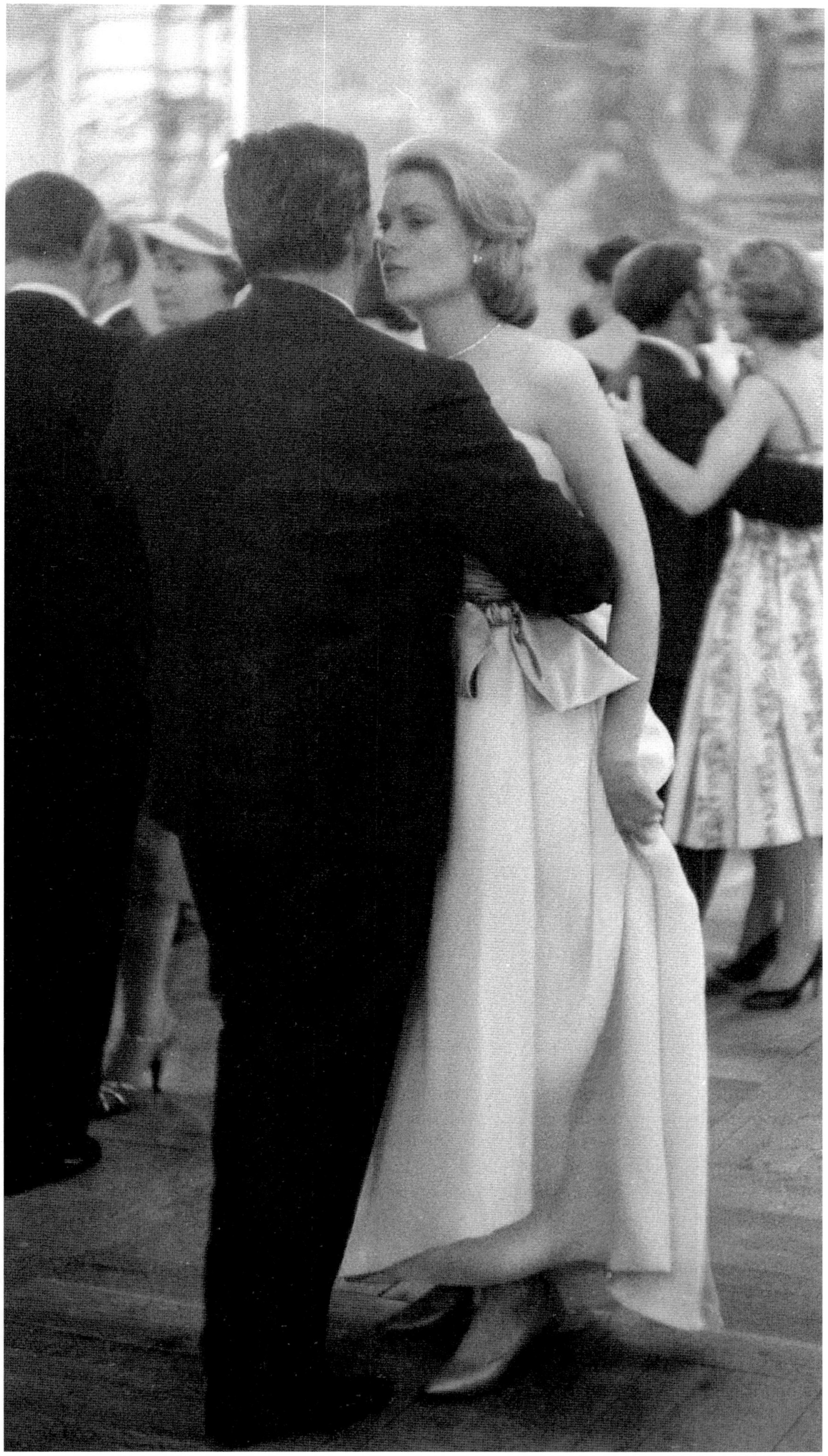

Fürstin Gracia und Fürst Rainier tanzen bei der Gala des Grand Prix einen „Slow“.

Princess Grace and Prince Rainier enjoy a slow dance together cheek to cheek at the Grand Prix Gala.

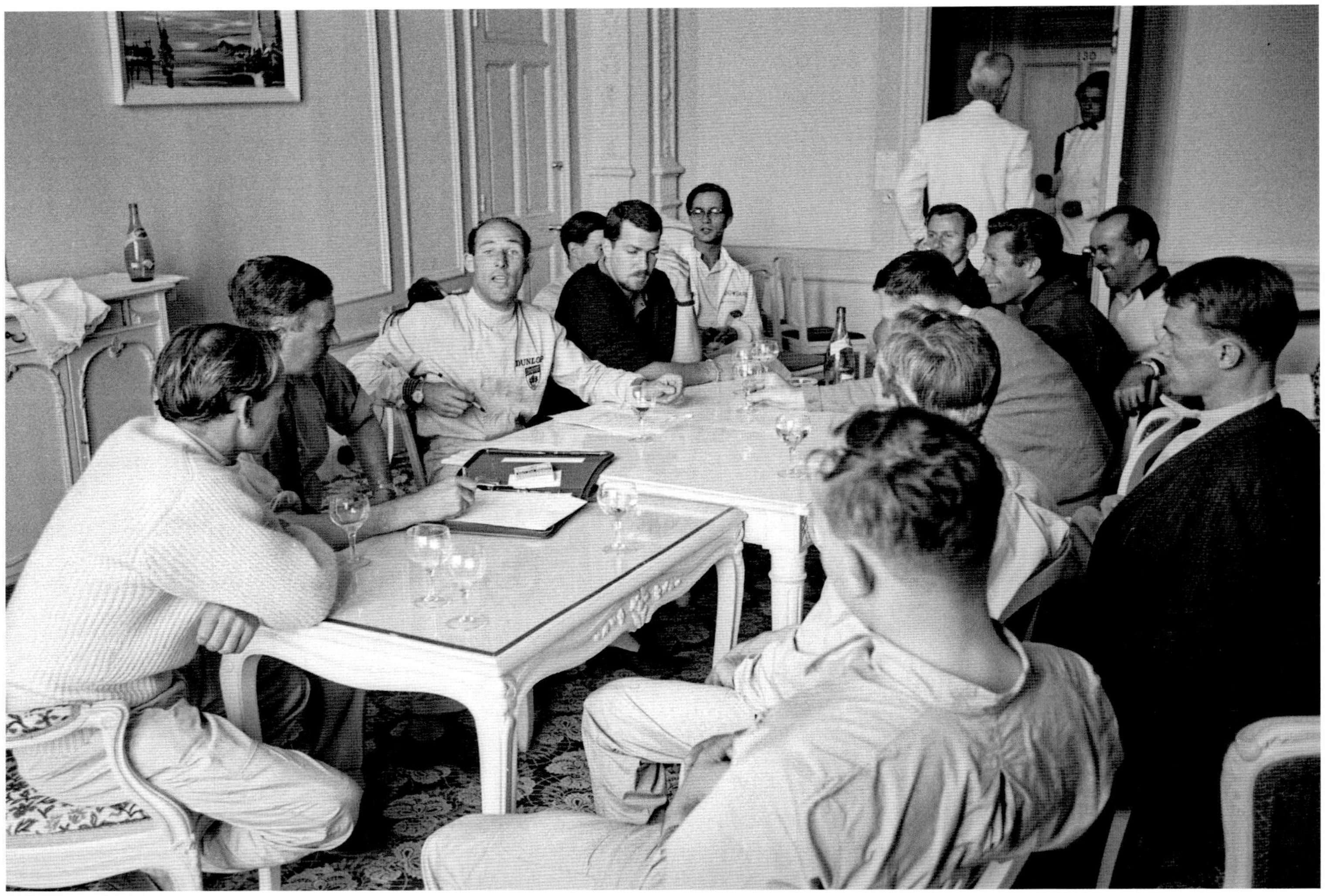

Seltenes Foto: die Eröffnungssitzung der neuen Rennfahrervereinigung (Grand Prix Drivers' Association) in Zimmer 183 des Hotels Metropole in Monte Carlo. Von links Innes Ireland, Sekretär Peter Garnier, Vorsitzender Stirling Moss, Jo Bonnier, Jim Clark, Masten Gregory. Auf der anderen Seite des Tisches von links John Surtees, Cliff Allison, Dan Gurney, Henry Taylor, Olivier Gendebien, Maurice Trintignant und Tony Brooks.

Rare photo: The inaugural meeting of the new racing driver association (Grand Prix Drivers' Association) in room 183 of Monte Carlo's Hotel Metropole. From left Innes Ireland, secretary Peter Garnier, chairman Stirling Moss, Jo Bonnier, Jim Clark, Masten Gregory. On the other side of the table from left John Surtees, Cliff Allison, Dan Gurney, Henry Taylor, Olivier Gendebien, Maurice Trintignant and Tony Brooks.

1961

Und wieder Stirling Moss

In diesem Jahr starten die ersten Rennen der neuen Formel mit einer Beschränkung des Hubraums auf 1½ Liter statt bisher 2½ Liter. Die britischen Konstrukteure hatten dagegen protestiert, da sie wegen den schwächeren Motoren unspektakuläre Rennen befürchteten, blieben aber erfolglos. Sie hätten die Zeit wohl besser für die Entwicklung neuer Motoren genutzt. So müssen sie sich mit Coventry-Climax-Motoren der F2 begnügen. Ferrari ist dagegen besser vorbereitet: Die Scuderia verfügt über einen überlegenen V6-Motor, der rund 20 bis 30 PS mehr leistet als der englische Rivale, und beschäftigt die Top-Piloten Ginther, Phil Hill und von Trips.

Porsche profitiert vom neuen Reglement und kann seine F2-Wagen fast ohne Änderung in der neuen Formel 1 einsetzen. Dan Gurney erreicht den fünften Rang, während sich Hans Herrmann und Jo Bonnier, die anderen Porsche-Fahrer, immerhin qualifizieren.

Aber wieder ist es Stirling Moss, der dominiert. In einem älteren Lotus 18 setzt er sich in Training und Rennen gegen die drei viel stärkeren Ferrari durch. „Ich denke, das war wahrscheinlich meine beste Fahrt in einem Formel-1-Rennen." (Moss in *All My Races,* Somerset 2009)

Stirling Moss wins again

This year's race was the first in the new formula with a restriction on engine capacity to 1½ liters instead of the previous 2½ liters. Fearing less spectacular races because of the reduced engine performance, British manufacturers mounted an unsuccessful protest. They would probably have been better advised to use the time to develop new engines. As things stood, they had to make do with Coventry Climax engines from F2. Ferrari, on the other hand, was better prepared: the Scuderia had a superior V6 engine that produced around 20 to 30 hp more than its British rivals and employed top drivers Ginther, Phil Hill and von Trips.

Porsche benefited from the new regulations and was able to field its F2 cars in the new Formula 1 with almost no changes. Dan Gurney finished fifth, while Hans Herrmann and Jo Bonnier, the other Porsche drivers, also qualified.

But yet again it was Stirling Moss who dominated. In an older Lotus 18, he prevailed in practice and in the race itself against the three much stronger Ferraris. "I think this was probably my greatest drive in a Formula 1 race." (Moss in All My Races, *Somerset 2009)*

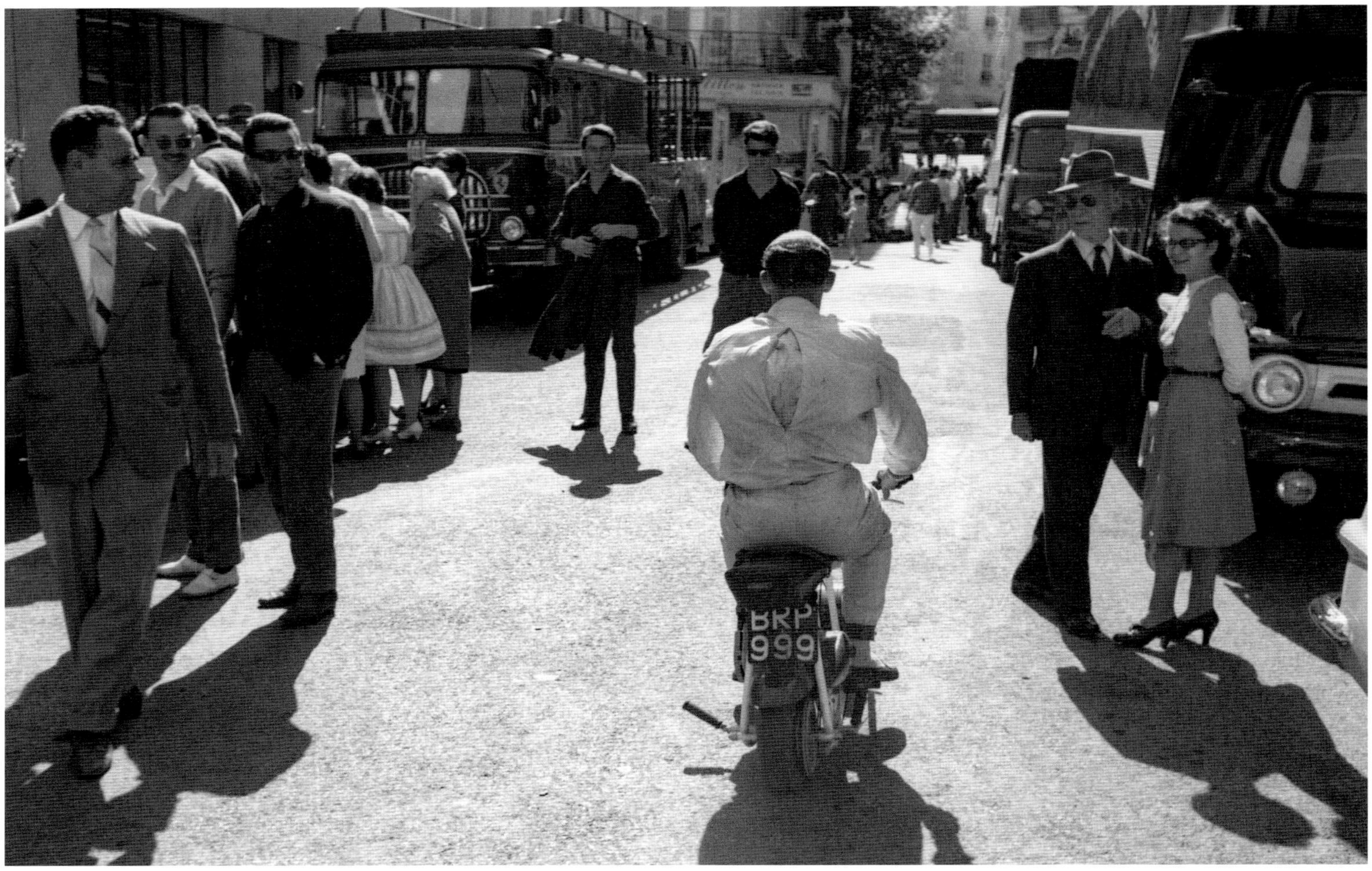

Stirling Moss genießt es, mit seinem Trojan Trobike herumzufahren.
Links der Ferrari-Transporter.

Stirling Moss enjoys riding around on his Trojan Trobike.
On the left, the Ferrari truck.

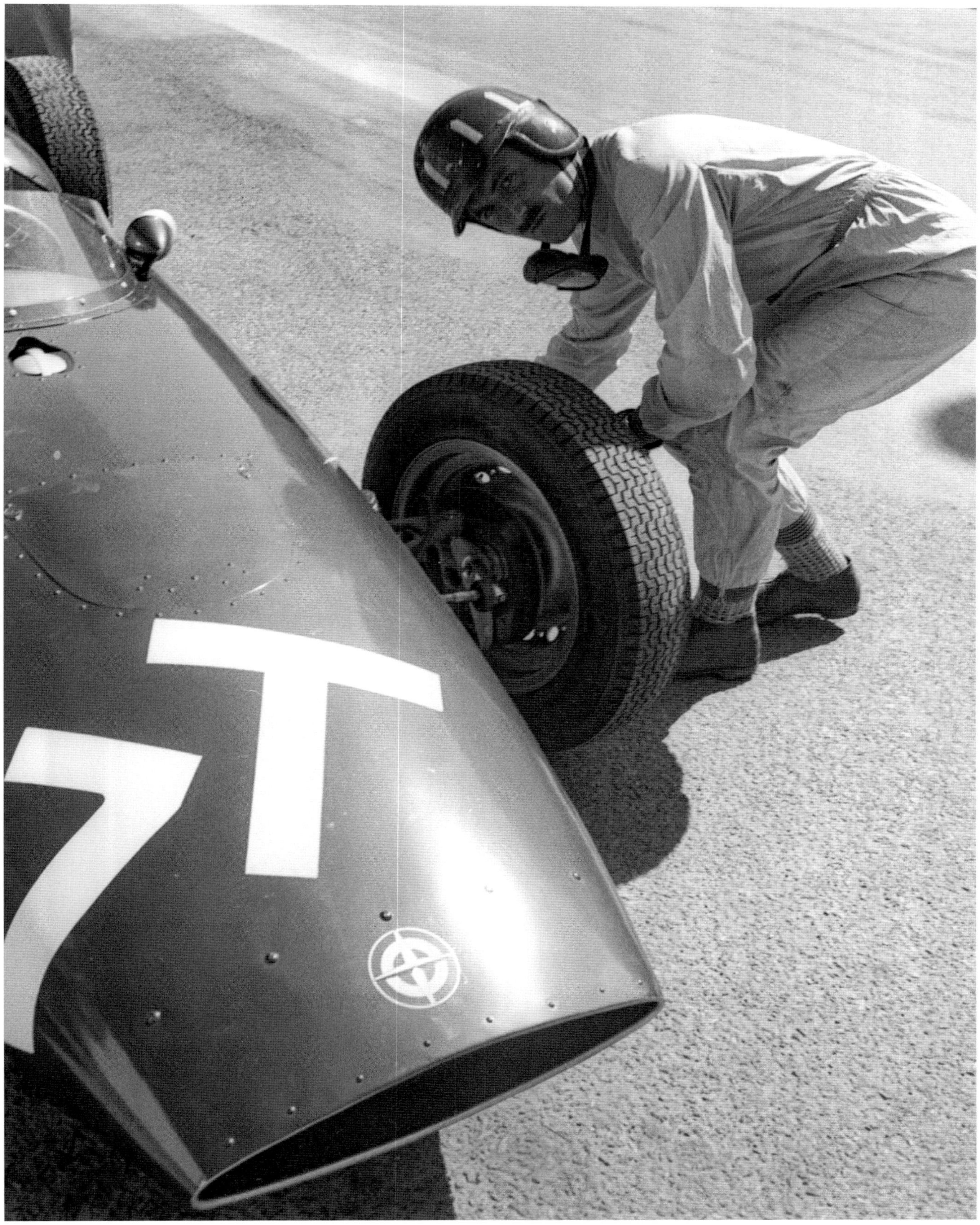

Graham Hill mit dem Reserve-BRM P48
(T für Training)

*Graham Hill with the spare BRM P48
(T for training)*

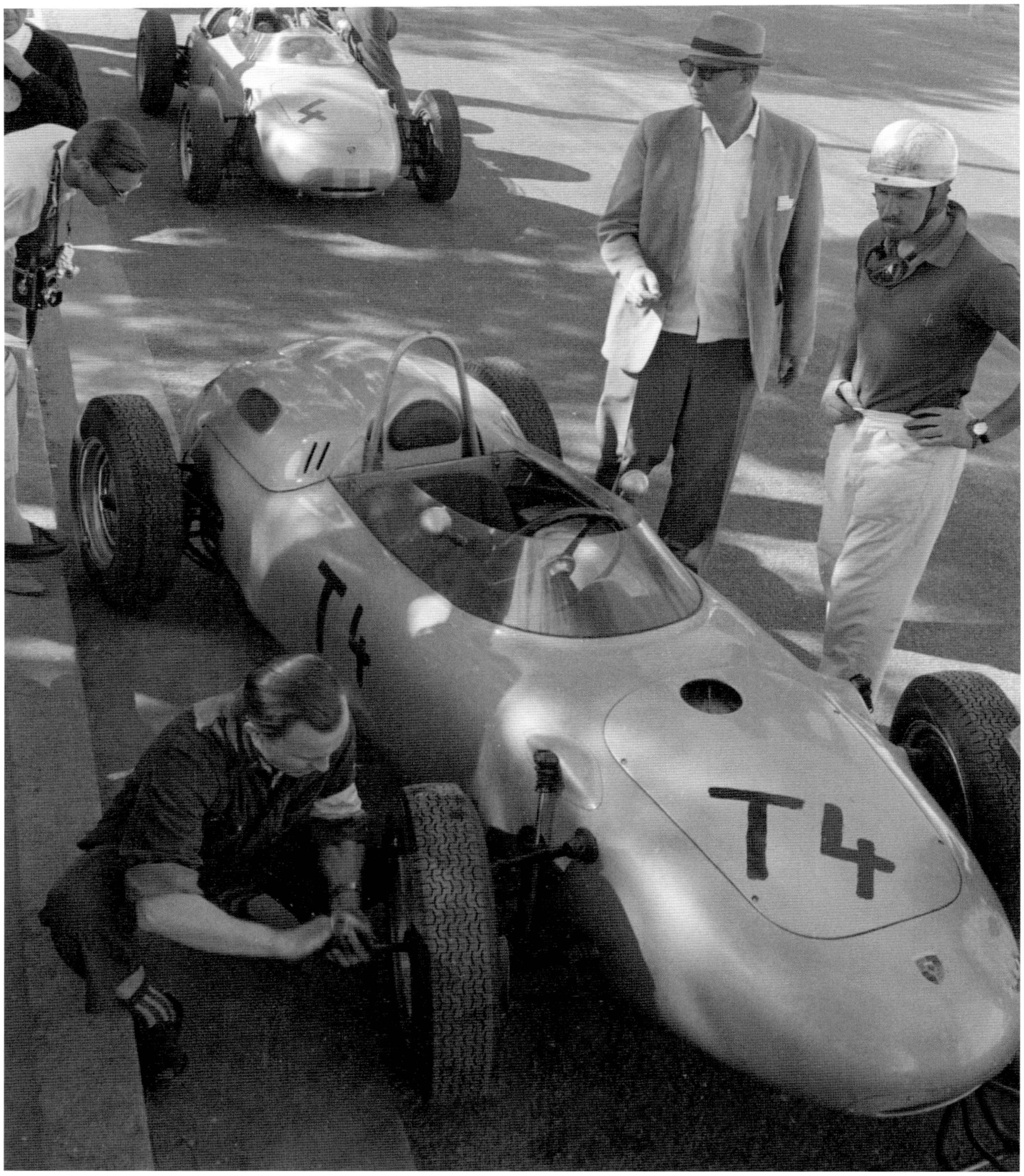

Rechts Joakim Bonnier mit dem Ersatzwagen Porsche 718/2 T4, im Hintergrund der Porsche 718/2 N° 4 von Dan Gurney. Zum ersten Mal sieht man den hinteren Überrollbügel, der ab 1961 vorgeschrieben ist.

Joakim Bonnier on the right with the spare car Porsche 718/2 T4, in the background Dan Gurney's Porsche 718/2 N° 4. This was the first appearance of the roll bar, which became mandatory in 1961.

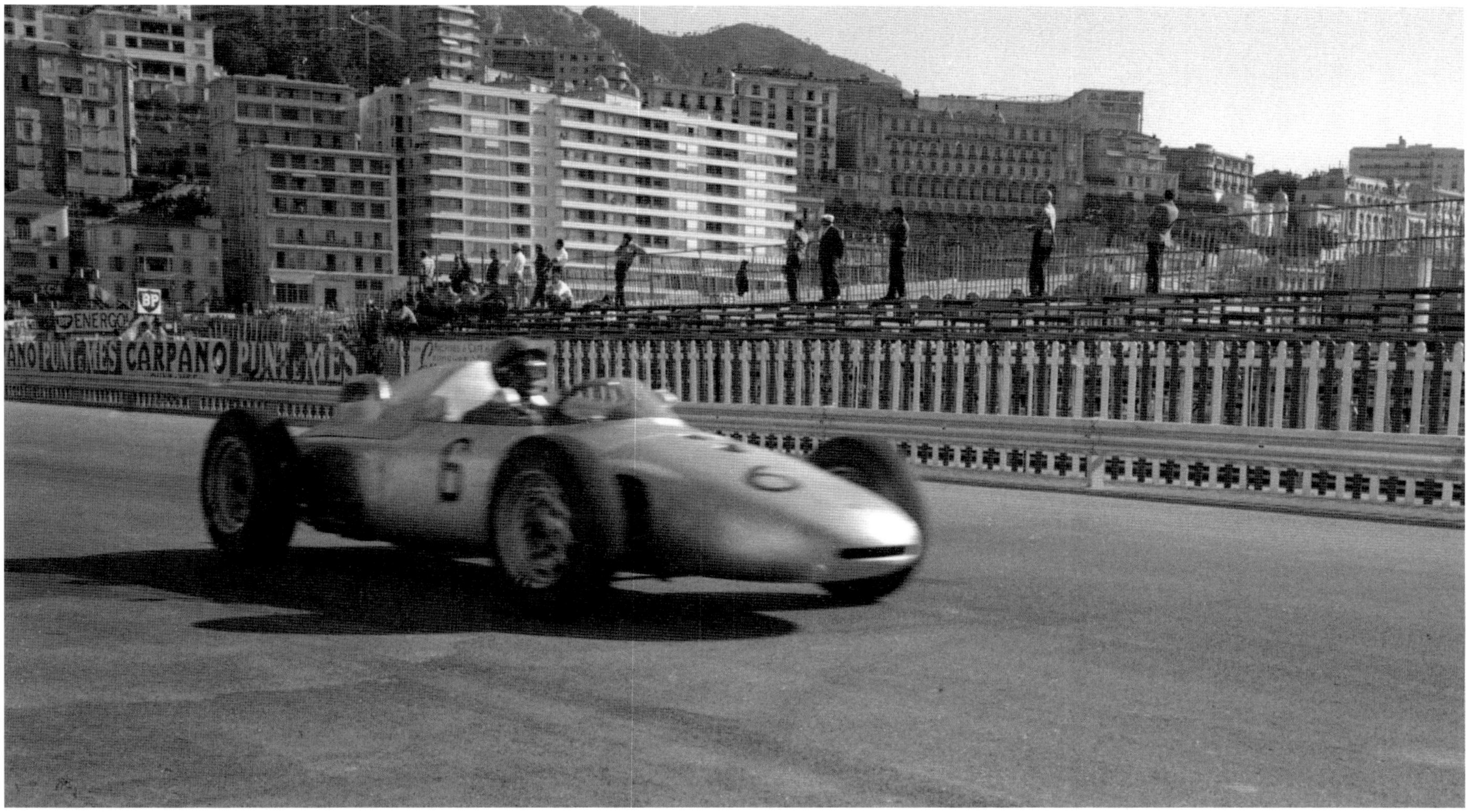

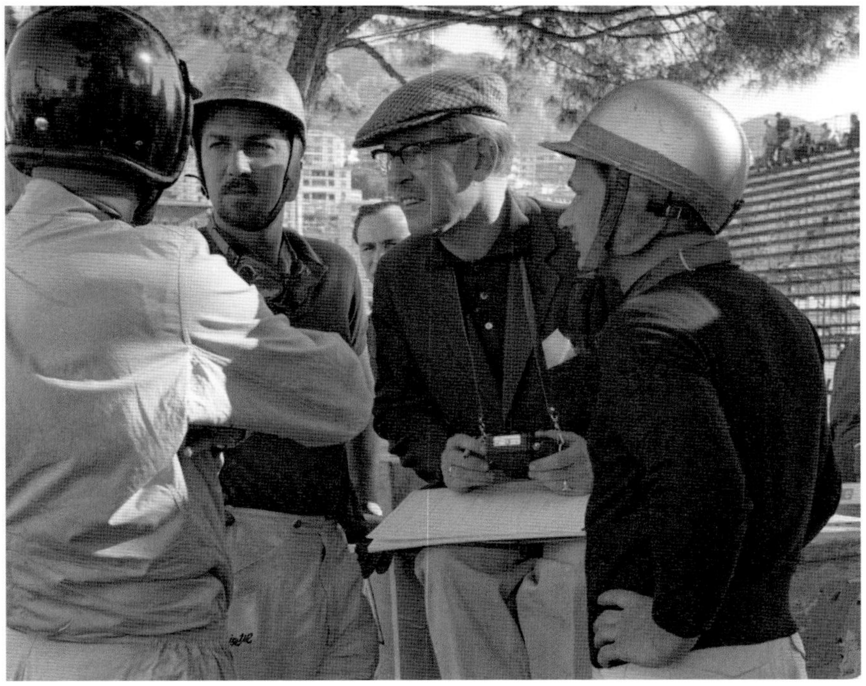

Hans Herrmann, Porsche 718/2 N° 6, mit neuer Karosserie.

Hans Herrmann, Porsche 718/2 N° 6. with a new body.

Von links: Dan Gurney, Joakim Bonnier, Porsche-Manager Huschke von Hanstein, Bruce McLaren.

From left: Dan Gurney, Joakim Bonnier, Porsche manager Huschke von Hanstein, Bruce McLaren.

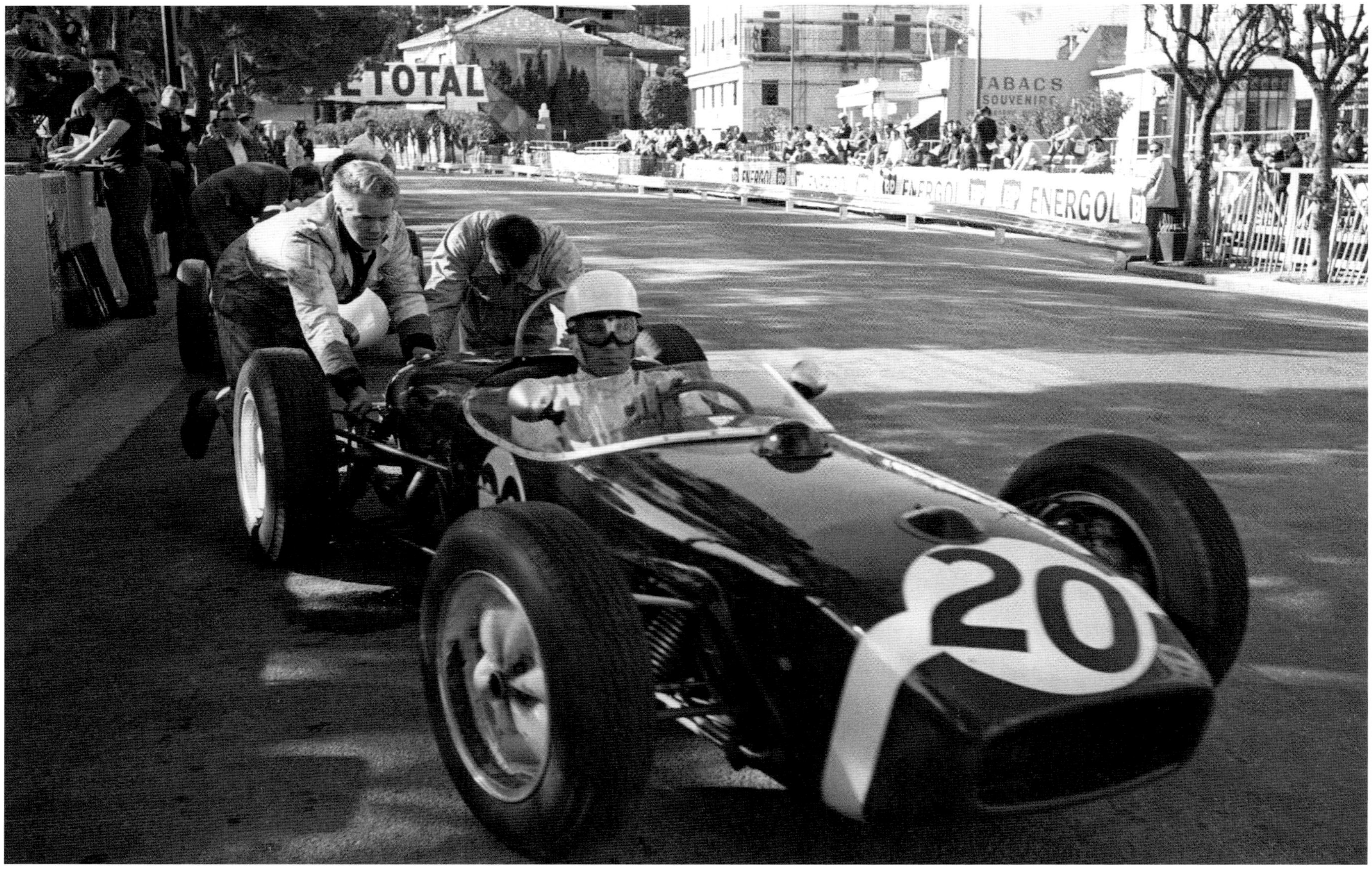

Stirling Moss, Lotus 18 N° 20. Rechts schiebt Alf Francis,
Chefmechaniker des Rob Walker Racing Teams.

Stirling Moss, Lotus 18 N° 20. Pushing on the right Alf Francis, chief mechanic for the Rob Walker Racing Team.

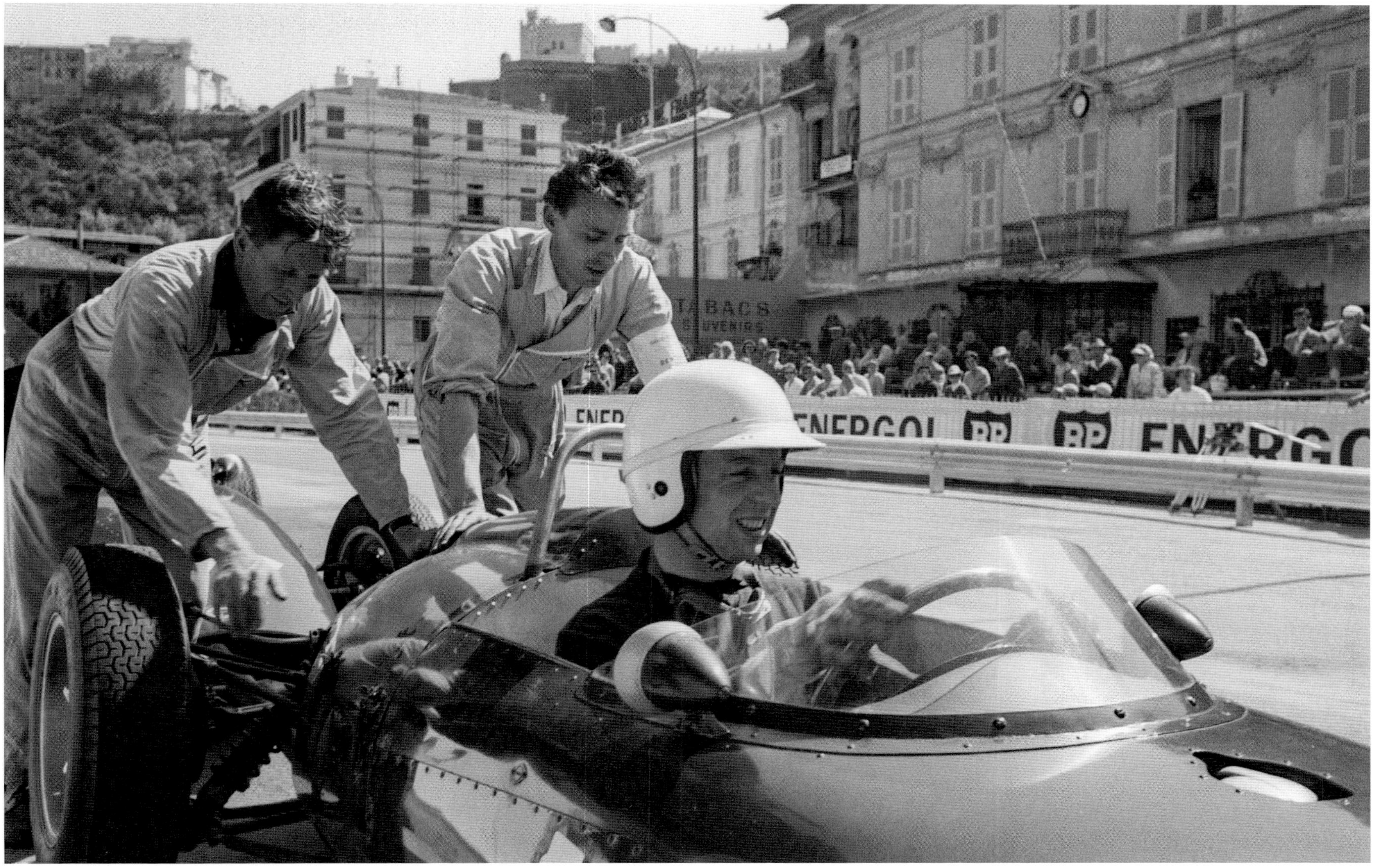

Tony Brooks, BRM P48/57 N° 16.

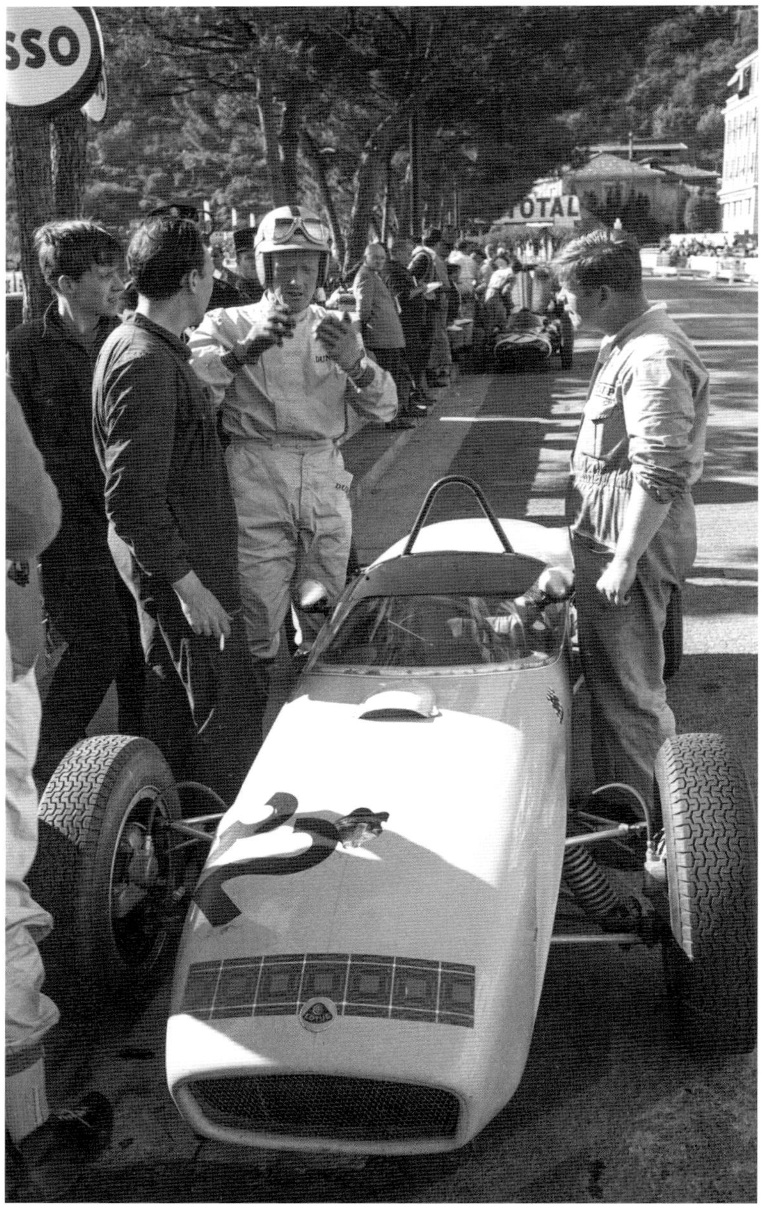

Cliff Allison, Lotus 18 N° 32.

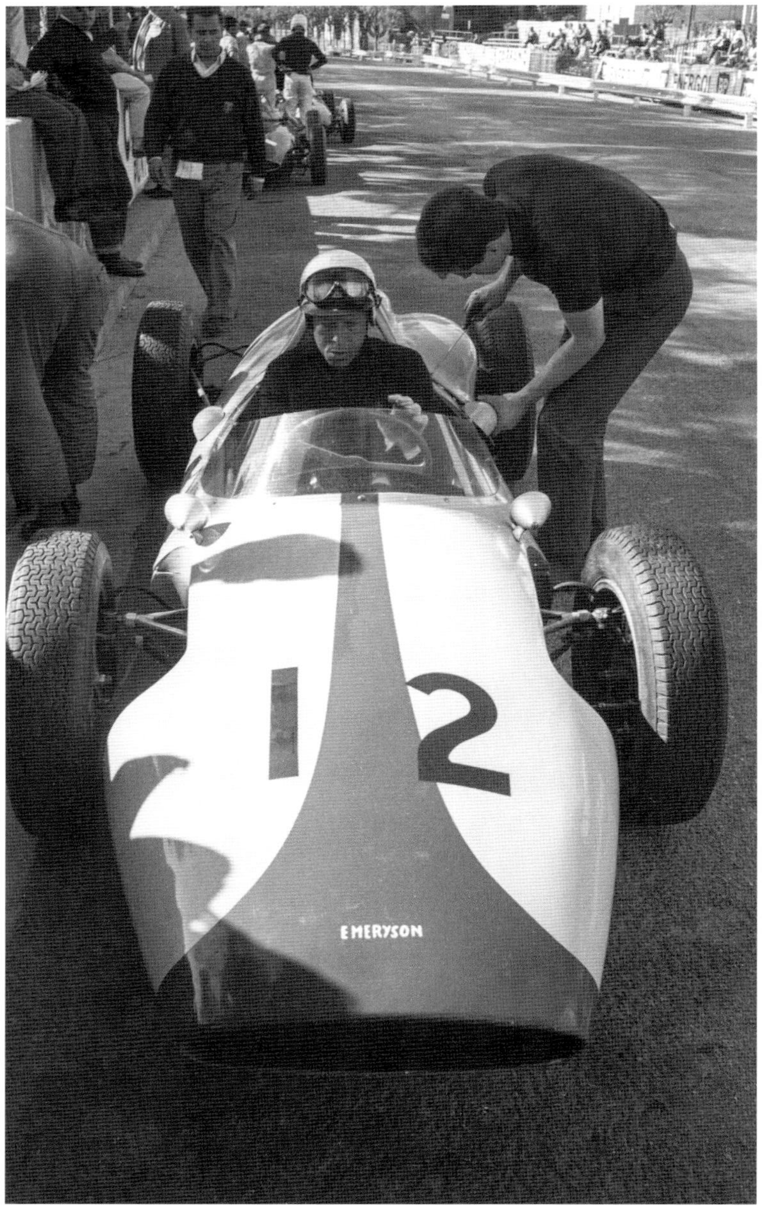

Olivier Gendebien, Emeryson-Maserati 1003 N° 12 (not qualified).

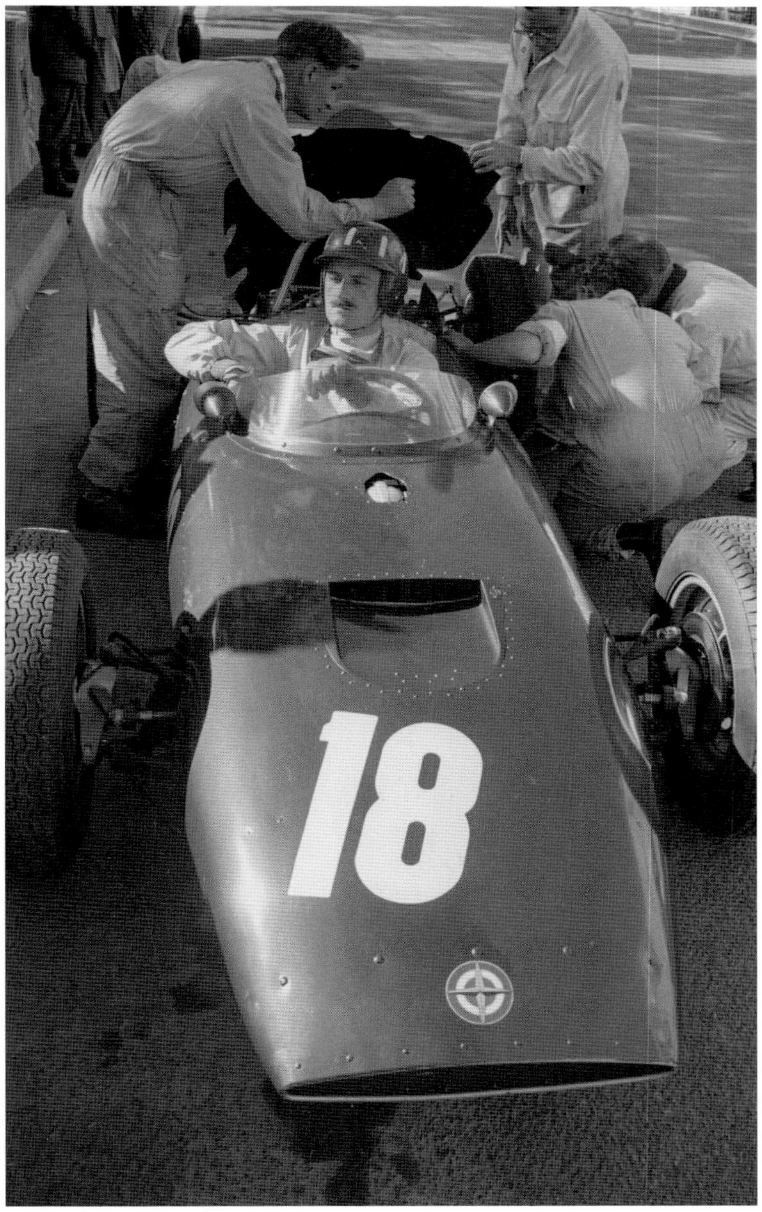

Graham Hill, BRM P48/57 N° 18.

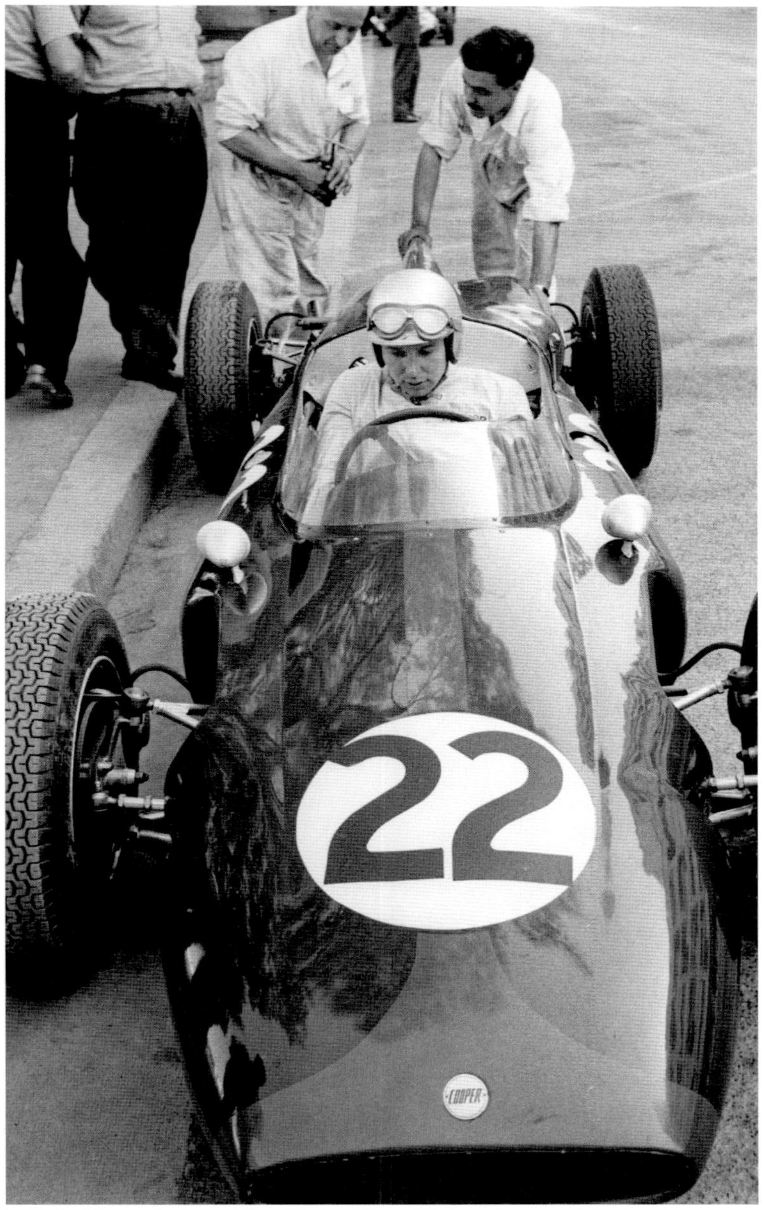

John Surtees, Cooper T53 N° 22.

Final Result of the Monaco Grand Prix 1961

1. Stirling Moss, Lotus 18
2. Richie Ginther, Ferrari 156
3. Phil Hill, Ferrari 156

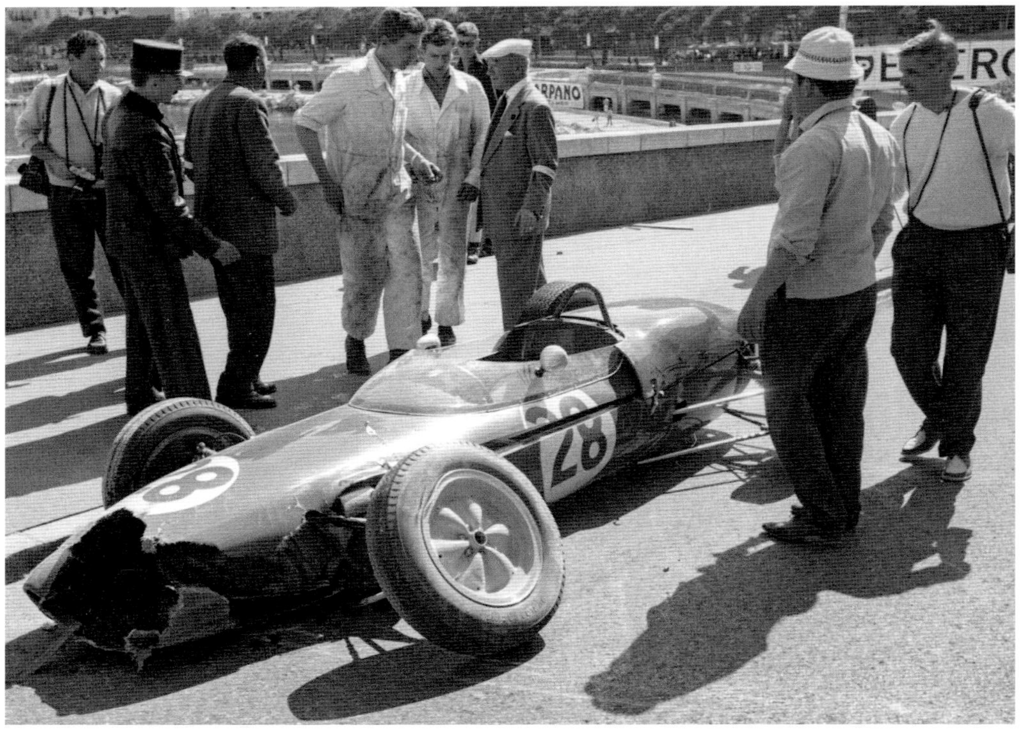

Im Training beschädigte Jim Clark nach Bestzeit seinen Lotus 21 in der Sainte Dévote schwer.

In practice, Jim Clark badly damaged his Lotus 21 in Sainte Dévote after setting the best time.

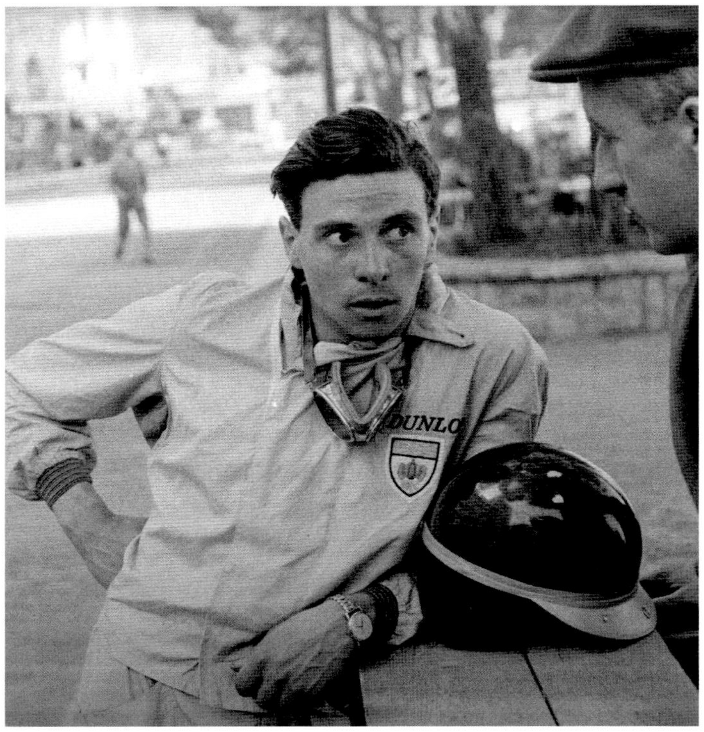

Ein enttäuschter Jim Clark mit Esso-Competition-Manager Geoff Murdoch.

Disappointed Jim Clark with Esso Competition Manager Geoff Murdoch.

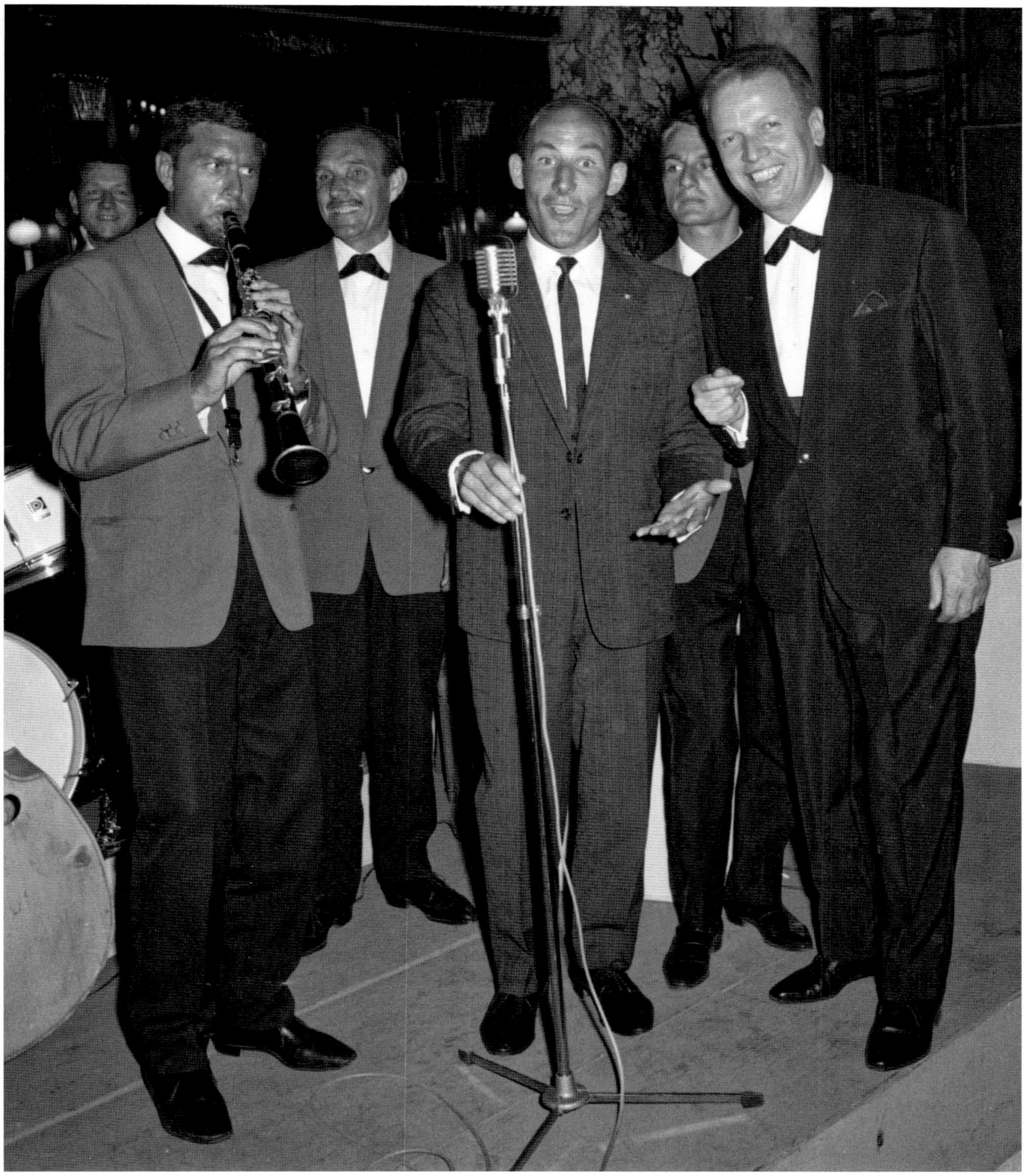

Ein Ständchen von Stirling Moss, als er nach dem Grand Prix in einem Nachtlokal in Monaco mit der Tanzband von Bandleader Louis Frosio (rechts) auftritt.

A snatch of song from Stirling Moss as he joins in with band leader Louis Frosio's (right) danceband in a Monaco nightspot after the Grand Prix.

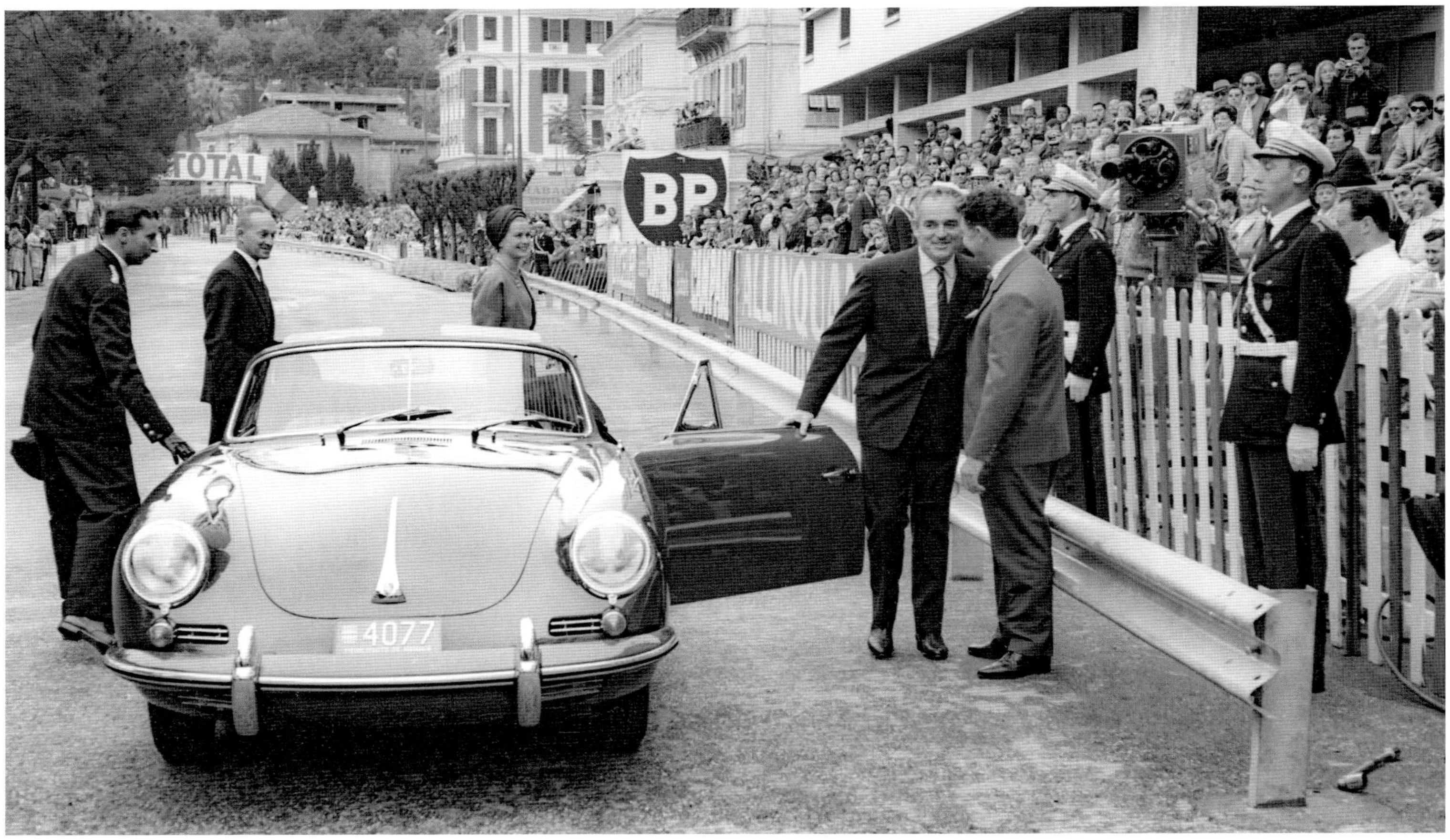

Fürst Rainier mit Fürstin Gracia nach der Ehrenrunde zur Streckeneröffnung mit ihrem Porsche 356. Wer hat den Radmutter-Schraubenschlüssel ganz rechts im Bild vergessen?

Prince Rainier with Princess Grace after the circuit-opening tour of honour with their Porsche 356. Who dropped the wheel nut spanner on the far right of the picture?

1962

Der große Abwesende

Einen Monat vor dem 20. Grand Prix von Monaco erleidet Stirling Moss bei einem Unfall während eines Rennens in Goodwood schwere Verletzungen. Trotz seiner Genesung bedeutet dies das Karriereende für einen der größten Rennfahrer aller Zeiten. Auch Tony Brooks ist nicht mehr dabei. Er zieht sich mit 30 Jahren vom Rennsport zurück und eröffnet eine Autowerkstatt.

Nachdem Ferrari die Saison im Vorjahr – abgesehen von Monaco – dominiert hatte, zeigt sich nun die Überlegenheit der britischen Chassis. Und die Engländer sind mit neuen V8-Motoren von Coventry-Climax und BRM auch leistungsmäßig wieder konkurrenzfähig. Ferrari ist zudem geschwächt nach dem Exodus der wichtigsten Techniker am Ende der Saison 1961.

Die wichtigste Neuentwicklung ist der Lotus 25. Colin Chapman revolutioniert mit der Monocoque-Bauweise, der selbsttragenden Karosserie, auch „Badewanne" genannt, das Design der Grand-Prix-Wagen. Das Konzept dafür hatte er während eines Nachtessens auf einer Serviette skizziert. Er erreicht mit dem seit langem erprobten Prinzip höhere Steifigkeit, mehr Sicherheit, weniger Gewicht und die Möglichkeit, Gummi-Tanks einzusetzen. Clark schafft mit dem Lotus 25 zwar die Pole-Position, scheidet im Rennen aber mit Kupplungsschaden aus.

Bruce McLaren holt seinen dritten Grand-Prix-Sieg in Europa im neuesten Cooper T60.

Absent friends

A month before the 20th Monaco Grand Prix, Stirling Moss suffered serious injuries in an accident at a race in Goodwood. Despite his recovery, this brought an end to the career of one of the greatest racing drivers of all time. Tony Brooks was also missing. He retired from racing at the age of 30 and opened a car repair shop.

After Ferrari had dominated the season the previous year – except in Monaco – the superiority of the British chassis was now becoming apparent. New V8 engines from Coventry-Climax and BRM brought the British into competition again in terms of performance. Ferrari was also weakened after the exodus of its most important technicians at the end of the 1961 season.

The most important new development was the Lotus 25. Colin Chapman revolutionised the design of Grand Prix cars with the monocoque construction, the self-supporting body, known as the "bathtub". This achieved greater rigidity, less weight and more safety, also allowing the use of rubber tanks. Clark managed to attain pole position with the Lotus 25, but retired from the race with clutch damage.

Bruce McLaren took his third Grand Prix victory in Europe in the latest Cooper T60.

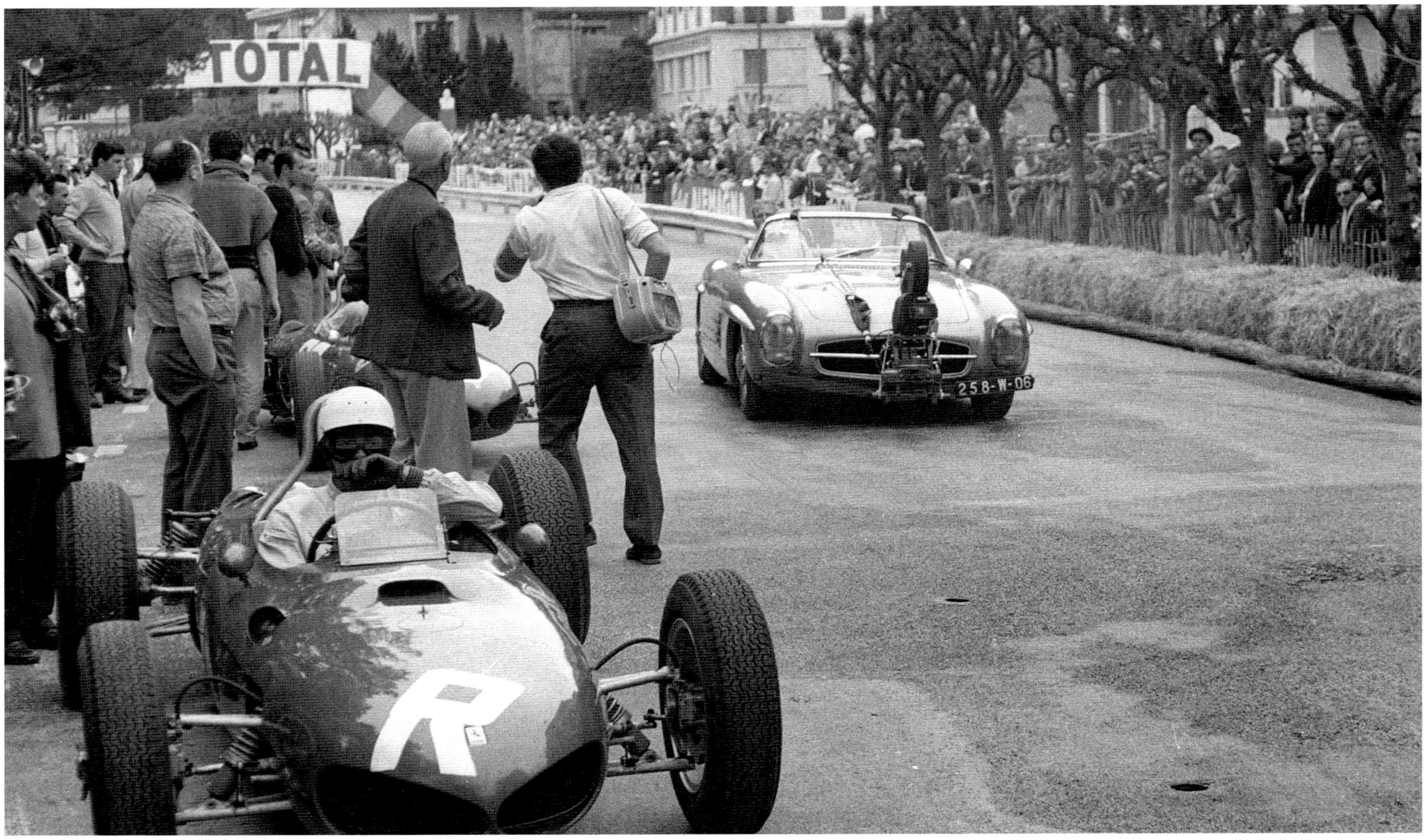

Der Mercedes 300 SL Kamerawagen für den deutschen 70-mm-Dokumentarfilm *Flying Clipper* oder *Mediterranean Holiday* von 1963. Phil Hill im Ferrari 156 „Sharknose".

The Mercedes 300 SL camera car used for the 1963 German 70mm documentary Flying Clipper *aka* Mediterranean Holiday. *Phil Hill in the Ferrari 156 "Sharknose".*

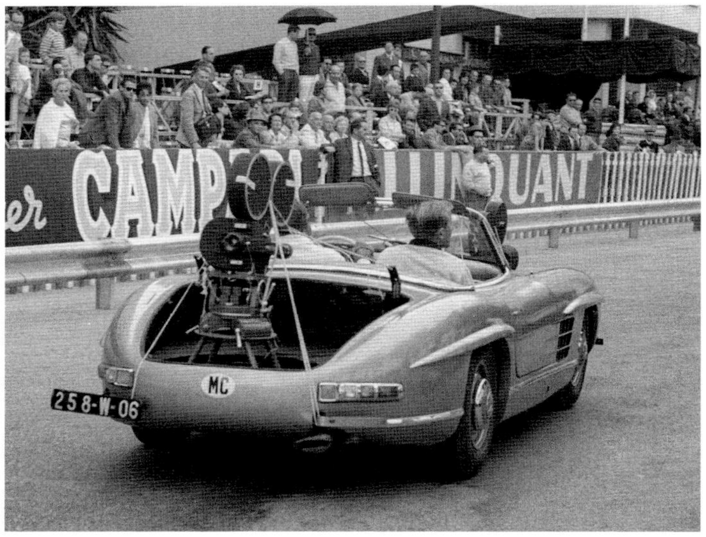

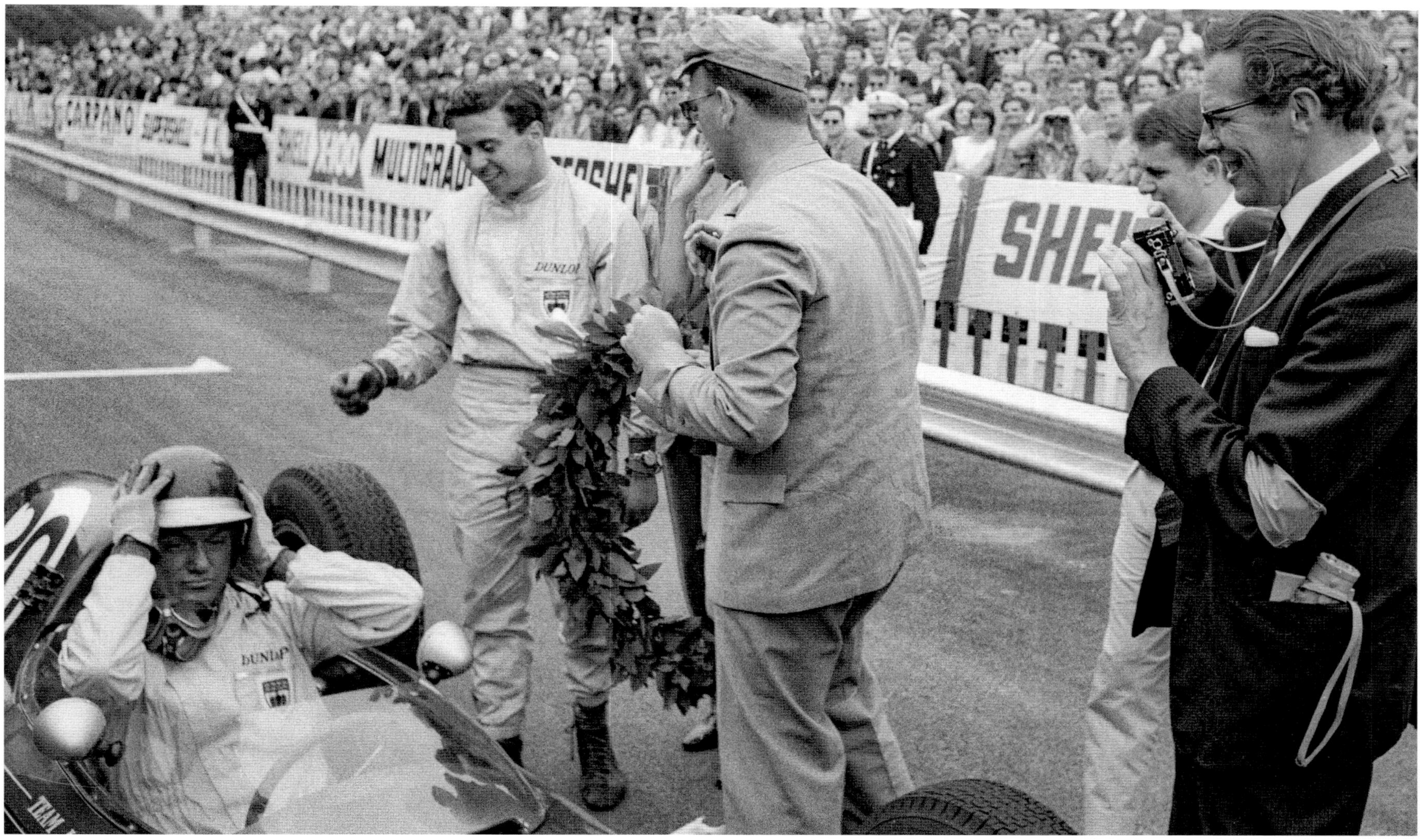

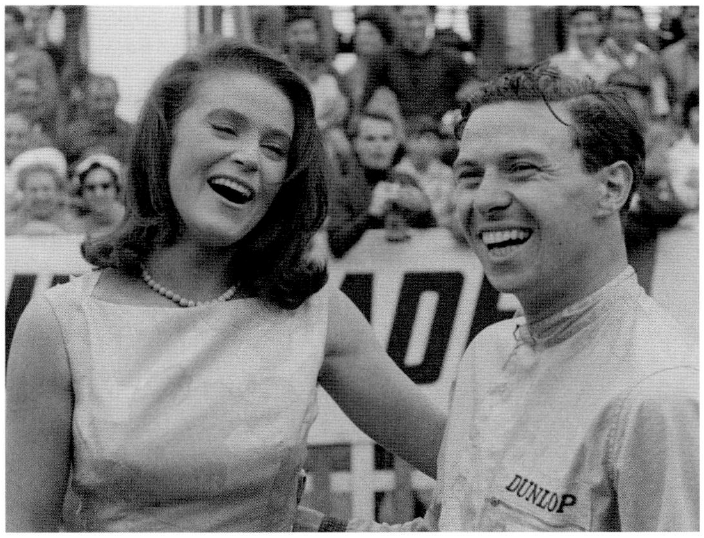

Regisseur Roger Corman, der den Film *The Young Racers* dreht, nutzt das Rennen, um einige Szenen während des Trainings zu drehen. Jim Clark mit dem Schauspieler William Campbell. Er sitzt im Cockpit des Lotus 24 von Trevor Taylor.

Director Roger Corman, making the film The Young Racers, *took the opportunity to use the race as a backdrop and shot some scenes during practice sessions. Jim Clark with actor William Campbell. He can be seen in the cockpit of Trevor Taylor's Lotus 24.*

Die französische Schauspielerin Béatrice Altariba amüsiert sich mit Jim Clark.

French actress Béatrice Altariba shares a joke with Jim Clark.

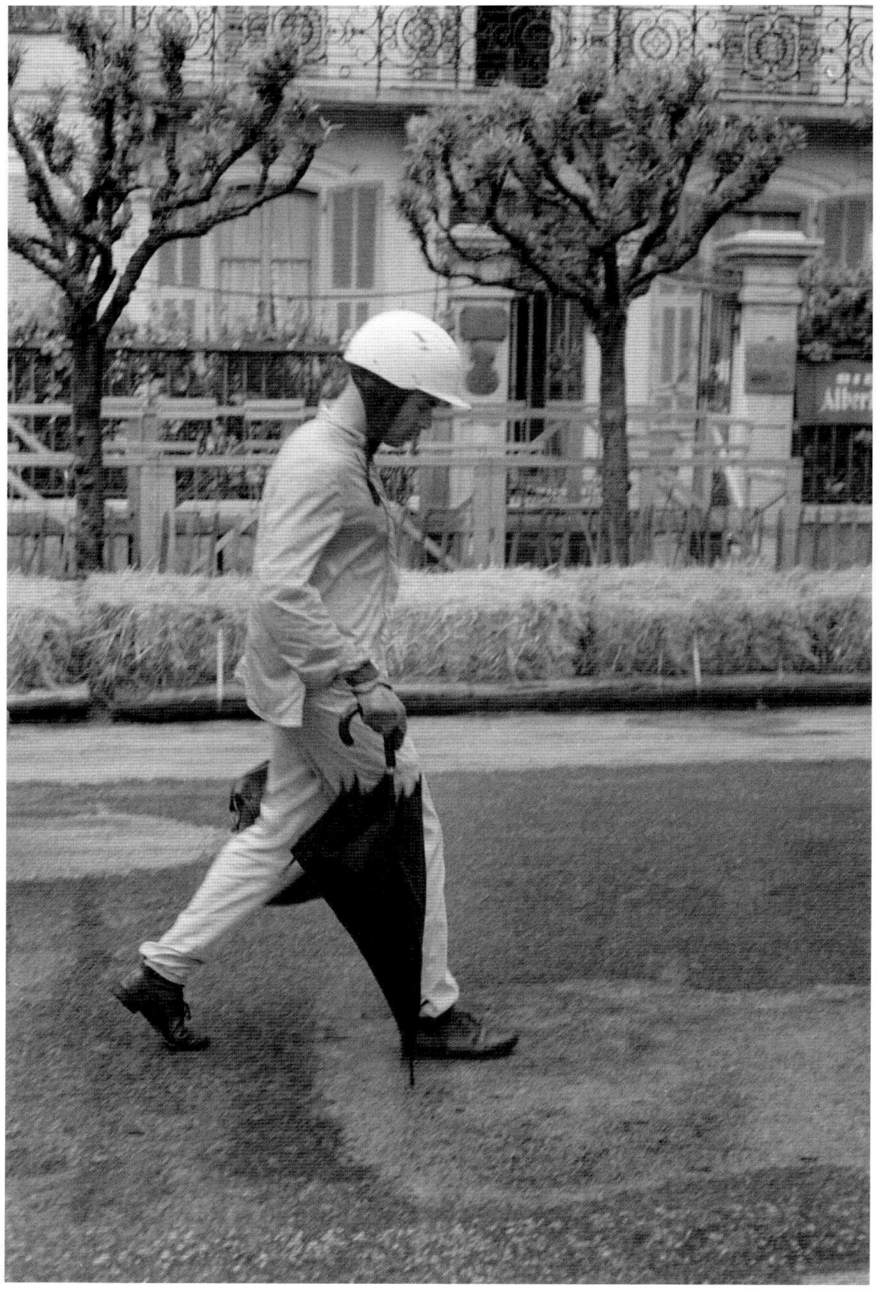

Ein heftiger Regenschauer beeinträchtigt das Training.
Phil Hill mit Regenschirm.

A heavy rainstorm marred practice.
Phil Hill is seen carrying an umbrella.

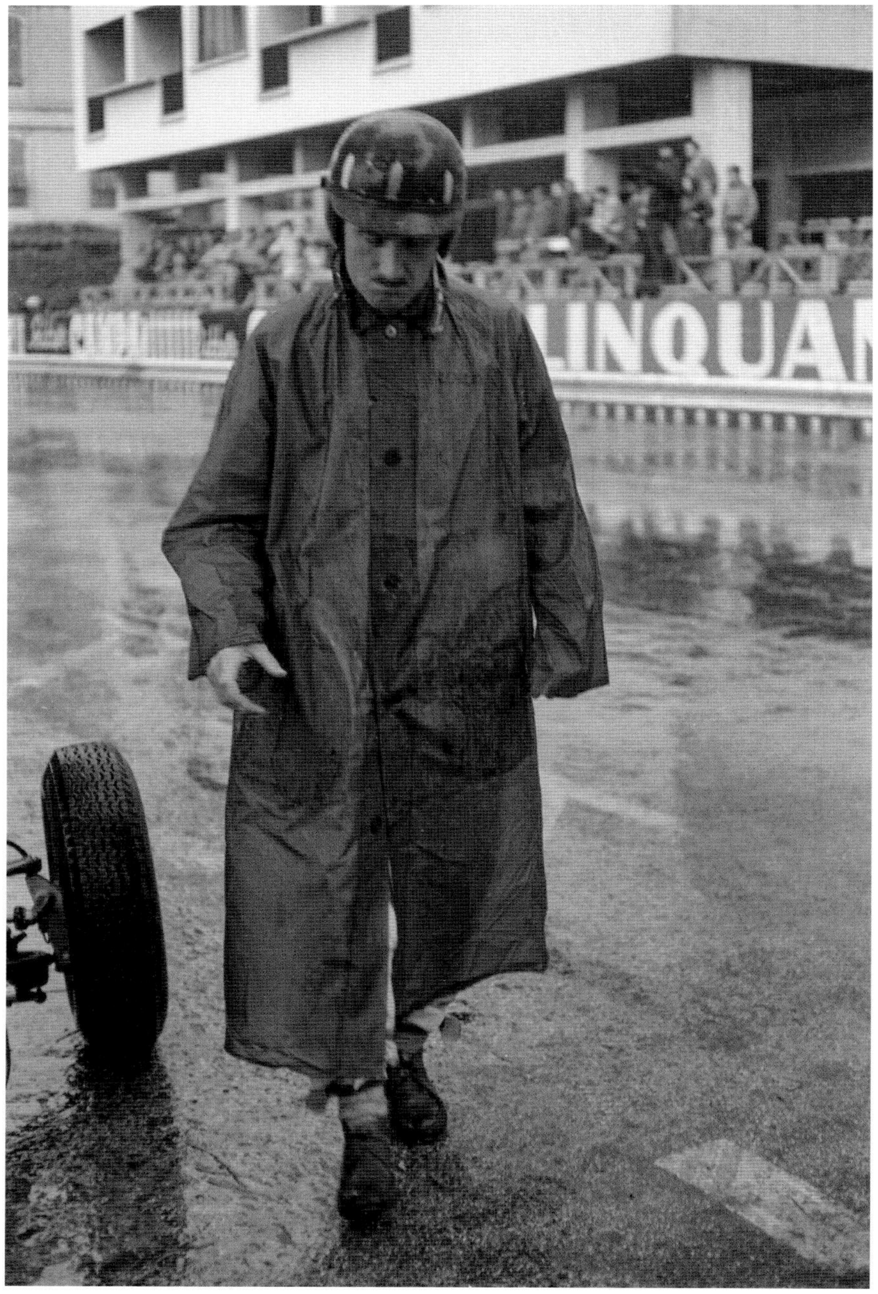

Graham Hill

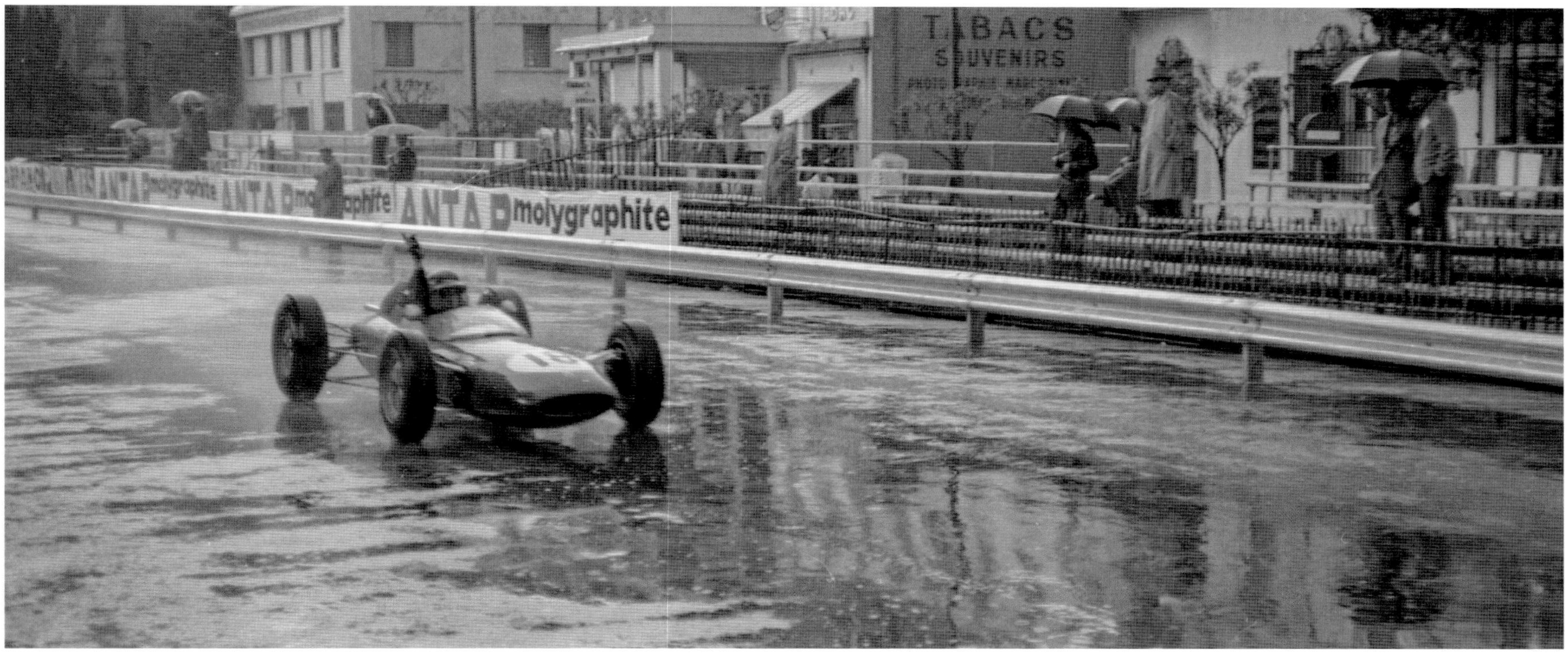

Jim Clark, Lotus 25 N° 18.

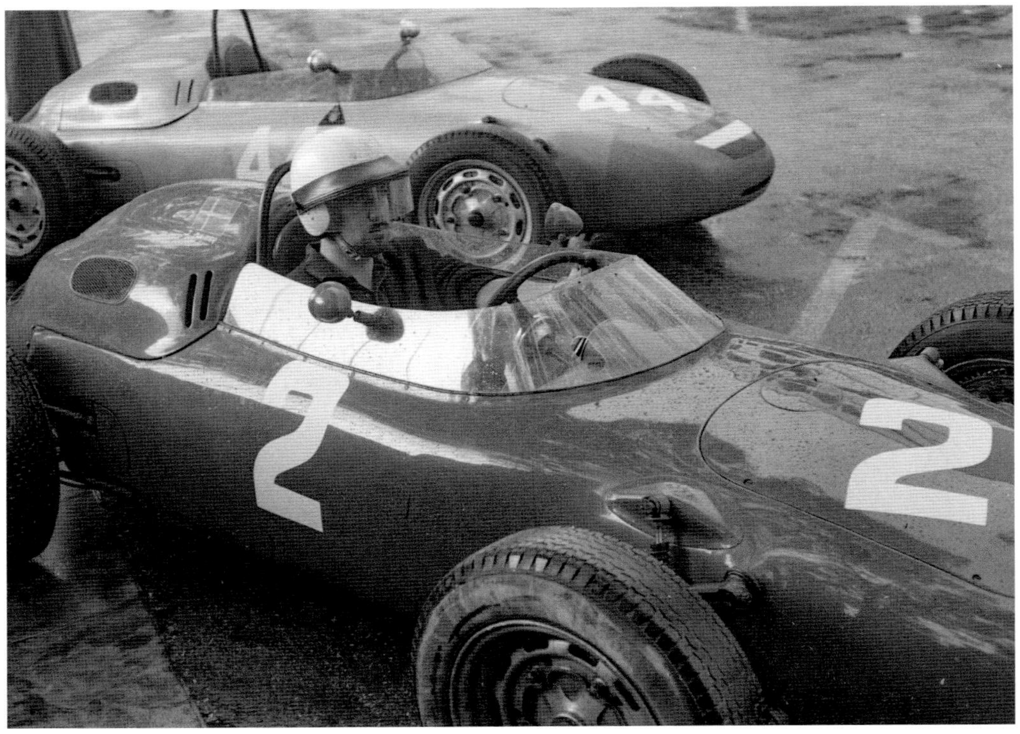

Jo Bonnier, Porsche F2-718 N° 2, und das Auto von Carel Godin Beaufort, Porsche F2-718 N° 44.

Jo Bonnier, Porsche F2-718 N° 2, and the car of Carel Godin Beaufort, Porsche F2-718 N° 44.

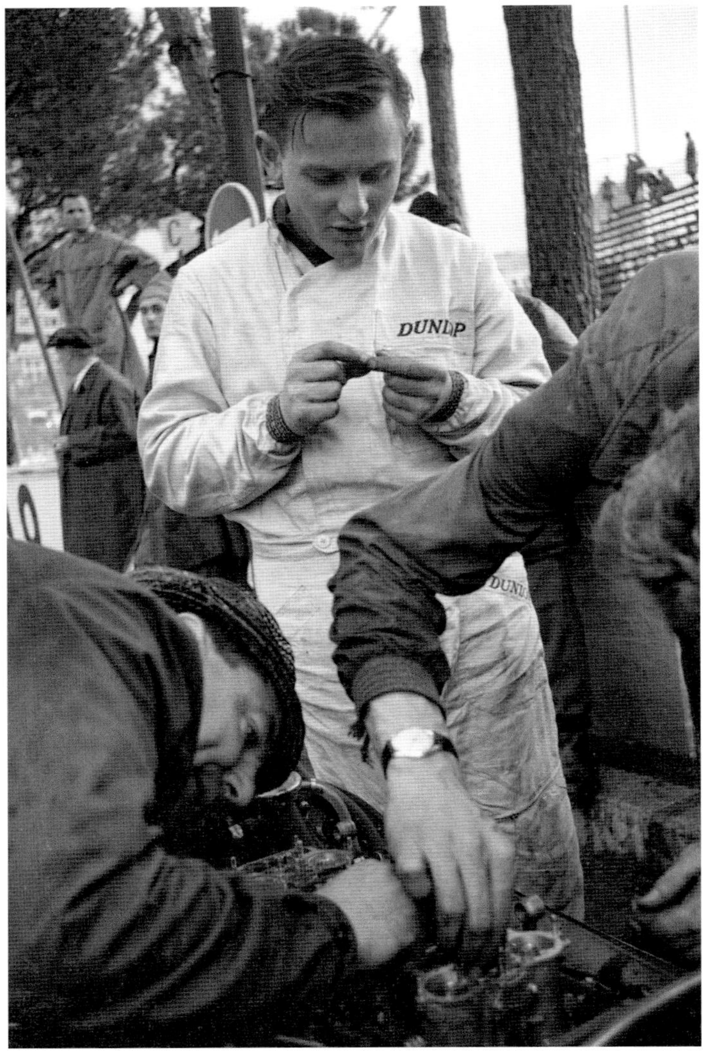

Bruce McLaren, Sieger des Rennens.

Bruce McLaren, winner of the race.

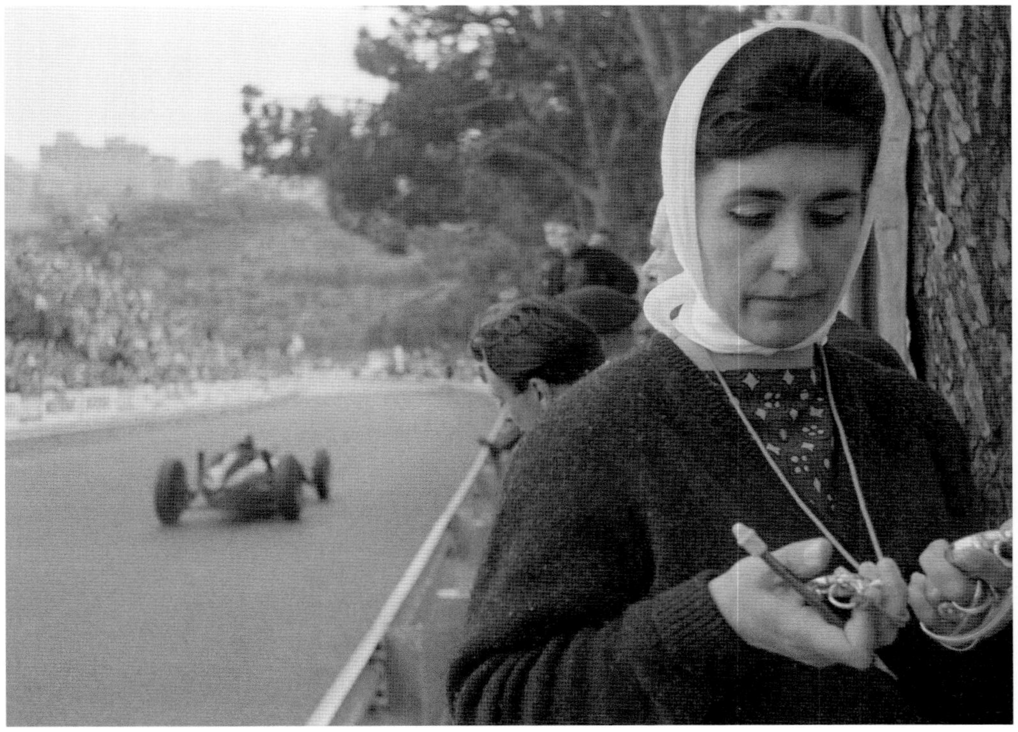

Bette Hill, Ehefrau von Graham Hill,
bewaffnet mit Stoppuhren.

*Bette Hill, wife of Graham Hill,
armed with stop watches.*

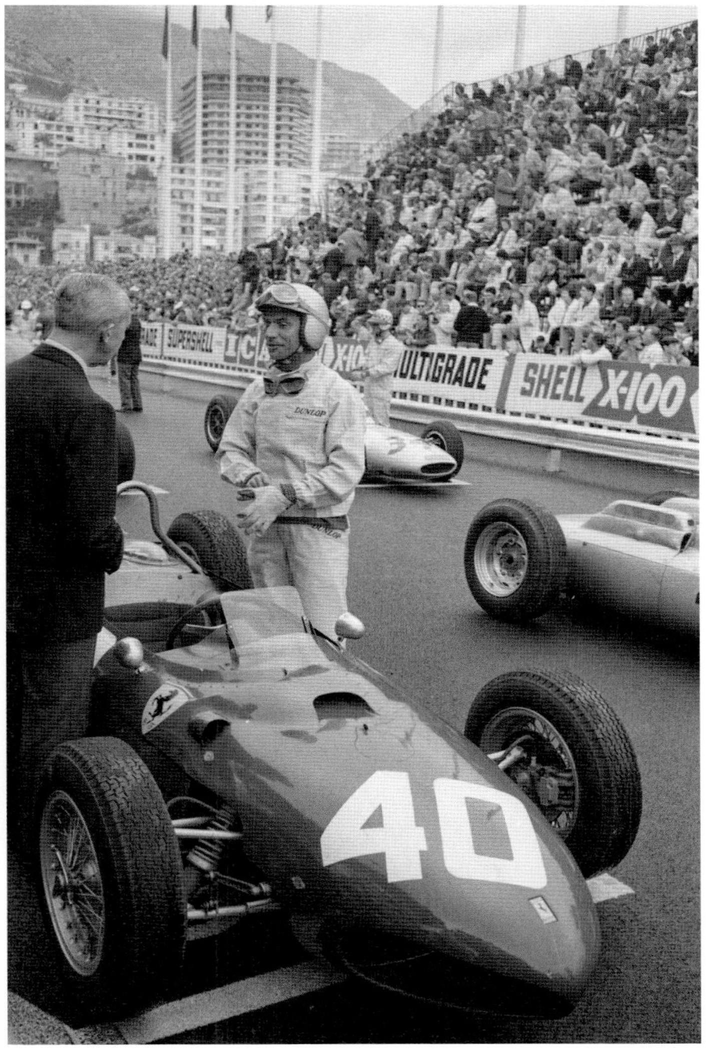

Willy Mairesse, „Kamikaze Willy“ oder
„Wild Willy“, Ferrari 156 „Sharknose“ N° 40.

*Willy Mairesse, "Kamikaze Willy" or
"Wild Willy", Ferrari 156 "Sharknose" N° 40.*

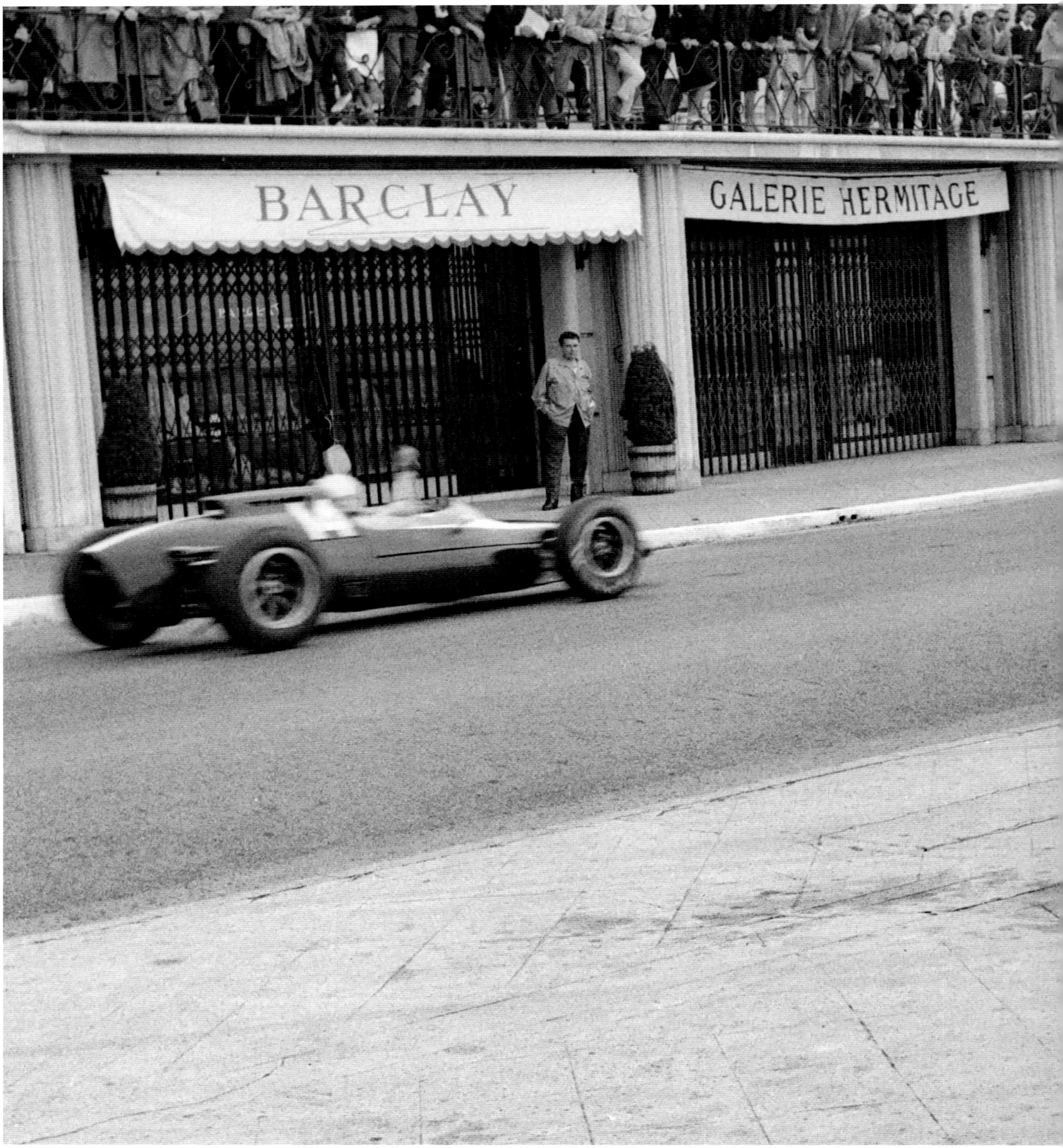
BARCLAY
GALERIE HERMITAGE

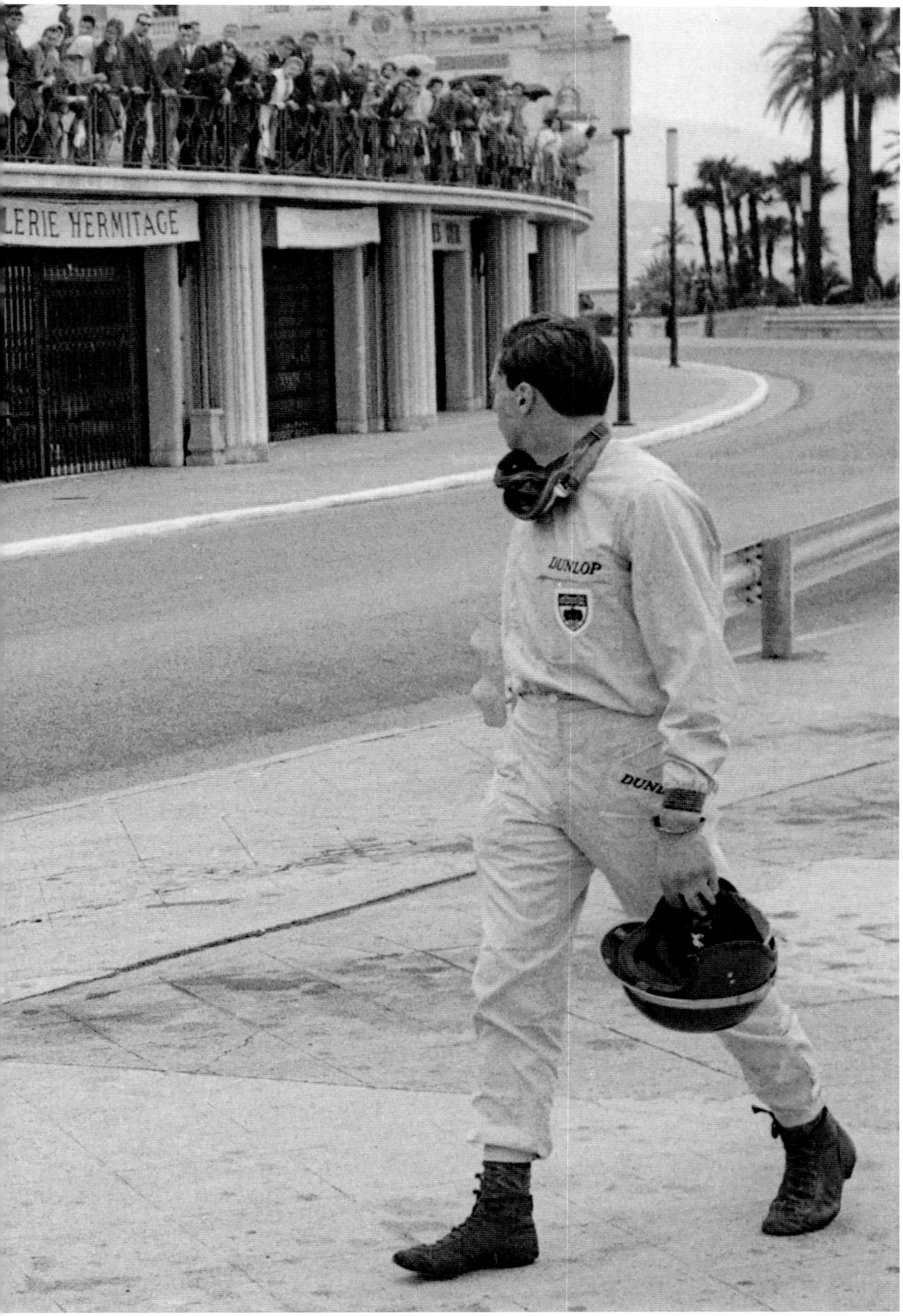

Jim Clark. Entweder gewinnt er ein Rennen oder er muss zurück an die Box, weil etwas kaputt ist. Am Beau Rivage Hill, dem Anstieg zu Massenet, fährt Bruce McLaren auf dem Cooper T60 N° 14 dem Sieg entgegen.

Jim Clark. Either he wins a race or he has to run back to the pits because something has gone wrong. At Beau Rivage Hill, the climb to Massenet, Bruce McLaren drives towards victory on Cooper T60 N° 14.

Final Result of the Monaco Grand Prix 1962

1. Bruce McLaren, Cooper T60
2. Phil Hill, Ferrari 156
3. Lorenzo Bandini, Ferrari 156

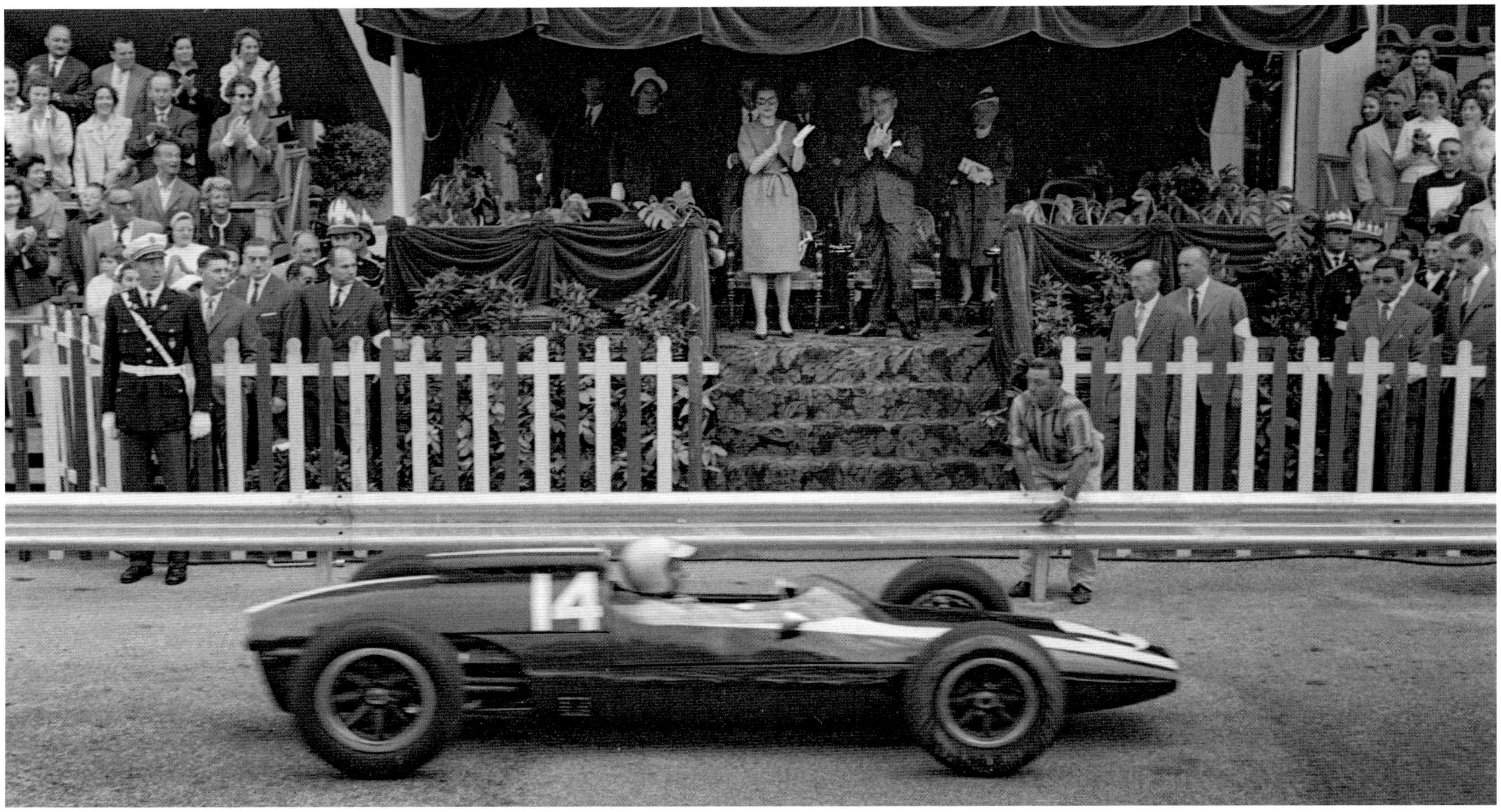

Bruce McLaren, Cooper T60 N° 14, Sieger des Rennens,
vor der Ehrentribüne.

*Bruce McLaren, Cooper T60 N° 14, winner of the race,
in front of the Royal box.*

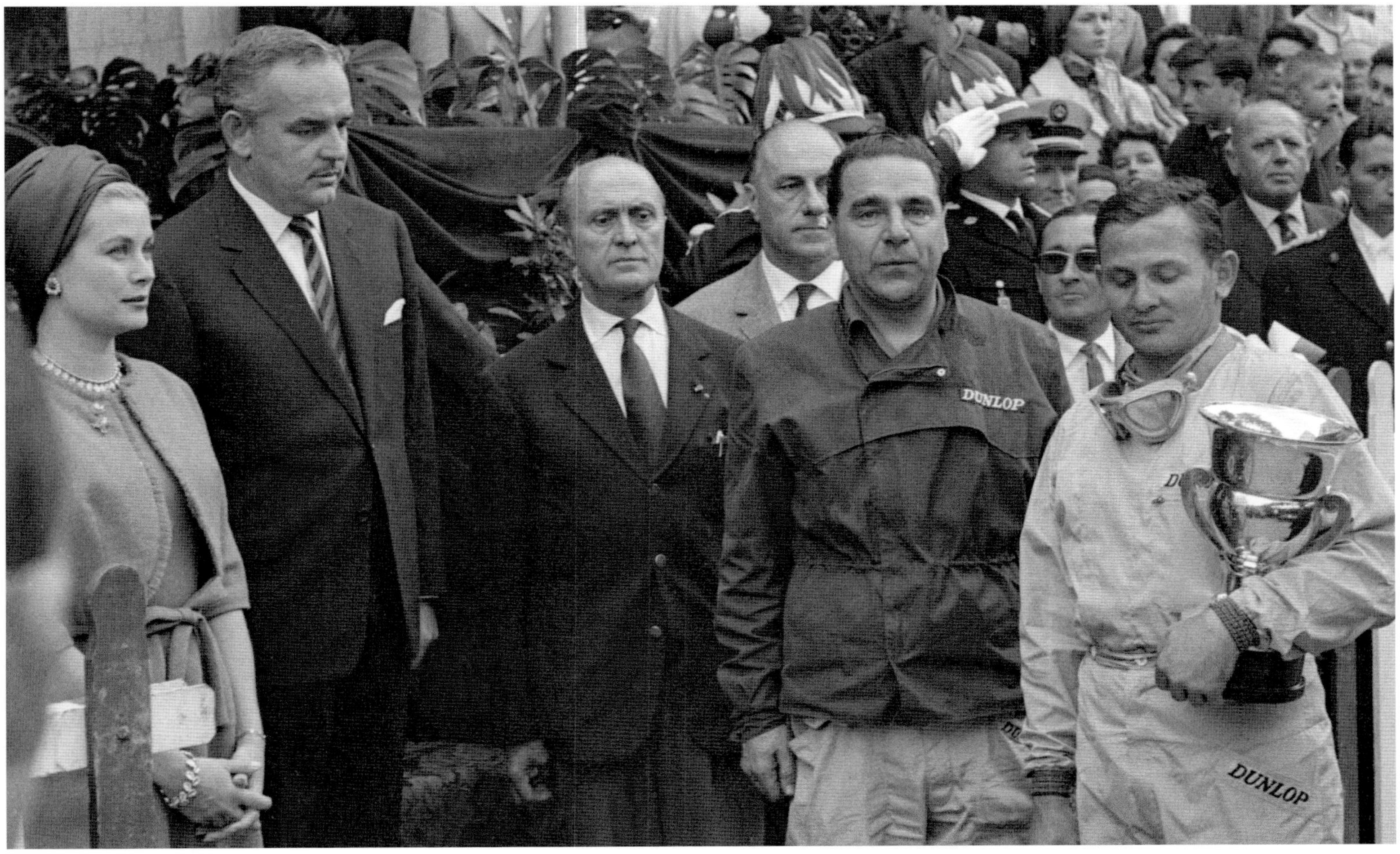

Die Nationalhymne Neuseelands erklingt für den Sieger Bruce McLaren. Von links Prinzessin Gracia, Prinz Rainier, Louis Chiron, John Cooper, Bruce McLaren.

Standing for the national anthem of New Zealand in honour of the winner, Bruce McLaren. From left Princess Grace, Prince Rainier, Louis Chiron, John Cooper, Bruce McLaren.

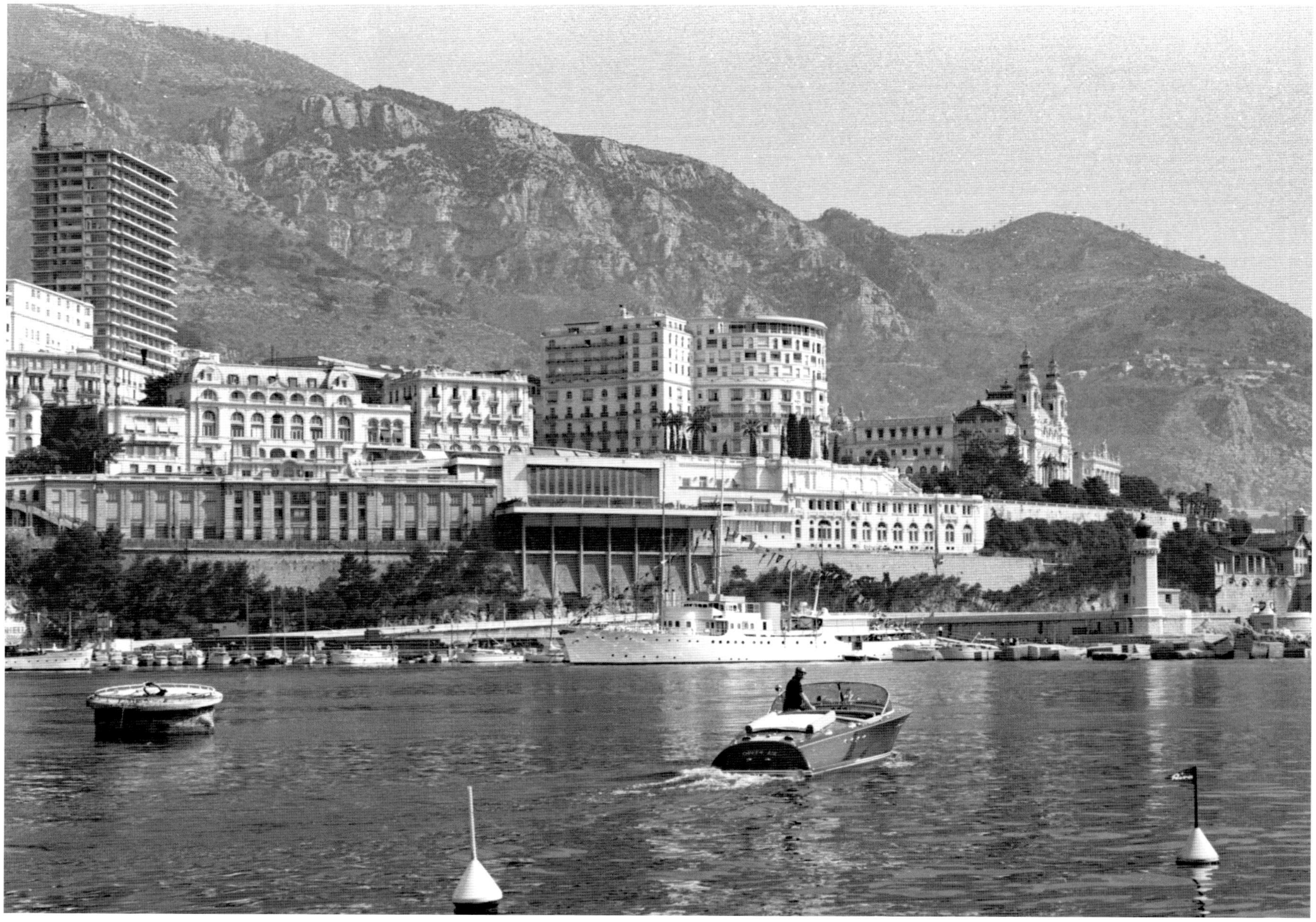

Monaco ist auf dem Weg vom verträumten romantischen Städtchen zur mondänen Stadt. Die Skyline verändert sich, es wird in die Höhe gebaut.

Monaco is being transformed from a dreamy romantic town to a glitzy city. The skyline is changing, and the city is climbing higher and higher.

1963

Der Fahrer und der Wagen, die es zu schlagen gilt

Die diesjährige Formel-1-Saison dominiert eindeutig Jim Clark auf dem überlegenen Lotus 25. Dieses Gespann gewinnt 7 von 10 Rennen – aber nicht den Monaco Grand Prix. Clark fährt zwar die schnellste Runde und steht wie im Vorjahr auf der Pole-Position. Doch in Runde 79, noch in Führung liegend, blockiert sein defektes Getriebe: Der 2. und 4. Gang werden gleichzeitig geschaltet. Er bleibt nach einem Dreher in der Gasometer-Kurve stehen. Wie immer geht er in Monaco leer aus; Graham Hill holt auf BRM seinen ersten von vier Monaco-Siegen.

The racer and the car to beat

This year's Formula 1 season was clearly dominated by Jim Clark in the superior Lotus 25. This team won 7 out of 10 races – but not the Monaco Grand Prix. Clark set the fastest lap and was in pole position, just as he was the previous year. Still in the lead on lap 79, his gearbox seized up: 2nd and 4th gear shifted at the same time. He stopped after spinning on the gasometer bend. As always, he came away empty-handed in Monaco; Graham Hill took the first of four Monaco victories in a BRM.

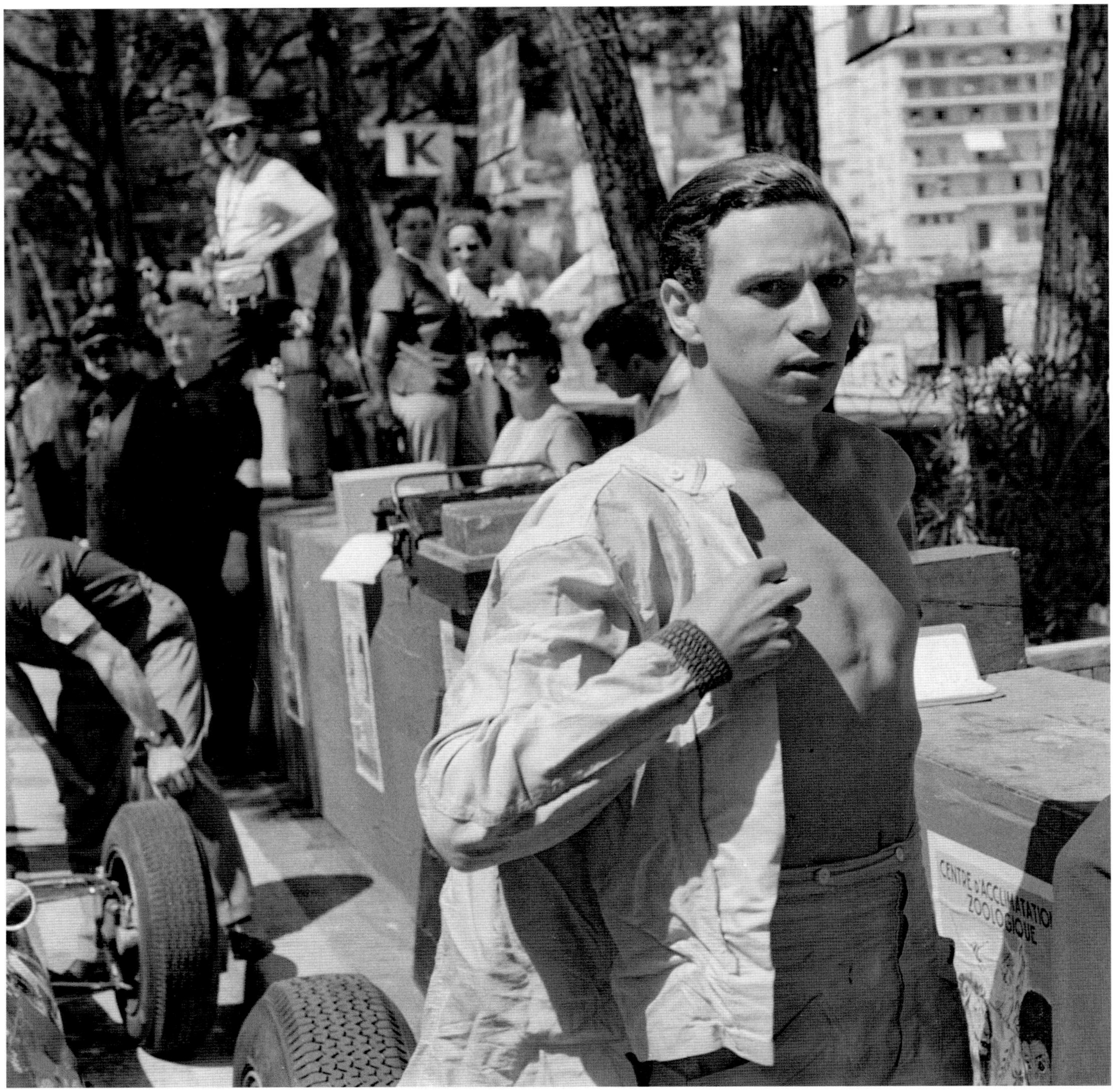

Und wieder ein Ausfall von Jim Clark.
Er startet von der Pole und fällt in Führung liegend mit technischen Problemen aus.

*Yet another retirement for Jim Clark.
He started from pole position and retired in the lead with technical problems.*

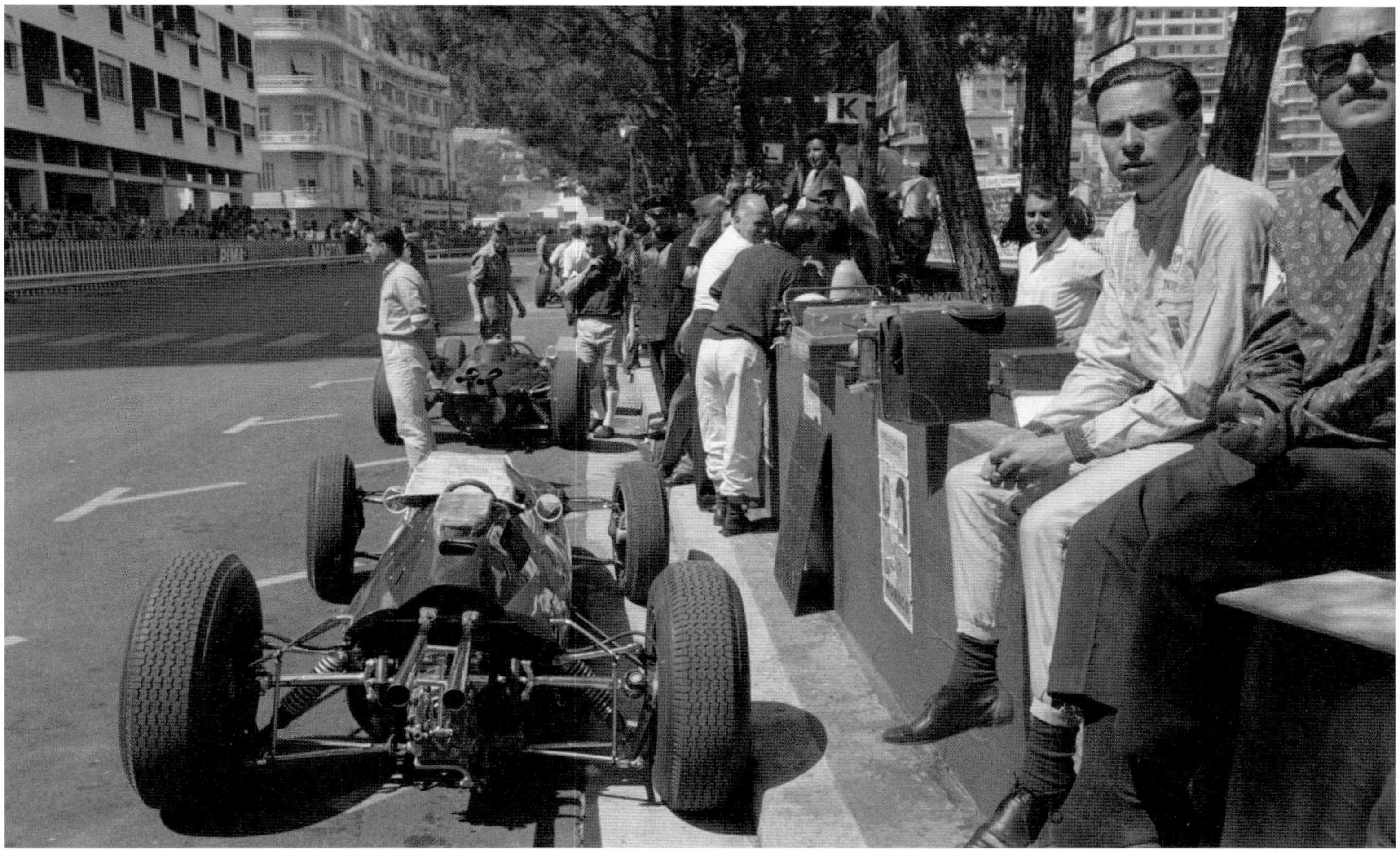

Jim Clark, Lotus 25 N° 9, und Colin Chapman (rechts), Gründer von Lotus Cars.

Jim Clark, Lotus 25 N° 9, and Colin Chapman (right), founder of Lotus Cars.

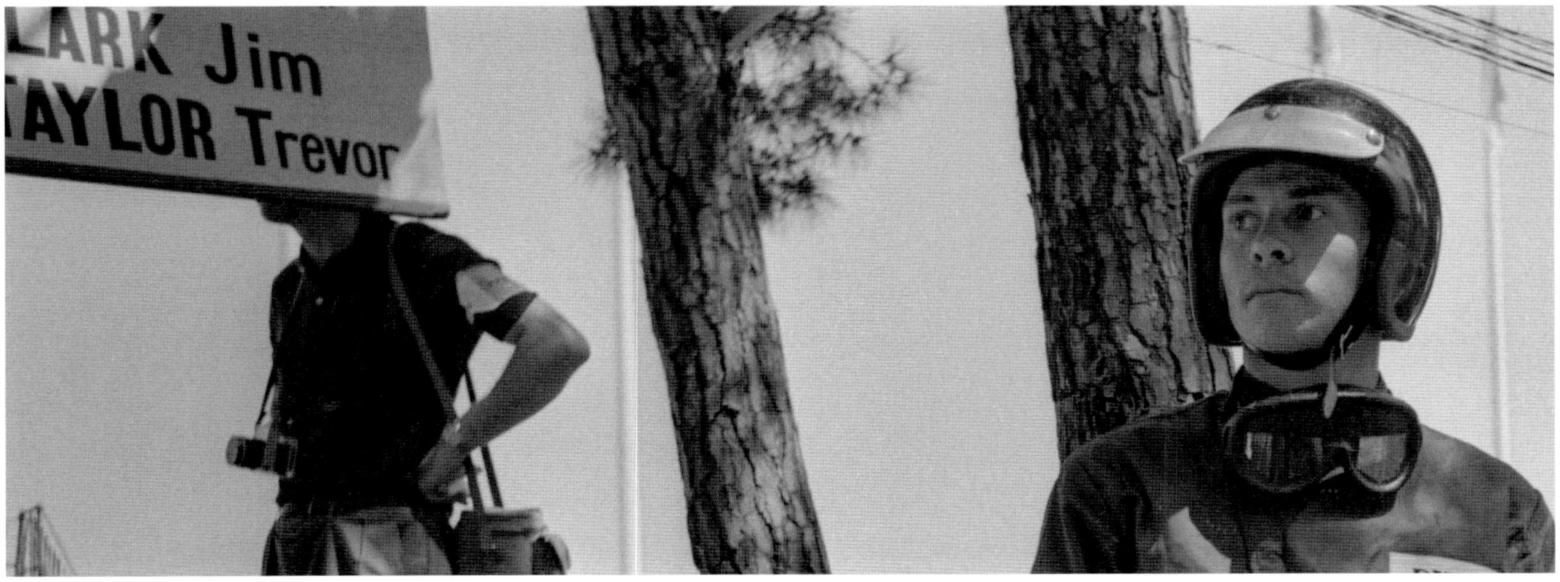

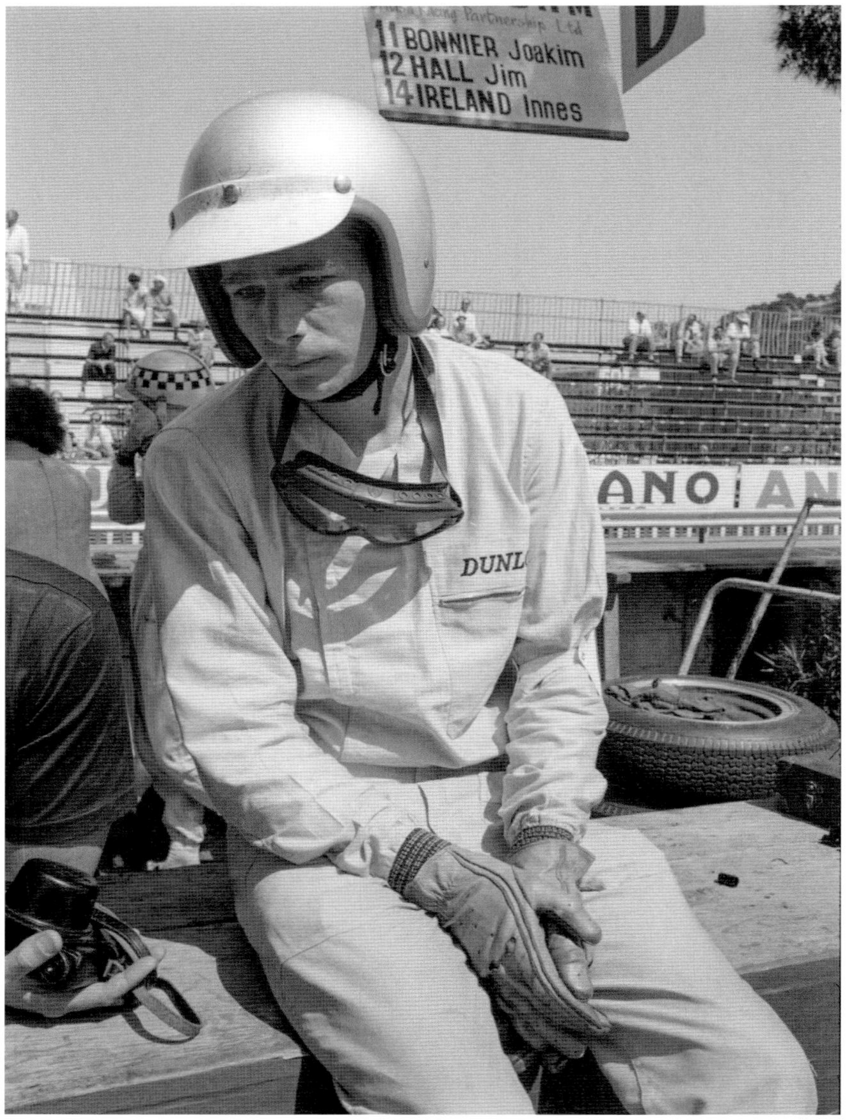

Jim Hall

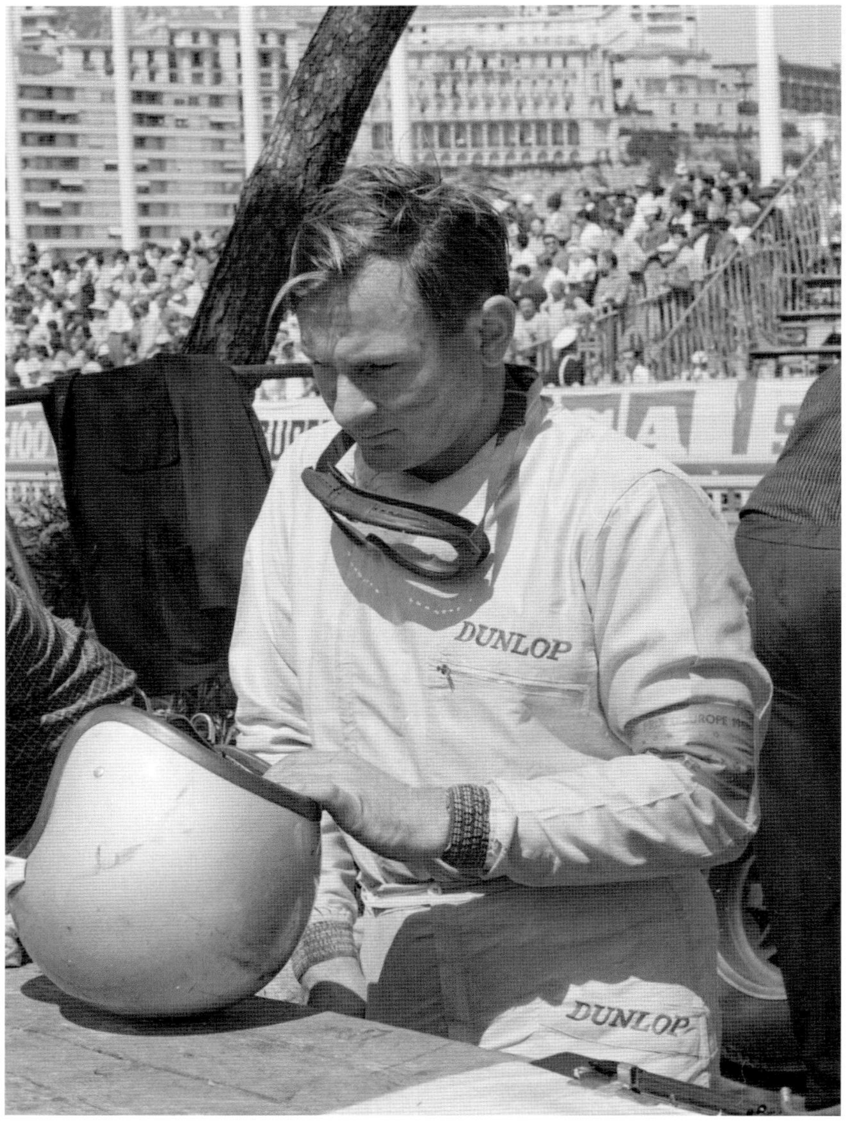

Bruce McLaren

Final Result of the Monaco Grand Prix 1963

1. Graham Hill, BRM P57
2. Richie Ginther, BRM P57
3. Bruce McLaren, Cooper T66

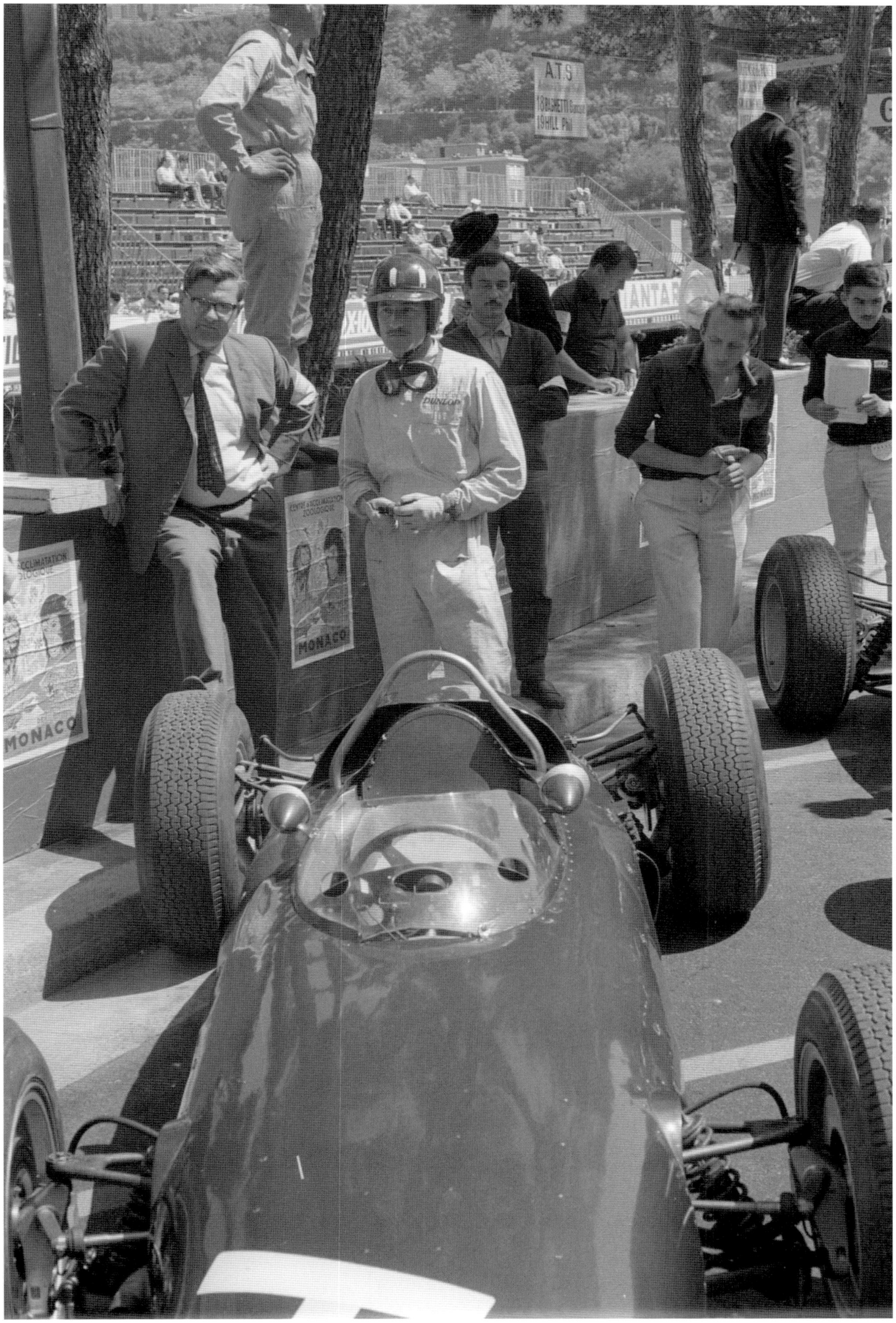

Der Sieger:
Graham Hill, BRM P57

Winner of the race:
Graham Hill, BRM P57

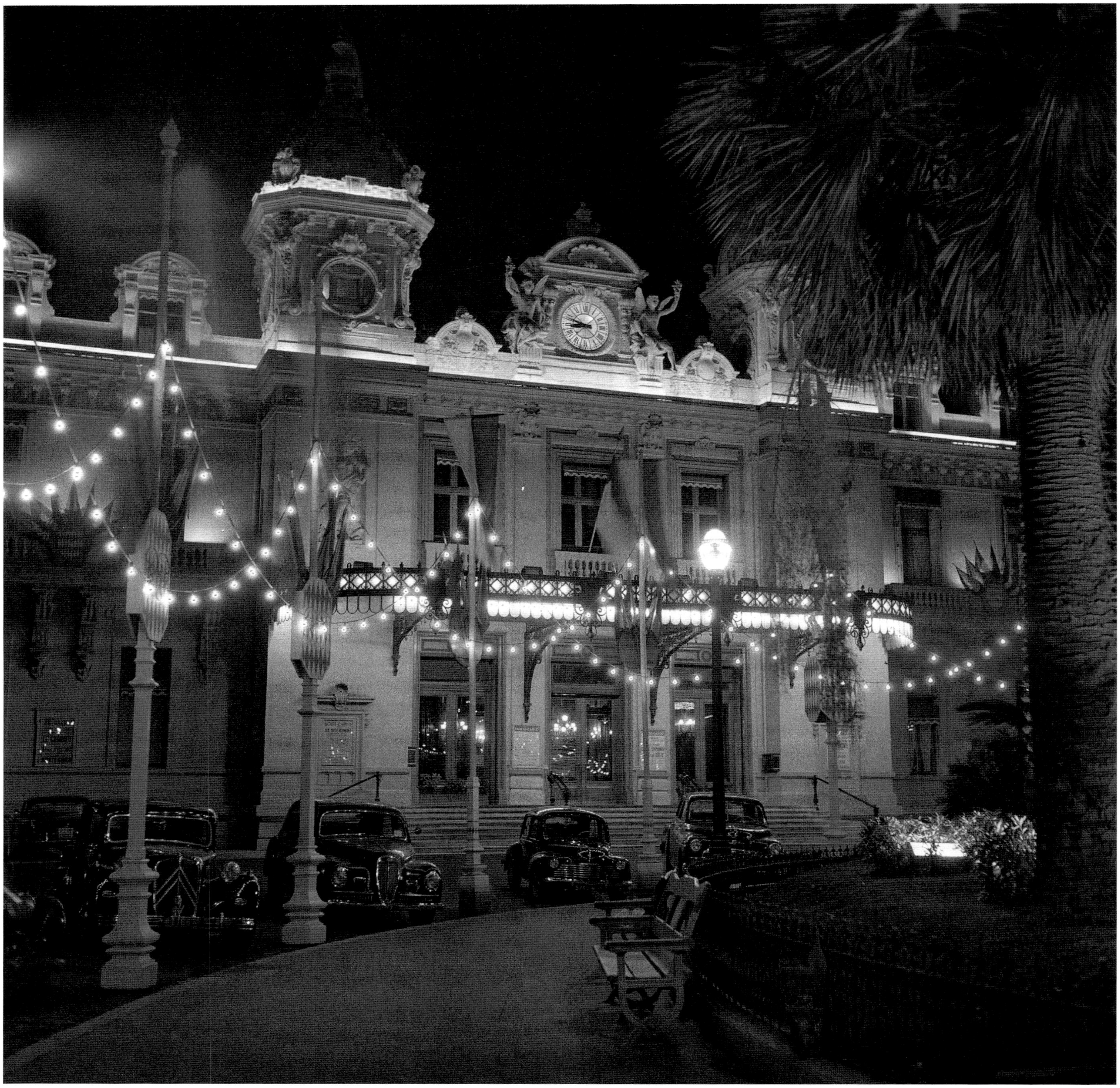

Erinnerung an vergangenes Monaco-Flair:
das Casino Monte Carlo.

*A reminder of the Monaco style of the past:
the Monte Carlo Casino.*

1964

Déjà-vu

Wie im Vorjahr holt Graham Hill den Sieg und Richie Ginther wird Zweiter, wiederum beide auf BRM. Es ist das erste „double double“ von Monaco, der erste doppelte Doppelsieg.

Und auch bei Jim Clark zeigt sich ein Déjà-vu: Er startet mit dem Lotus 25 wieder von der Pole und scheidet zum dritten Mal mit technischem Defekt aus. In der viertletzten Runde bleibt er mit fehlendem Öldruck stehen.

Den ersten Auftritt in Monaco hat der neue Ferrari 158. Dieses erste Monocoque wurde entwickelt unter dem Technikchef Mauro Forghieri, dem genialen Ingenieur bei der Scuderia. John Surtees wird mit dem V8 Tipo 158 in diesem Jahr Weltmeister und damit der einzige Weltmeister sowohl auf zwei als auch auf vier Rädern, denn 1956 hatte er die 500-cm³-Motorrad-Weltmeisterschaft gewonnen. In Monaco muss er mit Getriebeproblemen aufgeben.

Déjà vu

As in the previous year, Graham Hill took the title and Richie Ginther finished second, again both driving BRMs. This was the first “double double” victory in Monaco.

And Jim Clark also has a déjà vu: he started from pole position again with the Lotus 25 and was forced to retire for the third time with a technical defect. He came to a stop on the fourth last lap when the oil pressure failed.

A new kid on the block in Monaco was the new Ferrari 158, the first monocoque developed under technical director Mauro Forghieri, the brilliant engineer at Scuderia. John Surtees became world champion that year with the V8 Tipo 158, making him the only world champion on two and four wheels, because in 1956 he had won the 500cc motorbike world championship. In Monaco he had to retire with gearbox problems.

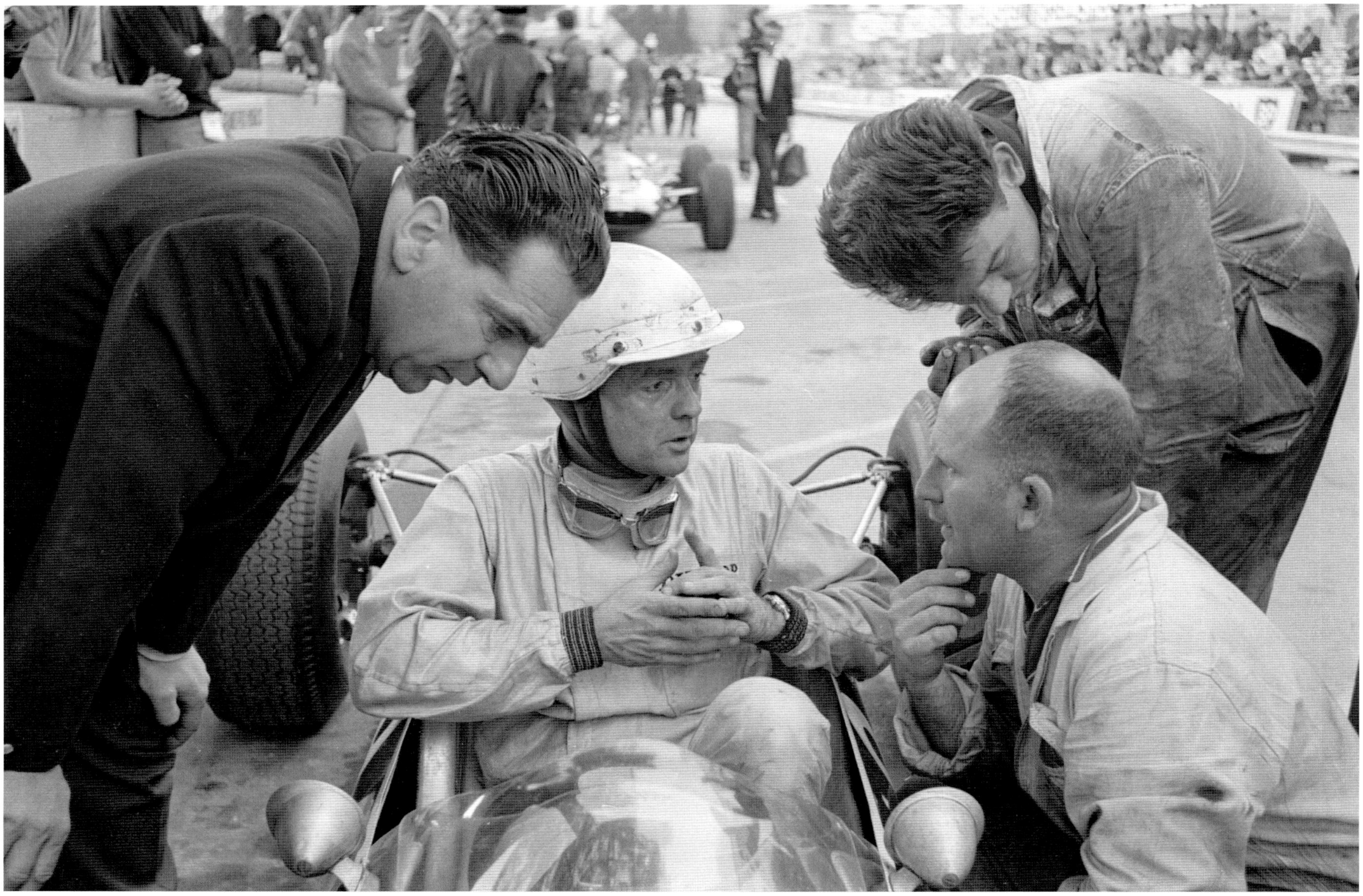

Phil Hill, Cooper T73 N° 9, im Gespräch mit
John Cooper (links) und Mechanikern.

*Phil Hill, Cooper T73 N° 9, in discussion with
John Cooper (left) and mechanics.*

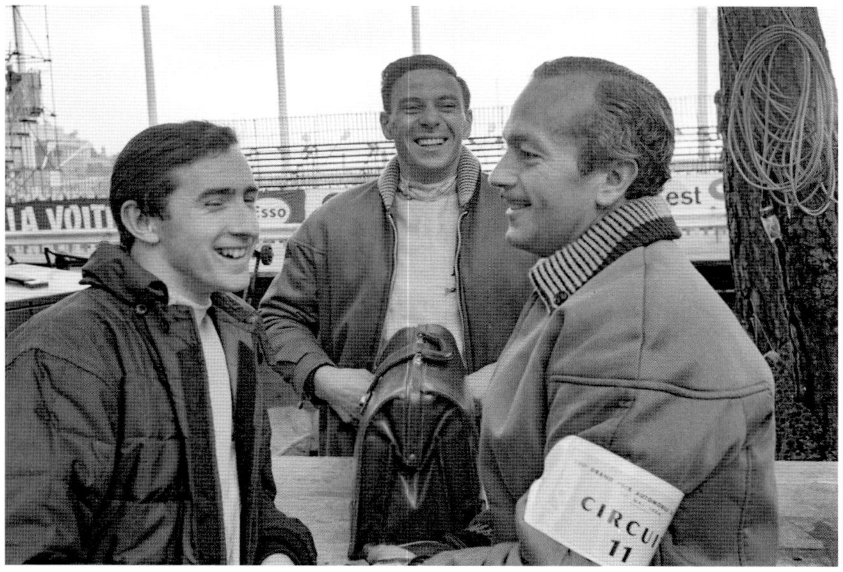

Jim Clark, Jackie Stewart,
Colin Chapman.

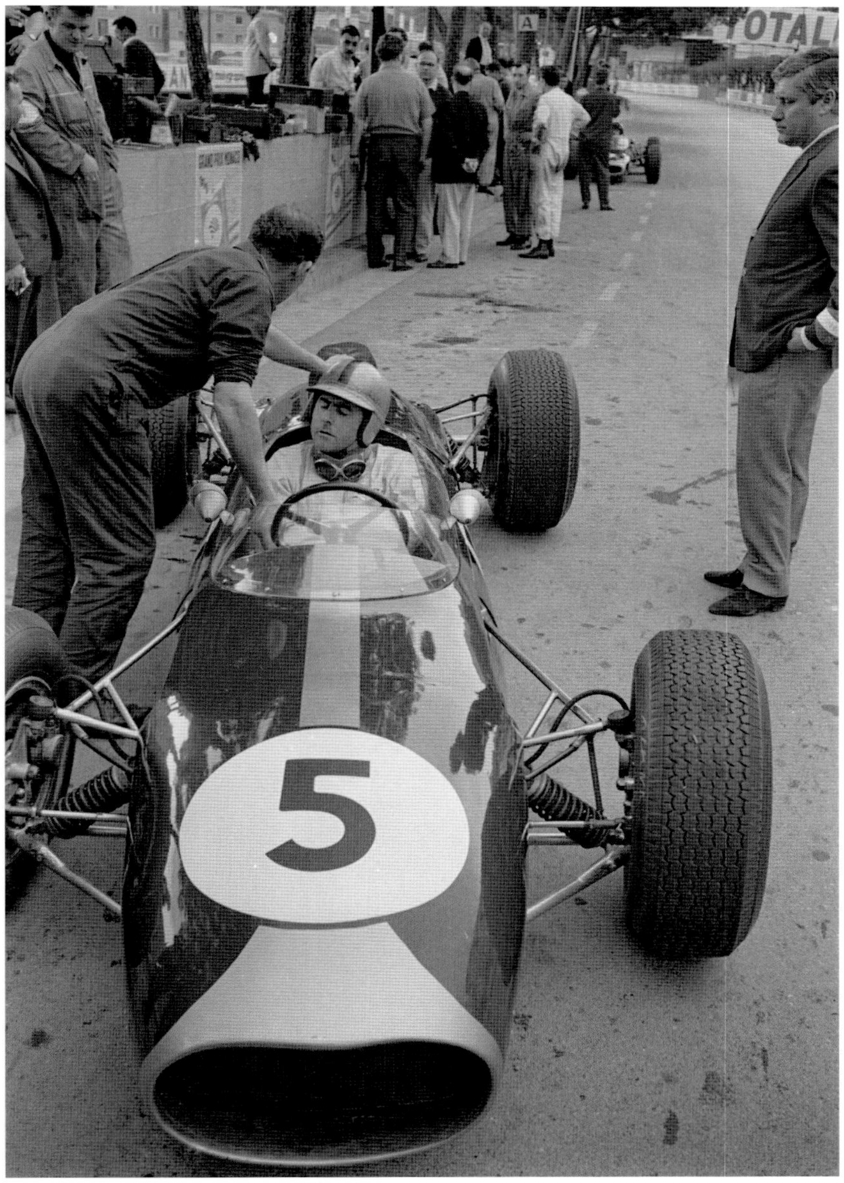

„Black Jack" Brabham auf Brabham BT7 N° 5.
Der einzige Rennfahrer, der im selbst konstruierten Wagen Weltmeister wird (1966).

"Black Jack" Brabham on Brabham BT7 N° 5.
The only racing driver to become world champion in a car he designed himself (1966).

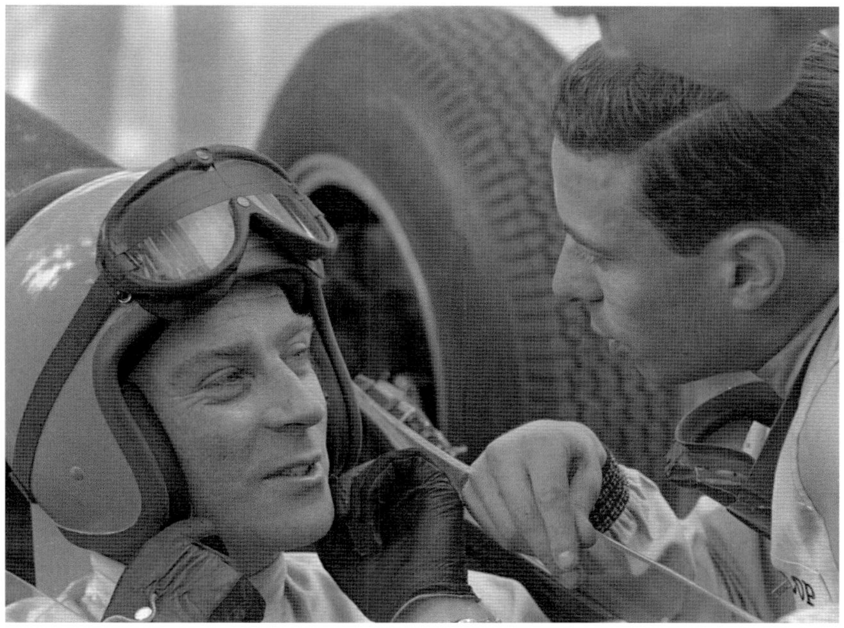

Peter Arundell, Jim Clark.

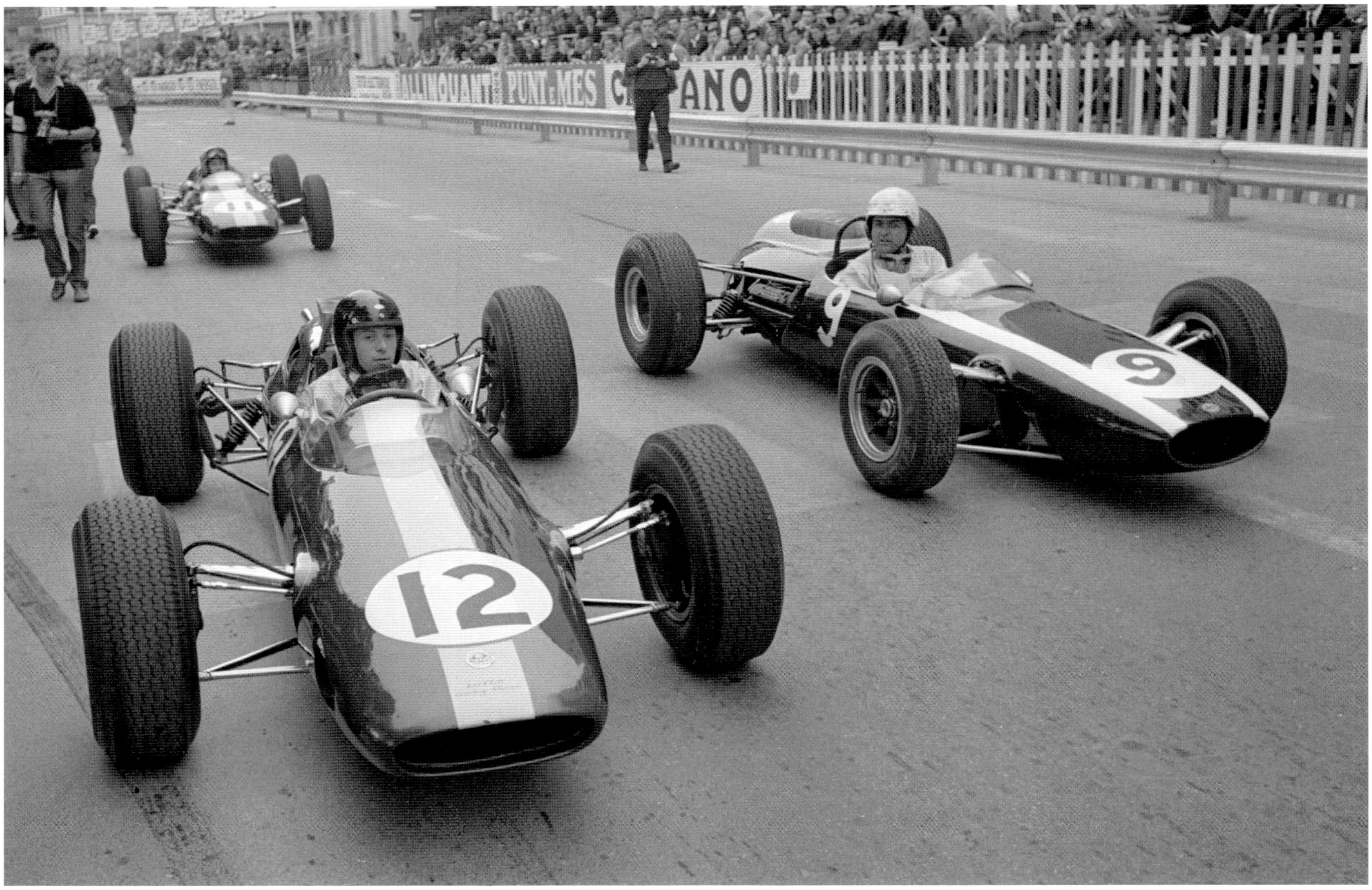

Immer noch ohne Gurte: Jim Clark, Lotus 25 N° 12,
Peter Arundell, Lotus 25 N° 11, und Phil Hill, Cooper T73 N° 9.

*Still no safety belts: Jim Clark, Lotus 25 N° 12,
Peter Arundell, Lotus 25 N° 11, and Phil Hill, Cooper T73 N° 9.*

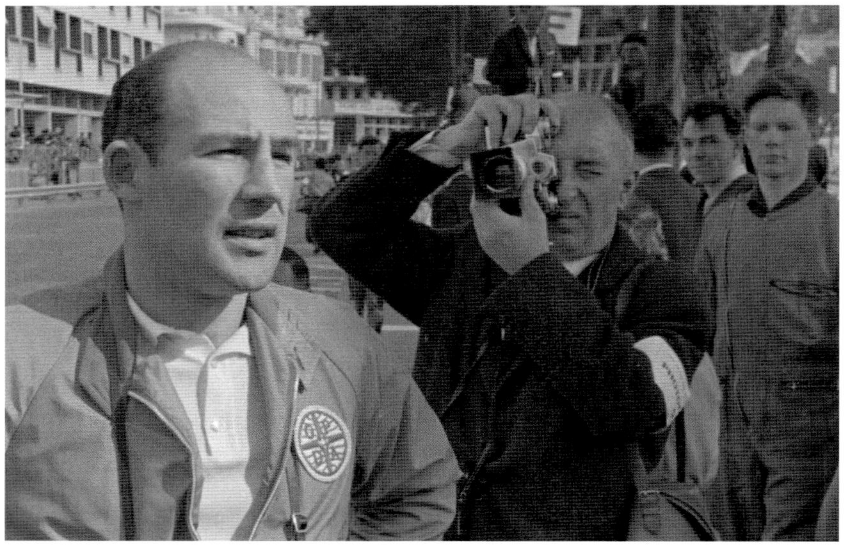

Wieder dabei: Stirling Moss, als Kommentator für das
amerikanische TV-Programm ABC Wide World of Sports.

*Back again: Stirling Moss, as commentator for the American
TV programme ABC Wide World of Sports.*

Final Result of the Monaco Grand Prix 1964

1. Graham Hill, BRM P261
2. Richie Ginther, BRM P261
3. Peter Arundell, Lotus 25

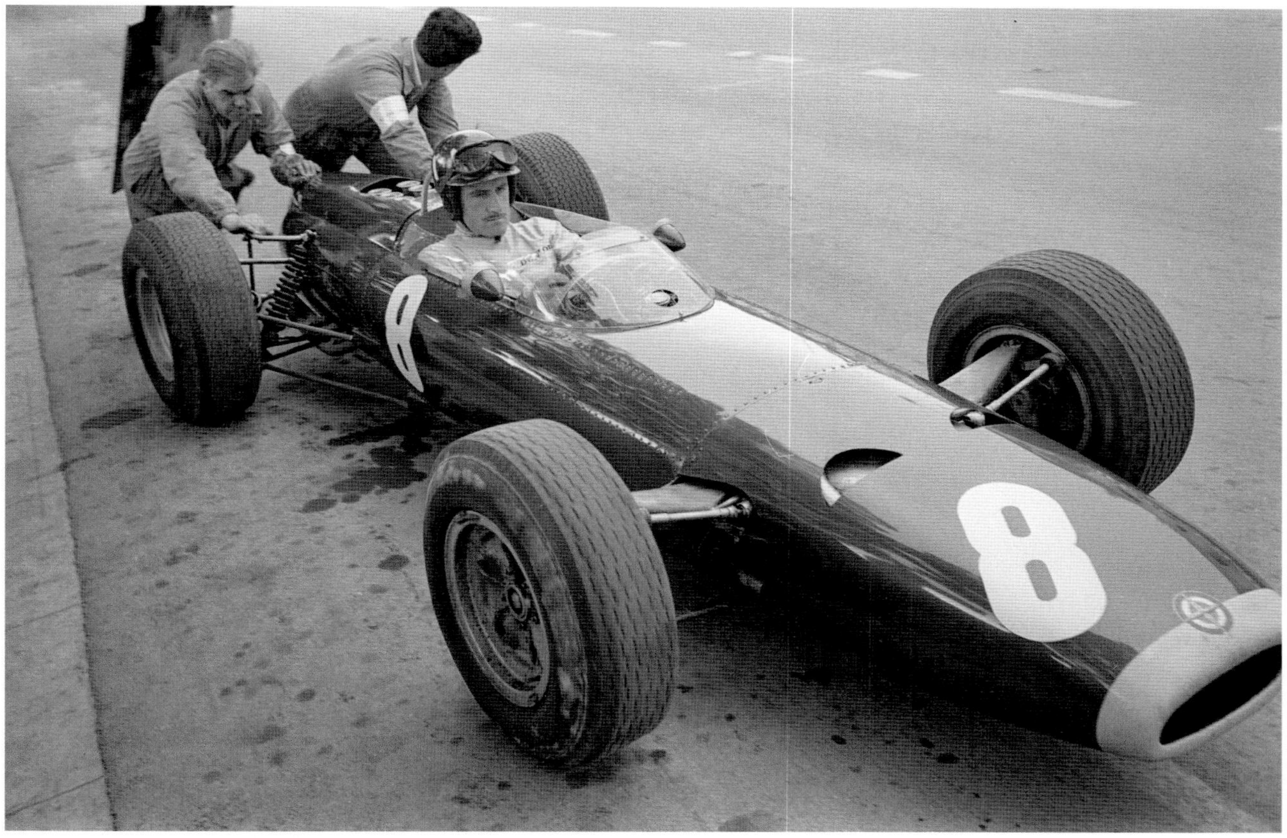

Graham Hill, BRM P261 N° 8,
Sieger des Rennens.

*Graham Hill, BRM P261 N° 8,
winner of the race.*

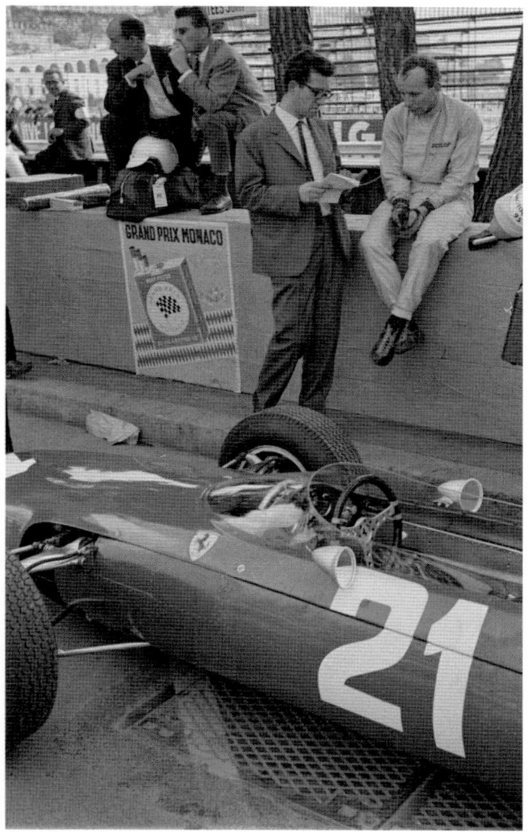

„Il Grande John“ Surtees,
V8-Ferrari 158 N° 21,
mit Ferrari-Renndirektor
Mauro Forghieri.

*“Il Grande John” Surtees,
V8-Ferrari 158 N° 21, with
Ferrari racing director
Mauro Forghieri.*

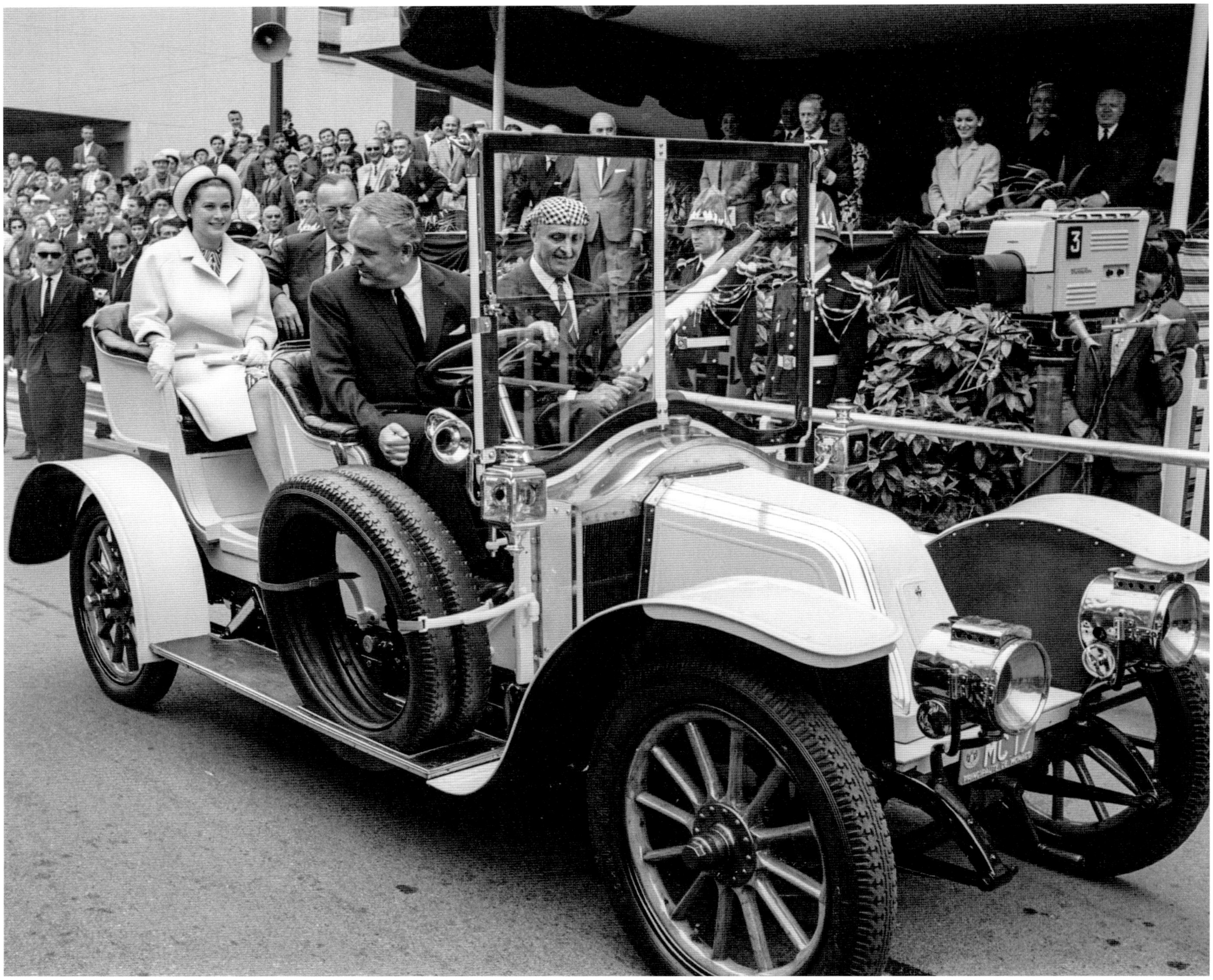

Fürst Rainier am Steuer eines Renault von 1910,
Beifahrer Louis Chiron und auf der Rückbank Prinzessin Grazia
von Monaco und Fürst Bernhard der Niederlande.

*Prince Rainier at the wheel of a 1910 Renault, Co-driver
Louis Chiron and in the back seat Princess Grace of Monaco and
Prince Bernhard of the Netherlands.*

1965

Zum dritten Mal Mr. Monaco

Zum letzten Mal wird mit dem Limit von 1,5-Liter-Motoren gefahren. Die Wagen gleichen sich immer mehr, weil die Monocoque-Konstruktion und der Mittelmotor Standard geworden sind. Zum ersten Mal startet Honda mit einem quer eingebauten 12-Zylinder-Motor in Monaco.

Jim Clark fehlt in diesem Jahr. Er zieht es vor, auf Lotus beim gleichzeitig stattfindenden Indy-500-Rennen in den USA zu starten und – er gewinnt das Rennen in Indianapolis als erster Nicht-Amerikaner seit 1916.

Graham Hill gewinnt das Rennen in Monaco zum dritten Mal auf BRM und verdient sich so den Spitznamen „Mr. Monaco".

Steve McQueen besucht den Grand Prix und kündet den Drehbeginn seines Films *Day of the Champion* an. Er trifft hier Stirling Moss, der als Production Consultant engagiert ist. Der Film wird nie realisiert.

Erstmals sieht man etwas Werbung auf den Overalls der Fahrer, aber nur mit Bezug zur Branche, zum Beispiel für Treibstofffirmen oder Reifen. Auf den Autos gibt es nach wie vor keine Werbung.

Mr Monaco for the third time

This was the last time, the limit of 1.5-litre engines was imposed. The cars were becoming more and more alike because the monocoque construction and the mid-engine had become standard. For the first time in Monaco, Honda started with a 12-cylinder transverse engine.

Jim Clark was absent this time. He preferred to start in the Indy 500 in the USA on Lotus at the same time and – he won the race at Indianapolis, the first non-American to do so since 1916.

Graham Hill won the Monaco race for the third time in a BRM, earning himself the nickname "Mr Monaco".

Steve McQueen visited the Grand Prix to announce the start of filming of his movie Day of the Champion. *He met with Stirling Moss, who was engaged as production consultant. The film was never made.*

Some advertising appeared for the first time on the drivers' overalls, but only related to the industry, for fuel companies or tyres for example. There was still no advertising on the cars themselves.

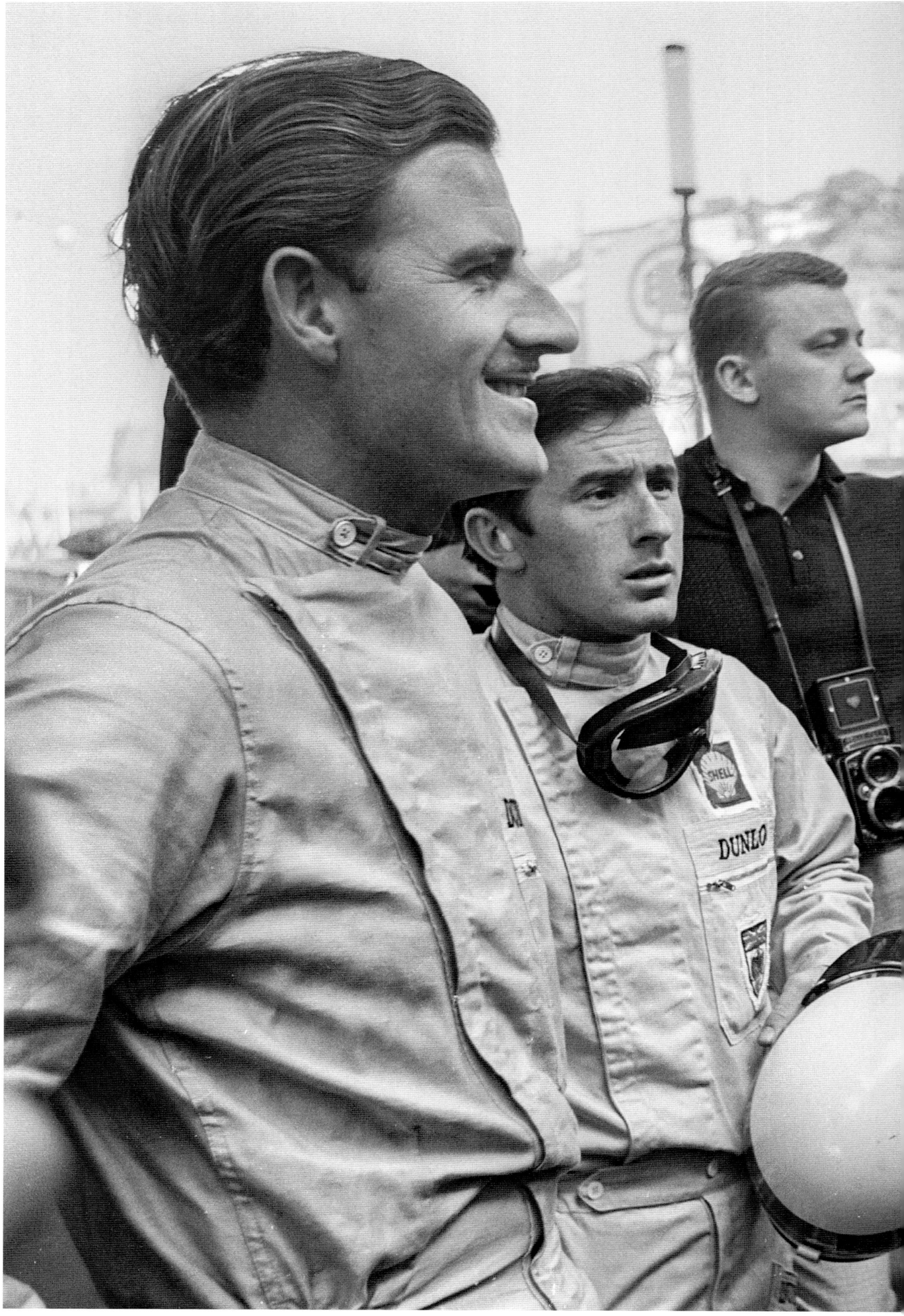

Mr. Monaco und der Cooler King: Graham Hill und Steve McQueen. Im Hintergrund Jackie Stewart. Steve McQueen kam nach Monaco, um den Start der Dreharbeiten für sein Traumprojekt, den Film *Day of the Champion* anzukündigen. Der Film wurde aber nie realisiert.

Mr Monaco and the Cooler King: Graham Hill and Steve McQueen. Jackie Stewart in the background. Steve McQueen came to Monaco to announce the start of filming for his dream project, the film Day of the Champion. *But the film was never realised.*

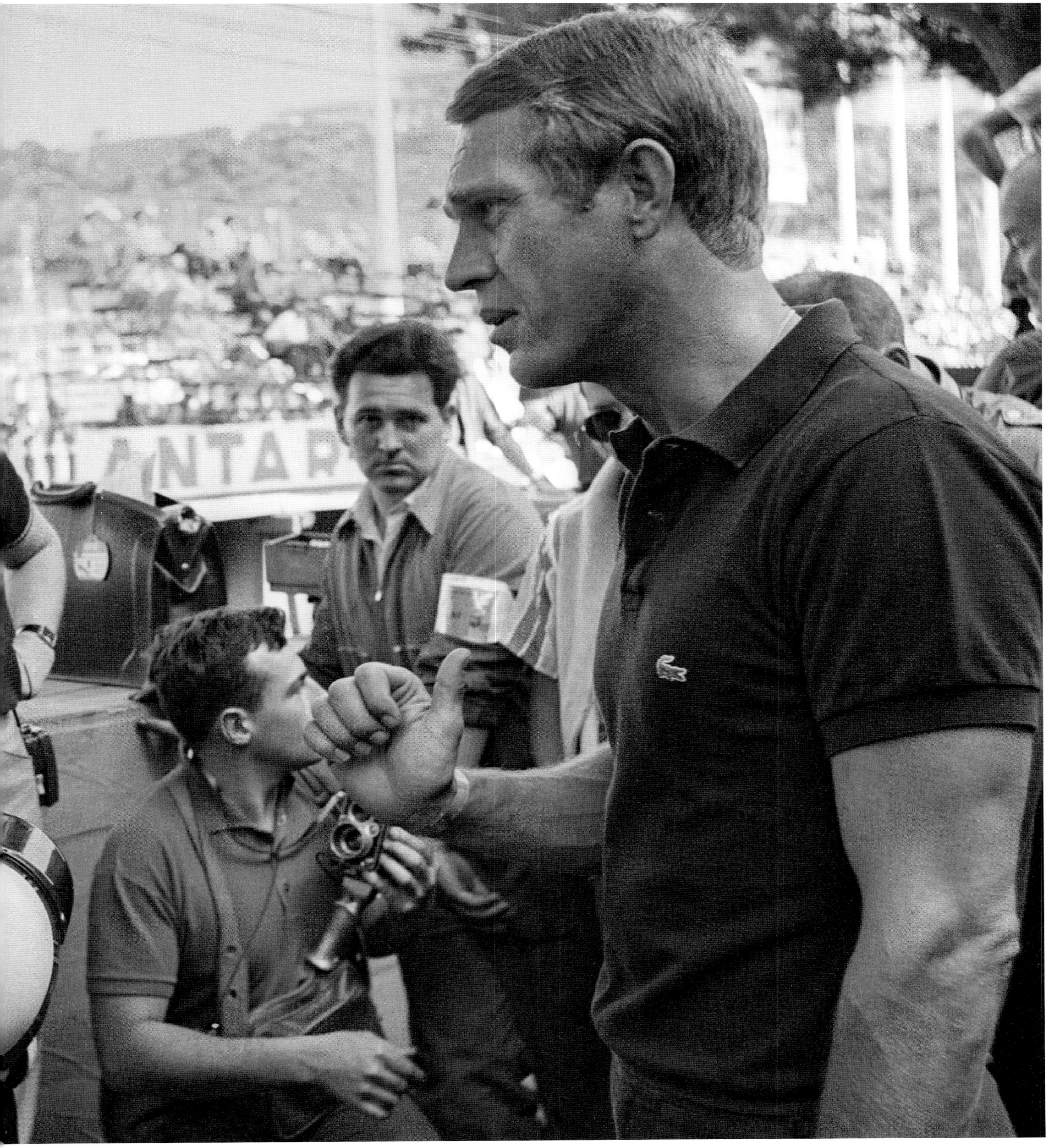

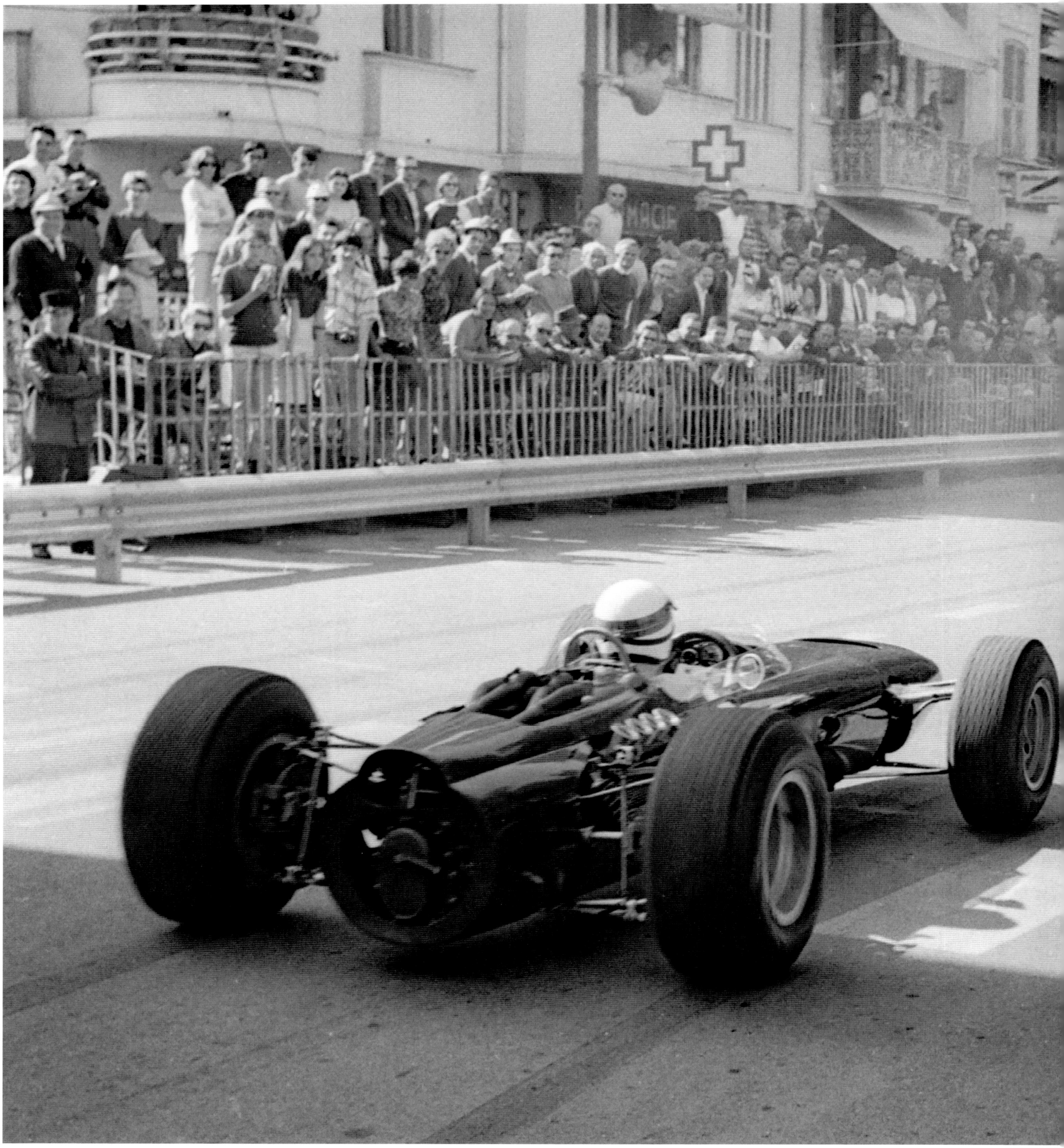

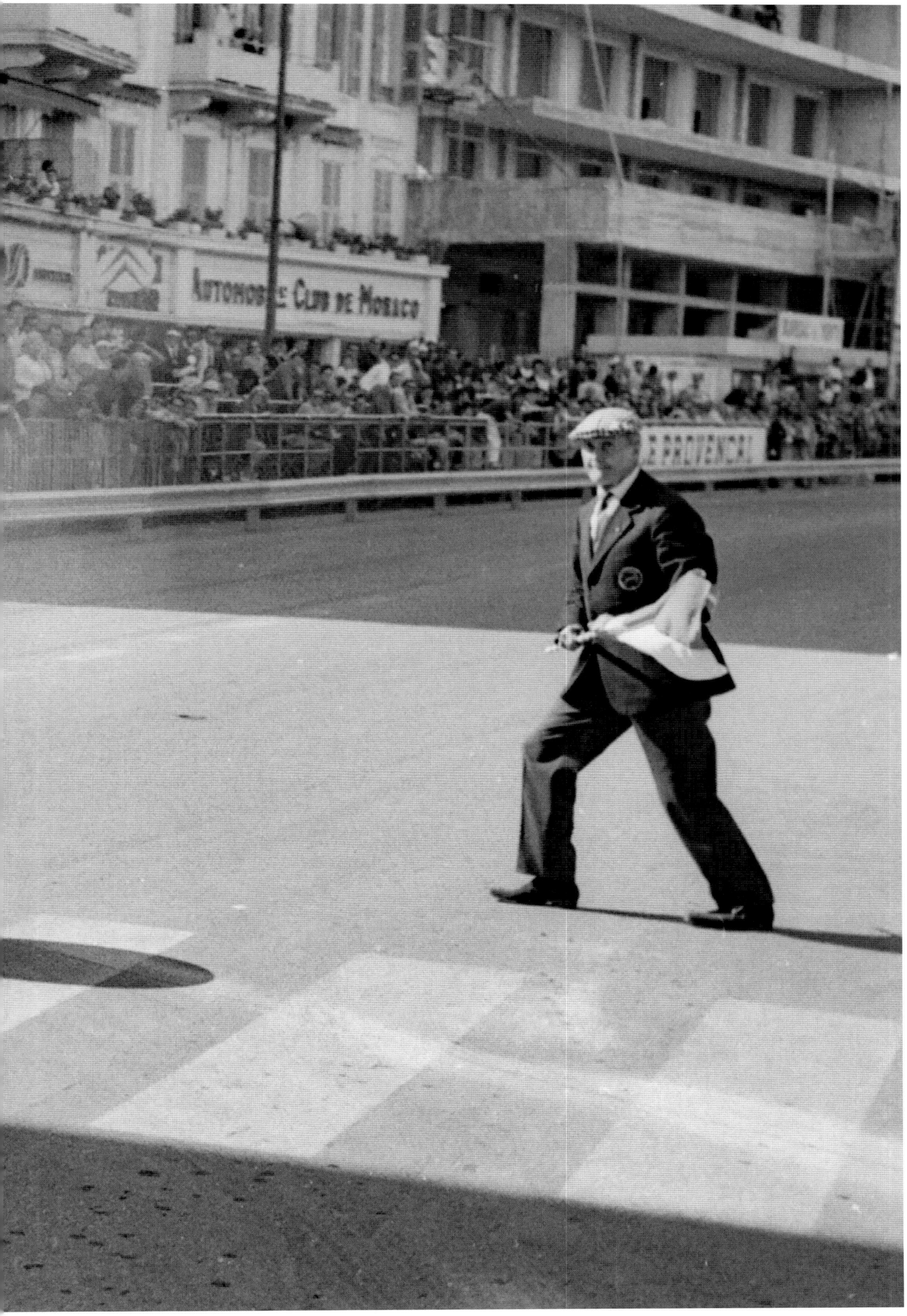

Auf der Ziellinie: Louis Chiron schwenkt die Flagge für Jackie Stewart, BRM P261 N° 4.

At the finish line: Louis Chiron waves the flag for Jackie Stewart, BRM P261 N° 4.

Final Result of the Monaco Grand Prix 1965

1. Graham Hill, BRM P261
2. Richie Ginther, BRM P261
3. Peter Arundell, Lotus 25

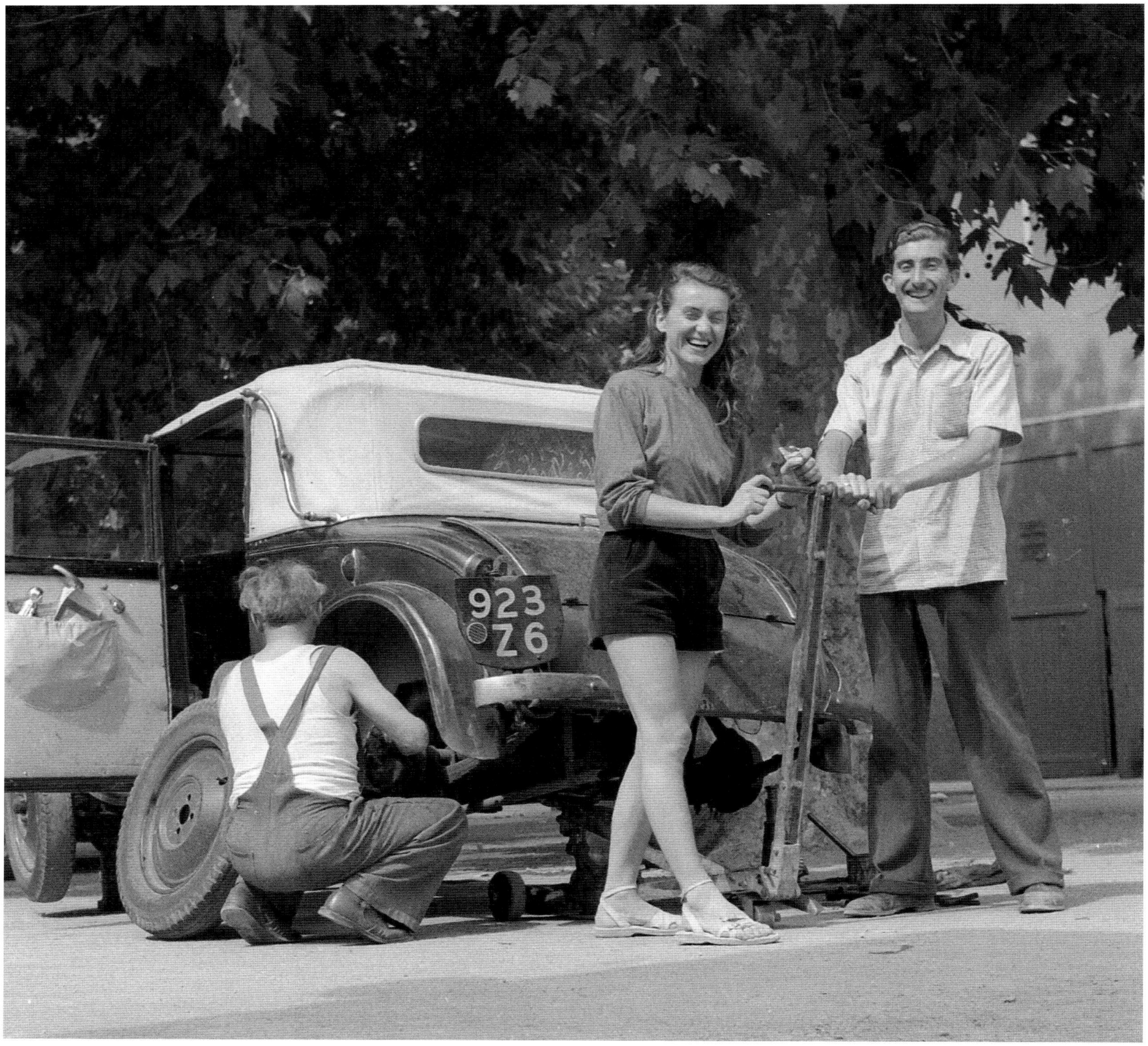

„Boxenstopp" im Sommer 1951: Edward und Gret Quinn sind gut gelaunt, obwohl sie in der Nähe von Arles zwei Tage auf einen Mechaniker warten mussten, der ihren Mathis reparieren konnte. Unbekannter Fotograf.

"Pit stop" in the summer of 1951: Edward and Gret Quinn are in good spirits, even though they had to wait two days for a mechanic to repair their Mathis near Arles. Unknown photographer.

EDWARD QUINN

Edward Quinn wurde 1920 in Irland geboren. Ab den 1950er-Jahren lebte und arbeitete er als Fotograf in Monaco und Nizza an der Côte d'Azur, die in den „Golden Fifties" ein Tummelplatz für Prominente aus der Welt des Showbusiness, der Kunst und der Wirtschaft war. Die Reichen und Berühmten kamen an die Riviera, um sich zu entspannen. Quinn war zur richtigen Zeit am richtigen Ort und schaffte es, spontane und bezaubernde Bilder einzufangen, die den Charme, die Raffinesse und den Chic einer legendären Ära dokumentierten.

1951 lernte Edward Quinn Pablo Picasso kennen und fotografierte ihn zum ersten Mal. Ihre Freundschaft dauerte bis zu Picassos Tod im Jahr 1973. Diese Begegnung mit Picasso beeinflusste Quinn nachhaltig, sowohl persönlich als auch in Bezug auf sein späteres Werk. Quinn ist der Autor mehrerer Bücher und Filme über Picasso.

Der Journalist Wolfgang Frei ist der Neffe von Quinn. Er realisierte zusammen mit ihm verschiedene Projekte, darunter das Buch *James Joyce's Dublin.* Er leitet das Edward Quinn Archiv, edwardquinn.com.

Edward Quinn was born 1920 in Ireland. Starting in the 1950s, he lived and worked as a photographer at Monaco and Nice on the Côte d'Azur, which was a playground for celebrities from the world of show biz, art and business during the "Golden '50s". The rich and famous came to the Riviera to relax. But the movie stars recognized the importance of their off-screen image, and Quinn was in the right place at the right time, managing to capture spontaneous and enchanting images that documented the charm, sophistication and chic of a legendary era.

In 1951, Edward Quinn met and photographed Pablo Picasso for the first time. Their friendship lasted until Picasso's death in 1973. This encounter with Picasso had a lasting influence on Quinn, both personally and in regard to his subsequent work. Quinn is the author of several books and films about Picasso.

The journalist Wolfgang Frei is Quinn's nephew. He worked on various projects with him, including the book James Joyce's Dublin. *He manages the Edward Quinn Archive, edwardquinn.com.*

IMPRESSUM

Bibliografische Information der Deutschen Nationalbibliothek
Die Deutsche Nationalbibliothek verzeichnet diese Publikation in der Deutschen Nationalbibliografie; detaillierte bibliografische Daten sind im Internet über http://dnb.dnb.de abrufbar.

Bibliographic information published by the Deutsche Nationalbibliothek
The Deutsche Nationalbibliothek lists this publication in the Deutsche Nationalbibliografie; detailed bibliographic data are available in the Internet at http://dnb.dnb.de.

1. Auflage / 1st edition
ISBN 978-3-667-12510-1
ISBN 978-3-667-12509-5
(limitierte Sonderausgabe)

Besonderer Dank geht an Adam Ferrington für die Durchsicht von Texten und Bildlegenden.
Special thanks to Adam Ferrington for reviewing the texts and captions.

Text und Konzept/
Text and concept:
Wolfgang Frei

Muttersprachliche Betreuung/
Native speaker review:
James O'Neill

Lektorat/Editor:
Hanno Vienken

Creative Director Design:
Michael Geisler

Lithografie/Lithography:
Mohn Media

Druck/Printed by:
Firmengruppe APPL – aprinta druck, Wemding
Printed in Germany 2022

Falls ein Leser im Buch auf Fehler stößt oder einen Kommentar abgeben möchte, möge er/sie sich bitte an archive@edwardquinn.com wenden. Wir veröffentlichen Korrekturen und Bemerkungen gern auf edwardquinn.com/racing.

If a reader finds any mistake or wants to comment, he/she is kindly asked to send a message to archive@edwardquinn.com. We will gladly publicize these comments at edwardquinn.com/racing.

Delius Klasing Verlag,
Siekerwall 21, 33602 Bielefeld,
Germany
Telefon/Phone
+49 (0)521 559-0,
Telefax/Fax
+49 (0)521 559-115
Email: info@delius-klasing.de

www.delius-klasing.de

INDEX

INDEX